MANAGEMENT OF IT, CHANGES, RISKS, WORKSHOPS & EPISTEMOLOGY

ISBN: 978-1-84753-147-6

1. Information Technology, Page 3
2. Changes In I.T., Page 127
3. I.T. Risks, Page 303
4. Programme Workshop, Page 403
5. Epistemological Concepts. Page 468

Short description of the five books. Page 692

The compilation of five Management related books by

Andreas Sofroniou *DSc PhD PsD ExecMBA CEng FIoD*

Copyright © Andreas Sofroniou

2007

ISBN: 978-1-84753-147-6

Andreas Sofroniou

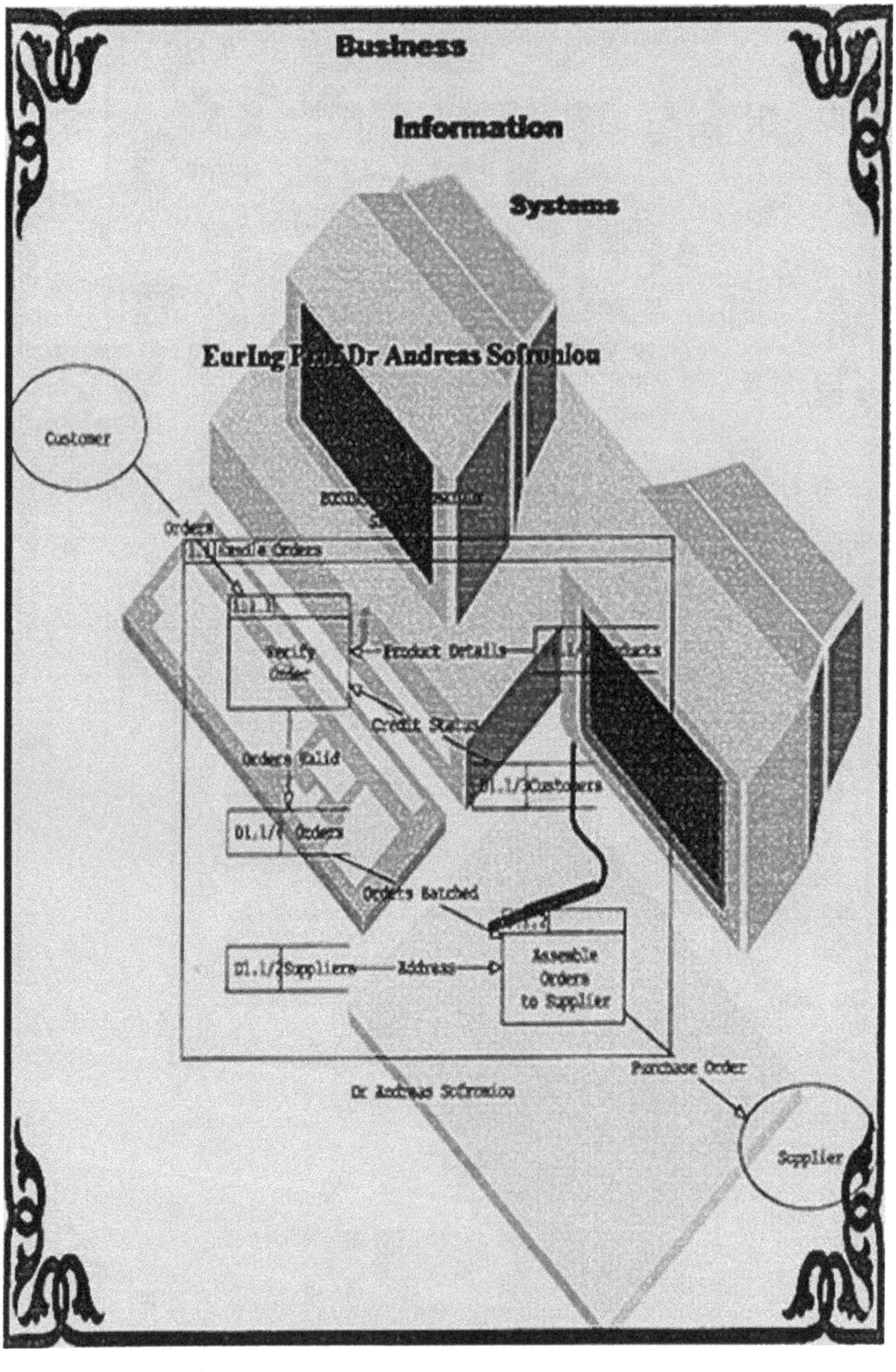
Business
Information
Systems
Customer
Orders
Product Details
Credit Status
Orders Batched
Assemble
Orders
to Supplier
Address
Purchase Order
Dr Andreas Sofroniou
Supplier

FOREWORD

There can be little doubt that information systems and computing in general, will become increasingly important in the years ahead. This book is, therefore, aiming to fill a gap in the current business and tutorial literature.

The Business Information Systems book has been designed for the business person, for the student and the computer professional who needs a detailed overview of Information Technology and the systems involved.

The book explores the fundamental aspects of operational computing, the development of new information systems, the choice of packages and the structured methodologies used. Current systems are discussed according to their structure and the book focuses on further developments in information technology, the year 2000 compliance and their planning.

In writing the book, the author is mostly concerned with the development and the managing of systems and people in multi-national corporations, software houses, government departments, the European Union Commissions and academia.

EurIng Dr Andreas Sofroniou has close links with business systems and their development, as well as the system engineering profession as a whole. He has developed numerous systems and managed a variety of applications and systems people, including Year 2000 projects.

It is the author's wish that the reader thoroughly enjoys reading the contents of this book.

Andreas Sofroniou

Contents

Foreword

Preface

1: Background
1.1 Introduction
1.2 Background of Information Systems
1.3 Computer Background

2: Systems Engineering
2.1 The Diagrammatic Representation Of Systems
2.2 Information Systems Diagram
2.3 Systems Architecture
2.4 Designing Systems
2.5 Security and Systems Assurance
2.6 Software Considerations
2.7 Relational Database
2.8 Distributed Systems Processing
2.9 Personal Computing
2.10 Network
2.11 Intranet
2.12 Teleworking

3: Object Oriented Methodology
3.1 Object Oriented System Development
3.2 Object Oriented Lifecycle
3.3 Analysis And Design Modelling
3.4 Construction and Reuse
3.5 Rapid Business Modelling
3.6 Benefits And Disadvantages
3.7 Experience-based OOM

4: Structured Systems Analysis And Design
4.1 The Background Of Structured Analysis
4.2 The Need For Structured Analysis And Design
4.3 Tools For Analysis
4.4 Drawing Dataflow Diagrams
4.5 Explosion Conventions
4.6 Using The Methodology
4.7 Bringing Structured Analysis To Companies
4.8 The Rapid Building Method
4.9 Structured English

5: Managing Systems Development
5.1 Systems Management

5.2 Structured Management Methods
5.3 Management Of Projects
5.4 Recruitment And Interviewing In Computing
5.5 Project Control In Developing Systems
5.6 Systems Development Procedures
5.7 Systems Specification
5.8 Process Analysis
5.9 System Reviews
5.10 Physical Design
5.11 Quick Dataflow Diagramming
5.12 Program Design

6: Commercial Systems Packages
6.1 Packages
6.2 Commercial Off-the-shelf (COTS)
6.3 The Integration Of Packages
6.4 Experience In COTS
6.5 The Commercial Off-the-shelf Studies
6.6 Reusability
6.7 Open Standards
6.8 Superhighway
6.9 Modelling And Prototyping
6.10 Review And Selection Of COTS
6.11 COTS Advantages And Disadvantages

7: Artificial Intelligence (AI)
7.1 Expert Systems
7.2 Applications Of Expert Systems
7.3 The Short History Of Artificial Intelligence
7.4 The Fifth Generation Language
7.5 Techniques
7.6 Meeting The Needs Of Industry

8: CASE Tools And Methodologies
8.1 The Overall Objectives
8.2 The CASE Tool And The Encyclopaedia

9: Systems Specification
9.1 The Highlights Of The Case Study
9.2 The Diagrammatic Representations

10: Information Systems Explained
10.1 Information Systems Now
10.2 Commerce And The Internet
10.3 Internet In Business
10.4 The Mainframe
10.5 The Mainframe As A Data Server

10.6 The Use Of PCs And Mainframes
10.7 The Mainframe For Management Services
10.8 The Client Server
10.9 Flexibility To The Users
10.10 Tools For Effective Systems
10.11 Inherited Systems
10.12 Data Warehousing
10.13 Accessing Data

11 Re-Engineering
11.1 Re-engineering The Business
11.2 Systems In the Future
11.3 Interrelating Sciences Diagram

12: Project Planning
12.1 Managing The Plan
12.2 Project Control
12.2.1 Planning Function
12.2.2 Initiation And Maintenance Of Plans
12.2.3 Plans For Management
12.2.4 Time Recording
12.2.5 Reviews
12.3 Quality Of Plans
12.3.1 Plans Assurance
12.3.2 Project Activities
12.4 Planning Office Preparations
12.4.1 The Planner
12.4.2 Deliverables
12.4.3 Monitoring
12.5 Settings
12.5.1 Outputs
12.5.2 The Stages
12.5.3 Tasks
12.5.4 Actuals
12.5.5 Baseline
12.5.6 Milestones
12.5.7 Tracked Time And Estimates
12.5.8 Resource Loading
12.5.9 Sub-totals
12.6 Planner's Responsibilities
12.7 Planning Objectives
12.7.1 Plan Completeness
12.7.2 Standards
12.8 Policies
Four Examples Of Plans

Preface

This book is mostly concerned with the development and the management of systems and the people involved in such development. The individuals who work on their own and those who work in groups to design systems applicable to users. The system practitioners who may be employed by multi-national corporations, software houses, government departments, European Union Commissions, or academia.

Computing as a service is given to all types of businesses, in any environment. As a tool at work, a systems department deals with individual problems, ranging from difficulties within job responsibilities, rifts and business inadequacies, including systems, operational problems and the people involved in such activities.

The book will assist operational groups of people, in various sections of commercial computing. Based on the contents, training courses can be prepared to suit the candidates, mainly workshops concerned with human-computer interactions, systems development and systems methodologies.

The modern Information Technology Executive attempts to merge the latest developments in human sciences and advanced technology. The combination of both, gives a service applicable to the systems user and his/her working surroundings.

In computing, the major theme is the responsibility to the system user, the individual and the company; to help with their problems and requirements in system development. The emergent technologies and the pace of change are placing increasing importance upon organisations and individuals being finely tuned, in performance terms. This does not just happen, but has to be worked at.

The Information Technology Manager's role is to provide a service in computing which will assist in developing skills, diagnose and treat discontinuities which affect the performance of the systems. In computing, the commercial, industrial and human expertise embrace the whole range of services. Technology in business environments, directing and management techniques, systems designing, personnel selection, counselling, training and individual development, production methods and artificial intelligence.

Many organisational and personnel problems may be solved. The system engineer offers advice and undertakes assignments relating to all aspects of information technology, including strategic, business and data analysis, systems and database designing, networking, hardware and software selection and systems users training. Within an organisation, the computing expertise can be offered as an ad-hoc advisory service, as a short term systems specialist, or on a long term project basis.

This book will prove very useful to the Executive who wishes to use modern skills, such as the human aspects of system management and directing, setting of tasks, project management and the state-of-the-art in computing, as a tool.

The responsibilities within information technology and the systems engineering areas, include the understanding of user personality, human-computer interaction and comparative methods within structured systems designing.

On the academic, educational and training aspect, the importance of a person as a whole system engineering professional must be emphasised, this being the major factor in dealing with organisational, system and personal problems. In the last few years, modern universities prepare their courses to suit the business environment and towards the professional accreditation of the appropriate computing institution and the engineering council. The whole venture of academia and the engineering institutions is seen by businesses as a pro for a continuous human development policy. This ensures high quality employment opportunities, secured in growth industries at the forefront of technological changes.

1: Background

1.1 Introduction

In the past, the majority of data processing has been carried out by companies using batch style computer systems. With the cost of hardware rapidly reducing and with the hardware power and facilities increasing inversely, on-line systems are now becoming easier to justify and develop.

The objectives of data processing are to capture data, process it and present the information. Because of the widespread use of computers within business, it is sometimes assumed that data always refers to some type of financially oriented transaction.

In fact, data has a more general meaning. In general terms, data can be used to denote any or all facts, numbers, letters and symbols that refer to, or describe an object, idea, condition, or any other function. But data can only be of value if it can be organised in some way, so that it becomes meaningful to somebody - this is information.

The data must be checked for integrity, to ensure that errors have not arisen during any data capture processes. Data are compared to establish relationships, similarities and differences. By now the data should have been completely processed, but to be proper information the processing results must be presented in such a way that it has relevance and meaning. Finally, the information must be produced on a medium that is legible.

In years bygone, on-line systems of any form have been difficult to justify because of the cost of:

- additional hardware needed to sustain speedy response times,
- systems software needed to support individual terminal activity,
- additional design overhead for systems assurance.

With hardware power increasing and their costs reducing rapidly, these objectives are now disappearing.

Indeed, the justification for modern applications must be much easier now, when their benefits include:

- speedier data entry,
- reduced data error rates,
- faster processing cycles,
- quick response to user enquiries.

1.2 Background of Information Systems

Of all the major problems encountered in computing, the most difficult is the management of the systems and their development. Unlike any engineering or architectural drawings, the systems cannot be visibly represented as a model. Any building or machine can be shown as a set of drawings and as a three dimensional model, but the design and the build of the system cannot be seen, nor can it be represented on top of a desk.

In the case of an architectural concept, the designer will draw the plans and will supervise and delegate the tasks to builders to construct in a fashion, as close to perfect logistics as possible.

In modern computing, structured methodologies are used, where dataflow diagrams can be drawn, data can be modelled and at the end of the logical phase, the system can be prototyped and programmed.

This brings forward the problem of managing, delegating, and guiding those who analyse the business requirements and the data on which the information is based, the professionals who proceed with the design based on the requirements and those who program and implement the required system.

In most cases, these activities are under one roof. Mainly, three different professions passing details to each other at the end of each developmental stage; Analysis, Designing and Programming. The Information Technology Manager will need to know what each step of development involves and at every phase what the professional system engineer is doing. As in every other project, tasks need to be based on timescales and the financial implication to remain close to the budgets.

In commercial computing the financial costs for developing a new system are in six figures and in many cases where additional hardware and software are to be acquired, one project can be in the region of millions of pounds. To cope with such enormities of resources and the correct availability of business information, an organisation relies completely on the professional knowledge of its system engineers and those who manage the projects.

The media frequently report failures of systems and frustrations in computers at large. More often within companies, disappointments in systems are such that

the computer department is totally isolated from other business activities. Yet, there are those companies whose total running of their business is based on the smooth running of their computer systems. The profitability and the revenue always ahead of their competitors.

But, it is also true to say that with all modern computing and devices, industry still suffers, or outputs could be improved, if only the computer department could design and operate a system the way the users work and based on the company's requirements.

The systems person is aware of these problems and yet cannot stretch his/her know-how any more than is already done. Imagine the various professionals under one roof, the complexity of designing and constructing systems, of the housekeeping involved, of the running and maintenance of all these sections.

If an organisation has many departments to enable it to function, so does the computer environment. In a superimposed mode, the Information Technology Manager has just as many sections to look after, admittedly on a smaller scale, but just as complex. Humans, machines, finances, stresses, productions, outputs, man-machine relationships, all in one department, just as much as any overall organisation is facing.

The I.T. Manager relies on management skills, systems knowledge and various other business methods in order to give a good service to everybody in the company. The subject covers business computing and its management, the development of new systems, the implementation and their running. The Manager in computing is aware of actual examples and will draw on projects and experience gained in building large and moderate systems based on what the users require, their problems, the solutions and their training in ensuring the success of the new system, or additional information technology modules.

In the first place, the expertise of those involved must cover the last generation of computing (which systems are still operating in many international organisations), its successes and its failures and the running in company environments. This includes the mainframe-based systems, the advent of PCs (Personal Computers) and their impact on networking and distributed processing, expert systems, shells and artificial intelligence.

These, inevitably will be supported by training and experience in Structured Methodologies, a comparative study into methods, the use of the predominant systems architectures and a method for 'Rapid Building' system engineering.

In the U.K. the structured methodology most of the systems people follow is

the Government and Defence companies preferred SSADM (Structured System Analysis and Design Methodology) version 4. Almost entirely, all the western organisations who create new systems use a structured methodology. The analysis of the logical stages, the use of CASE (Computer-aided Software Engineering) tools and the consideration of COTS, (Commercial Off The Shelf) systems, including GOTS (Government Off The Shelf) packages.

Modern systems engineering, concentrates on the training aspect, the psychology of users, motivation and delegating specific to the computer departments, the interviewing techniques in gathering the information on current systems, the cataloguing of the problems and requirements, the appropriate solutions and their incorporation into the design of the required system.

Regarding the newcomers to the commercial computing professions, organisations rely on aspiring young graduates. With all good will they bring with them and with all their ambitions for the yuppie incomes, graduates still need the specialised training in computing and systems applications to business requirements.

It must be said that academia has progressed enormously in computing during the last ten years, but business needs differ from that of university research and studies. Graduates who enter the companies surroundings find that they are unprepared for the demand of creating and using commercial systems in large organisations.

1.3 Computer Background

The early electronic computers of the 1940s had central processing units built up of banks of vacuum tubes, 'the glass bottles', also found in old wireless sets and television receivers. The CPUs (Central Processing Units), needed thousands of these tubes. The systems were cumbersome and unreliable, only hours between failures. There were heavy electrical power demands and the cooling plant was often as large as the computer.

The first computer of this type was ENIAC (Electronic Numerical Integrator and Computer), developed in the USA by J P Eckert and JW Mauchmy. ENIAC completed by 1946, was designed with the purpose of generating artillery firing tables. Built up of 18,000 vacuum tubes; it was immense, requiring a room 60 feet by 25 feet to hold it and weighing more than 30 tons.

In 1948, a transistor was first demonstrated by William Shockley, John Bardeen and Walter Brattain, working in the Bell Telephone Laboratory, in the USA. Transistors could do virtually all the jobs of the then conventional vacuum tube valves, but required much less electrical power, generated very little heat and were much smaller. They were considerably more reliable and made possible the development of computers as effective functional devices in an increasingly wide range of applications.

The computers of the fifties and early sixties, individually used thousands of transistors. The various electronic components, transistors, resistors, capacitors and diodes were mounted on printed circuit cards or boards. Copper was selectively edged from phenolic or fibreglass base to leave electrical connections between holes in which the wires of the components were inserted. A typical five-inch square printed circuit card would contain about a dozen transistors and a hundred or so other components.

Each computer (now second generation) comprised several thousand printed circuit cards. The cards, regarded as modules, were slotted into frames and interconnected by means of back-wiring. A typical large computer would be built up from several dozen specific modules, each of them being used up to several times in each computer.

In the sixties, the semi-conductor makers created a whole new technology, making possible the development of third generation computers. Using a more sophisticated version of transistor fabrication technology, it was possible to manufacture dozens of transistors together on a single small silicon chip. In this way an electronic circuit previously comprising many separate inter-connected components, could be manufactured as a single integrated unit.

By the early seventies, the basic components, transistors, diodes, etc. were assembled in a ten micro-millimetre thick surface layer in a silicon wafer. The components were then connected by metal layer evaporated on to the silicon. Subsequent etching produced a required inter-connection. Several of the integrated circuits could be mounted on a printed circuit card which could carry all the circuitry necessary for a central processing unit and the associated computer elements.

In recent years, integrated circuits were manufactured with a complexity of around one thousand transistors. The first micro-processor, produced by Intel Corporation in 1971, was based on a single quarter of an inch silicon chip which carried the equivalent of 2,250 transistors, all the necessary CPU circuitry for a tiny computer. By 1976, chips of this size using LSI (Large Scale Integration) could carry more than 20,000 components. Looking into the early part of the next millennium, the chip fabrication will allow larger chips to be built using smaller technology.

When a computer CPU is one integrated circuit, or a small number of circuits, the CPU is called a micro-processor. A micro-processor used with other integrated components forms a micro-computer.

The latest introduction of Intel's Pentium range, Motorola's and other manufacturers' equivalent PC-based capacity and speed, together with the personal computers software such as the Microsoft hold users in amazement and difficulty in following the development in computing.

In general, all modern computers and Personal Computers (PCs) have similar architecture features, functional elements equivalent to those of a large mainframe. The PCs may vary in performance according to their storage capacity. However, these are encroaching on many application areas, formerly the exclusive province of the larger computers.

The cost of computer hardware is expected to fall during the late nineties and it is expected that the resident software will be given free as part of the PC. Application software, in a packaged form and helpful in running commercial systems, will be of minimal cost.

Today, PCs are affecting work and leisure alike, increasingly involved in factory and business operations, networking, defence, medicine, education and the domestic environment. They are influencing attitudes to privacy, employment and other social issues.

2: Systems Engineering

2.1 The Diagrammatic Representation Of Systems

The reader must remember that the construction of a system is as complex as a house built in a swamp. It requires careful planning and design. Just as a house must have an architect's plan, so does a system. It must have requirements, system objectives and a blueprint.

In general, it must be well noticed that every system structured is an answer to the users problems and requirements. The solutions will be based on the studies of the current systems, manual and computerised and the problems and requirements catalogue.

The design of the system will be based on how the users work and what suits the overall business environment. Whilst analysing the users needs, the system engineer will proceed with the logical stages, by listening, interviewing and having Walkthroughs and reviews with users and colleagues.

Prior to proceeding into the physical stages, the system engineers and managers involved, will seek approval from the appropriate groups of people. Within the physical stages and during the construction of the system, the system builders will test and make the necessary alterations to the modules being implemented.

The users systems acceptance will include all the necessary documentation and all the training and support required to ensure that the new system, or module is successful.

The illustration of the overall computing environment, (on the following page) can help in unravelling these complexities. The hierarchical diagram represents computing in large organisations. Within IT five major modules are included in a structured mode. Every module is diagrammatically represented, at different levels.

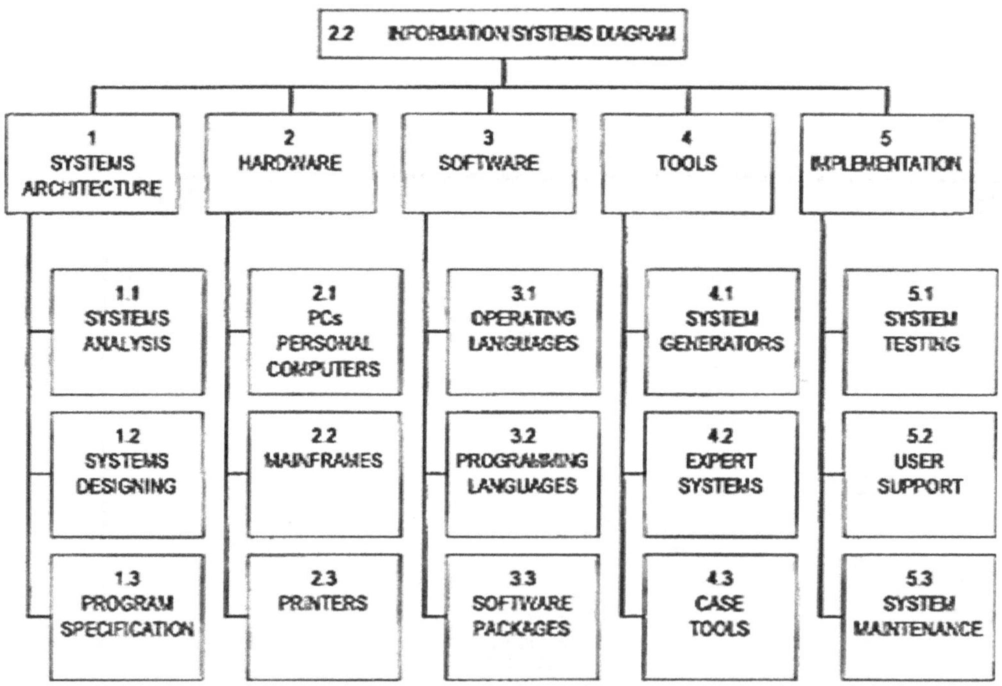

2.3 Systems Architecture

The background of structured analysis and designing as an information engineering methodology, a technique-driven approach, started in 1972. Between 1980 and 1982, Gane and Sarson and Yourdon methodologies were extensively used. In 1983, business started using the information engineering automated version. By 1989, the information engineering development paths underwent further evolution. In 1992, the business re-engineering and object-oriented versions were introduced.

The need to control and manage the ever-increasing amounts of all organisational data being created, particularly computer-generated data, has gained recognition. However, because data management automates the processes used within a company, implementation is not easy. Several data management suppliers have begun requesting that a full systems and business analysis is undertaken prior to system implementation.

This shows not only where existing processes need to be changed but determines exactly what the data management system needs to do within each unique organisation. It, therefore, provides the platform for successful systems architecture and management introduction and avoids the many pitfalls that so many companies have experienced in attempting to develop and install a new management system.

Rapid prototyping is gaining acceptance. Companies are using this method to obtain system design models in weeks rather than months, dramatically reducing lead-times and enabling better decisions and choice of system modules to be made.

A Systems Engineer in his/her approach defines the whole project, modularises it into manageable sections and proceeds in a logical manner according to the clear principles of user involvement.

The tasks are always broken down into a structured. goal-oriented, meaningful units of work. The end result of these structured sets of tasks are applicable to the development path of:

- Information Strategy Planning,
- Business Area Analysis,
- Business Design/Technical Design,
- Construction,
- Transition,
- Production.

The above stages can be used by Analysts, Designers, Project Managers, Directors and Trainers in information technology methods to suit the technical and the user environment.

New techniques have been introduced that dramatically reduce the time taken to solve business and system problems. The result is that it is now possible to take the requirements, analyse and view the results in days or weeks, rather than months. This, of course, makes analysis possible and cost-effective within the design process, rather than a special system task.

Recent years have seen further development in business and systems analysis software. Product releases of leading software houses, have not only made systems architecture easier for everyday system engineers, but faster too. Closer links to CASE (Computer-aided Software Engineering) systems have made analysis simpler, while new interfaces make analysis understandable to users.

The term systems analysis is used in many computer installations in different ways. In fact, for most development projects it means the following:

- fact finding,
- operational analysis,
- business system design.

System analysis for an organisation means that the analyst has more detailed work to do by establishing with the users that there is a justification for developing a new system.

2.4 Designing Systems

The interface between the user and a computer system has always been an important design factor. In interactive computer systems the interface (the dialogue) can influence not only the system's efficiency, but also its acceptability to the user.

The significance of effective dialogue design has its advantages and disadvantages:

- computer initiated dialogues are initially effective for the novice user, but quickly fall into disfavour when the user becomes more familiar with the system,
- equally, 'short-hand' user initiated dialogues can only be used effectively by an experienced user.

Therefore, the first aspect of interface design is to determine who will be using the system and how frequently they will be using it.

It may be necessary to have two sets of dialogues for the same system. One for the trainees and a 'short-hand' version for experienced staff.

The user psychology here is extremely important. The interface between the user and the system must be an extension of the way the user does his/her work. Any dialogue which causes deviation from this, will cause frustration and ultimately dislike for the system.

The second aspect of dialogue design is to ensure that the system is friendly and responsive.

Friendly means that:

- the screen formats are easy to read, data entry areas are clearly identified and error conditions are highlighted,
- the computer displays messages on the screens giving the status of user initiated functions.

Responsive means that the computer should react to a user's request within a given response time, which is normally a low number of seconds.

In summary, the design of the system is significant because:

- it affects the character of the overall systems design,
- it directly affects user acceptability,
- once committed to a design it is expensive to change.

The new technology is introducing techniques which are changing the way organisations work, as opposed to just addressing existing tasks. To successfully implement and apply the systems tools requires extensive education and it is this that is currently presenting the biggest hurdles for companies.

2.5 Security and System Assurance

Computer security has become a challenge dominated by the improvements to the technology of computers. Techniques are being developed to make access to systems harder. In recent years, much work has been done to make the computer recognise individual characteristics, unique to the user, such as a signature, a fingerprint, or even the genetic print of DNA.

With users and companies becoming more dependent upon computer systems, the privacy and reliability of such systems are becoming critical aspects of design. Systems Assurance, a term which is currently popular, of a system embraces the parts of systems design which reduce the risk of both the fraudulent use of the system and lengthy recovery times in the event of a system's failure.

In many companies, one of the few problems that has to be resolved quickly, is:

- privacy, the fraudulent entry of data,
- policing, a system must be more than reporting violation, it must include effective restricted access at varying levels, to different users,
- recording access violations.

Users and companies are becoming more and more dependent upon resilience of computer-based systems. Computer systems can fail for a number of reasons.

Failures due to:

- telecommunications,
- hardware,
- software.

Whichever the cause of the failure, the user will expect that the system can be recovered quickly and that the applications are free from data corruption.

Inconsistencies within applications can result in:

- the user losing confidence in the system,
- lengthy investigation into the cause of failure,
- protected systems down time whilst the data sets are reconstructed from source documentation.

Therefore, one significant aspect of recovery is the time taken to reconstruct application data sets. The most straightforward method of recovering is to duplicate them by backup. The advantage of a backup is that recovery after failure is extremely fast.

In various sensitive applications, frequent auditing is recommended. As a minimum, a daily control report should be produced, reconciling balances on the opening and closing versions of data sets. This report should, also, show in detail the origins of all transactions processed during the reporting period.

With the number of computer applications continuing to grow and with a similar increase in the number of people using them, a new type of back-up service is needed. To meet the demand, a number of companies have introduced guides to their applications, which include catalogues on CD ROM. The catalogue, in fact, serves as a comprehensive system engineering tool.

Details on system applications, specifications and service requirements are made available to all users. If a user is not sure what documents are needed, he/she can start by looking at the full index.

Companies are even making available dedicated internal e-mail messages and Internet pages. The latter being interactive and intelligent. Newsletters are published, which keep the users informed of new product developments, interesting applications and other IT activities.

The widespread use of computers throughout business and the rapid growth of Internet connectivity means that computer security should concern all organisations.

However, it involves more topics than might be supposed. Ranging from the technicalities of protecting networks, teleworking and mobile systems, through the legalities of computer crime and corporate responsibility, to the politics of registering and protecting encryption keys.

Many companies are rightly concerned about security in the teleworking environment. Security for the teleworker starts at ground level; whereas home PC users do not normally activate the password facility on their computer, this is necessary for the teleworker to prevent accidental damage to data by children, family, or visitors.

Extremely sophisticated identification systems now exist that can read retina patterns, fingerprints and infra-red emissions from faces..

One simple measure to prevent unauthorised outsiders dialling into the system is to install dial-back modems. However, this security measure is easy to side-step. Likewise, calling-line identification, which permits the computer to identify the calling number and refuse access if it not recognised, can be bypassed by the experienced people.

Encryption is essential for the transmission of any material passing down the line. A simple method is to employ software which uses the same code at either end to encode and decode data. The next level is to impose a code of the day, using an encryption device card which is synchronised with a similar calculator card within the network.

The most complex form of encryption available is the digital signature. Each user, or teleworker, has a private key linked to a public key made available on an electronic noticeboard. The user encodes the message with the private key and the message can be decoded by anyone holding the allocated public key. However, any message encoded with the public key can be decoded only by the holder of the private key.

2.6 Software Considerations

Developing large systems require a range of software to achieve the overall systems objective. Depending upon the application and hardware types, this range of software at best could be totally packaged, or at worst may need to be completely written specially for the system.

Software in a project is like a jigsaw puzzle. Each piece fulfils a role and each piece must integrate with other pieces to make the complete system.

The basic types of software used are:

- applications software,
- conversational software,
- database management software,
- system development software,
- network software,
- system support software.

Applying hardware and software knowledge to system engineering and the development of systems enables System Architects to choose individual applications from a range of developers and bring these together into a single system that best meets the needs of the company and its tasks, transparently, sharing data. It also enables standard software, such as spreadsheets, word-processing, presentation packages and databases, to be linked to engineering software.

The flexibility this gives is far better for users than the traditional closed systems environment that forms the basis of many engineering software packages. However, to take advantage of this environment the system developers must totally restructure their approach to system building, a complex and daunting task.

2.7 Relational Database

There have been considerable advances in data management systems. These are no longer just about storing simple groups of data for the Accounting department. The secured and controlled access to databases include work-flow applications which ensure that information is sent to the appropriate person at the appropriate time. Also,

introduced are the data configuration modules which take individual pieces of engineering information, such as drawings, models, test results, specifications and legal documentation.

The data storage of these applications enable the relationships between these information objects to be defined, manipulated and visualised. In practical terms they enable questions about changing and effect, or which suppliers meet deadlines. Information such as this, based on relational databases, can be answered in a fraction of the time traditional environments permit.

Not every company is large enough, or wants to undertake this complex process, but it may still want data management software. Several companies have launched lower-cost, object-orientated, but extremely powerful data management products that work within the PC and Windows environment.

While Windows has made the systems accessible to all, most of the products recently introduced into the knowledge-based environment, are software packages based on concepts that have been around for atleast ten years, with nothing more than a Windows-style interface. They do not exploit the new method of creating and utilising software and data that Windows and other operating systems offer. Two key elements to this, are the concept of data sharing between applications through 'object' technology and the dynamic linking of software such as packets, can be put together to create a single application suite specifically configured for a particular user.

Relational databases have now been around for some twenty years and have received much praise from system engineers who have seen their own productivity rate increase and systems easier to maintain and extend. Simultaneously, the end users are becoming proactive in deciding the appearance of their systems. They seek far greater control in customising their software.

To this effect, the users realise the simple fact that all computer systems need to store data and the simplest way to do so is to use flat files. The data are basically placed as a series of fields, grouped into records and stored sequentially on some magnetic media, usually tape or disk.

When writing logic to access these data the system engineer needed to understand where on the magnetic media the data were stored. This led to data and logic becoming inextricably linked, making it difficult to alter the system, should either change. Because of the way in which the data were stored, the developer often had to duplicate the storage of information, because different logic requirements needed different formats of data. Routines needed to access, update and delete information were not provided as standard routines and hence similar to access routines were frequently rewritten by various development teams.

Data could not be presented to the end user in an easily understandable format and the tools were very technical and demanded much training and computing expertise.

In answer to these problems, the first databases started to appear in the seventies. These were network and hierarchical types of database. In such systems the schema, or underlying data layout, had to follow strict rules such that it formed a hierarchy or network as the names suggest. The routines to access the data overcame some of the disadvantages of the flat file systems.

Currently, Data Warehousing is the term the technology organisations use to describe and to make sense of corporate data. It encompasses such diverse areas as Parallel Database Systems and Corporate Data Management.

Given the current advances in data acquisition and storage technologies, the problem of how to turn raw data into useful information is becoming ever more significant.

However, system developers using such systems have to understand fully the underlying and potentially complex data layout and navigate around the data structures very carefully to access the correct data.

The birth and growth of the newest type of database, the Relational Database Management System (RDBMS) changed the traditional way of storing data. The underlying data layout does not have to be contorted into any networks or hierarchies. Instead, the data mirror real life. Data are held in a series of tables, or data matrices and can contain any interrelationships which are required by the users. In short, relational databases give all the advantages of earlier database types, whilst remaining simple to use and design.

Another benefit of an RDBMS is that, instead of proprietary query languages, which are tied to one supplier's database, there is an industry standard query language called Structured Query Language (SQL - sometimes pronounced sequel), which is used by the majority of relational databases. Also, a 4th Generation Language (4GL) environment is normally wrapped around the database to provide such facilities as end user report-writers and screen-painters for rapid screen development.

The RDBMS is, basically, a number of spreadsheets, or tables, related to each other by fields, or keys in each table. An in-house system, or package based on the RDBMS, will contain many standard screens and reports, but also gives the user the added advantage of accessing the database directly with the SQL.

One advantage of an RDBMS is the ease with which extra data requirements can be accommodated. Any reports, or screens, that had previously been written would be unaffected by any additions. There is generally no limit to the number of tables, the number of columns in the tables and the number of records. A distinct advantage of an RDBMS is that totally ad-hoc queries can be made quickly on any data.

Of course, some end users may not wish to understand the logical structure of the RDBMS. However, many users are computer literate and may wish to make use of the powerful facilities of the SQL and other tools available within the RDBMS. Some users may even wish to have their own particular 'views' of the database.

'User views' may offer more frequent access and user friendliness, but they still give complete control over which data a user accesses, right down to the field level. When a user view is created via the SQL, the user's sign-on identity will be included in the SQL. Additionally, sophisticated packages use the power of the database to create very powerful security features.

Many systems engineers will have experienced the situation of being forced to change a system application because the company's computer hardware changed. This is not so with the modern RDBMS. An RDBMS will run on a number of platforms. The system application will look identical on different hardware, from mainframes to PCs, hence protecting the organisation's investment in software and user/staff training.

Many relational databases are supplied with a data dictionary as a standard facility. These dictionaries hold details about the database and any application held therein. These data dictionaries encompass such areas as design specifications, program logic and data structures. They even extend this facility to allow users to define their own specifications and validations.

As the data dictionary contains so much information, it is a natural progression for a system application to be generated automatically. Already some systems allow the system engineer to specify requirements in a detailed, structured fashion and then speedily generate the application.

It is expected, imminently, that these data dictionaries to be front-ended to the users, for them to generate and change their applications, without any technical, or data processing skills.

2.8 Distributed Systems Processing

Shortly after the personal computer was introduced, businesses became enamoured with the idea of connecting groups of PCs together to share information and other resources.

The Windows 95, NT and their successors enable this and the integration of existing mainframe applications with PC users. With the right connectivity and the Client Server technology, the PC users will begin to see a major improvement in multi-tasking and in automating applications and PC functions.

Over the last few years Client Server technology has become a well used phrase in the Information Technology industry. Client Server extends the server functions with on a LAN (Local Area Network), such as data and printer sharing. It enables the workstation (the user) to perform tasks in a co-operative way with the server. This makes the most of the strengths of both, user and server.

The user can have a very easy to use Graphical User Interface (GUI), exploiting the power of the PC to display information and provide some localised processing. Meanwhile departmental and corporate information can be held on and shared by one or more servers of varying sizes.

The sheer computing power which is now available on a single user's desktop has led to demand for ever-increasing degrees of sophistication for the user environment.

A modern user demands applications supporting:

- windows,
- icons,
- mice,
- pull-down menus,
- inter-applications enquiries,
- inter-person communications,
- database access,
- on-line help system.

Ever since computers were able to store data in large quantities, the software people thought of processing methods and ways of working in parallel modes. The idea, originally, came across to programmers at the time when transistors started to make their impact on the increased memory available on the larger mainframes.

Although the memory was there, parallel processing came to its infancy with the advent of distributed processing. In the mid-sixties, different types of work could be stored and processed on a number of different medium-sized computers. One such distributed processor would be dealing with sales and the other with manufacturing and both would be sharing information from one common database. In a real-time application, the same medium-sized computer would be updating the files independently.

Machines such as the DEC's VAX systems, Gould's SCI-CLONE/32 and Sequent Balance 8000 SPP systems and others were able to support, on an average, ten visual display terminals and a dedicated local printer. Each distributed processor was capable of tackling its own system and simultaneously, in a parallel mode (by being networked), it passed the results and the processed data to another distributed processor, or to a number of mainframes.

Universities followed the commercial lead with ambitions that led them to today's impact of smaller processors and more capacity. The industrial financial backing and support enabled the academic sector to move into a new era, thus, once more taking the lead in computer processing. This lead would have not be possible, had it not been for the new programming languages emerging from the university researchers.

Capacity wise, industry was still restricted. The performance in all the technological devices, until very recently, was thought of being inferior, in comparison to the know-how available. Parallel processing was not possible, because the chip with high capacity and the right language to program it, just did not exist. Many manufacturers and many academics collaborated to reach such an ideal. Inmos was one such environment where it was hoped that they achieved both - the superchip and the language to go with it. Human nature as it is, did not allow for further delays. The researchers not only worked on the idea of superchips, but also on networking these chips.

At the moment, parallel processing is being promoted by many computer manufacturers as an economic solution to the problem of long run-times inherent in many complex applications. Many computer systems may be configured as a collection of loosely, or tightly coupled processors, yet most do not support the concept of true parallel processing. It is, therefore, important to distinguish between multi-processing, or resilient computing (as in Cray systems) and parallel processing.

A multi-processing system utilises several processors connected together by some form of network, common bus structure, shared memory system, or a combination of these. At any instant in time, different progress may be running concurrently on different processors.

There are many advantages to a multi-processor approach. Expensive peripherals, such as disc drives may be shared between all processors; some systems allow simple plug-in of processor boards, rather than complete chassis assemblies minimising floor space consumed; more users may be supported as processing power increases. The principal advantage is that system throughput may be increased as processors are added, provided that input/output, or memory capacity do not become limiting factors.

In the ideal case, if a user application takes ten hours to run on a single processor, it could be made to run in one hour on a ten-processor system. Obviously, explicit parallelisation of any kind means that the programmer must grasp the principles of parallel operation on the machine, as well as understanding his/her application. By means of parallel processing tools, a user may have four processors, each responsible for concurrently dealing with respective quarters of the array.

As parallelism stands now, it is still unsatisfactory. Probably, with the emergence of smaller chips - smaller processors, more capacity, more inputs/outputs, more processing speeds, unlimited numbers being networked; true parallel processing, or perhaps concurrency can be achieved.

In the meantime, other innovations and other technological breakthroughs, together, with psychological and biological advances, may yet (collaboratively) solve the stagnation of parallel processing.

It is agreed that these systems point the way to the future of systems developing, providing open, highly sophisticated, but easily configurable, application suites. Using these new architectures and the speed at which they can be developed in these environments, the expertise and the benefits offered to users by these architectures could soon see companies strongly competing. Several major organisations world-wide already have committed themselves to these new architectures in distributed/parallel processing.

Parallel computers have been available for two decades. They offer a potentially much higher performance/cost ratio than conventional sequential computers. Yet, only a small fraction of computers in use are based on parallel technology. The parallel computers in commercial use, are mainly symmetric multi-processors systems in which parallelism is handled by the operating system scheduling independent tasks on different processors.

True parallel programs are rare, even on multi-processor systems. The main reason for this, is the difficulty in designing parallel software which can be architecture independent.

2.9 Personal Computing

Keeping up with computing technology is in itself almost a non-achievable task. The first comment most systems engineers make, is that technology is advancing because users are looking for these advances and not just for technology's sake. While many technologists express scepticism at the new techniques and tools on offer, there are companies in which successful implementation has led to significant business improvements. Consequently, they are continuously looking for the next areas of improvement.

The opportunities offered by Microsoft's Windows environment has not gone unnoticed by software developers. Windows is now standard on PCs and offers users a common interface to applications and resources. With the capabilities of PCs and work-stations becoming closely matched, engineering software developers have started to introduce applications normally associated with work-stations into this environment. Solid and assembly modelling are being introduced onto PC platforms.

Within this approach the terminals are placed into the user department and he/she enters the data. Any errors are immediately brought to the notice of the user, who can quickly respond and make any necessary corrections.

Modelling, as a tool on personal computers, provides a new way of undertaking system design, although is still viewed with scepticism by many system engineers. Yet there is a growing body of evidence that benefits of using such PC tools greatly outweighs the investment costs.

The improved quality of the information that such systems rapidly generate at the earliest stages of the design process enable better decisions to be made and errors reduced. Feeding these into downstream activities gives even greater benefits.

The specially designed computer devices with limited memory and storage facilities include internal modems to dial the Internet via a telephone line. This enables the exchange of e-mail and the use of conventional applications.

Data and documents created by users are stored on the network. This entails savings on the terminal and personal computer. This, some users maintain, may be the end of the use of conventional software such as Windows.

Computer companies such as Apple, Compaq, Phillips and the instigator of it all, the Oracle relational database experts, expect the design of the PC-like

device to last for years without becoming obsolete. Being a 'network computer' every time it is plugged in it will do the technical work for the user and whenever switched on the user will be accessing the latest version of applications.

2.10 Network

A network is a logical method of linking terminals to a computer. Today, because of the decentralised nature of most organisations, systems comprise terminals which are located away from the supporting computer. Most systems are supporting out-plant terminal equipment which is close to the computer as 400 meters and as distant as several hundred or several thousand kilometres.

One interesting aspect of system management that has seen increasing development, is the control of data between suppliers and customers. With many major organisations out-sourcing considerable amounts of systems development, they are recognising that suppliers need to become extensions of their own data management systems, connected via the latest telecommunications links.

Therefore, several companies have developed programs which request suppliers to use the same systems as they are using and which are directly connected to their own networks. This enables these organisations to extend the benefits of their technology throughout their whole systems environment and handle data flow in a dramatically more efficient manner than possible.

While compatible systems are seen as the only practical approach to data communication between supplier and customer, a new standard for transferring data between systems has become available from suppliers.

The supplier/customer communications systems are the first step in a networking revolution likely to occur in industry. The Internet, high-speed telecommunications links and video conferring will enable data to be communicated and discussed at speeds hitherto impossible, dramatically improving business efficiency.

When designing systems for this environment consideration must be given to the way data is transmitted between these out-plant locations.

The basic elements of a telecommunication network are:

- terminals, used in a network environment varying in speed and type, dependent upon the volume of traffic and the uniqueness of the application,
- transmission lines, which can be either simplex, half-duplex, or full duplex. Lines are, also, categorised by their transmission speeds, namely subvoice grade, voice band, or wide band,
- modems, which are required to translate digital signals used by computers and the analogue signals used on telecommunication lines.

Terminals used in a network environment vary in speed and type, dependent upon the volume of traffic and the uniqueness of the application.

The performance (and perhaps cost) of a network design can be improved by:

- sharing processing load, as in distributive processing and front end processing,
- sharing telecommunication facilities, thus taking away the network message handling from the host computer, allowing it to be dedicated to other processing,
- both.

2.11 Intranet

An Intranet is like a miniature Internet designed solely for the use of a company and its employees. It uses the same technology that built the World Wide Web,

but in the privacy of the organisation. A special network protocol called TCP/IP permits anyone on the company's network to access a set of documents which are stored on a dedicated computer called an Intranet Server. Hypertext links allow the user to 'surf' from one document to another.

An Intranet can put all of a company's information - from sales figures to the cafeteria lunch menu on one large, free-form database. Ideally, it captures and shares all the information in an organisation that was previously hoarded, or duplicated.

Intranet technology has all the benefits of the Internet; it is easy to jump from document to document, or to find a piece of information on a particular subject, or to access data quickly from any computer. But it does not have the Internet's disadvantages. Intranet use a network connection to data rather than the Internet's telephone-based connection, so they respond more quickly. The users control the information on an intranet, so they know that it is relevant. Because it exists behind the security screen of the company's computer network, known as the 'firewall', an intranet is as safe from hackers as the network itself.

Installing an intranet is cheap enough to make it easily affordable for small businesses, provided they use a local area network (LAN). In addition to the LAN, a company needs to install TCP/IP and a Web browser. The hardware cost involved is that of buying a dedicated computer to act as the storage point for all the intranet pages.

The key to a successful intranet lies in gaining the co-operation of its users who have to keep the information up-to-date and relevant. That means not only installing a culture of 'information sharing', but also managing the process of updating that information. Maintaining an intranet is more of a management task than a technical one.

Training is another area that requires careful planning, even though the browser software is relatively easy to use. Few companies attempt formal training programmes.

While the first stage of an intranet project can be no more dramatic than inputting a telephone book, an increasing number of firms are using intranet access to organise their structured information. This can be sales trends, or reports and financial information, automatically extracted from a company's database and placed on an intranet page. The software required to build these systems is more complex, because unless it updates automatically, the data quickly becomes useless.

A technology that can make the intranet useful, is likely to be what the industry calls 'push' technology. Push technology has conquered the problem of information overload on the Internet. Instead of going out and gathering information, the user can tell the software what he/she is looking for and it delivers the relevant data, automatically.

Push technology works just as well on intranet. Instead of searching the entire intranet for information, users can set their browser to find it by using a keyword, or other related data.

2.12 Teleworking

Advances in communications induce the IT department to rethink the way their staff conduct their business. New technology effectively deployed, permits the management of information systems to respond to the constant pressure to reduce costs while at the same time continuing to improve service to user departments.

For many organisations, the workplace itself is being transformed. In such an increasingly competitive business environment, a key success factor is the ability to access, collect, process, distribute and act upon information rapidly from anywhere in the world. New ways of working, such as teleworking, have made the workplace and source of information virtually location independent and are revolutionising the speed, cost and flexibility of the workforce.

A few years ago, teleworking meant staying at home occasionally to write a report and keeping in touch by telephone, or fax. Today, inexpensive and reliable communications solutions have transformed teleworking into a fast growing working practice that can bring substantial benefits to the IT department and its employees alike.

For systems development, the benefits include reduced overheads and improved productivity through using the time of key workers more efficiently and flexibly. For systems engineers it can mean greater control over their working environment and less stress. Advances in technology are enabling IT staff to do more for less. They can produce more systems and services of higher quality and with better user focus for less cost and with fewer people.

System engineers have eagerly invented labels for terms such as re-engineering, downsizing and outsourcing. But such jargon describes a genuine revolution in the systems environment. The latest buzzword, teleworking, refers to an equally substantive and growing method of work, namely, the ability (created by modern computing and telecommunications technology) of systems engineers to work when and where they can do so, most efficiently and effectively.

The challenges and the opportunities in both, the nature and location of work are particularly apparent. System engineers have more choice of where, when, how, with whom and for whom to work, than any generation in computing. System engineers can reach from almost any point, in seconds (by telephone, fax, or electronic mail) users and colleagues.

Faced with demanding users and intense competition from software houses, few IT departments can take success, or indeed survival, for granted. Constant renewal, regeneration and re-skilling are required.

Systems teams are re-engineering in the search for improvements in performance which will enable them to leap ahead, rather than merely catch up. They are aiming to reduce dependency upon fixed costs and particular locations, and are de-layering and slimming down in the search for greater efficiency, flexibility and responsiveness. By focusing upon core capabilities and key competencies, they are identifying areas of activity that can be outsourced, contracted out rather than performed by internal teams.

The relationships between people, information and tasks are also being reassessed critically and fundamentally. There are many ways in which IT departments can secure access to the skills they need. Work can be undertaken on a full or part-time basis, as a system engineer or contractor, for single or multiple projects, on a temporary or permanent basis. Teleworking represents a new way of working. A telecommunications link is used to secure access to people and information, and/or to interact with others.

The European Commission initiated a wide-ranging programme aimed at examining various aspects of teleworking. One such investigation is the COBRA (Constraints and Opportunities in Business Restructuring - an Analysis) project. A pan-European investigation of business restructuring by such means as delayering and re-engineering and the part played by teleworking.

For all the sophistication of available teleworking hardware, research shows that the telephone is still the most important device. The telephone has changed little in the last few years, atleast in terms of hardware. True, the cordless made an impact, but it still has its limitations. It has no real implications for teleworkers.

Where there have been significant developments is in the way calls are made and received. Many of the changes have been prompted by teleworking, particularly by the need to retain a seamless flow of communication between the home and other colleagues at the office.

While the telephone remains the pivotal teleworking device, it is almost impossible for most home-based workers to imagine life without the fax. With the ability to transmit documents and simple visuals in seconds its benefit is blindingly obvious.

Of course, the fax need not be a machine at all. It can be just a piece of software on a computer. In fact, more and more teleworkers send and receive all fax transmissions via their PCs. They do so with the addition of a modem. This device plugs into the PC to convert the computer's digital information into an analogue signal which can travel down telephone lines. It does the reverse for incoming faxes so that transmissions can be called up on screen instead of on a piece of fax paper.

The fax modem saves a great deal of time. Instead of printing out a document, loading it into the machine and dialling the number, the modem user simply keys in the fax number, clicks on send and gets on with his or her next job. The recipient downloads a 'living' document ready for editing without the need to re-type.

Like all the other hardware, modems are getting smaller, cheaper and faster. Most external models, which plug into the PC and have their own power supply, are no bigger than a pocket size radio.

The internal modem is the size of a credit card and fits into a slot found on most PCs and even laptops. When the internal modem is attached to a suitably equipped mobile phone, it gives the teleworker true mobility.

Many users already have e-mail facilities on their personal computers. Every e-mail user is given a personal address by the Internet access service, or work organisation and they send and receive messages using their computer and modem. Software makes it easy to do this. To send, simply key in a message, select an address and click on the appropriate icon. To call up a message just click on 'read' and everyone is displayed instantly.

E-mail is catching on fast because it is quicker and less cumbersome than the fax and cheaper. Messages are sent by the organisations to which the users belong so every e-mail (even one to an address on the other side of the world) is a local call.

The best way for the PC-using teleworker to be kept within the fold of his/her organisation is to be networked. Most companies already network the computers in their office so that every worker is hooked up to one printer and has shared access to information held on the master computer or server. It does not take much to expand this local area network (LAN) to a wide area network (WAN) so that remote workers have the same access.

The foundations of teleworking have already been laid, so it looks as if future changes will be incremental rather than revolutionary. The biggest development may well be a new kind of telephone line called ISDN (Integrated Services Digital Network). Because it is digital, ISDN allows huge amounts of data to flow between callers. It means that graphics and video (data-heavy for normal telephone lines to handle) can be transferred between teleworkers.

The applications are boundless. A home-based system engineer could remedy a system fault in another country. System architects could work on computer-aided tools together while hundreds of miles apart.

3: Object Oriented Methodology

3.1 Object Oriented System Development

Object-based technology is emerging as a development method that can lead to convergence between business processes and Information Technology systems, with some substantial benefits. An object in business or system terms has inputs, processes and outputs. Breaking complex business processes into identifiable, discrete objects is the first stage of business re-engineering, or process re-design.

Creating a matching object on the computer system (some call it 'fabrication') then linking them together (assembly) means that the system process should then mirror the business process. Subsequently, changes and improvements to a business process should be able to be matched quickly by an update to the corresponding system object.

Where common objects are used many times, this can lead to substantial savings of time and cost. Common objects are now becoming commercially available, to be incorporated into applications, rather like clipart and drawings are available for documents.

The idea of designing a system the data-driven way is probably best served by the Object Oriented Methodology (OOM). As a method for system development OOM allows the delivery of solutions to users' problems and requirements as close as possible to the real way the commercial world works. It assists the system engineers to represent and closely match the business functions.

It is claimed that OOM shortens the development lifecycle and that the system developed offers longer term benefits, less post-implementational costs, flexibility in building and reusability of the models created.

It is true to say that the terminology of OOM differs from that of the established methodologies, such as SSADM. It can be demonstrated though, that an object model can be considered as an entity model. Probably the most frequently cited model is that of the entity relationship model, where the 'real world' is represented in terms of entities, the relationship between entities and the attributes associated with entities.

Entities represent objects of interest, such as 'employees', 'department' and 'project'. Relationships represent named associations between entities. A department employs many employees. An employee is assigned to a number of projects. 'Employs' and 'is assigned to' are both relationships in the entity-relationship approach. Attributes are properties of an entity or relationship. 'Name' is an attribute of the entity 'employee'.

Associations is a form of abstraction in which instances of one entity are associated with instances of another entity. Association is implicit in the way relationships on entity models are defined.

The major difference between entities and objects is:

- An entity model gives a useful framework for painting the structured detail of a database system.
- Objects have more ambitious a purpose. An object is designed to encapsulate both, a structured and behavioural aspect.

Therefore, an object model gives a means for designing not only a database structure, but also shows how that database structure is to be used. An object models files and it also models constraints and transactions.

The easiest way to build an object model is to exploit some of the inherent strengths of entity modelling and extend them with some structural and behavioural abstractions.

3.2 Object Oriented Lifecycle

A typical lifecycle for the development of object oriented systems modelling consists of six stages, where all steps are fully defined.

These missions (stages) are:

- strategic modelling,
- analysis modelling,
- design modelling,
- implementation modelling,
- construction,
- delivery.

Each mission (stage) may be met by the introduction of new processes to meet objectives, or developing systems to support and supplement existing business processes. This type of strategic modelling maps directly to the domain decomposition used in analysis and design and is known as Business Re-engineering

3.3 Analysis And Design Modelling

The typical analysis and design for object orientation involves a number of stages:

- domain decomposition,
- static modelling,
- dynamic modelling.

In the domain decomposition, the identification of layers is a method of decomposing the problem domain. For example, a system representing a company may have layers for:

- marketing,
- sales,
- accounts,
- production.

The diagram on the next page represents the problem domain, including its constituents parts of Processing Hospital Patient:

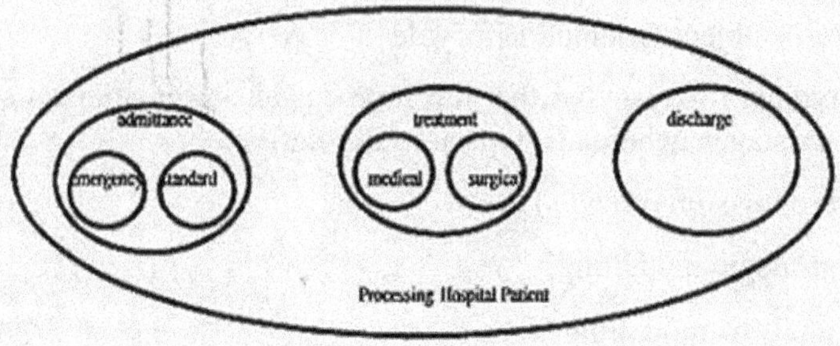

Static and dynamic models can now be created for the domain (or domains) of interest as defined by a domain diagram. Static object models of a sub-domain will generally be adequate to support all the business objects of interest with the particular domain.

Dynamic models will be unique at the higher level, but reusable events/objects may occur within the lower level system dynamic, hence some reusability.

The static model is represented by Entity Type Diagrams. The static modelling keys are: .

- object, represented by a rectangle, 
- message flow, shown as an unidirectional arrow, 
- bi-directional message flow, 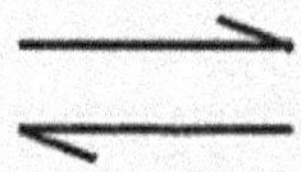

• classification inheritance,

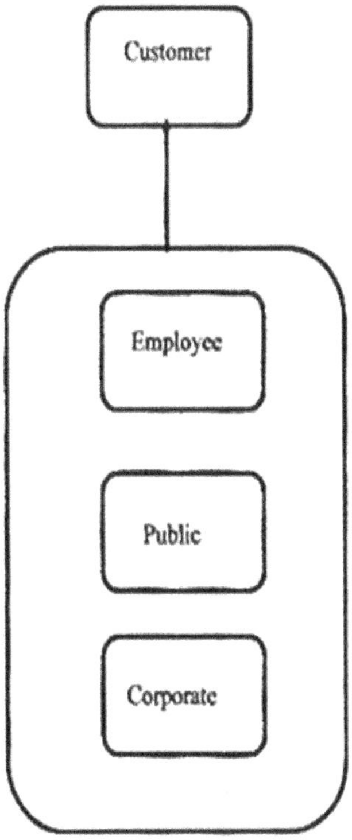

The dynamic aspects of a system can be modelled using another technique. These are known as Event Type Diagrams and as such represent the global finite state machine that gives instance to the inert or static objects as defined in the static model.

The components of the dynamic object model are:

• event:

- event showing that it exists as an instance of stative inheritance:

- event showing decomposition to additional events:

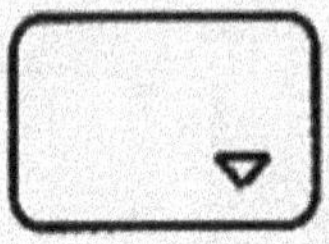

- recursive event:

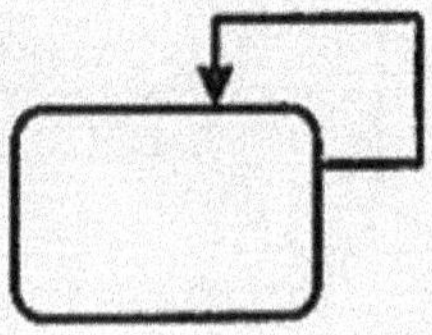

- event sequence:

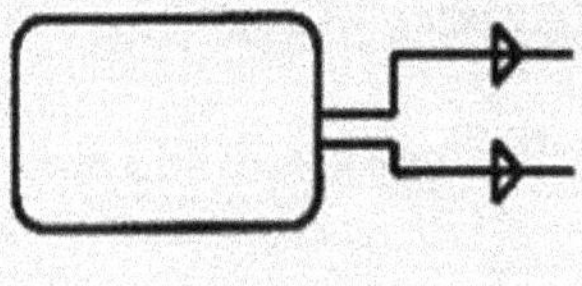

- compulsory and sequence:

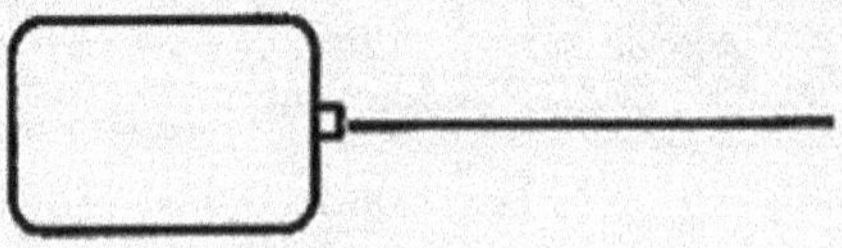

Events give rise to methods that support their existence. These methods are implemented by a series of rules. Instead of imbedding the rules within the body of a particular algorithm, these rules are defined in a set of methods that are attached to the relevant objects.

Rules may represent:

- business policy,
- regulations,
- triggers,
- exceptions,
- declarative descriptions of operations,
- control regimes.

Rules and Assertions:

- rules capture second order information about objects,
- rules can capture system control regimes,
- rules may be converted to assertions and class invariant at design time.

Assertions are:

- pre-conditions,
- post-conditions,
- invariance-conditions.

The deliverables from the analysis and design phase are:

- domain decomposition,
- static modelling (Entity Type Diagrams),
- dynamic modelling (Event Type Diagrams).

These are then taken forward to the implementation modelling phase.

The production of the method using a more formal and rigorous approach comes during the implementation modelling phase and requires all methods to be specified.

The generation of implementation specification methods must be performed in two directions. From the major events downwards through the atomic events and from the objects and sub-atomic events, so that the objects are mapped to the events and adhere to encapsulation.

3.4 Construction And Reuse

There are many different ways in which to build object oriented systems. These approaches fall into distinct groups. These major groups are formed due to the nature of programming languages and tools available:

- Hand carving, requiring large teams over extended periods of time. The languages that fall into this category are 3GLs and 4GLs. Both of these languages do not support inheritance of any kind, therefore, additional work is required.
- Semi-automated, relies on the use of languages that are fully compliant with the requirements of an object oriented environment in that they support all construct required for semantic modelling. The languages can be enhanced 3GLs and Object Oriented Database Management Systems (OODMS).
- Automated approach, makes use of CASE (Computer-aided Software Engineering) tools. These tool sets enable support for the semantic modelling deliverables of static and dynamic models. This approach, also, generates code, requiring minimal human intervention.

3.5 Rapid Business Modelling

The object oriented technology offers models that are intrinsically richer in their semantic content and therefore smaller and more easily digestible. The benefits of rapid modelling can be capitalised by using these models as a living requirements catalogue. The requirements catalogue becomes a much smaller textual document covering the area of strategic platforms and tools. Thus, the system functionality is described by a model and not text.

The true power of object technology can be seen in a model generated to capture and build the system for the IT and non-IT people. The rapid business modelling approach utilises the strength of the semantic modelling approach as a requirements catalogue is no longer a purely textual document.

Strategic requirements are entered into the requirements catalogue that describe:

- hardware,
- platform,
- operating systems,
- programming languages,
- tool set,
- volumetric,
- top level business area,
- critical business processes.

The in-depth functional requirements of the system are encapsulated within the object model that is now made part of the requirements catalogue. The object model acts as the design and the requirement. The object model is even more important in the rapid lifecycle approach.

An even bigger saving in terms of analysis and design can be made by using relational models that may already exist (based on structured methods). These existing models can be converted to an object oriented model (both static and dynamic) very rapidly that can encapsulate all the richness of the original model. The value of this approach is in maximising the original investment made in developing the model and speed taken to produce it.

If no existing relational structured model, or system exists, this approach must use the standard business modelling techniques to produce the first cut and subsequent refined object model. However, the conversion method is fully described below.

The conversion method is broken down into three main activities:

- identify the major objects,
- perform object identification,
- methods statement.

Each object (entity) shown on the main Entity Type Diagram must be further refined to show a greater level of class detail. However, to stop the model from becoming difficult to navigate, produce an Entity Type Diagram for every entity identified on the main Entity Type Diagram.

The general approach to produce an event model from a relational model is to review the appropriate dataflow diagram to find that dataflows across the boundaries to the processes that are of business interest. The Structured English that describes the processes of interest, will describe these events in much more detail than that shown on the process model (dataflow diagrams) as this model constitutes the full event model to a level of great detail.

The Human Computer Interface (HCI) consisting of screens, forms and letters is also of value to elicit the events occurring in a process, as these interactions points are the triggers for the event having occurred.

3.6 Benefits And Disadvantages

Object oriented technologies promise a number of significant benefits. It will lead to larger scale systems that organise information more effectively and adapt more easily to changing needs.

Possible benefits include:

- Faster production. The speed advantage comes from the reuse of existing objects, all the design work of the existing model of the processes and all the formal procedures that are bypassed by rapid prototyping.
- Higher quality. The increase in quality stems from the fact that programs are assembled out of existing proven components rather than being written from scratch. Also, the modularisation of object orientation reduces the interaction among components of a program, making it easier to verify functionality.
- Easier maintenance. Object oriented technology can reduce maintenance because it produces higher quality systems in the first instance. If errors occur, these can be easily located, because of the natural mapping between the structure of the software and the real world it models. Once located, the errors are generally confined to a small area of the problem, typically an object, so the effect of making a change has little or no effect on the rest of the system.

3.7 Experience-based OOM

Every analysis and design methodology gives directions on how to solve a problem and how to include the user requirements into an effective system and user accepted tool. Almost every method explains how to break up a problem, into two basic components: data structure and processes.

Simply stated, the OOM revolutionises the development of applications for personal computers. 4th generation application development products allow the Analyst to utilise the object oriented analysis and design (OOA/OOD) approach to computer application development.

The details of the OOM are brought to life by such readily available products, facilitating a visual, user friendly extension of OO programming design and implementation concepts. The use of Classes, Subclasses, Inheritance, Encapsulation and Polymorphism are an inherent part of such application development packages.

The OOM approach provides one of the important means with which to meet the pressures on the commercial systems function and to integrate IT with business objectives.

OOM concepts have been implemented in:

- programming languages,
- analysis and design methods,
- database management systems,
- operating systems,
- application development environments.

The basic conceptual elements of the object model are simple. Everything is treated as an object. Objects communicate by passing messages. A number of advantages accrue from the OOM approach with respect to software programming and systems development, in general.

A user and an Analyst can have a meaningful discussion on a given object, even though each will have a different view of the object. The user will be concerned with what it does, the Analyst with how it does it. This is in contrast to the traditional methods where the user's problems and requirements, their solutions and their incorporation in the design, involves distinct representation at each stage. Such that users and Analysts speak different languages in respect to the same problem.

Relating to the above, the OOM offers a set of clear conceptual and technical advantages which may go some significant way towards addressing most of the difficulties faced in developing a required system.

The computer languages (evolutionary) are divided into four generations:

1GL: includes the binary languages, sequences of the bits,

2GL: includes the assemblers,

3GL: high level languages, COBOL, PL/1,

4GL: The self-generating code languages,

5GL: The artificial intelligence, the non-procedural languages.

The OOM enthusiast place the non-procedural languages under 4GL and claim that the OO languages and methodology are the primary representative of 5GL.

The main fact remains, that the use of object oriented applications development is currently increasing and will influence the decisions regarding systems development, implementation strategies and software tool deployment during the remainder of this decade.

4: Structured Systems Analysis And Design

4.1 The Background Of Structured Analysis

As a background to structured methodology, it is worth mentioning that it all started with IBM and the problems this giant of computing was facing with the programming problems. IBM called in psychologist Larry Constantine who, as the story goes, diagnosed that the programmers were projecting their own individual perceptions of how the specifications were written.

Larry Constantine's write-up on a structured method included ideas from his psycho-physiological studies and terms such as afferent and efferent. His suggestions worked for IBM and soon after, others followed with variations. Names such as Gane and Sarson, Yourdon, James Martin and other gurus, who again were followed by BIS Modus, LBMS-LSDM and with CCTA the SSADM and many, many more familiar names.

The differences among the protagonists were not of any consequence. Gane and Sarson used to say that all details could be gather within a diagram and then modularise into smaller sections within boundaries. Yourdon maintained that anything bigger than an A4 paper was too complicated. Now-a-days, everybody is recommending five boxes on an average within a boundary, maximum seven and three the minimum. Any more than seven boxes and the analyst will take into consideration the possibility of decomposing to a lower level.

The point is that, instead of just picking up the keyboard of the dummy terminal and starting to program, everybody in the commercial world is now following a structured method. Whether the systems designed are successful or not, depends on the training and experience the systems engineers bear with them. In a similar way this is what the contents of this book are trying to assimilate.

4.2 The Need For Structured Analysis And Design

Systems Analysis consists of an evolving set of tools and techniques which have grown out of the success of structured designing. The underlying concept is the building of a logical model, a non-physical system, using a diagrammatic representation which enables the users and analysts to get a clear and common understanding of the required system. How its parts fit together and how it answers to the users' needs.

Since Computer-aided Software Engineering (CASE) tools are used to build a logical model, structured methodology involves building a system by successive refinement by:

- producing an overall system dataflow diagram (DFD),
- developing detailed dataflows,
- defining the detail of data structure and process logic,

The whole of the analysis and designing of the system is done by:

- analysing top-down,

- designing top-down,
- developing top-down,
- testing top-down.

It is recognised that good development involves iteration and an Analyst has to be prepared to refine the logical model and the physical design in the light of information resulting from the use of an early version of that model, or design. This may involve some reverse engineering of the processes of an earlier physical system, or an earlier version of the analysis exercise.

In many ways, systems analysis and designing is the toughest part of the development of an information technology system. The problems encountered by an Analyst in a company environment will include the:

- technical difficulty of the work,
- demand of knowledge of current technology,
- political difficulties that arise,
- several conflicting interest user groups,
- communication difficulties among people of different backgrounds,
- different views, requirements and priorities.

It is the compounding of these difficulties that makes systems analysis so demanding. The fact that the Analyst becomes the middleman between user groups and has the intuitive approach for the users' problems and their solutions. The Analyst must bring forward what is currently possible in an onrushing technology and what is optimum for the business run by people. Making the match in a way which is acceptable to all.

Even with the best CASE tool, no methodology will enable the Analyst to know what is in a user's mind and has no way of showing a tangible model of the system, apart from the diagrams of the logical phases and their short descriptions. On the other hand, it is hard for the users to imagine what the new system is going to do for them, until it is actually up and running, by which time it may be too late to perform any costly post-implementational repairs and additions.

To begin with, in order to ease the communication with the users, an Analyst can use the tools of structured systems analysis to prepare a functional specification which:

- is comprehended and agreed by the users,
- sets out the logical requirements of the system without dictating a physical implementation,
- expresses preferences and trade-offs.

The building of a logical model, which clearly communicates to users what the systems will and will not do, is crucially important. The users cannot afford to wait until the system is operational, before they see what they get. The analysing and designing of the logical phases are, therefore, of paramount importance in telling the users what to expect.

4.3 Tools for Analysis

At a general level, it can be said that just like an existing system, the new system will represent (for example) the processing of orders from customers, the orders will be checked against a file of products available, check on a file holding a customer's details and then dispatch the goods with an invoice.

This can be shown in a logical DFD:

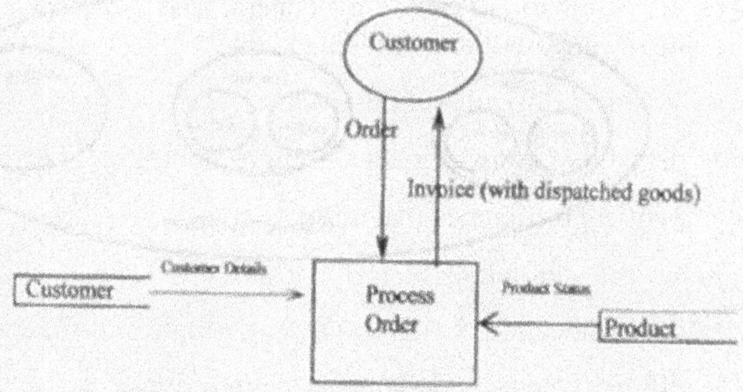

In this DFD four symbols were used:

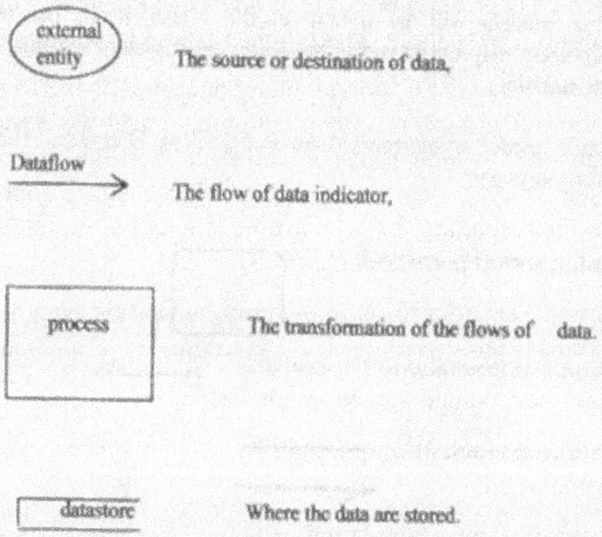

The symbols above and the concepts they represent, are at a logical level:

An external entity may represent a client/customer, or another entity/department from within an organisation.

- A flow of data may physically be contained in a letter, or an invoice; anywhere data pass from one entity or process to another.
- A process may physically be a clerk calculating charges, or a combination of manual and automated activities.
- A datastore can be a card file, a filing cabinet, or a file on a tape or disk.

Using the four symbols enables the Analyst to draw a diagram of the system without committing the system as to how it will be implemented.

The example of 'Process Order' can be expanded to show the logical functions within the present system. The checking of incoming orders can be shown. Once the orders have been validated, a supplier can be found who is willing to give discounts on large orders.

The DFD that follows shows the checking of each order and in return the assembling of bulk orders to the supplier, to benefit from a discount. In this DFD a boundary has been introduced to separate the external entities from the activities relating to the 'handling of orders'. In a way the boundary signifies the modularisation of the processes in the functions relating to 'verifying and assembling of orders' (within the 'handling'), the data flowing to and from various 'boxes' and the storing of the data in the datastores.

The example shown, is of course a summary of a lot of details regarding orders. Normally, the average of five boxes are shown within a boundary and further details are always shown in the exploded, lower level of the DFD. If necessary, each component process box can itself be broken down to a third level of detail.

Within the boundaries of the top level and the subsequent exploded second and third levels, other processes will be introduced. In elaborating the example of 'orders', processes such as 'invoicing', 'accounts receivable', 'assign shipment' etc. will be introduced.

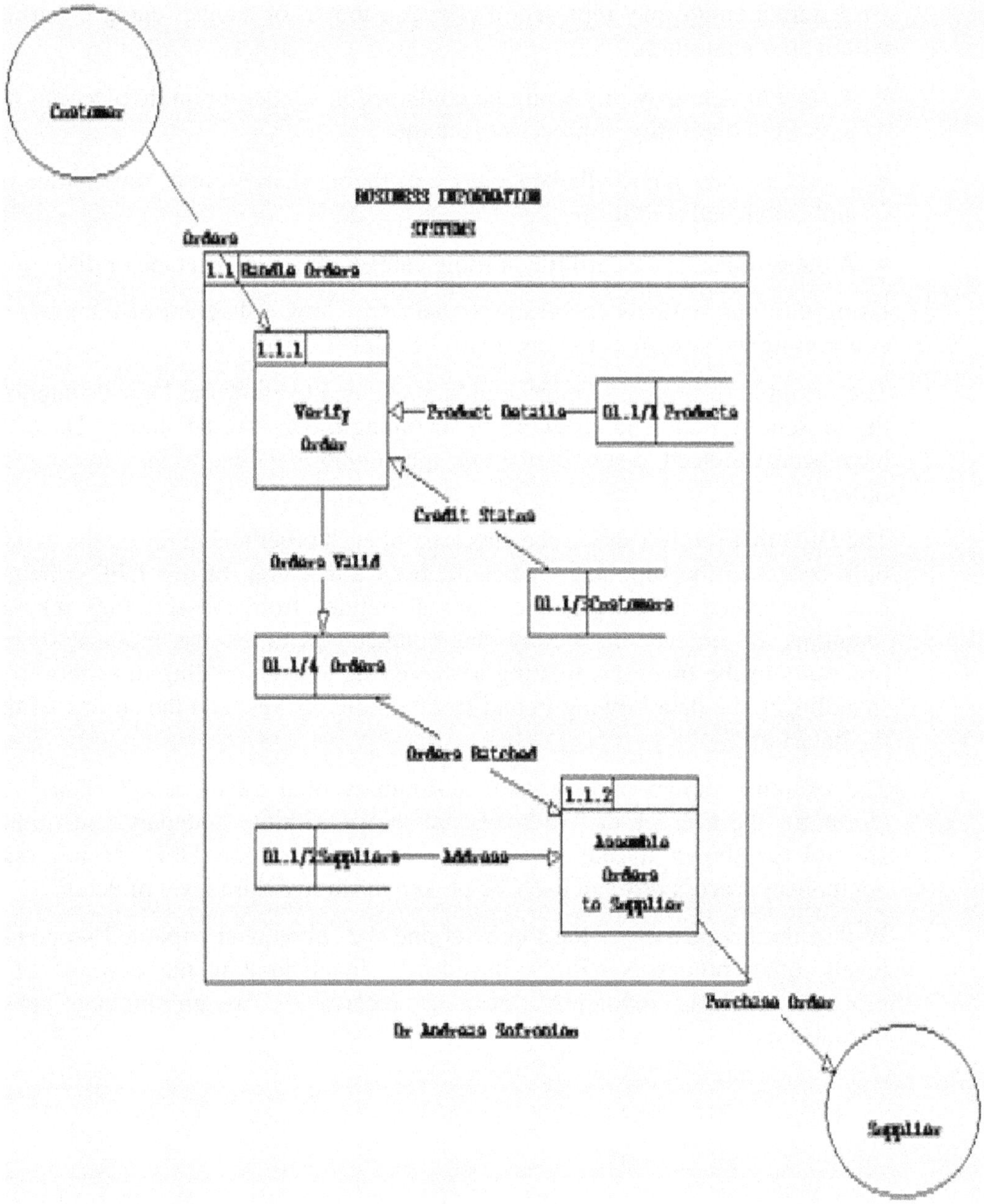
Customer
BUSINESS INFORMATION
SYSTEMS
Orders
1.1 Handle Orders
1.1.1
Verify
Order
Product Details
Products
Credit Status
Orders Valid
Customers
Orders
Orders Batched
1.1.2
Suppliers
Address
Assemble
Orders
to Supplier
Purchase Order
Dr Andreas Sofroniou
Supplier

4.4 Drawing Dataflow Diagrams

The idea of a chart for representing the flow of data through a system is not new. In analysing, as it was previously shown, symbols are needed together with their descriptions.

Herewith each symbol and its conventions are examined in detail:

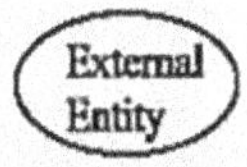

External entities are the logical classes of things, or people which represent a source/recipient of transactions, such as Customers, Employees, Suppliers, Taxpayers, Policy Holders. They may, also, be a source or destination within an organisation; Accounts Department, Warehouse, Factory. Where the system accepts data from another system, or returns data to it, that other system is an external entity.

The External Entity can be identified by a lower-case letter in the upper left-hand corner for reference.

To avoid crossing dataflow lines, the same entity can be drawn more than once on the same diagram; two or more boxes per entity can be identified by an angled line in the bottom right-hand corner, thus:

By designating a thing or a system as an external entity, it is implicitly stated that it is outside the boundary of the system being considered.

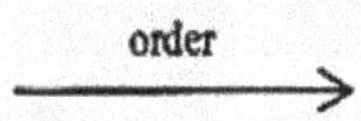

The dataflow is symbolised by an arrow, with an arrowhead showing the direction of the flow. In the top level of a diagram, a double-headed arrow may be used in place of two arrows.

Each dataflow is a 'pipe' which is used for data to be sent. Each 'pipe' has a meaningful description of the contents written alongside it. The description of the dataflow will include the attributes, as early in the design as possible.

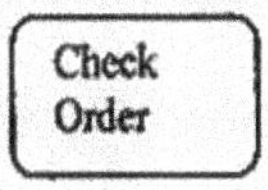

The Analyst needs to describe the function of each process and give each process a unique numerical identifier. Each time the process is exploded so is the number. For instance, the number of the process in the upper-most level is 1, where as the exploded process will have its boxes numbered 1.1, 1.2, 1.3 etc. At the lower level the process numbered 1.1, will now be numbered 1.1.1 and so on and so forth.

The description of the function should be an imperative sentence, ideally consisting of an active verb:

- Verify,
- Assemble,
- Compute,
- Extract.

followed by an object or object clause:

- Extract - monthly sales,
- Enter - customer details.
- Verify - stock availability.

Without a physical commitment, during analysis there are places where data are defined and stored between processes.

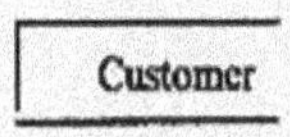

Datastores can be symbolised by a pair of horizontal lines, closed at one end. Each datastore can be identified by the letter 'D' and a number, in a box at the left-hand side.

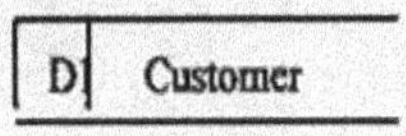

The name should be chosen to be most descriptive to the user.

To avoid complicating a dataflow diagram with crossed lines, the same datastore can be drawn more than once on the same diagram, identifying duplicate datastores by an additional vertical line at the left.

4.5 Explosion Conventions

Each process in the top level DFD can be exploded to become a lower level DFD. Each process at the lower level will need to be related back to the higher level process, by giving the lower level process box an identification number which is a decimal of the high-level process. Thus, box number 2 is decomposed into 2.1, 2.2, 2.3, 2.4, 2.5. Should it be necessary to go to a third level, 2.5 is decomposed into 2.5.1, 2.5.2, 2.5.3, 2.5.4, 2.5.5.

The lower level DFD is drawn within the boundary which represents the higher level process. All dataflows in and out of the higher level process must enter and leave the boundary. Datastores which are shown inside the boundary of the upper level, at the lower level DFD are shown outside the boundary.

Once the DFDs have been drawn and described, the Analyst has to decide whether a function should remain in the level shown, or identify lower level functions which are additions to the ones shown on the higher level processes.

To summarise the diagrammatic representation of an existing, or required system, identify the:

- External Entity. This involves a preliminary system boundary. Place the external entities outside the boundary, with dataflows into and out of the boundary, thus connecting the external entities with the processes inside the boundary.
- Inputs and the outputs (those arrows which represent the dataflows). What one expects in the normal course of any business. As the amount of dataflows increases invent logical groupings of inputs and outputs.
- Processes which represent the functions within the DFD boundary. The Analyst must remember that a process is triggered by a dataflow, the input of data which require a function. Once the process has undergone the transaction, the details are flowed out to be stored.
- Datastore, which can be the representative of a cupboard, a drawer, or a current system. The input of the data into a datastore can be on a temporary, or permanent basis. Whatever goes into a datastore must come out, otherwise the datastore will be the dead end of the information cycle.

4.6 Using The Methodology

As computers get cheaper, many companies are finding that they can gain from operating systems. Additionally, many organisation find the benefit of using structured methodologies for the development of new systems. Structured analysis is useful in investigating the existing systems, be it manual or automated. The structured methods help with the understanding of the problems faced by a business and the obstacles in running a profitable environment.

Structured analysis definitely helps in deciding whether to install a computer and what parts of the systems to develop and interface the automated system with manual systems, clerical procedures other systems and perhaps suppliers' systems - customer companies' systems.

To answer such questions, maybe an initial study will assist in making a decision. Most certainly the answers will be focused on the questions of:

- What is wrong with the current situation?
- What improvements are possible?
- What are the benefits?
- Who will be affected by the new system?

In an organisation of any size, there is usually a stream of requirements from user departments for improvements in information technology services. While some of these requests can be met by improving the current systems, such as better response time, some may still bear further enhancements of the existing operating systems.

Many companies prefer to start from scratch and develop new systems and bring new ideas in running their computer systems. In such cases, the development of new systems is overdone. Many organisations find that the demand for new systems is several times greater than the resources allow.

An initial study (lasting from two days to a couple of weeks), will help to decide the route to be followed. The Analyst should study the requests and meet with the managers to get the background and to begin to assess the costs and benefits of a possible new system.

It is useful to investigate the reasons for wanting to build a new system. It is fair to the analyst to remember that a new system may offer the opportunity to:

- increase revenue,
- avoid costs,
- improve service.

By the end of the initial study, the Analyst should be confident about the costs and the benefits resulting from a proposed system. The outcome of the initial study will be reviewed by the appropriate level of management or steering users group.

Once the go-ahead is authorised, a detailed study can begin. The detailed study builds on facts, current policies, functions and methods of transacting a business. The activities of the detailed study will include:

- who the users of a new system will be,
- the functional areas considered,
- collect views of objectives and preferences.

At this stage the building of a logical model of the current system starts and together with the refined estimates, a statement of possible increased revenue, avoidable costs and improved services will be included in the detailed study.

As a result of this phase of the study, reviews will follow and a decision is usually made to continue the project to the next set of steps.

The definition of alternative should follow. Until the advent of structured methods, the offering of a 'menu' has not been a practical proposition, because the presentation of alternatives to users has been difficult. With structured analysis and designing, the presentation of alternative solutions involves the users in making a business decision and offers the system as an answer to what the user community requires.

The activities involved in the development of alternatives include:

- deriving objectives from the current systems,
- cataloguing of the new requirements,
- developing a logical model of the new system,

Typically, the logical model by this stage consists of the overall DFD and the logical data structure. This logical model will be reviewed in detail with users and any feedback will be used to alter the documentation accordingly and will be incorporated in the design of the phase.

The analyst frequently acts as agent for the users in these phases, just like an architect will supervise the construction of a building, ensuring that the plans are being followed. The Analyst will keep the logical model up-to-date, through design and implementation, especially the DFDs (dataflow diagrams).

4.7 Bringing Structured Analysis To Companies

There are various steps which need to be taken in order to introduce the structured techniques into a systems development organisation, with consideration to the benefits expected, together with the problems that people experienced in using systems.

The main steps involved in implementing a structured methodology in a company, are:

1. Reviewing the method used for projects.

   The amount of work involved in assessing the procedures used in systems development will vary greatly, depending on whether a formal structured methodology has been adopted, or whether the organisation has created its own ground rules.

   Any method based on structured analysis will specify a sequence of activities to be followed in creating a system, the products to be developed at each stage and the management controls to be applied. Almost any established method will, in general, specify the conduct of a feasibility study. Following a feasibility study, a detailed design, followed by coding and testing.

   If such a methodology is already used, check that:

- it does not encourage pre-mature physical design. If so ensure that this is modified to allow for the logical stages to be introduced prior to entering the physical stage.
- The methodology in existence does not subscribe to over-documentation - the exhaustive narrative details. The DFDs and data modelling can easily replace the excessive writing and descriptions.
- The present method allows for top-down development. This point raises a more fundamental issue. That of the 'straight-line-approach'. Many systems engineers

assume that a well-managed development project goes in a 'straight line', from the feasibility study to the analysis, through design into testing and users acceptance. The path of such a project can be completed by using a 'spiral' approach.

The spiral concept reflects the reality of the problems faced in systems development. At each progressing phase a skeleton is built, this is then logicalised and walked through to see how well the logical phases work and then reverse to put more details into the study. Thus, the project control needs to accommodate the delivery of sensible products; dataflow diagrams, data structures and functional analysis, rather than the completion of activities.

2. Establish standards for the use of a CASE (Computer-aided Software Engineering) tool.

   A decision may have to be made to acquire a CASE tool. This is a good support for the Analyst's responsibilities in diagramming the system-to-be. It is very convenient to have a tool for diagrammatic representations for the maintenance and easy updating of diagrams and specifications in general.

   CASE tools are progressing so quickly, the latest versions include the facilities for quick prototyping and transforming the descriptions to structured English and in turn to 4GLs, coding.

3. The tools and techniques of structured systems analysis must be as simple and as realistic as possible. To use any system engineering techniques expertly needs experience; study and practice. While the rules and conventions can be learnt easily, the hardest thing appears to be at the logical level.

   Whatever the difficulty, a DFD showing sequence of events improves the understanding of the users and the analyst's tasks become much easier. In analysis and design users are asked to think about problems at a higher level of abstraction and this can take time and persistence.

   Apart from the fluency with the logical tools, the analysts need to become familiar with the emerging support software. If the ground rules for projects are to change, analysts will have to explain them to the users. Analysts need to be briefed on new methodology and think through its implications for users.

   If structured development is to be used, the Analysts must be thoroughly briefed on the concept and the implementation plan of each project with which they are concerned. The Analyst, most certainly, must be able to criticise a design in the light of the structured methodology principles.

4. As the new structured techniques and approaches improve communication with users and involve them more in setting the direction of the project, they are welcomed by the user community. At the same time, the new ideas represent a change in the rules of developing systems, in a positive way, as the implications and benefits are clearly explained in the process of designing.

   The communication with the users, as each 'structured' project starts, should cover the following points:

- the notation of the DFD,

- the concept of presenting a 'menu' of alternative systems for the users to consider,
- the briefing on the structured method,
- a warning on the participation and involvement required on the part of the users,
- reassurance that the new method for system development does not impose more effort,
- that the project will not generate more paperwork for the users.

In some companies, the users are trained to draw their own DFDs and their own descriptions in structured English. The Analyst ought to encourage this, provided the individual user wants to go ahead with this. This concept, in many organisations, proved very beneficial, in as much as the communication difficulties experienced prior to this method, they just disappeared. The users felt as if they were guiding the project the way it suited them.

Where specific executives are assigned as members of the Users Committee, it is desirable that they should be trained in structure methodology. This will give them the ability to present the business, their point of view and the requirements, and define them to the Analyst. The Executives trained in structured analysis can be more informed critics of the logical models produced by the system engineering area.

With structured training, the users will be able to quantify most of the benefits that result from improved productivity and the better management time and resources.

The benefits from using structured systems analysis, from the system engineering point of view, are even more profound:

- users get a much more vivid idea of the proposed system from logical DFDs, than they do from narratives and excessive descriptions,
- presenting the system in terms of logical DFD reduces the misunderstandings and issues,
- the interfaces between the new system and existing systems are shown clearly by the DFD and the data model,
- the use of logical models eliminates duplications,

The benefits, of course, are not free from potential problems. The problems may be partly due to the change in working procedures and partly the result of the discipline imposed by the logical phases. This type of problem can easily be reduced by:

- introducing training to the users and the analysts as early in the project as possible,
- the effort and degree of detail required, especially in building the data model is often resisted. The consolation here is that, if the data are right in the first attempt, then less effort will be needed in the latter stages of development,
- where structured English are introduced, programmers feel uneasy and often complaint that all fun is taken out of programming and that they become mere coders. The uneasiness goes away when the programmers see that structured

systems give them more work to do, by bringing forward their responsibilities, during the designing stage.

- introducing structured techniques for analysis, design and development, starting at any point in a project.

4.8 The Rapid Building Method

A quick method for building systems, using structured design techniques make for better systems, at lower costs, by providing techniques for detecting and correcting errors as early and as cheaply as possible.

Although quicker, it still means going through the structured analysis, designing, top-down development, structured coding and having structured Walkthroughs. What it means, is that the system engineer tries to cut down the unproductive use of professional time by matching what is possible with what is worth doing.

To manage such steps requires a lot of experience in the whole system development lifecycle and at each step the following thoughts ought to be raised:

- The system being built is of a technically excellent status, but is this what the users want?
- The users were given what they asked, but could the Analyst have done so much more for them?

In approaching the quick way of developing a system the analyst needs good

probing techniques. He or she must find out the factors which stand in the way of achieving the objectives. The factors which would be impacted by better, faster, richer information.

It is a fact, that unlike other engineering projects, system engineering cannot produce a model. In complex construction projects, a scale model is built and everybody concerned can get a vivid idea of what the final building will look and how their interests will be served.

In information technology this can be done by diagrammatic representation, demonstration of dataflow diagrams and screen prototypes.

'Boxes' as symbols are used as the tools of structured analysis in a DFD (Dataflow Diagram) form, where they fit together as a logical model of a system, at any level of detail.

The symbols involved are:

- External Entity (outside the boundary),
- Dataflow,
- Process (Each process within the boundary can be exploded),
- Datastore.

The quick building method relies heavily on the composition of Structured English, which in turn depends on the:

- functional decomposition,
- lowest level - decomposed DFD,
- entity diagram,
- descriptions.

The details extracted from all four above will 'sieve' into Structured English. These in turn, have their own conditions and actions:

IF condition - 1

THEN action - A

ELSE (not condition - 1)

action - B.

In nested 'Ifs', using 'AND-IF', the following example may help:

IF you need a holiday

AND-IF you can afford it

AND-IF you have somewhere to go

THEN take a holiday

ELSE (you have nowhere to go)

As a rule of thumb, in writing Structured English please do not nest more than three levels.

The role of the Analyst in all this is of great importance. A well trained, ethical individual with about five years experience will be able to:

- help in devising the system versions and speak for the users' interests,
- explain the top-down development concept to the user community,
- ensure management support for timely systems development,
- exert pressure for frequent, full integration of sub-systems,
- ensure that the sub-system is developed top-down,
- act as the users' representative in accepting each version.

Based on the procedures standards defined in the next chapter, the Analyst will carry out an analysis of the present systems operations and identify the problems. This exercise will include the:

- computer system,
- manual system
- combination of both.

This stage will be followed by the specification of the required system where the requirements are consolidated and the chosen option is defined in detail. In parallel to this, the required data structure is created.

4.9 Structured English

Sometimes known as 'pseudocode' and 'tight (or strict) English' this pre-programming tool bridges the gap between the logical and physical stages. Together with the processes, functional decomposition and the data structures, it serves as the 'sieve' into programming, especially if a 4th generation language (4GL) is to be used for constructing the system.

By following the structured English route, the programmers are given the opportunity to review the work, prior to accepting the design of the system. With the programmers' contribution and critique, the system stands a better chance by making any necessary alterations, before the actual implementation. Thus, less post-implementational maintenance and costly repairs.

In constructing the modules, programs can be made up out of suitable combinations of step-by-step instructions; like MOVE or ADD, binary decisions; IF, THEN, ELSE and loops. The logical processes defined in structured analysis are just that, programs for execution.

These few structures provide the basis for Structured Programming, which gets part of its effectiveness from the simplification and standardisation that comes from using structures, rather than the great variety permitted by a programming language. There are even more benefits, if the specifications can be written using the same approach, structured English.

As a rule, there are three main 'structures' in structured programming:

1. Sequential instructions: This structure covers any instructions which have no repetition, or branching, i.e.

   'multiply hours-worked by pay-rate to get gross-pay,

   dispatch products to customer's ship-to-address,

   add postage and package charges to total on invoice.'

   It is sometimes necessary to include descriptions of terms used, as in the above 'postage and package charges'.

2. Decision instructions: The standard format for a decision is the structure: IF, THEN, ELSE.

   Each action can be a set of sequential instructions, or loop, or another decision. To expand an earlier example:

```
IF        you need a break
  THEN IF    you can afford the break
             THEN  go on a holiday
         ELSE        (you cannot afford going away)
```

decorate the flat

ELSE you do not need the break carry on working.

3. Repetition (loop) instructions: This structure applies to any situation in which an instruction is repeated until some desired result is obtained.

   For instance, on an invoice with a number of items each listed on a separate line with quantity and unit price, it could be specified with 'REPEAT', as :

   REPEAT extend-item-line until all lines have been extended.

   The extend-item-line to be described as: Multiply quantity by unit price to get line total.

While the analyst should specify the repetitions as part of the logical function, it is wise to involve the programmer in setting up loops. As the analyst is concerned with the logical processing of each data structure, the programmer is concerned with the physical processing of a stream of structures. In this way, the definition of loops becomes more important.

When the logic is written in English sentences, using the capitalisation and indentation conventions, it is known as Structured English.

In summary, the conventions are:

- the logic of processes expressed as combination of sequential, decision, case and repetition structures,
- keywords IF, THEN, ELSE, REPEAT, UNTIL, should be capitalised and indented to show their hierarchy,
- blocks of instructions to be grouped and given a meaningful name describing their function.

At the beginning of this section, 'pseudocode' and 'tight English' were mentioned. It is only fair to add that these are not the same as 'structured English'. A process defined in structured English is not a computer program. The conventions of structured English, but without the detailed syntax of English and the 'almost-code' notation is known as 'pseudocode'.

To specify a program in pseudocode, a programmer needs to be able to handle initialisation and termination, read and write to files, handle end-of-file and specify counters and flags.

In pseudocode, the programmer distinguishes the DO-WHILE loop structure from the REPEAT-UNTIL loop structure. The DO-WHILE loop implies that the termination test is made before the body of the loop is executed. The REPEAT-UNTIL implies that the body of the loop is executed before the test is made.

It is important to note that the pseudocode represents a very detailed program design. Especially in an environment where all data structure and data elements are defined in a data dictionary, the task of translating pseudocode into COBOL, or similar languages, is relatively a simple one.

Where as pseudocoding can be beneficial where COBOL and other similar programming languages are present, the convention of 'tight English' can be poor for its use in programming environment.

The unfamiliar notation of tight English is not ideal for presentation to users. The main difficulty with tight English, is that it is hard to write until the logic of a process is worked out in structured English and understood in detail in terms of the structures; sequence, decision, case, repetition.

This section dealt with structured English and the Analysts together with Programmer as the professionals who are supposed to deal with this activity. The training of both should include structured English, as this will bring both closer in their work for the development of the system, in its full lifecycle; the logical and physical stages

5: Managing Systems Development

5.1 Systems Management

The majority of organisations recognise that the effective use of information is vital to their success. Successful companies build enormous knowledge bases that reside in their corporate files, their information centres and in the brains of their busy executives. This knowledge and experience is the organisation's power base and their competitive edge.

To remain competitive they must be able to find information at the right time, in the right place and in the format that is easy to use..

The management of the information systems must ensure:

- the availability of the information,
- the services that enable this,
- effective use of technology,
- the supply of the skills and time needed,

When the IT department manages the information derived from the systems, effectively, the company in turn gains real value from information. The IT department and its management of information must maintain a leading position in the specialised world of commercial computing.

The IT department will certainly benefit by having a network of specialists providing knowledge, experience and technical skills to suit most types of company demands.

In managing IT professionally, the benefits will include the:

- capturing of the knowledge already in the organisation,
- making this knowledge accessible to those running the company,
- developing the appropriate strategic plans and systems,
- protection of the information supplied by the systems,
- accuracy and recoverability of all data,
- recruitment, training and developing the system engineers.

Instant access to corporate information means better decisions, reduced costs and increased profits. To facilitate such a service, the IT department must work with a wide range of other departments and their staff. Many of the users are looking for help, or advice from the information management area.

This means that the IT staff must be prepared to undertake all sizes of projects, their development and the management of such systems. This entails a project management system which, together with the chosen methodology, will ensure the success of the information services.

5.2 Structured Management Methods

Many users believe that a project must involve computers in some way. However, a much broader view is required when one considers that a project is set up to deliver a business product. In other words, a projects temporary, which only exists to deliver something considered worthwhile to the business.

The resulting product may be for any application (manual or otherwise, clerical, management style, production of goods, engineering in general) , including a computer system. In this case, the environment created and the work done to deliver the product, is a project.

In some cases, projects may not deliver what was expected and costly investment produces few benefits. It is little wonder that things go wrong and projects fail, not because people are ineffective, but because of the sheer complexity of project management.

Some of the problems which may be familiar to management at all levels, are:

- no standard approach to project management,
- lack of communication,
- inadequate planning,
- unclear project objectives,
- uncontrolled change,
- shortage of experienced project managers,
- inadequate team building,
- inefficient staff motivation,
- poor quality standards.

Over the years it has become recognised that there is a common thread running through the management of projects. Much of this is common sense and it is the formulation of this rational thinking and management good practice, into a structure, which gives rise to project methods.

There are many project management methods available, each of which is characterised by the way in which it provides principles, procedures and techniques for the management of projects. Methods utilise existing standard techniques as well as introducing their own unique features.

The number of project failures can be dramatically reduced by the proper application of a structured project management method. A method which provides project management principles and processes to address the problems.

Structured management methods have evolved in private and government sectors since the late seventies. Such a management method is PRINCE (PRoject IN Controlled Environment). It is owned by the CCTA (Central Computer and Telecommunications Agency) and it is offered as a publicly available open product. This means that it is available to anyone and can be used without permission to apply it and without license, or fee of any kind.

A number of project management methods provide a variety of approaches. Traditional project management and other management methods plan and control against a list of activities. Some specially designed for the information systems project environment. Such procedures are applied to many types and sizes of project. This, therefore, gives the advantage of common standards being applied to the management of systems projects.

Using a management method will ensure that a system is built for the users and for the benefit of the business. Quality is of paramount importance to all IT departments. There are a few official national and international standards in information management, so an important feature of the structured management method approach is to create a de facto environment where standards can interrelate as they evolve.

The features of a structured management method can be summarised by a few basic facts:

- it brings together many standard procedures and techniques,
- provides a standard for management which can be applied to all types and sizes of a project,
- can be adapted to suit deferring projects, existing procedures and cultural attitudes,
- a quality approach to project management.

A structured management method provides management with the ability to react swiftly and efficiently to business and strategy changes, to understand what projects and studies are in hand and their interrelationships both, with each other and with the overall strategy. It, also, provides an effective way of controlling costs and resources at the business level.

All management methods demand the participation of senior management in any type of project. From the initial stage to the phase where a completed system is handed over to the user community. A project, also, needs the involvement of quality assurance and other support staff, where all the participants form the steering committee and the support groups.

The committee and all participating follow a project management method, comprising integrated procedures, based on a number of principles and documented in a set of procedural manuals.

The principles are:

- organisation,
- planning,
- controls,
- stages,
- product based approach,
- quality.

The overall objective of the structured management method is to enable the right people to make the right decision at the right time. This formally enforces the involvement and commitment of the business, users and technical interest in a project.

It creates a flexible organisational hierarchy of:

- people representing business and users,
- project manager, responsible to the committee for day to day management,
- project team members,
- people providing support and assuring delivery of quality products.

Plans are the basis of the management of any project. They provide the benchmark of information required for decision making, controlling, communicating and reporting.

Plans at each level address:

- scope,
- products,
- quality,
- risk management,
- timescale,
- resources,
- costs,
- controls.

Project control is carried out at two levels, by:

- formal assessment meetings,
- the project manager at checkpoint meetings.

The objectives of each meeting are defined and guidance is provided on the agenda and procedures. In certain projects, it is recognised that there may be a requirement to control the work of the project in more detail.

Project management methods are concentrating on the things to be produced, rather than the activities required to produce them. These things are called products and the approach ensures that all products are identified and clearly defined before proceeding with activity planning. It is a significant aid to better estimating and planning.

A structured management method, also, provides detailed guidance on the procedures and techniques required to apply the principles.

These procedures and techniques include:

- project initiation,
- product planning techniques,
- business case,

- quality review,
- configuration management,
- change control,
- documentation.

The application of the procedures and techniques is flexible and it is this aspect which makes a management method practical and successful.

5.3 Management Of Projects

A project management system should be utilised on all sizeable projects undertaken. A Project Manager should be appointed, responsible for the agreement and delivery of project products to agreed deadlines throughout the project's lifecycle.

The main project management issues include:

- proper user, staff and management training,
- management commitment,
- budgets,
- user and expert time,
- identify key users,
- schedule time for analysis and design,
- establish metrics,
- small teams.
- testing implementation and handover to users.

The Project Manager should produce a weekly Status Report which will be provided one day prior to a weekly Progress Meeting.

This report will have the following format:

- milestones, summary report of the current and previous status of milestones,
- progress, a narrative of progress,
- Changes to the project baseline, including change notices,
- issues, details reported for current week and the status of those previously reported,
- variances in either time, or effort for any milestone,
- resource usage for the week,
- external factors that may impact upon progress, but not within the control of the project management,
- cost reports of any costs incurred during the week, excluding resource costs and known regular costs,
- objectives and risks for the next period,

- recommendations and issues for discussion.

The weekly meeting should take place between:

- the user Project Manager, or representative,
- the system Project Manager, or representative.

During the project lifecycle, project issues can occur which require analysis, documentation and resolutions. Project issues fall into those that occur during the:

- development and delivery of the system,
- operational life of the system.

Any change to the requirements, or to any document once it has been formally agreed, is subject to the following change control procedures:

- a change control notice will be raised by the user requesting the change,
- an estimate of the impact of the change on the schedule and costing of the project will be prepared by the system Project Manager,
- the change details will be transmitted to the users representative for authorisation,
- if the change is authorised, then the change control notice will be annotated by the member of the project team, who implements the change to indicate that it has been completed. A copy will then be filed with the documentation affected,
- the documentation itself will be updated to reflect the change, with update pages sent to all nominated parties,
- all changes during the project, whether by the user, or system developer will be controlled by the IT project area.

Throughout the life of the project, reviews of critical documents are necessary. The procedures for review of these documents are as follows:

- all critical documents will be reviewed within the project team structure to ensure adherence to the project standards,
- the quality to be randomly selected and reviewed by the Assurance Manager,

In case of controlled documents, this will include a check that the documents have the following details:

- document identification,
- document name,
- name of system Project Manager,
- distribution list,
- current version.

The strategy of the system acceptance will be defined by the user. The subsequent plan and test scripts will be based upon the standards. As part of a quality management system, a senior manager undertakes the auditing of the project. The quality auditor operates outside the design and build team structures.

Before delivery of the system, a training schedule for the users will be agreed. Additionally, prior to any handing over, the system will be tested and should any problems arise, these will be reported and remedied before the users sign off.

5.4 Recruitment And Interviewing In Computing

With the state-of-the-art in commercial computing, the accelerated progress in technology and the demand made on more systems development, the IT management find themselves increasingly occupied in the selection of larger number of specialised staff. Such is the great weight on IT managers, to fulfill new job responsibilities and to replace those who leave for greener pastures.

The vacancies for system engineers are constantly increasing, at such a rate that a new industry has developed. Additional to the traditional recruitment, the demand for the supply of contractors, mainly for systems analysis and programming, has increased in proportions. Agencies for freelancers are now deeply rooted as a service to IT.

The contracting analysts/programmers are in their thousands and agencies in their hundreds. The cost to the organisation for such a service is huge, often enough remuneration paid being higher than what the business directors are paid. Frequently more than the IT manager gets. With such numbers of candidates involved and an unknown expertise at that, the systems managers are faced with the additional responsibility of frequent interviews and uncertainty as to what kind of know-how they will obtain from contractors.

The agencies do not have the knowledge to scrutinise every system engineer on their registers. It is a well known fact that the agents submit the CVs of individuals without even checking on the contractor's experience. The agencies arrange for the interviews between the company's managers and the freelancers over the telephone. For this kind of service the agencies receive between 20% and 40% of the contracting fees. The larger, established contracting agencies have a firm charge of 33% commission.

The IT management and their staff are faced with the overload of interviews. It is an under-estimated task. With all the pressures from within the systems areas, it is a wonder how systems can be developed and become operational within the quoted timescales and costs.

As an example, using the two extremes of the systems engineering professions of Analysts and Programmers. It is of paramount importance to use the right techniques for interviewing systems staff. In hiring systems engineers, it must be remembered that an analyst is the person who keeps in touch with the users and the programmer is the one that builds the system.

The analyst must be an out-going person, a good mixer. A person who can get on with other people, easily collect information and details and must be a good systems representative. The psychological personality type of an extrovert thinker.

On the other extreme, bear in mind that the programmer has to decipher the documents the analyst produces, in order to start constructing the required system. This makes the programmer the psychological personality of an introvert sensation type.

There are many other types of professionals within systems engineering. Designers, database administrators, operators, strategists, and a few more. In interviewing, therefore, the interviewer will be helped enormously if he/she makes a few notes beforehand regarding the type of person needed to fill in the responsibilities within the systems professions.

In interviewing, handing out a short narrative and asking the interviewee to turn it into diagrams and programming coding is not on. The candidate must be relaxed, made to feel wanted, important and then prompted to expand on items relevant to the vacancy.

Systems engineering is such a modern profession, its responsibilities and qualities are hardly known to psychologists psychometrists and professional recruiters. For instance, one cannot rely on aptitude testing alone, as there are no set rules. Experience in systems areas and knowing what is needed is the best guide and basis for the interview.

Within the various scales of recruitment are the newcomers to the professions of systems management. The graduates of IT 'hybrid' management and the MBAs, whose degree material is based on traditional management. Commercial computing demands organisational experience gained within business functions relating to systems.

The young graduates of the first degree education, can be recruited with the proviso that they get trained within the business parameters. It is true that the new universities in their computing sciences subjects cover methodologies, databases and programming, but the question still prevails. The extend of commercial experience embedded in the lecturers and their tutorials and those running the academic departments. Let it be stressed that this statement refers to the business computing and systems development in the commercial world.

Universities have progressed enormously in their research on artificial intelligence and other fields such as parallelism. The outside world still runs systems on mainframes and applications as required by the users. The modern construction of business systems and tools developed, suit the personalities and the abilities of those who use these applications.

Faced with such problems, the IT management pays a lot of attention to interviewing. After all, like any other recruitment, employing a human being (permanent or contractor) is still a big investment of time, costs and other resources.

It must be added, that the interviewing techniques in commercial computing are applied to applicants for vacant positions, as well as the users who ask for new systems, the repairing of an existing one, or the extraction of the data based information.

Interviewing is the most commonly used way of acquiring basic concepts and requirements from the users. It is an activity that needs careful planning and execution. It is crucial to plan an interview to ensure that it is as productive as possible.

Whether interviewing an applicant for a vacancy, or a user for his/her requirements, it is worthwhile bearing the following in mind:

- ensure that the interviewee is prepared for the interview,
- notify the subject to be covered,
- the time and location of the interview,

- probable length of the interview,
- ensure that a room is ready, away from the interviewee's workplace, thus minimising distractions,
- make the interviewee comfortable with the computing terminology and jargon,
- build a rapport, listen and show interest.

As an interviewer, practise the art of relaxation on you and then apply the technique to the candidate. Remember that the users interviewees may offer details on what they think you want to know. A good analyst will steer the discussion to the domain of interest. Whereas a job applicant will be nervous, anxious and feel as if on the receiving end.

5.5 Project Control In Developing Systems

Businesses have problems which they need to solve. They, also, have requirements which altogether enables the smooth running of their environment. To establish the appropriate running of the business organisation, projects need to be set.

An organisation is probably undergoing significant change. Changes span functional boundaries, case conflict and concern and present a major risk to the business and those managers responsible for the development of systems. Many companies are now adopting a project-based approach to managing the change of systems and their development.

Managers of today and of the future, require skills in managing projects. These skills are supplementary to the line management skills. A company needs to enhance business planning and control structures to explicitly link system implementation to business led projects and programmes.

A project in information technology is a temporary situation within the working groups (the system users) and the computing management, with the objective of delivering a product. The resulting product relies on the project progress and how it is approached in its scope to deliver.

For a project to be successful it needs:

- management at all levels,
- team building and staff motivation,
- planning and controls,
- quality standards to follow,
- communication between users and management,
- objectives and scope,
- adequate skills and experienced resources,
- explicit documentation and training.

Unlike existing systems operational management, where one deals with established computer services, project management encounters the unfamiliar, new problems and needs for change.

In managing a project, a list of activities will not be enough. The project must be product-based. A methodology needs to be followed, procedures to be applied. The appropriate procedures, therefore, give the advantage of common standards being applied to the management of all projects, with directional emphasis to meeting the corporate objectives.

Always remembering that a system is built with quality and that the application of the procedures and techniques must be flexible and practical:

- for the users,
- to fulfill a process,
- benefit the business function,

Project management supports the implementation of the business strategies with explicit link to the development plan. This provides management with the ability to react swiftly and efficiently to any changes, to understand the project stages and steps in hand and their relationship with each other. It, also, provides an effective way of controlling costs and resources at all levels.

The appropriate analysis and design methodology will assist the project team members to concentrate on the system components to be produced. It enables the management and the analysts to identify and clearly define all the development phases. It is, also, a significant contributor to quality, better estimating and planning.

This means that a systems manager and his/her team members need to establish project control standards, which will specifically include:

1. purpose,
2. scope,
3. input,
4. planning,
5. progress control.

1. Purpose:

   The purpose of the project control standards is to define the standard to be used within system development for managing the project in terms of project planning and progress control. The objectives of project management being:

- establish clear objectives and scope for a project,
- ensure roles and responsibilities are well defined and understood,
- break work down into schedules and deliverables,
- plan how an individual project will achieve the implementation of the required end product within a progressively refined and agreed schedule and budget.

A project control framework is necessary within which project management skills and techniques are exercised.

2. Scope:

This standard addresses Project Control in a new system development environment, i.e. a multi-team situation with Team Leaders and an overall Project Manager.

It covers the planning of each phase for each team and its members and the progressing of those plans.

3. Input:

The inputs will vary with the size and stage of development:

- Terms of Reference (ToR, for a new project) and Project Initiation Document (PID),
- key documentation from earlier phases (for an existing project)
- procedures manual

4. Planning:

The following steps describe a team leader's project control, carried out at the start of a project, or when rescheduling (as a result of supplying more tasks, or changing estimates).

- Task Identification. A source of information for this will be the overall project plan and the activities listed.
- Estimating. Estimating for project control planning is carried out using the bottom-up approach, starting with the steps involved and building upwards. When all tasks have been identified and estimated, an overall schedule can be drawn, which accounts for resource constraints, deadlines and overheads.
- Scheduling. The basics of scheduling are to take the information from task identification, sizing and resource allocation and to build a schedule which meets the necessary timescales.

5. Progress Control:

The Project Control system and progress meetings are the principal mechanisms for monitoring and controlling the progress of a project.

- Progress Meetings. Aside from the informal contact maintained between a team leader and team members, each person should receive a regular progress meeting, on an one-to-one basis. Also, each team leader should meet with the project manager on a similar basis.
- Team Meetings. A regular weekly meeting of all team members is important, in order to maintain communication and to resolve issues where input is required.
- Outstanding Issues. As projects progress, design issues may emerge which require a solution. At the end of the development, any loose ends not resolved can be passed to the support team for future enhancements to the system.

- Rescheduling. Even the best planned project may have its scope changed by changes in requirements, or late design changes. Changes of this type can cause disruption which outweigh the benefits they provide, so it is important to keep them to a minimum.

5.6 Systems Development Procedures

The system specification procedures form the basis within the conventional business environment for setting out the standards for system development. They describe a step by step approach to developing and implementing computer systems. They define the documents to be produced, the controls to be applied and the tasks to be performed.

The intention is that these procedures be applied flexibly. On the other hand, the phases are designed for sequential development, with the output from one phase being the input to the next, all leading to the eventual implementation of the system. Project plans should be drawn up to suit the particular project and then adhered to.

The procedures define the paths that will be followed in projects set up to develop computer systems. A project is, thus, described in terms of its major divisions (Phases), its Control Points, the Activities that are accomplished in each phase and the Tasks that go to make up those activities.

A project starts with an initiation and ends with a review and user training. The Project Initiation Document (PID) will incite the feasibility study and the terms of reference. The review will include the report to the users and the appropriate steps for the system training and the training manual distributed to all the users involved in the running of the system-to-be.

Otherwise, the project has the following phases:

1. Business Analysis: Users' business Problems and Requirements and the initial top level Dataflow Diagram.
2. Systems Analysis: System Proposal, Functional Decomposition, Dataflow Diagram, Logical Data Structure and Process Descriptions,
3. Design Options: Technical Design Options,
4. Functional Analysis: Process Model, Detailed Dataflow Diagram and Process Descriptions,
5. Data Analysis: Data Model, Entity Life History,
6. Physical Design/Build, System Specification, Program Code.

The system development lifecycle, in outlining the activities to be followed and the tasks to be carried out in a project, provides the framework for planning and defining a project.

The development lifecycle does not ensure that projects will meet a particular level of quality, nor does it ensure that work carried out will be both, efficient and effective. That is a matter of how people perform and it is the goal of project management to make sure that conditions exist for them to be efficient and effective.

The framework of the lifecycle with its different phases, offers some guidance on when project management should be applied. Each phase has a beginning, middle and end.

Project management procedures are ongoing and required to fit in with the dimensions of the workday and reporting cycles.

Project management is a series of activities that are carried out during a project by the leader:

- planning,
- estimating,
- monitoring,
- reporting,
- quality control,
- resource allocation,
- communication.

The performance of any computer department can only be judged by the service given to the system users. This clearly means business change through projects. It involves people and the experience they carry with them. Experience in system building when a company needs it most; when this type of people, the best in the organisation are in short supply and great demand. They are usually, therefore, not available when needed for a critical new project - to develop the long awaited system.

5.7 Systems Specification

The System Specification starts as far back as Systems Analysis and is not completed until programming begins. A standard is required for conducting systems design because a uniform approach is needed across all projects to ensure understanding and consistency.

The standard outputs are required as input to programming activities. The systems specifications, therefore, need to be written in a rigorous and consistent manner to ensure that all user requirements are catered for and all business processing is completely and accurately defined and documented.

The following may be input to system specification:

- current, systems documentation and specifications,
- user requirements documentation and proposals,
- system proposal from system analysis phase,
- process descriptions, dataflow diagrams and layouts from the functional analysis phase,
- minutes of meetings with users.

The System Specification is the phase where the lowest level dataflow diagrams and descriptions from process analysis are pulled together.

5.8 Process Analysis

The aim is to reach a detailed logical design sufficient for all specification work. A standard is required for conducting process analysis because a uniform approach is needed across all projects. It concentrates on processes rather than data. Thorough process analysis encourages understanding of the system and user environment. The outputs from the process analysis are required for the system design processes.

There can be many inputs into process analysis depending on the nature and complexity of the project. The following may be input to process analysis:

- systems documentation and specifications from the current system,
- user requirements and proposals
- decomposition of dataflow diagrams.

The dataflow diagram is a powerful input to design because it identifies the data flows, data stores and processing involved. The technique is top-down; an overview followed by increasingly lower levels of detail.

5.9 System Reviews

The purpose of a review is to define the process for understanding what is needed and as means of checking the quality of work throughout the systems development lifecycle.

The objectives of holding a review of a piece of work are to:

- ensure the work meets its requirements,
- trap errors as early as possible,
- provide a focus on outstanding issues which lie in the pathway to completion of a given task,
- check adherence to standards.

It is clear that in practice it would not be appropriate to subject all outputs to the same level of review and several variants of the review process are required.

The different levels of review allow for the:

- importance of the review material,
- authority of the attendees,
- level at which the review is documented,
- formality with which the review is held.

5.10 Physical Design

Physical design converts the results of process and data design into an implementable computer solution and defines the computer/clerical interface. This is evaluated against the requirements and amended as appropriate.

The scope of the physical design is to cover the technical design of application systems. It concentrates on the design of the system processes, rather than the design of databases.

The following may be input to systems design:

- current systems documentation and specifications,
- user requirements and solutions,
- system proposal from analysis phase,
- process descriptions, dataflow diagrams and layouts from functional analysis phase.

Requirements often change during the design phase and new ones emerge. In addition, it often raises more questions requiring further analysis. Therefore, the final design may only be arrived at through several iterations of logical and physical design.

5.11 Quick Dataflow Diagramming

Dataflow diagrams (DFDs) are used for process analysis, to show the logical:

- system processes, hierarchy and their relationships,
- datastores, the system's data 'at rest',
- data flows, the system's data 'in motion' between two processes, or between a process and a datastore.

To present a complete system description, additional documentation is necessary for each flow, each datastore, and each process.

It is the DFD which structures the analysis process and drawing the DFD helps the Analyst to:

- deal with the information collected during data gathering, in an orderly manner,
- avoid being overwhelmed by detail and losing sight of the overall picture,
- document the proposed system in a convenient format as input to design,
- communicate with users.

In diagramming, the following conventions apply to drawing dataflow diagrams:

- External Entity, usually represented by a circle outside the boundary. This is the source, or destination of data outside the area under study. If the circle has a line across the corner, then the external entity is used elsewhere and has been duplicated for diagramming convenience.
- Data Flow, depicted by an arrow and a description put alongside the arrow. The arrow shows direction of flow. Flows are labelled with a meaningful name describing content of the flow, not the document or report carrying the data.
- Process, usually represented by a rectangle, it can be a manual process or computerised. Processes are labelled with an appropriate and clear-cut name, which should be a verb followed by an object phrase. A process 'box' should be labelled for easy reference. This should reflect the top-down hierarchy. (Process: 1, 1.1, 1.1.1/1.1.2/1.1.3, Process: 2, etc.)

- Datastore, symbolised by an open-ended rectangle. A name for the datastore that is meaningful to users is written inside the symbol. Datastores should be numbered sequentially and prefixed by the letter 'D'.

In drawing a DFD the following must always be considered:

- The highest level picture of the system is called a 'context diagram' and consists of one box representing the system under study.
- External Entities are shown outside the boundary line, along with the flows between the study system and the externals.
- Having agreed a context diagram with the user management, a first level DFD is created containing high level functions.
- The functions on the first level DFD are then exploded by creating another DFD for each particular process. Each further level clarifies the activities within a system and shows an increasing level of detail in the activities themselves and the dataflows that connect them.
- In a new system partitioning should go to the level where each process box corresponds to a specific process. Partitioning is an iterative process. It takes several reviews to get to a perfect diagram.
- With partitioning it is always difficult to know when a sufficient level of detail has been reached.

  The following guidelines may help:

  - More than five flows into a process may indicate that the activity is over complex, although up to seven may be accommodated. Less than three, may indicate insufficient information.
  - The narrative description should not take more than a couple of pages.
  - The process should relate to units of work recognised by the user.
  - Generally, it should be possible to identify a single input that drives the process.
  - Often, there is only one major output.
- DFDs should be kept as simple as possible to avoid confusion. A good rule of thumb is no more than seven processes per page. If there are more than this, it probably means that there are more details than necessary. To be on the safe side, create another level by exploding one process into a lower level DFD.
- Symbols should be duplicated on the diagram to avoid crossing lines. A duplicate should be marked with a line on the left hand side of the symbol.
- Avoid partitioning according to company organisation, as the diagrams show functions not organisations.

5.12 Program Design

Before they are coded, programs need to be designed. There needs to be a structure which shows how and where the processes diagrammed in the DFD and described in the System Specification are to be performed.

Structured English is used to represent the design. This is a simplified form of English, presented in defined manner. Within the structure so formed, normal English is used, although in as succinct a form as possible.

The relevant systems specification proceeds to a program design ready for coding. To enable this, the following inputs are necessary:

- decomposition diagram,
- DFDs at the program or transaction level,
- system specification,
- system flowchart,
- data structure diagram.

A program design which is structured is easier to maintain and understand. The structuring of the design means principally that the design should be driven by the flows of input and output data.

The program designer or programmer should arrange for regular program and code Walkthroughs with another programmer/designer. The walkthrough session should check:

- adherence to programming standards,
- that the code matches the design structure,
- that the code performs the processing defined in the system specification,
- that database accessing is correct.

Program designing and programming in general, requires disciplined management since this needs clearly defined objectives to fulfill the overall project.

Project management must, therefore, ensure that the investment of resources, time and effort are fully justified and fulfilled. This includes program definition and the setting up of efficient structures. Whatever the requirements, experience is of major importance in helping and controlling programming

6: Commercial Systems Packages

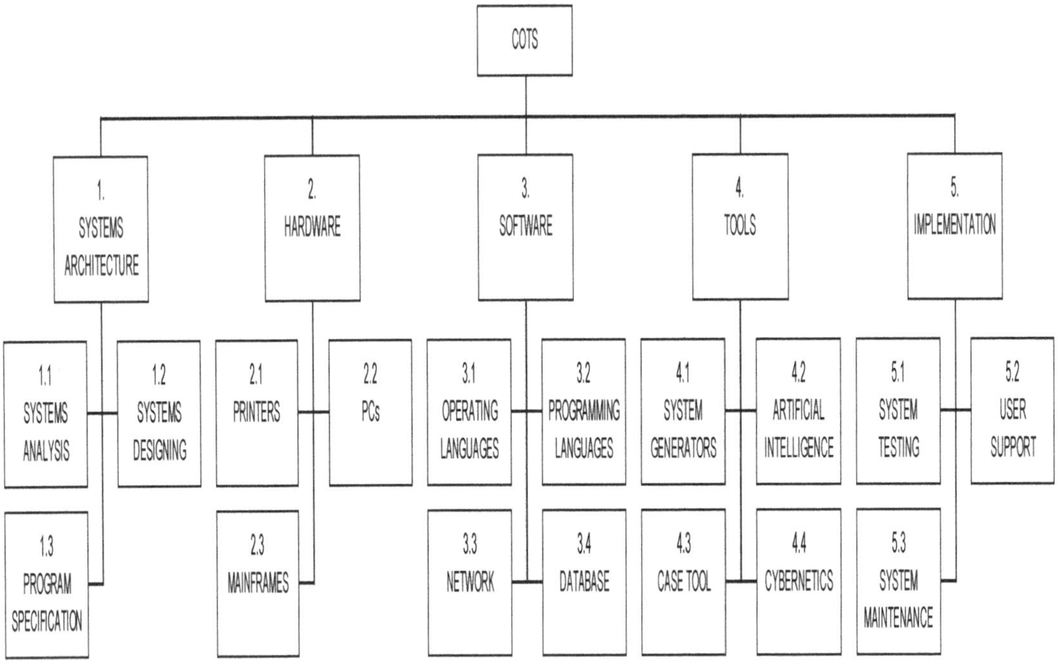

6.1 Packages

Some organisations have always followed the principle of 'build rather than attempt to buy'. Recent studies established that this trend has now started to change. Such studies have shown that the U.S.A. Department of Defense (DoD), the North Atlantic Treaty Organisation (NATO), the U.K. Ministry of Defence (MOD), the Central Computer and Telecommunications Agency (CCTA) and other government departments are seriously optimising the use of (Commercial Off-The-Shelf) COTS packages.

The USA DoD firmly explored the role of COTS software in the domain of large, real time, mission-critical systems. Regarding the networking of their hardware and software environments the DoD encouraged their suppliers to convene and resolve the communicational difficulties.

The NATO are establishing guidelines in the deployment of COTS software. COTS software provides a significant opportunity to NATO to control and lower software development costs, but with reservations regarding continuity of support, inconsistency among packages and integration with NATO specific software.

The UK MOD has not undertaken a firm commitment to the overall issue of COTS. Specific studies in large systems in the three forces have shown that there is a preferred route towards commercial packages. In the case of the Naval Logistics System of the

Upkeep project, having prepared the users requirements, it is hoped that the majority of the modules will be served by commercial packages.

The Central Computer and Telecommunications Agency (CCTA) has already established certain standards, regarding CASE Tools (System Engineer), Structured Methodology (SSADM - Structured System and Design Methodology) and the Project Control method of PRINCE. The guidelines are used by most Government Departments and CCTA expertise is made available in the form of consultative service.

6.2 Commercial Off-the-shelf (COTS)

COTS packages are developed by commercial companies for a variety of

applications and a wide range of users. The user market is increasing, therefore COTS will be cheaper to acquire. A procured package can be flexible and reliable, if based on well defined requirements. The chosen software are maintained by the vendor and can represent the state-of-the-art.

The usage of COTS packages have gained some acceptance in the U.K., as a cost effective approach. The supply and maintenance costs are lower than the bespoke developed systems. Originally COTS software was confined to operating languages and database management systems. Application-based packages, such as office automation and networking are now becoming standard, both in the large organisations and government departments.

By using COTS software, the development costs are lowered. But supplier support, inconsistency among packages and integration with other existing systems are difficult. Criteria for proper selection and management are required.

Some COTS packages are built for specific applications. This restricts portability and any attempt to change any of the facilities will jeopardise the set standards and affect the lower costs.

Therefore, there is a need to set a suite of rules regarding the selection of COTS. These would lead to the development of guidelines to the Project Managers and users at large. COTS products to be selected with the same level of effort as that input into the formal system analysis and designing exercises. Failure to do so, will cost as much, if not more, than the traditional system development.

It is of vital importance to remember that, the larger the system required, the more difficult it will be to choose the right COTS package and less the chances of fulfilling the system requirements. The smaller the amount of logical requirements, the easier it will be to select the appropriate ready-to-use product.

Wherever the requirements are of large proportions, especially where a mainframe-based system is needed, it is advisable to build rather than attempt to buy a packaged system.

6.3 The Integration Of Packages

Great importance is placed on the integration of packages and the re-usability of software. The basic system components will have to be carefully chosen and comply with the Open System Environment (OSE) base standards. As companies adopt new standards, the framework would need to be revised accordingly.

It is the large organisations' experience that COTS products do not always fulfill the requirements. Even if such products meet the set standards they do not always operate in conjunction with each other.

Many data entities (data types) need changing in order to communicate with each other. In addition, different data groups will require different storage, transmission and display strategies.

The COTS market is constantly changing. This creates new products, much faster than the commercial world would be able to acquire systems. Hardware and software become obsolete by the time a system becomes operational.

Although vendors claim standards compliance, in practice many problems have occurred. Conformance evaluation to test and validate standards, is recommended.

When COTS products have been selected, their evolution should be closely monitored. If these products are no longer meeting the state-of-the-art, the framework should allow easy replacement by other COTS products.

To approve any purchases of COTS packages, a company ought to take into consideration the following:

- The environment under which the package is to run,
- The quality and the maturity of the software,
- The standing of its supplier,
- The prospects for its long-term support,
- The adherence to OSE standards,
- Portability to other architectures.

In a bespoke system, security can be integrated as required. With COTS products, this is rather difficult and the system/s can become vulnerable.

The application of COTS software in smaller company systems can often be considered a more cost-effective approach across the whole life-cycle, than the development of new purpose-built software.

There are a number of issues which require investigation in order to facilitate the choice of the most appropriate COTS products. These issues must be considered in detail, in order to develop procurement guidelines, procedures and selection criteria for the use of COTS software.

In many larger companies, there is a preference to procure software rather than to develop software from scratch. The initial procurement costs do not necessarily determine the final savings. In order to achieve economies over a longer period, COTS procurement need to be well managed.

Current practice in international organisations for MIS software, calls for the use of COTS as far as practicable. This is based on the increase in reliability anticipated from software which have been succesfully used elsewhere and, secondly, a decrease in procurement cost compared with the development of a specifically tailored system.

6.4 Experience In COTS

In a recent presentation on COTS, the DoD Naval Undersea Warfare Center, U.S.A., explored the role of COTS software in the domain of large, real time, mission-critical systems.

In the case of networking hardware and software, the DoD encouraged the suppliers to achieve compatibility among themselves. Based on this, it is hoped that the DoD will establish a commonality in the various packages.

A presentation by the USA DoD NUWC, refers to COTS as the umbrella for:

- electronics,
- development Tools,
- graphics,
- network,
- equipment.

The DoD describes COTS as being items that can be purchased through commercial, retail, or wholesale distribution for use as is. The procurement of such items can be extended to cover government off-the-shelf and modified COTS products.

The main question as to whether COTS software is the answer, remains as an issue for the DoD. There is no doubt that there are disadvantages in using COTS. The major ones being:

- No control over future product availability,
- Rights-in-data issues must be confronted,
- COTS products not tailored to specific applications.

For COTS to be successful, they must be useful packages at reasonable costs and compatible with the rest of the system environment.

Specific performance requirements cannot be met. Where performance is critical, modelling and simulation is needed to confirm that a COTS product is capable of meeting the requirements.

The size of COTS software for real-time is small. The shelf size for re-usable real-time operational software is even smaller. COTS software may be unavailable for demanding military applications.

There is a confusion between COTS re-use and Open Systems. Users think that because they have bought something commercial, they have achieved re-usability or an open system. Open systems facilitate the use of COTS, but the presence of COTS does not constitute an open system.

It is, also, stipulated that COTS is not a synonym for 'reusable'. COTS does not imply re-usability. The DoD 'Reuse Vision' is to guide the software community to a process-driven, domain-specific and architecture centred environment.

The fundamental underlying principles are on the reuse in specific domains, reuse oriented architectures and utilisation of an interconnected network of reuse libraries.

The DoD's experience in COTS software reuse includes the COTS relational database, minor COTS mathematics functions and COTS development tools to produce a large real-time system.

Some COTS lessons learned include COTS licensing agreements and to avoid modifying such packages. The DoD underlines the allocation of additional time and resource for tool modification and for resolution of COTS interface/performance problems.

With recent events and trends, the DoD is satisfied that the growth in industrial consortia aimed at establishing standards will benefit the COTS software and reuse programme.

In order to avoid excessive costs of building new systems, the DoD is prepared to accept common operational requirements, but the safety and security of COTS should remain bespoke.

6.5 The Commercial Off-the-shelf Studies

In the commercial world, COTS products are available for a widespread use in the market place. Many of the large systems have made use of COTS and most procurements have a COTS element.

COTS software is built by commercial companies for a large user market. Although COTS software is of general applicability, by nature; flexible, reliable and state-of-the-art, it restricts the user to specific computer configurations.

Adapted COTS software can no longer be called COTS, Many COTS packages allow for the incorporation of, or interfacing to user specific software in a third ganeration language. Restrictions on calling routines between 4th generation languages (such as Ada) and COTS packages can exist.

As Ada is the 'defence' companies and government departments recommended 4GL for the development of new systems, it is important that an Ada interface is available. COTS packages can be categorised into four types and their interfacing with Ada is listed below:

- Ada COTS packages. These packages developed in Ada are easy to integrate with Ada application software,
- COTS packages with Ada interfaces. These packages are easy to integrate with Ada-based software,
- COTS software without an Ada interface. Many COTS packages provide interfaces to established languages like C, Fortran, Pascal, or COBOL, but not yet for Ada,
- COTS packages which do not require an Ada interface. Many COTS packages; word processors and spreadsheets run standalone and do not require an Ada interface.

British companies utilise COTS in the following application areas:

- accounting,
- CAD/CAM/CAE,
- configuration Management,
- costing/Cost Management,
- customer service,
- defence logistics,
- distribution,
- document management,
- executive information systems,
- human resources,
- library management,
- maintenance management,
- network management,
- logistics.

For some large systems there may be COTS packages which can fulfill some of the requirements. Experience shows that whatever the requirements, a substantial amount of work as a project is needed, prior to the acquisition of COTS.

As an example, a logistics project took two years, 50 people to establish the current method of work and the interpretation of the requirements into a logical documentation. Being a large required system, it will require a mixture of bespoke development with some modules replaced by COTS packages.

The reader will appreciate that the larger the system, the less the chances for an outright COTS solution. It must be stressed that the larger the system, the more difficult it is to select an appropriate COTS package.

Wherever the user requirements are of a substantial size the COTS solution will need to be looked into carefully, by collecting all relevant requirements, modelling these within a logical stage of development and then decide whether the required system can be:

- a complete bespoke system,
- partly bespoke and partly COTS,
- partly designed from scratch and partly modified COTS,
- divide the new system design into very small segments and then try COTS on a few individual small modules,
- modify the user requirements to suit the available COTS packages.

The latter may involve a totally new working method of what users are accustomed to. Therefore, the introduction of an extensive training course to cover the new modes of work, will be necessary.

The modification of requirements to suit COTS will reduce costs and substantially shorten the timescales. Large companies, from their experience, are preparing themselves for the adapt-your-requirements approach to COTS solutions.

In their current logistics exercises, known organisations have reached the point where the current systems and new requirements have been developed to stage 3 (the detailed study of what the users want), by using the SSADM (Structured

Systems And Design Methodology). The user accepted documentation has been presented for a possible COTS packages solution to a conglomeration of hardware, software and resourcing companies, who are currently looking for suitable COTS.

CASE (Computer-aided Software Engineering) Tools are already classified as COTS packages. A CASE tool, in turn, will assist in documenting and diagramming the COTS requirements. The MOD, almost all defence companies, many commercial organisations and financial institutions use the CCTA preferred System Engineer where the recommended methodology, SSADM, resides. The MOD is a dedicated user of SSADM, version 4, based on System Engineer. Certain sections of the DERA utilise the Object Oriented Methodology.

The challenge for the Information Technology, today, is to increase productivity, improve the quality of new applications and to maintain budget constraints. The solution can only be realised through a shared experience, with the companies developing COTS and the organisations who use the packages.

6.6 Reusability

Object technology, the Internet and information retrieval create new opportunities for software reuse. But there is always an up-front cost as reusable software costs more to build. Estimates show that reusable software requires three to ten times the development effort of one-off software. The payback for the vendor may not come for years. As a consequence, companies developing reusable products are not keen.

The search for reusable software is something that moved America's National Institute of Standards and Technology (NIST) Advance Technology Programme (ATP) to contribute $150 million into research on software reusability.

Approximately 200 software developers attended the third international conference on software reuse, held in November 1994, by the Institute of Electrical and Electronic Engineers.

Object-oriented programming can yield easily reused software components: class libraries and the pre-assembled kits of classes known as frameworks. The Internet enables software developers to distribute, advertise and search for software components worldwide. The problem is to find a business model of software distribution which works in the electronic environment.

Information retrieval presents the biggest technical challenge. What works for text will not necessarily work for software. English text consists of words with generally agreed meanings. Source code, however, is full of arbitrary names invented by programmers.

Interest in object-oriented programming (OOP) has soared. The biggest advantage of OOP is that objects can be re-used in different programs. Organisations and their policies on software reuse have generally adopted OOP languages, such as C++ or Smalltalk. But many companies strive for reuse without objects.

U.S. defence contracts often require the contractor to reuse software if suitable code exists and to make its own code available for reuse. Ada is the standard U.S. defence language and though it is strong on modularity and encapsulation, full OOP (object-oriented programming) will not be part of the language, until the adoption of Ada 9X, which currently, has Draft International Standard status.

Even COBOL may prove to be one of the more reasonable programming languages, for reasons unconnected with the planned OOP features of COBOL 97. Its verbose nature and English-like syntax tend to leave plenty of clues, not only to the mechanical function of a routine, but to its meaning and purpose. These clues might be picked up by information retrieval tools originally designed for use with natural-language text.

Object technology vendors such as Centerline Software and Hitachi Europe are among the first to deliver tools specifically designed to assist software reuse. This reflects customer demand who expect high rates of reuse when they adopt object technology. So the vendors have a powerful motive for making reuse work.

The re-use approach has obvious attractions in sharing development costs over a wider project base. Business process driven re-use may be a valid way of saving money. An agreement to evolve common procedures and approaches may prove beneficial for companies to join forces in utilising a common Information Systems strategy.

6.7 Open Standards

For the last twenty years institutions and government establishments in the western hemisphere have been pre-occupied with the standardisation of open systems. Systems in the 1980s were customised, in the 1990s governments accepted the commercial approach to systems development and in the year 2000, it is expected to proceed with open standards.

Open systems are receiving tremendous attention. Some of the claimed benefits from using open systems include:

- more competition leads to lower costs,
- the probability of schedule delay decreases,
- products are better tested, because they have more users,
- portable applications,
- interoperability in systems,
- faster technology insertion,
- foundation for system evolution.

The notion that open systems are a foundation for long-term system evolution is important. A goal to develop a disciplined framework for a system as that system evolves from new requirements, component upgrades and new technology. So open systems give a framework and the framework includes long-term supportability. Another related aspect to be listed is that the use open systems components represent a form of reuse.

An open system architecture is a collection of interacting software, hardware and human components, designed to satisfy stated needs. The American government policy is that 'agencies shall acquire commercial products and use commercial distribution systems whenever these systems satisfy the government's needs'. This serves to illustrate just how much the pendulum is swinging away from the government engaging in full-scale system development.

It is true that there are concerns about the use of open systems. Some of the claimed difficulties of open systems include:

- they cost too much,
- they are too risky (loss of control),
- they will never meet the exact user, performance and environment requirements,
- there are conformance and certification problems,
- there are supportability problems,
- they require continual investment,
- no prior experience in this field.

There are those who equate open systems with commercial products and believe that commercial products will not satisfy the requirements for performance. Hence, there are risks, including the risk of the quality of the implementation. This point has turned into a very interesting debate. One group believes that commercial products cannot meet performance and other requirements. the other group maintains that users at large have no unique requirements.

Open systems are driven by the modular use of components and modular creation of systems. Modularity is, also, a major feature in the development of programming languages and appears in the package construct of Ada. The interface to a component is defined and is visible to the users. The details of the component, what is on the inside, are not available, since the user does not need to know how it is done.

A new generation of applications is required to meet the business needs of the late 1990s. Client-server architecture, open systems and graphical-user interfaces are now able to offer cost-effective solutions for developing new systems.

To convert an existing information system into an open system one needs a strategic partner who understands the business and has the right expertise. A company developing open systems requires assurance from a supporting partnership.

The general open criteria and the areas where standardisation is expected, covers:

- operating systems. The language/s enabling the system to work,
- item-operability. The ability of two or more systems to exchange and use information,
- Relational Database Management Systems (RDBMS). Where the data are kept and the way these are sorted,
- project support,
- graphics language interfacing,
- multi-system interconnect,
- multi-processor Interconnect,
- portability. The ease with which an application, or hardware component can be transferred from one hardware or software environment to another,
- compatibility. Ability of two applications to co-ordinate with one another in their operation,
- re-usability. The ability to reuse portions of one application's software/hardware in the generation of another application,
- interfacing. The 'connection' to existing systems,
- maintainability. The qualities that improve the ability to maintain the application by eliminating interface uniqueness for parts of application code,
- performance.

The organisations and government departments as consumers of products, developed by others, needs guidance as to how to consider products. The term 'product' is used to denote, either a hardware product, a software product, or a combination of both. This can be called a 'consumer model':

- define system requirements,
- identify components and interfaces,
- select standards,
- select implementations,
- integrate and test,
- deploy system,
- perform maintenance.

The international standard (ISO 9126), defines quality characteristics for products and guidelines for their use. The characteristics include:

- functionality,
- reliability,

- usability,
- efficiency,
- maintainability,
- portability.

Other groups have, also, defined quality attributes. The MITRE Guide to Software Quality is based on the following attributes:

- efficiency,
- reliability,
- maintainability,
- expandability,
- inter-operability,
- re-usability,
- integrity,
- survivability,
- correctness,
- verifiability,
- flexibility,
- portability.

The world is moving to open systems, components and modular architectures. The user must understand this world and be able to deal with it intelligently.

6.8 Superhighway

The chapter on COTS packages will not be complete without the inclusion of the communication and information derived from the 'superhighway'. The term itself is controversial. So is the concept of such a utility being part of COTS. On the other hand COTS can be utilised to bring into effect the management of information derived from or via the superhighway.

In the business world, a new kind of supporting infrastructure is necessary, because groups can only function properly when they can be supported by shared communications and applications.

The infrastructure of the new frontier is beginning to fall into place and, although the information superhighway is not open yet, the paths it will eventually follow are being laid now. The information superhighway is not a single communication method, or route. It is a combination of technologies and packages drawn from many different areas, which are converging to create a new global information infrastructure.

New type of software, such as 'groupware' have been designed to do just that. Equally, the development of tailored applications has been speeded up, either by a process of refinement to off-the-shelf applications, or by employing new development tools.

Not only are new products introduced faster, but new companies can come into existence as a result. The convergence of computers and telecommunications has already shown itself to be a powerful driving force in the economy. New technologies create new opportunities.

The premium on the management of information, not data, but information, is now huge. Often though, organisations have vast data resources, but make little real information available to those who might utilise it most. Often too, there is a flood of data, but little information.

The information superhighway is a complex, growing mesh of thousands of computer networks, joined together by a common computer language. It allows the computer finally to realise its potential, with the seamless global exchange of text, superhighway represents a powerful tool with the potential to revolutionalise the way business is done.

Today's leading information highway is the Internet, a worldwide network of computers that has grown rapidly as more and more organisations recognise the value of sharing and exchanging information. The Internet works because it is based on the principles of open computing and networking, which allow many different types of computer to work together.

The Internet will deliver anything that can turn into digits. These days that includes text, graphics, voices, music, radio broadcasts, digitised photographs, art in general, formulae and moving video. When it is complete, the information superhighway will be the fastest route to the new frontier of an information based society.

All that is known for certain about the new technology, is that it will have much more powerful and cheaper computing. The Internet consists of computers and the cables that connect them and their users together. It must seem astonishing that such huge network has apparently grown up in a couple of years. In fact that is not how it happened. The Internet's roots go back 25 years through Arpanet, a network sponsored by the U.S. DoD.

The Internet already has over three million computers connected to it, in 146 countries. It is the requirements of the business world that are shaping the future of 'the Net'. The number of commercial users is growing at 92% a year, significantly faster than any other segment of the Internet user base. The technology required to gain access to the Internet today can consist of anything, from a laptop personal computer to a fully configured multi-user computer network.

The developments toward the information superhighway present the business community, government departments, educational establishments and individual users with unlimited opportunities for growth. The superhighway has the power potentially to revolutionise the way in which we communicate, educate, share information and conduct business.

The information superhighway will bring a range of services to businesses and the home. Despite the opportunities it offers, however, the information superhighway should be treated with care. The Internet used to be difficult to use and technologies must become more sophisticated and standards established before it can deliver its full potential. Security must be improved too, before the Net becomes a fully accepted trading channel.

The changeover to new ways of doing business, inevitably demands a heavy investment in staff training. With electronic mail increasingly taking the place of postal and facsimile services, administrative staff will have to become acquainted with more features on their personal computers, than just word processors and spreadsheets.

The European Union is committed to the creation of an information society. The recent 'Banggemann' report provides the basis upon which Europe's politicians will move forward. Progress in acting on their recommendations is slow. However, Europe is to build competitive advantage based upon the information revolution. Whereas the progress of Europe's political institutions is hampered by beaurocratic legislative processes, business leaders face no such obstacles.

The information superhighway has inspired many visions of the future, ranging from the utopian to the terrifying. The one clear message that comes from all the prophetic visions, however, is that the world will change radically. Successful 21st century businesses will be those that can adapt to the new electronic global infrastructure that the information superhighway will help to create.

The concept of a global 'macro-computer' evolving from the convergence of computers and telecommunications is not new. In the last 30 years, fiction has been augmented by more plausible, factually based predictions about the future impact of global computer networks. The emergence of the Internet as an early manifestation of the information superhighway allows us to see the shape of the future.

The innovative services available on the Internet give us a clue to the marketplace of tomorrow and the demands it will place both on suppliers and consumers. Work still needs to be done to turn the Internet into a genuine information superhighway, but the structure is there. So, indeed, are the long term implications.

The issue of access security is attracting more attention as the commercial potential of the information superhighway is recognised. The government wants to see its operational data fully secured from unauthorised users. The availability of industrial-strength encryption techniques such as public key encryption is an important first step towards a fully secure environment.

The cause of security is further served by other technical innovations in software, especially the concept of object-oriented design. Objects can package data and process together in such a way that they are inaccessible to the user or other programs. This means, that information packages from the network can be examined safely without the fear of security breaches.

6.9 Modelling and Prototyping

Modelling is a theme usually associated with COTS integration. COTS as a prototyping tool can be used for Human-computer Integration (HCI) exercise mock-up. Once requirements are prototyped and agreed that the mock-up is representing what is needed, the prototyped development can be the start of the operational system.

The prototyping exercise can be based on a COTS package, which itself can interface with other COTS products. Prototyping can serve as system architecture where changes to needs can be inexpensive and the risks of development can be minimised. As in manufacturing procurement, prototyping will serve as a prompt for 'just-in-time' COTS products.

By prototyping, various COTS components can be 'glued' together to produce integrated systems. Many COTS products can serve as applications on a single computer, where all screen records can access and retrieve data for a COTS Relational Database Management System (RDBMS). At this co-operative level, COTS components know that other COTS exist for data exchange and transfer.

By integrating COTS at various levels, COTS components are submerged into larger applications, where they work together efficiently and transparently that they lose separate identities to end-user.

Many COTS products come with Application Programming Interfaces (API). With sets of procedures, functions, routines, or sub-routines which can be called from the application. Linked into application code, like any other routines, it is possible to build applications that simply call COTS APIs to produce desired functionality.

The proper way to acquire a COTS package for prototyping and modelling is to go through the exercise of collecting the requirements and subsequently, follow the various stages of development techniques and structured methodology.

The various stages of development as recommended and supported by the CCTA (The Central Computing and Telecommunications Agency, Millbank, London), are:

- current systems and requirements analysis,
- systems analysis, being the logical representation of the functions and requirements,
- systems designing, the detailed study of what the users want,
- package selection (if the COTS route is chosen),
- software testing,
- integration,
- user training.

In selecting a package, COTS requires evaluation on performance and inter-operability. Therefore, the following need to be checked:

- operating language/system,
- compilers,
- graphics software,
- project support environment,
- relational Database Management Systems,
- prototyping and the Human-computer interaction.

The increased use of COTS for prototyping is inevitable. So are the technologies and themes related to COTS integration.

COTS integration as a means to cut costs, is probably the premier motivation to use COTS. The cost reductions can be measured in the areas of shortened development schedules and cheap COTS software. The latter, in turn, ensures inter-operability and portability.

6.10 Review And Selection Of COTS

This section of the book serves as a draft guidance. It brings forward a methodology for the expansion of the study and suggests ways of approaching the selection of products by the users.

Currently, the available COTS studies are concerned with software, which can be purchased through the commercial, retail and wholesale distributors. Such procurements can include GOTS (Government Off-The-Shelf) and modified COTS (customised products).

The major point to be remembered is that COTS is a packaged product on which modification must be avoided. The COTS package in this case, will be used as is, in its intended format.

It is imperative that various checks are made prior to purchasing a COTS package. The initial enquiry will be based on the possible compatibility and interfacing of the package to the existing technical environment. As in every system development, the reliability, accuracy and security of the package is of importance.

The first draft will utilise information readily available. This, in turn, will prompt the necessary feedback from the reviewers. The comments and requirements received will be catalogued and incorporated in the COTS exercise.

Upon the receipt of comments and requirements, the study will encompass all aspects of computing. Within this subject, the choice of modules to be represented diagrammatically in a top-down structure, which will include all components of computing:

- system architecture,
- hardware,
- software,
- tools,
- implementation

Thus, COTS as a selection system, will assist in choosing the package appropriate to the following criteria:

- vendor independence, where competition will benefit economically,
- user productivity, through established consistency and predictability in services,
- reduced life-cycle cost, with minimum duplication of functionality,
- technology insertion. Stable vendor target paths for technology and modular insertion,
- scalability. Ability of applications to be configured,

- networking of hardware. Allow operations of platforms ranging from micros to mainframes.

Another goal that may be important, is the recognition that the use of COTS represents a shift in the way that systems will be built in the foreseeable future. If this is accepted by the Project Managers, then the users will want to:

- understand basic terms and concepts,
- recognise programmatic issues,
- recognise potential benefits of COTS and difficulties to be faced in creating systems based on COTS components,
- feel better equipped to deal with the requirements,
- recognise that there are no easy solutions. COTS systems are not the answer to everything.

6.11 COTS Advantages and Disadvantages

COTS Advantages	COTS Disadvantages
Avoidance of development costs	Not tailored to specific applications
Use of established products	Entities (data) may not match
Latest, state-of-the-art	No control over future availability
Shorter development cycle	No authority over latest version
More sources	May not be the product required
Newer technology	May change to meet demands of others
Cheaper implementation	Vendor may stop supporting it
Easier interconnection	Discontinuation of a component
Technological advances as they occur.	

COTS will prove beneficial for the selection of small packages. It must be remembered that the bigger the system, less the chances for a shelf product. In the case of Open Systems, it may be beneficial to 'build' rather than to attempt to buy.

An advantage of COTS is the wide user base which helps expose problems and leads to products as an answer in a comparatively short time. Equally, obsolescence comes rapidly, which is hard to cope within the organisational culture used to long computing lifetimes.

The use of COTS is widely seen as a method of reducing costs. The reduction in costs is so sticking that all opportunities, where COTS can easily be applied, are vigorously pursued. The use of COTS is becoming extensive, but there are difficulties in extending COTS into combat and embedded systems deployed in war fighting roles.

The book is concerned with the use of COTS products in meeting operational information systems needs. There is already extensive use of COTS in strategic IS where the computer systems and the core operating software are fully commercial or based on commercial derivatives.

These trends are certain to continue as the capability of COTS to meet needs improves. Some of the constraints on COTS applications can be expected to diminish with time. The following are a few points :

- COTS producers sell packages for generic classes of users, not a single user,
- the consumer has no visibility into development or cost of COTS development,
- the evolution of software is driven by market forces,
- there will be compromising with requirements,
- COTS components may have no knowledge of each other.

Perhaps it is true that within many companies, the development of systems is always behind schedule and over cost, so why not make it someone else's problem? With this in mind, allow various vendors to compete with COTS offerings and through reduced duplication of functionality, meet the requirements.

Implementation of COTS architecture is probably the best method of reducing development time and system cost while using leading technology and improving compatibility between company departments and industry at large.

The integration of information appears to be the emerging goal in information management today. To achieve this, a realistic assessment of COTS is necessary and which level of the system architecture the COTS will satisfy. If information and information systems performance are critical to organisations, then a process for assessing emerging technology should be developed.

It is difficult to assess a COTS product line, but it is an important task. Such issues reflect the planning and accounting for the future. While the assessment of products has played an important role in determining the standards, standardisation on the products must be avoided.

The COTS system products provide a framework for the technical environment and vendor independence. Transition to the method of choosing the appropriate COTS based on the user requirements can be accomplished, but it needs skills to overcome the difficulties of the current business environment.

It must be remembered that COTS packages in their current development and evolution are not ready to cope with huge required systems, nor can they, just like that, replace the running systems. To replace existing operational systems and/or to develop new ones, based on user requirements, the proper development cycle must be followed.

This needs investigations into the current computer and manual systems, as a first step, followed by the analysis of the requirements, the documentation of both into a stage three logical design and then compare the modules of the new architecture with those offered by COTS packages.

COTS modules, in their present developmental state can only satisfy what the market at large needs. Tendencies towards information technology have always been individualistic. Perhaps a new culture needs to be nurtured. That of modifying the requirements to suit what is available in the COTS market.

Should the COTS route for systems be followed, the biggest obstacle will be the system training required by the users prior to running the COTS packages. Mistakes in industry have been made. One good example is that of an international company who went for a computer-aided manufacturing (CAM) package. The system was fine, but it nearly bankrupted this company and had to be rescued by other companies in the Group. The users of the CAM system were not prepared, or trained appropriately, to know how to operate the system.

It is stipulated that the larger the required system, the more difficult it will be for COTS to satisfy such needs. Modularising the architecture will help. It will be easier to select and compare COTS with sections of the required system.

Guidelines for the correct selection of COTS, its implementation and user training will have to be developed. For such a COTS selection system and guidelines to be developed, the System Architect must base this on what the users want. It is imperative, before proceeding with the guidelines, that comments and requirements are gathered and accordingly design the COTS selection package.

For the COTS selection system-to-be, this book suggests five major sections; System Architecture, Hardware, Software, Tools and Implementation. Each of these will be divided into various components which, in turn, will guide the Project Managers and other users in choosing the COTS package.

Such a guiding system for the selection of COTS packages has not been developed by anyone. Many are preparing standards and have a good idea of what they want, but guidelines as a system does not exist. Large organisations tend to work separately, therefore, very difficult to establish one common set of standards.

For small software needs, a COTS selection system can be implemented to suit all requirements. For large systems, perhaps a joint exercise will help. The know-how of the software houses and the experience of the commercial environment can be used in collaborative projects, which can include the concern with the software standards.

By the turn of the next millennium, it may be feasible (eventually), for COTS, the open systems and the standards that are associated with it, to assist in the integration of information technology and the sciences; computing, human behaviour and the specific sciences.

The diagram with the title 'Identify Customisation & Interface Needs Of Preferred Package', on the following page, incorporates four processes which may help the business in choosing an appropriate package.

1. In the first process, the business areas requiring the service are identified. The functions will include the study into the::

- timescales,
- interfaces,
- hardware,
- users' input.

2. In the second process, the vendor's features are identified. This needs the vendor's input for the:

- package features,
- costs,
- timescales,
- matching to users' requirements.

3. Process number three is used to match the package features to the business/users' requirements.

This includes the:

- additional hardware required,
- any possible changes to the package features.

4. In this process, all the costs are added together. The total costs will include the charges for the:

- implementation,
- customisation,
- matching the final costs with those already agreed.

The diagram on next page shows the processes for the selection of packages (COTS). A DFD format has been used to show the simplicity in using diagrams.

7: Artificial Intelligence (AI)

7.1 Expert Systems

Until recently, computers have been concerned with handling numbers and data. Today, many fields of human endeavour express our ideas and problems in non-numeric (symbolic) terms. An Expert System is concerned with concepts and methods of symbolic inference and representation of knowledge. Special computer languages, principally LISP and Prolog, have been developed to process symbolic information. Computer programs written in these languages can be much shorter and clearer than their conventional equivalents. The penalty which is paid, is that on conventional computers the programs are much less efficient and a new generation of computers and languages have and still are being developed to improve their execution.

In October, 1981, the Japanese announced their intention to embark on a research programme to develop fifth generation computer systems. This programme, jointly undertaken by universities, independent institutes and major Japanese companies, aims to move the whole basis of computing from data to knowledge processing. What they hope to achieve, is simply the development of knowledge-based systems, which will be the future driving force of their economy.

Faced with this threat, most of the technologically advanced countries have launched vigorous research programmes of their own. In the U.S.A., both the public (via the Defense Research Projects Agency) and the private sector are investing heavily in artificial intelligence research tools.

The UK's response was the Alvey Programme, a collaborative research project involving academic and industrial effort. What all activity shows, is that the future of computing lies in Artificial Intelligence (AI) systems. Today, many products have computer systems as integral components; these systems can only benefit from artificial intelligence, so products with 'added AI value' will give a considerable market advantage to companies which produce them.

Many companies in the fields of defence, electronics, communications and manufacturing are already planning AI programs for this reason. In the financial sector, as well, market pressures will leave organisations with little choice. Without the power and versatility of AI, survival will be difficult.

The areas of expert systems is fashionable at the moment. Over the past fifteen years, interest in expert systems has increased dramatically, especially in the

commercial field. In practice, it must be understood that expert systems are not threatening traditional computer skills.

The objective in constructing an expert system is to program into the computer a representation of human knowledge. There is an area of controversy over what exactly constitutes the definition of an expert system. Basically, this rests on artificial intelligence, or computing science, to form the base on which such systems are founded. That is, whether the primary stress should be put on knowledge, or logic.

Expert systems deal with knowledge which is accepted and certified, rather than working at a point where new knowledge can then be refined and checked pragmatically, against a recognised specialist.

Problems occur where there is controversy over what constitutes knowledge. If statistics are involved, there can be more than one interpretation of any results of which are obtained.

The applications of expert systems are wider in scope, than mathematical techniques, because heuristics can be used in situations which are not precisely defined, such as decision making.

7.2 Applications Of Expert Systems

There has been steady growth in the commercial adoption of expert systems, although the number of firms employing them is still small, compared to the total number of companies using computers. Those organisations using these systems have been surprised at the progress that can be made in this area, if the requirements are not excessively ambitious at the outset. Companies that have introduced expert systems, have done so, not to replace the work of existing computer systems, but to add to the functions that can be done automatically for the firm.

Expert systems can be employed for a range of relatively simple operations, such as fault diagnosis, where they can marginally improve on the performance of the average fitter. Other areas of applications which are being currently used are for sales advice, customer order handling and some aspects of training.

Although such systems would benefit smaller firms, it is the larger companies which employ their own research groups and have larger budgets to accomplish the latest technical advances.

Much of the early development work was done through academic research. The business community has been particularly active in investigating knowledge communication systems, a branch of expert systems which concentrates on eliciting and distributing knowledge for human consumption other than using it for programming.

Research concentrates on defining that part of human knowledge and skill which passes on verbally, or is taken to be tacit knowledge by the practitioners. The technology is being used to write down, check and define this type of knowledge. In some cases, the resulting programs can be used for training purposes.

Applications of expert systems to medicine have already been given much publicity. Although there are not many systems in routine use, as yet. The potential of prototypes has been demonstrated and are now close to the flowering of expert systems as an aid to doctors and physicians.

There are limitations which are under investigation at the moment and it is clear that applications of this technology will continue to develop rapidly. Expert systems are potentially an extremely useful aid to many human activities, not least, because they aim to utilise nothing more elaborate than plain common sense.

7.3 The Short History Of Artificial Intelligence

Artificial Intelligence (AI) has been a recognised, although somewhat dispersed field of endeavour since the mid-fifties; the term 'expert system' is quite recent. Its main force for popularity is derived from two major sources. First, the recognised inflexibility of established commercial computing and second, the promise given by new insight that intelligent machine behaviour could be achieved. The solution proposed to eliminate many evolving difficulties, is to refocus attention on the 'knowledge', rather than the 'data'.

Among the outstanding problems of knowledge engineering and expert systems development, are those relating to the difficulty of transferring their 'knowledge' from the human expert to the machine. It has been suggested, that one solution to the difficulty, lies in the use of inductive method for transfer, which would allow the expert to input examples from which the program can infer the rules, i.e. the inductive method should allow some automation of the knowledge engineer's task.

The resulting expert system must, of course, conform to the:

- agreed expert systems requirements,
- extend over a reasonable domain of expertise,
- give reliable decisions,
- its 'reasoning' must be accessible, both for the expert and non-expert user.

A further constraint, could require the expert system to deliver new knowledge, recognisable by the human expert, as such.

When faced with a complex task, the experienced programmer splits it into sub-problems. Each sub-problem is then programmed as a procedure and procedures can be nested to any level. The precise choice and hierarchical order of sub-problem in the province of top-down design is called 'structured induction'.

7.4 The Fifth Generation Language

The next generation of computer systems - the fifth generation language (5GL) - seeks to develop artificial intelligence (AI), which will greatly expand the applicability of computer systems from data processing into knowledge processing.

Since the fifties, computer researchers have believed that it is possible to make computers which can, to a limited extend, be considered to be capable of reasoning. The technical problems are enormous and it is only the last ten years, or so, that commercial organisations have begun to exploit artificial intelligence technology.

In its simplest form, artificial intelligence represents the ability of a computer to encompass the knowledge and problem-solving skills of experts from a range of disciplines; it helps the computer user to interpret information from several viewpoints, presenting that information in a form which allow a well informed decision about a particular problem to be made.

7.5 Techniques

Artificial intelligence techniques play a major part in improving the interface between humans and computers - image and speech understanding and robotics have all benefited from AI research.

By the end of the year 2000, it is forecast that more than thirty percent of existing computer applications will use artificial intelligence techniques and an even greater volume of new applications of computers will have arisen, addressing complex problems, which cannot currently be solved using today's computers.

Many of the world's largest companies are already developing AI-based applications. These are frequently called 'expert', or 'knowledge-based' systems. They seek to assist, or even replace 'experts', thus releasing manpower for more creative tasks.

To develop these complex systems quickly and efficiently, a new type of computer is needed. This is because the computer language normally used for AI applications requires much more processing power, than most conventional computers and more importantly, the computer power is used in a different way.

The principal difficulty lay in the fact that the fifth generation languages, which are most suitable for AI applications are very processor intensive and require novel computer architectures for efficient execution. Since commercial AI applications need, almost without exception, to interact with 'conventional' data processing systems, this imposes a serious limitation in their use. One solution is to network these 'machines' to a more general purpose computer.

7.6 Meeting The Needs Of Industry

Applying artificial intelligence techniques to industrial applications is not very easy. Some of the most useful AI-based solutions, such as continuous speech recognition, will not be practicable until later in the decade. However, a number of useful applications have already been developed to the extend that they show a substantial commercial benefit. The most commonly discussed application is the expert system.

The expert system seeks to encapsulate the knowledge and skills of highly qualified individuals (usually a scarce resource) and increase productivity by applying these skills equally and consistently throughout the organisation. Expert systems are particularly applicable where the task is repetitive, but low level. For example, configuring large computer systems is a good application for an expert system, but designing computers is not.

One of the most frequent mistakes which is made in designing expert systems is to under-estimate the size of the knowledge base which is required.

The major use of expert systems is for the rapid prototyping and development of complex software systems. Programmer productivity using the window-oriented graphics work-station and the high level software tools shows a ten-fold productivity increase over conventional programming language on a good quality super-personal computer.

Although 5GLs are generally associated with symbolic computing, many AI applications, also, require good performance for non-symbolic processing. Image-processing, model-based expert systems and systems accessing conventional databases are some examples.

In recent years, shell-based application packages have increased in many areas of systems. As a result, many companies explain how they have been using shells as tools to create complete 'virtual' models of their products and manufacturing processes and the benefits in cost, money and quality that shells have given them.

The installation of CAD\CAM\CAE\CASE technology, within a framework of concurrent engineering, has resulted in improvements in the design-to-manufacture lead-times for the producers of goods at large. The world of manufacturing and computing technology continues to advance at breakneck speed and keeping up can be difficult for those technology is intended. This year has seen the launch of numerous new products for expert systems in engineering.

8: CASE Tools And Methodologies

8.1 The Overall Objectives

As organisations strive to increase productivity, to reduce costs, to shorten cycle times, to improve product and service quality, so the demands made on systems for modifications and for new information increase. Being able to make better decisions based on quality information and having the flexibility to respond to new opportunities increasingly, depends on having the right systems in place at the right time.

Applications developed based on older technologies may well not meet current requirements in some or many areas, such as:

- functionality,
- ease of use,
- data access,
- maintainability,
- flexibility,
- robustness,
- costs.

With the wide range of application environments and building blocks now available, it is still possible to have an affordable system designed and built to meet specific business requirements. This gives the flexibility and control to define the system the way the users want it and then to change and adapt the system to support the business over coming years.

Computer-aided Software Engineering (CASE) tools address the application design stage. For business systems they can be extremely useful to assist in the design of both, the application and the data structure.

Rapid Application Development (RAD) techniques incorporate a series of steps which business people and Information Technology professionals work through together to develop a prototype of the application representing the business process before full scale development.

The objectives of analysis is to understand what a particular area of the business does and how information is exchanged, created and modified by business processes.

With a clear understanding of the information needs of a business area, the system engineer can determine which business activities to automate and then develop those systems so they meet end user requirements.

The design helps users move from a logical representation of 'what' a given system is to perform, into the physical specifications for 'how' the system will actually be implemented.

In order to handle the complex nature of a system, it is often helpful to break down the processes and data of the system into manageable pieces. Decomposition diagrams are an easy way to partition the data and process requirements of the system, by analysing and application, refining high level business processes into lower level processes. These processes can then be broken down further until the analyst reaches a level of detail where a process can best be described in terms of its procedural logic.

The decomposition diagram helps to create and maintain diagrams for :

- process decomposition; depict the analysis of processes into subprocesses,
- data decomposition; show how general groupings of data break down into more specific data entities,
- organisational decomposition; describe the hierarchical structure of the organisation.

The analysis stage is unique in its approach to integrating the process model with the data model. The analyst can build the application data model by defining, one at a time, the data model for each individual process.

Dataflow diagrams can help describe how a business area or system functions. They show how data flows into and out of the business area or system, how processes transform data and the external agents (recipients/sources) that interface with the system.

Entities are the subjects of information (people, places, things) about which a business needs to keep data. An entity diagram provides a graphic way of describing the data requirements of a system and how they interrelate. The entity diagram, also, helps describe and characterise the relationships among these entities.

In many Information Technology (IT) departments, the complexity of applications often dictates that development responsibilities be divided among members of a project team. The ability to share information is a fundamental requirement for systems development tools.

Such tools, Computer-aided Software Engineer (CASE - some system engineers describe them as ‘System’, instead of ‘Software’) tools are designed to offer unequalled flexibility in combining and reconciling the work of multiple users. The analyst can selectively consolidate and separate, either whole, or partial encyclopaedias, or selected objects and maintain multiple encyclopaedias for different projects or users.

8.2 The CASE Tool And The Encyclopaedia

For an IT department to be a valued contributor to the company’s success, its staff must be supplied with tools to respond effectively to business opportunities, where CASE tools can assist in the full life cycle of the applications development.

Applications which reduce costs and add value, effectiveness. For IT to be a valued contributor in business, its functions and service to users must be highly adaptive, in planning, manufacturing, products design, marketing and the overall company culture. To succeed in such concepts, IT conducts an inter-departmental analysis of its information systems, to assess its assets and capabilities.

Based on the investigation, the IT department may recommend COTS packages as a solution to the applications demand made by the company, or IT may recommend systems developed internally.

Whichever the choice, new concepts and advanced technologies will be introduced to the organisation. These cost money, but properly approached, the IT will be able to design new systems, or apply COTS packages in a much easier and less costly way.

As part of the new concepts, IT will bring forward a long range strategic plan for business systems. Evolve from a business system planning to an overall technical architecture planning approach. Tools, including CASE, are the key to the success of the overall technical architecture.

From the user perspective, the analysis of problems is critical. Detailed analyses of the operating systems, the manual systems and the functional relationships will serve the purpose of the overall architecture. A CASE tool is highly instrumental, in being able to present the numerous applications to management and users and to gain consensus among the staff..

One of the strengths of the CASE tool is its ability to hold information, definitions and comments. With a user-friendly tool, the analyst finds it easier to start and modify the diagrams. The users understands what the IT is doing. Pictures generated out of the tool are shown to the users for consensus and where necessary the diagrams get back into the tool to redraw.

The tool makes it easy. Diagrams are redrawn quickly and using the tool causes the analysts and users to question the analysis more. The result is a better quality system.

The CASE tool will prompt the analyst to begin with a decomposition of the areas that are involved and then a global data model which can be used as the starting point for the data model side of the project. These are explained to the users. In doing so, the design tool makes things easier. The analyst can move things around on the screen, which encourages modular design techniques.

As explained, the IT project team is responsible for the research and development of the advanced concepts and technologies in support of the company's information systems. The IT is not only responsible for the traditional data administration duties, but also for the introduction of the CASE tools and the building up of the encyclopaedia.

The successful introduction of the CASE tool and its encyclopaedia the following are strongly recommended:

- standardisation of methodology throughout the organisation,
- substantial investment in training IT staff and users,
- pilot the overall technical architecture.

It is fair to say that until recently, software development was more art than science. Applications were implemented in an undisciplined manual process that seemed to take for ever. Application backlogs got worse instead of improving.

Today, applications can be engineered and with the assistance of vendors and their products, applications are constructed to suit the users within realistic timescales. Users of CASE tools should develop better systems in less time.

CASE tools are used for planning, analysis, design and allow for the capturing of the user system requirements. All the specifications as diagrams and descriptions. Following on, application generators can then process these pictures to create complete applications for most environments.

If the application has been fully specified, this will include the source code, plus database definitions, the database access routines, screen maps and system level documentation. In short, everything a system engineer needs to compile and test the application.

Some vendors offer CASE tools which are tied to a specific methodology. This means that the system to be developed will be the vendor's way, no matter what the type, size, or scope of the project. A good CASE tool should not be constrained to a specific methodology.

Some CASE tools on the market are:

- IEF,
- IEW,
- Excelerator,
- LBMS System Engineer,
- Select, etc.

The IT should be free to choose and use any of these methodologies:

- James Martin's Information Engineering,
- Yourdon,
- DeMarco,
- Gane and Sarson,
- Arthur Young,
- Constantine,
- War-Mellor,
- BIS Modus,
- LSDM,
- SSADM,
- Prototyping, etc.

The application development lifecycle is common to almost all established methodologies and is often broken down into four major phases:

- planning,
- analysis,
- design,

• construction.

Developers will typically invest the most time in the first three phases. This emphasis on the front-end assures that the application being developed will be the right one and that it will be constructed the right way.

In the three front-end phases, relationships and system requirement specifications are most clearly and concisely represented as diagrams. In the back-end construction phase, a good CASE tool offers application generator solutions that can transform pictures into working systems.

One of the secrets to the success of the good CASE tool is the encyclopaedia and the consistency through it. The CASE tools with one common encyclopaedia ensure that the data are shared and that the diagrams and their meanings are always consistent with each other.

Each time a diagram is requested, the expert system within the CASE tool automatically generates it from knowledge contained in the encyclopaedia. Likewise, each time information is entered, the encyclopaedia interprets the meaning and can represent it in many different diagram forms.

As the content of the encyclopaedia is updated, the tools automatically update all the diagrams that are affected by the change. So there is no need for manually auditing the consistency among diagrams for every revision.

When system engineers are drawing diagrams on paper, it is not easy to see how all the parts of a large application will come together. As a result, diagrams may be missing inputs, relationships, or outputs that go nowhere.

CASE tools automatically guide the analyst through fundamental principles that are common to all methodologies. The CASE tool calls attention to errors, inconsistencies and checks for completeness. This automatically assures that the systems requirement specifications and designs created with the tool, can be transformed into real systems.

As has already been seen, the CASE tools include PC-based diagramming tools and application generators, all driven from a common encyclopaedia. The encyclopaedia is, also, the key to integrating the work of planning, analysis and design. Information captured with analysis is also available to the design phase and vice versa. This way the work of one phase can become the foundation for work in the next phase. Changes made during design will be reflected automatically back to the analysis diagrams.

By capturing all of the details in a single encyclopaedia the analyst can develop a shared resource of integrated information. This will be based on the user's needs. It will support the entire system specification and the system lifecycle. It will, also, have all the details needed to generate applications and databases. This way the systems can be maintained at the design level instead of at the coding stage.

If the IT has more than one person on a project, or multiple of modules or projects going on simultaneously, the CASE tool and its common encyclopaedia allows this automatically, while preserving the integrity of the diagrams and the knowledge they represent. The CASE tool combines the encyclopaedias, removes all redundancies and detects all potential conflicts and discrepancies.

The CASE tools use the latest user interface and are mouse-driven, with full windowing capabilities. The screens let the user point at commands, instead of remembering what the commands are and when they are to be used.

Several diagrams can be displayed on the screen at one time. This lets the user see the flow of information from one diagram to the next. Because diagrams are so easy to create and modify, analysts are more willing to exchange ideas with end-users and explore alternative paths to the best solution of the problems and the requirements.

CASE tools are a fairly new technology and systems engineers are still finding many ways to implement the potentials offered. Some CASE tools are design to be modular with separate tools for planning, analysis, design and application generation. These tools can work together as a single integrated product, or separately as individual ones.

To be practical, a CASE tool must be able to work with many other packages. These should include such things as:

- data dictionaries,
- databases,
- 4GLs,
- standard repositories,
- code generators,
- software testing platforms,
- compilers
- purchased COTS applications.

At the end of the day, no matter what anyone may say, a CASE tool, or any product may fail the IT department and the business as a whole, unless a properly documented system requirements specification is produced. A specification upon which everything will depend - to deliver what the user asked.

9: Systems Specification

9.1 The Highlights Of The Case Study

The documentation of the system requirements specification is concerned with the overall definition of the recommended system and the production of the required system, following the selection from the business systems options.

This stage of the project delivers the:

- functional decomposition (hierarchical diagram),
- processes (dataflow diagrams),
- data structure (model and relationships),
- data inventory,
- functions, transactions, events,
- requirements catalogue,
- problems solved,
- menus and screen reports,
- associations of all above,
- definitions of all above,
- activity plan (with the steps for each phase of development).

The case study presented in this chapter, is that of an imaginary retailer specialising in the selling of products through branches. The study incorporates logistics ideas as part of the electronic point-of-sale overall architecture. The fictional study shown in the following pages, is just one module of an overall retailing system. The company has inventories in warehouses as well as in the branches.

This exercise will look into the function of recalled goods by suppliers/manufacturers and how the branches return the recalled stocks. The specification will include the returning of excessive stocks from the branches to the designated company warehouses. The requirements, also, cover cases where goods need to be transferred from branch to branch.

The diagrammatic representations, descriptions and associations were produced by the LBMS System Engineer. This CASE tool can easily accommodate the methodologies of LSDM and the British government preferred SSADM. In order to illustrate the similarities of the many methodologies on the market, the study tried to cover many concepts of as many methodologies as possible.

This exercise deals with the excessive stock of products within the 'company' (and its 'branches') and the attempt to reduce the stockroom size.

The ordering algorithm to improve the re-ordering of stock to the branches is already established within the purchasing practices. Overstocks occur and unwanted goods still need to be returned to manufacturers and own warehouses. Further on, stocks have to be redeployed, by transferring the goods to other branches.

Due to the inability of the current systems, to cope with the demand made upon them, the company is losing quarter of all reclaimable moneys from recallable items.

The main problems of the current systems are, the:

- branch being unable to complete the returns any quicker,
- speed of goods travelling through the supply chain,
- timescales of goods being sorted and credit requested.

The implementation of this module will enable the substantial reduction stockroom space and savings in cashflow.

The major processes of this module, include:

- the receiving of instructions to return goods; which details can be generated by the external recipient/sources Centre (Head Office), Supplier, Area Manager, or another Branch,
- the Branch seeking authorisation to return unwanted stock,
- following the instructions to return or transfer, the Branch selects the products listed,
- the dispatching of items from the Branch to the Warehouse, or Supplier,
- following the dispatch of stock, the Branch verifies the credits and debits allocated by the Centre.

The data model subset represents nine major entities, which hold the appropriate attributes.

The entities involved are:

- Recall,
- Return,
- Inter-branch Transfer,
- Item,
- Stock Adjustment,
- Branch,
- Supplier,
- Warehouse,
- Claim.

Other aspect for consideration, regarding the specification of this module are:

- The Problems and Requirements Catalogue of the current fictional systems holds requirements applicable to the development of this module.
- The solutions to every problem listed has been found, agreed by the users and accordingly, the necessary associations to the CASE objects have been made.

- The fictional people who may participate in the production of the imaginary required system, are the members of the users consultative committee, the Head Offices (Centre) staff and representatives from the branches.

Additionally, there are a number of constraints which the senior management need to make a decision; company policies and methods of working.

Some of the issues are:

- different types of instructions procedures,
- various types of returns,
- different sets of delivery standards,
- inaccurate collation of the recalled products,
- other topics which involve a number of different departments.

In this case the users consultative committee, chaired by a senior manager, undertakes to resolve the issues, outside the scope of this system specification.

9.2 The Diagrammatic Representation

By now, all the phases, starting from the Project Initiation Document (PID), right through to the required analysis, the users problems and requirements cataloguing, their solutions and the specification of the required system, all are complete. The next step, is for the users to sign off this phase of the module, prior to starting on the building of the system.

The reader will appreciate that the volume of the documentation of the complete study of this fictional module may consist of more than one thousand pages. In view of this, only a few examples are selected as extracts of the system requirement specification. The full documentation of a module such as the example presented usually takes a small team of people a few months to complete.

Therefore, only one example of each one of the following is included in this book:

- Decomposition Diagram and Report,
- Data Model Subset Diagram and Components,
- Data Inventory,
- Dataflow Diagrams Set and Descriptions,
- Functions,
- Transactions,
- Events,
- Problems and Requirements Catalogue,
- Solutions,
- Menu And Screens Reports.

Once all above are inserted in the CASE tool, the automatic outputs, included in the specifications, individually show the listing of all the components, within each picture, with the appropriate descriptions for each component. Every one of the components is associated to each other.

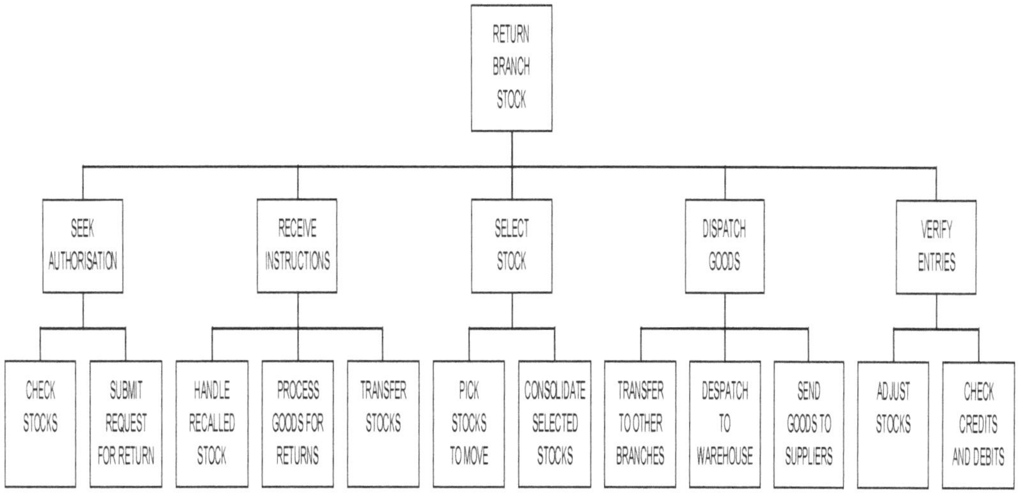

10: Information Systems Explained

10.1 Information Systems Now

It is hard to imagine business today without information systems. Information Technology in general is an important part of business and everyday life. It has become very important for individuals and organisations, in the ability to compete, perform and prosper.

As a support structure and as a tool for business, systems can deliver a number of significant benefits. Costs can be reduced, productivity increased, services improved and profits enhanced.

People at the sharp end of business, want a better understanding of the way that systems are developed and function. It is hoped that in this book systems issues are explained and that computing helps people to comprehend the broad aspects of technologies available to assist in achieving personal and business objectives.

Systems ought to be about enabling business and personal change.

10.2 Commerce And The Internet

The term 'Electronic Commerce' is commonly used to mean doing business electronically. It is the paperless exchange of critical business information between companies and their suppliers, government departments, financial institutions, customers and companies, even within organisations.

Business today see the electronic commerce as a way to streamline operations, reach new markets and serve their clients more efficiently. It can often be a catalyst for business change through business process re-engineering. A streamlined new process nearly always entails some degree of automation. Since many business processes cut across boundaries between departments, divisions and even companies, electronic commerce is a natural way to automate these processes.

A popular method of communication for exchanging data is Electronic Data Interchange (EDI). EDI may be defined as the 'exchange of standardised structured information between computer systems'.

EDI lends itself to the exchange of high volumes of information in a fixed format agreed by industry groups. This includes invoicing and payments, retail point-of-sale, bank transactions and manufacturing inventories. Because information is created and transferred electronically, there is no need for paperwork. This eliminated the need for re-keying data, which saves labour, speeds up processes and reduces details errors. Significant cost savings and reduced lead times can be achieved.

Processes can be automated and re-structured so that maximum operational efficiency is obtained. EDI operates by direct connection between users and over private and public data networks, ensuring privacy and security. As it uses highly structured formats, transmission speeds can be increased and overall costs reduced.

An electronic commerce business solution relies on a network to act as a conduit for the transfer of data. Often, a 'value-added network' from a commercial provider is used, to provide the infrastructure required to transfer data securely and reliably among trading partners.

One of the ideas brought forward, is whether the Internet will replace these value-added network services. The Internet is one methods of exchanging business data, but not the only means. A commercial network eliminates many of the technical matching issues and provides services not available on the Internet, such as security, tracking and audit ability. The Internet is an important element of an electronic commerce solution, but is not the only one.

10.3 Internet In Business

Until a few years ago, the Internet was not well known. One could scarcely have predicted the impact it would have on the world of systems and computers communications.

From its inception in the 1960s, the Internet evolved into a global network of business, academic and government computers. In recent years, businesses and individual users have recognised its potential as a way of communicating. By exchanging electronic mail, transferring files, accessing information services and communicating via bulletin boards and computer conferencing.

The communication has been accompanied by the emergence of a part of the Internet known as the World Wide Web, which allows information to be presented in a graphical format; incorporating text, images, video and sound.

Any user with a suitable personal computer can access the Web through a connection to the Internet using the normal telephone line and view information using low cost software tools, known as browsers.

Businesses are now setting up electronic shop-fronts and information sites on the World Wide Web and starting to realise the immense potential for reaching a global audience.

However, this open access to the vast storehouse of information raises a number of issues. The openness of the Internet leads to concerns over security. The Internet is a public set of networks that interconnect and are not inherently secure. As a consequence, there is a demand for effective software security tools known as 'firewalls'. These act as a secure gateway to limit outsiders' access to a company's data systems and provide control over staff access to the Internet.

Companies and individuals are reluctant to transmit and exchange sensitive details over the Internet, such as credit card information. The problem is now being addressed by developing effective encryption tools. The combination of firewalls and encryption will enable the realisation of the Internet's full commercial potential.

One genuine limiting factor on Internet usage is data transmission speeds. Although these have improved in recent years, for most users they remain painfully slow. It takes a few minutes to download and read even a basic Web page. Transferring large data files is often impracticably slow. These and other management issues associated with security, training and implementation, should be taken into account when considering the Internet as part of a business strategy.

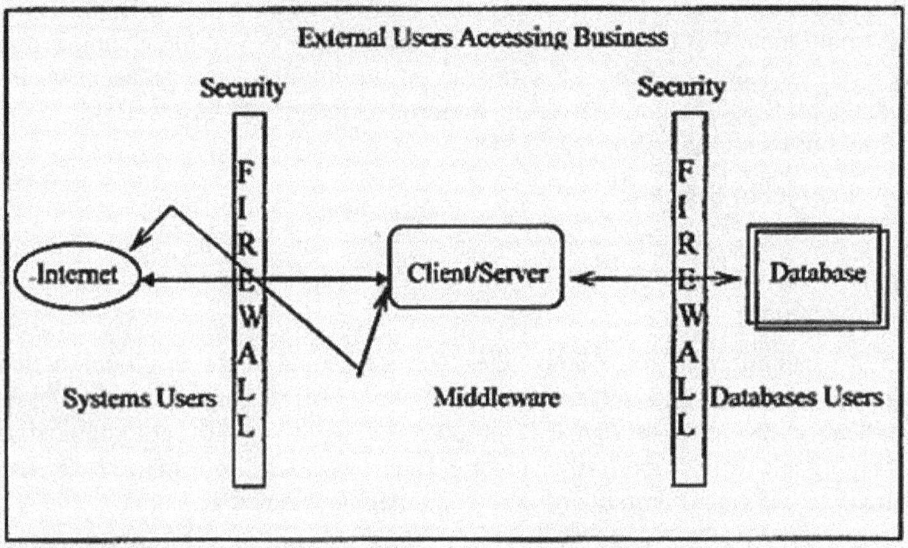

10.4 The Mainframe

Over the years, the word was that the mainframe computer was on the way out. The growth of the personal computers on the desk-top was claimed to replace the mainframe as the preferred business information technology platform, well before the end of the century.

The reports of the mainframe's death have turned out to be greatly exaggerated. The fact that mainframes have been around for so long helps explain why companies still use them.

Historically, data has been safe and secure on a mainframe. The cost and benefits of moving it to another type of system are difficult to justify. The longevity of the mainframe means that it is a mature environment as far as security, structure and disciplined operational processes are concerned. Innovations in computing may appear to be more sophisticated, but lack the tools to deliver the integrity, security and availability of data required to run critical business systems.

Mainframes are still perceived to be the best place for sensitive information and for running data intensive centralised systems, such as personnel, payroll, accounts and inventories.

10.5 The Mainframe As A Data Server.

In modern computing environments, the mainframe assumes a new role. Additional to its running of large systems, it is becoming a large-scale data server. Companies recognise the need to provide centralised management and protection for critical data distributed throughout the organisation. In fact, the amount of data storage on the mainframe is growing and so is the data held on systems elsewhere. This gives the systems function the added responsibility of storing, organising, managing and distributing the data.

The concept of managing data across an organisation requires the facility to manage its storage in a uniform manner, implementing consistent policies and standards and enforcing the protection of critical data. This is achieved via the use of software tools, which offer an overall view of the data stored.

The concept of storage management is well established in the mainframe environment and has been the basis for the replication of those disciplines across the business enterprise, leading to more efficient use of resources, greater ease of management and security of information.

10.6 The Use Of PCs And Mainframes

Desk-top personal computers have become extensively used alongside mainframes. The emergence of the PC led to a different perception of computing. Users expect systems which are easy to build, operate and use, with highly graphical and intuitive screens. These facilities have not been a strength of the mainframe in the past.

Many organisations have rationalised a requirement for centralised control with the need for end user autonomy by creating links and networks, utilising the strengths of both mainframes and personal computers. In effect, the mainframe is used to collect, store and process business information from a variety of sources, with individuals and work groups then accessing the centralised data using PCs.

Software houses have risen to this challenge by developing a range of software tools which allow PC users to access and analyse mainframe data and integrate it with desktop systems, such as spreadsheets, word processors and other business software tools. They need to be able to locate relevant information easily, using everyday PC language rather than specialised computer commands and are not interested in where the information lies and how it is retrieved.

The users expect to be able to search all available data sources in one go without worrying about the different structures and systems used by the various databases they are searching. Alternatively, links can be created between the PC and mainframe applications enabling automatic update of desk-top data whenever the source is changed on the mainframe.

10.7 The Mainframe For Management Services

The longevity of the mainframe means that the management of services it provides to the business is well understood and consequently more controllable. The mainframe acts as a hub, linked to many other areas of the organisation's systems and provides a central viewpoint for ensuring that users have systems up and running when they need them.

Consequently, a range of tools to manage the operational side of providing these services has evolved. These allow a high degree of automation and relate the services to their importance to the business. Hence, if a part of the system, or network fails, the services which are most critical to the running of the business can be addressed first, whilst less critical services assume a lower priority. In today's business environment, when organisations trade round the clock, management of systems to this sophistication is vital to business success. This type of service, simply cannot be managed without the control available with mainframe systems.

The mainframe plays an important part of the evolution of an organisation's systems and often provides the most logical platform to run business systems effectively. If the mainframe did ever die, it has certainly risen again.

10.8 The Client Server

A client/server system is a 'modular' approach to computer systems. Instead of all aspects of the system being held in one place, a server holds applications and data which can be accessed from a number of 'clients' who have their own processing capability.

In the most advanced systems, any computer on the network could act as a server for some applications and as a client for others. This is significantly different to the conventional local area network (LAN), where typically one computer will control the network and hold data, although applications tend to be held on each PC or workstation.

Client/server systems were conceived when the personal computer emerged as a credible platform for business systems. Users became accustomed to powerful desk-top applications and the ease of use provided by graphical user interfaces, such as Windows and OS/2. By linking these computers, it was reasoned, mainframe-based business systems could be replaced with groups of computers which were collectively as powerful, but individually easier and more flexible to use.

10.9 Flexibility To The Users

The new-style systems support greater integration and collaboration between corporate-wide and single user desk-top applications. Employees at all levels of an organisation have access to a company's systems, but do not need the support and training associated with traditional text-based programs. This wider use of graphical interfaces across the enterprise has enabled the implementation of better reporting tools and more flexible access to data through sophisticated information systems.

One of the reasons for the evolution of the client/server philosophy was the growth of power on the desk-top, via the personal computer. However, organisations soon realised that a huge amount of data resided elsewhere in the business, often collected and collated over many years and held in a secure and controlled environment, such as mainframe computers. There seemed to be little reason to migrate or relocate these systems on to a different type of computer, especially if the underlying business processes they would support were to remain fundamentally the same.

For this reason, the client/server concept encompasses all sizes of computers and not just the PC. However, a business structures its systems and data, the most important business benefit to be delivered is increased ease of use and flexibility of data access. Often, the best returns on investment in client/server have been achieved when personal computers have provided an interface with existing systems, but with the retention of the underlying programs and processes.

When implementing client/server systems, organisations can, therefore, choose between developing simple graphical interfaces to enable a personal computer to access mainframe data, or they may decide on a totally new application built from scratch. In each case, effective software tools are needed to develop the new interfaces and support the integration of new and old systems.

10.10 Tools For Effective Systems

Software tools are available which cover virtually every aspect of building and implementing client/server systems. The best are easy to use, typically running on PCs. Structurally incorporating rapid application development concepts and processes which involve the input of business users into the building of effective systems to support business needs. Usually, tools of varying kinds are required to make the most of computing elements already in existence.

Systems re-engineering software enables existing mainframe applications to be transferred to other computer types without losing the original investment in programming. Connectivity tools and terminal emulation software enable computers to access information on different platforms. Graphical development tools assist users to create new screen layouts and applications. Alternatively, fast productivity gains can be achieved from the use of integrating software, which takes older-style, text-based applications and creates an easy to use graphical screen for the user. Not only is this easier to use and, therefore, more productive, but it means that a number of applications can be combined on the desk-top.

Users of the systems need access to data wherever it is located, without having to be concerned with where it is, or techniques of accessing it. Sophisticated software tools are available to locate data stored in multiple locations and to allow it to be extracted in a common format for compilation of reports and integration into other applications.

It would be true to say that, in many organisations, client/server is happening despite IT and not because of it. The amount of technology and skill accumulating on the desk-top is growing exponentially , as is the need to connect to shared resources such as databases and mail services. A move to client/server should deliver concrete business advantages, integrating the PC and the corporate mainframe, thus increasing flexibility.

Such corporate integration leads to more direct business involvement in the use of information technology. However, there is often increased cost associated with client/server over a traditional centralised computing structure. A complete realignment of the IT function is needed to provide managed support to the distributed systems which are now running the business.

10.11 Inherited Systems

Most organisations have an inherited legacy of systems. These inherited systems will have been in operation for a number of years, on mainframes and running bespoke systems which were written in house, or by a contracting consultant. At first sight, legacy systems appear to have limited use in a modern organisation, with the exception of one very important fact. Their longevity means they hold a huge amount of vital, critical data. The business processes which they support, have been developed over the years and investment made in getting the systems right.

With the industry hype on the demise of the mainframe, organisations started to wonder whether the mainframe and the legacy systems running on it were declining and whether they should be replaced with new workstation and client/server systems. However, reality shows that this vast change is not easily achieved, that companies still depend upon legacy systems for the vast majority of their operations and that new systems continue to be built for the mainframe.

It has transpired that most of the conflict between the new client/server technologies and legacy applications is based on misconceptions. Companies can gain significant advantages by incorporating new features into legacy systems. Re-use of legacy code significantly reduces cost and risk, while spending the time taken to deliver new business systems.

Sophisticated software tools enable IT departments to inspect, assess, document and record their legacy applications scientifically and objectively. Further tools can then be used, if required, to extract the best of the application code and provide the basis for migration to new developments.

Since legacy systems may have been constantly developed over the years, it is also important to use the relevant software tools to re-document their structure, to ensure that they can be supported and maintained. This ensures that the vital business processes they support are not threatened.

One current issue requiring this attention is the 'Year 2000' issue. Many legacy systems were envisaged to have a short life and needed to minimise the use of computer storage which was relatively expensive in the early days of systems building. These systems were written to hold only last two digits of the year in the date field and have endured and played a vital role in running the business.

It is now necessary to use appropriate software tools to identify all occurrences of 2-digit fields and change them to 4-digit, otherwise systems will assume that the date is reset to 1900, when the new millennium is reached. An example of this would be a financial loan application, which would mature before it started, interest due would be impossible to calculate and chaos would reign.

The typical computer user today needs to access and use information throughout the organisation to produce business plans, reports and presentations. The users need to draw information from a variety of sources to help them make the sort of high quality informed decisions that give their business competitive edge, greater efficiency and improved productivity.

Many organisations have realised that their legacy systems can have a prolonged life if the information they hold can be made available to this new type of user. For this reason, legacy systems are often incorporated into client/server systems, where PC users have direct, but controlled access to mainframe data.

In these situations the mainframe is used as a secure gateway to corporate mission-critical systems and as a centralised repository for enterprise data. As an example, retailers and financial institutions are continuing to use legacy systems to control most of their on-line transactions for hole-in-the-wall cash machines, or electronic point-of-sale data collection and processing.

With this new understanding of legacy systems and the tools that now exist to leverage their potential, their future is assured. Legacy systems can be integrated effectively with new systems, so that the data they hold and business functions they support are available throughout the enterprise. This not only prolongs their cost-effective life but also reduces costs through minimising the need to acquire new skills and purchase new hardware, software and infrastructure.

10.12 Data Warehousing

In this 'information age', making the best possible use of data is one of the biggest challenge facing the international organisation.

Historically, companies have acquired and managed data using separate computer systems for each application, with each optimised for its particular use. For this reason, data relating to sales, inventory, financial controls, customer service, personnel and other parts of the organisation is often held in a variety of locations and formats. Where links do exist among different applications, they often identify connections, or relationships between two different pieces of data. For example, linking a sale to a payment received.

While understanding this data is important, businesses need to make analyses in more complex ways. Managers and executives need to be able to make informed judgements and effective decisions in order to keep their business competitive, efficient and profitable.

This requirement is addressed by the an executive information system (EIS). Designed to help managers perform their responsibilities better, this system allows them to assess current and future business requirements by providing sophisticated analytical tools, such as trends analysis and what-if scenarios.

Because EIS enables effective decision making based on higher quality data, it is often classified as a business intelligence system (BIS), decision support systems (DSS), or management information system (MIS). While this may be true, it does not mean that these terms apply exclusively to EIS. They are, in fact, more often used to describe generic business information systems, while EIS has a more precise meaning.

If data from a variety of sources is placed in a central repository, it can all be accessed and analysed by an information system at the same time. This concept is known as a data warehouse. The key strength of data warehousing is the information advantage. All businesses, especially service businesses, want to know more about their customers. Data warehousing technology gives users instant access to data about all aspects of the company's business, without having to re-write applications to find it.

The data warehousing concept started out on the mainframe. The aim was to build large databases of historical information that could be extensively analysed, without affecting the performance of production systems. On a smaller scale, companies also built multiple management information systems, but they did not pull together data from across the enterprise and many were built using conventional tools which made them difficult for unskilled users.

The data warehouse addresses the IT department's need to manage data that, with the rise of client/server distributed computing, is now dispersed across different platforms and is in varied and often incompatible forms. The arrival of new technologies such as client/server and cheaper hardware systems, make building a data warehouse a much more affordable exercise.

With the introduction of more powerful PCs and advances in software, data in the warehouse can be processed whenever a business user needs to analyse information. This concept, known as on-line analytical processing, or OLAP, means that up-to-date information is always available, so long as it resides in the data warehouse.

Another characteristic of an EIS is that data is stored and processed in a multi-dimensional format. This means that information can be viewed in a number of ways, so that interactions and relationships between data that are not obvious with conventional database tools can be identified and assessed. This can only be achieved by EIS. For example, a store might analyse sales of a particular product line by store, region or globally, enabling managers to identify anomalies in performance very quickly and in a high graphical format.

As the core application is commonly held on a powerful server, which undertakes the processing, with users accessing information from PCs connected across the corporate network, EIS is a prime example of an application based on a client/server principles.

The creation of a data warehouse takes considerable amount of management and planning to achieve successfully and, in the interim, the use of data access tools on the PC can provide a step towards the availability of the information needed to make the best business decisions.

10.13 Accessing Data

Next to its employees, data is the most important asset that a company has. Without data and easy access to it, a business cannot function properly.

When business computing systems were based on mainframes, virtually all data was stored centrally in a secure and well managed environment. Operators made

sure data was safe, secure and easily accessible by authorised users. They, also, carried out mundane, but nevertheless important, storage management functions such as data backup.

With the advent of distributed computer systems, such as client/server networks, this has changed. A large proportion of a business' data is now acquired, processed and stored throughout the enterprise on many PCs and file servers. This leads to duplication of effort, wasted resources, poor or non-existent disaster recovery planning and inconsistencies in data. Conversely, executives and managers have also changed the way they perceive data. When mainframes ruled, organisations saw little value in comparing information from different applications.

Even small organisations will hold data in a variety of formats. Sales information on one system, stock control on another, financial data elsewhere. Modern business systems require the analysis and comparison of this data. Executives and managers are now required to create sophisticated business plans, reports and presentations using data which might be located anywhere on the enterprise. They need to locate information intuitively and without complex computer instructions, retrieve and then integrate it with the systems they run on their own PC.

The need for greater control and improved security while enabling enterprise access to information has led to the concept of corporate data which can be accessed by any authorised user. Data mining is a term used to describe the process of sifting through data to identify trends and, therefore, opportunities. Data mining is used to extract information from the databases.

The data in a data warehouse is information created and used by an organisation's core business applications. Vast amounts of data exist in different forms and different databases, including traditional operational data, such as sales, cost, inventory, payroll and accounting data, external data such as industry sales, forecasts and macro-economic data. The data can also be meta-data, which is 'data about the data itself'.

Some data is in unstructured format, examples include electronic mail and bulletin board entries, letters and journal articles. The challenge is to organise, analyse and present this data in a manner meaningful to decision makers. The primary benefits of data mining are to determine the patterns among data elements and enable the summarising, categorising and analysis of data from almost any conceivable viewpoint.

Data mining provides a significant competitive edge beyond that available from traditional operational systems and allows the determination of patterns amongst products, customers and resources.

The latest data mining software can search across different databases. Seek out relevant data, interpret the format and then retrieve it into the desk-top applications used by executives and managers. The most advanced software of this type runs on PCs and incorporates graphical user interfaces such as Windows, or OS/2 for easy operation. Users can search for data using simple business language terms and keywords, then integrate it into their own programs for further processing, or manipulation.

Data warehousing and data mining are concepts which many organisations are working towards. However, there are also many simpler and powerful data tools on the market which can provide a fast solution to the problems of gathering and manipulating data from distributed platforms. In the absence of a data warehouse it is particularly important to consider the management aspects when using these tools, as users making uncontrolled queries can impact the mission-critical applications which run the business. This problem can be overcome by the selection of an appropriate tool with management facilities to control access, provide security for confidential data and to restrict uncontrolled queries on operational systems.

The concepts of data access, data warehousing and data mining are being used successfully by many organisations to gain insight into their customers. Implementing these technologies will enable staff to make informed decisions using the best quality information to ensure their organisation remains competitive, efficient and productive.

11. Re-engineering

11.1 The Business

Business Process Re-engineering (BPR) is the strategic application of analysis and change at a departmental or corporate level to deliver business benefits such as cost savings and efficiency gains. Information technology is often applied to BPR projects, but it is not in itself the BPR. It is more accurately the method enabling business change.

Effective re-engineering starts with assessing operations at a corporate, departmental or even functional level. Each of the business processes involved is analysed to see how it works, how it interrelates with other processes, what it achieves and what it costs. The next stage is to investigate whether each process

is necessary and how it might be improved. Finally, new processes are developed and implemented so that improvements are made to overall efficiency, with reduced costs and increased productivity. All of this can be achieved without any information technology whatsoever.

However, in most organisations it is likely that IT can be used to help automate certain processes, eliminate others and introduce new ways of working. For these reasons, it is closely associated with re-engineering and the allied area of workflow, which addresses the need to improve the management of the passage of information through an organisation. Software modelling tools can also aid the process of documenting business work flows in order that the processes are comprehensively understood before considering change.

The key benefits of the business process re-engineering are typically the elimination of wasteful or costly processes, improved customer service, better efficiency and higher productivity. However, BPR should not be viewed as the mere automation of existing processes. Effective BPR will eliminate the wasteful elements of the process and then, if it appropriate, apply systems to deliver the automation and better overall efficiency.

Many of the most successful re-engineering projects have involved the introduction of electronic or paperless trading. Banks and building societies have introduced document image processing, where forms and letters are converted to digital images and processes using computers and work flow practices. There is no need to handle paper. Work loads can be balanced and managed so that maximum productivity and responsiveness to customer requirements is achieved.

In the retail and industrial sectors, examination of the processes involved in the manufacturing and supply chains have led to the application of electronic commerce concepts to streamline the supply chain. Concepts such as Electronic Data Interchange (EDI) have been applied to speed up communications between trading partners, effect the rapid payment of invoices, reduce other lead times and eliminate the cost and potential of errors associated with handling and processing huge amounts of paper.

Organisations considering embarking on re-engineering projects are well advised to talk to consultants and solutions providers with widespread experience in business analysis and re-engineering. These are most likely to have the breath of skills to make a holistic assessment of business processes and to deliver cost effective solutions based on the best available practices and technologies. As with so many parts of business life, careful planning and a clear set of objectives are also essential

11.2 Systems In The Future

The diagram on the following page attempts to show the inter-relationship of various sciences and other academic fields, which includes computing and systems, not only as tools but as a science in its own right.

The illustration shows how easy it is for an experienced analyst to use a CASE tool to diagram nine different fields of any subject and their contributions to each other.

No attempt is made to indicate any firm relationships among the 'boxes'. This is an example of how various subject can function with each other and together, in order to exchange information of common interests.

Undoubtedly, computing has become one of the most important tools of modern times and will continue to be just as influential in the future, for ever and ever. Every student, pupil, academic, professional, at home or in the office, use it in order to show improvement in his/her work, to speed things up, to calculate or illustrate. The time will come when every human being will end up using a system, or develop a system to accommodate his/her thoughts, problems/solutions, methods, business, statistics and predictions.

With computerised systems, things can only improve. More education and training is required at the beginning of life, when children can understand and are able to hit the keyboard and use the systems. With an early introduction to computing, the conditions of current phobias of computers will only improve and within a generation, most probably eliminated.

Computers, their systems and their applications do not get rid of people. All they do is to improve life - imagine life without the computerised systems! After all computers as tools, systems used for a multiple of functions and applications for any kind of work, are only an extension of human brains, knowledge and experience.

It is hoped that the diagram on the following page will prompt more inclusions and thoughts for the future. Computerised systems can be so enjoyable, in developing them, using them and playing with them.

INTERRELATING SCIENCES DIAGRAM

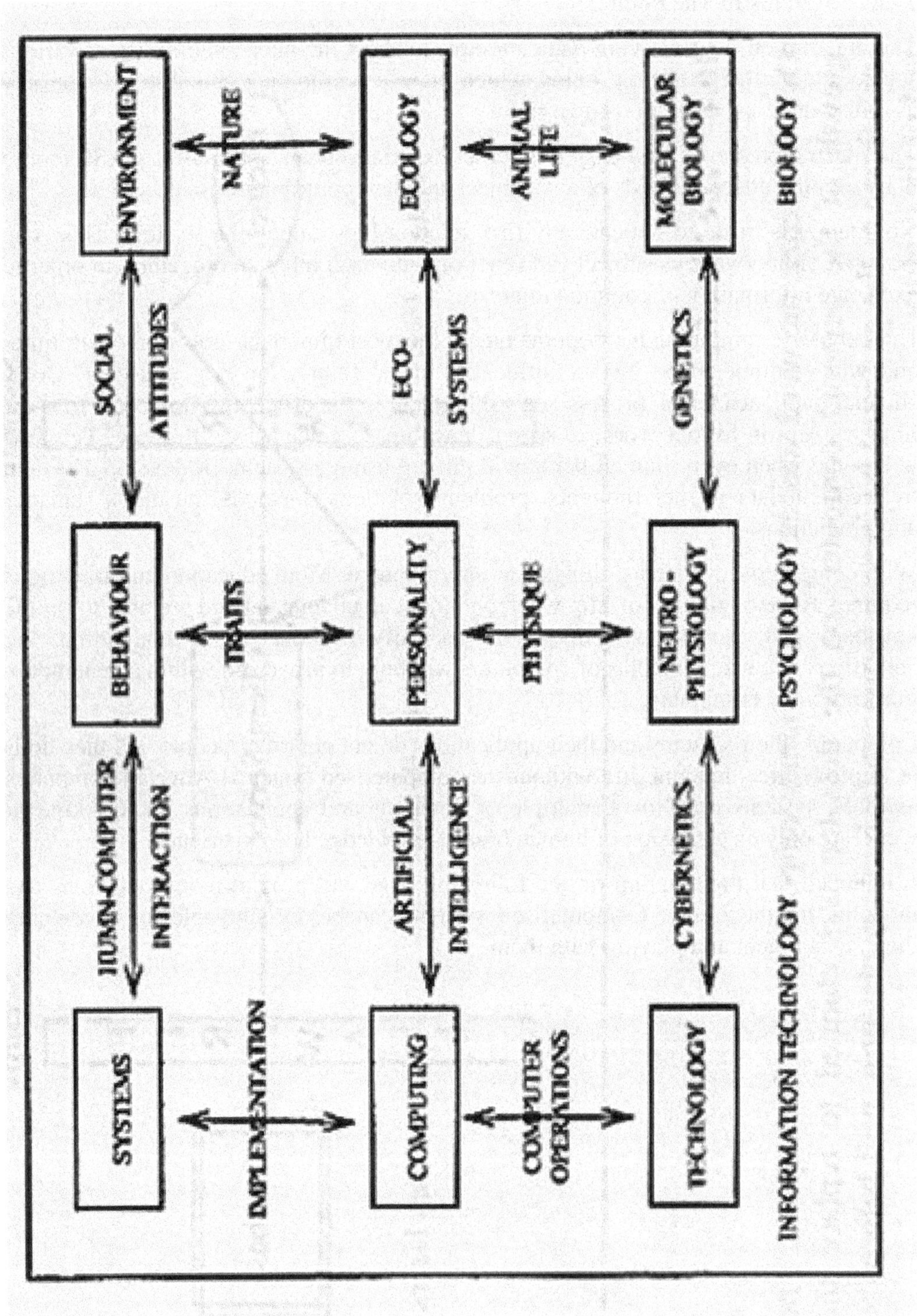

12: Project Planning

12.1 Managing The Plan

There are many PC-based tools and software which help with the management of a project and the allocation of responsibilities to software engineers. For the examples of the plans in this chapter, the PMW package has been used. It must be noted that the selection of a package depends on what the IT department's study has highlighted; the usage and tasks the project control software package is supposed to cover.

The stages of development and the steps within each stage are recorded, together with the timescales and the staff involved. A Gantt chart is produced showing the dates applicable to the steps completed and those outstanding. The updating is done regularly, preferably once a week and all participants become the recipients of various reports. Meetings are then held to discuss outstanding tasks, or issues arising.

12.2 Project Control

To maintain an effective project control, the overall planning activity is supported by the project managers. The management forum sets priorities, allocates resources, resolves issues and deals with risks.

12.2.1 Planning Function

The planning function relies on receiving up-to-date plans from individual project managers. As such, the planning office is responsible for the overall plan and the identification of risks and issues. Further on, the individual project plans, their monitoring, the transference of the actual resources and the reporting are handled by the planning office.

12.2.2 Initiation And Maintenance Of Plans.

The plans are initiated by the Project Manager. These are then set up by the Planner. Once approved, the plans are maintained by the Planning/Project Office. The Planning Office personnel define the standards. Additionally, the planners are responsible for the development and maintenance of the integrated baseline plan.

12.2.3 Plans For Management

Vital to the effective management of the programme are the plans with milestones, which:

- Set priorities,
- Allocate resources,
- Highlight issues,
- Assist in managing risks.

12.2.4 Time Recording

Timesheets are submitted on a weekly basis by the individuals in the project teams. Their completion is checked by the Project Manager. The details entered in the timesheets are transferred on the plans as actuals. The status of the plans is monitored by the Planning Office.

12.2.5 Reviews

Regular reviews are held with the Project Managers. Following the reviews, the planner makes the necessary adjustments to the plans. When the adjustments are completed, copies with the appropriate changes are submitted to the Project Managers for approval.

12.3 Quality Of Plans

The quality of the overall plan depends on the state of the plans of the individual teams and the commitment of the Project Managers to support this approach. With the outputs generated, the Project Manager identifies the resource requirements, the skills required to meet the targets and the costs incurred within the approved budget.

12.3.1 Plans Assurance

The Project Managers ensure that the:

- Plans are fit for the project,
- Current plans are logged,
- Plans and work completed match the project deadlines,
- Plans show adequate resources,
- Progress to date is in line with the expectations.

12.3.2 Project Activities

The project activities can include all the:

- IT applications,
- Embedded systems,
- Infrastructure,
- Equipment.

12.4 Planning Office Preparations

The Planning Office is responsible for the:

- Consistent standards on plans,
- Site plans development and maintenance,
- Agreement on milestones,
- Baselining of plans against actuals,
- Inter-projects dependencies.

12.4.1 The Planner

The Planner works with individual Project Managers for the:

- Estimated and actual project costing,
- Planning training needs for the project teams,
- Monitoring of progress against milestones,
- Identification of contentions,

- Project issues and risks,
- Proposes solutions and corrective actions.

12.4.2 Deliverables

The planning tool deliverables include the:

- Plans with milestones (based on the individual team plans),
- A register of issues and risks and their impact on target dates.

12.4.3 Monitoring

The monitoring by the Planning Office enables the:

- Viewing,
- Tracking,
- Reporting.

12.4.3.1 Viewing:

- Production of Gantt charts,
- Fields to create new plans,
- Gantt by resource,
- Viewing of dependencies,
- Creation of new resources,
- Setting up and viewing of fixed loading patterns,
- Assigning of categories.

12.4.3.2 Tracking:

- Hours worked from time sheets,
- Actual end dates, Status and Complete,
- Timesheet per person,
- Timesheets for all resources,

12.4.3.3 Reporting:

- Gantt chart at task level,
- Gantt chart at phase level,
- Actuals against baseline effort,
- All project milestones,
- Total loading of resources in days per week,
- Tracked time by week,
- Estimate to complete,
- Subtotals by project within group.

12.5 Settings

In addition, the planner prepares all plans to show the following settings:

- Project,
- Phase activity,
- Task,
- Milestone.

12.5.1 Outputs

Based on these settings the Planning Office outputs the following:

- Check list,
- Hierarchical chart,
- Programme flowchart,
- Weekly timesheets modifications,
- Individual project plans,
- Main plan.

12.5.2 The Stages

The various stages of work within the projects are classified by site. Systems and tasks are allocated within the stages.

12.5.3 Tasks

The tasks for the testing of the systems are uniform to all of the plans in the projects. These are:

- Investigation,
- Risk Assessment,
- Review,
- Site Test Plan,
- Contingency Plan,
- Test,
- Documentation,
- Sign off.

12.5.4 Actuals

The actuals recorded are based on the entry from the timesheets received from the Project Managers.

12.5.5 Baseline

The start and end dates are locked and baselined. The baselining on the plans are:

- Non-production time,
- General project time,
- General project management tasks,
- Activities.

12.5.6 Milestones

Where visits or tests on the sites have been completed, they are marked as milestones on the plans. Milestones are agreed with the Project Managers.

12.5.7 Tracked Time And Estimates

Based on the project managers' assumptions, estimates are entered on the plans. These estimates are initially baselined to show variances. The actuals are compared against these estimates.

12.5.8 Resource Loading

All resources are allocated on the planned tasks. To enable quick tracking of loading, the resources are uniquely abbreviated.

12.5.9 Sub-totals

The following sub-totals can be extracted from any of the project plans:

- Resource loading,
- Elapsed time against phases,
- Sites,
- Systems.

12.6 Planner's Responsibilities

The following responsibilities are part of the planning service offered by the individual planners to the project in general:

- Liaison with Project Managers,
- Co-ordination of all plans,
- Equal responsibility to all teams,
- Regular reviews with all Project Managers,
- Individual reviews,
- Global reviews (of all plans, at least every three months),
- Ad hoc presentations,
- Monitoring of:

    -Actuals,

    -Appropriate dates,

-Project milestones,

-All planning modifications.

- Training on planning:

  -Filtering,

  -Production of plans,

  -Timesheet entries,

  -Conversions.

- Collection of all estimates:

  -Resource,

  -Costs,

  -Timescales.

12.7 Planning Objectives

The objective of using a planning tool, such as the Microsoft Project, PMW, or spreadsheets, is to produce plans and reports based on details submitted by the Project Managers. Some plans may already exist in a draft format, at detailed and summary level.

12.7.1 Plan Completeness

The completeness of the plans at the end of each period largely relies upon the input from the project teams. The Planner's responsibility is to verify the plans received and consequently standardise, rationalise and consolidate the plans entered by the individuals.

12.7.2 Standards

All project plans can be developed to a constant standard. Although there is a certain degree for local site control, the milestones can be agreed and all project plans can be baselined and monitored against actuals.

12.8 Policies

The planner demonstrates and advises on what already exists on the planning tool/s. Any changes to the planning practices rely on policy decisions made by senior management.

END

ISBN: 978-1-84753-147-6

CHANGE MANAGEMENT IN I.T.

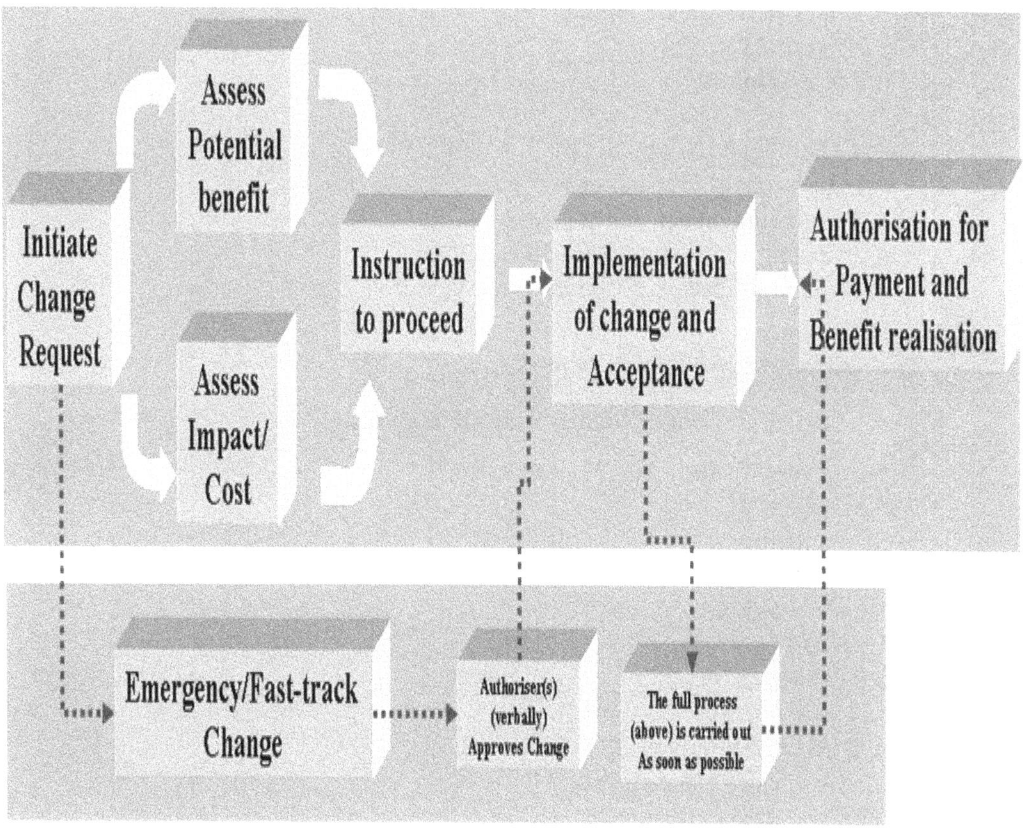

Andreas Sofroniou

CONTENTS

1. THE MANAGEMENT OF CHANGE
1.1 Change Management: The Concept
1.2 Programme Management
1.3 The Change Management Methodology

2. CHANGE MANAGEMENT IN IT PROGRAMMES
2.1 The Substitution Of Conditions
2.2 Change Management Leader
2.3 The Change Management Cycle
2.4 The Integration Of Methodologies
2.5 The Inter-relationship
2.6 Managing the Change Programme
2.7 Impact On Business

3. THE OBLIGATIONS OF A CORPORATION
3.1 Inter-dependency On I.T.
3.2 Internal Control
3.3 Staff Training

4. CHANGE MANAGEMENT ANALYSES
4.1 Assessment Of Changes
4.2 Communication
4.3 Change Management Practice
4.4 The Full Change Management Cycle

5. SAFEGUARDING INFORMATION SYSTEMS
5.1 Correct Software Control And Maintenance
5.2 Access Control And Maintenance
5.3 Firewalls
5.4 Vulnerability Assessment
5.5 Intrusion Detection Systems (IDS)
5.6 Cryptography
5.7 Virus Protection
5.8 Content Security

6. BUSINESS RELATED OVERVIEW
6.1 Business Responsibilities
6.2 Corporate Governance
6.3 Business Continuity
6.4 Reputation Management
6.5 Good Corporate Reputations
6.6 Preparing For A Crisis
6.7 Information Assurance
6.8 Information Availability

6.9 Interdependency And The Critical Information Infrastructure
6.10 Internet Commerce
6.11 World Wide Web (WWW)
6.12 Business Case
6.13 Global Networked Business
6.14 Implementation Of A Change Management Strategy
6.15 Monitoring

7. THE METHOD EXPLAINED
7.1 The Programme Objectives
7.2 The Suggested Method
7.3 The Change Management Cycle
7.4 Features And Benefits Of The Approach
7.5 Assessment Analysis
7.6 Strategic Cost Analysis
7.7 Change Administration System Tool
7.8 Work Plan Analysis
7.9 Communicating The Changes
7.10 How To Use The Contents

8. THE PRINCIPLES OF CHANGE MANAGEMENT
8.1 Team Approach
8.2 The Definition Of A Change
8.3 Approaches to Change Management
8.4 Events And Change Registers
8.5 Individual Interviews
8.6 Group Brainstorming
8.7 Change Analyses And Quantification of Changes
8.8 Change Control And Lack Of Follow-through
8.9 Change Transfer
8.10 Change Management vs. Project Management

9. BASIC PRINCIPLES OF CHANGE MANAGEMENT
9.1 The Process
9.2 Communication Of Assessments
9.3 The Current Project Plan Is The Baseline
9.4 Uncertainty Equals Risk In Changes
9.5 Judging The Quality Using The Scale
9.6 Process Overview
9.7 Project Prioritisation
9.8 Changes Prioritisation
9.9 Change Control

10. Initiating the Process
10.1 Organisational Culture

10.2 Organisational Structure And Stability
10.3 Effect Of Current Project Status
10.4 Project Fully Planned And Proceeding
10.5 Project In Trouble
10.6 Interviews With Key People
10.7 Choosing A Suitable Change Assessment Team.
10.8 Change Review Meetings

11. PROJECT PRIORITISATION
11.1 The Project And/Or Programme
11.2 Project Inclusion In Process
11.3 Prioritisation
11.4 The Project Prioritisation Process
11.4.1 The Standard Reference Matrix
11.4.2 Positioning and Prioritising New Projects
11.4.3 Project Approval and Resources
11.4.4 When Projects Change Position on the CC Diagram
11.4.5 Deciding which Projects Require Formal Change Management
11.5 Change Identification and Analysis
11.5.1 Assessment Analysis
11.5.2 Identify the Sources of Assessments
11.5.3 Prioritise Assessments
11.5.3.1 Sensitivity
11.5.3.2 Stability
11.5.4 Convert Key Assessments Into Changes
11.5.5 Categorisation Of Assessments — Change Drivers
11.6 Strategic Cost Analysis
11.7 Work Plan Analysis
11.7.1 Quality Review of Plans
11.7.2 Locate Hot Spots in the Plans
11.7.3 Project Readiness Walkthroughs
11.7.3.1 Basic Objectives Of A Project Readiness Walkthrough
11.7.3.2 Process follows a standard structure.
11.7.3.3 The Project Team meets
11.7.3.4 The Walkthrough is scheduled for (say) 3 hours.
11.7.3.5 The typical participants
11.7.3.6 The Walkthrough starts
11.7.3.7 The Walkthrough is completed
11.7.3.8 The matrix is updated
11.7.3.9 Changes reviewed regularly
11.7.4 Pre-selected Assessments
11.8 Change Prioritisation
11.8.1 Assessments and Changes Register
11.8.2 Positioning Changes
11.8.2.1 Criticality
11.8.2.2 Positioning in time

11.8.2.3 Controllability
10.8.3 Change Register Reports
10.9 Change Control
10.9.1 Strategic Approaches
Technical
Milestone
Decision
Resources
Red, Amber, Green
11.9.2 Tactical Approaches
11.9.3 Following Through on Actions
11.9.4 The Need for Change Plans
11.9.5 Essential Components of a Formal Change Plan
11.9.6 Devising Change Plans to Attack Changes
11.9.6.1 Developing Change Plans
11.9.6.2 Plans for Attacking Assessment Based Changes
11.9.6.3 Plans for Attacking Planning-Type Changes
11.9.6.4 Selecting Particular Change Plans
11.9.7 Project Change Organisation And Responsibilities
11.9.7.1 Change Ownership and Change Action Managers
11.9.7.2 Selecting Change Action Managers
11.9.7.3 Selecting Change Owners
11.9.7.4 The Change Review Board
11.9.7.4.1 Representation
11.9.7.4.2 before the meeting
11.9.7.4.3 during the meeting
11.9.7.4.4 After the meeting
11.9.7.5 Running Change Plans
11.9.7.6 Closing Change Plans
11.9.7.7 Stopping a Change Plan
11.9.7.8 Closing a Change Plan
11.9.7.9 Configuration Control
11.10 Applying The Process - Practical Considerations
11.10.1 Project Prioritisation Considerations
11.10.1.1 Using software tools to maintain the project inventory
11.10.1.2 Assessment Analysis Considerations
11.10.1.3 Getting To The Right Assessment
Self-analysis:
Forms:
Workshops:
11.10.1.4 Preparation For The Interview
11.10.1.5 During The Interview
11.10.1.6 At The End Of The Interview

11.10.1.7 Review Assessments And Changes Regularly
11.11 Sponsorship And Ownership
11.11.1 Identifying The Process Champions
11.11.2 Identifying The Process Owners
11.11.2.1 Affording Time For The Process
11.11.2.2 Enthusiasm And Attention To Detail
11.11.2.3 Access To Key Players In The Organisation
11.11.2.4 Avoiding The Split-up Approach
11.12 Hand Over Process
11.12.1 Training
11.12.2 Parallel Interviews
11.12.2.1 Consultant Leading Interviews
11.12.2.2 Client Leading Interviews
11.12.3 Procedures And Supporting Documentation
11.12.4 Software Tool Support
11.13 Ongoing Quality Management
11.13.1 Can they Continue To Do It Themselves?
11.13.2 Applying Change Management To The Hand Over Phase
11.14 Integrating Methodologies

12. INTERFACING
12.1 The Diagrammatic Representation Of The Desired Integration
12.2 Suggested Interfacing
2.3 Using The Existing Methods
12.4 Connection Of Project Management To Change Management

13. MANAGING THE CHANGE MANAGEMENT PROGRAMME
13.1 The Diagrammatic Representation Shown.
13.2 O: Sigma Change Management Decomposition
0: Manage Change Programme,
1: Manage Change Process,
2: Facilitate Change Programme,
3: Practise Change Methodology.
13.3 Relationship Of Dataflow Diagrams

14. MANAGING SUCCESSFUL PROGRAMMES
14.1 A Management Framework
14.2 Management Science
14.3 Automation
14.4 Deskilling
14.5 Database
14.6 Information Technology
14.7 Metamorphosis
14.8 Production Management

14.9 Hegemony
14.10 Time

15. CONFIGURATION MANAGEMENT
15.1 Identification Of Assets
15.2 Change Control And Release Procedures
15.3 Business Critical Projects

16. VALUATION OF FIXED ASSETS
16.1 Tangible Fixed Assets
16.2 Operational Assets
16.3 Not For Profit Activities
16.4 Disposal Of Assets

17. RELEASE
17.1 Prepare and Test Release
17.2 Release Plans
17.3 Documentation
17.4 Definition Of Products
17.5 Procurement
17.6 Reviews
17.7 Audit
17.8 Dual Key Review Process
17.9 The Difference Between A Programme And A Project
17.10 'Traffic Lights'

18. BENEFITS MANAGEMENT
18.1 Definition Of Benefits Management
18.2 Identification Of Benefits
18.3 Benefits And Performance Management
18.4 Benefits And Risks
18.5 Achieving Benefits
18.6 Key Factors For Success
18.7 Value Of Benefits
18.8 The Role Of Benefits Management
18.9 Scope Of Benefits Management
18.10 Management Commitment And Support

19. MANAGING CHANGES TO REQUIREMENTS
19.1 Managing The Requirements Changes
19.2 Partnership Arrangement
19.3 Requirements For Change
19.4 Change Control Procedure
19.5 Authorisation
19.6 Planned Change
19.7 Proactive Change Programmes
19.8 Unplanned Change

20. SECURITY AND PRIVACY OF INFORMATION
20.1 Investment Protection
20.2 Vulnerability
20.3 Privacy And Data Sharing
20.4 Legislation
20.5 Security Policy Processes
20.6 Securing Assets
20.6.1 Personnel Security
20.6.2 Physical Security
20.6.3 Document Security
20.6.4 Technical Security
20.7 Security Incidents
20.8 Good Practice In Security

21. A CASE STUDY IN CHANGE MANAGEMENT
21.1 Purpose Of Case Study
21.2 Principles Of Report
21.3 Scope And Assumptions
21.4 Summary Of Analysis
21.5 Overview Of Recommendation
21.6 Review Of Current Change Management (CM) Processes
21.7 Change At A Client Site
21.8 Changes In Scope Within The Programme
21.9 Release Management
21.10 Configuration, Release, Assets, Change (CRAC) Diagram
21.11 Current CM Procedures For A Client (Legacy and Modernisation)
21.12 Current Procedures For Activity Requests (Legacy and Modernisation)
21.13 Current CM Procedures For Major Hardware (Legacy and Modernisation)
21.14 Current CM Procedures For Other Sites
21.15 Current Incident Management Procedures for Desktop/Network
21.16 Current Service Request Procedures
21.17 Current New Business Procedures
21.18 Configuration Management
21.19 New Business process
21.20 Business and Capacity Planning
21.21 Contract Management and Management Accounting
21.22 An example of various phases involved for a multi-sites client
21.23 Options
Governance:
Culture:
Process:

Tool:
21.24 Recommended Option
21.25 A New Single Process For Change Management
21.26 Adoption Of One Existing Process For Change Management
21.27 Virtual Change Management Community
21. 28 Wait for DWP to take lead on Change Management processes
21.29 Improve Visibility
21.30 Next Step For Recommended Option
21.31 Immediate Action
Client Owned Change Boards
Explicitly Identify Change Co-ordinators
Pipeline owners:
Further identification/mapping
21.32 Next Phase of CM Process Development
Process Re-engineering and Assurance:
Communication:
Form and IT toolsets used by teams:
Management Information System (MIS):
Training and guidance notes
21.32.1 Governance
21.32.2 Culture
21.32.3 Process
21.32.4 Tools
21.33 Reports Availability
21.34 Long Term Aim
21.35 A Major Consultancy Study
21.36 People Stop Change

22. PROJECT MANAGEMENT IMPROVEMENTS
22.1 Programme Management
22.2 The Use Of Programme Management
22.3 Programme Management Organisation
22.3.1 Programme sponsorship
22.3.2 Programme management
22.3.3 Programme support
22. 4 Programme Planning
22.5 Benefits Management
22.6 Stakeholder Management
22.7 Issues Management And Risk Management
22.8 Quality Management
22.9 Configuration Management
22.10 Audit

23. THE PROCESSES OF PROGRAMME MANAGEMENT
23.1 Identifying A Programme

23.2 Defining A Programme
23.3 Establishing A Programme
23.4 Managing The Project Portfolio
23.5 Delivery Of Benefits
23.6 Closing A Programme

24. PROJECT PLAN
24.1 Producing Plans
24.2 Sub-Products
24.3 Quality Control
24.4 Project Plan Example (In Microsoft Format)

25. WEAKNESS IN PROJECT MANAGEMENT
25.1 Weakness Of Individuals
25.2 Process Steps Required
25.3 Collection Of Information
25.4 Agreement On Resources
25.5 Project Management
25.6 Project Management Element
25.7 Project Management Functional Skills

26. LIFE CYCLE COSTING
26.1 Whole Life Costing
26.2 The Importance Of Life Cycle Costing (LCC)
26.3 Option Evaluation. LCC Techniques
26.3.1 Improved Awareness
26.3.2.Improved Forecasting
26.3.3 Performance Trade-off Against Cost
26.4 People Involved
26.5 Principles Included
26.6 The Process
26.7 The Methodology of LCC
26.8 Cost Breakdown Structure (CBS)
26.9 Cost Estimating
26.10 Discounting
26.11 Inflation
26.12 Risk Assessment
26.13 Sensitivity

27. REMEMBERING THE MAIN CHANGE MANAGEMENT POINTS
27.1 Change, An Uncertain Event
27.2 Identification Of Risky Projects
27.2.1 Systematic
27.2.2 Interaction
27.2.3 Generic Approach
27.2.5 Applications
27.3 Management Qualities Required

27.4 Decomposition Of Management Attributes
27.5 Project Management Points For Improvement
27.6 Process Steps Required
27.7 Collection Of Information
27.8 Agreement On Resources
27.9 The Score Graph
27.10 Acknowledgement

1. THE MANAGEMENT OF CHANGE

1.1 Change Management: The Concept

Change Management and the changes to Configuration, Release and Assets as a whole group of activities have traditionally been concerned with finding effective solutions to specific operational problems. The purpose of this book is to look at current problems and new, better methods, techniques, and tools for processing changes. In the past, it has been found that too many of the solutions are not implemented and, of those that are, too few survive the inclination of client functional areas to return to familiar ways of doing things. Therefore, Change Management personnel have gradually come to realize that their tasks should not only include solving specific problems but also designing problem-solving and implementation systems that predict and prevent future problems, identify and solve current ones, and implement and maintain these solutions under changing conditions.

As an Executive in multi-national organisations and Government Departments, the author has come to realise that most problems do not arise in isolation but are part of an interacting system. The book, in principle, is seeking for a process of simultaneous interrelated solutions to a set of interdependent problems. Further more, substantial effort has been devoted in recommending a rational methodology for one, or the least possible processes, for future change management. Businesses need to find better ways of doing things, is often not nearly as great as is the need to maximize use of what is already operational. This book, therefore, has been addressing itself more and more to determining how to produce the willingness to change procedures suitable to the way people are willing to work and with processes that they are familiar with.

The book, which follows various consultancy assignments, considers the additional, more detailed recommendations, including strategic changes, training, convincing resources, meetings with people, development of workshops and exchanges of new ideas. The reader, therefore, must consider such points that absorb resources, excessive costs and incur a heavy workload for existing staff.

In the areas in which technology advances fastest, new products and new materials are required in a constant flow, but there are many client areas in which the rate of change can be gentle. Although each process considered may be trivial, the total effect is many times as large as the margin between success and failure in an operational situation. These efforts to improve existing processes have been formalised under the various sections of this book.

The legacy processes and their procedures have had a dramatic impact on the management of changes. The speed and data-handling capabilities of experienced staff, enables the realistic changes and because of their know-how they get meaningful solutions to those changes through the use of long standing techniques. The changes occurring under such circumstances consist of calculating the performance of a system by evaluating a model of it for randomly selected values of variables contained within a unique process and its procedures. Most changes under such operations are concerned with "stochastic" variables; that is, variables whose values change randomly within some probability distribution over time.

There is still considerable difficulty, however, in drawing inferences from operational legacy processes to the real world of smooth Change Management. Additionally, the growing number of changes in the information-processing applications is currently on the increase. To this effect, the recommendations made in this book may be the optimum solution to the problems of adopting new processes. The procedures recommended as processes, will improve the cost-effectiveness of changes and their management. In the realm of the economy, they may be expected to lead to higher productivity, particularly in the service sectors and related processes, decision-making, problem solving, administration, and support of clerical functions.

Awareness that possession of information on any changes is tantamount to a competitive edge is stimulating the gathering of information at national levels. Similarly, concern is mounting over the safeguarding and husbanding of changes to the proprietary and strategic information within the confines of a client, as well as within outsourcing companies. Administration-oriented information systems and the management of changes in client sites have as their objective the husbanding and optimisation of corporate resources, namely; employees and their activities, inventories of materials and equipment, facilities, and finances.

A client's administrative information systems and the Management Information Systems (MIS) focus primarily on resource administration and provide top management with reports of aggregate data. Executive information systems may be viewed as an evolution of administrative information systems in the direction of strategic tracking, modelling, and decision-making. Typically, Change Management consists of a number of processes, each supporting a particular function and changes, which may occur any day of the year.

Change Management processes concentrate on resource allocation and task completion of organized activities. They usually incorporate such scheduling methods as the Critical Path Method (CPM) or Program Evaluation and Review Technique (PERT).

The processes, with which the book is concerned, are first of all man-made. Second, some of them are small and simple to manage, or they are large and complex, depending on the changes required. Their component parts sometimes interact so extensively that a change in one part is likely to affect many others. It is, therefore, of primary importance that all the Change Management processes interact with all the functionalities. Otherwise, Change Management as a tool is of no significance. Processes may also vary depending on the amount of human judgment that enters into their operation.

1.2 Programme Management

Programme Management may have many responsibilities, but the most important of all is the ability to identify and positively execute plans to manage the changes threatening the objectives.

Through a process of structured interviews and plans the Assessment Analysis is used to highlight the specific requests for changes, which may turn into risks. During the interviews Assessment Analysis is used to capture the key changes from the interviewees.

In turn, the Assessment Analysis provides a life-cycle process, which highlights the primary prioritisation of the changes. In large, complex and critical programmes, it is essential that a true prioritised report is available so that the imminent changes can be managed first.

The process commences by identifying the most important changes, which may become threats to a project. These are given priority, support and management expertise. Once the prioritisation exercise is completed, the participating people are notified and subsequently interviewed to bring out and capture any possible changes they may have.

Within a programme, projects are prioritised to ensure that those most critical to the programme's success are given priority to scarce resources.

1.3 The Change Management Methodology

The Management of Change allows the capture of collective knowledge and expertise from those involved on the project, in a form that facilitates the communication of changes, their assessments and the pro-active management of the changes requested.

In essence, this is the mechanism by which the functions of Information Technology programmes and projects are held together as a result of the principles operating within the methodology for the management of change:

- Systematic: The varied Changes, their Assessments and the consequential Risks relating to or consisting of a system. Methodical in procedures and plans, these are addressed to those involved and deliberating within the parameters of their systems development responsibilities.
- Integration: The results being dependable on the mutual or reciprocal action which encourages those involved in the programmes and projects to communicate with each other and to work closely with a view to solving the threatening changes before they impact on the development of the system.
- Generic: The individuals involved maintain an approach, which relates and characterises the whole group of those involved in assessing the changes and attacking any threatening ones before they become risks to the development of the system. The end result being the avoidance of apparent problems within the pre-defined users systems requirements.
- Methodology: Following the system architects and the change management practitioners enable this. Simply follow the approved body of systems development methods, rules and management procedures employed by their organisation. For practical or even ethical reasons, it must be noted that with such a philosophy, it is seldom possible to fulfil all requirements of very large organisational systems.
- Applications: As such, Change Management is administered by putting to use such techniques and in applying the Change Management principles in the development of various applications will involve numerous and varied activities. A concrete issue in developing new applications is the problem of communication among the people involved, the motivation constantly needed for generic work, the ability to interact systematically and in using Change Management.

2. CHANGE MANAGEMENT IN IT PROGRAMMES

2.1 The Substitution Of Conditions

In general, the Management of Change, deals with the substitution of one thing or set of conditions for another, thus making something different from its previous condition, be it an alteration in state or quality, variety, variation, mutation.

More specific, in the Information Technology environment anything that becomes different, be it the performance of a system, the planning of new enhancements, the development of new systems and their various phases, the complete configuration and its assets, releases, all this require a structure approach.

Change Management in Information Technology Programmes Management, therefore, includes and enables any:

- Alteration,
- Modification,
- Conversion,
- Variance,
- Transformation,
- Remodelling,
- Reconstruction,
- Re-organization,
- Substitution,
- Replacement.

Any kind or type of change which may occur and affect a systems configuration, releases and assets, be it hardware, software or whatever the term of IT may represent.

This process spans the whole life cycle from initial concept and definition of business needs through to the end of the useful life of an asset or end of a services contract. Both conventionally funded and more innovative types of funded projects are included. This definition is consistent with modern supply chain management practices. The process is not limited to the purchasing function in companies and departments and is inherently multi-functional especially in large, complex and/or novel procurements.

2.2 Change Management Leader

The Change Management Leader proposes and agrees the scope of the Change Management processes, function, the items that are to be controlled, and the information that is to be recorded.

Develops Change Management standards, Change Management plans and procedures. Evaluates Change Management tools and recommends those that best meet the organisation's budget, resource, timescale and technical requirements.

Creates and manages the Change Management plan. Performs audits to check that the physical IT inventory is consistent with the Change Management Database Initiates actions needed to secure funds to enhance the infrastructure and staffing levels in order to cope with growth and change

2.3 The Change Management Cycle

The concept being a simple one as shown in the diagram below:

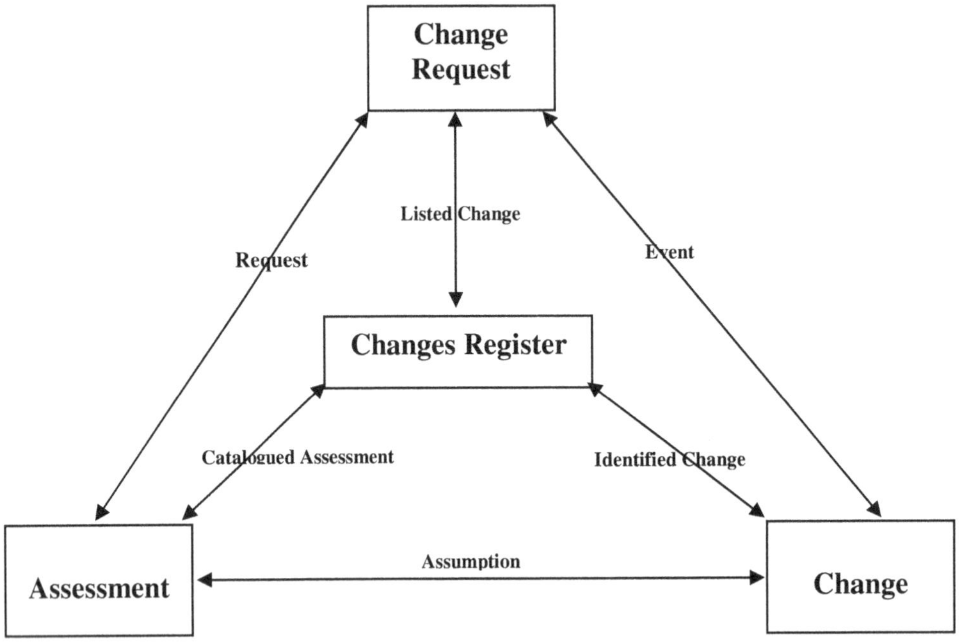

Change Management Cycle

The Change Management principles explained in this book were developed by the author whilst employed by *PsySys Limited,* over a period of twenty four years. The methodology was used for PsySys' international clients, from 1980 onwards. The idea of a structured approached to organisational requests for changes and their management proved beneficial to customers and users who integrated the full process with other methodologies, such as Structured Systems Analysis and Designing methods and Project Management procedures

.

2.4 The Integration Of Methodologies

The comprehension of how to integrate the three methodologies can be achieved, simply by following the concept as shown below:

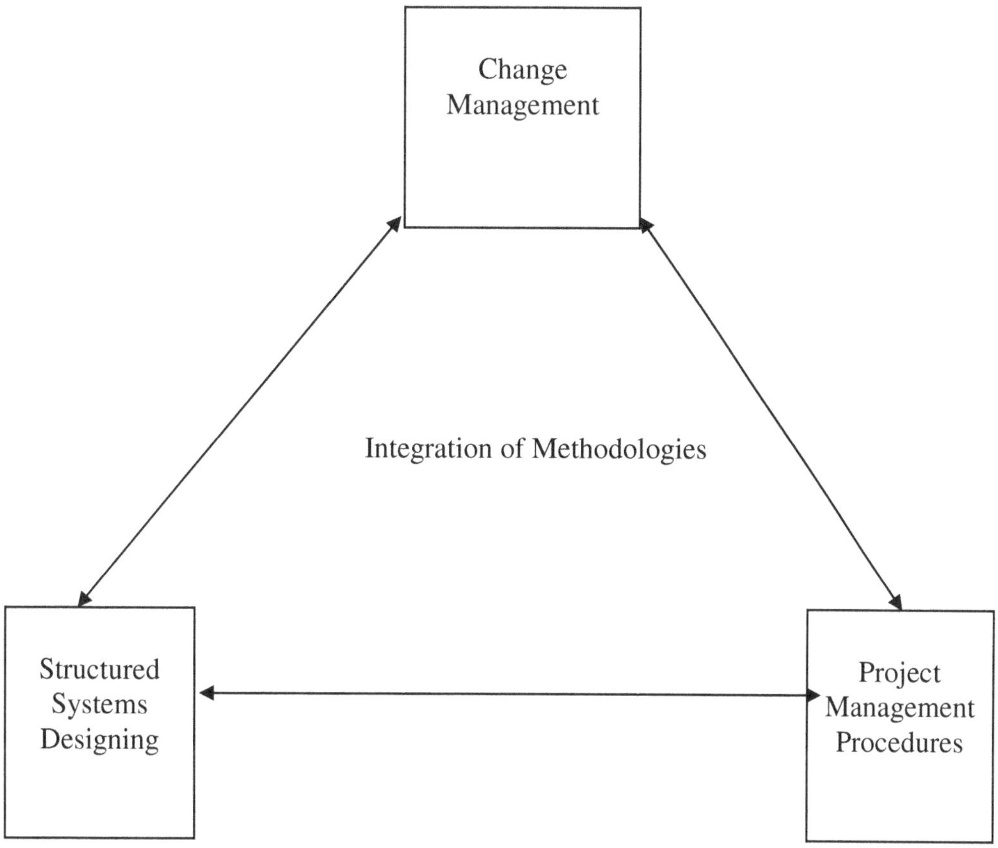

2.5 The Inter-relationship

The various steps included in each of the methodologies are named in the next diagram. Or, to a further extent, the various stages of system development and the steps taken to manage projects and adopt the change management cycle, are shown on the next page:

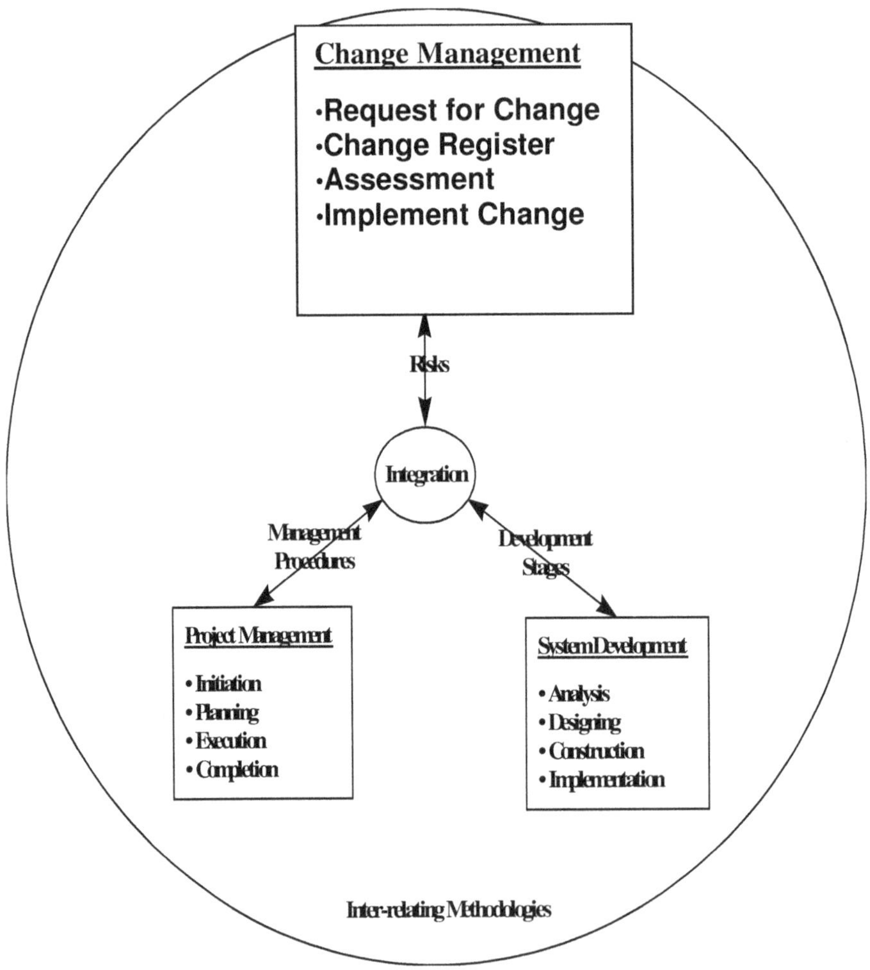

2.6 Managing the Change Programme

It is basic business sense to identify, assess, manage and monitor changes that are significant to the fulfilment of an organisation's business objectives. In recent years businesses have been transformed by Changes many cases heavily dependent on I.T.

The financial consequences of a breakdown in controls or a security breach are not only the loss incurred, but also the costs of recovering and preventing further failures. The impact is not only financial: it can affect adversely reputation and brand value as well as the business' performance and future potential.

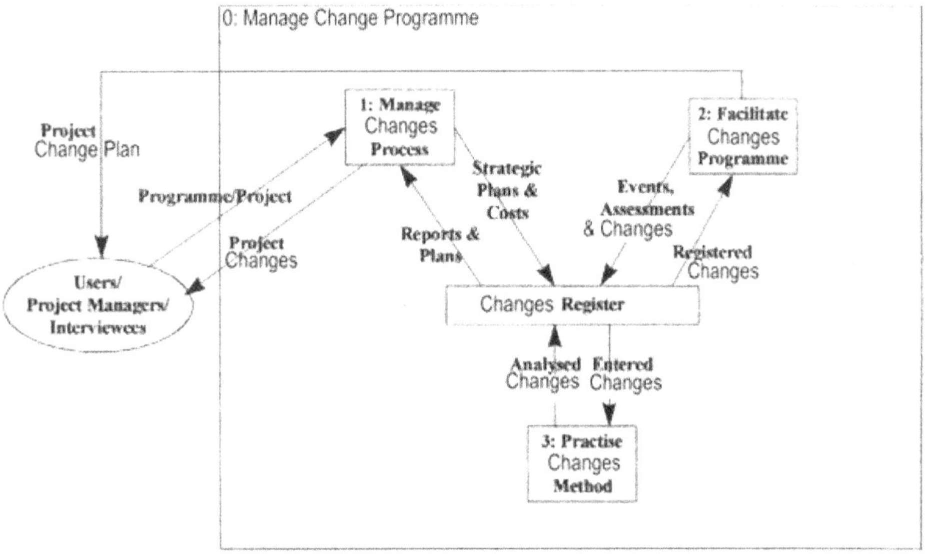

2.7 Impact On Business

Boards can regard inadequate system development as a significant risk, and where directors feel that this may be the situation in their organisations, they may need to ask tough questions of themselves and their management teams. Systems development and their changes is an issue that boards may need to recognise should regularly be on their agenda, and not delegated to I.T. technicians.

Business in the past was primarily confined to assessment of the change and its associated risk surrounding fire, flood and Acts of God. In business today we have become high dependent on information systems. Failure to build computer systems as required and the changes requested thereafter, by the users has a major impact on our business to function. The inability of companies to provide adequate systems can cause potential problems to customers, suppliers, employees and an all round havoc to information.

3. THE OBLIGATIONS OF A CORPORATION

3.1 Inter-dependency On I.T.

During the last fifty years, the governments of the industrialised countries and the global businesses have become increasingly inter-dependent on Information Technology systems, to the point where many organisations would cease to function if these systems were unavailable.

Creating a strategy to ensure business continuity is, therefore, a prime consideration and whilst we are all familiar with the threat to the operations of corporations, such as system failures, badly developed and running systems, we are less aware of the potential risks to our I.T. systems and their costly development.

In the early days of I.T. few people envisaged the level of complexity and connectivity that would be achieved by the end of last century, particularly through the explosive growth in the use of the Internet. In the last ten years the number of the individuals and organisations that are connected to each other electronically has risen exponentially, thus increasing the risks of substantial loss through internal and external threats, some of which can paralyse distributed systems.

More and more transactions and communications will be carried out electronically and therefore the conditions to create risk free systems are essential to build confidence in information, communications and technology.

3.2 Internal Control

A further complication is that organisations are now subjected to a number of new laws and requirements that add further burdens to the hard-pressed executive. Specifically, these relate to the prevention of unauthorised access to information stored about the general public and employees, as well as allowing them to access information stored about them.

Furthermore, the importance that is placed on the protection of the information base of an organisation is emphasised by the rules on corporate governance being strengthened to ensure that protecting the electronic assets is taken seriously by Senior Executives.

Compliance with all of the influences that can affect the construction of new systems in your business or organisation is best achieved by the development of a methodical changes management practice. This includes the collection of events, the cataloguing of the assessments leading to the identification of threatening changes and the plan to assist in the execution of various tasks. Thus, securing the building of the I.T. system as per target, with the least possible changes.

To achieve such standards, the following elements should be included:

- The concept of changes planning and their control to be managed by a Changes Management Practitioner,
- A vulnerable part of the management of changes is the Changes Management system itself and the data stored in it,

- The changes plans as reported by the Changes Management system is, also, of a significant importance, in evaluating the events and in the execution of actions.

3.3 Staff Training

One of the greatest threats in Change Management is the non-acceptance of it or misuse of the system by the organisation's own personnel. Obtaining their buy-in is essential. It is obvious that someone is going to be appointed to ensure that the change management principles are adhered to and the system maintained throughout the organisation. It is, also, important that if information leaves the organisation by its transference to others for use on the company's behalf, that they have adequate systems to protect the set standards. The successful implementation of Change Management is reliant upon people and in particular the employees whose contracts of employment may need adjustment to protect the company and the adequate management and execution of plans for the solution to the threats caused by the changes identified.

To build a complete picture of what the Change Management cycle includes, please refer to the diagram drawn below:

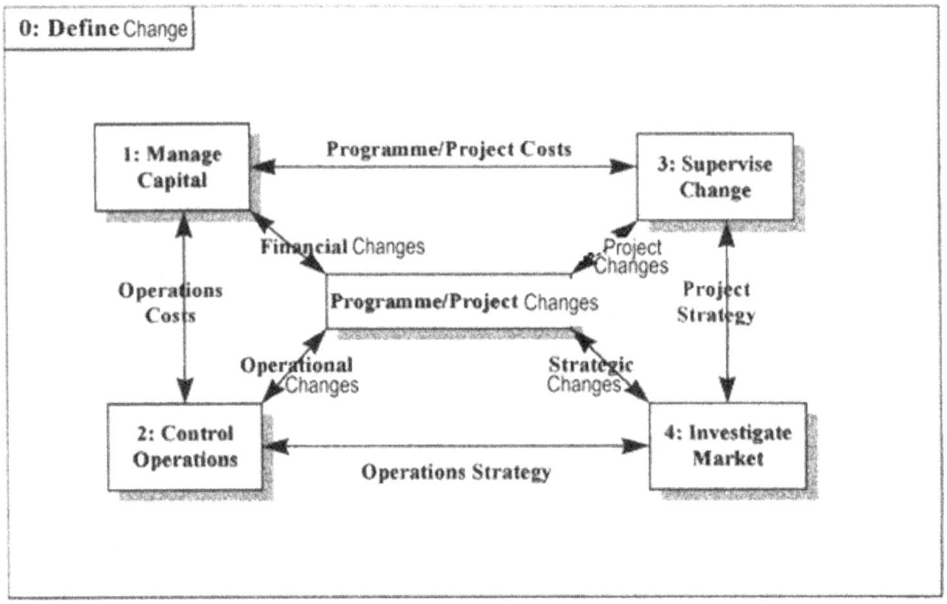

The Comp[onents Of The Total Business Changes

Computer and Network Management ensure that we secure the processing facilities and generally prevent loss, modification or misuse of the Change Management information entered on the changes systems. Computer based changes classification and control of the written changes policy allows management to have direction to control and monitor the information output by the changes system.

There are two ways in which you can approach the creation and implementation of change management. By:

- Completing the process internally, or
- Utilising the services of external Changes Management Consultants.

4. CHANGE MANAGEMENT ANALYSES

4.1 Assessment Of Changes

Fundamental to the creation of a Change Management system is the assessment of the changes (Changes Analysis) to your business and the potential loss that could accrue if things go wrong. Change Assessment software tools are available in the market, which can be used by consultants, or by internal staff. What is important is the ability to assess the change to your business and the cost to protect it against the change. The end result is that you have to make the valued judgement on the amount the business spends, on the implementation and the monitoring of a change policy.

Products and systems are available to counter the threats and changes that have been identified. There is a wide range of options available, but remember that anything chosen will require expertise to design and complete a system, taking into account how the various solutions will inter-react with each other. Like all things to do with I.T., the design and implementation of systems, change solutions are only as good as the people installing them.

4.2 Communication

The most important factor in the success of any management style is the ability to communicate with each other, one to one or in groups of people. The art of communication is just as important to the whole process of the management of changes. More so, where the changes identified have become a threat because of the problem of human communications.

This is where the appointment of an experienced and trained Change Practitioner is worth the effort put into securing such individual/s.

4.3 Change Management Practice

A trained Change Management Practitioner will have enough knowledge to run and maintain the system, as well as ample experience to be able to communicate with all levels of employees, hold meetings and ensure the plans executed.

In brief and as the diagram on the next page shows, the Practitioner will be responsible for the complete Change Management cycle.

4.4 The Full Change Management Cycle

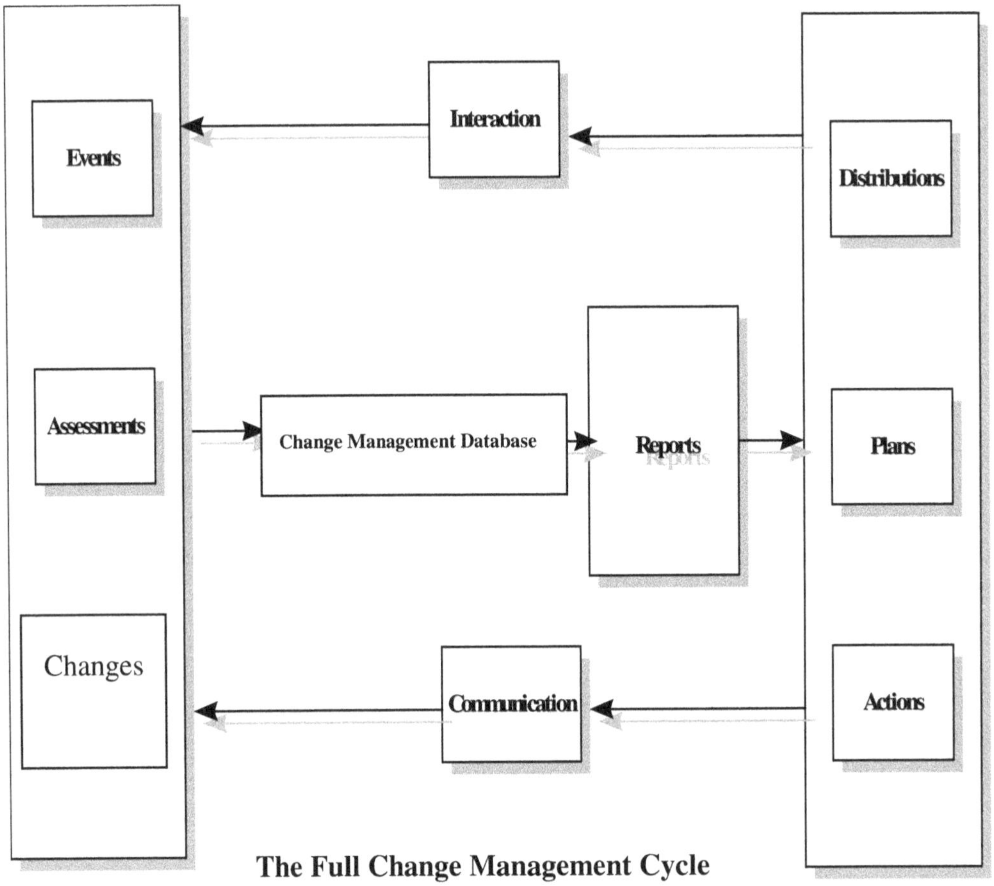

The Full Change Management Cycle

In analysing changes, certain counter measures may have to be looked into. The mechanisms for safeguarding the construction of your information system is by managing changes and avoiding the threat of failing to build the required system.

5. SAFEGUARDING INFORMATION SYSTEMS

5.1 Correct Software Control And Maintenance

Writing software is not a precise science and software companies are continually updating their software as information is received from users on their experiences.

They also become aware of the ways in which hackers are breaking into their systems and produce 'fixes' to prevent this happening. Regular monitoring of your suppliers' web sites and contacts with them will allow your organisation to keep up to date with the changes.

The mechanism for safeguarding your information systems include:

- The simplest and most important information security safeguard,
- Removal of known bugs,
- Updates with latest revisions,
- Secure 'back doors' into your systems.

5.2 Access Control And Maintenance

Access control is one of the fundamental parts of the security policy as it defines the employees, customers, suppliers or partners who are allowed to access information stored on your computer system.

Achieving the balance between security and practicality takes time and deals with people's own perception of the right to access information and their perceived position in the organisation.

The following are a few steps, which will help:

- Deter hackers through use of access screens and passwords,
- Authenticate users by use of passwords and/or token,
- Protect sensitive systems by special authorisation,
- Ensure passwords are secure,
- Revoke all passwords.

5.3 Firewalls

A Firewall is a security mechanism that allows limited access to your stored information, allowing approved traffic access according to a well thought out plan. A Firewall in its normal context prevents the passage of fire for a given period, but as stated above a Firewall in computer security does not prevent access in its totality.

Your security policy will have decided the traffic that is allowed in from the outside world on to your servers where information and programmes are stored.

A Firewall:

- Should be used on any system connected to the Internet,
- Can block communications likely to cause damage,

- Must be correctly configured and constantly monitored.

5.4 Vulnerability Assessment

The analysis of a network to identify points of weakness, if done manually from scratch, is an extremely time consuming operation. Therefore, software has been developed to complete this task. Experience in understanding the results is important to ensure implementation of the right solutions to cure any weaknesses.

- Network scanning:
    - Looks at entire network from hacker's perspective,
    - Looks for poor configuration and maintenance.
- Host scanning:
    - Looks at individual systems to ensure technical standards and business needs are maintained
- Covers software configuration, passwords and auditing on individual systems.

5.5 Intrusion Detection Systems (IDS)

Intrusion detection is the art of detecting inappropriate, incorrect or irregular activity.

There is often a distinction between misuse and intrusion detection. The term intrusion is used to describe attacks from outside, where as misuse is used to describe an attack that originates from the internal network.

The purpose of an intrusion detection system is to detect unauthorised access or misuse of a computer system.

- IDS monitor intrusions into a network and detect potential attacks:
    - Network IDS
        - Detect attacks from outside,
        - Must be carefully configured to avoid false alarms,
    - Host IDS
        - Can look for unwanted 'graffiti' on web sites
        - Can detect attempts to steal passwords and data and tamper with audit trails.

5.6 Cryptography

Cryptography has been used for centuries to provide a means of sending messages in code so that they mean nothing to the casual reader.

It was an obvious extension to use cryptography to secure data held on or transmitted by computers. As computers become more powerful it is necessary to increase the power of the encryption so that the codes used cannot be broken within a reasonable time scale.

Cryptography:

- Provides the most effective way of ensuring confidentiality, integrity and authentication of data,
- Should be used for secure transmission of data both internally and externally,
- Must utilise digital signatures for important electronic documents.

5.7 Virus Protection

'Virus' is used as a generic term covering any of the various forms of malicious software code that circulates freely on the Internet. Malicious code can cause immediate and obvious damage to a system, by tying up network resources or by destroying data.

Or, it can work in a more insidious way by causing cumulative deletions from, or insertion into, databases. Even more dangerously, it can open back doors into your system.

These may enable hostile outsiders to take control of parts of the network:

- Virus:
  - Covers any malicious software –whether damaging or not,
  - Circulates freely on the Internet, but can be on any floppy disc or CD,
  - Can tie up resources, destroy data, or change it subtly,
  - Can allow hostile outsiders when you have been attacked.
- Virus protection can:
  - Alert you to possible attacks,
  - Provide you with protection,
  - Give you solutions when you have been attacked.

5.8 Content Security

Content security/filtering is the management of the content of digital communications.

For legal reasons companies need to control the content of the material created, stored and forwarded on their networks. Content filtering software will permit scanning of e-mail and Internet sites for criminal, defamatory or racist material.

Such software must be carefully configured and companies should have a clear policy on its use.

The software should:

- Enable you to control the content of e-mails and Internet downloads,
- Reduce legal liability for illegal or damaging material,
- Be carefully configured and monitored,
- Enable a policy to be clear to all employees and third parties.

6. BUSINESS RELATED OVERVIEW

6.1 Business Responsibilities

There are now a host of legal and regulatory definitions detailing Board/Business Owner's responsibilities to ensure that information stored on computer systems, particularly with reference to people's personal information, be they employees or customers, is protected from improper access or use.

Corporate Governance defines Business Continuity and the management of the organisation's reputation as being the responsibility of the Board within public quoted companies. Compliance with the policies laid down is equally applicable to non-quoted companies, as it ensures best practice and safeguards all of our businesses. To comply, it must be shown that the risks to the organisation have been assessed and policies have been enacted to ensure that, as far as practicable, the potential for damage or loss has been reduced to realistic levels.

In the electronic age every aspect of our lives is becoming interdependent on others for computer-based transactions, especially in the business world. Around half of the interruptions to Business Continuity are now as a result of a failure in areas related to computers.

6.2 Corporate Governance

It is basic business sense to identify, assess, manage and monitor changes that are significant to the fulfilment of an organisation's business objectives. In recent years businesses have been transformed by, and are in many cases heavily dependent on I.T. The financial consequences of a breakdown in controls or a security breach are not only the loss incurred, but also the costs of recovering and preventing further failures. The impact is not only financial: it can affect adversely reputation and brand value as well as the business' performance and future potential.

Boards can regard inadequate system development as a significant change, and where directors feel that this may be the situation in their organisations, they may need to ask tough questions of themselves and their management teams. Systems development and their changes is an issue that boards may need to recognise, should regularly be on their agenda and not delegated to I.T. technicians.

6.3 Business Continuity

Business in the past was primarily confined to assessment of the change surrounding fire, flood and Acts of God. In business today we have become dependent on information systems. Failure to build computer systems as required by the users has a major impact on our business and how the company functions. The inability of organisations to provide adequate systems can cause potential problems to customers, suppliers, employees and an all round havoc to information.

6.4 Reputation Management

The management of a company's reputation is a vital issue for any business. It is the responsibility of directors to ensure that the issues are fully understood at board level and that time is spent putting in thorough, but flexible, plans to deal with them.

A good reputation can:

- Put you above competition,
- Attract better staff,
- Attract business partners,
- Attract investors,
- Open doors to different markets,
- Protect your business during a crisis.

6.5 Good Corporate Reputations

According to research carried out by MORI and Fortune magazine, the seven key aspects for a good corporate reputation are:

- Financial performance, profitability and long term investment value,
- The chief executive and senior management team,
- Quality of your products and services,
- Treatment of staff,
- Social responsibility,
- Customer service,
- Ability to communicate.

6.6 Preparing For A Crisis

A crisis is an event that can damage the company, its product, service or reputation. Crises include natural disasters, man-made disasters, product recalls, sudden and serious financial problems, and closures and strikes.

Preparing for a future can appear a mundane task, but in essence is necessary for the safe-keeping of a company's reputation.

Companies should:

- Identify and prepare a crisis management team,
- Form a crisis management plan,
- Remind board members that more is at stake than their own reputation.

6.7 Information Assurance

Information Assurance is becoming the term to denote the protection of information and information systems by ensuring their confidentiality, integrity and availability, as well as providing for authentication and non-repudiation.

A comprehensive strategy will assure those with whom you wish to do business electronically, that you have taken all reasonable precautions to ensure that your business is safe to connect to. In order to be able to prove that a contract exists between organisations both sides must be able to prove that the electronic communications have not been tampered with and you have to know that the person/organisation with whom you are doing business is who they say they are.

Information Assurance is the practice of developing and maintaining a secure, effective information risk management system that protects the information infrastructure as well as the data held within it. This is not merely good business practice, but for public quoted companies, a legal mandate, against which businesses must be audited.

6.8 Information Availability

Imagine a company being denied access of information (including its own) by the activity of others. This would be irritating at best, but for those that rely on time-sensitive information, it could be catastrophic. Let us face facts: today's purchasers have less and less time and patience. If they cannot reach their preferred supplier instantly, they will seek an alternative, if at all possible. So, a company's ability to provide specific, accurate information, on demand, will directly affect its success.

6.9 Interdependency And The Critical Information Infrastructure

The drive for greater efficiency in the global economy has created a situation where there is a highly sophisticated network of dependency on others and their systems, which enables us all to live and work. A failure on the system of delivery has a significant effect on the total operation.

The infrastructure interdependency, the onward march of information technology and the drive for more efficient business systems, demands an increasingly complex and sophisticated infrastructure, for the modern industrialised nation state. Systems such as transportation, power, banking, food distribution and telecommunications, to name but a few, are each crucial to a nation's well being in a highly competitive age.

Each of these systems, however, relies on some of the others for continued and efficient operation. For example, food distribution relies on transportation and telecommunications need power, conversely power needs telecommunications for the efficient control of its engineering operations. The reliance of each vital system upon one or more of its peers is known as infrastructure interdependency.

The more business driven and sophisticated a nation, the greater its vulnerability to infrastructure damage due to the compounding effects in a crisis of infrastructure interdependency. Whilst one cannot turn against the business drive for greater efficiency that enhances such vulnerabilities, it behoves governments to take an overview on infrastructure and insist on sufficient robustness to safeguard the nation, particularly in view of the potential exploitation of such weakness by terrorism and information warfare.

6.10 Internet Commerce

Internet Commerce is a key component of the Global Networked Business model, providing a company's customers and partners with end-to-end solutions to conduct business transactions and exchange of information.

As a background, probably the main driver for building the Internet Global Commerce model has been the need for continuous business improvement, leading to cost savings achieved by changes in the supply chain.

Global businesses and manufacturing techniques now ensure that the business works twenty-four hours, by seven days, by fifty-two weeks basis, which can only be effectively managed by the integration of computer systems on the equivalent global basis. The computer industry is reacting by introducing further interoperability between computer systems with the introduction of new software and bigger capacity technological devices.

Further on, the Internet, this network of networks stretches around the world and makes it possible for every computer to connect to every other computer. It is the biggest network in the world.

6.11 World Wide Web (WWW)

Often confused with the Internet, this is the most widely used means of publishing and accessing information that is stored on the computers, which are connected to the Internet.

The web allows you to link to many sites on the Internet. The basic concept is the page or collection of screens that it displays on your monitor. Within each page are links to related pages and other web sites. Each of these links is known as a hypertext link.

The web was originally used for text links only, but as it was further developed multimedia links were added. The web now contains pictures, audio and video links. With the addition of sound and graphics the web soon became the most popular way of linking to resources on the Internet.

Most organisations are worried by threats presented in using the web. Viruses are one of the main concerns, although these are unlikely to occur in normal surfing, except perhaps where Word and Excel documents are downloaded. Unauthorised access by outsiders is another.

Many organisations are also concerned about the employees wasting time surfing inappropriate web sites. To overcome this problem some companies choose to install a Content Security product that checks for ratings, profanity and legal disclaimers.

6.12 Business Case

The business case for justifying the expenditure on implementing a Change Management system and the practising procedures to go with it in the early days of system development was more a leap of faith than a carefully evaluated financial case, and in many cases this may still be so.

Consultancy assignments and studies show that only a small percentage of organisations worldwide are taking this subject seriously. It is hoped that the information in this book will encourage you to review the Change Management policy within your company.

6.13 Global Networked Business

A Global Networked Business is a company, of any size, whose networked infrastructure and use of technology speeds up the process of communication, and the sharing of knowledge-between prospects, customers, employees, partners and suppliers.

A Global Networked Business uses networks and information technology to:

- Empower people to use and share information and to act more decisively,
- Transcend traditional barriers – including geographic, financial or organisational barriers,
- Increase responsiveness to customer needs and business opportunities,
- Compete more effectively in the global marketplace,
- Enables its customers, partners, employees and suppliers to access information, resources and services in ways that work best for them.

6.14 Implementation Of A Change Management Strategy

The success, or failure, surrounding a Change Management Strategy depends almost entirely on people, those who are designing and developing it and those who are expected to implement it. If the system is designed in such a way as to be too complicated to understand and comply with, or in such a way that makes it almost impossible to do ones job, then it will be rejected by those who should implement it.

Implementation of the policy is likely to involve modification of employment contracts. Monitoring the passage of information in and out of the organisation will involve human communication as well as technological means of communicating, such as the analysis of e-mails sent by employees, which can infringe their human rights, as can monitoring which sites are accessed on the Internet.

Care in selecting those who implement the Change Management principles can substantially influence the level of confidence attained. The programmes require parameters to be set and therefore the level of understanding of your business requirements and the software will influence policies success or otherwise.

The communication exercise to the employees is probably the most important part of the implementation. If left to the I.T. department, it may be delivered in seem-technical language or in terms of the needs of the business, rather than in terms and language to which employees can relate. Failure to allocate sufficient budgets to this area can put the success of a change management policy in jeopardy. It is also important to remember to include training in this area as part of the employees' induction.

Adoption of a Code of Ethics can be a useful adjunct to the process, as can the use of an external communication company.

6.15 Monitoring

For reasons of corporate governance you are required to monitor the success or otherwise of your Change Management process and to review at Senior Management/Board Level any significant shortcomings on a regular basis. It is recommended that in order to protect themselves and to ensure that the development of their systems are demonstrably risks free Senior Management should consider employing external monitoring and health check services.

Having implemented your Change Management procedures and method of working, it is necessary to have a system review and reporting to ensure satisfactory communication among those involved and satisfactory compliance to the practice of change management. The methodology will have been agreed during the specification and implementation process.

The review should include a list of all breaches of the system, the potential exposure because of the breach, actions taken as a result of the breach including the implications of the Change Management.

It is the intention of this book to provide an insight into the subject of change management together with sufficient background information to be able to enter into discussions on the subject, in order to determine the state of your policies on change analysis. In addition to the financial and other benefits, one has also to consider the effects on the reputation of your organisation in the event that changes 'explode' into an uncontrollable situation.

7. THE METHOD EXPLAINED

7.1 The Programme Objectives

It is a fact that most large, complex projects and programs fail to meet their planned objectives and as a consequence, most organisations are undertaking one or more aggressive programs at any point in time. These may fundamentally change the way the company conducts its business and failure to meet objectives on time may lead to a catastrophic loss of business.

Some projects or programmes can be chaotic at times. Objectives are evolving and plans and priorities are constantly changing. There is a temptation to accept this chaos as a necessary 'nature of the beast'. However, it is essential to move the programme forward in a traditional project management way by making sure that objectives and plans move forward.

Once we have clear objectives and plans, programme managers must control two fundamental factors if they are to be successful:

- The business plan must be clearly identified,
- The implementation of the program must be made explicit.

This can be answered by isolating the fundamental cause of most, if not all-major project problems. It can be argued that projects only fail due to two fundamental reasons:

- The plans are proven to be incorrect,
- The significance of these plans is misunderstood.

The capture, analysis and communication of such assessments are, therefore, critical to the success of any project. This forms the basis of the Change Management method. This method has been applied by PsySys Limited to help many diverse organisations to deliver large, complex projects and programmes on time, to budget and in meeting the expectations of demanding users.

7.2 The Suggested Method

The focus of the method is based on he capture and analysis of the critical events and their assessments within the project plans, processes and procedures.

The method is essentially a framework process that allows the capture of collective knowledge and viewpoints from those involved on the project, in a form that facilitates communication of events, assessments and ensures the pro-active management of changes. This is accomplished by dramatically improving communications, risks (which may be caused by changes) are avoided or managed to the optimum and project objectives are delivered on time.

In essence, this is the mechanism by which the functions of programmes and projects are held together as a result of the principles operating within the method.

This, in effect, includes the varied events, their assessments and the consequential changes relating to or consisting of a system. Methodical in procedures and plans, these are addressed to those involved and deliberating within the parameters of their systems development responsibilities.

The results being dependable on the mutual or reciprocal action which encourages those involved in the programmes and projects to communicate with each other and to work closely with a view to solving the threatening events before they impact on the development of the system.

The individuals involved maintain an approach, which relates and characterises the whole group of those involved in assessing the events and attacking the threatening ones before any changes become risks to the development of the system.

Following the system architects and the change management practitioners enables this. Simply follow the approved body of systems development methods, rules and management procedures employed by their organisation. For practical or even ethical reasons, it must be noted that with such a philosophy, it is seldom possible to fulfil all requirements of very large organisational systems.

As such, the suggested method is administered in the various applications. Putting to use such techniques and in applying the change management principles in the development of various applications will involve numerous and varied activities. A concrete issue in developing new applications is the problem of communication among the people involved, the motivation constantly needed for generic work, the ability to interact systematically and in using a structured systems methodology.

7.3 The Change Management Cycle

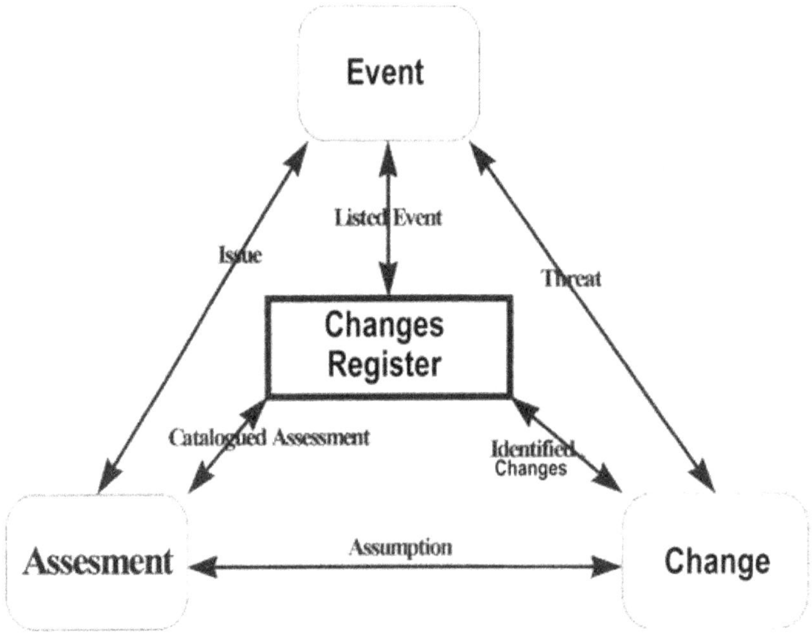

Change Management Cycle

7.4 Features And Benefits Of The Approach

The key features and benefits of the PsySys Limited approach are:

- *Communication* — Provides a simple, common, language for the communication of risk up, down and sideways within the organisation, whilst avoiding the normal problems of political sensitivity and risk aversion.
- *Control* — Enhances project control by exception management and achieves an overview of change at senior management levels.
- *Information* — Encourages the sharing of change information, establishing common objectives, discouraging change transfer and hence reducing the overall risk to all involved parties.
- *Flexible* — An adaptable process, which is rigorously applied to ensure that all significant changes are identified and controlled at the appropriate time.
- *Acceptable* — The non-intrusive/non-bureaucratic management process improves management discipline across the organization and is readily accepted by project teams.

7.5 Assessment Analysis

The core of *Change* is in the Assessment Analysis. This uses structured techniques to analyse project plans and identify the most sensitive events that are potentially unstable, and therefore the source of greatest change.

Everything is rated on a GAR principle: *G*reen, *A*mber and *R*ed scale; where G is always "good" and R is always "bad". This provides an instantly understood assessment on each stage: Events, Assessments and Changes in relationship with the time scales as used in the plans. This, effectively, provides guidance on how best to handle the change.

7.6 Strategic Cost Analysis

Costing is a process within the approach that can be used to define the cost of a requested change within a project or business area from as early as the proposal stage. It works by adding a 'quality' dimension to the estimating process so that high quality estimates, based on relevant experience, are treated differently from low quality estimates, which are little more than guesses.

The output takes the form of a probability distribution diagram and a set of assessments, which need to be managed in order to move the curve to the left and squeeze it (i.e. reduce the likely cost and the uncertainty).

Costing is particularly useful in the early stages of a project when the final cost of the project is subject to great uncertainty. The process has also been effectively used to define business budgets for re-structured business areas.

7.7 Change Administration System Tool

A Microsoft Access based tool or any type of an ordinary spreadsheet can be utilised to allow the events, assessments and changes to be captured and reviewed by all stockholders in the program. In this way changes that would have been missed are captured through the identification of events.

7.8 Work Plan Analysis

Work Plan Analysis is a set of techniques that enables a rapid change assessment to be undertaken on a complex project, which is already in progress.

It is always difficult to focus on the right areas when the project organisation is large and the plans are extensive and likely to be multi-levelled. Using Work Plan Analysis, the 'poor quality' areas of a project are quickly highlighted for further investigation.

One very successful application of this approach has been through the use of Project Readiness Assessment Walkthroughs. These are structured review meetings held just prior to major project milestones or deliverables. Initially the project team explain their self-evaluation of the project status and are questioned by an independent review team. Potential changes arising are captured using the Assessment Analysis process.

7.9 Communicating The Changes

The technique summarised above will only deliver its full benefits to any business if a suitable governance structure is quickly established to communicate the change information and set suitable actions to mitigate the changes. The mapping of the process onto an organisation is the key step to ensuring that the investment in the process is fully realised.

7.10 How To Use The Contents Of This Book

The level of treatment of the material in this book assumes that the reader has already understood the principles already explained. With this in mind, the author attempts to explain the:

- Basic principles of change management and contrasts the more traditional approaches with the theories that underpin the thinking behind the process,
- Practicalities of launching a process into a new project and/or organisation,
- The process described includes some of the practical considerations of applying the popular approaches of Project Prioritisation and Assessment Analysis,
- Process of transferring ownership and embedding the method into the client's organisation.

8. THE PRINCIPLES OF CHANGE MANAGEMENT

8.1 Team Approach

An enterprise must escape from a culture based on transfer of changes between parties, to a team approach that is focused on implementing changes. Methods must be effective without the need for detailed time-consuming analysis.

8.2 The Definition Of A Change

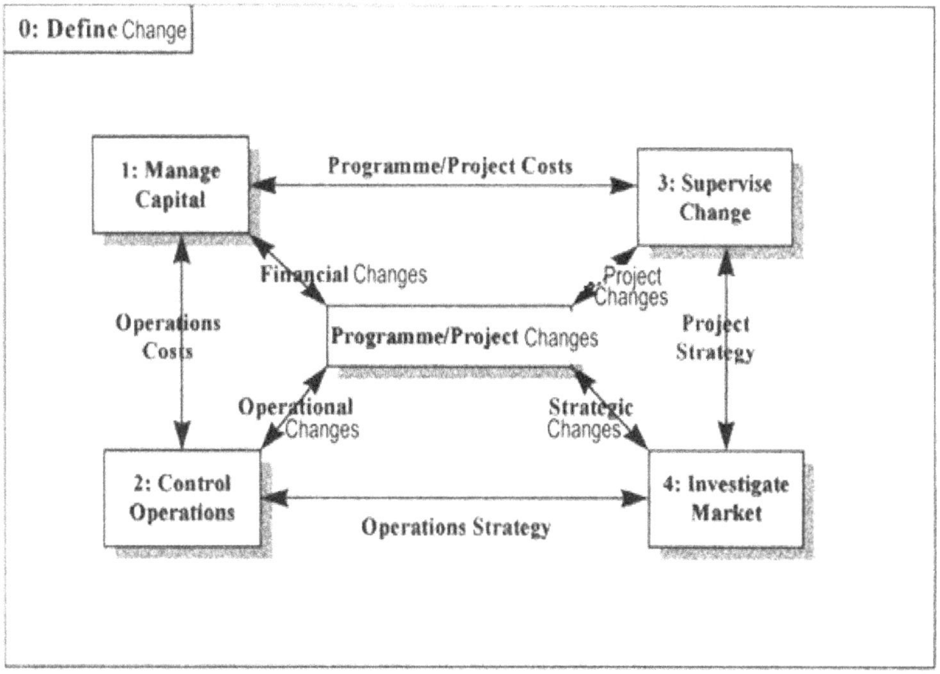

The Comp|onents Of The Total Business Changes

A change may be perceived as a possible loss. A change is individual to a person or organisation because another as a minor change may perceive what one individual as a major change perceives.

A change is linked very strongly with competitiveness. Each decision has the possibility of resulting in loss. Each decision to introduce a new product into the marketplace can result in varying degrees of loss or gain. To be entrepreneurial is to accept change, that is, the possibility of loss. A good entrepreneur's strength, however, is to make decisions which maximise possible gain. Hence minimise possible loss, which constitutes effective change management.

Change is inherent in all aspect of an organisation and may be viewed from four primary directions: financial, operational, programme/project and portfolio/products. Many changes are related to the running of the operations and its processes but are often in trying to change operations that the greatest change is experienced. It is the management of change in such 'change' projects that the method (explained earlier) addresses.

A project can be described in its simplest terms as: Planning to achieve specific objectives and then executing the plans. The emphasis is on the word 'plan' as without a plan we have no project. So in the context of a project, a change is something, which might disrupt the plans such that the objectives of the project are not met. The discipline of Project Change Management is thus a framework of techniques, which allows the project manager to pro-actively identify and manage changes before they develop into problems, which will impact the project plans.

8.3 Approaches to Change Management

In recent years we have seen large projects in many areas of business suffering from a lack of control. The size of cost and time over-runs do not seem to be decreasing, despite the amount of management time which is being dedicated to analysing and quantifying the potential problems and selecting suitable personnel and processes. One may conclude that management, either do not have the correct methods and tools in place to attack the potential problems, or that they are not using, or do not understand, those which they do have.

In the early 1970's, the concepts of formal project change management began to emerge. Hailed as the saviour of project managers, in practice the results have been mixed. Change management has proved highly effective in certain mature industries - e.g. the Petrochemical or construction industry where project managers can base their estimates on years of similar engineering experience. Difficulties seem to be encountered when these traditional Change Management methods are applied to innovative and fast evolving areas such as Information Technology.

8.4 Events And Change Registers

Most projects will have an Events Register and some may have what they call a Change Register. In effect, this tends to be a list into which anyone can input the concerns. It will contain references to current problems, questions, and assessments, difficult activities about which there is reasonable confidence and the odd real change.

In any large project the Events or Change Register quickly becomes swamped with items that require very different actions and many which do not require any action at all. All this leads to an inevitable loss of focus. Further, the content tends to be biased towards current problems rather than future potential problems.

8.5 Individual Interviews

One-on-one interviews can be an effective way of capturing changes. When management and peers do not inhibit people, they tend to be far more open about their concerns. Unfortunately, most use very unsophisticated approaches such as "what do you see as your changes?" or "what keeps you awake at night?" Thus, if the person being interviewed is sensitive to discussing changes it may prevent the capture of any valuable information. At best the changes captured will tend to lack structure, as they are not focused onto the future objectives that the project plans to achieve.

8.6 Group Brainstorming

Can be a very effective technique for opening up a very complex situation. However, information can be subconsciously suppressed by peer pressure, which may bias the discussion on one area at the expense of the rest of the project. Inevitably the mass of information captured is often difficult to focus, prioritise and allocate ownership.

In general, it should be remembered that the quality of the output is only as good as the quality of the input data.

8.7 Change Analyses And Quantification of Changes

Changes may be difficult to capture reliably and concisely but further problems are likely to be experienced when trying to analyse them. Virtually all approaches to change analysis are based on estimating the factored impact of the change. This exposure to change is a combination of the chance (probability) of an event happening and the consequences (impact) if it does occur i.e.:

- Change Exposure = Potential Impact x Probability of Occurrence

Fundamental problems arise when individuals are required to estimate, numerically, the impact and then predict (numerically) the probability. Estimates, which are often little more than guesses, result in a single point estimate of Change Exposure, which is then given undeserved credibility in the detailed analysis of the change and used as the basis for many major project decisions. Also, it is often the case that part of the change impact can be quantified but often not the major part. An example can be based on an attempt to quantify bad publicity, quality and relationship.

Some processes add complexity by rating the impact of changes in terms of financial, time scales, quality, performance etc., which quickly become very tedious to maintain.

8.8 Change Control And Lack Of Follow-through

Many change management systems fail due to a lack of follow-through on actions. There is a surprising tendency to identify changes and then watch them happen!

This is caused by:

- Failure to use the change register to set appropriate action plans,
- Lack of regular updates/maintenance of the change register,
- Absence of named owners and deadlines (lack of ownership),
- Tracking generalities rather than specifics,
- Concentrating on what can be done if the change occurs rather than stopping the change happening (pro-active),
- Trying to transfer the change elsewhere, without considering the consequences.

8.9 Change Transfer

Change transfer often occurs because the partner who knows most about the level of change within the enterprise (i.e. the supplier/purchaser relationship) is encouraged to transfer this to the other partner. Once accomplished, the party with the most knowledge of the change relaxes and the most ignorant partner inherits the change. An example of this is the Purchaser insisting on a fixed-price contract in a poorly defined contract when they know that the supplier does not understand the scope of the contract.

The supplier then has a tendency to deliver the minimum possible and obtain sign-off for everything, irrespective of quality. The effect of this type of commercial 'table-tennis' is actually to increase the level of change within the enterprise as the real changes pile up without intervention.

What is needed is a method that identifies and encourages the attack of real change at source. Such a method would force projects within the enterprise to become pro-active by attacking risky changes, rather than waiting for events to unfold and then counting the cost, as recorded in the previous month's financial returns.

8.10 Change Management vs. Project Management

There is often a tendency to treat change management as no more than another necessary evil of project management. Thus, it often becomes an additional administrative burden for the Project Manager and consequently does not get the quality attention to make it work effectively.

In order to make change management work, a shift in philosophy is required. This must lead the project team to view the process not just as another component of project management, but more as the communication stabiliser that holds the project together.

9. BASIC PRINCIPLES OF CHANGE MANAGEMENT

9.1 The Process

The Change Management method described in this book aims to provide an effective means of managing changes within all types of projects. The process grew out of a thorough assessment of the problems often encountered in project management and the techniques of the traditional change management approaches that have been used to try and improve the situation.

Both good and bad principles were noted and new techniques were introduced to address key deficiencies. The resulting change management process has a proven track record of delivering tangible results in large projects across a diverse range of organisations.

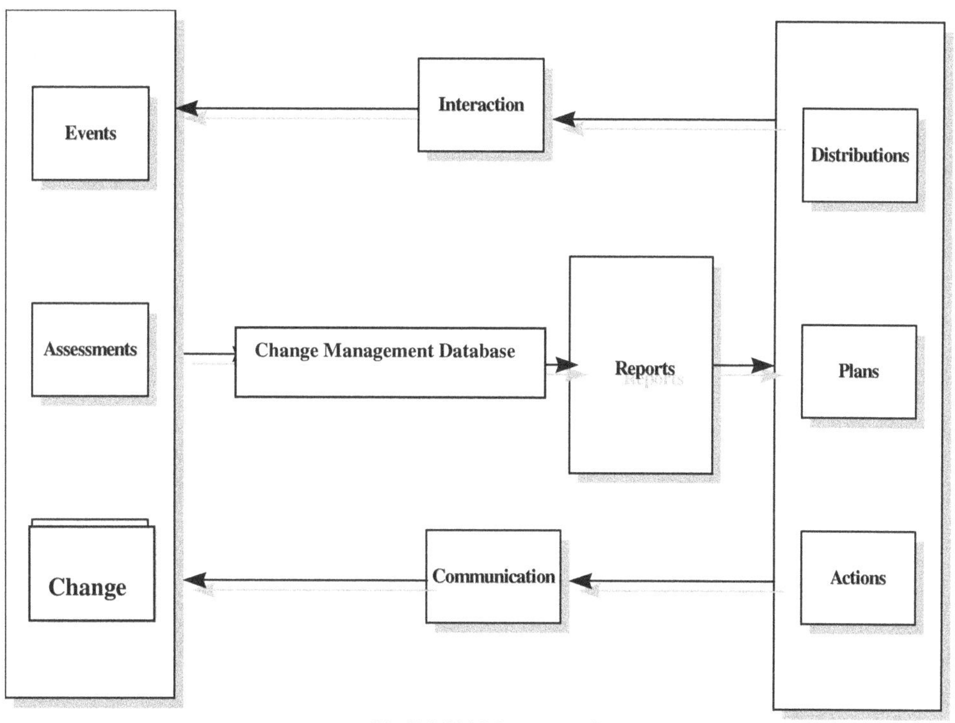

The Full Risk Management Cycle

9.2 Communication Of Assessments

As already highlighted, a fundamental reason for project failure is the lack of quality communications both within the project and between the programme and its environment. Most problems incurred by projects could be avoided if information was effectively communicated in a timely fashion. The problem is that there is so much information that it is difficult to decide what needs to be communicated and to who. This is where assessments come in.

Everything important associated with a project can be captured and tracked as an assessment:

- Activities are sized on the basis of assessments,
- Milestones are set according to assessments,
- Dependencies are based on assessments,
- Plans are executed by making assessments.

Therefore, the capture, analysis and communication of assessments are critical to the success of any project, and this forms the core of the Project Change Management process.

9.3 The Current Project Plan Is The Baseline

Capturing the critical assessments in the project plans are uncertain identifies changes. In other words, whatever might stop the objectives, time scales and budget of the project plan being achieved? In this way, all assessments are effectively referenced to the project plans. Consequently, the plan provides the focus for the change management process.

This approach keeps the changes specific, forward looking and ensures that the plan is always sufficiently detailed and up to date.

9.4 Uncertainty Equals Risk In Changes

Risk in changing is inherent whenever there is uncertainty. The best judges of uncertainty are those who are asked to make estimates for the plans and, in most circumstances, the people who will actually have to do the work make the best estimators.

Combining this principle with the assessments captured from the project plans leads us to rate assessments for quality/uncertainty. Analysis is concentrated onto the areas of the project about which little are known and particularly the inter-dependencies that often represent the highest risk.

9.5 Judging The Quality Using The Scale

To capture this vital information about how sure the estimator is, each estimator is asked, not only for assessments or the value of any estimate, but also, what quality he or she considers the assessment or estimate to be. This is not a judgement of the skill of the estimator. It is a self-assessment of the current quality of the basic information, upon which the project plans are based.

The scale is defined for multiple uses throughout the process. It always means effectively the same thing i.e. 'A' is always good and 'C' is always bad. 'B' expresses tendencies to the two extremes.

- A (Green) means very good, high confidence, not important
- B (Amber) means fairly good, reasonable confidence, not very important
- C (Red) means very poor, little or no confidence, and critically important.

It should be noted that the method does not allow the estimator to say that the estimate or assessment is of average quality. The whole principle is that we should be forced to make a choice between good, high confidence and bad, low confidence estimates and cannot 'sit on the fence'.

Using these simple A, B, C terms to express degrees of uncertainty, it is possible to encourage the estimator to reveal a wide range of uncertainty. Also, it is often possible to persuade him or her to make estimates when not normally prepared to do so. Being able to qualify an assessment or estimate with a C quality, often assures the estimators that they will not be forced into a given value or statement. We can thus gain vital information about the uncertainty and therefore the risks if one goes ahead with a change that may lie at the heart of the project.

9.6 Process Overview

The process consists of an integrated closed loop method, which logically progresses through:

- Project Prioritisation (for multiple project environments),
- Change Assessment (consisting of Assessments Analysis plus Strategic Cost Analysis and/or Work Plan Analysis, if appropriate),
- Changes Prioritisation (to decide the 'order of attack'),
- Change Control (to put the mitigation plans into action and monitor their effectiveness).

9.7 Project Prioritisation

A large organisation may have, at any one time, hundreds of projects of varying sizes, and nature. Yet many organisations have no formal mechanism for prioritising projects leading to problems such as:

- Not knowing which projects should be approved/resourced,
- Uncertainty as to which projects should be formally assessed for Changes Assessment.

Once the critical and potentially changes to the projects have been identified, the book offers three change assessment techniques to identify and analyse the specific changes within each project.

The Assumption Analysis technique provides a backbone onto which the Strategic Cost Analysis and/or Work Plan Analysis approaches can be built.

In this respect Assumption Analysis would always be applied, Strategic Cost Analysis would be used in the early stages of a project or proposal to address the uncertainty in the cost/pricing of the project and Work Plan Analysis may be used to assess a very complex project which is well progressed.

9.8 Changes Prioritisation

The specific changes captured from each project assessment needs to be prioritised in order to allocate resources and decide the order in which the risks should be addressed.

The book provides a simple framework, which rates each change for Criticality, Controllability and Impact Timing. The resulting list of changes is captured in a Microsoft Access Change Register (or any type of spreadsheet) and the changes are summarised in a diagram, which provides an executive overview of the project change profile.

9.9 Change Control

The book provides a framework for change control based on taking both strategic and tactical views of implementing changes. The strategic approach is achieved by applying trend analysis to the underlying assessments to identify any strong Change Drivers, which can be neutralised together.

Tactical approaches match the complexity of the change action plan to the complexity of the change to minimise bureaucracy for simple-to-manage changes, whilst maintaining the necessary formality for complex changes.

10. Initiating the Process

10.1 Organisational Culture

Some organisations are very change aversive. Senior management who suppress the open discussion of changes and create an organisation where stressing progress is the basis of management meetings often sets this culture unknowingly. In this environment, nobody has any changes until they suddenly become problems!

In such situations, it may be necessary to re-sell the benefits of using change management i.e. the worse thing that they can do is suppress a change, whilst the best thing that they can do is to identify changes and explain how they will be managed. Senior management need to be re-oriented from worrying about their current problems towards managing the changes within the plans that are designed to fix problems.

If the organisation has any previous experience of using formal change management techniques, it may be necessary to stress the particular benefits of a properly managed change process. Effective change management and plans:

- Provide a common, apolitical language for the communication of changes,
- Enhance project control by exception management,
- Achieve an overview of changes at senior management levels.

Project teams must concentrate on facts and trust that this method of non-intrusive, non-bureaucratic management process improves management discipline across the organisation.

In order to make the process work, the senior level sponsor must believe in the process and communicate with the organisation that they expect them to play a full role in the process. Buy-in must be both top-down and bottom-up.

10.2 Organisational Structure And Stability

When establishing the change management process, the organisational structure and its stability need to be considered.

Once the first round of change identification interviews have been completed and the first Change Review meeting is scheduled, it is essential to ensure that the meeting representation covers the changes being discussed and has the authority to take action. Often such actions require re-prioritisation of resources and this may mean that very senior representation is required to resolve conflicts.

The interview list and review meeting may be based on a project organisation, which may change imminently. It is, therefore, always worth checking with senior level management on the likely organisational stability. If there is a re-organisation planned, do not remove people from the interview list on this basis alone. They may still provide valuable insights and certainly more than their replacement, if new to the project.

Perhaps one of the unstable environments in which to conduct a change assessment is within a merger or acquisition scenario and it is worth noting that the process described in this book has proved extremely effective in this type of environment.

10.3 Effect Of Current Project Status

The stage and status of the project will have a strong bearing on the change management initiation process. Although all situations are unique, the following may give some helpful guidelines. Such a status may make a Strategic Cost Analysis very attractive. If there are no plans it may be difficult to undertake a full Assessment Analysis, but a high level assessment of issues or assumptions based on major milestones should be possible. Expect to identify a high proportion of changes that relate to missing or inadequate plans and resources problems. Projects just starting tend to have many events and few assessments (due to the lack of documented plans).

10.4 Project Fully Planned And Proceeding

Once the project has been substantially planned and is active, Assessment Analysis becomes the primary change identification process. If the planning is very detailed and/or complex, some of the techniques of Work Plan Analysis may prove useful. For example, if there were a requirement to produce a first-cut of a change register very quickly, for a rapidly approaching milestone, a Project Readiness Walkthrough would be an ideal approach.

10.5 Project In Trouble

The key aspect of a project in trouble is that it requires re-planning to put it back on track. Thus, the timing of the change assessment relative to this planning process is very important.

If the re-planning process has not started there will be very little of the new approach to assess. It may be possible to influence this new approach by undertaking a change assessment of the options being considered. To do this an Assumption Analysis of the alternative high-level plans can provide a useful framework for decision-making.

If the project has been re-planned, then an Assessment Analysis of the new plans, possibly supplemented by Work Plan Analysis, is an appropriate way forward.

10.6 Interviews With Key People

Identifying the right people to interview is critical to producing a comprehensive and coherent picture of the changes facing a project. So, to decide on who should be interviewed, start with the project or programme organisational structure.

Depending on the scope of the change assessment (i.e. single project, programme of multiple projects, portfolio of business projects etc.) it may be necessary to map the organisational hierarchy to ensure that the right people are interviewed and that the changes arising are reviewed at an appropriate level.

Working with the Programme or Project Manager, try to identify the 'key players'. A key player is someone within the programme/project who is likely to have either specific expertise in a particular area and/or insight into the environment in which the project is being implemented.

Key players tend to be Project Managers for a programme or Team Managers for a project with the addition of Users involved in the requirement capture and other activities. This group would likely form the initial interview list.

During the interview, these people should decide who else is needed to participate. Interviewers need to exercise their judgement when evaluating the responses to this question. Typically it is necessary to go down at least one level below the Project/Team manager unless the team size is small.

One of the key features of this process is that of obtaining counter viewpoints within the organisation. Thus, the more people interviewed, the better. However, if many projects are being assessed for change within an organisation, resource constraints will inevitably lead to reducing the interview pool. Under these circumstances at least two counter viewpoints must be obtained within each project. (Business manager and technical manager) so that the assessment ratings can be compared.

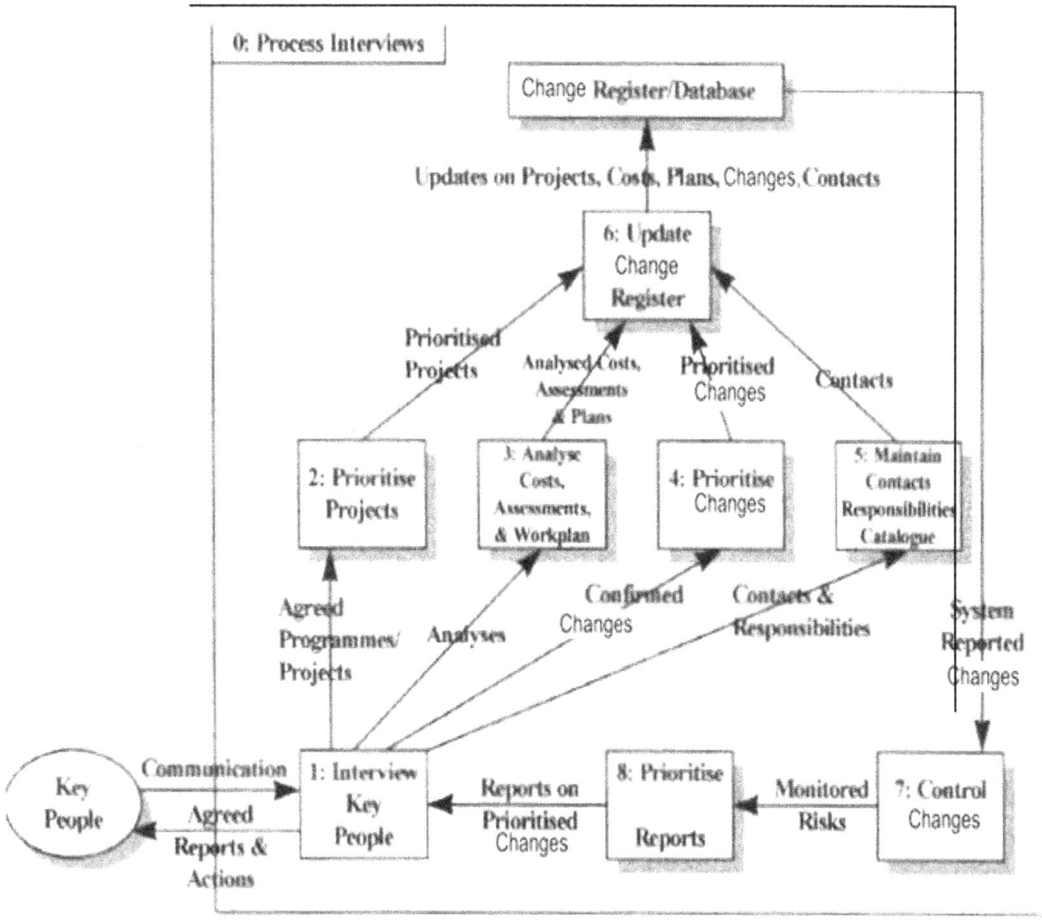

THE INTERVIEWING PROCESS

10.7 Choosing A Suitable Change Assessment Team

- The team that will operate and manage the process requires a particular set of skills and background to be successful:
- Experience of working in large (preferably non-consulting) projects and managing (preferably) medium sized projects (say 10-20 people).
- Understanding of project planning principles and some exposure to associated tools.
- Forceful personalities to ensure quality data captures in difficult client situations.
- IT background, in order to understand the issues in IT projects and to help with using the support tools.
- Some understanding of the clients business.

Note that it can sometimes be a disadvantage to have too much knowledge of the clients business in applying the process. This is because there may be a tendency for the interviewer to get into too much detail in non-risky areas and take too much of the client's time in the process.

10.8 Change Review Meetings

After the initial round of interviews, a suitable forum must be established to discuss the changes identified. The client may suggest that the changes are discussed as part of the regular project meeting. This should be resisted unless the changes are an early agenda item and there will be sufficient time to get through the agenda with this additional discussion.

Typically, a minimum of an hour will be required for discussion of the changes - all if possible but just the most critical if not. If discussion of the changes is left to the end there will often be little time (or concentration) left to do the process justice. Also, it is likely that some events will end up being discussed twice. If discussed first, the changes tend to focus the meeting and get away from talking about progress onto the things that need to be discussed - i.e. what threatens the success of the project.

The best method is to establish a specific Change Review Meeting with a representation consisting of the Change Owners and chaired by the Programme Director, or the process 'champion' in the client organisation.

11. PROJECT PRIORITISATION

11.1 The Project And/Or Programme

Only complex and critical projects need to have a fully structured change management process in place.

A project is the controlled change of an enterprise. Projects are defined as having their own project plans and can be clearly distinguished from other projects (as opposed to being part of another identified project). For example, a rollout of a major system to individual countries with a specific plan for each country would only be identified as individual projects at a country level if they were effectively independent of each other.

The terms 'project' and 'programme' tend to be used very loosely. Sometimes the terms are used interchangeably or a programme is considered to be a large project. The definition preferred here is that a programme is a collection of inter-dependent projects.

From a change management viewpoint the structure is important, as it will dictate who is interviewed and where the key dependencies are likely to be. In addition, there may be a requirement to set up a multi-level change management system where the project changes feed up into a programme Change Register where there is a programme wide impact or the change needs to be managed at the programme level.

11.2 Project Inclusion In Process

Basic criteria are required to decide which projects should be included in the project prioritisation process. Such criteria may be developed to suit the organisation but guidelines would include:

- Size and duration of project (i.e. must be big enough to use significant resources for a significant period),
- Projects agreed by the business sponsor responsible for their implementation,
- Projects managed by the department/organisation and making use of their resources,
- Projects not managed by the department/organisation, but making use of their resources.

11.3 Prioritisation

The objective of prioritising projects is to ensure that the right projects have the appropriate resources and that appropriate management attention is paid to the most complex and critical projects. These projects are inherently risky, and in most cases will require a formal change management process to support the other project management disciplines.

Therefore, there is a need for a process which:

- Produces a prioritised and agreed project inventory that can be used when allocating resources to projects,

- Helps management to focus attention on the critical projects which are inherently risky,
- Highlights the projects, which require formal change management to guarantee timely delivery.

Project Size. An objective scale where A, B, and C are ranges of cost which are set by the business areas. The project is allocated to a cost range based on the anticipated total development and implementation costs over the life of the project.

Example, criteria could be:

- C = More than ten equivalent resources,
- B = Five to ten equivalent resources,
- A = One to five equivalent resources.

Technical Complexity. How advanced or unknown are the engineering techniques, which are needed to design and build the solution.

- C = Highly complex, new technology, or scale never attempted before,
- B= Some degree of complexity, some experience of proposed technology or manageable scale,
- A = Straightforward, familiar technology, small implementation.

Business Complexity. Many functions, areas of the business are involved in the project or impacted by the project.

- C = Global system/involves many parts of the customer's business
- B = Multi department/user groups
- A = Single department/user group

Note that these scales are examples and must be re-defined to reflect the business objectives of the organisation under review.

11.4 The Project Prioritisation Process

11.4.1 The Standard Reference Matrix

In order to help refine the appropriate positioning of projects, each business area must identify two or three current key projects with which management are familiar. After agreement between the senior client and supplier managers, these will be positioned to make up a standard reference matrix. This matrix will then be used as the baseline.

11.4.2 Positioning and Prioritising New Projects

The supplier and client project managers should undertake initial positioning of the new project, together, as early as possible in the project. Complete consensus is not always possible at this stage, due to incomplete understanding of the business and technical issues involved.

However, it is essential that consensus is reached before any approval boards, or it is clear that the project is not ready to proceed. Lack of consensus can result in biased project ratings. Too high a rating will waste resources and cause frustration within the project team due to excessive management attention. Too low a rating will result in management neglect and consequently, increased risk.

11.4.3 Project Approval and Resources

In practice, the primary factor that is taken into consideration when approving a project is the Business Criticality. There are many projects that could be undertaken and only a finite resource pool available, so only the projects that will most improve the organisation's business should be approved.

Once management endorsement has been obtained, the results of the positioning exercise should be published to the teams and senior management.

11.4.4 When Projects Change Position on the CC Diagram

Once a project has been positioned it will be subject to review at least once every phase and certainly before progressing to the next stage. The most significant event in the life of a project is likely to be if it moves within either matrix.

A project may move because it is discovered that it is more or less complex than previously thought. It may have grown or been reduced in size. It may have become more or less critical to the client's business.

If a project moves, it is indicating something about the management approach required in the future. In particular, the approach to change management should be reviewed and projects moving towards the top-right corner of the matrix should be assessed whilst projects moving towards the bottom left corner may be dropped from the change assessment process.

11.4.5 Deciding which Projects Require Formal Change Management

The position of a project on the diagram is also used to determine which projects should be assessed formally for change going forward. The threshold can be set at any appropriate level. For example, some organisations work on the principle that any project judged to be a C, on either matrix, should be assessed for change using the process. Projects falling below this threshold are still encouraged to use a formal method for change assessment, but it is not mandated.

11.5 Change Identification and Analysis

The process uses three windows; Assessment Analysis, Strategic Cost Analysis and Work Plan Analysis, to obtain a clear view of the source of any change.

Although it is possible to create a change by poor planning and management, an element of risk is inherent in any enterprise. The main problem is to find a method of identifying the sources of the changes in time to allow specific actions to be taken to avoid or reduce the impact.

The nature of the project changes varies with the nature of the tasks, the size and the development phase of the project. Later phases may make use of methods for identifying change based on the project's experiences to date. In early phases, good quality information and experience is scarce. Thus, using different techniques and tools best looks at different phases and different types of change.

By using all these windows over the life of a project we increase our chances of identifying the major changes, which lie within the project and to understand the nature of each change. The process ultimately allows us to represent each change in terms of:

- The potential criticality of the change in terms of impact on the core project objectives,
- The point in time that the change will impact the project if unresolved,
- The likelihood of the change occurring.

Using these three analysis techniques; Strategic Cost Analysis, Assessment Analysis and Work Plan Analysis, it is possible to generate a single list that contains all the fundamental changes to the project. This list can then be used to decide which elements represent important changes and should thus be subject to proactive Change Management by the creation and execution of dedicated Change Plans.

11.5.1 Assessment Analysis

Fundamentally, projects only fail due to two reasons: either the wrong assessments were made, or the significance of the assessments was not understood.

The plans for any project are based on a few facts and many assessments. If the final out turn cost and time scales are excessive, it is obvious that either the assessments were wrong, or the estimators did not understand their significance.

It is important to note that these assessments are made due to the inevitable lack of total understanding or information, which is inherent, particularly in the early stages of any project. Assessments are made to allow us to proceed with the project design or plans, but if they are important and prove incorrect, they will jeopardise the success of the project. Thus low quality assessments are at the heart of the risks in a project.

Assessment Analysis is the backbone of the change methodology, and as such is at the core of Strategic Cost Analysis and Work Plan Analysis. It can be used at any stage in a project. However you should start the analysis as early as possible in the project to capture open events.

11.5.2 Identify the Sources of Assessments

Assessments come from a wide range of sources. At the beginning of a project all these sources are external to the project. As the project progresses it develops its own, internal assessments, while drawing on an increasingly larger set from its interfacing business and technical systems.

Assessments are captured by interviews with the key players in a project and its interfacing environment. Detailed interviews are conducted to kick-off the process and follow-up interviews are scheduled to track the status of the assessments captured and capture assessments over the life of the project.

Assessments may be explicit and be recorded in specifications, standards, plans or regulations. Many assessments will be implicit and only revealed by detailed questioning of the interviewee. Assessments may be made by the project, interfacing projects, the organisation or, they may relate to national standards and laws within the affected countries. Most assessments are made specifically to close open events, so that plans and estimates can be made and progressed.

At the start of a project there are likely to be many open events and few assessments. However, once the planning process is underway, the event is effectively closed by the assessments being made in the plans. Consequently, a project that is under way with reasonable quality plans will have few open events, if any.

11.5.3 Prioritise Assessments

Many assessments made on a project are considered to be high quality as they are based on relevant knowledge or sound experience. Other assessments are insignificant when compared with the overall project objectives. Neither of these types of assessments is likely to be the source of changes and we therefore require a method to filter out high quality or unimportant assessments, so that we can concentrate on low quality or very important cases.

This change identification method uses the knowledge of the key players in the interviews to assess two vital parameters, which we have to know about assessments.

- The Sensitivity of the project to the assessments (i.e. How much does it matter if the assessments prove incorrect),
- The Stability of those assessments. How likely are they to change during the course of the project, (i.e. How confident are we that the assessment will prove correct?).

11.5.3.1 Sensitivity:

- A: would mean that the assessment being incorrect would have a minor impact on the project.
- B: would indicate a manageable impact.

11.5.3.2 Stability:

- A: would mean that there was high confidence that the assessment will turn out to be true,
- B: would be fairly confident,
- C: would mean a total lack of confidence in the assessment (i.e. it would almost certainly be wrong.)

Using this method it is possible to conduct a systematic analysis of the assessments on which a project is based. We can represent this assessment on a Sensitivity/Stability diagram.

11.5.4 Convert Key Assessments Into Changes

Assessments are identified through employing Assessments Analysis, Strategic Cost Analysis and Work Plan Analysis. Essentially, the assessments captured, which are important to the project (i.e. C Sensitivity) and are considered to be unstable (i.e. C Stability), represent significant changes to the project.

These changes require action to bring them under control. The most effective way of achieving this is by raising the changes to a suitable body in the organisation that have the power to make the necessary decisions, set the actions and make sure that they are followed through.

Communicating changes to senior management groups is always difficult as they are often not familiar with the detail of the project. Subsequently, the changes need to be presented in a concise, clear way that explains what is causing the change (and therefore indicates what needs to be done) and what would be the consequences if the change were allowed to impact the project.

Thus assessments are converted into changes using the form:

- *If (the assessment proves incorrect)*
- *Then (describe the consequences to the project or business).*

It is important to express the full consequences of the change or it may fail the 'so-what', test when submitted to senior management. A good principle is to describe at least the immediate impact and the ultimate impact on the project programme or business.

An alternative representation of a change is to leave the assessments stated in the positive and add the impact. The advantage of this is that the change can still be expressed in a positive sense. Some people find this very important.

If the Sensitivity/Stability ratings are AA, AB, BA or BB we have an assessment, which is not crucial to the project and is likely to prove correct anyway. This does not require further action at this time, but it should be re-assessed at regular intervals to make sure that the quality ratings are still good.

If another combination of Sensitivity/Stability ratings are assessed (e.g. BC, AC, CB etc.) these are called potential changes. Such assessments need at least to be monitored carefully for change. Retain the data and re-assess these assessments with the originators at regular intervals to check that their status has not changed significantly.

It is important to remember that this assessment is only made at a point in time and will change as the project progresses. For this reason Assessments Analysis must be an ongoing process with regular interviews and review meetings throughout the life of the project.

11.5.5 Categorisation Of Assessments — Change Drivers

When capturing assessments, it is often useful to identify what is driving the Sensitivity and Stability ratings allocated to it so that the source (or "driver" of the change) is clear. This is simply achieved by categorising assessments into one of three types:

- Policy where the assessment relates to a business decision or policy, standards, resource priorities etc. The assessment requires management intervention to bring it under control.
- Milestone where the timescales of the activities are being 'squeezed' or timescale dependencies on other projects, suppliers etc. The assessment would be no problem if more time were available.
- Technical where the complexity of the undertaking is driving the ratings (e.g. untried design, hardware and software constraints, complex organisations etc.). The complexity is such that mistakes are likely irrespective of the time available.

Categorising assessments in this way can make the selection of appropriate Change Plans easier by ensuring that the true source of the change is addressed. Further, it can allow a strategic view of the changes to be obtained but only when a statistically large number of changes are being tracked.

11.6 Strategic Cost Analysis

Strategic Cost Analysis provides a means of assessing the cost change in a project in its very early stages and commences the change management process.

Strategic Cost Analysis is a process, which can be used to define the cost of a change within a project or business area. It works by adding a 'quality' dimension to the estimating process so that high quality estimates, based on relevant experience, are treated differently from low quality estimates, which are little more than guesses.

The output takes the form of a probability distribution diagram and a set of assessments, which need to be managed in order to move the curve to the left and squeeze it (i.e. reduce the likely cost and the uncertainty).

Strategic Cost Analysis is particularly useful in the early stages of a project when the final cost of the project is subject to great uncertainty. The process has also been effectively used to define business budgets for re-structured business areas.

Its main aim is to highlight the possible range of final project cost, set contingencies, suggest a suitable Change Budget and identify the fundamental uncertainties in the form of open events and critical assessments which can be converted into statements of changes.

The output of a Strategic Cost Analysis is a range of final project costs, the degree of risk in the project and open issues or assumptions that are linked to the poor quality estimates.

The main steps in performing Strategic Cost Analysis are to:

- Break up the project into modules and allocate ownership,
- Estimate time and/or cost of each module with the owner and attach quality ratings,
- Use a software tool to process the data,
- Analyse the results.

In essence the shape of the curve is dictated by the uncertainties (changes) in the cost estimates. Conversely, by managing these specific changes the curve can be compressed, increasing the certainty in the final project cost.

11.7 Work Plan Analysis

Work Plan Analysis may be used to focus on the risky areas of detailed, multi-level project plans when time is of the essence.

The final window for viewing potential changes to a project is through the detailed analysis of project work programmes and plans.

Work Plan Analysis is a set of techniques, which enables a rapid change assessment to be undertaken on a complex project, which is already in progress.

It is always difficult to focus on the right areas when the project organisation is large and the plans are extensive and likely to be multi-levelled. Using Work Plan Analysis, the poor quality areas of a project are quickly highlighted for further investigation.

One very successful application of Work Plan Analysis has been the use of Project Readiness Assessment Walkthroughs. These are structured review meetings held just prior to major project milestones or deliverables. Same kind of walkthroughs as used in structured systems, analysis and design. Initially, the project team explain their self-evaluation of the project status and are questioned by an independent review team. Potential changes arising are captured using the assessments analysis process.

11.7.1 Quality Review of Plans

One would normally expect high quality detailed plans to be available for the current and next stage of the project, with the quality and detail decreasing progressively into the future. Thus the high level (Level 0 and Level 1) plans should normally be well defined with the definition becoming progressively lesser accuracy at the lower levels.

Remember that a high level of detail is not always equivalent to quality. It is possible to produce very detailed plans that are based on very poor quality assessments.

If the analysis of the plans shows areas of poor quality or incomplete planning in the current phase or at the higher levels, it is likely to indicate the presence of changes. These should be investigated for their root causes using Assessment Analysis.

Using a dedicated checklist, which is specific to the type of project being discussed, can produce an overview like this. However, it can often be achieved by self-assessment from a number of the project's key players.

Further high-level views of potential project changes can be obtained from conducting a Contingency Analysis and/or a Timescale Change Analysis using project management software packages.

11.7.2 Locate Hot Spots in the Plans

While project management packages are effective in producing likely cost profiles of the type produced by Strategic Cost Analysis, they are not very effective at identifying specific underlying changes within the project.

Skilled analysis of plans will reveal sensitive areas, which cannot be avoided. These Hot Spots may occur because of sensitive or multiple inputs to work packages, because of resource conflicts between packages, or through the difficulty of getting the output of the packages genuinely approved and agreed, or multiple output which all rely on the completion of one work package.

The assessments in such areas of the plans may be analysed. Once identified as changes, the *If/Then* statement should be used to express the source and possible consequences.

11.7.3 Project Readiness Walkthroughs

Project Readiness Walkthroughs are a highly effective way of ensuring that all changes have been captured from the assessments analysis process. When used independently from, or prior to, an Assessments Analysis, the walkthrough provides a start to the change assessment process, which is particularly useful when time is short.

11.7.3.1 Basic objectives of a Project Readiness Walkthrough are:

- Assess the readiness to meet milestones for high-priority projects,
- Identify any corporate resource contention that may exist, and assist with prioritisation,
- Identify common events and changes, and communicate information to support other project teams,
- Help project teams achieve their goals by identifying and/or providing resources for assistance as needed,
- Assess enterprise-wide change through the evaluation of multiple projects.

11.7.3.2 Process follows a standard structure.

The project team are briefed and provided with a self evaluation form:

Ref.	Project Area	Pre-Milestone	Milestone	Post-Milestone
1.	Data conversion process			
2.	Data volumes/sizing			
3.	Operations changes			
4.	Systems changes			
5.	Test plans/test execution			
6.	Contingency plans			
7.	Staffing and resources			
8.	Controls and standards			
9.	Metrics and benchmarking			
10.	Training/education			
11.	Cross project communication			
12.	Customer impact			
13.	Problem reporting/escalation			

Form for Capturing Confidence Levels

11.7.3.3 the project team meets and fills in their confidence levels (A-C) against each category. The most pessimistic score is logged in each case to produce an entry matrix.

11.7.3.4 The Walkthrough is scheduled

- For (say) 3 hours.

11.7.3.5 the typical participants are:

- The project team (key players),
- Key players from associated projects,
- An independent review team of senior management,
- An independent facilitator,
- Secretarial support.

11.7.3.6 The Walkthrough starts by concentrating on the Cs to find out what is driving them. Appropriate assessments and changes are captured in real time.

11.7.3.7 The Walkthrough is completed by going through the As and Bs and asking for them to be (briefly) justified. Any additional assessments or changes are logged.

11.7.3.8 the matrix is updated to reflect the changes identified to produce an exit matrix.

11.7.3.9 Changes reviewed regularly and actions stated to ensure that they are brought under control.

11.7.4 Pre-selected Assessments

This is a process very similar to the Walkthroughs, where the assessment criteria are a set of pre-selected assessments. A set of high-level assessments are defined on the basis that this is what is needed for the project to be successful. These assessments are then agreed with the sponsor before undertaking short focussed interviews with as many team members as possible. In essence, the team members are asked for their opinion on the Sensitivity/Stability of each assessment.

The results are collated to show trends across the team. The strength of this approach is based on the team's perspective and not on what the reviewer assumes.

11.8 Change Prioritisation

Prioritisation allows the Project Manager to direct limited resources at the most critical project changes.

The objective of the change prioritisation is to identify the most significant changes out of all those, which have been identified by the various analysis methods used. Once all the changes have been collected in a consolidated list or register, they should be placed in order of priority and attacked via a logical, planned programme. The problem is to decide how to place changes in an appropriate order.

11.8.1 Assessments and Changes Register

All assessments captured should be held in an Assessments Register. Only critical assessments will be converted into changes and held in a Change Register. Filtering the assessments and consolidating them into changes do this. All information captured will be rationalised and details of their source and consequences will be traceable.

11.8.2 Positioning Changes

The primary criteria used for prioritising changes are:

- Criticality
- Timing
- Controllability

11.8.2.1 Criticality

In certain instances the change may undermine the basic objectives of the project and no amount of money will save the project if such a change impacts. If not resolved, the uncertainty may halt the progress of the project. Such a change may be related to the overall programme, a part of the programme, an individual part of the design, or even a particular module of software. This, also, provides a way of representing the effect of such changes on the overall project, where cost impact is small or meaningless.

To satisfy this need a Criticality index is defined. Criticality is in effect a multi-dimensional change impact rating. Once again, we use the assessment A, B, C. C being dangerous, while A impacts the edge of the system design or the programme. Something that may be important in itself, or to one group of users, or designers, but will not stop progress on the rest of the project.

In most applications, Criticality has been the primary means of prioritising changes and has been described in terms of traffic-light ratings of Red, Amber or Green. This can be very effective at concentrating on the project impacts and/or avoiding confusion with ratings of assessment Sensitivity.

11.8.2.2 Positioning in time

One of the most important things we need to know is *when* we have to do something about an event, assessment, or change. In the case of a project we need to know when the change will start to impact the work. Then we must determine when we have to take action to prevent it happening or to reduce its impact. The timing of a change should always equate to the latest time to start the first necessary action. In this respect, it is analogous with trying to stop a cancer. This must be done at the point that it starts to grow, not when it can be first be seen.

11.8.2.3 Controllability

Controllability is a measure of confidence that the change will be managed. It should not be confused with the probability of the change occurring, which is a measure of how likely the change is to occur if nothing is done. The controllability grade cannot normally be assigned until the change has been reviewed and discussed by senior management, whereby an agreement is reached as to their confidence that the change can ultimately be managed. A ‘C’ grade means that no change plans are in place and no action has been taken, whereas an ‘A’ grade indicates that change plans or actions are well under way with a very high confidence of success.

11.8.3 Change Register Reports

Impact Diagrams provide an overview or change profile of the project. However, the detail of the changes is required for the change review meeting in order that the detail of the changes can be seen, discussed and actions taken.

The order of the changes in the report is important so that senior management can focus on the key changes first.

If the impact diagram is used to prioritise the change register the time element can be easily included. For instance there may be an urgent AMBER criticality, C controllability change that needs attention that is not an obvious priority if the Change Report is prioritised by Criticality and Controllability alone.

In essence the easiest way to prioritise is to use the Impact Diagram and to treat the highest priority change as the one nearest to the origin, the next nearest being number two and so on. The intention is to order the risks so that they are roughly in the right order.

11.9 Change Control

Changes may be attacked at both the strategic and tactical levels. Strategic approaches look for trends and underlying causes for groups of changes. Tactical approaches take each change at face value.

11.9.1 Strategic Approaches

A strategic viewpoint is achieved by using the Change Driver approach. Each assessment and subsequent change is categorised into Technical, Milestone, Decision or Resource to reflect what is driving the poor quality ratings:

- Technical relates to assessments of a technical or complexity nature (e.g. the pure complexity of providing an interface)
- Milestone that applies to assessments regarding timescale dependencies on other projects, or external suppliers, and can be used to identify linkages to project milestones (e.g. an activity which is not inherently complex but may not be feasible due to timescale constraints).
- Decision that is used to describe assessments that require business decisions, business policies or standards (e.g. organisational announcements).
- Resources that relate to resource deficiencies or priorities (e.g. insufficient training resources).

Note that with this categorisation, Policy has been split into Decision and Resource categories. This is necessary when the resource constraints are external to the programme/organisation. When the resource constraints are internal, a simple Policy Driver will cover this.

Categorising assessments and changes in this way identifies the main change drivers, can simplify the identification of trends and assist in the development of appropriate change plans.

For example, Red Decision and Resource changes are "show-stoppers" which generally require senior management action. Red Milestone changes are an indication of how tightly the programme is being "squeezed" and Red Technical changes indicate the complexity of the planned activities.

The Change Driver chart indicates where particular effort is required. In the example below the relatively high number of Decision based changes suggests that the project is being put at risk by having to wait for decisions, probably from within the organisation. A steering committee meeting could potentially resolve most of these changes. If the project is in the early stages, it is already showing signs that the time scales are too ambitious by the high number of milestone changes.

	Technical	Milestone	Resource	Decision	Total
Red	7	15	4	19	*45*
Amber	12	19	15	26	*72*
Green	10	6	12	12	*40*
Total	29	40	31	57	157

It is important to note that noting that the "normal" Change Driver profile trends with the phase of the project. i.e. "Normal" would be (using relative terms):

Phase	Technical	Milestone	Resource	Decision
Start of project	Rising	Min.	Max.	Max.
Middle of project	Max.	Rising	Falling	Falling
End of project	Falling	Max.	Min.	Min.

11.9.2 Tactical Approaches

Most changes will need to be addressed specifically (i.e. one action plan for each change) to address the underlying assessment. Assessments that are placed in the C area of the Sensitivity/Stability matrix are unreliable, represent significant risks, and it is dangerous to continue with the project without taking action. We must do at least one of two things:

- Stabilise them by escalating the assessment to senior management and obtaining agreements that increase confidence that the assessment will turn out to be true.
- Make the project less sensitive to the assessment i.e. Reduce sensitivity by redesign, re-planning or having acceptable fallback plans in place.

The actions taken to attack the problem may be very different, depending on whether we are trying to reduce Sensitivity or Stabilise. It is normal to try to stabilise the assessment first before trying to handle sensitivity, which is usually more difficult.

11.9.3 Following Through on Actions

Just as it is possible to introduce change by planning a project badly, it is possible to address many changes by using normal project management methods, as long as the risk has been identified early enough.

Changes generally come from two areas activities that have not been planned adequately or planned activities that are likely to go wrong. Therefore, the first filter to apply to the changes is to identify those that can be tackled by just improving the plans. Obviously, if there is no project plan the change is unbounded and the first action must be to create a plan.

11.9.4 The Need for Change Plans

Changes, which cannot be resolved by improved planning, must be tackled individually through the use of dedicated Change Plans. Ultimately, the plans for reducing the changes must be incorporated into the main project plans.

Change Plans may be divided into "Simple" or "Complex", irrespective of the potential impact of the change. Simple means that it is possible to resolve the change quickly say by a simple phone call or single task. For such changes, monitoring the status on the Change Report is sufficient and minimises bureaucracy. Complex changes require significant resources and time to resolve them and for these a formal Change Plan is required.

11.9.5 Essential Components of a Formal Change Plan

For Complex changes, it is essential that a structured plan be formulated. This will clarify thinking, provide the necessary visibility and feed directly into the main planning process:

The basic components of a Change Plan are:

- The change statement and its ratings,
- Change Owner and Change Action Manager,
- The driving statement and its ratings,
- Assessment Originator,
- Objectives of the Change Plan i.e. Stabilise the assessment,
- Criteria i.e. how will we know when the objectives have been met,
- Change Plan summary i.e. what are the steps to meet the objectives,
- Reference to project plans,
- Additional resources required,
- Monitoring process i.e. how often and by whom,
- Re-assessment of the driving assessment (completed after execution of the Change Plan)
- Fallback plans i.e. what we do if the Change Plan fails.

11.9.6 Devising Change Plans to Attack Changes

11.9.6.1 Developing Change Plans

It is preferable to develop a number of alternative Change Plans before a decision is made to implement any one of them. The analysis technique used to identify changes can be used to help understand what type of plans may be appropriate. There are no firm rules that govern the way we approach Change Plans but, if a simple logic is followed, it becomes easier to be sure all the possible strategies have been considered.

11.9.6.2 Plans for Attacking Assessment Based Changes

Two approaches should be considered for each critical assessment:

- Stabilise the assessment to ensure that it will be right,
- Reduce Sensitivity to the assumption, and make it matter less.

It can, also, be useful to analyse the Change Driver to understand what sort of assessment is being considered:

- Technical assessments that may relate to the complexity of the design, implementation and the technical interfaces with other systems and projects.
- Milestone assessments that are based on timing constraints and co-ordination with other projects. Appropriate Change Plans normally result in re-planning and the addition of new milestones to the project plans to check that external deliveries will be met.
- Policy based assessments (including Decision and Resource Drivers) that are caused by the business environment, its policies and the decisions or lack of decisions. Change Plans aimed at stabilising the assessment are normally appropriate (e.g. gaining high-level commitment to a policy or standard).

11.9.6.3 Plans for Attacking Planning-Type Changes

A Work Plan Analysis of the project plans may reveal changes that are related to:

- Areas where the plans are of poor quality (C), where we should expect good quality,
- Areas where high probabilities that the contingencies will be used have been identified,
- Areas where large contingencies have been added.

Change plans addressing changes that have been identified by an analysis of the project plans often involve the same type of process as that used in main project planning:

- Detailed (re) planning of sensitive areas,
- Re-timing modules and activities,
- Re-structuring the work breakdown,
- Re-allocation of responsibilities for elements of the work within the project,
- Exporting certain elements to other agencies,
- Forming sub-projects,
- Constructing models and prototypes,
- Resolving resources,
- Special programme control procedures,

- Planning parallel activities,
- Identification of linked milestones in other projects,
- Monitoring external dependencies.

11.9.6.4 Selecting Particular Change Plans

The selection of a particular Change Plan is normally a simple process; as the plan, which is most likely, to succeed is often obvious. Occasionally it is necessary to analyse the Return On Investment (ROI) of each plan in order to make a decision.

Having generated a number of alternative Change Plans for each important change, we now have the task of deciding which plan to put into operation. It will normally be obvious which of these plans should be employed first. Our own experience and judgement will be enough, in most circumstances, to choose the plan on the basis of simplicity, cost, time to implement or chance of success.

Often, some selection criteria for Change Plans will be used before the plans are prepared and this will obviously have a bearing on the plans proposed (e.g. on a tight time scale, only plans which can be implemented quickly will be considered).

Circumstances may change, however, and it is a good idea not to limit plans to those that may be appropriate at the time of initial selection. After all, the first plan that is tried may fail.

When we consider the merits of various Change Plans, there are a number of factors that must be assessed:

- The time available before the last action date by which the change must be reduced to an acceptable level,
- The duration of the proposed plan,
- The cost impact of the change, which may limit the allowable cost of the Change Plan to produce an acceptable rate of return,
- The remoteness of the change, which also affects the minimum acceptable rate of return required of the plan,
- The collective judgement in the project team will have to be used to assess many of these factors. However, cost and time scales factors can be approached in a more structured manner, if the choice of plan is not immediately obvious,
- When considering how much to invest in a Change Plan it is important to know how much time is available before the change may impact the project. If the change is a long way away, and remote from the heart of the project, we should think very carefully before immediately implementing a Change Plan, which will expend a lot of effort.

The expected Return On Investment that may be required before the project manager sanctions a Change Plan tends to vary with time. Experienced project managers expect returns as high as 50 to 1 if the change is beyond the planning horizon.

The reason for this is that:

- Any Change Plan contains its own change that it may fail,

- Remote changes may disappear of their own accord,
- The fact that we are aware of a remote change may allow us time to modify our plans to avoid them, without taking any special measures,
- The change may not be as big as it looks at long range,
- It may be wise to find out more about a change with a modest plan before we launch the full attack,
- If a modest plan succeeds we have saved resources,
- If a modest plan fails we still have time to launch another, more aggressive, attack,
- If an expensive plan is launched and fails we may not have the time or resources to carry out a further plan,

Also, as a change moves through the planning horizon - i.e. when the change is still there after detailed plans have been developed, it is essential that suitable Change Plans be prepared quickly to maximise the Return on Investment. Time becomes the essential decision driver.

As the change approaches, the acceptable rate of return drops rapidly, until plans with very low Returns on Investment may have to be implemented in order to save the project. If the change is not high Criticality, it may become more cost effective to accept the impact in terms of cost or loss of functionality, and perhaps launch a sub-project later.

However, in these circumstances, we either failed to identify the change in time to act, or we finalised the Change Plan too late for it to be effective.

11.9.7 Project Change Organisation And Responsibilities

The definition of Change Management roles and responsibilities is crucial to the success of the Change Management process.

Each change a Change Owner and every Change Plan must have a dedicated Change Action Manager, to ensure that the change is properly attacked. Each of these roles should have published responsibilities. The roles may be full or part time, as appropriate to the size complexity and criticality of the project. The individuals may be drawn from within the project team, from either the supplier or client personnel, or from an outside source, if this is appropriate or the resources are not available within the project.

11.9.7.1 Change Ownership and Change Action Managers

It is common practice in traditional change management methods to assign a single Change Action Manager/Owner for each change. This is normally the person who knows most about the area in which the change would impact and also actions the change.

The main problem with this approach is that, particularly on large projects, changes stop being identified effectively as the change Owner/Manager of a risky area becomes overloaded with Change Plans.

To avoid this situation, it is recommended that, on all but the smallest of projects (i.e. less than 10 people in the combined supplier/client project team), separate Change Owners and Change Action Managers should be assigned for each change.

The allocation of separate tasks to Change Action Managers and Owners, whenever possible, produces a system of checks and balances.

The Change Owner:

- Sets the overall objectives for the plan,
- Certifies that the Change Plan selected will work,
- Certifies that progress is on schedule and that the plan has succeeded in reducing the change.
- The Change Action Manager:
- Plans the detail,
- Applies for any necessary resources,
- Carries out the plan and ensures that time and effort is not wasted on activities not strictly associated with the specified Change Plan.

The Change Action Manager will tend to be, naturally, efficient at such tasks, as they will be busy with their own part of the project.

Separating the Owner of the change from the Change Management task is thus very desirable on large projects and ensures that Change Plans do just enough to effectively attack the changes. It relieves the Project Manager of much of the monitoring effort associated with controlling a large number of different plans and permits him or her an overview of the changes to the project and the Change Management process.

11.9.7.2 Selecting Change Action Managers

The choice of Change Action Manager depends upon the task in hand. Quite junior staff can manage many changes. Motivated systems engineers and administrative staff can be empowered to carry out a simple plan which may have very significant effects on the project (e.g. Collecting the latest information from Policy making bodies).

Using junior staff is very cost effective, it is very good training and it can be a very effective motivator. Allocating junior staff tends to prevent the Change Plans dominating other routine activities, and thus disrupting the rest of the project.

Change Action Managers should be drawn from outside the project for external changes. In this case the Project Manager identifies suitable candidates, but the project Steering Committee or advisory board appoints them. One of these groups is also responsible for ensuring that any external Change Action Managers are correctly empowered and controlled by their own line management.

11.9.7.3 Selecting Change Owners

The choice of Change Owner is critical to the success of a plan. A person must be chosen who is:

- Knowledgeable about the project area that the change will impact,

- Informed about the nature of the change,
- Motivated to see the problem solved,
- Able to see when the plan has been successful,
- Able to recommend that the plan should be stopped.

Care is required to ensure that the Change Owner is suitably senior and first-line reports to the Project Manager are normally appropriate. This is because the senior members of the project team will normally review changes and it is essential that all key changes can be discussed in such a forum.

It is perfectly possible to have an external Change Owner. The only problem with this external arrangement is ensuring that there is sufficient motivation in supporting the project that will be affected by the change.

11.9.7.4 The Change Review Board

The focal point of the Change Control process is the Change Review Board. This body ensures that the roles and responsibilities are set; the changes are understood at the appropriate level in the organisation, action plans are set and followed through and the communication flows at the senior level in the organisation.

The basic terms of reference of a Change Review Board are:

11.9.7.4.1 Representation

The senior managers (e.g. Project Managers in a Programme) normally form the core of this meeting. In addition any (senior) Change Owners will be required to attend. The meeting should be chaired by the Programme/Business Director and facilitated by a Change Management expert.

11.9.7.4.2 before the meeting

The Change Team will undertake interviews of all agreed key players to capture important and assessments. All data will be captured in the Change as database from which the Change Register and report will be produced.

The Change Register will be circulated to all Change Owners one day prior to the meeting. It is the responsibility of each Change Owner to review their changes before the meeting and to make sure that they fully understand the change, agree with the ratings and are clear about any actions underway. To achieve this it may be necessary for the Change Owner to communicate with the Assessment Originator and/or the Change Action Manager.

In addition, each Change Owner should review the Assumption Register (or relevant part of it) to check agreement with other people's assessments and ratings. Any major disagreements should be raised in the Change Review Board. Minor queries should be fed back to the Change Team.

11.9.7.4.3 during the meeting

The changes will be discussed in priority order as indicated by the Impact Diagram. The process for each change will be:

- The Change Owner will clarify the change briefly (if necessary),

- The meeting will endorse or change the ratings for Criticality, Controllability and Impact Timing.
- For new changes, suitable action/s will be agreed and a Change Action Manager will be assigned to undertake the action plan.
- For existing changes, the Change Action Manager will report on mitigation progress and when the change is considered as resolved, the Change Owner will agree the closure proposal. Note that the change is not formally closed until the Assessment Originator agrees to down-rate or close the associated assessment.

At the end of the meeting there will be time to raise any urgent assessment queries and discuss them as changes, if appropriate.

11.9.7.4.4 After the meeting

The Change Register and Impact Diagram will be updated from the meeting and re-issued, within one week, to all Change Owners as a formal record of the meeting and actions agreed. Change Action Managers are then responsible to undertake the actions agreed in the Action Status section of the Change Register, while Change Owners are responsible for making sure that actions are followed through in a timely fashion.

Immediately following the meeting, the Change Team will commence the next cycle of interviews.

11.9.7.5 Running Change Plans

Once the Change Plan has been agreed and approved, the running of the Change Plan should be straightforward. The plan should be followed and progress reported to the Change Owner and Project Manager against time and the resources expended.

Simple action plans (e.g.: phone calls, one day investigations etc.) should be noted quickly and tracked in the Action/Status field of the Change Report. Complex Change Plans that extend over a longer period (say more than 5 man-days) should be detailed in the Change Plan section of the database and ultimately incorporated into the main project plan.

The decision on whether to incorporate a Change Plan into the main project plans is a judgement based on the relative duration of the Change Plan relative to the main plans. For example, there is little point in including a 3 man day Change Plan in the project plans if the planning has only been carried out down to 20 man day activities.

11.9.7.6 Closing Change Plans

There is a significant difference between closing a plan and just stopping it. Change Plans should be stopped if they are not succeeding. Closure is only authorised when the objectives have been met. It is critical that Change Plans are closed or stopped at the appropriate time in order to avoid wasting effort.

Further on, there is no point in expending effort on identifying changes, deciding which to attack, formulating alternative Change Plans, and then conducting them, if the plan is not properly closed when it is complete or has failed.

11.9.7.7 Stopping a Change Plan

A Change Plan must be stopped when:

- Either it is seen to be failing,
- Or it is no longer necessary.

It is essential that money is not wasted on ineffective Change Plans or the value of the entire process may be questioned.

11.9.7.8 Closing a Change Plan

It is always best to err on the side of caution when closing a Change Plan i.e. if in doubt, leave it open. When the Change Plan is thought to have met its objectives:

- Obtain agreement from the Change Owner to close the plan,
- Trust a statement or promise only when it is fully endorsed and recorded at the right level in the enterprise,
- Ensure that all the necessary changes resulting from the Change Plan are incorporated into the main project plans, documentation and specifications,
- Check that any revised practices are reflected in the business area,
- Evaluate if there is any remaining (residual) Change that may still need to be addressed.

Then document the closure in the Change Administration System.

11.9.7.9 Configuration Control

To allow the Project Management process to be effective, the main projects and management concerned must have an effective change and configuration control system in place. To support the Change Management element, some form of Change Administration System will be required, in either a manual format for small projects, or a software based tool (such as Change) for larger projects.

11.10 Applying The Process - Practical Considerations

11.10.1 Project Prioritisation Considerations

It is important that the project inventory is updated regularly. Ensure it relies on high quality information; otherwise the Change Management exercise will quickly become meaningless (i.e. projects currently being assessed for risks may meet their objectives whilst a new, more critical project flounders because it has not been identified for Change Assessment.)

It is, also, important that all relevant contacts are involved in the process (i.e. technical and business). The projects should be prioritised from the overall business perspective, not that of a single department.

11.10.1.1 Using software tools to maintain the project inventory

A sophisticated system is not always necessary for maintaining the project inventory. A simple Word document or spreadsheet can do the job adequately. The main questions to ask when deciding how to record project information, including data for the Criticality/Complexity matrices, are:

- What is the inventory going to be used for?

The inventory is useful for deciding on resource allocation, as well as which projects are approved to go ahead and which should be assessed for change. The inventory will need to be sorted by various criteria, for example by business criticality, start date, department, even by project manager. If the inventory is going to be used in this complex manner, it may be worth using Microsoft Project or Access database, or something similar.

- How large is the inventory going to be?

  A documented list of projects and their attributes has been used for an inventory of up to 50 projects, without recourse to more complex software.

- Is there a system for prioritising projects already in place at the client? Can this easily be adapted?

  Some clients have been found to have sophisticated yet disparate and unconnected lists of projects, prioritised through departmental influence and politics, rather than by a sensible business level view.

Overall, the purpose of the project prioritisation process is to ensure that there is a sensible, business-level view of which projects contribute most to the business strategy and which need a formal risk management process to increase their chance of successfully meeting their objectives.

Further value can be added through improving resource allocation and the client's general management of projects.

It is not always necessary to visually represent projects using the CC Diagram. Some clients prefer to prioritise projects based solely on the business criticality, and use the other parameters for deciding which projects require formal change management.

Even then, other management systems can lead senior management to highlight particular projects for formal change management. For example, through own discussions with the project managers. Even in these circumstances, plotting the projects on a CC Diagram can help to focus priorities and ensure consistency across the business.

11.10.1.2 Assessment Analysis Considerations

It is important to identify the right people to interview in order to capture assessments. You will need to interview people from the project organisation and the customer/users departments.

These people tend to be:

- Project managers (smaller projects):

  If the project organisation is relatively small, the project manager is likely to be a rich source of information. The project manager should have a good understanding of the project plans and the activities taking place within the project. He should be able to speak on behalf of his direct reports on the project.

- Project managers (larger projects):

In larger projects, the Project Manager will tend to identify his Team Leaders for interview. The Project Manager will be able to provide assessments relating to the project as a whole and the events it faces relative to overall business objectives whilst the Team Leaders will tend to concentrate on their own area.

A project manager looking at assessments raised by the project team will be able to provide feedback and further assessments.

- Team members:

  Down to a certain level, team members should be interviewed to capture assessments. They have the front line view and more detailed knowledge of the events and potential problems they could face in delivering the project.

  Clearly it is not necessary to interview everyone including the student on work experience. There is a pragmatic cut-off point where you have to rely on the communication mechanisms within the team ensuring the more senior members have a good idea of what is going on.

  Having said that, if you are getting assessments that are clearly lacking in detail and specifics, it may indicate that you do need to interview more people further down the project organisation.

- Customers/Users:

  Interview those who would suffer most from the failure of the project to deliver, and those who will need to provide resources to the project in the form of finance or future users

11.10.1.3 Getting To The Right Assessment

The process is designed to capture and analyse a substantially complete set of critical project assessments.

To achieve this the following criteria must be met:

- The key contacts in the organisation are interviewed to capture the assessments,
- The interviews are conducted by a team trained in the methodology,
- Someone with experience of the business and project management is involved, to help capture assessments that are not implicit from the plans,
- The assessments captured are disseminated around the key players to gather counter/multiple viewpoints on the ratings,
- The key players are re-interviewed on a regular basis to review the assessments and to capture new assessments.

In practice, interviewing is the most efficient and successful method of capturing high quality assumptions. Other methods have been tried. However, it is far more difficult to ensure that high quality data is captured.

For example:

- Self-analysis:

Every Key Player needs to be fully conversant in Change Management and its underlying principles, be knowledgeable about project management, and apply a degree of objectivity to their own thinking.

Furthermore, people tend to need prompting to perform this exercise, even if they think it's a great idea, a separate facilitator ensuring regular review would be required. Great caution is required with this approach if quality problems are not to negate all benefits.

- Forms:

  A structured form, which allows project team members to fill in their assessments and rate them is clearly a form of self-analysis and, in practice, a very ineffective means of identifying changes. The form will be seen as an administrative burden and will not receive the attention it deserves.

  The information will inevitably be brief incomplete and unclear and the ratings will be meaningless without the challenge of a facilitator to ensure that the assessment is the right one and the ratings are fully understood and allocated relative to the project and business objectives.

- Workshops:

  If led by an expert, workshops can produce a lot of data in a short space of time. The data quality however tends to be low, unless significant extra time is spent improving it. People may become more reticent in divulging potentially sensitive information, and assessments tend to be generic, embodying the group point of view and losing much of their specific value.

  One effective way to run a change assessment workshop is to use a Project Readiness Assessment Walkthrough.

Compared with other approaches, the primary benefits of the interviewing approach are:

- Only a small number of interviewers need to be experts and have experience of project management to generate high quality output,
- Key contacts do not need to be highly trained in Change Management. They only need to understand how information is graded and how the process works (at a high level),
- Key contacts will talk more openly and provide higher quality information in a one-on-one situation, and differences of opinion are made visible to the interviewer,
- The interviewer is not a stakeholder and can be completely objective,
- The interviewer can judge that the right contacts are regularly interviewed to maintain a complete assessments register.

11.10.1.4 Preparation For The Interview

Key contacts are interviewed not only to capture their assessments and changes, but also to communicate relevant information captured from other key contacts. This can actually lead to further assessments and changes being captured as the interviewee reacts to the new information. Thus, a decision has to be made as to what other assessments should be shown to the Key Player being interviewed.

Ideally each key contact should be aware of assessments and changes raised by all key contacts for the project, and would benefit from the latest report of these on each visit. Should the project prove too large for this to be practical, assessments and changes can be categorised and a sub-group of these reported to each key contact. The changes database facilitates this process.

11.10.1.5 During The Interview

If this is the first time the interviewer has seen the person, they should talk through the Assessment Analysis approach, and determine the correct role of this person in the process.

It is also important for the interviewer to understand the person's role in each project they are a key contact for, so that questions can be directed effectively.

There are a number of key activities that should take place during the interview:

- Check that plans exist for the project and at least for the current phase. Work from a high-level milestone plan if it is available or the plan that they are carrying around in their head at the very least.
- Walk them through the plan asking the question "what is your next milestone and do you have any concerns in achieving it?"
- Ask questions based on what planned activities need to take place, focusing on weak areas, activities that are not in the plans and suggest potential problems the interviewee may not have thought of.
- Capture important assessments that have been made explicitly in the plans, or that the interviewee has revealed as a result of your questions.
- Should an assessment be graded as C,C., it will be necessary to capture the change statement straight away. Ask the interviewee what the consequences will be if the assessment does not happen, and capture all other details required to describe the change.
- Existing assessments and changes should be reviewed with the interviewee. This may lead to a change in grading, wording, timing, or any other attributes of an assumption or change. The assessment and change wording and ratings must be the Key Player's and not the interviewer's, if ownership and buy-in are to be encouraged.

11.10.1.6 At The End Of The Interview

There are a number of steps to take in completing an interview:

- Review the assessments and changes to ensure the interviewee is happy with the wording and ratings,
- Make sure they represent what they believe to be their major changes/concerns,

- Explain that you will revisit these assessments the next time you visit, and that meantime their changes will be reviewed and action taken by senior management.

11.10.1.7 Review Assessments And Changes Regularly

It is important to review assessments and changes on a regular basis because:

- There should be a constant communication of this information between key contacts and senior management,
- The quality of the assessments changes over time; they may become more or less stable as further information is made available, or the project may become more or less sensitive to it as planning decisions are made,
- Action to control changes and assessments needs to be communicated back to the originators and any resulting changes to the list made according to the originator's feedback.

There are a number of tools that can be used to manage this:

- The Assessments and Changes Register,
- A matrix of key contacts against projects being tracked for change,
- An interview schedule for all key contacts,
- An interviewing template to provide structure during the interview.

These must be maintained on a regular basis in order that the change management process remains focused.

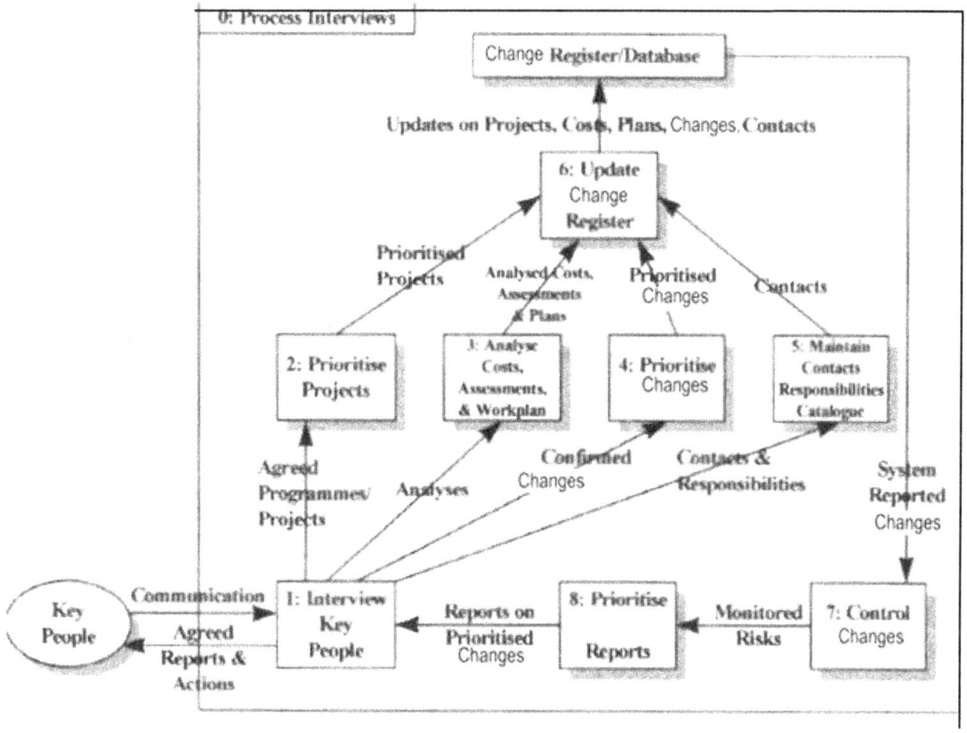

THE INTERVIEWING PROCESS

11.11 Sponsorship and Ownership

The Change Management process can only be effectively handed over to the client organisation, or users when two primary criteria are met:

- A clear sponsor (champion) and new process owners are identified,
- The process is fully up and running and is stable.

11.11.1 Identifying The Process Champions

It is important to ensure that the future sponsor and key people who will be using the process have been involved in it and can testify to the value that it adds. It may still be necessary to continue selling the benefits of the process throughout the hand over period.

The choice of sponsor is critical, since they will have to be able to keep the process on track, reinforcing it where necessary and ensuring it remains focused on what is important to the business.

Their main responsibilities would be:

- Enable the necessary interviews and break down any local resistance,
- Ensuring the senior management change review process is kept focused, action-oriented and timely,
- Managing any conflict between senior management in the process,
- Applying pressure on those who try to subvert or hijack the process.

11.11.2 Identifying The Process Owners

Equally important as the choice of sponsor is the choice of client process owners. No matter how strongly the sponsor champions the process, ineffective process owners can allow the quality of information from the method to slip, rendering the functions almost valueless in a matter of weeks following hand over.

There are several critical success factors for ensuring the effective management of the process:

- Affording time and resources for the process,
- Enthusiasm and attention to detail,
- Access to key players in the organisation.

11.11.2.1 Affording Time For The Process

The amount of effort associated with the process will be far greater than the new process owner will expect.

There may be a tendency to treat the process as a low priority activity to be done in the process owner's spare time. If care is not taken the process will not receive the necessary attention and will quickly fall down the priority list when compared with other direct business responsibilities.

Sometimes the new process owner will see this new responsibility as a poor career move. Under these circumstances there are a number of benefits that should be emphasised:

- Personal exposure to senior management on a regular (trusting) basis,
- Access to all relevant areas of the organisation, affording a much improved cross-functional view of the organisation and a larger network of contacts,
- Greater understanding of the projects being undertaken and the business problems they face,
- Greater appreciation of project management principles and the business as a whole.

11.11.2.2 Enthusiasm And Attention To Detail

An essential ingredient of a successful implementation of the process is high quality data. The process owner should be able to demonstrate a meticulous attention to detail. If senior management cannot understand the changes or the changes are not presented to them in a consistent manner, they will quickly lose interest and question the value of the process.

Typical groups within an organisation, which could provide suitable process owners, are:

- Internal consulting groups,
- Programme Offices,
- Quality management groups,
- Audit departments,
- Organisation-wide project/programme management groups.

However, care must be taken with how positively these groups are perceived within each organisation.

11.11.2.3 Access To Key Players In The Organisation

The process owners have to be in such a position as to be able to access:

- Key Players: project sponsors, project managers and key project contacts,
- Senior Management contacts: process sponsor, senior managers involved in change review and control,

The process champion will need to intervene quickly in any access problems.

11.11.2.4 Avoiding The Split-up Approach

There may be a temptation to split up the process across the organisation to spread the load and allow part time involvement of the new process owners. Great care is required here as one the key benefits of Change Management that of providing a cross-organisational communication mechanism, may be undermined.

11.12 Hand Over Process

11.12.1 Training

The training must cover both the theory and practical application of Change Management. Theory without practice inevitably leads to poor quality data and practice without theory extends the learning curve considerably.

11.12.2 Parallel Interviews

One of the most important parts of the hand over programme is the parallel interview sessions. After the training course, a series of parallel interviews are held where the consultant and new process owner conduct a number of interviews together.

This achieves the following:

- The new process owner can learn first hand how the interviews are conducted and how the different interviewees behave,
- The new process owner can practice the interviewing process with a degree of comfort that they can make mistakes,
- The interviewees can visibly see the handover process at work and meet their future interviewers.

Past experience has shown that approximately 15-20 parallel interviews are required to get the average candidate up to speed.

It is useful to arrange for the new process owner to conduct an interview with each of the Key Players during the parallel interviewing process. This allows them to establish a dialogue with each of their contacts by the time the hand over is complete.

It is also useful to interview some new Key Players, so the new process owner can learn how to explain the process and its benefits to the individual.

Parallel interviews should be conducted with the consultant leading for the first few interviews, and then with the new process owner leading in later interviews. Prior to each interview, the consultant should review with the client the documentation required for the interview. This avoids the client losing valuable learning time in the interview being unable to understand the language used or the relevant project background.

11.12.2.1 Consultant Leading Interviews

The main skill learnt by the client through this activity is how to capture high quality assumptions and changes.

The new process owner should have a copy of all the materials that the consultant has to conduct the interview. The consultant conducts the interview as normal. The new process owner will learn how interviews are conducted, and practice capturing assumptions and changes as the consultant asks the questions. When the captured data is recorded in a Change Register, the consultant can correct the client's notes after the interview. About 5 to 10 interviews should be sufficient.

11.12.2.2 Client Leading Interviews

One of the most difficult aspects of the interviewing process is asking the right questions and maintaining a dialogue with the interviewee whilst at the same time following a strict code in documenting the assessments and changes and their associated grading. The client will have acquired changes in the mechanics of capturing assessments and changes, and will now have the opportunity to practice asking the right questions to obtain that information.

The consultant should allow the client to run the interview by him or herself as much as possible, intervening only where quality is compromised to ensure the best results from the interview are obtained. The consultant should concentrate on asking any questions at the end that may have been missed due to lack of experience.

The consultant should spend time with the new process owner after the interview to discuss what went well (so the client knows they are progressing) and what could be improved.

More time should be spent on this stage of the hand over with the client leading the interviews since they have more to learn at this stage. About 10 to 15 interviews should be sufficient.

11.12.3 Procedures And Supporting Documentation

The client process owners have a lot to learn in a short hand over time i.e.: a complete methodology, the current process, the interviewing technique and using the software support tools. All this needs to be supported by some form of procedures, to provide a reference point during the hand over and to act as supplementary training material should the process owners need to train further people in their organisation.

11.12.4 Software Tool Support

Not only do the new process owners have to learn to use the changes software, but someone will have to be trained in maintaining the software, as it is likely at some stage that they will need to add new fields or categories, or modify the report formats.

The ideal way to achieve this is to provide good documentation of the system, combined with at least half a day's worth hands-on demonstration with the chosen system maintainer. This person should be able to 'play' with the database by himself (trying to add fields/modify reports etc.) and be able to come back and ask questions before the hand over is complete.

11.13 Ongoing Quality Management

11.13.1 Can they Continue To Do It Themselves?

No matter how well the hand over has been managed the process can still start to fail quickly when the consultants depart if the new process owners do not fully understand all the subtleties of the application of Change Management. A way of minimising this risk is to consciously involve the new process owner in all decisions, discussions, changes etc. during the hand over period.

When adjustments need to be made to the process, involve the new process owners - ask how they would deal with it first. Such adjustments may include:

- Reassessing the list of key contacts where necessary,
- Changing the format of change reporting to senior management,
- Adjusting interviewing approach or timing,
- Changing the format of the change review meetings,
- Managing political hiccups that can disrupt the process,
- Seizing opportunities that can enhance the process,

- Provide them with a 'troubleshooting guide' that highlights typical symptoms, what it is that may be going wrong, and ways to correct the problem.

    For example:

    - Not identifying many changes,
    - Senior management do not understand the changes,
    - Key Players start to lose interest in the process,
    - The Change Review meetings become irregular.

11.13.2 Applying Change Management To The Hand Over Phase

A highly effective way of ensuring a successful hand over within agreed timescales is to apply the process to the hand over activities. This means treating the hand over as a project and forming a simple Change Register that is communicated to the client at regular intervals.

If the Process Sponsor is regularly updated with changes to achieving successful hand over, he will be able to take actions to support the consultants. Furthermore, if the hand over is impeded by factors outside the consultants' control, for example late sign-off, problems accessing the right people, and so on, the change register can provide a valuable audit trail backing up promises to deliver, or supporting any explanations as to why there were delays.

11.14 Integrating Methodologies

In handing over and in applying any Change Management method, as in any other Management tool, the integration of all existing methodologies is of primary importance.

In choosing the new owner of the methodology, consideration must be given regarding the experience possessed by the new proprietor. Preference should be given to the people with systems methodology and management procedures training and experience.

12. INTERFACING

12.1 The Diagrammatic Representation Of The Desired Integration

The diagrammatic flow shown below is the desired overall integration of related top-level processes:

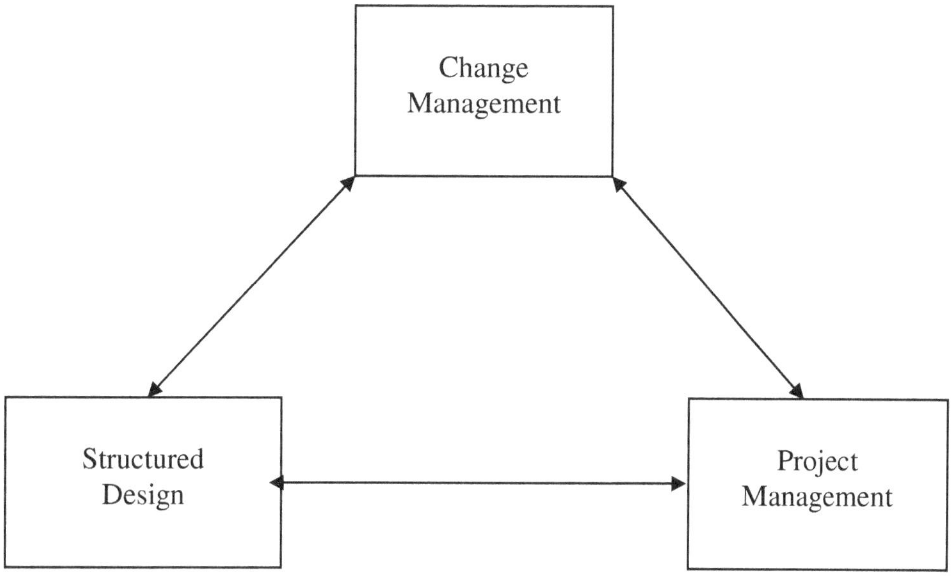

Integration of Methodologies

12.2 Suggested Interfacing

The suggested interfacing of the Structured Systems Analysis and Design methodology and the Project Management procedures to the Change Management processes may be done separately.

12.3 Using The Existing Methods

In interfacing the various processes from the different existing organisational methodologies, the main steps of Project Management and the Structures Systems Analysis and Designing methodology, will be incorporated in this exercise.

Namely, the four main stages of system development:

- Analyse,
- Design,
- Construct,
- Implement.

The identified processes of Project Management procedures and Structured Systems Analysis and Designing to be linked to the Change Management processes of:

- Events,
- Assessments,
- Changes,
- Plans.

The actual points of interfacing the stages of development, the procedures of managing projects and the assessments analysis of the methodology are explored in this book.

12.4 Connection Of Project Management To Change Management

Regarding the connections of the project management procedures to change management, it is suggested that the link be from the higher level of project management work elements, such as:

- Initiate Change Management,
- Adjust Project Approach to Change,
- Control Change,
- Complete Change Management.

This is as far as most users drill into the process and generally as far as they are required to by structured analysis and designing methodologies guidelines.

13. MANAGING THE CHANGE MANAGEMENT PROGRAMME

13.1 The Diagrammatic Representation Shown.

- O: Change Management Decomposition,
- O: Management of the Change Programme,
- 1: Managing of the Change Management Process,
- 2: Facilitation of the Change Management Programme,
- 3. Practising the Methodology.

13.2 O: Change Management Decomposition

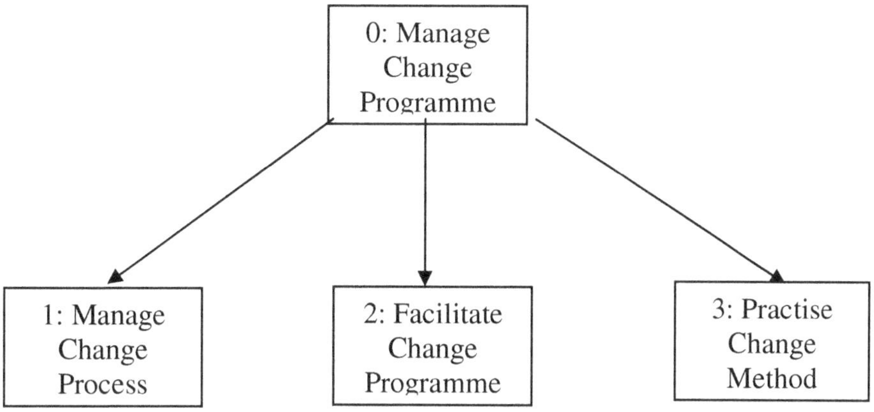

The Change Management Decomposition

The next four Dataflow Diagrams are shown on the following two pages and are:

0: Manage Change Programme,

1: Manage Change Process,

2: Facilitate Change Programme,

3: Practise Change Methodology.

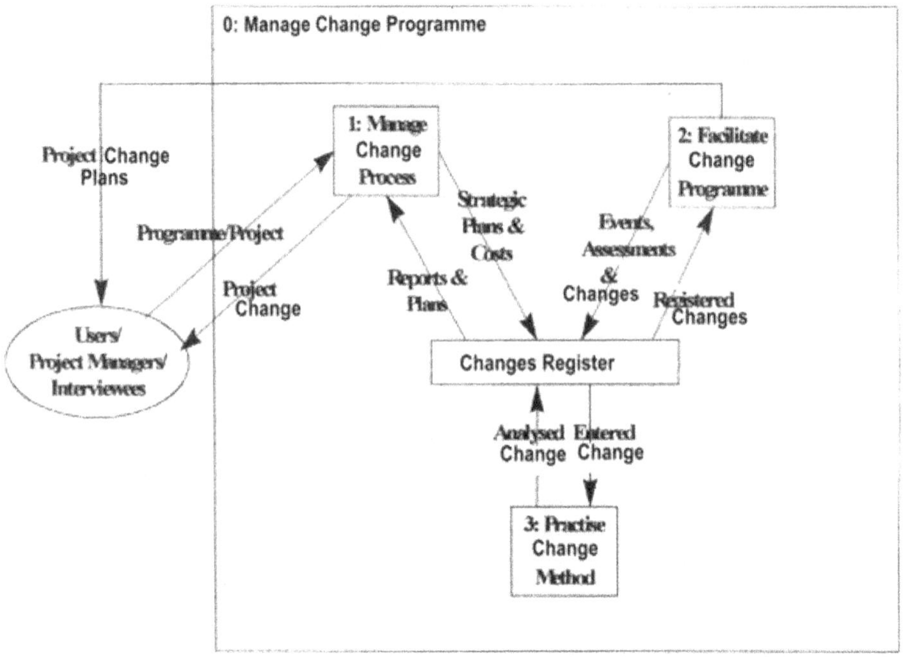

13.4 1: Managing of the Change Management Process

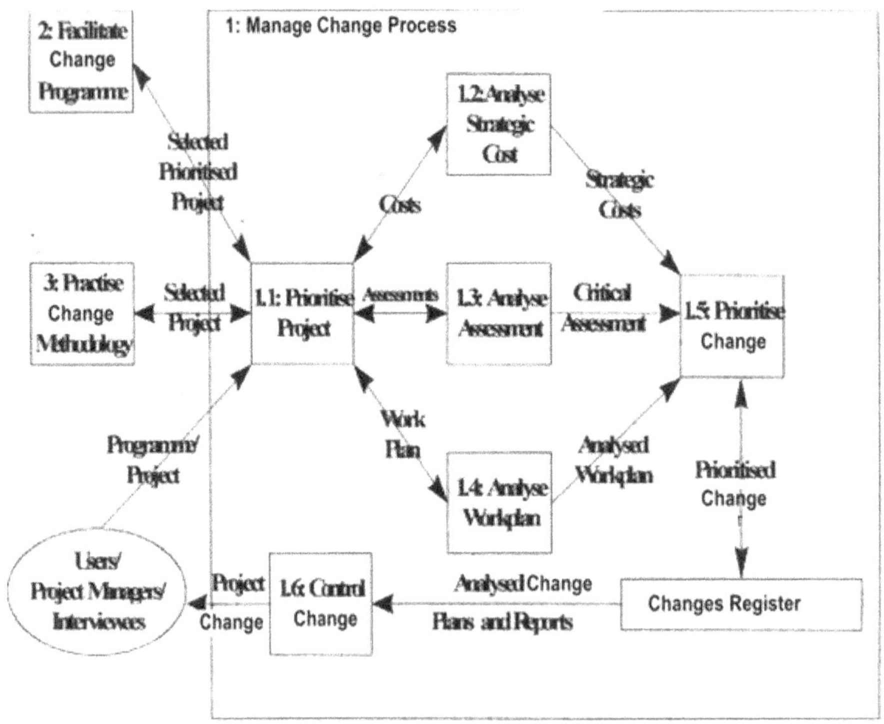

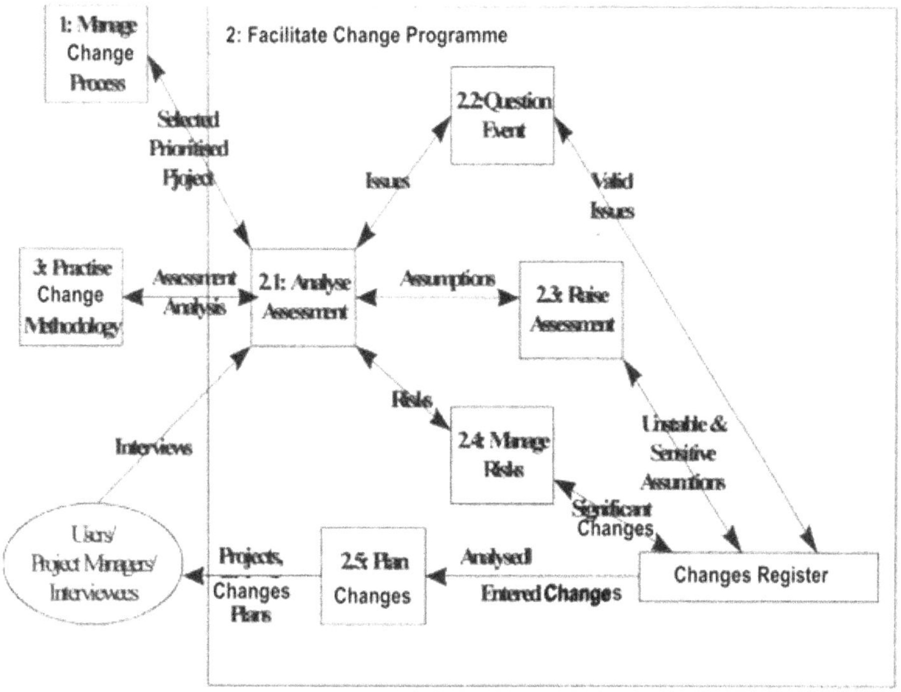
1: Manage Change Process
2: Facilitate Change Programme
2.2: Question Event
Selected Prioritised Project
Issues
Valid Issues
3: Practise Change Methodology
Assessment Analysis
2.1: Analyse Assessment
Assumptions
2.3: Raise Assessment
Risks
2.4: Manage Risks
Unstable & Sensitive Assumptions
Interviews
Significant Changes
Users/ Project Managers/ Interviewees
Projects, Changes Plans
2.5: Plan Changes
Analysed Entered Changes
Changes Register

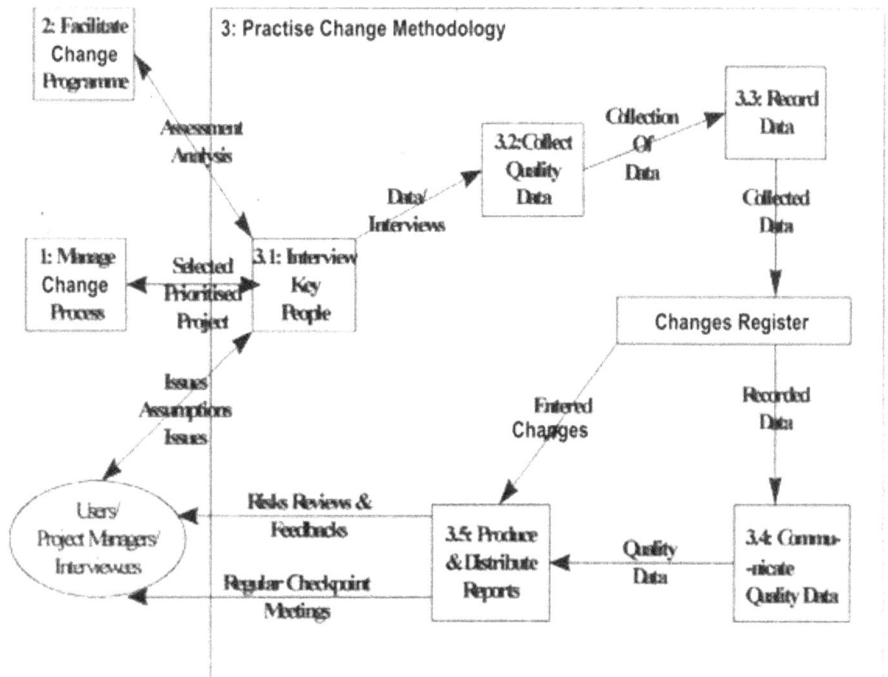
2: Facilitate Change Programme
3: Practise Change Methodology
3.3: Record Data
Collection Of Data
3.2: Collect Quality Data
Assessment Analysis
Data/ Interviews
Collected Data
1: Manage Change Process
Selected Prioritised Project
3.1: Interview Key People
Changes Register
Issues Assumptions Issues
Entered Changes
Recorded Data
Users/ Project Managers/ Interviewees
Risks Reviews & Feedbacks
3.5: Produce & Distribute Reports
Quality Data
3.4: Communicate Quality Data
Regular Checkpoint Meetings

13.3 Relationship Of Dataflow Diagrams

All dataflow diagrams shown in above pages are based on the PsySys Limited manuals and handouts as used for the training.

DATAFLOW DIAGRAMS:	*DESCRIPTION OF DIAGRAMS AND THEIR PROCESSES.*
0: Manage Change Programme	• Project: something complex that you want (plan) to happen. • Change: Something that you don't want to happen. • Project management: Planning and making things happen. • Change management: Attacking anything that might disturb the plans
1: Manage Change Process	The process consists of an integrated closed loop method which logically progresses through: 1.1 Project Prioritisation, 1.2 Strategic Cost Analysis, 1.3 Assessment Analysis, 1.4 Work Plan Analysis, 1.5 Risk Prioritisation, 1.6 Change Control.
1.1 Prioriti Project	Only complex and critical projects need to have a fully structur Change Management process in place.
1.2 Analyse Strategic Cos	Strategic Cost Analysis provides a means of assessing the cos Change in a project in its very early stages and "kick-starts" th Change Management process.
1.3 Analy Assessment	Fundamentally, projects only fail due to two reasons either t wrong assumptions were made or the significance of t assumptions was not understood.
1.4 Analyse Work plan	Work Plan Analysis may be used to focus on the risky areas o detailed, multi-level project plans when time is of the essence.
1.5 Prioriti	Prioritisation allows the Project Manager to divert limited resourc

Change	at the most critical project change.
1.6 Contro Change	Changes may be attacked at both the strategic and tactical levels Strategic approaches look for trends and underlying causes fo groups of Changes. Tactical approaches take each Change at fac value.
2: Facilitate Change Programme	The Change Management Programme is essentially a framewo process that allows the capture of collective knowledge a viewpoints from those involved on the project, in a form th facilitates communication of events, assessments and ensures pr active management of changes. By dramatically improvi communication, Changes are avoided, or managed proactively a project objectives are delivered on time.
2.1: Analys Assessment	The core is Assessment Analysis. This uses structured technique to analyse project plans and identify the most sensitiv assumptions that are potentially unstable, and therefore the sourc of greatest change.
2.2: Questi Event	Events are open questions, which are holding plans/implementation. An Event is any open question, which has been asked at the rig time to which a high quality answer cannot be provided witho escalation.
2.3: Rais Assessment	Making Assessments in plans closes many Events. An Assessment is a single, simple, positive or negative statement
2.4: Mana Changes	Unstable/sensitive assumptions create changes. Significant changes need to be managed formally. Definition: A Change is a simple statement of the form: "IF" Assumption proves incorrect, "THEN" Describe the impact.
2.5: Pla Changes	Change Plans impact project plans. Events, Assessments and chamges are inherent in the projec

plans.

Population of assessment and risks registers by progressin Change Plans/Main/Project Plans.

3: Practi Change Methodology

The Role of a Change Management Practitioner includes:

- Interview 'Key People' within the project,
- To collect 'Quality' data,
- Ensure the data collected is recorded in the Change Registe
- Communicate the 'Quality' data to Project staff,
- Produces accurate and timely reports for meetings:
    - Weekly Check Point Meetings,
    - Change Review Boards.

3.1: Interviev Key People

Identifying the right people to interview is critical to producing comprehensive and coherent picture of the changes facing project. So, to decide who should be interviewed, start with th project or programme organisational structure. Depending on th scope of the change assessment it may be necessary to map th organisational hierarchy to ensure that the right people ar interviewed and that the risks arising are reviewed at a appropriate level.

3.2: Colle Quality Data

This function requires to:

- Interview 'Key People' within the project,
- Collect 'Quality' data.

3.3: Recor Data

Having Interviewed the 'Key People' within the project an collected the 'Quality' data:

- Ensure the data collected is recorded in the Chang Register.

3.4: Communicate Quality Data

The interviews of 'Key People' within the project have be completed, the 'Quality' data recorded in the Change Register a communicated to Project staff, the next function is:

- Facilitate and ensure the Change Management process sta on track.

3.5: Produc After the initial round of interviews, a suitable forum must b

Reports

established to discuss the changes identified.

The best method is to establish a specific Change Reviev Meeting with a representation consisting of the Change Owner and chaired by the Programme Director or the proces 'champion' in the client organisation.

The main function is to:

- Produce accurate and timely reports for meetings,
- Weekly Check Point Meetings,
- Change Review Boards.

Database Of Events, Assessments and Changes Register Description.

Data Store:

Changes Register

All events, assessments and changes captured should be held in : Changes Register.

Remember, only critical assessments will be converted int(changes and held in a Change Register.

Thus, by filtering the assessments and consolidating them int(changes, all information captured will be rationalised and detail of their source and consequences will be traceable.

14. MANAGING SUCCESSFUL PROGRAMMES

14.1 A MANAGEMENT FRAMEWORK

Managing successful programmes provides a management framework and long term strategies so that a range of change projects can be looked at in relation to the benefits they can all bring to the organisation, and handled accordingly.

It takes you through the entire process, starting with defining and establishing an effective programme environment, through managing the project portfolio, then onto delivery, realisation of measurable benefits, and finally close-down.

It describes the framework you need to manage programmes successfully: understanding, planning, implementing and controlling the process. It encourages everyone involved in the programme to take a holistic view, and pay close attention to interactions between the environment, the organisation, its people and all supporting information systems.

14.2 Management Science

This is the application of quantitative techniques (those involving making measurements) to business decision-making. Management science covers the whole range of decision-making by management, for example, operations research, production management, marketing, personnel management, and cost accounting. Management science operates by forming a quantitative representation of a business problem that is by putting a numerical value on the factors involved. This modelling process enables the major elements of the decision to be identified and considered in relation to the whole problem. Alternative solutions can then be put forward and evaluated and an optimum solution found.

There is always a need to balance the quantitative approach with behavioural considerations, keeping in mind that business decisions involve people. Whilst past experience can be used to suggest how people might react in the future, conditions change and consequently people's future reactions are not always predictable. Thus management science techniques should be used as an aid to business decision-making not as a substitute for it.

14.3 Automation

This applies to the use of automatic machinery and systems, particularly those manufacturing or data-processing systems, which require little or no human intervention in their normal operation. Although the term was first used in 1946 to describe machinery being developed by the Ford Motor Company to move automobile components and work-pieces automatically to and from other machines, the origins of the concept are much older.

During the 19th century a number of machines such as looms and lathes became increasingly self-regulating. At the same time transfer-machines were developed, whereby a series of machine tools, each doing one operation automatically, became linked in a continuous production line by pneumatic or hydraulic devices transferring components from one operation to the next.

In addition to these technological advances in automation, the theory of 'scientific management', which was based on the early time-and-motion studies of Frederick

Winslow Taylor in Philadelphia, USA, in the 1880s was designed by Taylor to enhance the efficiency and productivity of workers and machines. In the early 20th century, with the development of electrical devices and time switches, more processes became automatically controlled, and a number of basic industries such as oil refining, chemicals, and food processing were increasingly automated. The development of computers after World War II enabled more sophisticated automation to be used in manufacturing industries, for example in iron and steel production.

The most familiar example of a highly automated system is perhaps an assembly plant for automobiles or other complex products. Such a plant might involve the automatic machining, welding, transfer, and assembly of parts, using equipment and techniques such as numerically controlled machine-tools, automatically controlled robot arms, and guided vehicles, automated warehousing, materials handling, stock control, and so on.

Advances in automation have been the result of a combination of many factors, including modifications to the physical layout of production or processing facilities to ease handling; improvements in materials to facilitate manufacturing processes; increasing mechanization of individual processes (the carrying out of tasks by machine rather than human actions), which often necessitates changes to the processes themselves; changes in product design to aid mechanization and mass production; more advanced instrumentation and control systems for both individual machines and for plants as a whole; and the adoption of information technology as an integral part of the production process, leading ultimately to the concept of computer-integrated manufacturing.

Over the last few decades, automation has evolved from the comparatively straightforward mechanization of tasks traditionally carried out by hand, through the introduction of complex automatic control systems, to the widespread automation of information collection and processing. Whereas in the past automation has involved a high degree of standardization and uniformity in production, the increasing use of information technology has now made it possible to develop more flexible manufacturing systems.

14.4 Deskilling

Deskilling refers to the loss of skills or responsibility resulting from mechanisation and automation. The change in printing from typesetting by hand, using heavy metal type, to the use of computer-based equipment linked to automated production of printing plates is one example. H. Braverman in *Labor and Monopoly Capital: The Degradation of Work in the 20th Century* (1974) contended that the result was the degradation of human labour, and that deskilling was a deliberate management strategy to reduce the bargaining power of employees.

Much research has been done, but there is no agreement. It is unclear, for example, how to weigh the boredom of work on an assembly line against the exhaustion of hard physical work that carries responsibility. Furthermore, some writers and official statistics suggest that technological change has resulted in a greater demand for skills. While some traditional skills disappear, new ones are in demand: automated industries need highly skilled maintenance technicians; the service industry sector (see tertiary industry), in which individual skills are important, is growing in relation to heavy industry. Market forces and competitive pricing result in standardized and uniform products. In reaction there is a renewed demand for products requiring skill in their manufacture.

14.5 Database

A computer-based database is a logically organised collection of related data, generally accessed by a set of programs known as a database management system (DBMS), which oversees the creation and use of the database and controls access to the data. The organization of a database obviates the need to duplicate information to meet the various requirements of different groups of users, and ensures that the data always remains consistent. A large database requires extensive storage facilities.

In some organizations and services databases can be accessed over networks from microcomputers or as videotex. 'Relational' databases and hypertext techniques include extensive and complex cross-reference facilities so that information on related items may be retrieved. Many database programs have been designed to run on microcomputers. Some of these contain computer languages that enable users to change the operation of the database to suit their requirements. For example, a mailing list on a microcomputer constitutes a simple database in which--if the information were available in a structured format--the DBMS could be instructed to print out the addresses of all the people called Smith, or of everyone on the mailing list living in Melbourne, Australia.

14.6 Information Technology

IT, as is often called, is the umbrella term used to describe the practical applications of computer systems. The term has become prevalent with the increasing use of computers such as word processors for office systems, but it also embraces the more traditional areas of data processing and information retrieval. Key factors in the recent rapid spread of microelectronics and information technology (often known simply as 'new technology') have been the drastic reduction in electronic hardware costs during the 1970s and 1980s; the so-called 'convergence' of computing and telecommunications (sometimes denoted by the term telematics); and the emergence of various formal standards and informal agreements within the IT industry.

The mass production of microprocessors and other electronic components at low unit cost has made it possible to incorporate digital electronics into a wide range of products for commerce, industry, and the home. New technology has made an enormous impact on the design and performance of consumer goods, for example, cameras, video and hi-fi equipment, and personal computers. In offices and business, new technology was introduced for text processing, using dedicated (special-purpose) word processors. Now, however, it is usual to find general-purpose small computers and workstations being exploited for a much wider range of office applications using special-purpose application software such as financial planning packages, management support software, information storage and retrieval applications, desk-top publishing, and so on. Expert systems using artificial intelligence techniques to aid decision-making can also be run on suitable personal computers.

The combination of computing with private and public telecommunication networks has been particularly significant in retailing and banking. Bar codes on products can be read automatically at checkouts, and the information used both to print a customer's receipt and to reorder necessary stocks. Electronic funds transfer using an 'intelligent' cash register or point-of-sale terminal can then complete the cycle of electronic information flow by automatically debiting the customer's bank or credit-card account by the appropriate amount. Sales records held by the store's central computer can be used to develop overall retailing strategies; records of the purchasing patterns of particular customers can be exploited for direct marketing of goods or services.

The IT revolution has been just as great in the manufacturing and processing industries. An early application was the numerical control of machine tools, in which digital electronics were used to control lathes and other equipment. Now it has become common for a wide range of industrial equipment (sensors, control systems, robots, and so on) to incorporate microelectronics and to be interconnected (networked) so that information can be gathered, communicated, and processed in order to optimize the activity. Artificial intelligence, in which computer programs mimic certain aspects of human behaviour, is beginning to play a role in areas such as process control, as well as in mechatronic products combining aspects of electronic, mechanical, and software engineering. Again, the convergence of telecommunications and computing has been a vital factor, allowing the computer to become fully integrated into the manufacturing or other processes (see computer-integrated manufacturing), thus transcending individual applications such as computer-aided design.

The introduction of new technology into areas, which have not traditionally used computers, has had a great influence on working practices. Some traditional tasks--or even whole categories of tasks--have disappeared completely and new ones have appeared. In some sectors (printing in the UK, for example), adoption of new technology has led to serious industrial conflict.

Once it became commonplace for information retrieval and data processing to be carried out by digital computers in business and industrial settings, it was also natural for such information to be transmitted digitally using a range of new services; telecommunications has therefore become an essential part of many working environments. Small computers are often linked by means of local area networks within an office or company, so that expensive resources such as laser printers or databases can be shared; a further advantage of such networking is that in-house communication can then include electronic mail, computer conferencing, or even voice messaging, as well as the traditional telephone and memo. Digital telecommunication links extend such facilities to the outside world, providing electronic communication between widely dispersed organizations or individuals, as well as access to external databases or information services. It is even becoming possible for certain employees to work partially or entirely from home, communicating with colleagues via a computer and modem. In the home, information is available electronically through teletex services such as Ceefax and Oracle as well as call-up videotex such as Prestel. More recently, with a growth in the ownership of home computers, individual users have linked into the Internet. In the future, the combination of telecommunication services (including television), home computer, and new storage media such as videodisc and CD-ROM is likely to form the core of domestic entertainment and educational applications of IT.

All the above applications of new technology are based upon a computer architecture, which has remained virtually unchanged since the early days of the digital computer. Alternative structures such as neural networks are currently arousing much interest, particularly for their potential in artificial-intelligence applications, while parallel computing offers possibilities for faster processing. In the immediate future, however, further exploitation of new technology is more likely to result from a continuing expansion of telecommunications services and economies of scale in the provision of hardware than from radical changes to computer design. Information technology raises problems of privacy and freedom of information, as data is gathered about citizens who may not have access to records held about them.

14.7 Metamorphosis

As the book refers to 'Change Management', the word metamorphosis may also be used in changing 'things' within IT. The word is normally used for the scientific subjects, but the author would like the broader aspect of metamorphosis to cover the needs of change in technology.

Anyway, academically speaking, metamorphosis refers to the change of form, and often of physiology as well, during the life history of an animal. Such changes are distinct from changes in mere size and those associated with sexual maturity. Metamorphosis is described as either complete or incomplete and it may be abrupt or gradual. In a complete metamorphosis, as between a caterpillar and a butterfly, an intermediate stage called the pupa is found. In incomplete metamorphosis, as in a grasshopper, the young resemble the adults except that they have wing-buds in place of wings, and the feeding habits are the same.

The most abrupt changes are also found in insects: a legless crawling maggot may turn into a housefly in the course of a few days. The transformation from tadpole to frog is an example of gradual metamorphosis, with the development of legs, and loss of gills and tail, taking place over a considerable period. Metamorphosis does not imply an increase in complexity; many parasitic adult animals are much less structurally complex than the free-living larvae from which they come.

14.8 Production Management

Strictly speaking this refers to the planning, co-ordination, and control of the processes involved in the manufacture of products in an organization. It plans how raw materials are to be transformed into products and services efficiently and effectively by the work force. The choice of production method enables an organization to produce the right amounts of each of its products to fixed deadlines.

Similar processes exist in the building of IT systems, hence the reason why the author introduces the term.

14.9 Hegemony

As Change Management relies on Leadership, the explanation of the term hegemonia (from Greek, 'leader') deserves the broader meaning of leadership. In this case, Hegemony/Leadership/Management usually applies to the directing of a state, which exercises dominance within an international system.

Within the study of international relations, the term is exclusively applied to the industrialised nations of the developed world. According to the hegemonic stability theory developed by US theorists in the 1970s, stability within international economic relationships is dependent on the dominance of one power, which establishes a framework of rules and expectations, and encourages compliance with them. Recent discussion has concerned the decline of US hegemony in the political and economic world order.

In *War and Change in World Politics* (1984), the US political theorist Robert Gilpin used the term hegemonic war to denote major wars which occur when the leading power in the international system changes. In another sense, hegemony is the dominance of a class within the state over the remaining classes. The latter sense is due chiefly to the Italian Marxist Gramsci. According to Gramsci, the ruling class exercised hegemony by manipulating the institutions of civil society (such as the media, the schools, the churches) so that its own beliefs and values were foisted upon the rest of society.

14.10 Time

The concept of the duration between events or of any process, such as the period it takes an object to change. As such, the term 'time' in this book will mainly refer to the time as used in the plans of Change Management.

Academically, time may be measured astronomically either with reference to the stars or to the Sun. The former, called sidereal time, is conceptually simpler. Local sidereal time is defined with respect to the stars. For example, the sidereal day is essentially the time of one apparent revolution of the celestial sphere. More precisely, sidereal time is the hour angle of the vernal equinox. The precession of the equinoxes and sometimes mutation are allowed for but these effects are very small, so that sidereal time is almost entirely dependent on the Earth's rotation.

Whatever the scientific, or the philosophical conceptual understanding, the process of Change Management in IT, does require the use of time, in plans for any changes required in Configurations, Assets and Releases.

15. CONFIGURATION MANAGEMENT

15.1 Identification Of Assets

The purpose for this process is for the identification of those assets of the project that need to be made into configuration items, and to control those items throughout the lifecycle. Also, to follow the Configuration Management procedures defined for the project and to ensure the version of each configuration item that applies to the development, test and live environments is known.

Configuration Management ensures that any changes applied to any configuration item are tracked and are auditable. It allows periodic baselines to be drawn where configuration items synchronise and the whole project is in a 'known state'.

The level of formality required, to be applied to configuration management must be commensurate with the size, nature and importance of the project. The approach to configuration management will be documented in the Project Plan and must be in place before major development starts, that is, at the end of Business Study.

15.2 Change Control And Release Procedures

Configuration management has a close relationship with change control and release procedures. If a configuration management tool is used, then ensure that staff is trained in its use. Define which products from each phase are to be placed under configuration management. Involve the release management team as early as possible as they will have an interest in the Configuration Management strategy adopted for the project.

Configuration Management is particularly important throughout development when using an iterative approach. Therefore, how staff will be made aware of the configuration management tools, procedures, etc. when they join the project.

At the end of the Business Study the Prioritised Requirements List, Business Area Definition and System Architecture Definition should all be base-lined. These products will still evolve through the remainder of the project. Keep the Trace ability Matrix from the beginning. If projects are developing iteratively, consider producing a daily software build as a way of base-lining the system and identifying integration problems.

15.3 Business Critical Projects

Consult the Configuration Management Team before and during your project. Use the database under the care of the Configuration Management Team and follow the instructions in the guidelines especially concerning configuration baseline contents and the minimum baseline. Project technical documents may be stored and published.

16. VALUATION OF FIXED ASSETS

16.1 Tangible Fixed Assets

Tangible fixed assets should be valued at the lower of replacement cost and recoverable amount. Recoverable amount is defined as the higher of net realisable value and value in use. This can be expressed diagrammatically. The replacement cost for different classes of assets is described in the following paragraphs.

Impairment occurs where the recoverable amount falls below replacement cost. The replacement cost for operational land and buildings exists use value. In the case of specialised properties or properties not normally traded on the open market, valuation on this basis may be inappropriate and/or impractical and such property should be valued on the basis of depreciated replacement cost.

16.2 Operational Assets

Other (non-property) operational assets should be valued on the basis of depreciated replacement cost. The normal basis of valuation may not be appropriate if a modern substitute is markedly different in its cost, life or output, or where technological advances have resulted in likely replacements having significantly improved quality or quantity of outputs. Under such circumstances, it will be necessary to undertake an "equivalent asset" calculation to arrive at a replacement cost the asset.

Impairment occurs where the recoverable amount of an asset is lower than its replacement cost.

16.3 Not For Profit Activities

The not-for-profit nature of the vast majority of activities means that value in use is not measurable in terms of income. In these cases, value in use will be assumed to be at least equal to the cost of replacing the service potential provided by the asset, unless there has been a reduction in that service potential.

Such a reduction can arise for various reasons, including:

- The purpose for which the asset was acquired is no longer carried;
- Out and there is no alternative use for the asset;
- The asset is to be sold;
- The asset cannot be used;
- The asset is otherwise surplus and has no alternative use;
- The asset is over-specified for its current use.

The recoverable amount will be the asset's net realisable value, i.e. the amount at which the asset could be disposed of, less any disposal costs.

Consideration should also be given to the residual value of assets created during the project, at the end of the appraisal period.

16.4 Disposal Of Assets

Disposal of assets, especially high value assets and property, needs to be conducted with the same scrupulous rigour as the acquisition of those assets. For major assets, the process of disposal follows the stages where decisions about investment are made in the context of achieving an appropriate return for the release of the asset.

17. RELEASE

17.1 Prepare And Test Release

The purpose for this activity is to group all the individual products of the project (code, training docs, new business procedures etc) together into a coherent configured whole. The ultimate purpose for this is to perform the final test on the configured release.

Testing must be integrated throughout the lifecycle. This is not the first time the whole system has been system tested. As long the previous testing has been integrated properly this final test should be very quick and not find many additional bugs.

The final test must address all elements of the product. This will include code, installation procedures, and training documents, changed business procedures.

The process to be used for release will differ, depending on the type of application being delivered by the project. For example: Electronic Self Service programme have defined a process suitable for their applications.

17.2 Release Plans

The release plans should provide the ability to indicate where a particular requirement has been designed, built and tested. The Project Configuration Management Plan (sub-product of Project Plan) should document the approach the project will take to manage the project's assets.

As such the following activities should be included:

- Identify the roles to be involved in performing configuration management;
- Identify any tools that may be used to facilitate the management procedures;
- Describe the procedures that will be used to perform configuration and change management.

17.3 Documentation

Project documentation that satisfies the Change Management process must be included and identified. Definitive documents must be visible to the project and Reviewers. If it is to be a model for others it must be visible programme wide and all documentation must be under version control. All changes must be documented and there must be a register of published documents.

Project Software Repository Source code should be readable by only those who need to know and such software should be subject to an audit trail of who has, who amended etc. All software should be uniquely identifiable and versioned.

The level of formality required, to be applied to configuration management must be commensurate with the size, nature and importance of the project. The approach to configuration management will be documented in the Project Plan and must be in place before major development starts, that is, at the end of Business Study. Configuration management has a close relationship with change control and release procedures. If a configuration management tool is used then ensure that staff is trained in its use.

17.4 Definition Of Products

Define which products from each phase are to be placed in configuration management. Involve the release management team as early as possible as they will have an interest in the Configuration Management strategy adopted for the project.

17.5 Procurement

'Procurement' means the whole process of acquisition from third parties (including the logistical aspects) and covers goods, services and construction projects. This process spans the whole life cycle from initial concept and definition of business needs through to the end of the useful life of an asset or end of a services contract. Both conventionally funded and more innovative types of funded projects are included. The process is not limited to the purchasing function in organisations and is inherently multi-functional especially in large, complex procurements.

17.6 Reviews

Any Process will define review points throughout the lifecycle of acquisition projects. Reviews are undertaken for procurement projects of all levels of change. Requests for Reviews are initiated by Senior Responsible Owners.

Additional interim Reviews may sometimes be carried out during the life of a procurement project. For a big project that has a long time span between Reviews, an additional Review may be arranged before a significant decision point e.g. the announcement of a preferred supplier). Additional reviews may also be beneficial where added assurance is needed or where there are specific areas of concern. These reviews are often referred to as Peer Reviews.

A Review is held before key decision points in the lifecycle of a procurement project. The review teams are made up of independent experienced practitioners who bring their prior knowledge and skills to bear to identify the key issues that need to be addressed for the project to succeed. The review criteria are established and published in a set of workbooks available on an intranet and website. The work of a Review team is for the project, and ownership of the review report and recommendations lies with this team.

A Review is carried out over a period of 4-5 days at the most with the review report presented and discussed with the team before the review team leaves the client premises.

17.7 Audit

Internal Audit primarily provides an independent and objective opinion to the Accounting Officer on change management, control and governance, by measuring and evaluating their effectiveness in achieving an organisation's agreed objectives. In most organisational bodies Internal Audit reports go directly to the Accounting Officer (Chief Executive). In order for Internal Audit to provide the Accounting Officer with an objective opinion, the Chief Executive and the Audit Committee develop an audit strategy in consultation with, and subject to approval.

The audit plan is circulated to senior members of the organisation and advance notice will be given prior to the commencement of a review. Under normal circumstances

Terms of Reference will be produced for each audit assignment and these will be discussed and agreed with management. The views and opinions of management will be obtained at the end of each review and the final report will contain an agreed action plan, which will contain the name of the of the officer responsible for each recommendation and a target date for full implementation.

17.8 Dual Key Review Process

In short, to secure the release of dual key monies, it has to be demonstrated that:

1. The programme is aligned with the strategy,
2. They are implementing the recommendations in the report for the projects within each programme,
3. They have plans in place to realise the benefits of the investment.

Much of the evidence needed to meet these criteria is capable of being derived from two complementary processes:

1. The development of business strategies,
2. The various Reviews.

The Change Management process is designed as an aid to companies rather than as an external audit of projects.

17.9 The Difference Between A Programme And A Project

A project is a particular way of managing activities to deliver specific products over a specified period of time and within defined cost and resource constraints. A programme is a management framework for co-ordinating related projects and work-streams to deliver strategic outcomes and benefits over timescales that are often less well defined.

A strategic assessment is designed to apply at the start of an acquisition programme and may be repeated at subsequent key decision points. A Review can confirm that the appropriate project structure is in place and that interdependencies have been recognised.

Reviews apply to each of the procurement projects within the programme. A repeat Review later in the life of a programme can be helpful to re-visit and confirm the business case, the management of the programme changes and interactions between the projects and the delivery of benefits for the programme as a whole.

Financial value is only one of the factors to consider when deciding on the level of change faced by a programme or project. This is recognised within the Change Assessment. The fact that a programme or project environment has been deemed appropriate indicates that there is uniqueness to the programme or project, which, in turn, indicates a level of inherent change. For example, the programme or project could be of low cost but, if unsuccessful, could have a major impact upon staff morale within an organisation. Reviews are scaleable. Acquisition programmes and procurement projects should, therefore, receive a level of Review appropriate to the level of change associated.

Organisations should use Change Management and Assessment to determine the change level of their programmes and projects and to understand the nature of the changes associated with them in a structured and systematic way. Programmes or projects classified as needing small change are likely to contain significant procurements.

In certain cases, a Process was originally set up to help procurement projects that involve external (actual) expenditure. However, even on projects being "developed in house", there would normally be additional expenditure on hardware, software, licensing, increased network capacity, consultancy support. The change analysis would, of course, indicate whether to involve further reviews, or whether it is small change and carried out by in house staff (and of course it is arguable that "in house developments/solutions" are smaller changes given that the client has to retain financial, technical and managerial changes compared to outsourced deals).

To summarise, technically non-procurement activities are out of the scope, but this takes a very narrow view of the benefits that can arise from a review (assurance that the project likely to be successful or, if not, remedial actions proposed).

Pilot procurement projects have the same characteristics as other procurement projects. The fact that a pilot is being managed within a project structure itself indicates that there is a unique environment, which, in turn, indicates a level of inherent risk. An assessment review should be completed in the usual way to determine the risk associated with the project.

Projects utilising existing contractual arrangements will still benefit from the added value provided by the process of reviewing and assessing, in that the majority of the issues addressed will still apply. In these cases Reviews may be scaled down where the procurement strategy is largely predetermined and standard procedures exist for the take on of new work packages.

As usual reviews start up operability and the results achieved and lessons learnt. There is evidence that anything less than a well disciplined use of framework contracts with sound management processes akin to any project leads these contracts to becoming a leaky sieve for companies and a source of high margins to suppliers. With the growth of framework arrangements it is mandatory for such call offs in central civil government and international organisations to be exposed to the appropriate level of Reviews.

A successful company would provide sufficient staff to the pool to cover the resourcing of procurement reviews. Staff will need to be trained and accredited as reviewers. You need to assign a coordinator to administer the reviews, the process roll out of changes within projects, the staff provision and the communications and training programme in house. Changes are undertaken by the Review Team Leader and nominated members.

> The Project Manager should arrange an initial assessment meeting. The purpose of the assessment meeting is to agree the change level of the project (low, medium or high), to enable those responsible for the individual changes to gain an understanding of the programme/project and to establish readiness for solutions to the problems.
>
> Notice is required following the assessment meeting in order to assemble a review team and hold the necessary prior Planning Meeting. The revised assessment may indicate a change to the change level associated with the

programme or project and therefore a change to subsequent handling within the process. In that eventuality the team will discuss the way forward.

The Review Planning Meeting has, following senior staff support, been established as essential to the delivery of reviews of changes I the various projects. It is designed as a facilitated workshop at which the Senior Responsible Owner, review team and project team jointly plan their approach to the review. The planning meeting is envisaged as a mandatory part of all new reviews of changes.

The value of these planning meetings is such that only (as an example) the Programmes Director/Manager for the project/s has the authority to modify this policy. The Programmes Director/Manager may recommend earliest and continued intervention to increase the likelihood of success. The team/s involved will then agree an overall traffic light assessment for inclusion in the report at the end of each review.

17.10 'Traffic Lights'

The definitions of the traffic lights are:

Red – To achieve success the programme or project should take remedial action immediately. It means 'fix the changes/key problems fast', not 'stop the project'.

Amber – The programme or project should go forward with actions on recommendations to be carried out before the next review.

Green – the programme or project is on target to succeed but may benefit from the uptake of the recommendations.

Reports and reviews should be conducted on a confidential basis. This approach promotes an open and honest exchange between the programme/project and review teams delivering maximum added value. Responsibility for the quality of the workshop and ownership of the materials used will remain with Programmes Director/Manager.

An interim review can be conducted between two major reviews, where there are interim decision points e.g. one at preferred bidder stage and the other at best and final offers. For property/construction projects, the interim reviews could be at outline design and detailed design.

18. BENEFITS MANAGEMENT

18.1 Definition Of Benefits Management

Benefits Management is concerned with the definition or articulation, at a broad level, of the size of the anticipated benefits and the main beneficiary stakeholder group(s), together with an indication of the timescales over which the benefits will be realised. This includes identification and/or setting up of key measures. Key measures and key milestones established here will need to be clarified and detailed at subsequent Programme level.

There is also the overall scope of the business change proposed, the implications for benefits management processes and performance measurement for governance of the changes, together with any benefit assumptions. Initiatives may need to demonstrate improvements in the organisation's Key Measures as part of the business case approval process.

18.2 Identification Of Benefits

Benefits management is the identification of potential benefits, their planning, modelling and tracking, the assignment of responsibilities and authorities and their actual realisation as a result of investing in business change. It is usually carried out as a key part of programme management; otherwise it needs to operate in the context of a management methodology, such as project management.

Benefits management complements and overlaps investment appraisal in the business case. While investment appraisal provides the justification for the investment, benefits management allows organisations to plan for and achieve the benefits. Costs and benefits cannot be viewed in isolation and you should plan the benefits management process and the overall investment appraisal together.

18.3 Benefits And Performance Management

Benefits management also interfaces with performance management, a means of measurement and management that monitors and reports achievement of outcomes.

A benefits management approach:

- Identifies expected benefits,
- Identifies contributions to business objectives and stakeholders,
- Establishes a benefits management structure defining functions, relationships, communications, roles and responsibilities,
- Develops models of benefits, including intermediate and final outcomes,
- Defines the benefits, including their attributes and measures, owners and changes,
- Assesses value and organisational impact, dependencies and changes,
- Shows how the benefits are interrelated,
- Develops a benefits realisation plan, including a schedule for delivery, assessment or review points, alignment/linkage/inter-dependencies with other modules, projects or programmes, and business change processes for implementation and delivery,

- Establishes accountability for realisation and a means of tracking benefit realisation, including any performance management requirements.

18.4 Benefits And Risks

Many business change projects fail to deliver the benefits on which the investment was originally justified. An estimated 30 - 40 % of systems to support business change deliver no benefits whatsoever. The ongoing costs and risks will usually be monitored - but the anticipated benefits are not so easy to define and quantify.

Benefits management ensures that business change achieves the expected results by translating business objectives into identifiable measurable benefits that can be systematically tracked.

Without benefits management the risks are:

- Failure of business areas to commit to the benefits or their delivery,
- Any required changes in business and working methods lack focus,
- Unrealistic benefits claimed in terms of scope and value,
- Failure to identify wider contribution,
- Benefits are difficult to realise, with uncertainty of delivery,
- Achievements not tracked or recorded,
- Lack of positive activity for benefits realisation or harvesting, giving failure to deliver business benefits sought from investment,
- No clear linkage between business case, outcomes and measurement processes.

18.5 Achieving Benefits

While programme and project teams will be involved in projects deliver business change, the responsibility for managing and realising benefits rests ultimately with business users and managers.

The Senior Responsible Owner (SRO/Project Owner) is responsible for ensuring the management of the process and realisation of benefits. A business change manager who is responsible for enabling the organisation to realise the benefits delivered from the product, service or change may support the SRO/PO. Individual managers of business areas will be responsible for actual benefits delivery.

18.6 Key Factors For Success

Benefits management needs to be part of, and not separate from, programme, project and business management activities.

To achieve this, there needs to be:

- Clear definition and acceptance of accountability of those involved, including users, managers and the wider organisation, in terms of governance, roles and responsibilities
- A benefits management structure and organisation

- An effective process or methodology and techniques for benefits planning, management and harvesting
- Relevant practical measures, a performance measurement and management system to track benefits and act on the results
- Effective use of change management
- Staff training in benefits identification, analysis and techniques.
- In addition, you need to be able to identify the totality of potential benefits
- Recognise the components of the benefits (business, technology, organisation, people and processes),
- Identify measurable benefits from the investment,
- Assess their relevance and priority to the organisation,
- Focus on the people aspects that will achieve the benefits,
- Recognise if the benefits are being achieved, by benchmarking current performance,
- Identify the risks in achieving them,
- Identify the risks in not achieving them.

Considerations when addressing these factors are: the 'people' aspects are a high priority. You must ensure that enough time is allowed to prepare staff for new ways of working, and that everyone affected by the change is included collecting information to support the management of benefits costs money and consumes resource.

18.7 Value Of Benefits

The value of managing benefits will need to be agreed and demonstrated over time communicate the reasons for doing it, especially where benefits and costs cross organisational boundaries. Responsibilities must be clear and agreed the simple way to assess benefits is to compare actual and planned results measurement information is used to determine what actions need to be taken, if any.

Any shortfall or over-achievement must be evaluated and action taken to continue to harvest maximum benefits from the investment commit to delivery of measurable benefits within realistic timescales, costs and risks.

18.8 The Role Of Benefits Management

Successful benefits management is not an overhead or separate activity conducted at "arm's length" from programme or project management. For it to be effective, it needs to be part of good management practice throughout the business change lifecycle - from strategic business planning through to eventual disposal of the service or asset.

As part of this cycle, benefits management performs an important function in capturing lessons over a longer time-span from a series of comparisons between what was anticipated (in terms of benefits) and what actually happened after project deliverables were brought into operational use. The lessons learned in the application of benefits management are also fed back as modifications to the benefits management process itself.

Set out below is a high-level representation of the relationship between key management processes and the business lifecycle for programmes and projects of business change.

18.9 Scope Of Benefits Management

The scope of the process for managing the benefits from business change will vary according to the type and size of the programme or project under consideration and the organisation in which it is being implemented. There is however a set of fundamental principles that will apply to all investments involving business change.

There must be full investment in business change. There may be many different types of benefit accruing to an organisation the scope of the benefits management exercise must be clear at the outset achieving the planned benefits depends on the people who will be working in new ways as a result of the business change.

Benefits arise from a full investment in business change, not just investment in a new building, an information system and the associated training. There are no construction or IT projects in isolation; they are always part of business change. This change needs to be managed carefully and requires change management skills and resource.

18.10 Management Commitments And Support

It is primarily the responsibility of business (user) management and requires commitment and support from management with the authority to resource it. Many different types of benefit may accrue to an organisation, enabled by the introduction of new ways of working. The importance attached to individual types of benefit will depend on what the organisation is trying to achieve.

Benefits fall into three categories:

- Those which can be quantified and valued (direct financial benefits),
- Those which can be quantified, but are difficult or impossible to value (direct non-financial benefits),
- Those that can be identified but cannot easily be quantified (indirect benefits).

Financial and direct non-financial benefits are relatively easy to identify and quantify. Direct financial benefits can be compared with each other in cost terms or to other ways of spending the money.

19. MANAGING CHANGES TO REQUIREMENTS

19.1 Managing The Requirements Changes

This briefing looks at an issue that is fundamental to the success of any commercial relationship that is to succeed over time, the ability to accommodate change successfully. Managing the change at the end of the requirements contract is perhaps the biggest challenge of all.

Changes to requirements can be small adjustments to existing service specifications, planned modular/incremental developments, major business change leading to completely new services - or anything in between. In the context of this briefing, changes are significant enough to require management involvement.

The need to negotiate change is a continuing and ongoing component of service contracts. The ability to accommodate change successfully is fundamental to the success of any commercial arrangement that is to succeed over time; partnerships are increasingly seen as a way of coping with uncertainty, as their purpose is to accommodate change effectively and efficiently. The need to negotiate change is a continuing and on-going component of partnerships. It may be an important issue too in more conventional contractual arrangements.

19.2 Partnership Arrangement

This briefing assumes a partnership arrangement, but the principles apply generally. Maintenance of existing systems involves ongoing changes to requirements. It is a major cost that requires careful attention.

Business managers and service providers are responsible for identifying the need for change in response to user demand or changes in the business. Service providers manage the implementation and provision of new or updated services. There may be an informed customer role providing the interface between the customer and provider. In addition, there may be programme/project teams who are involved in modular or incremental change.

19.3 Requirements For Change

The requirements/drivers for change during the term of the requirements contract can derive from a range of internal or external sources.

Internal change could include:

- Evolving business requirements,
- Changes in the customer's roles/responsibilities,
- Statutory developments,
- Boundary of responsibility changes,
- Rationalisation of roles,
- New developments,
- Provider restructuring, merger or acquisition,
- Revised management, reporting and/or approvals chains,
- Significant revisions to the corporate strategy/business,

- External sources of change, such as developments in technology,
- Economic trends which affect the profitability/value for money,
- The need to provide electronic forms of service delivery,
- Meet customer expectation.

19.4 Change Control Procedure

A single change control procedure should apply to all changes, although there may be certain delegated or shortened procedures available in defined circumstances – such as delegated budget tolerance levels within which a manager would not have to seek senior management approval. However, flexibility needs to be built into this procedure to deal with issues such as emergencies.

A change control procedure should provide a clear set of steps and clearly allocated responsibilities covering:

- Requesting changes,
- Assessment of impact,
- Prioritisation and authorisation,
- Agreement with provider,
- Control of implementation,
- Documentation of change assessments and orders.

19.5 Authorisation

Responsibility for authorising different types of change will often rest with different people, and documented internal procedures will need to reflect this. In particular, changes to the overall contract, such as changes to prices outside the scope of agreed price variation mechanisms must have senior management approval.

In many cases it will be possible to delegate limited powers to authorise minor changes, which affect particular services or Service Level Agreements using agreed processes.

Change during the term of a contract can be categorised as follows:

- Planned/routine change,
- Proactive change programmes,
- Unplanned change.

19.6 Planned Change

This could include modular and incremental developments, such as planning for changes to user requirements, refurbishment of workspace, maintenance/enhancements to existing systems or planned technology refreshment. This type of change is most easily accommodated under, and is best suited to, formal change management processes.

Well-constructed contractual agreements should express provisions detailing the procedures to be adopted in initiating, discussing and delivering change through:

- User groups,
- Change control boards,
- Formal approvals processes,
- Benefits management regimes.

The procedures to be adopted for the escalation and resolution of disputes that may arise, such as:

- Defined escalation routes and timescales,
- Alternative dispute resolution procedures (neutral advisors, expert determination, arbitration),

The procedure for making amendments to the contract documentation:

- QA procedures (including legal QA),
- Authorisations (individual authorised signing powers)
- Audit trail.

19.7 Proactive Change Programmes

Change need not necessarily always be reactive in nature. It can be initiated deliberately as a proactive approach. There could, for example, be an element of business transformation to drive forward a change programme. In this way the contract is used as a vehicle to deliver efficiency improvements and associated cost savings from the re-engineering of the customer's internal business processes, facilitated by the use of technology.

The details of approaches taken in each project to date have been different, but a typical partnership arrangement might be (in summary):

- Step 1: provider proposes business change project to customer,
- Step 2: customer approves project on basis of agreed cost/benefit model,
- Step 3: provider develops and implements new service to support new business process (at provider's risk),
- Step 4: implement and adopt new business processes,
- Step 5: both parties measure resultant cost savings to customer using agreed cost/benefit model,
- Step 6: provider's service charges calculated as a percentage of realised cost savings to customer.

Recent contracts show an emerging trend. Over the life of partnership as a whole, the expectation of the parties, sometimes underwritten by contractual guarantees from the provider, is that the aggregate cost savings to the customer over the term of the partnership may in fact exceed the aggregate 'core' service payable by the customer. The viability/appropriateness of approach outlined above of course depends on the nature of the partnership, the customer organisation (in terms of its receptiveness to change, potential for improvement in existing business processes etc), and the services to be delivered.

19.8 Unplanned Change

Unplanned change is imposed on the partnership from outside (for example, resulting from a change in some aspect of the external environment). This is the most difficult type of change to manage and accommodate. It is also potentially the most damaging to the partnership. It can hit the partnership unannounced and require immediate action by both parties. At worst it can serve to invalidate the deal for one or both parties, resulting in unplanned conclusion of the programme or even the partnership.

Unplanned change will test the strength of the partnership relationship, and the capabilities of its management. The response to un-planned change is crucial and must be structured. In response to unplanned change, the partnership (that is both parties in co-operation), must undertake the following analysis:

- Step 1: understand and assess the impact of the change on partnership. Can this be dealt with under the existing change management procedures or does this require specialised management?
- Step 2: escalate within both partner organisations as appropriate,
- Step 3: review the basis of the deal – does the original deal remain viable for both parties?
- Step 4: assess the extent of change required to the deal,
- Step 5: negotiate the required amendments.

From the customer's perspective as the public sector partner a key decision point is often reached at Step 4 above. It may be necessary for both partners to make real, and sometimes significant, concessions in the resulting negotiations in order to make the deal work for the future. A complete audit trail of developments is essential to ensure public accountability, but you must be prepared to make bold judgments where necessary to ensure the survival of the partnership (subject to the overall deal remaining viable to the public sector partner). Your decision-making must be driven by clear business objectives of the organisation.

20. SECURITIES AND PRIVACY OF INFORMATION

20.1 Investment Protection

It is good management practice to protect your investment from others. The most important asset of an organisation is the people, closely followed by information. Ensuring these assets are protected is a major responsibility for any organisation.

Security and privacy are related in that:

- Security is the state of being secure (certain to remain safe).
- This can be interpreted as an adequate level of protection of the organisation against espionage, theft or other danger.
- Privacy is concerned with ensuring information is only available to those who should have access to it.

Assets need to be suitably protected to ensure business continuity, minimise business damage and maximise Return on Investment and business opportunities. Today everyone is more dependent on technology in the management of their information and so the range of security issues that need to be considered is broadened. Apart from the commercial reasons for protecting information, businesses have legal obligations to take care of personnel and information entrusted to them.

Information and its supporting processes, systems and networks are important business assets. Confidentiality, integrity and availability of information are essential features of organisation's interaction with the citizen and business. Information should be stored in a way that makes it readily accessible to those inside and outside the organisation that have the right to access it.

20.2 Vulnerability

Increasing dependence on information systems and services means that organisations are more vulnerable to security threats, especially where public and private networks are interconnected. The key issue is that the nature of security requirements changes when end-customers are connected over whom you have no control. There are also issues relating to rapid take up of e-commerce and the Internet, especially the increasing number of external users over whom your organisation has no control.

Your security policy must evolve to take account of:

- Internal users and infrastructure entirely under your control,
- Controlled formal relationships with third parties,
- Completely unknown end-users and infrastructure, where you want to offer choice and a range of channels through which they interact with you.

If the public is to use company services that are delivered electronically, there must be genuinely secure communication between the citizen and the vendor, even though use is made of public channels. Some organisations have developed a security framework, which sets out a staged approach so that security levels reflect the real risks associated with a service. The issues for providing a suitable mechanism for a service include not only the need for a secure channel but also transparency for the user and authentication that parties at both ends of the communication channel are who they claim to be.

20.3 Privacy And Data Sharing

An organisation should address concerns about privacy and to provide a proper and lawful basis for data sharing where this is desirable, but there is public wariness about the sharing of personal data across government. Top management support is essential for information security since it involves investments in both infrastructure and organisation.

Everyone within an organisation has a responsibility for security in some form. People need to understand that responsibility, level of accountability and the procedures that apply to them.

Notwithstanding, certain people may be specifically tasked with various aspects of security and privacy these would include business managers and service providers who need to work closely together to agree appropriate measures for security and privacy, consistent with the guidelines in the e-government frameworks. Senior management must be involved in setting policy for security and privacy.

20.4 Legislation

There is an increasing amount of legislation, which is relevant to security, including:

- Data Protection Act (DPA) 1984 and 1998,
- The Copyrights, Designs and Patents act 1988 (amended by DPA),
- Computer Misuse Act 1990,
- Public Records Act 1958 and 1967,
- Human Rights Act,
- Electronic Communications Act,
- Freedom of Information Act,
- Official Secrets Act.

Health and safety legislation relates to all aspects of people within a working environment. This is a specialist area and requires adequate training as well as fully assigned responsibility for ensuring adequate controls are in place. In the area of health, safety and welfare there are various regulations and sets of legislation.

These include:

- Workplace (Health and Safety and Welfare) Regulations 1992,
- Buildings related regulations (for example, Electricity at work),
- Regulations (1989) covering, among other things, ergonomics, lighting, noise levels and air quality),
- Fire Precautions (1997),
- Control of Hazardous Substances (1998),
- Working Time Regulations (1998 based on EU Working Time Directive),

- EU Part-time working Directive (2000).

The Health and Safety Executive produce much guidance in this area including specific guidance on the prevention of work related illness.

20.5 Security Policy Processes

The organisation needs to adopt a structured approach to ensure that an appropriate security policy is devised and adopted for the organization. The approach to changes should follow the same overall process as for the adoption of risk management:

- Set the overall policy for managing security,
- Identify the changes,
- Evaluate the changes,
- Identify possible responses/countermeasures,
- Implement responses,
- Monitor effectiveness of responses,
- Review effectiveness of security measures.

Some processes still need to be undertaken but as many of these issues will be organization-wide these are likely to be included within the security policy statement. Aspects here are identifying probable risk owners and setting the acceptable level of change.

20.6 Securing Assets

The main areas that need to be considered for security purposes are:

- Personnel,
- Physical,
- Document,
- IT,
- Information.

There are overlaps between some of these categories – in particular, technical and document security. These overlaps may sometimes be difficult to clarify. Key areas to consider are outlined below.

20.6.1 Personnel Security

Organisations will wish to make arrangements to check staff and consultants that are to work for them. There may be different levels of clearance required for security purposes. The levels and circumstances to which they apply should be clearly documented. The required security check should be undertaken as part of the recruitment process. In many cases this will simply involve taking up a number of references. These references may relate to personal or business associations. Additionally, when a persons role within the organisation changes this may also require a change of clearance level.

20.6.2 Physical Security

Access to buildings; this should cover ensuring access at a business location; it should take account of the impact of fire, flood, terrorism, risks to transport infrastructure. It should also ensure that only authorised people gain access to the building or parts of the building. Arrangements should cover staff, consultants or other visitors.

Access to information; only those people with appropriate authority are allowed access to the organisation's information. An important consideration is the Data Protection Act, which requires suitable controls for the handling of personal information.

Availability of resources; people or equipment must be available at the right time and place to fulfil the business requirement. It should take account of the facilities people need and whether the building is adequately heated, supplied with water, sewerage systems and so on.

20.6.3 Document Security

The Data Protection Act requires that:

'Appropriate security measures shall be taken against unauthorised access to, or alteration, disclosure or destruction of, personal data and against accidental loss or destruction of personal data.'

Documentation needs to be maintained to ensure confidentiality, availability and integrity.

20.6.4 Technical Security

This aspect needs to consider the security requirements of technology related assets, in particular IT networks, systems and equipment. This has to be balanced with enabling staff to make appropriate use of equipment so they can perform their designated business function.

Topics that require specific consideration for IT equipment include:

- Use of internal networks,
- Internet access,
- E-mail,
- Viruses,
- Hacking,
- Remote working,
- Backing up information (particularly from laptops).

20.7 Security Incidents

A security incident is any deliberate or accidental event which leads to an actual or possible:

- Breach of confidentiality – when information is disclosed to people who have no permission to have it,
- Breach of integrity – when access to information is changed without permission,

- Breach of availability – anything that restricts or hinders the ongoing business functionality.

There must be policies and proven procedures in place to deal with security incidents as they arise.

20.8 Good Practice In Security

Adopting good practice in information security management and the critical success factors for adopting information security management include:

- Establishing a clear security policy, objectives and activities, that reflect business objectives,
- Ensuring the policy is owned and supported by senior management,
- Building a good understanding of security risks (the threats, probability and impacts), ensuring this is based on the value and importance of the assets,
- Effective marketing of the security policy and associated issues to all managers and employees,
- Distribution of comprehensive guidance on the security policy and standards to all employees and contractors.
- Supported by appropriate training, this should ensure everyone understands their responsibilities and actively follows the guidance.

The British Standard, BS 7799, has been widely adopted as a business-led approach to best practice on information security management.

21. A CASE STUDY IN CHANGE MANAGEMENT

21.1 Purpose Of Case Study

The purpose of this book is to illustrate the findings of Change management teams within various business accounts.

The aim of the book is to build a foundation of facts about Change Management Processes and Systems within Information Technology Programmes Management, which can be used to develop a consolidated process, to be deployed in international organisations and government departments.

21.2 Principles Of Report

The purpose of Change Management is to ensure that potential changes are reviewed in terms of their efficacy to meet the Information Technology business requirements and that the impact on service quality is managed.

The recommended Change Management processes are best implemented concurrently with Configuration Management, Release and Asset Management. In preparing this book and in recommending approaches to improve Change Management practices in the business environment, the following principles were considered:

- The facilitation and the introduction of all types of change via simple, clear, and effective procedures and tools across the various organisational needs;
- Assessment of changes on the basis of sound business and technological advice;
- The provision of a framework within which those initiating changes will retain accountability and ownership for the change;
- Support for Programme/Project Management and their co-ordination with staff,
- The prevention of changes which represent an unacceptable risk to the reliable delivery of services;
- Prevention against the introduction of unauthorised changes.

21.3 Scope And Assumptions

The scope of Change Management is assumed to be such that all changes, including business, hardware and software products; changes in new versions of the provision of IT services, and the inclusion of new items into the live environments, will be subject to change control procedures.

These controls would include:

- Business Change,
- Hardware,
- Communications equipment,
- System software,
- Live applications software,

- Together with all documentation and procedures associated with the running and the support needed.

To this effect, this book is based on actual business studies, which include investigations with people, involved in the current processes and took into consideration the various points highlighted below:

- Change Management processes established in a business organisation;
- Procedures for raising and issuing requests for change;
- Standards, or other quality criteria for the raising and registering of changes;
- Mechanisms for maintaining formal change records;
- Assessment of the business and technical impacts of changes;
- Procedures for approving, verifying and scheduling of changes;
- Change Management reports produced;
- Suitable training for personnel responsible for Change Management activities,
- Regular meetings with interested parties, in which Change Management matters are discussed;
- Checks with the relevant teams to ascertain whether activities performed by Change Management adequately support their business needs.

21.4 Summary Of Analysis

The table, below, shows the highlight issues found throughout the investigations. Each issue has a resolution suggested, which is outlined in more detail at the 'Next Step For Recommended Option' section.

ID	Title	Priority	Detail	Suggested Resolution
1	Governance	High	Although senior people, decisions at later stages, govern the early stages of the change process, Procurement of Work and changes to contract, austerely such as release to live environment are not monitored closely.	Encourage change boards (e.g.: Release Board, etc.) to take ownership of decisions at these later stages.
2	Importance categorisation of changes	High	With the current volumes of change, it is very difficult to spot the change that is of high importance.	A rigorous and precise set of importance categories is required as standard for all changes.
3	Impact Assessment	Medium	It is sometimes difficult to find everyone that may be affected by a change, especially in an account as large as those in international organisations.	Introduction of Change Co-ordinators (perhaps within each programme). These co-ordinators will be responsible for managing the list of impact assessors for the projects involved.
4	Prioritisation of changes	Medium	With the number of changes in their thousands, the priority of each one can be distorted, by the "Who shouts loudest" factor.	A rigorous and precise set of priority categories is required as standard for all changes.
5	Culture	Medium	Individually, all the people/teams work hard to provide an integrated and efficient set of Change Processes. As an organisation the culture, possibly from legacy systems days, is to work in silos, instead of working in partnership with	Encourage through a business account team cross communication and better ways of working with the customers.

			projects.	
6	Leveraged organisation	Medium	As an organisation, which has technical resources dispersed at solution centres, the union of technical project teams is often non- existent. As such, it is difficult to have a technical overview across the account.	Develop Virtual Teams to integrate across internal organisational boundaries, where and whenever necessary.
7	The manual and other paperwork processes take too long	Low	Currently, after the change has been assessed and approved by those in authority, it takes prolonged period to implement.	Further investigation is required to understand why the process takes this amount of time. It is possible that some of the activities could be moved further up the process.

21.5 Overview Of Recommendation

In this case study, the recommendation is to initiate a project to develop Virtual Change Management Communities (VCMC). With an implementation team of 6, this can be set up and operational in a very short period. This involves nominating and training Process Leaders, defining the Change Management Landscape for the business estate and building a Management Information System for the Virtual Change Management Communities.

The primary objective is to facilitate and encourage all Change Management teams on the business estate to join the VCMC. Hence a significant amount of effort will be spent on communication and auditing of change management processes.

The secondary objective is to improve visibility of changes across the organisation. In order to accomplish this part of the team will build a Management Information System, which will provide an overview of all changes (including other suppliers).

Details of such a recommendation is outlined later on in this chapter.

21.6 Review Of Current Change Management (CM) Processes

Each of the Processes is described below. Each team as depicted below, uses the standard five-stage process. The five stages consist of: Initiating a change, assessing the change, obtaining authorisation for the change, Implementing change and Post-change processing (such as invoicing and benefit realisation). In almost all cases, a fast-track process will exist for changes that need to be implemented quickly, in an emergency.

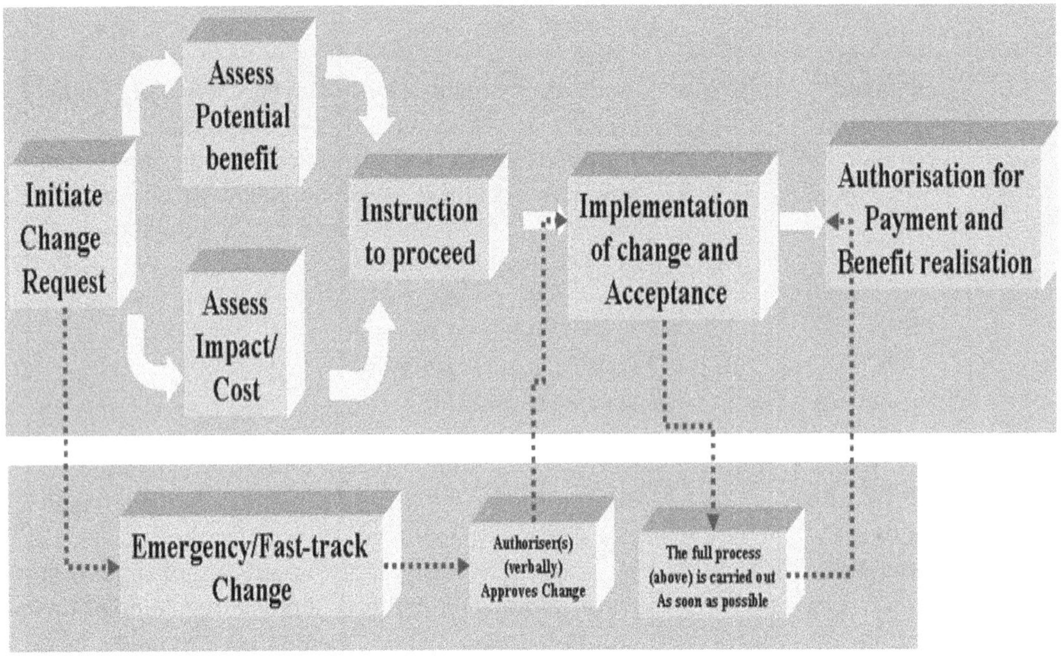

21.7 Change At A Client Site

At a very high level the following process is carried out for a new change:

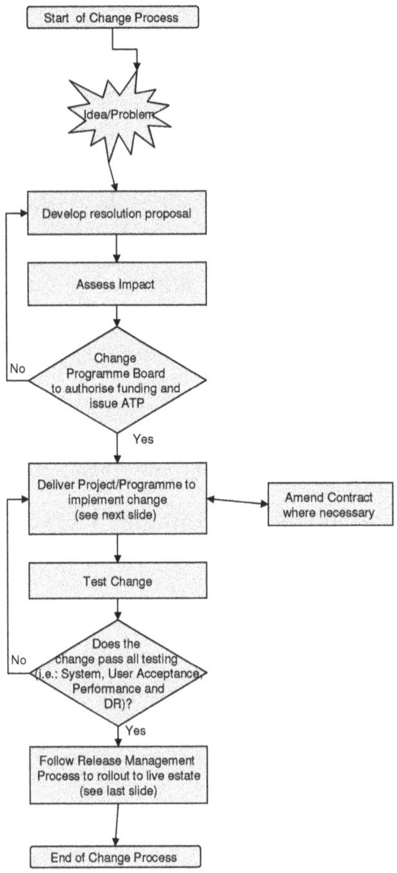

As the diagram, above shows, the initial step after and idea/problem is identified is to work with the client to cultivate the idea into a proposed solution/resolution. This proposal is then distributed to all relevant parties for impact assessment. The impact assessment, which would include estimates of cost and benefit, is put to a Change Programme Board. The Board would usually have an annual budget to distribute to projects/programmes and will have overall visibility of changes within its scope. If the CPB does not approve the change, the proposal is usually amended and re-impact assessed. Once the CPB has approved funding and the issue of an "Authorisation to Proceed" (ATP), then a project/programme is initiated.

The next diagram shows how changes are managed within the scope of a project. In certain cases, a contractual change is also required to support the change overall. After the change has been implemented, it must be tested and released to the live environment. The third slide explains the release management process.

21.8 Changes In Scope Within The Programme

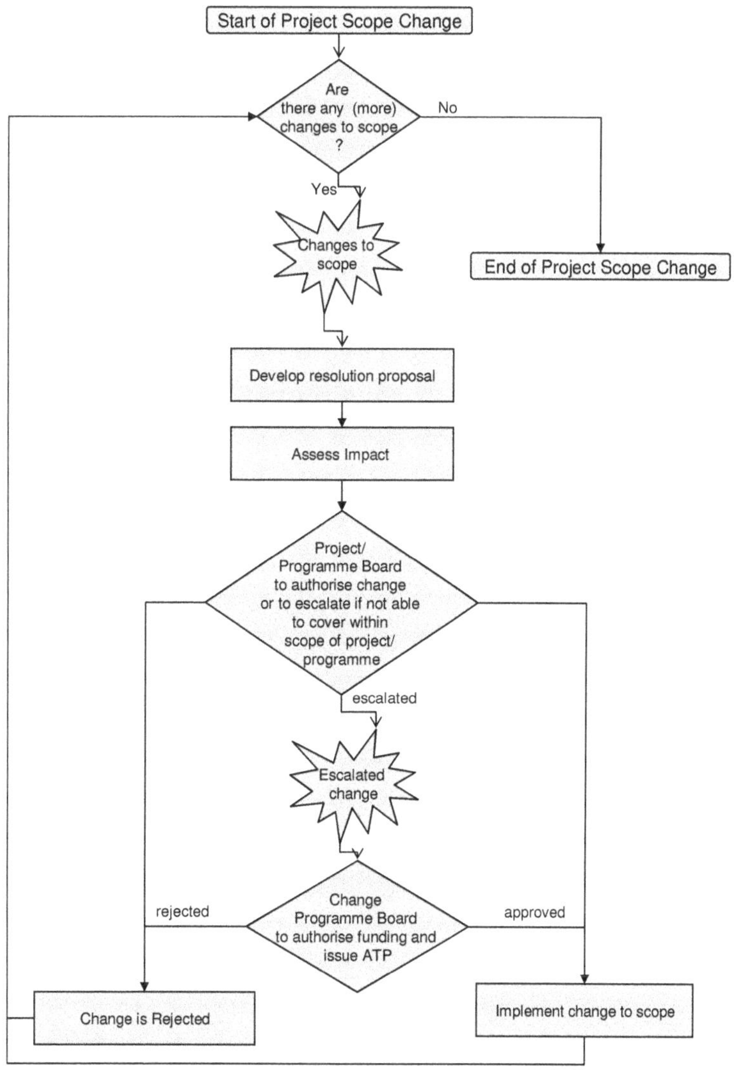

Once the Project has started, a project change management team manages all changes. If there are any changes, a proposed solution is constructed and sent to all relevant teams (internal and often external to the project) for impact assessment. If the change has limited impact and can be funded from existing authorised funds, the Project/Programme board or director can authorise the change. It is up to the Project/Programme board to decide that the change needs to be escalated, either as funding is required or because of the impact it may have on other projects/programmes.

If the change is approved, it would be implemented and if the change is rejected, the change notification/details will reflect the reason it is rejected. This cycle of changes to Project/Programme scope is continued for each change that is required, until the implementation is complete.

21.9 Release Management

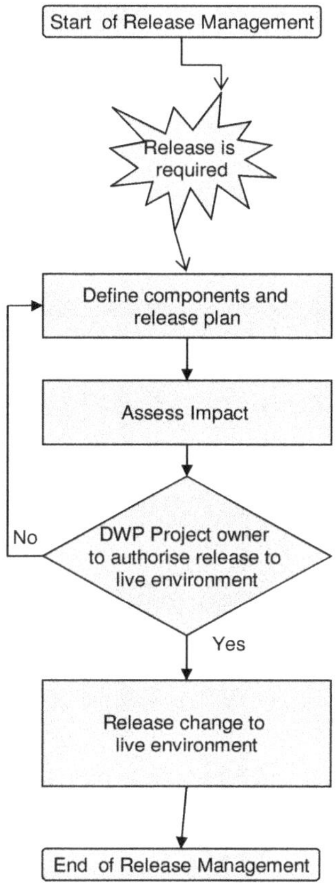

Once the implemented change has been tested, it must be released to the live estate. In order to ensure that the scope of the release is clearly identified, the project team will create a release plan or at least a definition of release items. This is then issued to all relevant parties for impact assessment. Once all assessment has been collated, the ultimate decision resides with the client change leader. Once this authorisation is given, the change is rolled out to the live estate.

21.10 Configuration, Release, Assets, Change (CRAC) Diagram

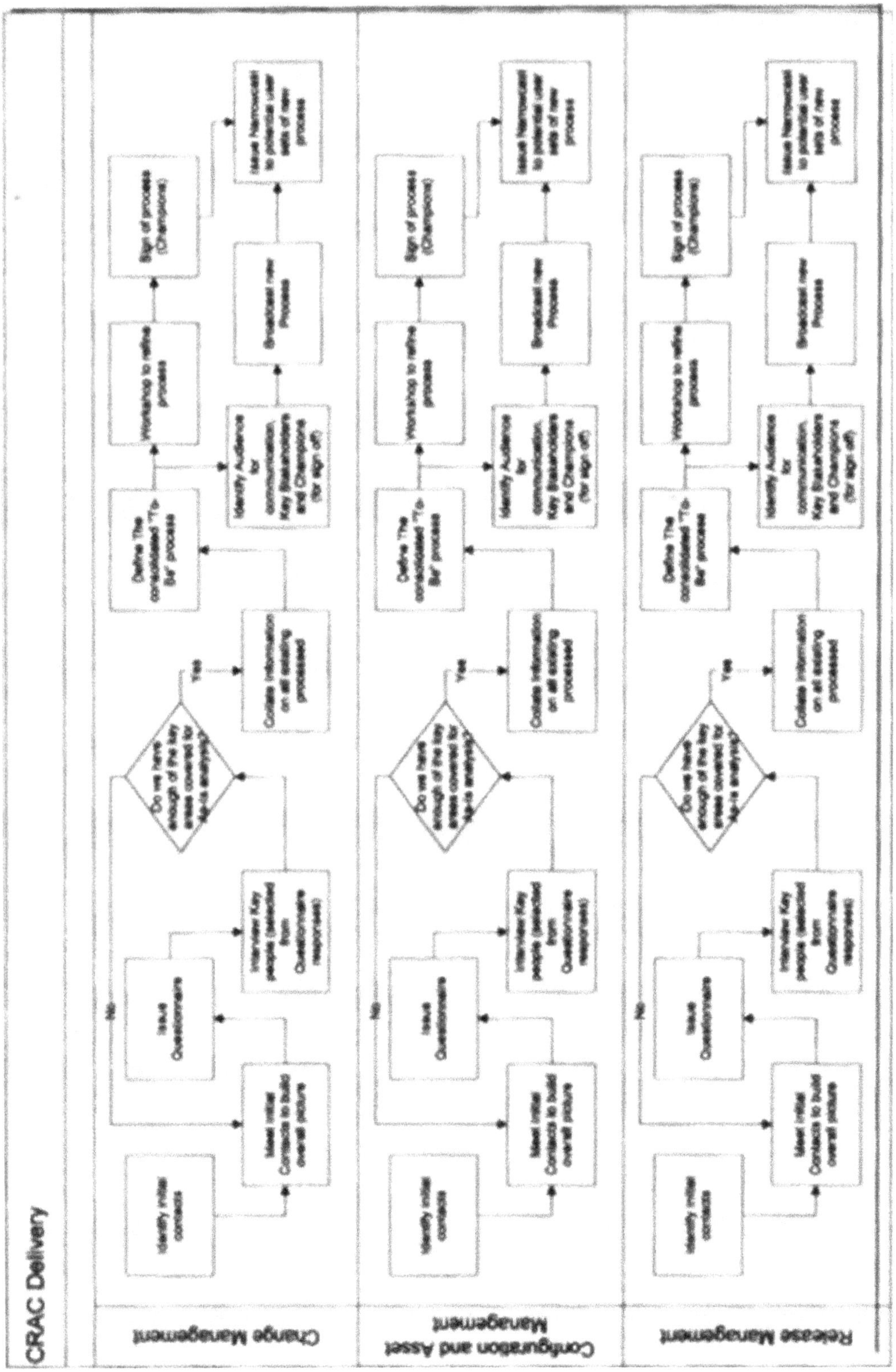

21.11 Current CM Procedures For A Client (Legacy and Modernisation)

Requests for Change (RFCs) are changes initiated by a development team, possibly on behalf of the customer/user representative of the system in development. The aim of the RFC is to manage changes to agreed product specifications and the impact of such changes on other developments and the live production environment.

The scope of an RFC is to manage the technical impact of a change, within the client account/infrastructure. Hence, there is no need for funding authorisation or contractual instruction to proceed. The Change Management team gives the authorisation, if all impact assessment replies have given the go-ahead.

RFCs exist for both Legacy and the Modernisation development areas. Once the RFCs are approved, and they need to hit the live production environment, they are scheduled in for one of two releases to the live environment (scheduled in for several months of each year).

In this case, a workflow system called AMS has been developed bespoke for the client. It resides on the client's network. Each Product, supported by this process, is recorded on the system, with a set of Impact Assessors that need to see a change to a specific product (both sign-off and for information).

21.12 Current CM Procedures For Activity Requests (Legacy and Modernisation)

ARs are effectively changes to live environment. This could be immediate fixes or releases of fixes, developed packages, new versions of existing systems. ARs cover a release of new product, new version of an existing product or small changes that are applied directly to the live environment.

Any person on the account can initiate an AR. The AR is sent for impact assessment to all teams that could be affected by that live environment. The scope of an AR is to manage the technical impact of a change, within the client's account/infrastructure. Hence, there is no need for funding authorisation or contractual instruction to proceed. The Change Management team gives the authorisation if all impact assessment replies have given the go-ahead. There are a group of Impact Assessors that must have returned a "Yes", before the AR is considered approved. ARs exist for both Legacy and the Modernisation development areas.

A workflow system called AMS has been developed bespoke for the client. It resides only on the client's network. Each Product, supported by this process, is recorded on the system, with a set of Impact Assessors that need to see a change to a specific product (both sign-off and for information). There is a new system, which is the client's Global solution for RFCs and ARs, being rolled out to this team. The project is currently in the Gap Analysis phase.

On a number of occasions, due to Business Needs, the client has had to push through an AR, even when one or more of the impact assessments have advised against it. This has caused significant issues and repercussions.

21.13 Current CM Procedures For Major Hardware (Legacy and Modernisation)

Major Hardware changes, as opposed to minor infrastructure changes, will be initiated by project teams, and processed through the Digital Infrastructure (DI) team. The team is interested in component changes rather than new business, which are handled through the business team.

All infrastructure changes are sent to the DI team, including those from other branches. Changes are usually copied to the DI team for information.

The process usually uses a specific form, but other forms are often accepted. The changes are managed through an excel spreadsheet, although there is an ongoing move to a bespoke system.

The changes are assessed and in essence authorised if the change has no unacceptable adverse effect.

21.14 Current CM Procedures For Other Sites

The procedures here are for the project responsible for delivering new desktop and network infrastructure across the business estates. In this case, the scope of the Change Management team is:

- Live Implementation Dates, which are roll out dates pertaining to an project plan;
- Changes to the existing rollout, such as changes to the desktop set-up and network configuration;
- Work Requests, such as additional work to configure or amend and application, or to resolve a conflict between applications.

These types of changes are often generated either by authorised groups on the account, an Incident, or through a New Business Change request.

The system used for managing this system is an extensively developed bespoke system. Although other teams are currently not using it, discussions are taking place for it to be made available for others. A standard list of assessors exists within the system. This includes members of the Technical Architect and other communities.

Work Requests are always pre-funded, due to existing contract arrangements. Change Requests will usually require a funding authorisation from the client group.

All CRs and WRs are given technical approval based on the result of impact assessments.

21.15 Current Incident Management Procedures for Desktop/Network

As an example, the various client's sites used for this purpose, in this book, has approximately 180 thousand desktops being rolled out as part of the project. The scope of this project also includes upgrades to the network, to support the rollout of the new service. The most common incidents relate to conflicts between installed software, within the varying builds expected of the project/service.

The scope of this team is to manage the problems that result from the rollout. An incident is usually raised via the Request Management Centre (RMC). The RMC team is responsible for ensuring that each raised Incident is routed to the appropriate team.

A meeting is held once per month to monitor the outstanding Incidents. On average 5-8 incidents are raised each week with a rolling stack of 160 unresolved incidents.

Once a fix has been identified for the problem, a Fix form is raised with the team. This is then sent to TCP for assurance and then to the client for approval. Thirdly, release form is used for impact assessment via email and the fix is then sent to the client to authorise the release. Finally it is sent to the Original requestor to inform them that the fix will be released.

21.16 Current Service Request Procedures

A typical Service Request (SR) would be a non-catalogue Infrastructure change (e.g.: moving more than 20 PCs, telephony and big IMACS). SRs can generate TWRs (see above) and can be sent for approval from the TCP if required.

They are usually generated by the client, or escalated from a standard catalogue IMAC. Each SR will expect to have a funding authorisation; hence potential funding details will be recorded even at the stage of the initial request.

The Service Request Control Team will route the request form for impact assessment via well-established routes. The Bespoke Database system has contact information for most common routes, while irregular requests are managed on a one on one basis.

As there is a funding element for all Service Requests, authorisation will be required for both Funding and Contractual Instruction to Proceed. As per rules this means signature from two customers, one for each.

21.17 Current New Business Procedures

A typical New Business Request (NBR) would be a project that is required to implement a change. NBRs can generate TWRs and SRs (see above). They are usually generated by the client, or escalated from an SR or TWR. Each NBR will expect to have a funding authorisation; hence potential funding details will be recorded even at the stage of the initial request.

The most common first step in an NBR is to define the requirements with the customer and to produce a proposal, which is essentially a statement of requirements and planned deliverables. The Service Request Control Team will ensure that the appropriate resource will work with client to define this.

The Service Request Control Team will then route the Request Form for impact assessment via well-established routes. The Bespoke Database system has contact information for most common routes, while irregular requests are managed on a one-on-one basis.

As there is a funding element for all NBRs, authorisation will be required for both Funding and Contractual Instruction to Proceed. As per rules this means signature from two client-authorised signatories (i.e.: one for each).

21.18 Configuration Management

The Configuration Management Team is a leveraged group. The team's other remit, is to investigate and encourage/incorporate Configuration Management activity at client centres, without interfering with the progression of live projects. The team have found that there are no organisational policies with regard to Configuration Management, and so have written a Configuration Management Plan which includes references to Release/Asset Management etc. this has been used in a 'Global Replace' fashion at a number of client centres.

Although their policies do not seem to include Change Management, in its purest sense, it will interface with any work.

21.19 New Business Process

The team's primary responsibility is for the resourcing of and contribution to New Business Bids coming through, usually where the contract value of the Bid is >$1m. This team does not cover legacy changes. The focus of the team is to contribute parts to a proposal from a Delivery, rather than sales, point of view.

Although each area (legacy changes and modernisation new business) has their own change management procedures, for new business, there is little communication between the streams due to the considerable complexity and differences between them. Impacting cross-program or projects has proved to be difficult.

Regarding the programmes and projects in existence, there is no definitive list of client work. Each specific area will have their lists, but there is no central repository. Examples of groups, which will have significant visibility of projects and so considerable lists of work include: Legacy, Commercial, Client Groups and other centres.

Bids under $1m are processed through a similar process, even though at least three other teams in place who deal with these. Consultancy is treated differently, and these teams would not usually deal with consultancy bids. Third Parties would have input where necessary as impact assessors and possibly a part of the delivery of the solution. However, they would not be involved in sign-off processes.

The SDEs, SC Managers, Programme Directors and others where applicable, all have to approve a proposal before it is sent to the customer. It is one of the main goals of the team to put together a comprehensive Stakeholder list.

21.20 Business And Capacity Planning

The team's main role is to carry out Business Planning and Capacity Planning (specifically in terms of human resources). The team was originally a client team that worked directly for the company. Since the outsourcing their role has changed little, although they are now part of outsourcing organisation.

Within the scope of Business Planning, the team supplies man-day resource/capacity information to the client. The client's plan is baselined annually in March and the information is gathered to measure against that baseline. Its aim is to allow the client to identify the future budgets of projects.

21.21 Contract Management And Management Accounting

This section covers how two teams, Contract Management and Management Accounting, interact with the New Business element of the Change Management process. The Contract Management team's main responsibility is to supply cost models for Fixed Price. When a proposal for the Data Centre Operations contract is being put together, the Management Accounting team receives the estimates and the cost of hardware for the proposed piece of work. This is then matched against the relevant rates and turned into a cost model for the proposal.

The proposal is then developed and goes through a Value Review Board (VRB), which is internal. This is the last chance for teams to stop the proposal, before it is put to the client.

After the client has approved the change and funding has been allocated, an Authorisation to Proceed (ATP) is sent to the Contract Management team, who store the physical copy.

The ATP will usually specify when the work will be invoiced. A copy of the ATP is sent to the invoicing team to accomplish this.

21.22 An Example Of Various Phases Involved For A Multi-sites Client

The team consists of two components: a core team of 20 Change Analysts and a larger group of Subject Matter Experts (SMEs) who are involved in requests, as and when required. The main purpose of the team is to take an initial request from the client through one or more iterations.

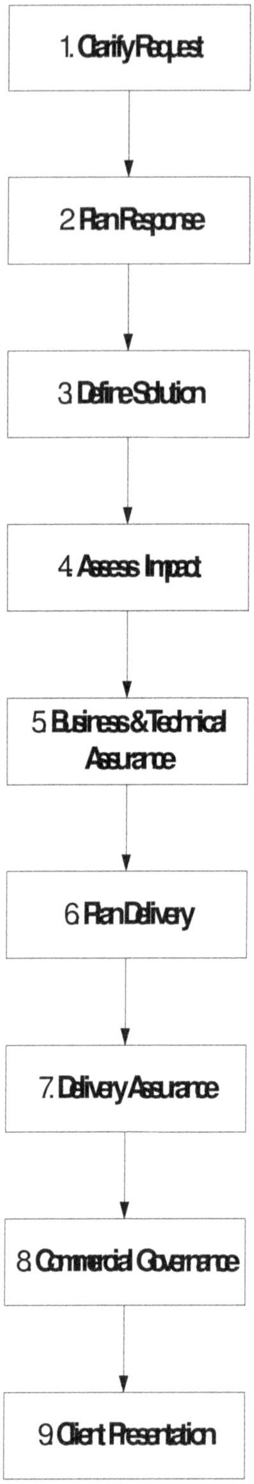
1. Clarify Request
2 Plan Response
3 Define Solution
4 Assess Impact
5 Business & Technical Assurance
6 Plan Delivery
7. Delivery Assurance
8 Commercial Governance
9 Client Presentation

In order to ensure that the correct list of people impact assess each change, a set of impact assessment co-ordinators are identified, who should ensure that this happens.

The main input of requests, to this team, is through projects and programmes.

21.23 Options

The purpose of this section is to identify and outline the main options available for Change Management. A recommended option will be developed further into a plan for how the proposed solution will be implemented. Each solution for managing change across the account can be characterised under the following four categories:

Governance: The method in which changes are approved. It is possible that a single change may require budget approval. It is usually Governance that causes the biggest delays in any process and not obtaining necessary sign off can be disastrous, hence getting the hierarchy and escalation processes right is essential.

Culture: The way in which people work together. The ideal culture for changes to be managed effectively is a true partnership. Hence each option must strive to drive the teams to work together better.

Process: The steps people take to manage change. This is a purist point of view, of what activities take place in order to manage a change from a concept to an implemented product. This would include standards for forms and communication guidelines.

Tool: Whether there is one tool to support a single process, or a number of tools that interface well with each other, the right tool(s) have to be developed to meet the established Process requirements.

21.24 Recommended Option

The recommended option is to develop a set of Virtual Change Management communities. All the options are outlined below. The recommended option is developed into a high-level implementation plan in the next section.

21.25 A New Single Process For Change Management

In order to control change effectively, the ideal solution is to use a single process for all types of Change Management. If a single process was introduced, which is consistent and can be used across the account, then there would be no issues regarding conflicting approaches and procedures and guidelines can be made clear and available to all.

	What needs to change	Pros	Cons
Governance	This aspect needs to be completely merged or at least joined up. In addition, it needs to be as static as possible throughout the account.	If possible, this would solve a number of the issues on the account relating to and beyond Change Management.	This may be too much of a step from the current governance structure.
Culture	The team needs to be joined up with a single focus and vision to develop better relationship with the customer.	The customer will undoubtedly be impressed if this is achieved.	This may be too much of a step from the current cultural status.
Process	A single process needs to be created for all changes, across all 8 contracts, which will need to fit all contractual requirements.	It would make the contractual relationships much more open and easy to navigate through.	This may be too much of a step, as the contractual requirements are very different.
Tools	One single IT tool needs to be developed for all changes.	One IT system for all changes would give everyone a full overview of all changes across the account.	Although developing this system would be easy, as it already exists using a product called Peregrine, getting teams to adopt it effectively would be very difficult.

21.26 Adoption Of One Existing Process For Change Management

Some sites have very well developed processes and procedures. One of the Client Service Groups could be chosen as the most mature process within the account and all other CSGs would take up the processes and procedures.

It would be possible to mix and match the different procedures. If this option is chosen, then the next step must be to identify which processes should be picked for each area.

	What needs to change	Pros	Cons
Governance	One of the governance structures must be chosen. This needs to be completely merged or at least joined up. In addition, it needs to be as static as possible throughout the account.	If possible, this would solve a number of the issues on the account beyond CM and the chosen CSG will not need to change.	This may be too much of a step from the current governance structure
Culture	The team needs to be joined up with a single focus and mission to develop better relationship with the customer.	The customer will undoubtedly be impressed if this is achieved.	This may be too much of a step from the current cultural status.
Process	As one single process for all changes, across all 8 contracts, the process will need to fit all contractual requirements.	It would make the contractual relationships much more open and easy to navigate through and the chosen CSG's processes would not need to change.	This may be too much of a step, as the contractual requirements are very different.
Tools	One single IT tool to be developed further to accommodate requirements for all changes across the organisation.	One IT system for all changes would give everyone a full overview of all changes across the account.	Although developing this system would be easy, as it already exists, in one area, non chosen areas will not be happy and/or able to change.

21.27 Virtual Change Management Community

The client account is vast and very dispersed, both geographically and organisationally. This means that trying to merge the teams together physically would be very difficult in the short-medium term. Hence one alternative is to create Virtual teams. The scope of these teams would be to:

- Have a Process Leader (PL), who would own the standards, protocols, processes and procedures. The Process Leader will have a number of Subject Matter Experts (SMEs), who although will not report directly to the PL, will own their respective processes, which must meet the set out quality standards.
- Have across the Virtual Teams (VTs) join into a Virtual Change Management Community (VCMC) in order to ensure that each process, which belongs to, the respective VT is up to the standards defined in it.
- Meet on a regular basis to share information across the VTs, to ensure that lessons learnt are shared.
- Have a regular feed of changes into centralised MIS system, which is owned and maintained by the QA team supporting the VTs.

	What needs to change	Pros	Cons
Governance	No change in governance, except to ensure that there is a minimal standard of governance for each process.	Only governance structures that need improvement will change.	There is no single governance structure, to take ownership of processes.
Culture	Small changes are required to the culture of some teams, to seek a method for improving working relationships across virtual process communities.	A small step will make it much easier to adopt across the account. A number of teams are already interested.	This is only a small change and ultimately, the teams will still be separate and working for different sections.
Process	All processes will need to be identified and the VCMCs will need to be created. After which the PLs will be responsible for continuous process improvement.	A phased and continuous improvement is much more likely to have an effect then a big bang approach. Also, VCMCs will enable best practise to be adopted and shared across the account.	This is only a small change and ultimately, the teams will still be separate and working on different processes. A team of 3 analysts, for 6-8 months, will be required to create the VCMC
Tools	All individual tools will be required to have an automatic feed of changes. This will be collated in a central MIS system.	A central system will be able to provide MIS of all changes.	The MIS system will need to be developed for all VTs. A team of 3 developers will be required to create the MIS system.

21. 28 Wait For Client To Take Lead On Change Management Processes

In order to change effectively, the most ergonomic method would be to enable and await merger of change processes across the different Client Service Groups.

	What needs to change	Pros	Cons
Governance	Would lead the changes in governance and take ownership of the processes.	Should lead in any governance change and they are best placed to take ownership of processes.	This may be a long-term option, which is not possible to implement within the short-medium term.
Culture	Would merge the outsourcing and IT related departments of each CSG to ensure that changes are managed across the department as a single outsourcer as opposed to 5 separate units.	The true merger would make it much easier for any supplier to ensure that his or her own processes are joined up.	This may be a long- term option, which is not possible to implement within the short-medium term.
Process	Would take over ownership of the processes.	Ownership of the process should lie with whoever has better visibility across the account to take decisions where necessary.	This may be a long-term option, which is not possible to implement within the short-medium term.
Tools	Decide what tool to develop and how the data should be populated.	This depends on the tool chosen by client.	This may be a long-term option, which is not possible to implement within the short-medium term.

21.29 Improve Visibility

As there are a number of Change Management Processes that interact well with each other, the option to leave things as they are could be considered plausible. Instead of interfering with the current system, as there is still the perception that there isn't a working Change Management process for client account, the visibility of Changes should be improved and communicated.

The best method for achieving this is to take more of an active part in the existing Change Management Boards and sub-groups;

- To ensure that all decision boards are chaired by a senior person;
- To ensure that all changes are approved and owned by the client;

21.30 Next Step For Recommended Option

The purpose of this section is to delineate the proposed plan, for improving Change Management visibility across the client estate. The plan is based on the assumption that the Virtual Change Management Community option is chosen.

The purpose of the plans is to identify a set of activities that can take be accomplished within agreed timescales.

21.31 Immediate Action

The following resolutions, to issues identified in the Management Summary, need to be actioned in the short term:

- Client owned change boards: In order to provide the client with visibility and control over the different parts of the change lifecycle, the client must own and chair boards which will authorise changes (such as releases to the live environment). In order to ensure that the client sites have adequate visibility and control, they must create a board to authorise all ARs and therefore own the releases. Due to high volumes of ARs, only ones with high importance are authorised individually and others are authorised on bulk.
- Explicitly identify Change Co-ordinators: For each area, this Change Co-ordinator is required to be the single point of contact. Their role will involve them at two stages of the process: Impact Assessment and authorisation. Therefore, they must hold an up-to-date, documented and accurate list of Assessors and Authorisers. All changes must then be sent via these co-ordinators to ensure that changes are assessed and authorised by the right people.
- Pipeline owners: The introduction of Pre-Live Service Line Managers is endorsed as an essential step to provide assurance of consistency across the Change Management Process.
- Further identification/mapping of all routes for change: In order to improve the way in which change of all types are managed (including Configuration Control and Release Management), we should join the elements of Configuration, Release and Assets, and build a detailed map of routes a change can take from developing the client idea to releasing it into the live environment. One of the main deliverables of this would be to identify a set of change management groups, which can be turned into Virtual Change Management Communities.

21.32 Next Phase of CM Process Development

The more medium term plan for this proposal is to develop the Virtual Change Management Communities (VCMC) for each of the change management groups we have identified.

Various activities need to take place in order to implement VCMC. The proposal is that a project team of 6 (2 Process analysts, 3 Analyst/Programmers and 1 team leader) will implement the VCMC proposal as described in this section. At a high level, they can be summarised as:

Process Re-engineering and Assurance: Although a single process cannot be imposed on all teams, they must have a documented and mapped out process. The implementation team's first role will be to facilitate and aid the teams wishing to join the VCMC in developing these. The sections, below define how the implementation team will need to carry out their assurance role.

Communication: The essence of change control/management is communication. Hence the team will need to develop broadcast and narrowcast communication material to teams wishing to join the VCMC and other Department and supplier that could be affected.

Form and IT toolsets used by teams: Each team may wish, for very valid reasons, to use a form specific to the needs of their process. In order to ensure that adequate information is captured on these forms, the team will facilitate and assist the teams wishing to join the VCMC in developing these.

Management Information System (MIS): In order to provide key stakeholders and customers of the VCMC with relevant and up to date information about changes processed by member teams, a bespoke system will need to be developed. This system will take in electronic feeds and turned them into easily accessed and manipulated reports.

Training and guidance notes: As with any change, new processes and IT systems, there will be the requirement to train both users of these new processes/IT systems and the VCMC administrators.

The impact of the move to adopt and implement the introduction of a Virtual Change Management Community (VCMC) is expected to have the following impact:

21.32.1 Governance

In order to ensure that the client has the visibility and control over these processes within the estate, a set of change control boards will need to be established and chaired/owned by the client. A high priority example of this is the Release Boards. The client should have Release Managers, possibly one for Legacy and one for Modernisation, where releases to the environment can only be authorised (even if authorised on bulk) by these Release Managers.

As with any large and organically grown account, ensuring that teams that there is cross-Client Service Group communication can be a challenge. In order to improve the communication between staff/teams, which carry out similar activities, Process Leaders (PL) will need to be appointed to lead a Virtual Team for that activity. The PL is preferably one of the people already in the Virtual Team (VT), partly, as it is a part time role and partly, as the aim is to lead the VT to improve standards, processes and tools.

The PLs will not have line management responsibility for any of the Virtual Team members and will not have any change to their direct line management. The VTs will be a part of the Virtual Change Management Community, which will be supported by a small team of administrators. These administrators are responsible for supporting the Management Information System.

21.32.2 Culture

The aim of Virtual Change Management Communities is to:

- Communicate with staff/teams that carry out similar tasks;
- Improve and ensure consistency of processes across the account;
- Improve toolsets, where appropriate and possible;
- Improve management information;

It is hoped that a well-established VCMC will teleconference every two weeks and physically meet every month (to 6 weeks).

In order to ensure that the right changes are escalated, a standardised set of categories is proposed. The purpose of prioritisation is to ensure that the urgency of a change is considered when processing it.

The following categories are recommended:

- Showstopper (change must be implemented immediately);
- Immediate (change must be implemented within a day);
- Critical (change must be implemented within 48 hours);
- Urgent (change must be implemented within 5 working days);
- Imperative (change must be implemented within 2 weeks);
- Strategic. Change implementation can take longer term.

21.32.3 Process

It will not be possible to impose a single process or a centrally based team for managing changes across the estate. Having said this, there must be a set of standards and requirements for all processes that pertain to a VCMC. In order to define these set of standard, a detailed process mapping exercise will need to take place.

The objectives of this exercise are:

- To map each process at a detailed level;
- To develop the VCMC teams and their stakeholders;
- To develop (for each VCMC team) the minimal requirements for governance, processes, and toolsets;
- To identify the gaps between the minimal requirements and each individual process;

In order to gain membership to a VCMC, the team will need to:

- Produce documentary evidence of existing processes. Special emphasis will be brought to ensuring that the team maintains good interface links with teams at different stages of the change lifecycle;
- Ensure that the data collected (i.e.: on forms) meets minimum requirements;
- Ensure that governance bodies and boards have been identified (and have been documented);
- Ensure that the tools to register and track changes exist and have been documented. In addition the ability to produce the electronic feed of changes as defined below;
- Ensure that all members of the team and key users of the processes involved are trained adequately. Training packs and user guides are usually adequate documentary evidence of this;
- Ensure that adequate communication has been dispensed to both a narrowcast and broadcast audience.

The role of the implementation team will be to facilitate the induction of each team into the VCMC. The method for this is to carry out an audit of the team, in question. The DWP/OSM member of the VCMC will be asked to approve the result of the audit and the recommendation that the change process is given the VCMC certificate.

21.32.4 Tools

In order to become a stakeholder in a VCMC, the team will have to ensure that a regular electronic feed of changes, process by the team. This batch file of changes will be imported into the VCMC Management Information System (VCMC MIS). The batch file will need to contain the following information:

- Details of which team has sent the information (including a unique identification for the team);
- Details of where in the VCMC the team sits;
- Unique identifier for the change;
- Title;
- Current Status of Change (predefined list of agreed statuses);
- Description of the requirements;
- Definition of change deliverables;
- Priority (including a specific deadline requirement);
- Importance;
- Dependencies and Constraints;
- Original requestor (i.e.: usually an authorised client contact);
- Date of original request and date received authorisation to assess request;

- Outline benefits of change;
- List of teams that have impact assessed change and details of assessments;
- Authorisation received for change. This can be one of a predefined list (i.e.: Authorised for Impact Assessment; Authorised for Implementation, etc.);
- Closure details.

The idea is that as a unique identification, will identify each change; a team is encouraged to send regular updates for a change. For example at first the team can send a "registration" of change with only the bold attributes completed. After more information is available and updated on the team's toolset, the updated record can be sent to the VCMC MIS system and the record on the database will replace the original version of the record with the new details, using this unique identifier.

21.33 Reports Availability

The following reports will be available from the system:

- Highlight Priority Report: Details of changes which are Priority A or B;
- Highlight Importance Report: Details of changes which are Importance 1 or 2;
- Changes Per Status: List of all changes grouped by their status;
- Inactive Change Report: Open changes that have not changed status and open changes that have not been updated for a period of time;
- Changes processed by team: List of changes currently open for a team;
- Detailed report of each change;
- Other ad-hoc queries will be available via the administrators.

21.34 Long Term Aim

The purpose of the plans so far, as described above, is to identify a set of activities that can take be accomplished within the short and medium timescales.

The aim is to ensure that the medium and short-term actions are progressing in line with the strategy for Change Management, that is:

- To have a single process for all types of Change Management;
- To ensure that the client has the visibility and ownership of all Change Management checkpoints and boards;
- To encourage a joint working relationship between the client and its suppliers;
- To ensure that process related knowledge is retained by the client and to ensure that movement staff do not hinder existing processes;
- To ensure that there is less reliance on informal networks and named individuals;
- To have a single toolset for registering and tracking change;

- To share change management activities.

21.35 A Major Consultancy Study

A major consultancy's survey, focusing on large change programmes in 500 multinationals and public sector companies covering all industry sectors in North America Europe, Far East, has shown the following results:

Top 10 Barriers	% of 500 companies	Top 10 Success Factors	% of 500 companies
Competing resources	48%	Ensuring top sponsorship	82%
Functional boundaries	44%	Treating people fairly	82%
Change skills	43%	Involving employees	75%
Middle management	38%	Giving quality communications	70%
Long IT lead times	35%	Providing sufficient training	68%
Communication	35%	Using clear performance measures	65%
Employee opposition	33%	Building teams after change	62%
HR (people/training) issues	33%	Focusing on culture/skill changes	62%
Initiative fatigue	32%	Rewarding success	60%
Unrealistic timetables	31%	Using internal champions	60%

21.36 People Stop Change

As the statistics above shows, people stop change.

It is recommended that the client and its suppliers work together to develop a transformational change programme to address the issue of fragmented change management across the client estate.

22. PROJECT MANAGEMENT IMPROVEMENTS

22.1 Programme Management

A programme is a portfolio of projects and activities that are co-ordinated and managed as a unit such that they achieve outcomes and realise benefits. Further on, Programme Management is a structured framework for defining and implementing change within an organisation. It provides a framework for implementing business strategies and initiatives through the co-ordinated management of a portfolio of projects that change organisations to achieve benefits that are of strategic importance.

This briefing summarises the key principles and processes of programme management. For further details see "Managing Successful Programmes", which is OGC's recommended structured approach to programme management.

22.2 The Use Of Programme Management

Using a structured approach will allow the coordination of a set of activities and projects to achieve a strategic goal (or vision) for the organisation. Both programmes and projects are about change, and this involves risk. A structured approach to programme management ensures that the interdependencies between projects are coordinated and the risk managed across these interdependencies.

It will also enable more efficient use of resources through project prioritisation and with other programmes and the interface to business strategy. Clearly assigned responsibility for the delivery of business benefits, the organisation has appropriate personnel available with relevant skills and experience to set up, manage and deliver the programme. The organisation is capable of achieving the change required by the programme.

22.3 Programme Management Organisation

Once the Programme Management and support processes are in place, the organisation structure for a programme should have clear lines of sponsorship, authority and management while being flexible enough to react to changes. Responsibilities of staff engaged in programme roles should be matched against required individual skills, competencies and experience.

Training and on-going mentoring may be required to support individuals and the team. Recommended roles are the following:

22.3.1 Programme sponsorship

Programmes require sponsorship from the most senior executives of the organisation or group of organisations committed to the programme to ensure support of the business case and its fit into organisational objectives. Sponsorship also includes senior management support for the changes introduced by the programme and commitment to achieve the required outcomes.

22.3.2 Programme management

There are three primary roles for managing a programme:

The Programme Director who provides overall leadership and has ultimate responsibility for the successful delivery of the programme.

The Programme Manager who carries the responsibility for day-to-day management of the programme's portfolio of projects and for ensuring these is focused on delivery of the required capabilities.

The Business Change Manager(s) who is responsible for realising the required outcomes through the integration of the new capabilities into the business operation.

22.3.3 Programme support

For most programmes, a Programme Support Office should be established to assist with the management of programme information, i.e. budget control, status reports, programme documentation. A Programme Support Office can serve both the programme and the individual projects within a programme.

22.4 Programme Planning

Programme planning is not simply project planning on a larger scale but requires an overall management of quality, risk communications and benefits whilst to reconciling project objectives with overall programme goals. Using a Programme Plan ensures that control is established and maintained. Major decision points must be built into the programme plans to ensure that the continued viability of the programme can be reviewed.

22.5 Benefits Management

Benefits management is the activity of identifying, optimising and tracking the expected benefits from business change to ensure that they are achieved. It is a core activity and a continuous management process running throughout the programme supported by the Business Change Manager (see also Benefits Management).

22.6 Stakeholder Management

Programme success relies on co-operative contributions and support from all involved. A continuing and two-way approach to communications is essential between the programme and its stakeholders to secure commitment and maintain momentum.

22.7 Issues Management And Change Management

The programme must have a clear strategy covering how issues will be handled, and in particular, how changes will be identified, monitored and managed throughout the running of the programme. The programme must use and maintain a Change Register or Change Log to document the actions and responsibilities associated with managing change.

22.8 Quality Management

Quality management ensures that the deliverables from the programme are fit for purpose and are delivered within an overall quality management strategy for the programme.

22.9 Configuration Management

Configuration management helps keep related programme information about the programme up-to-date and accurate by continuous review, monitoring, and controlled changes.

22.10 Audit

Audit involvement with the programme will help to assure the programme's sponsors and stakeholders that the programme is being managed effectively and the delivery of changes is aligned with the required outcomes.

23. THE PROCESSES OF PROGRAMME MANAGEMENT

23.1 Identifying A Programme

This is a typically short process, whose purpose is to define the scope for the programme, which is derived from the organisation's business strategy and triggered by a need for change.

It initiates development of initial thoughts on the vision, anticipated benefits, risk and estimated costs, timescales and effort required which help to determine whether the programme should go ahead. This includes establishing the Programme Mandate which provides the high level requirements of the programme and the benefits required by the organisation, establishing a Sponsoring Group formed by senior executives from the organisation and appointing the Programme Director to translate the Programme Mandate into a Programme Brief, which defines the aim and envisaged benefits to the organisation.

23.2 Defining A Programme

If the programme appears to be justified and senior management agrees to proceed to the Defining a Programme process then the initial vision is refined into the Vision Statement and the Blueprint prepared, which is a description of the transformed organisation as a result of delivering this programme of change.

Activities during this phase provide the detailed information that establishes the definition of the new capabilities, they way the are going to be delivered, details of how the programme will be run, changes be implemented and benefits delivered. The programme is thereby clearly defined and the Sponsoring Group decide whether to formally commit to the programme or not.

23.3 Establishing A Programme

If approval to proceed has been obtained, this process is used to appoint individuals to programme management and support roles and to set procedures and infrastructures in place to support the programme.

23.4 Managing The Project Portfolio

Once the programme is established, this process will provide an effective monitoring and management regime for the project portfolio such that the required outputs from the projects are delivered. This process covers the prime areas of interaction with project management and requires active coordination of programme's components, the relationship with other programmes and the interface to business strategy. This also means that programme documentation need to be updated and revisited regularly to reflect any changes.

23.5 Delivery Of Benefits

The programme activities, work streams and projects will deliver new capabilities, services or business operations. The purpose of this process is to track the specific outcomes, which were identified at the start, and to drive through the process of achieving these outcomes within the business operations during the life of the programme. Throughout the programme, progress is reviewed at defined milestones and the benefit profiles and benefits plan adjusted to reflect any changes. This process also manages the transition old and new ways of working. The responsibilities for achievement of outcomes must be clearly assigned.

23.6 Closing A Programme

In order to establish and maintain a clear focus on achieving the end-goal, a programme should have a pre-determined end-point and a formal process of close down. This includes confirmation that the changes defined in the Blueprint have been delivered and the programme's vision achieved. Benefits management (delivery of required outcomes) may need to continue beyond the formal closure of the programme, particularly if the achievement of measurable improvements is to be part of on-going business operations. The Programme Management Workbook breaks down this process into a manageable stage-based method.

24. PROJECT PLAN

24.1 Producing Plans

The Project Manager to refine the information in the Outline Plan in order to provide a firm foundation for the Development/Deployment phase of the project.

This refinement should include:

- Define what project products will be produced and when.
- Provide the project team with a strategy for carrying out the development work.
- Define how the project team intends to deliver products, which are fit for business purpose and meet the defined quality standards.
- Identify individuals who will take on the various roles and responsibilities on forthcoming phases of the project.
- Define the necessary project control procedures, including change and risk management.
- Identify which items are to be subject to configuration management and to outline how configuration control is to be applied.
- Define the approach to maintain quality, including what types of tests are to be run, how they are to be specified and how results are recorded.
- Identify the required project standards and guidelines, and to identify which of them already exist in a suitable form.

24.2 Sub-Products

Any of these sub-products would be generated as a separate document when the procedures and processes they describe are too complex to be made an integral part of the Project Plan.

The Product Topics included under the Plan/s are:

- Change Management Plan; Covers the procedures that will manage changes to the project scope or objectives. These changes are those, which tend to come from outside the project, such as, new requirements, changes in business direction, changes to technical architectures or platforms.
- Configuration Management; Will also address "change control" issues, but these are more applicable to changes occurring from inside the project such as defects discovered during testing. However there is a fair degree of overlap between these two processes.
- Communications Plan; To define all parties with an interest in the project and the means and frequency of communication between them and the project. This includes any marketing material that will be produced to sell the system to potential customers/users
- Project Configuration Management Plan; Covers all the details as to how Configuration Management is to be performed during the project, including how

changes to the configuration are made, how configuration items are identified, and which items are to be considered as configuration items. The change control parts of CM bear a close relationship to the Change Management procedures.

- Change Management Plan; Explains how risks to the successful outcome of the project are identified and managed.

- Test Strategy; For projects that are going to require a significant amount of testing to be done on the products (especially projects with IT aspects to them), this document explains how that testing will be performed and what sort of tests are needed.

24.3 Quality Control

The Quality Criteria questions the following points:

- Are the roles and responsibilities clearly defined and owned?
- Are the project standards, and the approach by which they will be adhered to, clearly defined?
- Are quality control and audit processes clearly defined and in operation?
- Does the plan clearly define ways in which the users' quality expectations will be met?
- Have acceptance criteria been defined by the support team and the business?
- Are the timescales consistent with the business objectives in the Feasibility Report and the Business Area Definition?
- Does the order of activities within the plan reflect the list of prioritised requirements?
- Does the plan reflect the need to address areas of risk at appropriate times?
- Are all affected classes of users identified in the plan?
- Is the proposed user effort consistent with the needs of both the existing business processes and the development?
- Will the necessary effort (from all personnel) be available when required?
- When prototypes are used, is the selection of categories of prototypes feasible within the expected development environment?
- Are the configuration items appropriate to the functionality in the Business Area Definition and to the deliverables in the Outline Plan?
- Is the method of configuration management appropriate to the environment?
- Are the proposed extent, depth and formality of testing appropriate?

24.4 Project Plan Example (In Microsoft Plan Format)

Management of Change Plan. Page

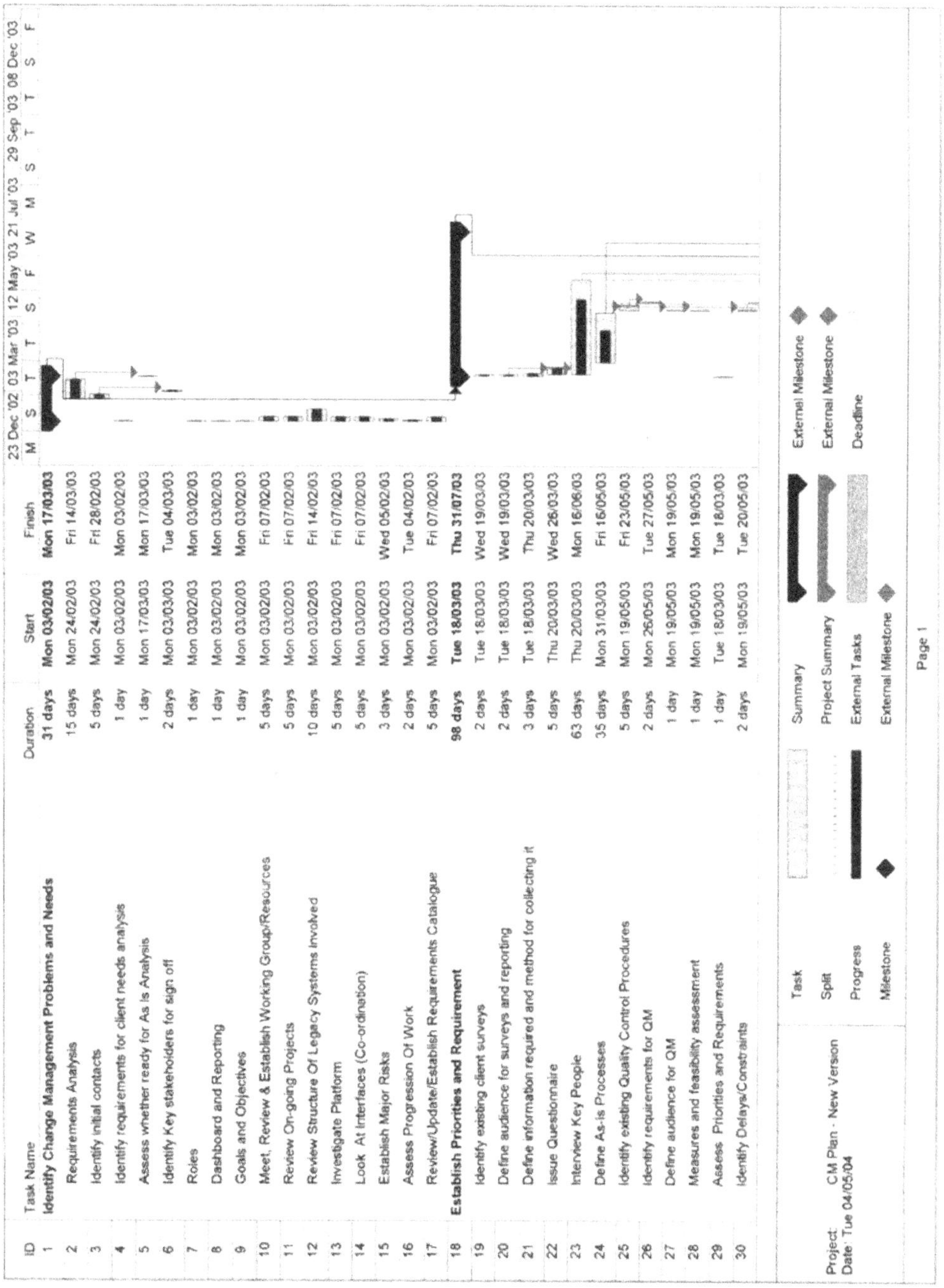

ID	Task Name	Duration	Start	Finish
1	**Identify Change Management Problems and Needs**	**31 days**	**Mon 03/02/03**	**Mon 17/03/03**
2	Requirements Analysis	15 days	Mon 24/02/03	Fri 14/03/03
3	Identify initial contacts	5 days	Mon 24/02/03	Fri 28/02/03
4	Identify requirements for client needs analysis	1 day	Mon 03/02/03	Mon 03/02/03
5	Assess whether ready for As Is Analysis	1 day	Mon 17/03/03	Mon 17/03/03
6	Identify Key stakeholders for sign off	2 days	Mon 03/03/03	Tue 04/03/03
7	Roles	1 day	Mon 03/02/03	Mon 03/02/03
8	Dashboard and Reporting	1 day	Mon 03/02/03	Mon 03/02/03
9	Goals and Objectives	1 day	Mon 03/02/03	Mon 03/02/03
10	Meet, Review & Establish Working Group/Resources	5 days	Mon 03/02/03	Fri 07/02/03
11	Review On-going Projects	5 days	Mon 03/02/03	Fri 07/02/03
12	Review Structure Of Legacy Systems involved	10 days	Mon 03/02/03	Fri 14/02/03
13	Investigate Platform	5 days	Mon 03/02/03	Fri 07/02/03
14	Look At Interfaces (Co-ordination)	5 days	Mon 03/02/03	Fri 07/02/03
15	Establish Major Risks	3 days	Mon 03/02/03	Wed 05/02/03
16	Assess Progression Of Work	2 days	Mon 03/02/03	Tue 04/02/03
17	Review/Update/Establish Requirements Catalogue	5 days	Mon 03/02/03	Fri 07/02/03
18	**Establish Priorities and Requirement**	**98 days**	**Tue 18/03/03**	**Thu 31/07/03**
19	Identify existing client surveys	2 days	Tue 18/03/03	Wed 19/03/03
20	Define audience for surveys and reporting	2 days	Tue 18/03/03	Wed 19/03/03
21	Define information required and method for collecting it	3 days	Tue 18/03/03	Thu 20/03/03
22	Issue Questionnaire	5 days	Thu 20/03/03	Wed 26/03/03
23	Interview Key People	63 days	Thu 20/03/03	Mon 16/06/03
24	Define As-is Processes	35 days	Mon 31/03/03	Fri 16/05/03
25	Identify existing Quality Control Procedures	5 days	Mon 19/05/03	Fri 23/05/03
26	Identify requirements for QM	2 days	Mon 26/05/03	Tue 27/05/03
27	Define audience for QM	1 day	Mon 19/05/03	Mon 19/05/03
28	Measures and feasibility assessment	1 day	Mon 19/05/03	Mon 19/05/03
29	Assess Priorities and Requirements	1 day	Tue 18/03/03	Tue 18/03/03
30	Identify Delays/Constraints	2 days	Mon 19/05/03	Tue 20/05/03

Management of Change Plan. Page

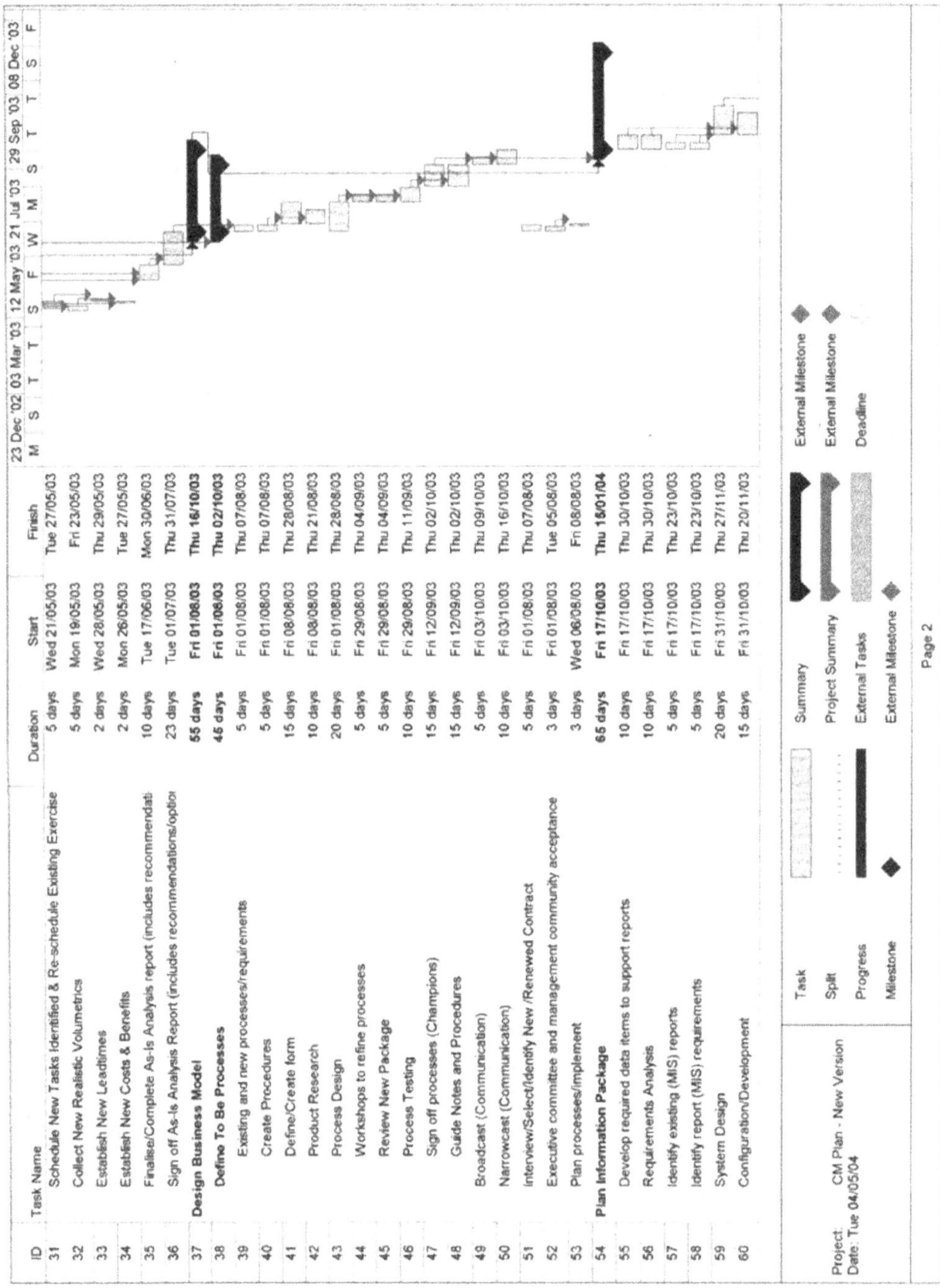

ID	Task Name	Duration	Start	Finish
31	Schedule New Tasks Identified & Re-schedule Existing Exercise	5 days	Wed 21/05/03	Tue 27/05/03
32	Collect New Realistic Volumetrics	5 days	Mon 19/05/03	Fri 23/05/03
33	Establish New Leadtimes	2 days	Wed 28/05/03	Thu 29/05/03
34	Establish New Costs & Benefits	2 days	Mon 26/05/03	Tue 27/05/03
35	Finalise/Complete As-Is Analysis report (includes recommendati	10 days	Tue 17/06/03	Mon 30/06/03
36	Sign off As-Is Analysis Report (includes recommendations/optio	23 days	Tue 01/07/03	Thu 31/07/03
37	**Design Business Model**	**55 days**	**Fri 01/08/03**	**Thu 16/10/03**
38	**Define To Be Processes**	**45 days**	**Fri 01/08/03**	**Thu 02/10/03**
39	Existing and new processes/requirements	5 days	Fri 01/08/03	Thu 07/08/03
40	Create Procedures	5 days	Fri 01/08/03	Thu 07/08/03
41	Define/Create form	15 days	Fri 08/08/03	Thu 28/08/03
42	Product Research	10 days	Fri 08/08/03	Thu 21/08/03
43	Process Design	20 days	Fri 01/08/03	Thu 28/08/03
44	Workshops to refine processes	5 days	Fri 29/08/03	Thu 04/09/03
45	Review New Package	5 days	Fri 29/08/03	Thu 04/09/03
46	Process Testing	10 days	Fri 29/08/03	Thu 11/09/03
47	Sign off processes (Champions)	15 days	Fri 12/09/03	Thu 02/10/03
48	Guide Notes and Procedures	15 days	Fri 12/09/03	Thu 02/10/03
49	Broadcast (Communication)	5 days	Fri 03/10/03	Thu 09/10/03
50	Narrowcast (Communication)	10 days	Fri 03/10/03	Thu 16/10/03
51	Interview/Select/Identify New /Renewed Contract	5 days	Fri 01/08/03	Thu 07/08/03
52	Executive committee and management community acceptance	3 days	Fri 01/08/03	Tue 05/08/03
53	Plan processes/implement	3 days	Wed 06/08/03	Fri 08/08/03
54	**Plan Information Package**	**65 days**	**Fri 17/10/03**	**Thu 15/01/04**
55	Develop required data items to support reports	10 days	Fri 17/10/03	Thu 30/10/03
56	Requirements Analysis	10 days	Fri 17/10/03	Thu 30/10/03
57	Identify existing (MIS) reports	5 days	Fri 17/10/03	Thu 23/10/03
58	Identify report (MIS) requirements	5 days	Fri 17/10/03	Thu 23/10/03
59	System Design	20 days	Fri 31/10/03	Thu 27/11/03
60	Configuration/Development	15 days	Fri 31/10/03	Thu 20/11/03

Management of Change Plan. Page

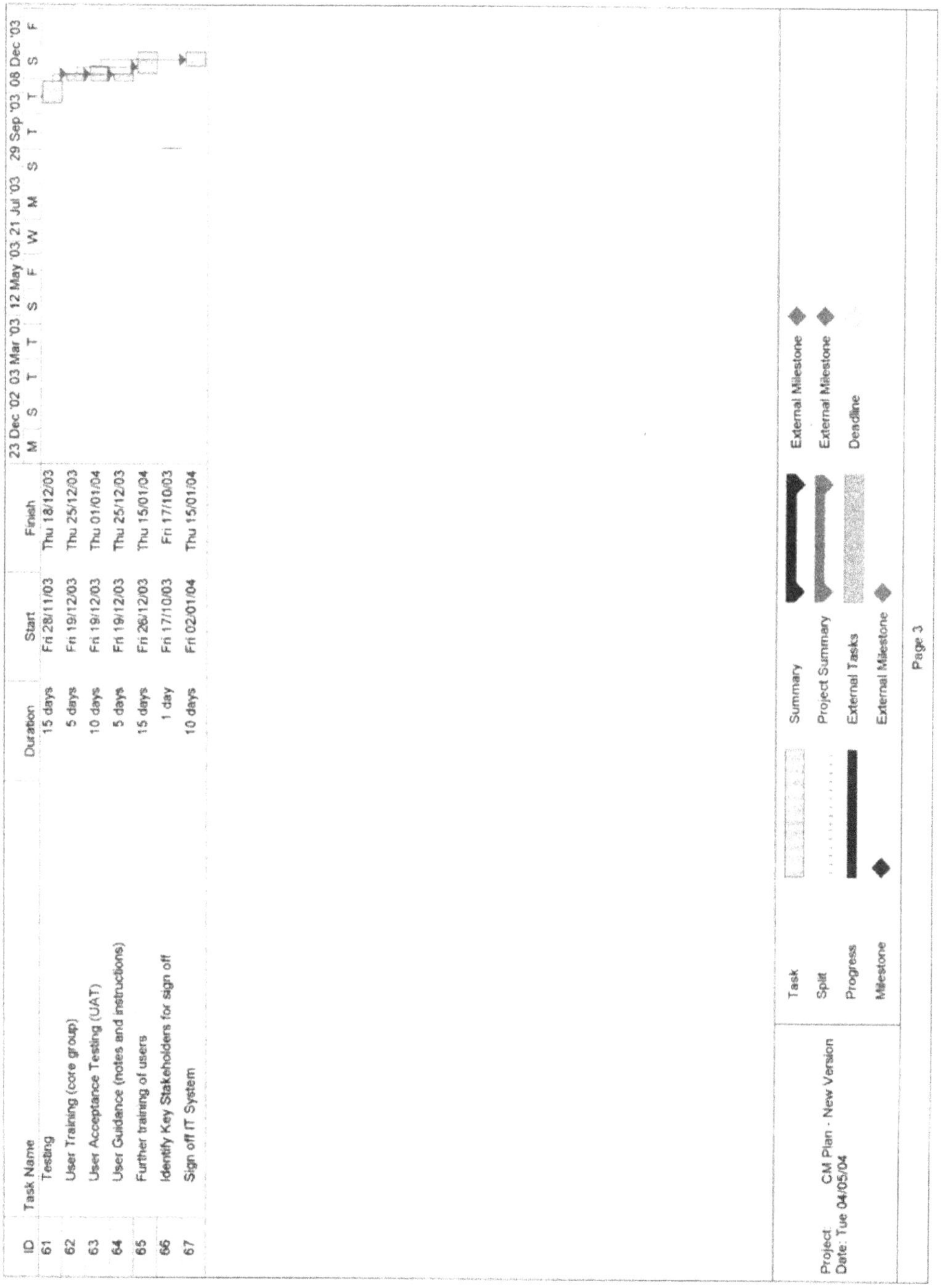

ID	Task Name	Duration	Start	Finish
61	Testing	15 days	Fri 28/11/03	Thu 18/12/03
62	User Training (core group)	5 days	Fri 19/12/03	Thu 25/12/03
63	User Acceptance Testing (UAT)	10 days	Fri 19/12/03	Thu 01/01/04
64	User Guidance (notes and instructions)	5 days	Fri 19/12/03	Thu 25/12/03
65	Further training of users	15 days	Fri 26/12/03	Thu 15/01/04
66	Identify Key Stakeholders for sign off	1 day	Fri 17/10/03	Fri 17/10/03
67	Sign off IT System	10 days	Fri 02/01/04	Thu 15/01/04

25. WEAKNESS IN PROJECT MANAGEMENT

25.1 Weakness Of Individuals

In the process of using Change Management, it will soon become apparent that probably the main cause for the threatening changes is project management, or perhaps the weakness of individual/s to manage the growth of a system.

Even if you used Change Management in its fullest, your experience will soon enable you to identify the real cause for the failure in implementing your system. In such cases, your programme/project management may need further support, assistance, training, better communicational ability and proper delegating, or even some listening to other people involved in the on-going project. Employing the expertise of a consultancy may help.

The main point is to try to reduce potential project caused loss by providing efficient *Event* driven project reviews for the critical project/s. Such project consulting steps will create and utilise virtual group of experienced project managers. As a panel of experts they will assess critical projects and provide consulting being perceived as helpful by the project team, the management and the users/clients.

25.2 Process Steps Required

For such a project consulting programme implementation, various process steps are needed:

- Select critical project,
- Understand project status,
- Plan project review,
- Create reviews agenda
- Execute project review,
- Implement change plan,
- Conclude the project review.

25.3 Collection Of Information

The project manager of the project pending the review should gather the requested information from the existing project documentation. If such documentation is not available, the project manager should collect as much an as possible from verbal discussions.

Such a preparation should include details of:

- Communication plans,
- Project organisation plan,
- Contacts and scopes,
- Background and status of finances,
- Schedules,

- Status and history of resources plans,
- Quality plan,
- System documentation,
- Brief description of the project environment,
- Change Register prioritisation/s and other reports,
- Last project review minutes.

25. 4 Agreement On Resources

The final outcome of all communications, discussions and reviews should enable the team members to produce an agreed score on the various project management resources.

The list for such a scoring agreement should include:

- Quality management,
- User participation,
- Requirements management,
- Communications,
- Business orientation,
- Project team,
- Project planning,
- Change Management,
- Technical environment.

25.5 Project Management

The typical project development stages and the project management procedures are shown in the diagram below:

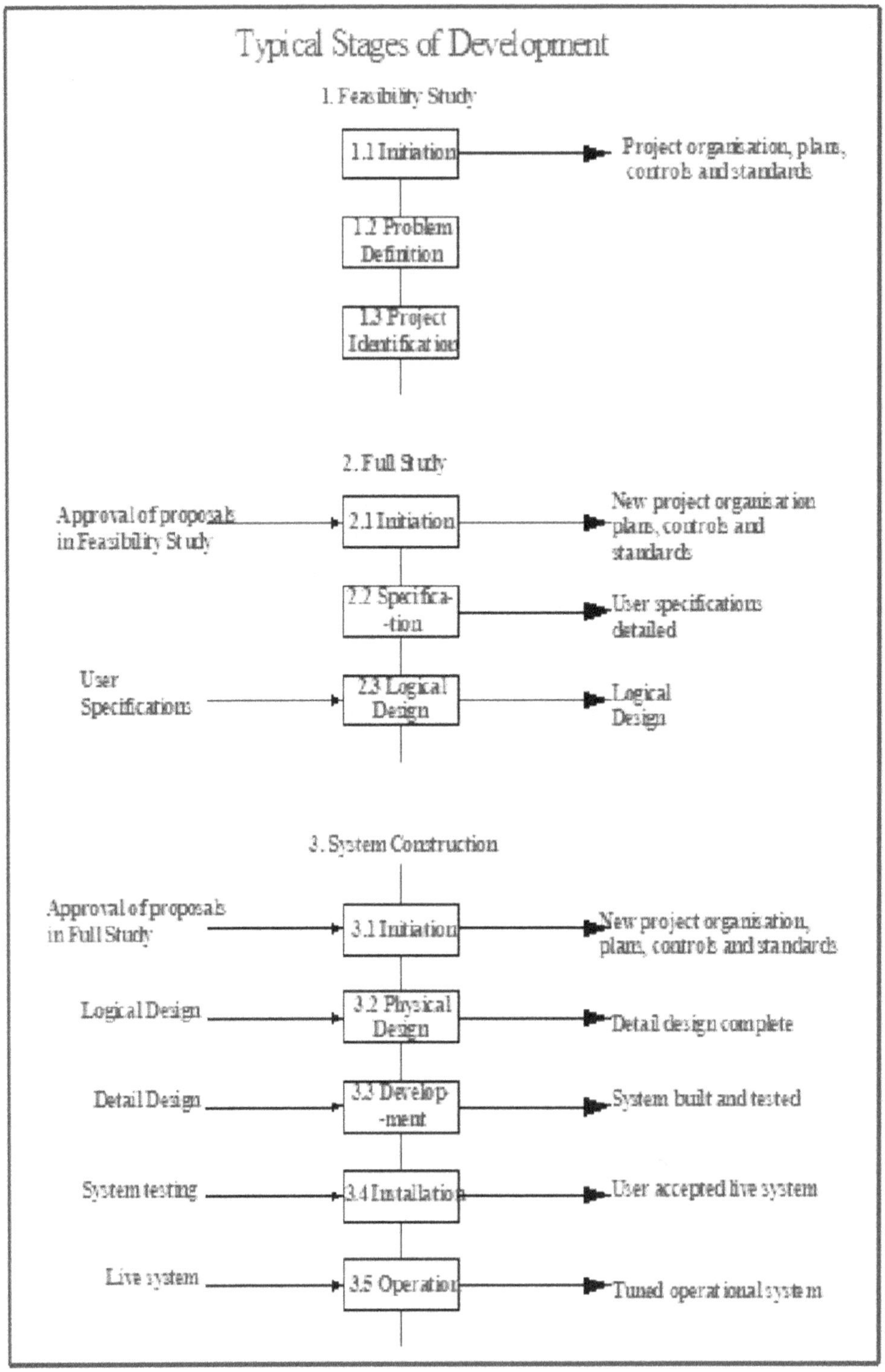
Typical Stages of Development
1. Feasibility Study
1.1 Initiation
Project organisation, plans, controls and standards
1.2 Problem Definition
1.3 Project Identification
2. Full Study
Approval of proposals in Feasibility Study
2.1 Initiation
New project organisation plans, controls and standards
2.2 Specifica- -tion
User specifications detailed
User Specifications
2.3 Logical Design
Logical Design
3. System Construction
Approval of proposals in Full Study
3.1 Initiation
New project organisation, plans, controls and standards
Logical Design
3.2 Physical Design
Detail design complete
Detail Design
3.3 Develop- -ment
System built and tested
System testing
3.4 Installation
User accepted live system
Live system
3.5 Operation
Tuned operational system

25.6 Project Management Element

As shown in the following table, every stage of development is divided in various elements and every element in sub-elements:

Project Management Element	Project Management Sub-element
Start-up	
Establish Initial Project Team	Determine Initial Roles and Responsibilities
	Determine initial skill and experience needs
	Select Initial Team Members
	Roles and Responsibilities Definition
Establish Project Relationship with Customer	Develop Partnership with customer
Create Initial Project Plan	Communications Plan
Conduct High-level risk assessment	Determine Project Approach to Risk
	Assess risk
	High-level Risk Assessment
Planning	
Identify, Assess and Plan for project risk	Apply Risk Plan to Project Plan
	Assess and Prioritise Risk
	Create Risk Plan
Refine Project Environment	Refine Risk Plan

Project Management Element	Project Management Sub-element
Update Project Budget	Risk Identification List
Review and Baseline Project Plans	
Execution	
Acquire Project resources	
Execute the Project	
Monitor the Project	Assess and Prioritise Risk
Communicate Progress Information	
Close Down	
Complete Project Plan and requirements Documentation	
Identify Improvement Opportunities and Incorporate	
Close-down Project	

25.7 Project Management Functional Skills

Project Management Key Area	Module	Functional Skills
1. Integration Management	1.1 Components	1.Goals/performance measurements 2.Project variances (Earned Value, Service Performance Indicators)
	1.2 Integrated Change Management	3.Change control plan 4.Assess ongoing project status 5.Interpret and handle variances as part of project control

Project Management Key Area	Module	Functional Skills
2. Scope Managem ent	2.1 Scope Control	6.Analyse impact on project scope, time, budget, staff etc. 7.Analyse scope change within existing contract or contract addendum 8.Facilitate change control board where applicable 9.Assess alternatives of scope change outcomes 10.Decide how to escalate
	2.2 Estimating	11.Define and manage the appropriate estimating process usage
	2.3 Requiremen ts and project scope	12.Agree and manage requirements, expectations, opportunities (acceptance criteria and sign-offs)
3. Time Manag ement	3.1 Schedule	13.Create and maintain appropriate multiple schedules 14.Define appropriate measurements 15.Identify and consider stakeholder needs 16.Balance the need for details against comprehensiveness (detailed versus summarized schedule) 17.How to handle the dynamics of changing baselines also according to performance measurement
	3.2 Time Recording	18.Establish time tracking as an element of the project outlook 19.Perceive time recording as part of an overall reporting process 20.Manage planned effort vs. actual effort, 21.Define and control appropriate thresholds

Project Management Key Area	Module	Functional Skills
		22.Create and interpret CATS reports 23.Define required project (administrative) profiles
4. Cost Managem ent	4.1 Cost Model	24.Create appropriate project cost model. (Considering inventory costing) 25.Manage Cost Centres (cross charging) 26.Handle purchasing and billing procedures
	4.2 Outlook	27.Manage cost variances and adapt outlooks 28.Define performance measures 29.Handle expense reporting
	4.3 Budget	30.Define/manage project budgets within the business model context
5. Quality Managem ent	5.1 Quality Plan	31.Manage the Quality Plan(s) and the QA processes 32.Define/implement actions for optimising project performance
	5.2 Configurati on Managemen t. Plan	33.Manage CM Plan(s); usage of results to optimise project and/or perform corrective actions of the overall project change control
	5.3 Project Standards & Procedures	34.Control effectiveness of project standards and procedures
6. Human Resource Managem ent	6.1 Managing Resources	35.Assess required skills and compile resource estimates 36.Utilize the Process for staffing the project 37.Utilize community and individual networks to identify required skills 38.Create skills inventory and resource estimates

Project Management Key Area	Module	Functional Skills
		39.Maintain Resource Plans
	6.2 Project team Developme nt	40.Create & maintain project team Development Plans 41.Organize appropriate team building activities
7. Communicat ions Management	7.1 Communicati on Plan	42.Define overall communication plan and strategy 43.Oversee relevant project internal & external communication 44.Decide about on 'marketing" activities
	7.2 Inter-group Coordinatio n, Affected Groups	45.Co-ordinate deliverables from external groups 46.Manage and escalate issues and risks 47.Push/pull necessary information on time 48.Manage virtual teams (what works / what does not work) 49.Differentiate between appropriate working practices in a multi-vendor environment
	7.3 Reporting (Status, Dashboard, Variance Analysis, Trend Analysis, Earned Value)	50.Manage project status for overall project (understand that project control does not simply equal project reporting) 51.Establish guidelines, summaries/filters or sub-reports when appropriate 52.Understand the effects of reporting to external sources
	7.4 Project Public Relations	53.Market outside immediate area (comfort zone)
8. Change Manageme	8.1 Change Managemen	54.Define appropriate change management process (prompting of management action)

Project Management Key Area	Module	Functional Skills
nt	t	55.Decide on the level of customer involvement on project processes 56.Decide about on central vs. de-central maintenance of changes.
9. Procurem ent Managem ent	9.1 Contract	57.Structure and manage contract deliverables 58.Issue and manage contracts within matrix organizations and with suppliers 59.Consider impact of contract type for projects (DU vs. Fixed Price contracts) 60.Negotiate contracts with third party supplier/contractor
	9.2 Purchase Scenario	61.Manage purchase orders with third party
10. Other	10.1 Strategic Value Selling	62.Assess the VRB process deliverables relative to project (input, deliverables, case scenario)
	10.2 Organisatio n-al Model	63.Consider shared practices from the Community
	10.3 Business Context	64.Consider existing business plan impact on project
	10.4 Risk Managemen t	65.Avoid all kinds of Risks to the various systems (existing and those being developed).

26. LIFE CYCLE COSTING

26.1 Whole Life Costing

Life Cycle Costing (LCC) also called Whole Life Costing is a technique to establish the total cost of ownership. It is a structured approach that addresses all the elements of this cost and can be used to produce a spend profile of the product or service over its anticipated life-span. The results of an LCC analysis can be used to assist management in the decision-making process where there is a choice of options. The accuracy of LCC analysis diminishes as it projects further into the future, so it is most valuable as a comparative tool when long term assumptions apply to all the options and consequently have the same impact.

26.2 The Importance Of Life Cycle Costing (LCC)

The visible costs of any purchase represent only a small proportion of the total cost of ownership. In many departments, different areas hold the responsibility for acquisition cost and subsequent support funding and, consequently, there is little or no incentive to apply the principles of LCC to purchasing policy.

Therefore, the application of LCC does have a management implication because purchasing units are unlikely to apply the rigours of LCC analysis unless they see the benefit resulting from their efforts.

There are 4 major benefits of LCC analysis:

- Evaluation of competing options in purchasing;
- Improved awareness of total costs;
- More accurate forecasting of cost profiles; and
- Performance trade-off against cost.

26.3 Option Evaluation. LCC Techniques

The Option Evaluation LCC techniques allow evaluation of competing proposals on the basis of through life costs. LCC analysis is relevant to most service contracts and equipment purchasing decisions.

26.3.1 Improved Awareness. Application of LCC techniques provides management with an improved awareness of the factors that drive cost and the resources required by the purchase. It is important that the cost drivers are identified so that most management effort is applied to the most cost effective areas of the purchase.

Additionally, awareness of the cost drivers will also highlight areas in existing items, which would benefit from management involvement.

26.3.2 Improved Forecasting. The application of LCC techniques allows the full cost associated with a procurement to be estimated more accurately. It leads to improved decision making at all levels, for example major investment decisions, or the establishment of cost effective support policies. Additionally, LCC analysis allows more accurate forecasting of future expenditure to be applied to long-term costing assessments.

26.3.3 Performance Trade-off Against Cost. In purchasing decisions cost is not the only factor to be considered when assessing the options. There are other factors such as the overall fit against the requirement and the quality of the goods and the levels of service to be provided. LCC analysis allows for a cost trade-off to be made against the varying attributes of the purchasing options.

26.4 People Involved

The investment decision maker (typically the management board) is accountable for any decisions relating to the cost of a project or programme.

The SRO is responsible for ensuring that estimates are based on whole life costs and is assisted by the project sponsor or project manager, as appropriate, together with additional professional expertise as required.

26.5 Principles Included

The cost of ownership of an asset or service is incurred throughout its whole life and does not all occur at the point of acquisition.

In some instances the disposal cost will be negative because the item will have a resale value whilst for other procurements the disposal, termination or replacement cost is extremely high and must be taken into account at the planning stage.

Acquisition costs are those incurred between the decision to proceed with the procurement and the entry of the goods or services to operational use Operational costs are those incurred during the operational life of the asset or service End life costs are those associated with the disposal, termination or replacement of the asset or service. In the case of assets, disposal cost can be negative because the asset has a resale value.

A purchasing decision normally commits the user to over 95 per cent of the through-life costs. There is very little scope to change the cost of ownership after the item has been delivered.

The principles of LCC can be applied to both complex and simple projects though a more developed approach would be taken for say a large PFI project than a straightforward equipment purchase.

26.6 The Process

LCC involves identifying the individual costs relating to the procurement of the product or service. These can be either "one-off" or "recurring" costs. It is important to appreciate the difference between these cost groupings because one-off costs are sunk once the acquisition is made whereas recurring costs are time dependent and continue to be incurred throughout the life of the product or service. Furthermore, recurring costs can increase with time for example through increased maintenance costs as equipment ages.

The types of costs incurred will vary according to the goods or services being acquired, some examples are given below.

Examples of one-off costs include:

- Procurement;

- Implementation and acceptance;
- Initial training;
- Documentation;
- Facilities;
- Transition from incumbent supplier(s);
- Changes to business processes.

Examples of recurring costs include:

- Retraining;
- Operating costs;
- Service charges;
- Contract and supplier management costs;
- Changing volumes;
- Cost of changes;
- Downtime/non-availability;
- Maintenance and repair; and
- Transportation and handling.

26.7 The Methodology of LCC

LCC is based on the premise that to arrive at meaningful purchasing decisions full account must be taken of each available option. All significant expenditure of resources, which is likely to arise as a result of any decision, must be addressed. Explicit consideration must be given to all relevant costs for each of the options from initial consideration through to disposal.

The degree sophistication of LCC will vary according to the complexity of the gods or services to be procured. The cost of collecting necessary data can be considerable, and where the same items are procured frequently a cost database can be developed.

The following fundamental concepts are common to all applications of LCC:

- Cost breakdown structure;
- Cost estimating;
- Discounting; and inflation.

26.8 Cost Breakdown Structure (CBS)

CBS is central to LCC analysis. It will vary in complexity depending on the purchasing decision. Its aim is to identify all the relevant cost elements and it must have well defined boundaries to avoid omission or duplication.

Whatever the complexity any CBS should have the following basic characteristics:

- It must include all cost elements that are relevant to the option under consideration including internal costs;
- Each cost element must be well defined so that all involved have a clear understanding of what is to be included in that element;
- Each cost element should be identifiable with a significant level of activity or major item of equipment or software;
- The cost breakdown should be structured in such a way as to allow analysis of specific areas. For example, the purchaser might need to compare spares costs for each option; these costs should therefore be identified within the structure;
- The CBS should be compatible, through cross-indexing, with the management accounting procedures used in collecting costs. This will allow costs to be fed directly to the LCC analysis;
- For programmes with subcontractors, these costs should have separate cost categories to allow close control and monitoring;
- The CBS should be designed to allow different levels of data within various cost categories. For example, the analyst may wish to examine in considerable detail the operator manpower cost whilst only roughly estimating the maintenance manpower contribution. The CBS should be sufficiently flexible to allow cost allocation both horizontally and vertically.

26.9 Cost Estimating

Having produced a CBS, it is necessary to calculate the costs of each category. These are determined by one of the following methods as described below.

Known factors or rates are inputs to the LCC analysis, which have a known accuracy. For example, if the Unit Production Cost and quantity are known, then the Procurement Cost can be calculated. Equally, if costs of different grades of staff and the numbers employed delivering the service are known, the staff cost of service delivery can be calculated.

Cost Estimating Relationships (CERs) are derived from historical or empirical data. For example, if experience had shown that for similar items the cost of Initial Spares was 20 per cent of the UPC, this could be used as a CER for the new purchase. CERs can become very complex but, in general, the simpler the relationship the more effective the CER. The results produced by CERs must be treated with caution as incorrect relationships can lead to large LCC errors. Sources can include experience of similar procurements in-house and in other organisations. Care should be taken with historical data, particularly in rapidly changing industries such as IT where can soon become out of date.

Expert opinion, although open to debate, it is often the only method available when real data is unobtainable. When expert opinion is used in an LCC analysis it should include the assumptions and rationale that support the opinion.

26.10 Discounting

Discounting is a technique used to compare costs and benefits that occur in different time periods. It is a separate concept from inflation, and is based on the principle that, generally, people prefer to receive goods and services now rather than later. This is known as 'time preference'. This guidance does not cover the topic in great detail, as it is a procedure common to many cost appraisal methods and well understood by purchasing officers.

When comparing two or more options, a common base is necessary to ensure fair evaluation. As the present is the most suitable time reference, all future costs must be adjusted to their present value.

Discounting refers to the application of a selected discount rate such that each future cost is adjusted to present time, i.e. the time when the decision is made. Discounting reduces the impact of downstream savings and as such acts as a disincentive to improving the reliability of the product.

The procedure for discounting is straightforward and discount rates for government purchases are published in the Green Book. Discount rates used by industry will vary considerably and care must be taken when comparing LCC analyses, which are commercially prepared to ensure a common discount rate, is used.

26.11 Inflation

It is important not to confuse discounting and inflation. The Discount Rate is not the inflation rate but is the investment "premium" over and above inflation. Provided inflation for all costs is approximately equal, it is normal practice to exclude inflation effects when undertaking LCC analysis.

However, if the analysis were estimating the costs of two very different commodities with differing inflation rates, for example oil price and man-hour rates, then inflation would have to be considered. However, one should be extremely careful to avoid double counting of the effects of inflation. For example, a vendor's proposal may already include a provision for inflation and, unless this is noted, there is a strong possibility that an additional estimate for inflation might be included.

26.12 Risk Assessment

Cost estimates are made up of the base estimate (the estimated cost without any risk allowance built in) and a risk allowance (the estimated consequential cost if the key risks materialise). The risk allowance should be steadily reduced over time as the risks or their consequences are minimised through good risk management.

26.13 Sensitivity

The sensitivity of cost estimates to factors such as changes in volumes, usage etc need to be considered Optimism bias. Optimism bias is the demonstrated systematic tendency to be over-optimistic about key project parameters. In can arise in relation to:

- Capital costs;
- Works duration;
- Operating costs; and

- Under delivery of benefits.

Optimism bias needs to be assessed with care, because experience has shown that undue optimism about benefits that can be achieved in relation to risk will have a significant impact on costs. A recommended approach is to consider best and worst case scenarios, where optimism and pessimism can be balanced out. The probability of these scenarios actually happening is assessed and the expected expenditure adjusted accordingly. For more on optimism bias see the Green Book.

27. REMEMBERING THE MAIN CHANGE MANAGEMENT POINTS

27.1 Change, An Uncertain Event

A change is an uncertain event, which may have an adverse effect on the project's objectives. Using Change Management should be very effective in the quest for identifying changes throughout the project lifecycle.

Remember, Change Management is:

- Forward looking, investigating problems and how to deal with threats,
- A tool enabling communication, getting people at all levels to talk to each other and to interact,
- A no blame team culture, bringing concerns into the open where actions can be taken and plans put in place, in order to stop a change occurring.

27.2 Identification Of Risky Projects

The Change Management process commences by identifying the enterprises most important and risky projects, as these must be given priority. Change Management is essentially a method that permits the collection of knowledge and experience from those involved, in a form that facilitates the Systematic Interaction and Generic Methodology for Applications:

27.2.1 Systematic: The varied events, their assessments and the consequential risks relating to or consisting of a system. Methodical in procedures and plans, these are addressed to those involved and deliberating within the parameters of their systems development responsibilities. The results will depend on interaction.

27.2.2 Interaction: The mutual or reciprocal action which encourages those involved in the programmes and projects to communicate with each other and to work closely with a view to solving the threatening events before they impact on the development of the system. The individuals involved maintain a generic approach.

27.2.3 Generic approach: Relates and characterises the whole group of those involved in assessing the events and attacking the threatening ones, before they become risks to the development of the system. The end result being the avoidance of apparent problems, within the pre-defined users systems requirements. This is enabled by following the establish methodology.

27.2.4 Methodology: The system architects and the change management practitioners simply follow the approved body of systems development methods, rules and management procedures employed by their organisation. For practical or even ethical reasons, it must be noted that with such a philosophy, it is seldom possible to fulfil all requirements of very large organisational systems. As such, the Change Management methodology ought to be obligatory and as such it should be administered in all applications.

27.2.5 Applications: Putting to use such techniques and in applying the change management principles in the development of various applications will involve numerous and varied activities. A concrete issue in developing new applications is the problem of communication among the people involved, the motivation constantly needed for generic work, the ability to interact systematically and in using a structured systems methodology.

27.3 Management Qualities Required

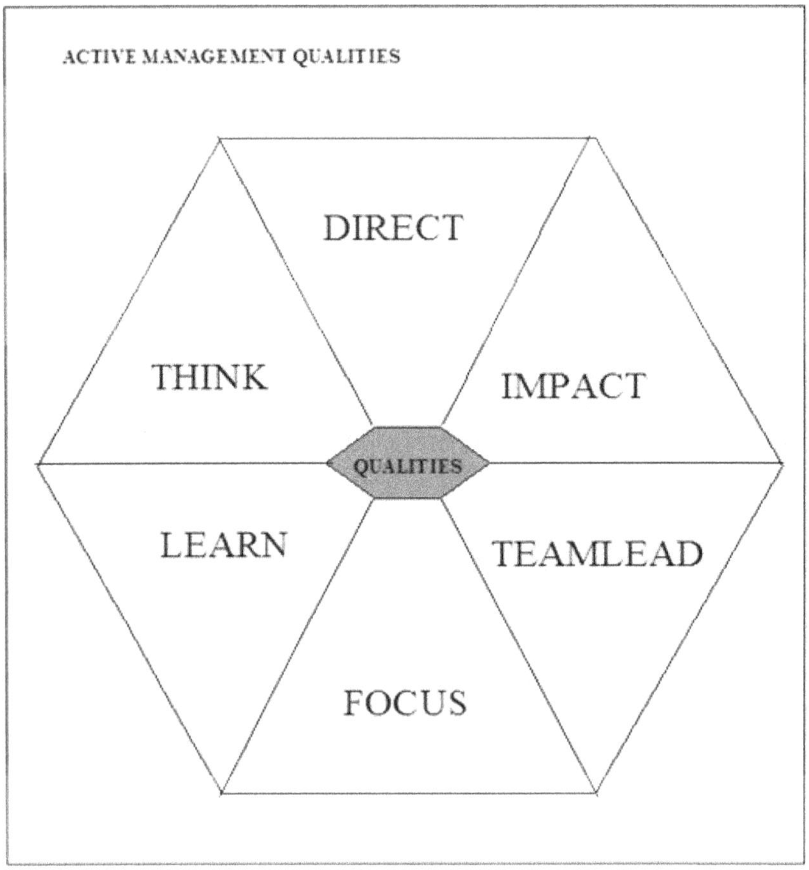

27.4 Decomposition of Management Attributes

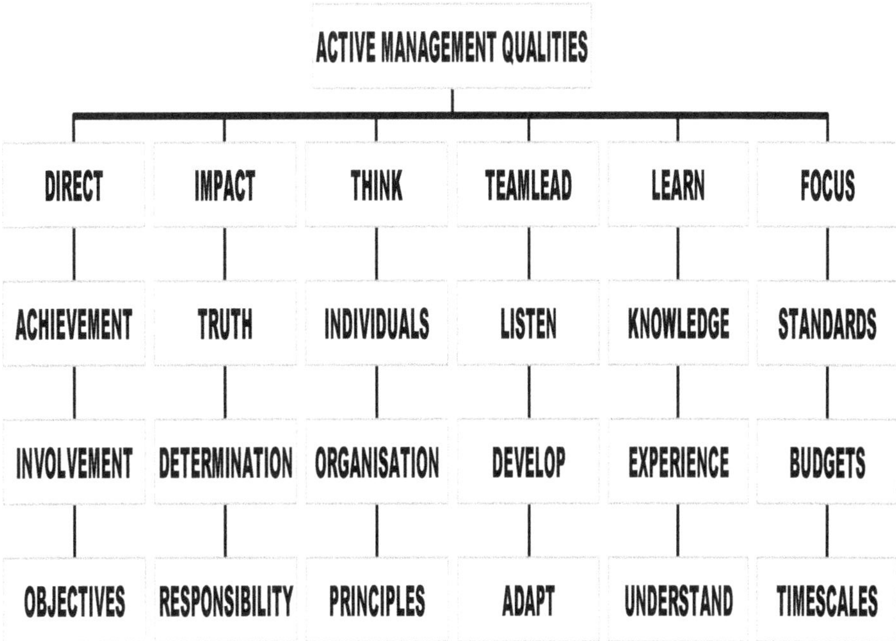

27.5 Project Management Points For Improvement

In the process of using Sigma, it will soon become apparent that probably the main cause for the threatening risks is project management, or perhaps the weakness of individual/s to manage the growth of a system.

Even if you used Sigma in its fullest, your experience will soon enable you to identify the real cause for the failure in implementing your system. In such cases, your programme/project management may need further support, assistance, training, better communicational ability and proper delegating, or even some listening to other people involved in the on-going project. Employing the expertise of a consultancy may help.

The main point is to try to reduce potential project caused loss by providing efficient *Event* driven project reviews for the critical project/s. Such project consulting steps will create and utilise virtual group of experienced project managers. As a panel of experts they will assess critical projects and provide consulting being perceived as helpful by the project team, the management and the users/clients.

27.6 Process Steps Required

For such a project consulting programme implementation, various process steps are needed:

1. Select critical project,
2. Understand project status,
3. Plan project review,
4. Create reviews agenda
5. Execute project review,
6. Implement change plan,
7. Conclude the project review.

27.7 Collection Of Information

The project manager of the project pending the review should gather the requested information from the existing project documentation. If such documentation is not available, the project manager should collect as much a as possible from verbal discussions.

Such a preparation should include details of:

1. Communication plans,
2. Project organisation plan,
3. Contacts and scopes,
4. Background and status of finances,
5. Schedules,
6. Status and history of resources plans,
7. Quality plan,
8. System documentation,
9. Brief description of the project environment,
10. Risk register prioritisation/s and other reports,
11. Last project review minutes.

27.8 Agreement On Resources

The final outcome of all communications, discussions and reviews should enable the team members to produce an agreed score on the various project management resources.

The list for such a scoring agreement should include:

1. Quality management,
2. User participation,
3. Requirements management,
4. Communications,
5. Business orientation,
6. Project team,

6. Project Team,
7. Project planning,
8. Change management,
9. Technical environment.

27.9 The Score Graph

A scoring card graph can easily be produced on a spreadsheet and it could look something like this:

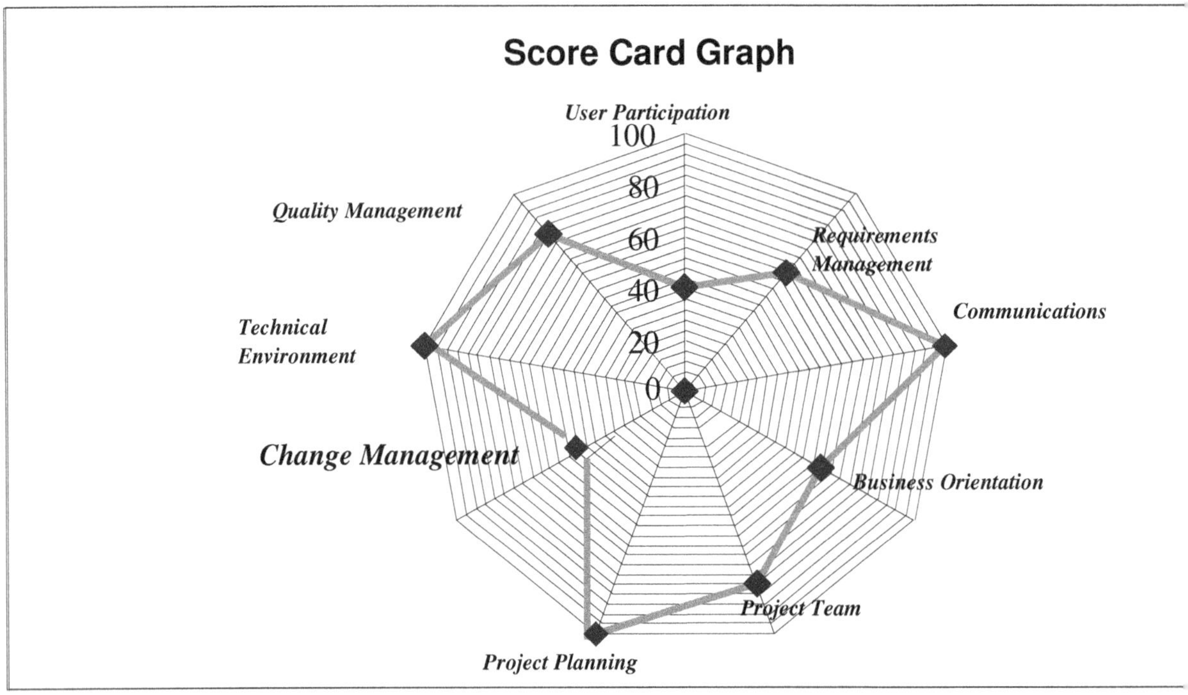

7.10 Acknowledgement

The method for the Management of Change, as explained in this book was developed by the author whilst employed by *PsySys Limited,* over a period of twenty four years. The methodology was used for PsySys' international clients, from 1980 onwards. The idea of a structured approached to organisational problems proved beneficial to clients and users who integrated the full process with other methodologies, such as Structured Systems Analysis and Designing methods, Risk management and Project Management procedures.

For the reader who wishes to use this book for training
Practitioners for Change Management In I.T.,
please note that 153 slides on the subject of
Change Management Training
are available on request.
To obtain the Microsoft PowerPoint version of these slides
please e-mail the author: mailto:sofroniou@aol.com

This will incur extra costs.

Change Management and the changes to Configuration, Release and Assets as a whole group of activities have traditionally been concerned with finding effective solutions to specific operational problems. The purpose of this book is to look at current problems and new, better methods, techniques, and tools for processing changes. In the past, it has been found that too many of the solutions are not implemented and, of those that are, too few survive the inclination of client functional areas to return to familiar ways of doing things. Therefore, Change Management personnel have gradually come to realise that their tasks should not only include solving specific problems but also designing problem-solving and implementation systems that predict and prevent future problems, identify and solve current ones, and implement and maintain these solutions under changing conditions.

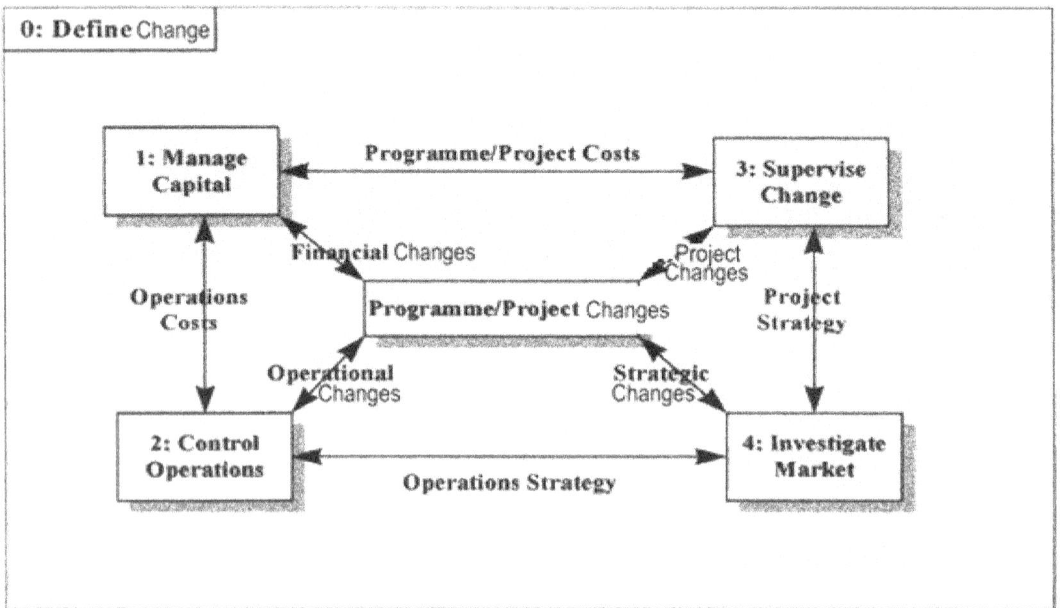

The Components Of The Total Business Changes

As an Executive in multi-national organisations and Government Departments, the author has come to realise that most problems do not arise in isolation but are part of an interacting system. The book, in principle, is seeking for a process of simultaneous interrelated solutions to a set of interdependent problems. Further more, substantial effort has been devoted in recommending a rational methodology for the management of change. This book, therefore, has been addressing the willingness to change procedures suitable to the way people are willing to work and with processes that they are familiar with.

Published by: Andreas Sofroniou,

RISK MANAGEMENT IN SYSTEMS DEVELOPMENT

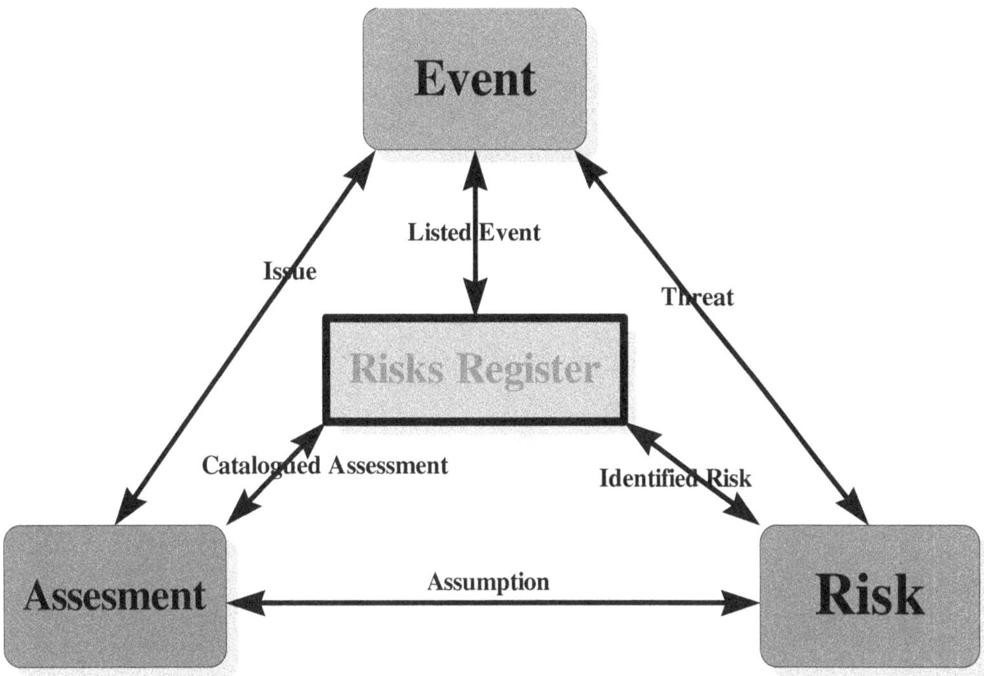

Risk Management Cycle

Andreas Sofroniou

Contents

1. Risk Management: The Concept
2. Programme Management
A. The Sigma Methodology
B. The Risk Management Cycle
C. The Integration Of Methodologies
D. The Inter-relationship
E. Managing the Risk Programme
F. Impact On Business

2. The Obligations Of A Corporation
A. Inter-dependency On I.T.
B. Internal Control
C. Staff Training

3. Risk Management Analysis
A. Assessment Of Risks
B. Communication
C. Risks Management Practice
D. The Full Risk management Cycle

4. Safeguarding Information Systems
A. Correct Software Control And Maintenance
B. Access Control And Maintenance
C. Firewalls
D. Vulnerability Assessment
E. Intrusion Detection Systems (IDS)
F. Cryptography
G. Virus Protection
H. Content Security

5. Business Related Overview

A. Business Responsibilities

B. Corporate Governance

C. Business Continuity

D. Reputation Management

E. Good Corporate Reputation

F. Preparing For A Crisis

G. Information Assurance

H. Information Availability

I. Interdependency And The Critical Information Infrastructure

J. Internet Commerce

K. World Wide Web (WWW)

L. Business Case

M. Global Networked Business

N. Implementation of a Risk Management Strategy

O. Monitoring

6. The Sigma Methodology Explained

6.1 The Programme Objectives

6.2 The Sigma Methodology

6.3 The Risk Management Cycle

A. Features And Benefits Of The Sigma Approach

Communication

Control

Information

Flexible

Acceptable

6.5 Assessment Analysis

6.6 Strategic Cost Analysis

A. Risk Administration System Tool

B. Work Plan Analysis

6.9 Communicating The Risks

6.10 How To Use The Contents Of This Book

7. The Principles Of Risk Management

A. Team Approach

•*7.2 The Definition of a Risk*

B. Approaches to Risk Management

7.4 Events And Risk Registers

A. Individual Interviews

B. Group Brainstorming

C. Risk Analysis And Quantification of Risks

D. Risk Control and Lack of Follow-Through

E. Risk Transfer

7.10 Risk Management vs. Project Management

8. Basic Principles of the Sigma Methodology

A. The Process

B. Communication Of Assessments

C. The Current Project Plan Is The Baseline

8.4 Uncertainty Equals Risk

8.5 Judging the Quality Using the Sigma Scale

D. Sigma Process Overview

E. Project Prioritisation

8.8 Risk Prioritisation

8.9 Risk Control

9. Initiating the Sigma Process

A. Organisational Culture

B. Organisational Structure and Stability

9.3 Effect Of Current Project Status

9.4 Project Fully Planned And Proceeding

9.5 Project In Trouble

9.6 Interviews With Key People

A. Choosing A Suitable Risk Assessment Team

9.8 Risk Review Meetings

10. Project Prioritisation

10.1 The Project And/Or Programme

10.2 Project Inclusion In Process

10.3 Prioritisation

10.4 The Project Prioritisation Process

10.4.1 The Standard Reference Matrix

10.4.2 Positioning and Prioritising New Projects

10.4.3 Project Approval and Resources

10.4.4 When Projects Change Position on the CC Diagram

10.4.5 Deciding which Projects Require Formal Risk Management

10.5 Risk Identification and Analysis

1 Assessment Analysis

2 10.5.2 Identify the Sources of Assessments

10.5.3 Prioritise Assessments

10.5.4 Convert Key Assessments Into Risks

1 Categorisation Of Assessments — Risk Drivers

10.6 Strategic Cost Analysis

10.7 Work Plan Analysis

10.7.1 Quality Review of Plans

10.7.2 Locate Hot Spots in the Plans

10.7.3 Project Readiness Walkthroughs

10.7.3.1 The basic objectives of a Project Readiness Walkthrough

1 The process follows a standard structure.

10.7.3.3 The project team meets and fills in their confidence levels (A-C)

10.7.3.4 The Walkthrough is scheduled
10.7.3.5 The typical participants
1 The Walkthrough starts by concentrating on the Cs
2 The Walkthrough is completed
10.7.3.8 The matrix is updated
10.7.3.9 The risks reviewed regularly
10.7.4 Pre-selected Assessments
A. Risk Prioritisation
10.8.1 Assessments and Risks Register
10.8.2 Positioning Risks
10.8.3 Risk Register Reports
10.9 Risk Control
10.9.1 Strategic Approaches
10.9.2 Tactical Approaches
10.9.3 Following Through on Actions
1 The Need for Risk Plans
10.9.5 Essential Components of a Formal Risk Plan
10.9.6 Devising Risk Plans to Attack Risks
10.9.6.1 Developing Risk Plans
10.9.6.2 Plans for Attacking Assessment Based Risks
10.9.6.3 Plans for Attacking Planning-Type Risks
10.9.6.4 Selecting Particular Risk Plans
10.9.7 Project Risk Organisation And Responsibilities
10.9.7.1 Risk Ownership and Risk Action Managers
10.9.7.2 Selecting Risk Action Managers
10.9.7.3 Selecting Risk Owners
1 The Risk Review Board

10.9.7.5 Running Risk Plans

10.9.7.6 Closing Risk Plans

10.9.7.7 Stopping a Risk Plan

10.9.7.8 Closing a Risk Plan

10.9.7.9 Configuration Control

10.10 Applying The Sigma Process - Practical Considerations

10.10.1 Project Prioritisation Considerations

10.10.1.1 Using software tools to maintain the project inventory

10.10.1.2 Assessment Analysis Considerations

10.10.1.3 Getting To The Right Assessment

10.10.1.4 Preparation For The Interview

10.10.1.5 During The Interview

10.10.1.6 At The End Of The Interview

10.10.1.7 Review Assessments And Risks Regularly

11. Transferring Ownership Of The Sigma Process

11.1 Sponsorship And Ownership

11.1.1 Identifying The Process Champions

11.1.2 Identifying The Process Owners

a) Affording Time For The Process

b) Enthusiasm And Attention To Detail

c) Access To Key Players In The Organisation

d) Avoiding The Split-up Approach

B. Hand Over Process

1. Training

2. Parallel Interviews

a) Consultant Leading Interviews

11.2.2.2 Client Leading Interviews

11.2.3 Procedures And Supporting Documentation

11.2.4 Software Tool Support

11.3 Ongoing Quality Management

11.3.1 Can they Continue To Do It Themselves?

11.3.2 Applying Sigma To The Hand Over Phase

11.4 Integrating Methodologies

12. Interfacing

12.1 The Diagrammatic Representation Of The Desired Integration

A. Suggested Interfacing

B. Using The Existing Methods

C. Connection Of Project Management To Sigma

13. Managing The Sigma Risk Programme

A. The Diagrammatic Representation Shown.

B. O: Sigma Risk Management Decomposition

C. O: Management of the Risk Programme

D. 1: Managing of the Sigma Process

E. 2: Facilitation of the Sigma Programme

F. 3: Practising the Sigma Methodology

G. Relationship Of Dataflow Diagrams and SIGMA

14 Project Management Improvement

A. Weakness In Project Management

14.2 Process Steps Required

A. Collection Of Information

B. Agreement On Resources

C. The Score Graph

15.Remembering The Main Risk Management Points

1. Risk Management: The Concept

A. Programme Management

Programme Management may have many responsibilities, but the most important of all is the ability to identify and positively execute plans to manage the risks threatening the objectives.

Through a process of structured interviews and plans the Assessment Analysis is used to highlight the specific Events which may turn into Risks. During the interviews Assessment Analysis is used to capture the key Events from the interviewees.

In turn, the Assessment Analysis provides a life-cycle process, which highlights the primary prioritisation of the risks. In large, complex and critical programmes, it is essential that a true prioritised report is available so that the imminent threats can be managed first.

The process commences by identifying the most important events which may become threats to a project. These are given priority, support and management expertise. Once the prioritisation exercise is completed, the participating people are notified and subsequently interviewed to bring out and capture any possible concerns they may have.

Within a programme, projects are prioritised to ensure that those most critical to the programme's success are given priority to scarce resources.

A. The Sigma Methodology

The Sigma methodology allows the capture of collective knowledge and expertise from those involved on the project, in a form that facilitates the communication of Events, Assessments and the pro-active management of Risks. Sigma can be applied to any type of project, or programme.

In essence, this is the mechanism by which the functions of programmes and projects are held together as a result of the principles operating within the *Sigma* methodology:

□ystematic: The varied Events, their Assessments and the consequential Risks relating to or consisting of a system. Methodical in procedures and plans, these are addressed to those involved and deliberating within the parameters of their systems development responsibilities. The results being dependable on:

Interaction: The mutual or reciprocal action which encourages those involved in the programmes and projects to communicate with each other and to work closely with a view to solving the threatening Events before they impact on the development of the system. The individuals involved maintain a -

Generic approach, which relates and characterises the whole group of those involved in assessing the Events and attacking the threatening ones before they become Risks to the development of the system. The end result being the avoidance of apparent problems within the pre-defined users systems requirements. This is enabled by following the -

Methodology: The system architects and the risk management practitioners simply follow the approved body of systems development methods, rules and management procedures employed by their organisation. For practical or even ethical reasons, it must be noted that with such a philosophy, it is seldom possible to fulfil all requirements of very large organisational systems. As such, the *Sigma* methodology is administered in -

Applications: Putting to use such techniques and in applying the Risk Management principles in the development of various *applications* will involve numerous and varied activities. A concrete issue in developing new applications is the problem of communication among the people involved, the motivation constantly needed for *generic* work, the ability to *interact systematically* and in using a structured systems *methodology*.

1.3 The Risk Management Cycle

The concept being a simple one as shown in the diagram below:

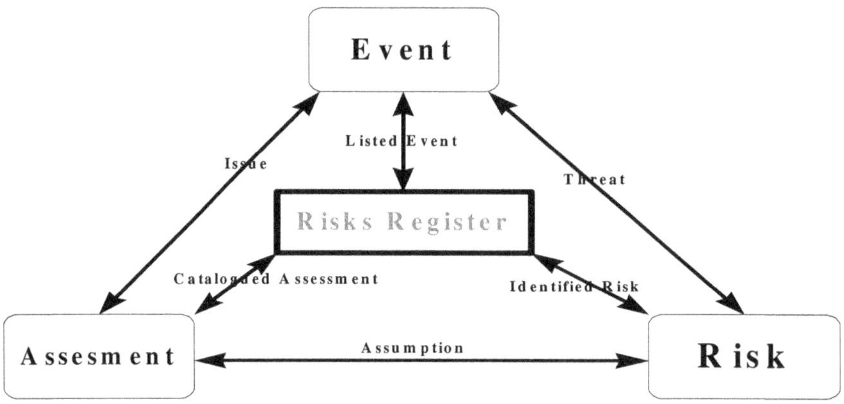

Risk Management Cycle

The *Sigma* (□ystematic Interaction and Generic Methodology for Applications) was developed by by the author whilst employed by *PsySys Limited,* over a period of some twenty years. The methodology was used for PsySys' international clients, from 1982 onwards. The idea of a structured approached to organisational problems proved beneficial to customers and users who integrated the full process with other methodologies, such as Structured Systems Analysis and Designing methods and Project Management procedures.

1.4 The Integration Of Methodologies

The comprehension of how to integrate the three methodologies can be achieved, simply by following the concept as shown on the following diagrammatic representation:

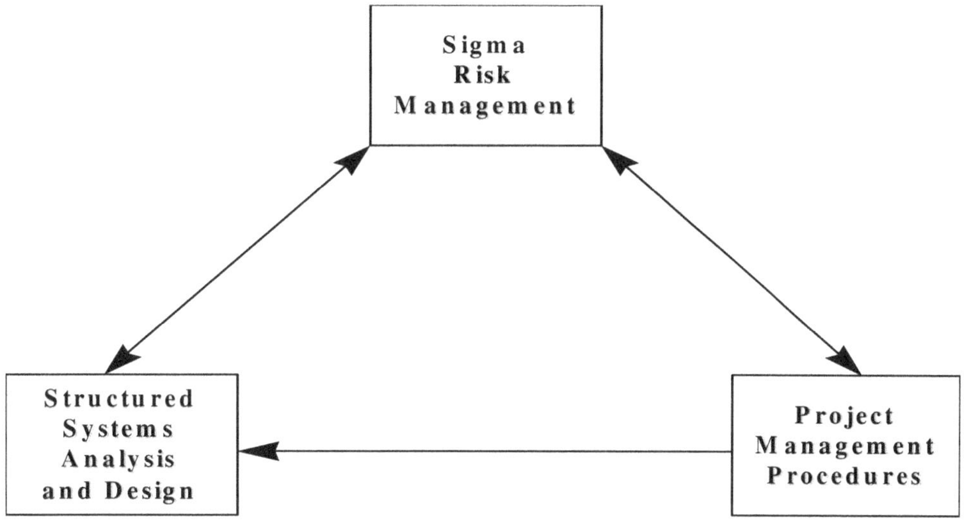

Integration Of Methodologies

1.5 The Inter-relationship

The various steps included in each of the methodologies are named in the next diagram. Or, to a further extent, the various stages of system development and the steps taken to manage projects and adopt the risk management cycle, are shown on the next page:

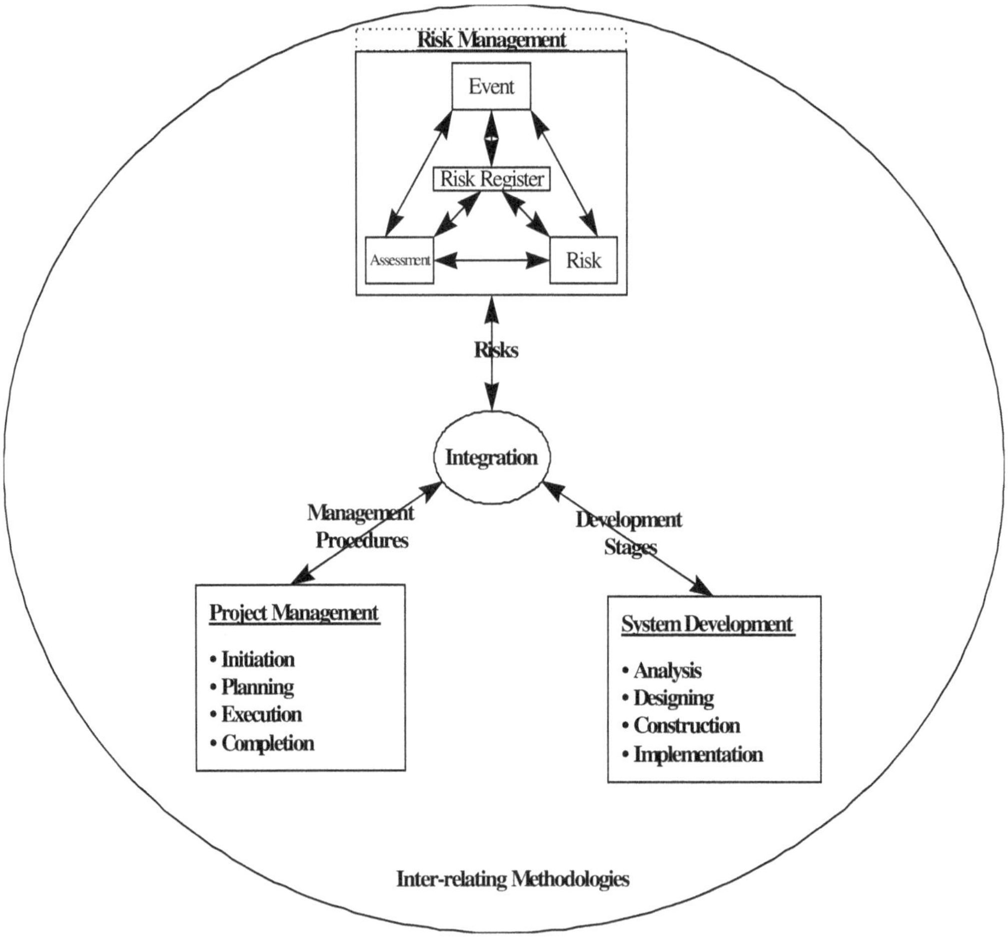

1.6 Managing the Risk Programme

It is basic business sense to identify, assess, manage and monitor risks that are significant to the fulfilment of an organisation's business objectives. In recent years businesses have been transformed by, and are in many cases heavily dependent on I.T.

The financial consequences of a breakdown in controls or a security breach are not only the loss incurred, but also the costs of recovering and preventing further failures. The impact is not only financial: it can affect adversely reputation and brand value as well as the business' performance and future potential.

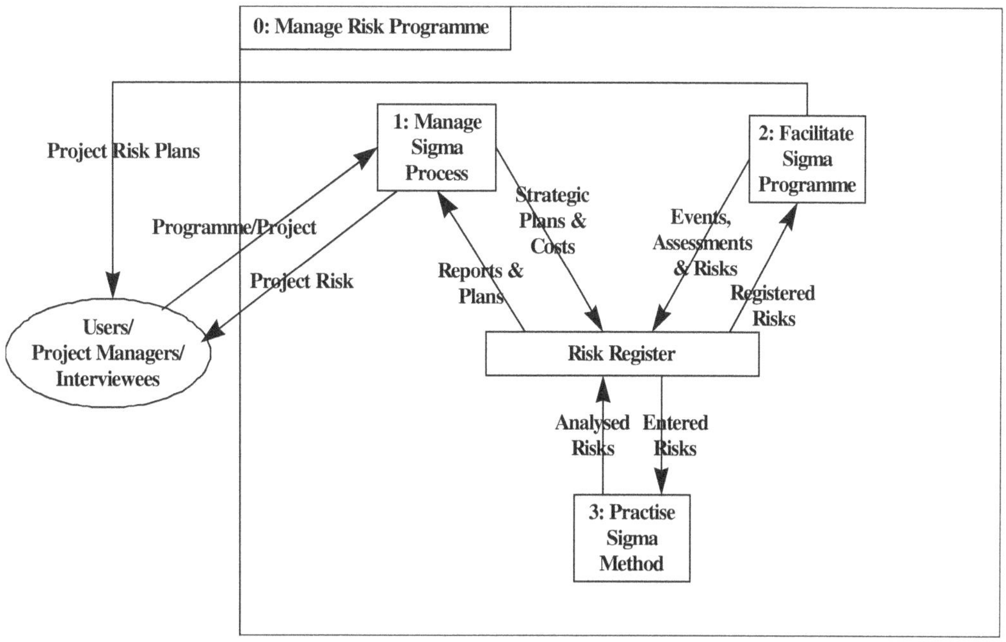

1.7 Impact On Business

Boards can regard inadequate system development as a significant risk, and where directors feel that this may be the situation in their organisations, they may need to ask tough questions of themselves and their management teams. Systems development and their risks is an issue that boards may need to recognise should regularly be on their agenda, and not delegated to I.T. technicians.

Business in the past was primarily confined to assessment of the risk surrounding fire, flood and Acts of God. In business today we have become high dependent on information systems. Failure to build computer systems as required by the users has a major impact on our business to function. The inability of companies to provide adequate systems can cause potential problems to customers, suppliers, employees and an all round havoc to information.

2. The Obligations of A Corporation

2.1 Inter-dependency On I.T.

During the last forty or so years, the governments of the industrialised countries and the global businesses have become increasingly inter-dependent on Information Technology systems, to the point where many organisations would cease to function if these systems were unavailable.

Creating a strategy to ensure business continuity is, therefore, a prime consideration and whilst we are all familiar with the threat to the operations of corporations, such as system failures, badly developed and running systems, we are less aware of the potential risks to our I.T. systems and their costly development.

In the early days of I.T. few people envisaged the level of complexity and connectivity that would be achieved by the end of last century, particularly through the explosive growth in the use of the Internet. In the last ten years the number of the individuals and organisations that are connected to each other electronically has risen exponentially, thus increasing the risks of substantial loss through internal and external threats, some of which can paralyse distributed systems.

More and more transactions and communications will be carried out electronically and therefore the conditions to create risk free systems are essential to build confidence in information, communications and technology.

2.2 Internal Control

A further complication is that organisations are now subjected to a number of new laws and requirements that add further burdens to the hard-pressed executive. Specifically, these relate to the prevention of unauthorised access to information stored about the general public and employees, as well as allowing them to access information stored about them.

Furthermore, the importance that is placed on the protection of the information base of an organisation is emphasised by the rules on corporate governance being strengthened to ensure that protecting the electronic assets is taken seriously by Senior Executives.

Compliance with all of the influences that can affect the construction of new systems in your business or organisation is best achieved by the development of a methodical risk management practice. This includes the collection of events, the cataloguing of the assessments leading to the identification of threatening risks and the plan to assist in the execution of various tasks. Thus, securing the building of the I.T. system as per target, with the least possible risks.

To achieve such standards, the following elements should be included:

1. The concept of risks planning and their control to be managed by a Risks Management Practitioner,
2. A vulnerable part of the management of risks is the Risks Management system itself and the data stored in it,
3. The risks plans as reported by the Risks Management system is, also, of a significant importance, in evaluating the events and in the execution of actions.

2.3 Staff Training

One of the greatest threats in Risk Management is the non-acceptance of it or misuse of the system by your own personnel. Obtaining their buy-in is essential. It is obvious that someone is going to be appointed to ensure that the risk management principles are adhered to and the system maintained throughout the organisation.

It is, also, important that if information leaves your organisation by its transference to others for use on your behalf, that they have adequate systems to protect to your standards. The successful implementation of your Risk Management is reliant upon people and in particular your employees whose contracts of employment may need adjustment to protect the company and the adequate management and execution of plans for the solution to the threats caused by the risks identified.

To build a complete picture of what the Risk Management cycle includes, please refer to the diagram drawn below:

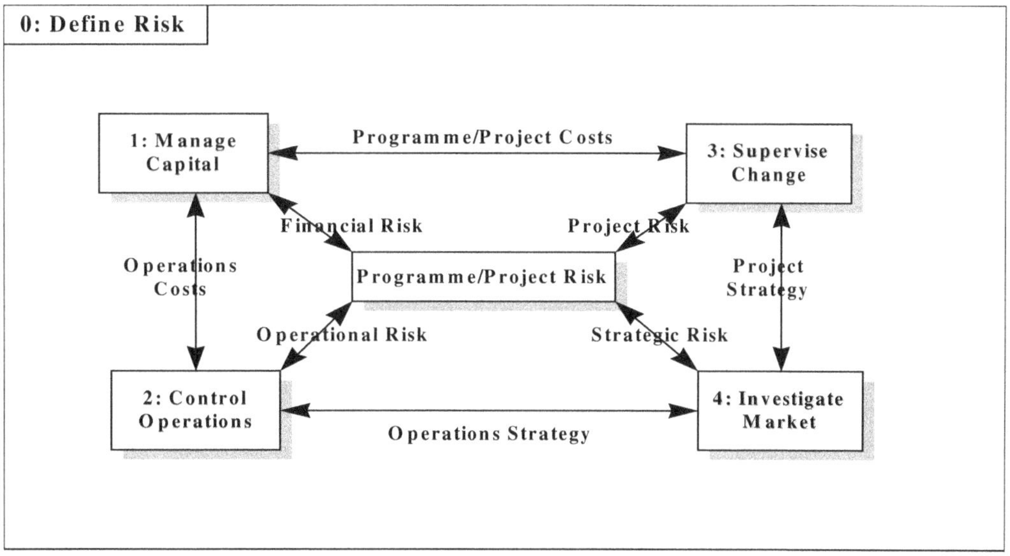

Programme/Project Risk: One Component Of The Total Business Risk.

Computer and Network Management ensure that we secure the processing facilities and generally prevent loss, modification or misuse of the Risk Management information entered on the risks systems. Computer based risks classification and control of the written risks policy allows management to have direction to control and monitor the information output by the risks system.

There are two ways in which you can approach the creation and implementation of risk management. By:

- Completing the process internally, or
- Utilising the services of external Risks Management Consultants.

3. Risk Management Analysis

3.1 Assessment Of Risks

Fundamental to the creation of a Risk Management system is the assessment of the risks (Risks Analysis) to your business and the potential loss that could accrue if things go wring. Risk Assessment software tools are available in the market, which can be used by consultants, or by internal staff. What is important is the ability to assess the risk to your business and the cost to protect it against the risk. The end result is that you have to make the valued judgement on the amount the business spends on the implementation and the monitoring of a risk policy.

Products and systems are available to counter the threats and risks that have been identified. There is a wide range of options available, but remember that anything chosen will require expertise to design and complete a system, taking into account how the various solutions will inter-react with each other. Like all things to do with I.T., the design and implementation of systems' risk solutions are only as good as the people installing them.

3.2 Communication

The most important factor in the success of any management style is the ability to communicate with each other, one to one or in groups of people. The art of communication is just as important to the whole process of the management of risks. More so where the risks identified have become a threat because of the problem of human communications.

This is where the appointment of an experienced and trained Risk Practitioner is worth the effort put into securing such individual/s.

3.3 Risks Management Practice

A trained Practitioner will have enough knowledge to run and maintain the system, as well as ample experience to be able to communicate with all levels of employees, hold meetings and ensure the plans executed.
In brief and as the diagram on the next page shows, the Practitioner will be responsible for the complete Risk Management cycle.

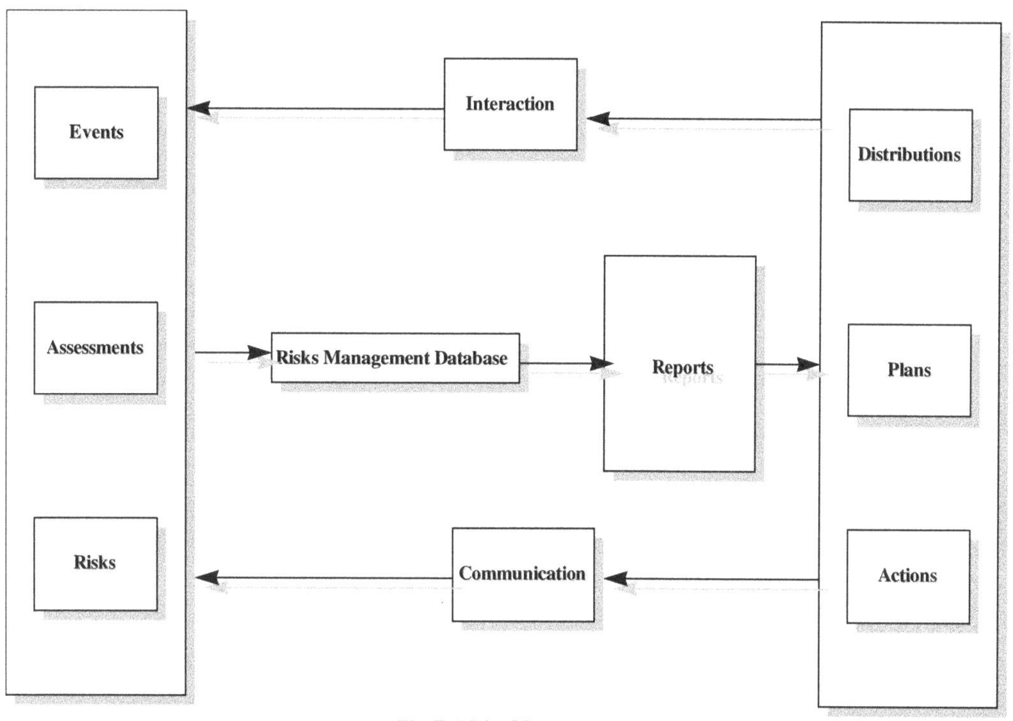

The Full Risk Management Cycle

3.4 The Full Risk management Cycle

In analysing risks, certain counter measures may have to be looked into. The mechanisms for safeguarding the construction of your information system is by managing risks and avoiding the threat of failing to build the required system.

4. Safeguarding Information Systems

4.1 Correct Software Control And Maintenance

Writing software is not a precise science and software companies are continually updating their software as information is received from users on their experiences.

They also become aware of the ways in which hackers are breaking into their systems and produce 'fixes' to prevent this happening. Regular monitoring of your suppliers' web sites and contacts with them will allow your organisation to keep up to date with the changes.

The mechanism for safeguarding your information systems include:

- The simplest and most important information security safeguard,
- Removal of known bugs,
- Updates with latest revisions,
- Secure 'back doors' into your systems.

A. Access Control And Maintenance

Access control is one of the fundamental parts of the security policy as it defines the employees, customers, suppliers or partners who are allowed to access information stored on your computer system.

Achieving the balance between security and practicality takes time and deals with people's own perception of the right to access information and their perceived position in the organisation.

The following are a few steps which will help:

- Deter hackers through use of access screens and passwords,
- Authenticate users by use of passwords and/or token,
- Protect sensitive systems by special authorisation,
- Ensure passwords are secure,
- Revoke all passwords.

4.3 Firewalls

A Firewall is a security mechanism that allows limited access to your stored information, allowing approved traffic access according to a well thought out plan. A Firewall in its normal context prevents the passage of fire for a given period, but as stated above a Firewall in computer security does not prevent access in its totality.

Your security policy will have decided the traffic that is allowed in from the outside world on to your servers where information and programmes are stored.

A Firewall:

- Should be used on any system connected to the Internet,
- Can block communications likely to cause damage,
- Must be correctly configured and constantly monitored.

4.4 Vulnerability Assessment

The analysis of a network to identify points of weakness, if done manually from scratch, is an extremely time consuming operation. Therefore, software has been developed to complete this task. Experience in understanding the results is important to ensure implementation of the right solutions to cure any weaknesses.

- Network scanning:
    - Looks at entire network from hacker's perspective,
    - Looks for poor configuration and maintenance.
- Host scanning:
    - Looks at individual systems to ensure technical standards and business needs are maintained
    - Covers software configuration, passwords and auditing on individual systems.

4.5 Intrusion Detection Systems (IDS)

Intrusion detection is the art of detecting inappropriate, incorrect or irregular activity.

There is often a distinction between misuse and intrusion detection. The term intrusion is used to describe attacks from outside, where as misuse is used to describe an attack that originates from the internal network.

The purpose of an intrusion detection system is to detect unauthorised access or misuse of a computer system.

- IDS monitor intrusions into a network and detect potential attacks:
    - Network IDS
        1. Detect attacks from outside,
        2. Must be carefully configured to avoid false alarms,
    - Host IDS
        3. Can look for unwanted 'graffiti' on web sites
        4. Can detect attempts to steal passwords and data and tamper with audit trails.

A. Cryptography

Cryptography has been used for centuries to provide a means of sending messages in code so that they mean nothing to the casual reader.

It was an obvious extension to use cryptography to secure data held on or transmitted by computers. As computers become more powerful it is necessary to increase the power of the encryption so that the codes used cannot be broken within a reasonable time scale.

Cryptography:

- Provides the most effective way of ensuring confidentiality, integrity and authentication of data,
- Should be used for secure transmission of data both internally and externally,
- Must utilise digital signatures for important electronic documents.

4.7 Virus Protection

'Virus' is used as a generic term covering any of the various forms of malicious software code that circulates freely on the Internet. Malicious code can cause immediate and obvious damage to a system, by tying up network resources or by destroying data.

Or, it can work in a more insidious way by causing cumulative deletions from, or insertion into, databases. Even more dangerously, it can open back doors into your system.

These may enable hostile outsiders to take control of parts of the network:

- Virus:
    - Covers any malicious software –whether damaging or not,
    - Circulates freely on the Internet, but can be on any floppy disc or CD,
    - Can tie up resources, destroy data, or change it subtly,
    - Can allow hostile outsiders when you have been attacked.
- Virus protection can:
    - Alert you to possible attacks,
    - Provide you with protection,
    - Give you solutions when you have been attacked.

4.8 Content Security

Content security/filtering is the management of the content of digital communications.

For legal reasons companies need to control the content of the material created, stored and forwarded on their networks. Content filtering software will permit scanning of e-mail and Internet sites for criminal, defamatory or racist material.

Such software must be carefully configured and companies should have a clear policy on its use.

The software should:

- Enable you to control the content of e-mails and Internet downloads,
- Reduce legal liability for illegal or damaging material,
- Be carefully configured and monitored,
- Enable a policy to be clear to all employees and third parties.

5. Business Related Overview

5.1 Business Responsibilities

There are now a host of legal and regulatory definitions detailing Board/Business Owner's responsibilities to ensure that information stored on computer systems, particularly with reference to people's personal information, be they employees or customers, is protected from improper access or use.

Corporate Governance defines Business Continuity and the management of the organisation's reputation as being the responsibility of the Board within public quoted companies. Compliance with the policies laid down is equally applicable to non-quoted companies, as it ensures best practice and safeguards all of our businesses. To comply, it must be shown that the risks to the organisation have been assessed and policies have been enacted to ensure that, as far as practicable, the potential for damage or loss has been reduced to realistic levels.

In the electronic age every aspect of our lives is becoming interdependent on others for computer-based transactions, especially in the business world. Around half of the interruptions to Business Continuity are now as a result of a failure in areas related to computers.

5.2 Corporate Governance

It is basic business sense to identify, assess, manage and monitor risks that are significant to the fulfilment of an organisation's business objectives. In recent years businesses have been transformed by, and are in many cases heavily dependent on I.T. The financial consequences of a breakdown in controls or a security breach are not only the loss incurred, but also the costs of recovering and preventing further failures. The impact is not only financial: it can affect adversely reputation and brand value as well as the business' performance and future potential.

Boards can regard inadequate system development as a significant risk, and where directors feel that this may be the situation in their organisations, they may need to ask tough questions of themselves and their management teams. Systems development and their risks is an issue that boards may need to recognise, should regularly be on their agenda and not delegated to I.T. technicians.

5.3 Business Continuity

Business in the past was primarily confined to assessment of the risk surrounding fire, flood and Acts of God. In business today we have become dependent on information systems. Failure to build computer systems as required by the users has a major impact on our business and how the company functions. The inability of organisations to provide adequate systems can cause potential problems to customers, suppliers, employees and an all round havoc to information.

5.4 Reputation Management

The management of a company's reputation is a vital issue for any business. It is the responsibility of directors to ensure that the issues are fully understood at board level and that time is spent putting in thorough, but flexible, plans to deal with them.

A good reputation can:

1. Put you above competition,
2. Attract better staff,
3. Attract business partners,
4. Attract investors,
5. Open doors to different markets,
6. Protect your business during a crisis.

5.5 Good Corporate Reputation

According to research carried out by MORI and Fortune magazine, the seven key aspects for a good corporate reputation are:

1. Financial performance, profitability and long term investment value,
2. The chief executive and senior management team,
3. Quality of your products and services,
4. Treatment of staff,
5. Social responsibility,
6. Customer service,
7. Ability to communicate.

5.6 Preparing For A Crisis

A crisis is an event that can damage the company, its product, service or reputation. Crises include natural disasters, man-made disasters, product recalls, sudden and serious financial problems, and closures and strikes.

Preparing for a future can appear a mundane task, but in essence is necessary for the safe-keeping of a company's reputation.

Companies should:

1. Identify and prepare a crisis management team,
2. Form a crisis management plan,
3. Remind board members that more is at stake than their own reputation.

5.7 Information Assurance

Information Assurance is becoming the term to denote the protection of information and information systems by ensuring their confidentiality, integrity and availability, as well as providing for authentication and non-repudiation.

A comprehensive strategy will assure those with whom you wish to do business electronically, that you have taken all reasonable precautions to ensure that your business is safe to connect to. In order to be able to prove that a contract exists between organisations both sides must be able to prove that the electronic communications have not been tampered with and you have to know that the person/organisation with whom you are doing business is who they say they are.

Information Assurance is the practice of developing and maintaining a secure, effective information risk management system that protects the information infrastructure as well as the data held within it. This is not merely good business practice, but for public quoted companies, a legal mandate, against which businesses must be audited.

5.8 Information Availability

Imagine a company being denied access of information (including its own) by the activity of others. This would be irritating at best, but for those that rely on time-sensitive information, it could be catastrophic. Let us face facts: today's purchasers have less and less time and patience. If they cannot reach their preferred supplier instantly, they will seek an alternative, if at all possible. So, a company's ability to provide specific, accurate information, on demand, will directly affect its success.

5.9 Interdependency And The Critical Information Infrastructure

The drive for greater efficiency in the global economy has created a situation where there is a highly sophisticated network of dependency on others and their systems, which enables us all to live and work. A failure on the system of delivery has a significant effect on the total operation.

The infrastructure interdependency, the onward march of information technology and the drive for more efficient business systems, demands an increasingly complex and sophisticated infrastructure, for the modern industrialised nation state. Systems such as transportation, power, banking, food distribution and telecommunications, to name but a few, are each crucial to a nation's well being in a highly competitive age.

Each of these systems, however, relies on some of the others for continued and efficient operation. For example, food distribution relies on transportation and telecommunications need power, conversely power needs telecommunications for the efficient control of its engineering operations. The reliance of each vital system upon one or more of its peers is known as infrastructure interdependency.

The more business driven and sophisticated a nation, the greater its vulnerability to infrastructure damage due to the compounding effects in a crisis of infrastructure interdependency. Whilst one cannot turn against the business drive for greater efficiency that enhances such vulnerabilities, it behoves governments to take an overview on infrastructure and insist on sufficient robustness to safeguard the nation, particularly in view of the potential exploitation of such weakness by terrorism and information warfare.

5.10 Internet Commerce

Internet Commerce is a key component of the Global Networked Business model, providing a company's customers and partners with end-to-end solutions to conduct business transactions and exchange of information.

As a background, probably the main driver for building the Internet Global Commerce model has been the need for continuous business improvement, leading to cost savings achieved by changes in the supply chain.

Global businesses and manufacturing techniques now ensure that the business works twenty-four hours, by seven days, by fifty-two weeks basis, which can only be effectively managed by the integration of computer systems on the equivalent global basis. The computer industry is reacting by introducing further interoperability between computer systems with the introduction of new software and bigger capacity technological devices.

Further on, the Internet, this network of networks stretches around the world and makes it possible for every computer to connect to every other computer. It is the biggest network in the world.

5.11 World Wide Web (WWW)

Often confused with the Internet, this is the most widely used means of publishing and accessing information that is stored on the computers, that are connected to the Internet.

The web allows you to link to many sites on the Internet. The basic concept is the page or collection of screens that it displays on your monitor. Within each page are links to related pages and other web sites. Each of these links is known as a hypertext link.

The web was originally used for text links only, but as it was further developed multimedia links were added. The web now contains pictures, audio and video links. With the addition of sound and graphics the web soon became the most popular way of linking to resources on the Internet.

Most organisations are worried by threats presented in using the web. Viruses are one of the main concerns, although these are unlikely to occur in normal surfing, except perhaps where Word and Excel documents are downloaded. Unauthorised access by outsiders is another.

Many organisations are also concerned about the employees wasting time surfing inappropriate web sites. To overcome this problem some companies choose to install a Content Security product that checks for ratings, profanity and legal disclaimers.

5.12 Business Case

The business case for justifying the expenditure on implementing a Risk Management system and the practising procedures to go with it in the early days of system development was more a leap of faith than a carefully evaluated financial case, and in many cases this may still be so.

Consultancy assignments and studies show that only a small percentage of organisations world-wide are taking this subject seriously. It is hoped that the information in this book will encourage you to review the Risk Management policy within your company.

5.13 Global Networked Business

A Global Networked Business is a company, of any size, whose networked infrastructure and use of technology speeds up the process of communication, and the sharing of knowledge-between prospects, customers, employees, partners and suppliers.

A Global Networked Business uses networks and information technology to:

1. Empower people to use and share information and to act more decisively,
2. Transcend traditional barriers – including geographic, financial or organisational barriers,
3. Increase responsiveness to customer needs and business opportunities,
4. Compete more effectively in the global marketplace,
5. Enables its customers, partners, employees and suppliers to access information, resources and services in ways that work best for them.

5.14 Implementation of a Risk Management Strategy

The success, or failure, surrounding a Risk Management Strategy depends almost entirely on people, those who are designing and developing it and those who are expected to implement it. If the system is designed in such a way as to be too complicated to understand and comply with, or in such a way that makes it almost impossible to do ones job, then it will be rejected by those who should implement it.

Implementation of the policy is likely to involve modification of employment contracts. Monitoring the passage of information in and out of the organisation will involve human communication as well as technological means of communicating, such as the analysis of e-mails sent by employees, which can infringe their human rights, as can monitoring which sites are accessed on the Internet.

Care in selecting those who implement the Risk Management principles can substantially influence the level of confidence attained. The programmes require parameters to be set and therefore the level of understanding of your business requirements and the software will influence policies success or otherwise.

The communication exercise to the employees is probably the most important part of the implementation. If left to the I.T. department, it may be delivered in seem-technical language or in terms of the needs of the business, rather than in terms and language to which employees can relate. Failure to allocate sufficient budgets to this area can put the success of a risk management policy in jeopardy. It is also important to remember to include training in this area as part of the employees' induction.

Adoption of a Code of Ethics can be a useful adjunct to the process, as can the use of an external communication company.

5.15 Monitoring

For reasons of corporate governance you are required to monitor the success or otherwise of your Risk Management process and to review at Senior Management/Board Level any significant shortcomings on a regular basis. It is recommended that in order to protect themselves and to ensure that the development of their systems are demonstrably risks free Senior Management should consider employing external monitoring and health check services.

Having implemented your Risk Management procedures and method of working, it is necessary to have a system review and reporting to ensure satisfactory communication among those involved and satisfactory compliance to the practice of risk management. The methodology will have been agreed during the specification and implementation process.

The review should include a list of all breaches of the system, the potential exposure because of the breach, actions taken as a result of the breach including the implications of the Risk Management.

It is the intention of this book to provide an insight into the subject of risk management together with sufficient background information to be able to enter into discussions on the subject, in order to determine the state of your policies on risk analysis. In addition to the financial and other benefits, one has also to consider the effects on the reputation of your organisation in the event that risks 'explode' into an uncontrollable situation.

6. The Sigma Methodology Explained

6.1 The Programme Objectives

It is a fact that most large, complex projects and programs fail to meet their planned objectives and as a consequence, most organisations are undertaking one or more aggressive programs at any point in time. These may fundamentally change the way the company conducts its business and failure to meet objectives on time may lead to a catastrophic loss of business.

Some projects or programmes can be chaotic at times. Objectives are evolving and plans and priorities are constantly changing. There is a temptation to accept this chaos as a necessary 'nature of the beast'. However, it is essential to move the programme forward in a traditional project management way by making sure that objectives and plans move forward.

Once we have clear objectives and plans, programme managers must control two fundamental factors if they are to be successful:

1. The business plan must be clearly identified,
2. The implementation of the program must be made explicit.

This can be answered by isolating the fundamental cause of most, if not all major project problems. It can be argued that projects only fail due to two fundamental reasons:

1. The plans are proven to be incorrect,
2. The significance of these plans are misunderstood.

The capture, analysis and communication of such assessments are, therefore, critical to the success of any project. This forms the basis of the Sigma Risk Management methodology. The Sigma method has been applied by PsySys to help many diverse organisations to deliver large, complex projects and programmes on time, to budget and in meeting the expectations of demanding users.

6.2 The Sigma Methodology

The focus of the ystematic Interaction and Generic Methodology for Applications (*Sigma*) is based on he capture and analysis of the critical events and their assessments within the project plans, processes and procedures.

The *Sigma* methodology is essentially a framework process that allows the capture of collective knowledge and viewpoints from those involved on the project, in a form that facilitates communication of events, assessments and ensures the pro-active management of risks. This is accomplished by dramatically improving communications, risks are avoided or managed to the optimum and project objectives are delivered on time.

In essence, this is the mechanism by which the functions of programmes and projects are held together as a result of the principles operating within the *Sigma* methodology:

Systematic: The varied events, their assessments and the consequential risks relating to or consisting of a system. Methodical in procedures and plans, these are addressed to those involved and deliberating within the parameters of their systems development responsibilities. The results being dependable on:

Interaction: The mutual or reciprocal action which encourages those involved in the programmes and projects to communicate with each other and to work closely with a view to solving the threatening events before they impact on the development of the system. The individuals involved maintain a:

Generic approach, which relates and characterises the whole group of those involved in assessing the events and attacking the threatening ones before they become risks to the development of the system. The end result being the avoidance of apparent problems within the pre-defined users systems requirements. This is enabled by following the:

Methodology: The system architects and the risk management practitioners simply follow the approved body of systems development methods, rules and management procedures employed by their organisation. For practical or even ethical reasons, it must be noted that with such a philosophy, it is seldom possible to fulfil all requirements of very large organisational systems. As such, the *Sigma* methodology is administered in:

Applications: Putting to use such techniques and in applying the risk management principles in the development of various *applications* will involve numerous and varied activities. A concrete issue in developing new applications is the problem of communication among the people involved, the motivation constantly needed for *generic* work, the ability to *interact systematically* and in using a structured systems *methodology*.

A. The Risk Management Cycle

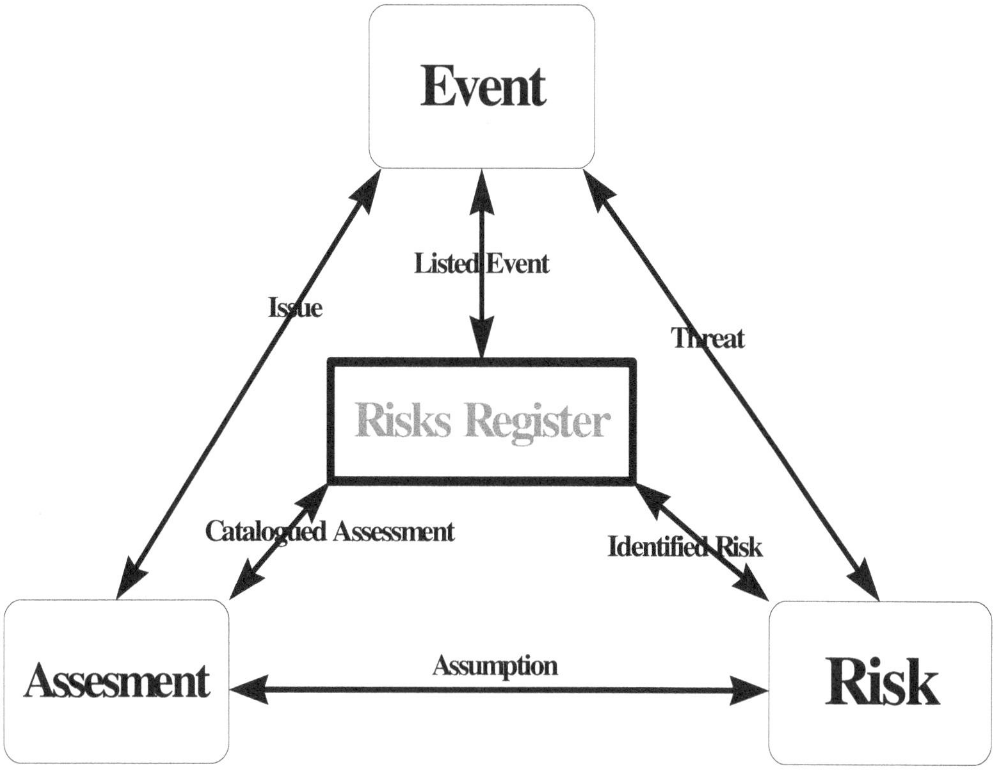

Risk Management Cycle

6.4 Features And Benefits Of The Sigma Approach

The key features and benefits of the PsySys approach are:

- *Communication* — Provides a simple, common, language for the communication of risk up, down and sideways within the organisation, whilst avoiding the normal problems of political sensitivity and risk aversion.
- *Control* — Enhances project control by exception management and achieves an overview of risk at senior management levels.
- *Information* — Encourages the sharing of risk information, establishing common objectives, discouraging risk transfer and hence reducing the overall risk to all involved parties.
- *Flexible* — An adaptable process which is rigorously applied to ensure that all significant risks are identified and controlled at the appropriate time.

- *Acceptable* — The non-intrusive/non-bureaucratic management process improves management discipline across the organization and is readily accepted by project teams.

6.5 Assessment Analysis

The core of *Sigma* is the Assessment Analysis. This uses structured techniques to analyse project plans and identify the most sensitive events that are potentially unstable, and therefore the source of greatest risk.

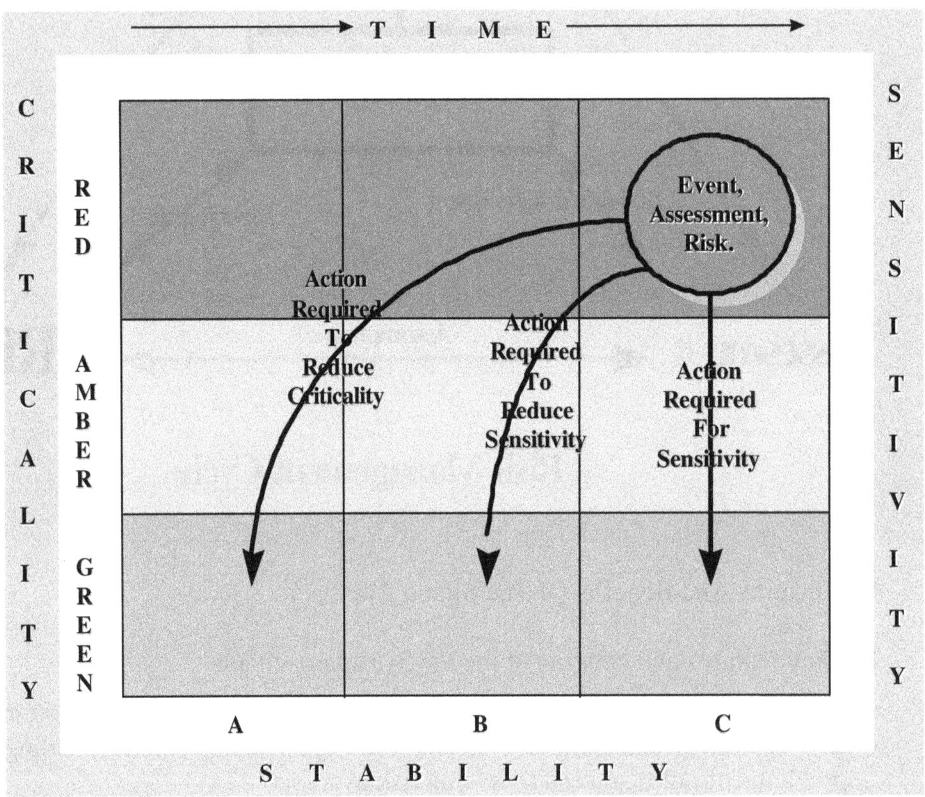

Project Criticality, Stability and Sensitivity: Measures To Be Taken To Reduce The Risk Impact

Everything is rated on a GAR principle: G̲reen, A̲mber and R̲ed scale; where G is always "good" and R is always "bad". This provides an instantly understood assessment on each stage: Events, Assessments and Risks in relationship with the time scales as used in the plans. This, effectively, provides guidance on how best to attack the risk.

6.6 Strategic Cost Analysis

Costing is a process within *Sigma* that can be used to define the cost of risk within a project or business area from as early as the proposal stage. It works by adding a 'quality' dimension to the estimating process so that high quality estimates, based on relevant experience, are treated differently from low quality estimates which are little more than guesses.
The output takes the form of a probability distribution diagram and a set of assessments which need to be managed in order to move the curve to the left and squeeze it (i.e. reduce the likely cost and the uncertainty).

Costing is particularly useful in the early stages of a project when the final cost of the project is subject to great uncertainty. The process has also been effectively used to define business budgets for re-structured business areas.

6.7 Risk Administration System Tool

A Microsoft Access based tool or any type of an ordinary spreadsheet can be utilised to allow the events, assessments and risks to be captured and reviewed by all stockholders in the program. In this way risks that would have been missed
are captured through the identification of events.

6.8 Work Plan Analysis

Work Plan Analysis is a set of techniques that enables a rapid risk assessment to be undertaken on a complex project which is already in progress.

It is always difficult to focus on the right areas when the project organisation is large and the plans are extensive and likely to be multi-levelled. Using Work Plan Analysis, the 'poor quality' areas of a project are quickly highlighted for further investigation.

One very successful application of this approach has been through the use of Project Readiness Assessment Walkthroughs. These are structured review meetings held just prior to major project milestones or deliverables. Initially the project team explain their self-evaluation of the project status and are questioned by an independent review team. Potential risks arising are captured using the Assessment Analysis process.

6.9 Communicating The Risks

The Sigma techniques summarised above will only deliver its full benefits to any business if a suitable governance structure is quickly established to communicate the risk information and set suitable actions to mitigate the risks. The mapping of the process onto an organisation is the key step to ensuring that the investment in the *Sigma* process is fully realised.

6.10 How To Use The Contents Of This Book

The level of treatment of the material in this book assumes that the reader has already understood the principles already explained. With this in mind, the author attempts to explain the:

- Basic principles of risk management and contrasts the more traditional approaches with the theories that underpin the thinking behind the Sigma process,
- Practicalities of launching a Sigma process into a new project and/or organisation,
- Theory of Sigma and includes some of the practical considerations of applying the popular approaches of Project Prioritisation and Assessment Analysis,
- Process of transferring ownership and embedding the method into the client's organisation.

7. The Principles of Risk Management

7.1 Team Approach

An enterprise must escape from a culture based on transfer of risk between parties, to a team approach that is focused on attacking the real source of the risks. Methods must be effective without the need for detailed, time consuming analysis.

•*7.2 The Definition of a Risk*

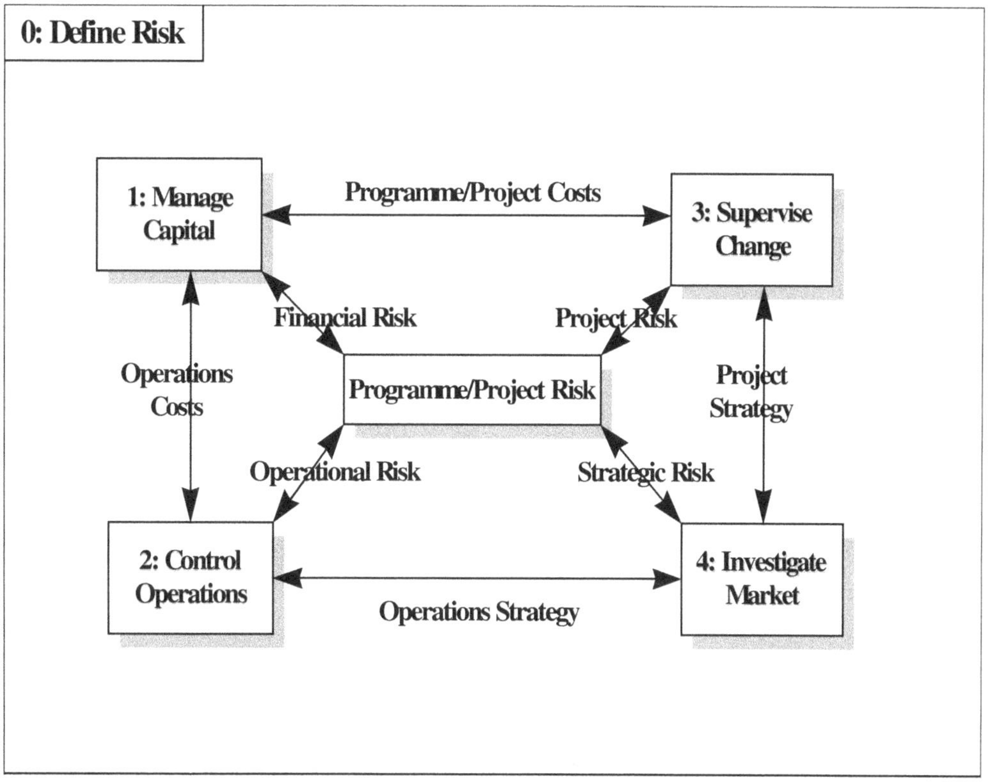

Programme/Project Risk: One Component Of The Total Business Risk.

A risk may be perceived as a possible loss. Risk is individual to a person or organisation because - what is perceived by one individual as a major risk may be perceived by another as a minor risk.

A risk is linked very strongly with competitiveness. Each decision has the possibility of resulting in loss. Each decision to introduce a new product into the marketplace can result in varying degrees of loss or gain. To be entrepreneurial is to accept risk, that is, the possibility of loss. A good entrepreneur's strength, however, is to make decisions which maximise possible gain. Hence minimise possible loss, which constitutes effective risk management.

Risk is inherent in all aspect of an organisation and may be viewed from four primary directions: financial, operational, programme/project and portfolio/products. Many risks are related to the running of the operations and its processes but is often in trying to change operations that the greatest risk is experienced. It is the management of risk in such 'change' projects that the Sigma methodology addresses.

A project can be described in its simplest terms as: Planning to achieve specific objectives and then executing the plans. The emphasis is on the word 'plan' as without a plan we have no project. So in the context of a project, a risk is something which might disrupt the plans such that the objectives of the project are not met. The discipline of Project Risk Management is thus a framework of techniques which allows the project manager to pro-actively identify and manage risks before they develop into problems which will impact the project plans.

7.3 Approaches to Risk Management

In recent years we have seen large projects in many areas of business suffering from a lack of control. The size of cost and time over-runs do not seem to be decreasing, despite the amount of management time which is being dedicated to analysing and quantifying the potential problems and selecting suitable personnel and processes. One may conclude that management, either do not have the correct methods and tools in place to attack the potential problems, or that they are not using, or do not understand, those which they do have.

In the early 1970's, the concepts of formal project risk management began to emerge. Hailed as the saviour of project managers, in practice the results have been mixed. Risk management has proved highly effective in certain mature industries - e.g. the Petrochemical or construction industry where project managers can base their estimates on years of similar engineering experience. Difficulties seem to be encountered when these traditional Risk Management methods are applied to innovative and fast evolving areas such as Information Technology.

7.4 Events And Risk Registers

Most projects will have an Events Register and some may have what they call a Risk Register. In effect, this tends to be a list into which anyone can input their concerns. It will contain references to current problems, questions, and assessments, difficult activities about which there is reasonable confidence and the odd real risk.

In any large project the Events or Risk Register quickly becomes swamped with items that require very different actions and many which do not require any action at all. All this leads to an inevitable loss of focus. Further, the content tends to be biased towards current problems rather than future potential problems.

7.5 Individual Interviews

One-on-one interviews can be an effective way of capturing risks. When people are not inhibited by management and peers, they tend to be far more open about their concerns. Unfortunately, most use very unsophisticated approaches such as "what do you see as your risks?" or "what keeps you awake at night?" Thus, if the person being interviewed is sensitive to discussing risks it may prevent the capture of any valuable information. At best the risks captured will tend to lack structure as they are not focused onto the future objectives that the project plans to achieve.

7.6 Group Brainstorming

Can be a very effective technique for opening up a very complex situation. However, information can be subconsciously suppressed by peer pressure, which may bias the discussion on one area at the expense of the rest of the project. Inevitably the mass of information captured is often difficult to focus, prioritise and allocate ownership.

In general, it should be remembered that the quality of the output is only as good as the quality of the input data.

7.7 Risk Analysis And Quantification of Risks

Risks may be difficult to capture reliably and concisely but further problems are likely to be experienced when trying to analyse them. Virtually all approaches to risk analysis are based on estimating the factored impact of the risk. This exposure to risk is a combination of the chance (probability) of an event happening and the consequences (impact) if it does occur i.e.:

Risk Exposure = Potential Impact x Probability of Occurrence

Fundamental problems arise when individuals are required to estimate, numerically, the impact and then predict (numerically) the probability. Estimates, which are often little more than guesses, result in a single point estimate of Risk Exposure, which is then given undeserved credibility in the detailed analysis of the risk and used as the basis for many major project decisions. Also, it is often the case that part of the risk impact can be quantified but often not the major part. An example can be based on an attempt yo quantify bad publicity, quality and relationship.

Some processes add complexity by rating the impact of risks in terms of financial, time scales, quality, performance etc., which quickly become very tedious to maintain.

7.8 Risk Control and Lack of Follow-through

Many risk management systems fail due to a lack of follow-through on actions. There is a surprising tendency to identify risks and then watch them happen!

This is caused by:

- Failure to use the risk register to set appropriate action plans,
- Lack of regular updates/maintenance of the risk register,
- Absence of named owners and deadlines (lack of ownership),
- Tracking generalities rather than specifics,
- Concentrating on what can be done if the risk occurs rather than stopping the risk happening (pro-active),
- Trying to transfer the risk elsewhere, without considering the consequences.

7.9 Risk Transfer

Risk transfer often occurs because the partner who knows most about the level of risk within the enterprise (i.e. the supplier/purchaser relationship) is encouraged to transfer this to the other partner. Once accomplished, the party with the most knowledge of the risk relaxes and the most ignorant partner inherits the risk. An example of this is the Purchaser insisting on a fixed-price contract in a poorly defined contract when they know that the supplier does not understand the scope of the contract.

The supplier then has a tendency to deliver the minimum possible and obtain sign-off for everything, irrespective of quality. The effect of this type of commercial 'table-tennis' is actually to increase the level of risk within the enterprise as the real risks pile up without intervention.

What is needed is a method that identifies and encourages the attack of real risk at source. Such a method would force projects within the enterprise to become pro-active by attacking risks, rather than waiting for events to unfold and then counting the cost, as recorded in the previous month's financial returns.

7.10 Risk Management vs. Project Management

There is often a tendency to treat risk management as no more than another necessary evil of project management. Thus, it often becomes an additional administrative burden for the Project Manager and consequently does not get the quality attention to make it work effectively.

In order to make risk management work, a shift in philosophy is required. This must lead the project team to view the process not just as another component of project management, but more as the communication stabiliser that holds the project together.

8. Basic Principles of the Sigma Methodology

8.1 The Process

The *Sigma* Risk Management method described in this book aims to provide an effective means of managing risks within all types of projects. The *Sigma* process grew out of a thorough assessment of the problems often encountered in project management and the techniques of the traditional risk management approaches that have been used to try and improve the situation.

Both good and bad principles were noted and new techniques were introduced to address key deficiencies. The resulting *Sigma* risk management process has a proven track record of delivering tangible results in large projects across a diverse range of organisations.

8.2 Communication Of Assessments

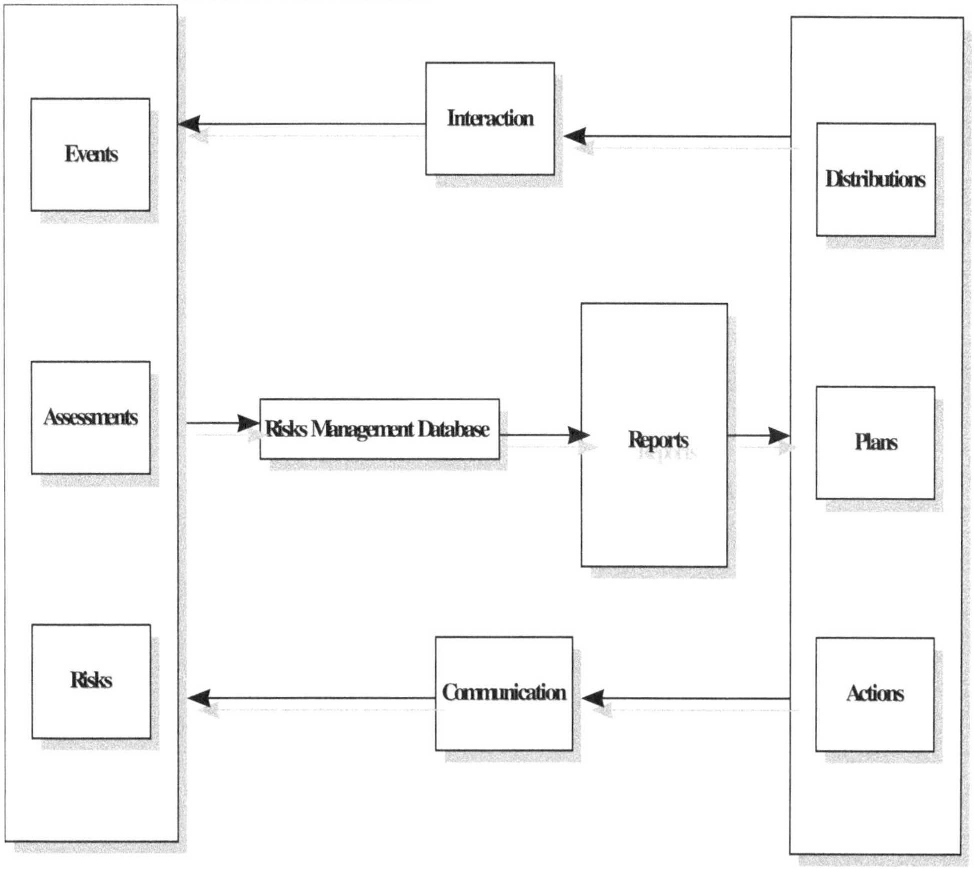

The Full Risk Management Cycle

As already highlighted, a fundamental reason for project failure is the lack of quality communications both within the project and between the programme and its environment. Most problems incurred by projects could be avoided if information was effectively communicated in a timely fashion. The problem is that there is so much information that it is difficult to decide what needs to be communicated and to who. This is where assessments come in.

Everything important associated with a project can be captured and tracked as an assessment:.

- Activities are sized on the basis of assessments,
- Milestones are set according to assessments,
- Dependencies are based on assessments,
- Plans are executed by making assessments.

Therefore, the capture, analysis and communication of assessments is critical to the success of any project, and this forms the core of the Sigma Project Risk Management process.

8.3 The Current Project Plan Is The Baseline

Risks are identified by capturing the critical assessments in the project plans are uncertain. In other words, whatever might stop the objectives, time scales and budget of the project plan being achieved. In this way, all assessments are effectively referenced to the project plans. Consequently, the plan provides the focus for the risk management process.

This approach keeps the risks specific, forward looking and ensures that the plan is always sufficiently detailed and up to date.

8.4 Uncertainty Equals Risk

Risk is inherent whenever there is uncertainty. The best judges of uncertainty are those who are asked to make estimates for the plans and, in most circumstances, the people who will actually have to do the work make the best estimators.

Combining this principle with the assessments captured from the project plans leads us to rate assessments for quality/uncertainty. Analysis is concentrated onto the areas of the project about which little is known and particularly the inter-dependencies that often represent the highest risk.

8.5 Judging the Quality using the *Sigma* Scale

To capture this vital information about how sure the estimator is, each estimator is asked, not only for assessments or the value of any estimate, but also, what quality he or she considers the assessment or estimate to be. This is not a judgement of the skill of the estimator. It is a self-assessment of the current quality of the basic information, upon which the project plans are based.

The *Sigma* scale is defined for multiple use throughout the process. It always means effectively the same thing i.e. A is always good and C is always bad. B expresses tendencies to the two extremes.

- A (Green) means very good, high confidence, not important
- B (Amber) means fairly good, reasonable confidence, not very important
- C (Red) means very poor, little or no confidence, critically important.

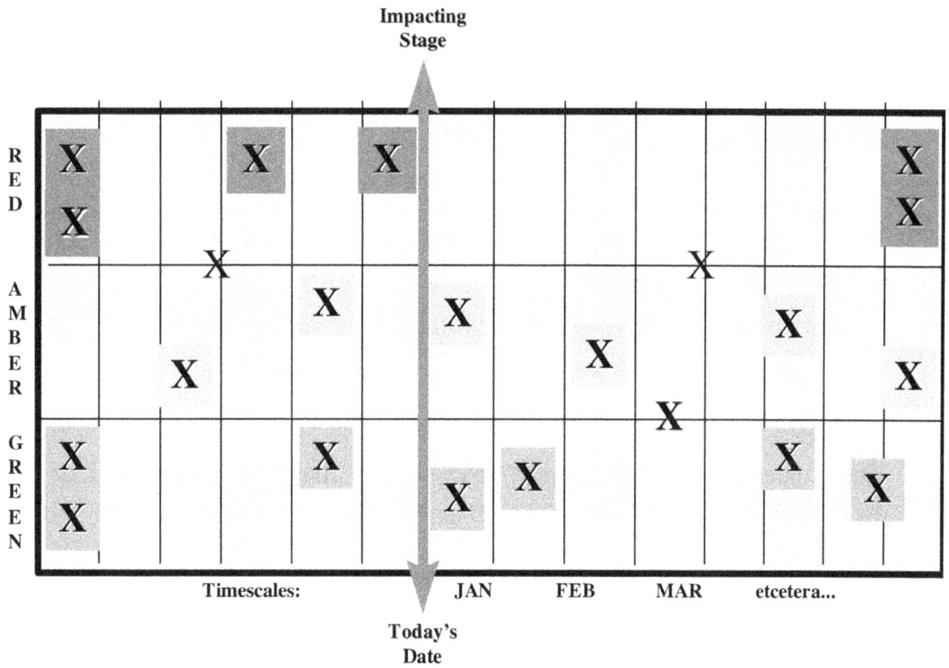

ImpactIng RIsks

It should be noted that the method does not allow the estimator to say that the estimate or assessment is of average quality. The whole principle is that we should be forced to make a choice between good, high confidence and bad, low confidence estimates and cannot 'sit on the fence'.

Using these simple A, B, C terms to express degrees of uncertainty, it is possible to encourage the estimator to reveal a wide range of uncertainty. Also, it is often possible to persuade him or her to make estimates when not normally prepared to do so. Being able to qualify an assessment or estimate with a C quality, often assures the estimators that they will not be forced into a given value or statement. We can thus gain vital information about the uncertainty and therefore the risks that may lie at the heart of the project without even asking for a risk.

8.6 *Sigma* Process Overview

The *Sigma* process consists of an integrated closed loop method, which logically progresses through:

- Project Prioritisation (for multiple project environments),
- Risk Assessment (consisting of Assessments Analysis plus Strategic Cost Analysis and/or Work Plan Analysis, if appropriate),
- Risk Prioritisation (to decide the 'order of attack'),
- Risk Control (to put the mitigation plans into action and monitor their effectiveness).

8.7 Project Prioritisation

A large organisation may have, at any one time, hundreds of projects of varying size, and nature. Yet many organisations have no formal mechanism for prioritising projects leading to problems such as:

- Not knowing which projects should be approved/resourced,
- Uncertainty as to which projects should be formally assessed for risk.Risk Assessment

Once the critical and potentially risky projects have been identified, Sigma offers three risk assessment techniques to identify and analyse the specific risks within each project.

The Assumption Analysis technique provides a backbone onto which the Strategic Cost Analysis and/or Work Plan Analysis approaches can be built.

In this respect Assumption Analysis would always be applied, Strategic Cost Analysis would be used in the early stages of a project or proposal to address the uncertainty in the cost/pricing of the project and Work Plan Analysis may be used to assess a very complex project which is well progressed.

8.8 Risk Prioritisation

The specific risks captured from each project risk assessment needs to be prioritised in order to allocate resources and decide the order in which the risks should be addressed.

Sigma provides a simple framework which rates each risk for Criticality, Controllability and Impact Timing. The resulting list of risks is captured in a Microsoft Access Risk Register (or any type of spreadsheet) and the risks are summarised in a diagram which provides an executive overview of the project risk profile.

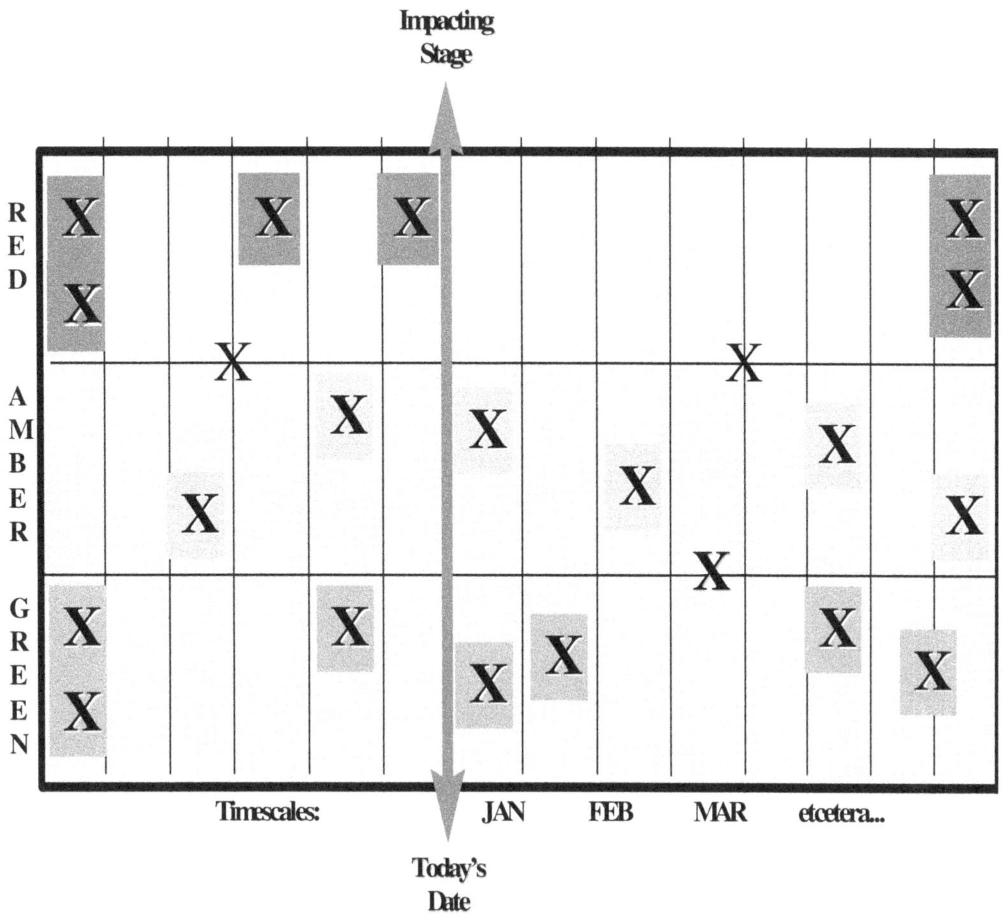

ImpactIng RIsks

The diagram shown in 8.5 is also appearing above, as this can be modified to include the list of impacting risks as reported by the Risk Register. Although this figure shows risks with the letter X, in reality, the Xs can be replaced by the actual system generated risks reports.

8.9 Risk Control

Sigma provides a framework for risk control based on taking both strategic and tactical views of attacking risks. The strategic approach is achieved by applying trend analysis to the underlying assessments to identify any strong Risk Drivers, which can be neutralised together.

Tactical approaches match the complexity of the risk action plan to the complexity of the risk to minimise bureaucracy for simple-to-manage risks, whilst maintaining the necessary formality for complex risks.

The purpose of the diagram below is to show to the reader that at a certain point of time, measures have to be taken to reduce the impact of a Critical, Unstable and/or a Sensitive event, assessment and/or risk.

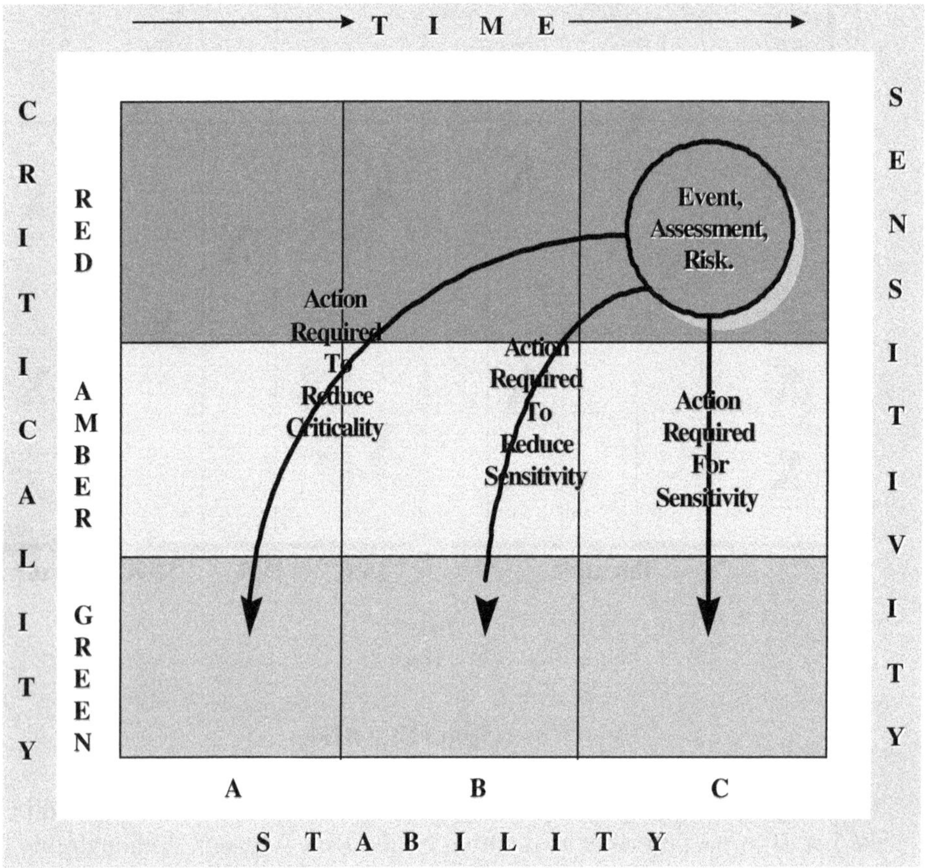

Project Criticality, Stability and Sensitivity: Measures To Be Taken To Reduce The Risk Impact

9. Initiating the Sigma Process

9.1 Organisational Culture

Some organisations are very risk aversive. This culture is often set unknowingly by senior management who suppress the open discussion of risks and create an organisation where stressing progress is the basis of management meetings. In this environment, nobody has any risks until they suddenly become problems!

In such situations, it may be necessary to re-sell the benefits of using risk management i.e. the worse thing that they can do is suppress risk, whilst the best thing that they can do is to identify risks and explain how they will be managed. Senior management need to be re-oriented from worrying about their current problems towards managing the risks within the plans that are designed to fix these problems.

If the organisation have any previous experience of using formal risk management techniques, it may be necessary to stress the particular benefits of a properly managed risk process. Effective risk management and plans:

- Provide a common, apolitical language for the communication of risks,
- Enhance project control by exception management,
- Achieve an overview of risks at senior management levels.

> The emphasis must be on fact that this method of non-intrusive, non-bureaucratic management process improves management discipline across the organisation and is readily accepted by project teams

In order to make the process work, the senior level sponsor must believe in the process and communicate with the organisation that they expect them to play a full role in the process. Buy-in must be both top-down and bottom-up.

9.2 Organisational Structure and Stability

When establishing the risk management process, the organisational structure and its stability needs to be considered.

Once the first round of risk identification interviews have been completed and the first Risk Review meeting is scheduled, it is essential to ensure that the meeting representation covers the risks being discussed and has the authority to take action. Often such actions require re-prioritisation of resources and this may mean that very senior representation is required to resolve conflicts.

The interview list and review meeting may be based on a project organisation which may change imminently. It is, therefore, always worth checking with senior level management on the likely organisational stability. If there is a re-organisation planned, do not remove people from the interview list on this basis alone. They may still provide valuable insights and certainly more than their replacement, if new to the project.

Perhaps one of the unstable environments in which to conduct a risk assessment is within a merger or acquisition scenario and it is worth noting that Sigma has proved extremely effective in this type of environment.

9.3 Effect Of Current Project Status

The stage and status of the project will have a strong bearing on the Sigma initiation process. Although all situations are unique, the following may give some helpful guidelines. Such a status may make a Strategic Cost Analysis very attractive. If there are no plans it may be difficult to undertake a full Assessment Analysis, but a high level assessment of issues or assumptions based on major milestones should be possible. Expect to identify a high proportion of risks that relate to missing or inadequate plans and resources problems. Projects just starting tend to have many events and few assessments (due to the lack of documented plans).

9.4 Project Fully Planned And Proceeding

Once the project has been substantially planned and is active, Assessment Analysis becomes the primary risk identification process. If the planning is very detailed and/or complex, some of the techniques of Work Plan Analysis may prove useful. For example, if there is a requirement to produce a first-cut of a risk register very quickly, for a rapidly approaching milestone, a Project Readiness Walkthrough would be an ideal approach.

9.5 Project In Trouble

The key aspect of a project in trouble is that it requires re-planning to put it back on track. Thus, the timing of the risk assessment relative to this planning process is very important.

If the re-planning process has not started there will be very little of the new approach to assess. It may be possible to influence this new approach by undertaking a risk assessment of the options being considered. To do this an Assumption Analysis of the alternative high-level plans can provide a useful framework for decision making.

If the project has been re-planned, then an Assessment Analysis of the new plans, possibly supplemented by Work Plan Analysis, is an appropriate way forward.

9.6 Interviews With Key People

Identifying the right people to interview is critical to producing a comprehensive and coherent picture of the risks facing a project. So, to decide on who should be interviewed, start with the project or programme organisational structure.

Depending on the scope of the risk assessment (i.e. single project, programme of multiple projects, portfolio of business projects etc.) it may be necessary to map the organisational hierarchy to ensure that the right people are interviewed and that the risks arising are reviewed at an appropriate level.

Working with the Programme or Project Manager, try to identify the 'key players'. A key player is someone within the programme/project who is likely to have either specific expertise in a particular area and/or insight into the environment in which the project is being implemented.

Key players tend to be Project Managers for a programme or Team Managers for a project with the addition of Users involved in the requirement capture and other activities. This group would likely form the initial interview list.

During the interview, these people should decide who else they need to participate. Interviewers need to exercise their judgement when evaluating the responses to this question. Typically it is necessary to go down at least one level below the Project/Team manager unless the team size is small.

One of the key features of the Sigma process is that of obtaining counter viewpoints within the organisation. Thus, the more people that are interviewed, the better. However, if many projects are being assessed for risk within an organisation, resource constraints will inevitably lead to reducing the interview pool. Under these circumstances at least two counter viewpoints must be obtained within each project. (e.g.: business manager and technical manager) so that the assessment ratings can be compared.

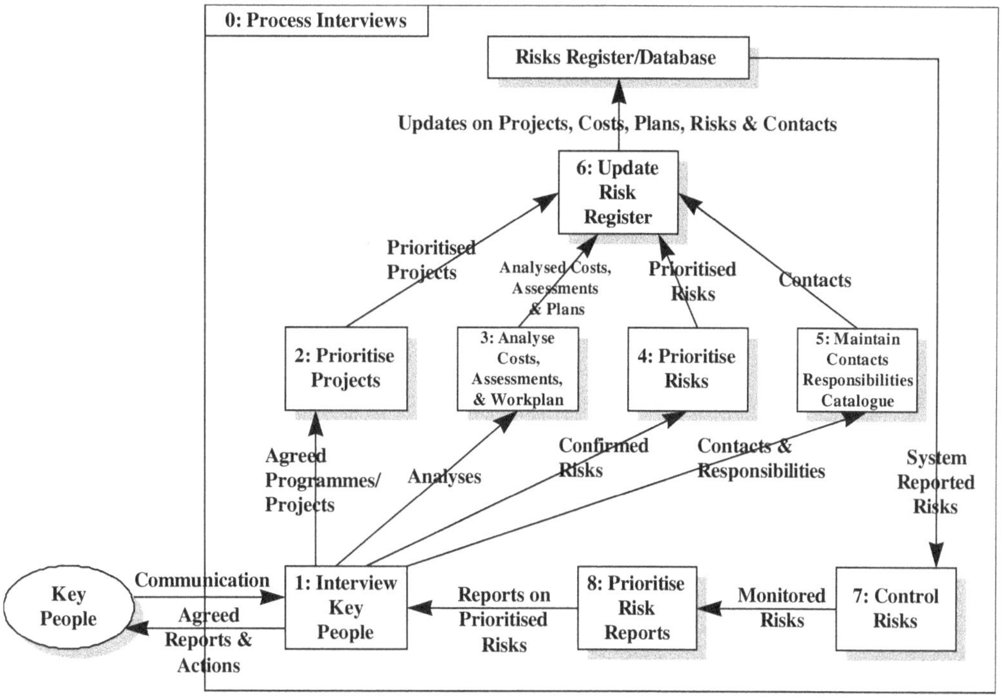

The Interviewing Process

9.7 Choosing A Suitable Risk Assessment Team

The team that will operate and manage the Sigma process requires a particular set of skills and background to be successful:

- Experience of working in large (preferably non-consulting) projects and managing (preferably) medium sized projects (say 10-20 people).
- Understanding of project planning principles and some exposure to associated tools.
- Forceful personalities to ensure quality data captures in difficult client situations.

- IT background, in order to understand the issues in IT projects and to help with using the Sigma support tools.
- Some understanding of the clients business.

Note that it can sometimes be a disadvantage to have too much knowledge of the clients business in applying the Sigma process. This is because there may be a tendency for the interviewer to get into too much detail in non-risky areas and take too much of the client's time in the process.

9.8 Risk Review Meetings

After the initial round of interviews, a suitable forum must be established to discuss the risks identified. The client may suggest that the risks are discussed as part of the regular project meeting. This should be resisted unless the risks are an early agenda item and there will be sufficient time to get through the agenda with this additional discussion.

Typically, a minimum of an hour will be required for discussion of the risks - all if possible but just the most critical if not. If discussion of the risks is left to the end there will often be little time (or concentration) left to do the process justice. Also, it is likely that some events will end up being discussed twice. If discussed first, the risks tend to focus the meeting and get away from talking about progress onto the things that need to be discussed - i.e. what threatens the success of the project.

The best method is to establish a specific Risk Review Meeting with a representation consisting of the Risk Owners and chaired by the Programme Director, or the process 'champion' in the client organisation.

10. Project Prioritisation

10.1 The Project And/Or Programme

Only complex and critical projects need to have a fully structured risk management process in place.

A project is the controlled change of an enterprise. Projects are defined as having their own project plans and can be clearly distinguished from other projects (as opposed to being part of another identified project). For example, a rollout of a major system to individual countries with a specific plan for each country would only be identified as individual projects at a country level if they were effectively independent of each other.

The terms 'project' and 'programme' tend to be used very loosely. Sometimes the terms are used interchangeably or a programme is considered to be a large project. The definition preferred here is that a programme is a collection of inter-dependent projects.

From a risk management viewpoint the structure is important as it will dictate who is interviewed and where the key dependencies are likely to be. In addition, there may be a requirement to set up a multi-level risk management system where the project risks feed up into a programme risk register where there is a programme wide impact or the risk needs to be managed at the programme level.

10.2 Project Inclusion In Process

Basic criteria are required to decide which projects should be included in the project prioritisation process. Such criteria may be developed to suit the organisation but guidelines would include:

- Size and duration of project (i.e must be big enough to use significant resources for a significant period),
- Projects agreed by the business sponsor responsible for their implementation,
- Projects managed by the department/organisation and making use of their resources,
- Projects not managed by the department/organisation, but making use of their resources.

10.3 Prioritisation

The objective of prioritising projects is to ensure that the right projects have the appropriate resources and that appropriate management attention is paid to the most complex and critical projects. These projects are inherently risky, and in most cases will require a formal risk management process to support the other project management disciplines.

Therefore, there is a need for a process which:

- Produces a prioritised and agreed project inventory that can be used when allocating resources to projects,
- Helps management to focus attention on the critical projects which are inherently risky,
- Highlights the projects which require formal risk management to guarantee timely delivery.

Project Size. An objective scale where A, B, and C are ranges of cost which are set by the business areas. The project is allocated to a cost range based on the anticipated total development and implementation costs over the life of the project.

Example, criteria could be:

- C = More than ten equivalent resources,
- B = Five to ten equivalent resources,
- A = One to five equivalent resources.

Technical Complexity. How advanced or unknown are the engineering techniques which are needed to design and build the solution.

- C = Highly complex, new technology, or scale never attempted before,
- B= Some degree of complexity, some experience of proposed technology or manageable scale,
- A = Straightforward, familiar technology, small implementation.

Business Complexity. Many functions, areas of the business are involved in the project or impacted by the project.

- C = Global system/involves many parts of the customer's business
- B = Multi department/user groups
- A = Single department/user group

Note that these scales are examples and must be re-defined to reflect the business objectives of the organisation under review.

10.4 The Project Prioritisation Process

10.4.1 The Standard Reference Matrix

In order to help refine the appropriate positioning of projects, each business area must identify two or three current key projects with which management are familiar. After agreement between the senior client and supplier managers, these will be positioned to make up a standard reference matrix. This matrix will then be used as the baseline.

10.4.2 Positioning and Prioritising New Projects

Initial positioning of the new project should be undertaken by the supplier and client project managers, together, as early as possible in the project. Complete consensus is not always possible at this stage, due to incomplete understanding of the business and technical issues involved.

However, it is essential that consensus is reached before any approval boards, or it is clear that the project is not ready to proceed. Lack of consensus can result in biased project ratings. Too high a rating will waste resources and cause frustration within the project team due to excessive management attention. Too low a rating will result in management neglect and consequently, increased risk.

10.4.3 Project Approval and Resources

In practice, the primary factor that is taken into consideration when approving a project is the Business Criticality. There are many projects that could be undertaken and only a finite resource pool available, so only the projects that will most improve the organisation's business should be approved.

Once management endorsement has been obtained, the results of the positioning exercise should be published to the teams and senior management.

10.4.4 When Projects Change Position on the CC Diagram

Once a project has been positioned it will be subject to review at least once every phase and certainly before progressing to the next stage. The most significant event in the life of a project is likely to be if it moves within either matrix.

A project may move because it is discovered that it is more or less complex than previously thought. It may have grown or been reduced in size. It may have become more or less critical to the client's business.

If a project moves, it is indicating something about the management approach required in the future. In particular, the approach to risk management should be reviewed and projects moving towards the top-right corner of the matrix should be assessed whilst projects moving towards the bottom left corner may be dropped from the risk assessment process.

10.4.5 Deciding which Projects Require Formal Risk Management

The position of a project on the diagram is also used to determine which projects should be assessed formally for risk going forward. The threshold can be set at any appropriate level. For example, some organisations work on the principle that any project judged to be a C, on either matrix, should be assessed for risk using the Sigma process. Projects falling below this threshold are still encouraged to use a formal method for risk assessment, but it is not mandated.

10.5 Risk Identification and Analysis

Sigma uses three windows; Assessment Analysis, Strategic Cost Analysis and Work Plan Analysis, to obtain a clear view of the source of any risk.

Although it is possible to create risk by poor planning and management, an element of risk is inherent in any enterprise. The main problem is to find a method of identifying the sources of the risks in time to allow specific actions to be taken to avoid or reduce the impact.

The nature of the project risks varies with the nature of the tasks, the size and the development phase of the project. Later phases may make use of methods for identifying risk based on the project's experiences to date. In early phases, good quality information and experience is scarce. Thus, different phases and different types of risk are best looked at by using different techniques and tools.

By using all these windows over the life of a project we increase our chances of identifying the major risks which lie within the project and to understand the nature of each risk. The process ultimately allows us to represent each risk in terms of:

- The potential criticality of the risk in terms of impact on the core project objectives,
- The point in time that the risk will impact the project if unresolved,
- The likelihood of the risk occurring.

Using these three analysis techniques; Strategic Cost Analysis, Assessment Analysis and Work Plan Analysis, it is possible to generate a single list that contains all the fundamental risks to the project. This list can then be used to decide which elements represent important risks and should thus be subject to proactive Risk Management by the creation and execution of dedicated Risk Plans.

10.5.1 Assessment Analysis

Fundamentally, projects only fail due to two reasons: either the wrong assessments were made, or the significance of the assessments was not understood.

The plans for any project are based on a few facts and many assessments. If the final out turn cost and time scales are excessive, it is obvious that either the assessments were wrong, or the estimators did not understand their significance.

It is important to note that these assessments are made due to the inevitable lack of total understanding or information which is inherent, particularly in the early stages of any project. Assessments are made to allow us to proceed with the project design or plans, but if they are important and prove incorrect, they will jeopardise the success of the project. Thus low quality assessments are at the heart of the risks in a project.

Assessment Analysis is the backbone of the Sigma methodology, and as such is at the core of Strategic Cost Analysis and Work Plan Analysis. It can be used at any stage in a project. However you should start the analysis as early as possible in the project to capture open events.

10.5.2 Identify the Sources of Assessments

Assessments come from a wide range of sources. At the beginning of a project all these sources are external to the project. As the project progresses it develops its own, internal assessments, while drawing on an increasingly larger set from its interfacing business and technical systems.

Assessments are captured by interviews with the key players in a project and its interfacing environment. Detailed interviews are conducted to kick-off the process and follow-up interviews are scheduled to track the status of the assessments captured and capture assessments over the life of the project.

Assessments may be explicit and be recorded in specifications, standards, plans or regulations. Many assessments will be implicit and only revealed by detailed questioning of the interviewee. Assessments may be made by the project, interfacing projects, the organisation or, they may relate to national standards and laws within the affected countries. Most assessments are made specifically to close open events, so that plans and estimates can be made and progressed.

At the start of a project there are likely to be many open events and few assessments. However, once the planning process is underway, the event are effectively closed by the assessments being made in the plans. Consequently, a project that is under way with reasonable quality plans will have few open events, if any. But, many assessments.

10.5.3 Prioritise Assessments

Many assessments made on a project are considered to be high quality as they are based on relevant knowledge or sound experience. Other assessments are insignificant when compared with the overall project objectives. Neither of these types of assessments are likely to be the source of risks and we therefore require a method to filter out high quality or unimportant assessments, so that we can concentrate on low quality or very important cases.

This risk identification method uses the knowledge of the key players in the interviews to assess two vital parameters which we have to know about assessments.

- The Sensitivity of the project to the assessments (i.e. How much does it matter if the assessments proves incorrect),
- The Stability of those assessments. How likely are they to change during the course of the project (i.e. How confident are we that the assessmentwill prove correct).

Sensitivity:

- A: would mean that the assessment being incorrect would have a minor impact on the project.
- B: would indicate a manageable impact.

Stability:

- A: would mean that there was high confidence that the assessment will turn out to be true,
- B: would be fairly confident,
- C: would mean a total lack of confidence in the assessment (i.e. it would almost certainly be wrong.

Using this method it is possible to conduct a systematic analysis of the assessments on which a project is based. We can represent this assessment on a Sensitivity/Stability diagram.

10.5.4 Convert Key Assessments Into Risks

Assessments are identified through employing Assessments Analysis, Strategic Cost Analysis and Work Plan Analysis. Essentially, the assessments captured which are important to the project (i.e. C Sensitivity) and are considered to be unstable (i.e. C Stability), represent significant risks to the project.

These risks require action to bring them under control. The most effective way of achieving this is by raising the risks to a suitable body in the organisation who have the power to make the necessary decisions, set the actions and make sure that they are followed through.

Communicating risks to senior management groups is always difficult as they are often not familiar with the detail of the project. Subsequently, the risks need to be presented in a concise, clear way which explains what is causing the risk (and therefore indicates what needs to be done) and what would be the consequences if the risk is allowed to impact the project.

Thus assessments are converted into risks using the form:

If (the assessment proves incorrect)

Then (describe the consequences to the project or business).

It is important to express the full consequences of the risk or it may fail the "so-what", test when submitted to senior management. A good principle is to describe at least the immediate impact and the ultimate impact on the project programme or business.

An alternative representation of a risk is to leave the assessments stated in the positive and add the impact. The advantage of this is that the risk can still be expressed in a positive sense. Some people find this very important.

If the Sensitivity/Stability ratings are AA, AB, BA or BB we have an assessment which is not crucial to the project and is likely to prove correct anyway. This does not require further action at this time but it should be re-assessed at regular intervals to make sure that the quality ratings are still good.

If another combination of Sensitivity/Stability ratings are assessed (e.g. BC, AC, CB etc.) these are called potential risks. Such assessments need at least to be monitored carefully for change. Retain the data and re-assess these assessments with the originators at regular intervals to check that their status has not changed significantly.

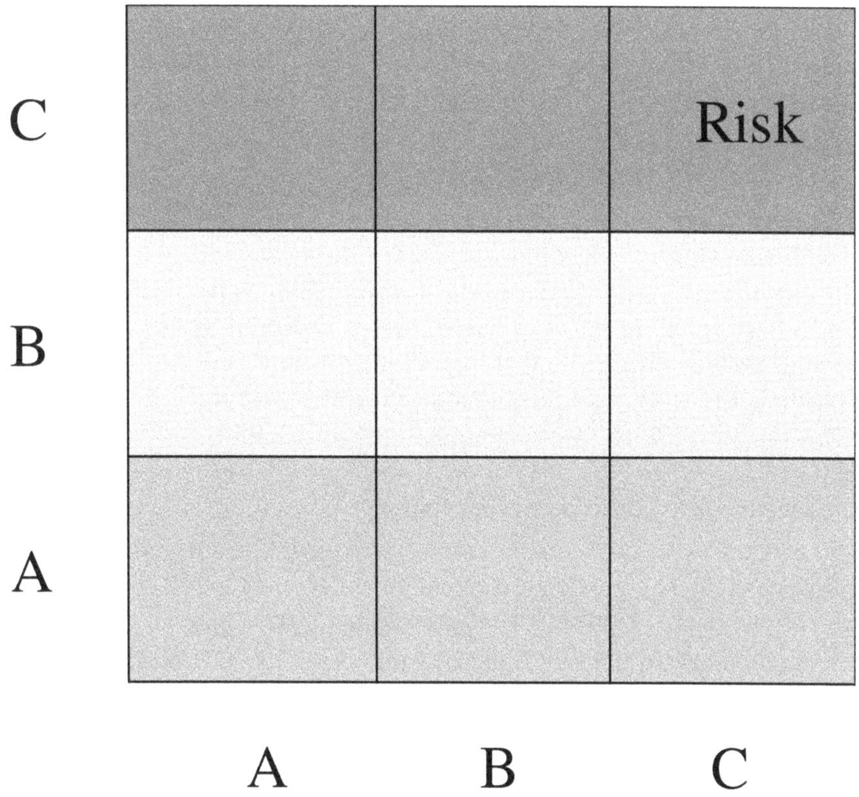

Table for Stability Sensitivity Ratings

It is important to remember that this assessment is only made at a point in time and will change as the project progresses. For this reason Assessments Analysis must be an ongoing process with regular interviews and review meetings throughout the life of the project.

10.5.5 Categorisation Of Assessments — Risk Drivers

When capturing assessments, it is often useful to identify what is driving the Sensitivity and Stability ratings allocated to it so that the source (or "driver" of the risk) is clear. This is simply achieved by categorising assessments into one of three types:

- Policy where the assessment relates to a business decision or policy, standards, resourcing priorities etc. The assessment requires management intervention to bring it under control.
- Milestone where the timescales of the activities are being 'squeezed' or timescale dependencies on other projects, suppliers etc. The assessment would be no problem if more time were available.
- Technical where the complexity of the undertaking is driving the ratings (e.g. untried design, hardware and software constraints, complex organisations etc.). The complexity is such that mistakes are likely irrespective of the time available.

Categorising assessments in this way can make the selection of appropriate Risk Plans easier by ensuring that the true source of the risk is addressed. Further, it can allow a strategic view of the risks to be obtained but only when a statistically large number of risks are being tracked.

10.6 Strategic Cost Analysis

Strategic Cost Analysis provides a means of assessing the cost risk in a project in its very early stages and commences the risk management process.

Strategic Cost Analysis is a process within Sigma which can be used to define the cost of a risk within a project or business area. It works by adding a 'quality' dimension to the estimating process so that high quality estimates, based on relevant experience, are treated differently from low quality estimates which are little more than guesses.

The output takes the form of a probability distribution diagram and a set of assessments which need to be managed in order to move the curve to the left and squeeze it (i.e. reduce the likely cost and the uncertainty).

Strategic Cost Analysis is particularly useful in the early stages of a project when the final cost of the project is subject to great uncertainty. The process has also been effectively used to define business budgets for re-structured business areas.

Its main aim is to highlight the possible range of final project cost, set contingencies, suggest a suitable Risk Budget and identify the fundamental uncertainties in the form of open events and critical assessments which can be converted into statements of risks.

The output of a Strategic Cost Analysis is a range of final project costs, the degree of risk in the project and open issues or assumptions that are linked to the poor quality estimates.

The main steps in performing Strategic Cost Analysis are to:

- Break up the project into modules and allocate ownership,
- Estimate time and/or cost of each module with the owner and attach quality ratings,
- Use a software tool to process the data,
- Analyse the results.

In essence the shape of the curve is dictated by the uncertainties (risks) in the cost estimates. Conversely, by managing these specific risks the curve can be compressed, increasing the certainty in the final project cost.

10.7 Work Plan Analysis

Work Plan Analysis may be used to focus on the risky areas of detailed, multi-level project plans when time is of the essence.

The final window for viewing potential risks to a project is through the detailed analysis of project work programmes and plans.

Work Plan Analysis is a set of techniques, which enables a rapid risk assessment to be undertaken on a complex project which is already in progress.

It is always difficult to focus on the right areas when the project organisation is large and the plans are extensive and likely to be multi-levelled. Using Work Plan Analysis, the poor quality areas of a project are quickly highlighted for further investigation.

One very successful application of Work Plan Analysis has been the use of Project Readiness Assessment Walkthroughs. These are structured review meetings held just prior to major project milestones or deliverables. Same kind of walkthroughs as used in structured systems analysis and design. Initially, the project team explain their self-evaluation of the project status and are questioned by an independent review team. Potential risks arising are captured using the assessments analysis process.

10.7.1 Quality Review of Plans

One would normally expect high quality detailed plans to be available for the current and next stage of the project, with the quality and detail decreasing progressively into the future. Thus the high level (Level 0 and Level 1) plans should normally be well defined with the definition becoming progressively lesser accuracy at the lower levels.

Remember that a high level of detail is not always equivalent to quality. It is possible to produce very detailed plans that are based on very poor quality assessments.

If the analysis of the plans shows areas of poor quality or incomplete planning in the current phase or at the higher levels, it is likely to indicate the presence of risks. These should be investigated for their root causes using Assessment Analysis.

An overview like this can be produced by using a dedicated checklist which is specific to the type of project being discussed. However, it can often be achieved by self-assessment from a number of the project's key players.

Further high-level views of potential project risks can be obtained from conducting a Contingency Analysis and/or a Time scale Risk Analysis using project management software packages.

10.7.2 Locate Hot Spots in the Plans

While project management packages are effective in producing likely cost profiles of the type produced by Strategic Cost Analysis, they are not very effective at identifying specific underlying risks within the project.

Skilled analysis of plans will reveal sensitive areas, which cannot be avoided. These Hot Spots may occur because of sensitive or multiple inputs to work packages, because of resource conflicts between packages, or through the difficulty of getting the output of the packages genuinely approved and agreed or multiple output which all rely on the completion of one work package.

The assessments in such areas of the plans may be analysed. Once identified as risks, the *If/Then* statement should be used to express the source and possible consequences.

10.7.3 Project Readiness Walkthroughs

Project Readiness Walkthroughs are a highly effective way of ensuring that all risks have been captured from the assessments analysis process. When used independently from, or prior to, an Assessments Analysis, the walkthrough provides a start to the risk assessment process which is particularly useful when time is short.

10.7.3.1 The basic objectives of a Project Readiness Walkthrough are:

- Assess the readiness to meet milestones for high-priority projects,
- Identify any corporate resource contention that may exist, and assist with prioritisation,
- Identify common events and risks, and communicate information to support other project teams,

- Help project teams achieve their goals by identifying and/or providing resources for assistance as needed,
- Assess enterprise-wide risk through the evaluation of multiple projects.

10.7.3.3 The process follows a standard structure.

The project team are briefed and provided with a self evaluation form:

Ref.	Project Area	Pre-Milestone	Milestone	Post-Milestone
1.	Data conversion process			
2.	Data volumes/sizing			
3.	Operations changes			
4.	Systems changes			
5.	Test plans/test execution			
6.	Contingency plans			
7.	Staffing and resources			
8.	Controls and standards			
9.	Metrics and benchmarking			
10.	Training/education			
11.	Cross project communication			
12.	Customer impact			
13.	Problem reporting/escalation			

Form for Capturing Confidence Levels

10.7.3.3 The project team meets and fills in their confidence levels (A-C) against each category. The most pessimistic score is logged in each case to produce an entry matrix.

10.7.3.4 The Walkthrough is scheduled for (say) 3 hours.

10.7.3.5 The typical participants are:

- The project team (key players),
- Key players from associated projects,
- An independent review team of senior management,
- An independent facilitator,
- Secretarial support.

10.7.3.6 The Walkthrough starts by concentrating on the Cs to find out what is driving them. Appropriate assessments and risks are captured in real time.

10.7.3.7 The Walkthrough is completed by going through the As and Bs and asking for them to be (briefly) justified. Any additional assessments or risks are logged.

10.7.3.8 The matrix is updated to reflect the risks identified to produce an exit matrix.

10.7.3.9 The risks reviewed regularly and actions stated to ensure that they are brought under control.

10.7.4 Pre-selected Assessments

This is a process very similar to the Walkthroughs, where the assessment criteria are a set of pre-selected assessments. A set of high-level assessments are defined on the basis that this is what is needed for the project to be successful. These assessments are then agreed with the sponsor before undertaking short focussed interviews with as many team members as possible. In essence, the team members are asked for their opinion on the Sensitivity/Stability of each assessment.

The results are collated to show trends across the team. The strength of this approach is based on the teams perspective and not on what the reviewer assumes.

10.8 Risk Prioritisation

Prioritisation allows the Project Manager to direct limited resources at the most critical project risks.

The objective of the risk prioritisation is to identify the most significant risks out of all those which have been identified by the various analysis methods used. Once all the risks have been collected in a consolidated list or register, they should be placed in order of priority and attacked via a logical, planned programme. The problem is to decide how to place risks in an appropriate order.

10.8.1 Assessments and Risks Register

All assessments captured should be held in an Assessments Register. Only critical assessments will be converted into risks and held in a Risk Register. This is done by filtering the assessments and consolidating them into risks. All information captured will be rationalised and details of their source and consequences will be traceable.

10.8.2 Positioning Risks

The primary criteria used for prioritising risks in Sigma are:

- Criticality
- Timing
- Controllability

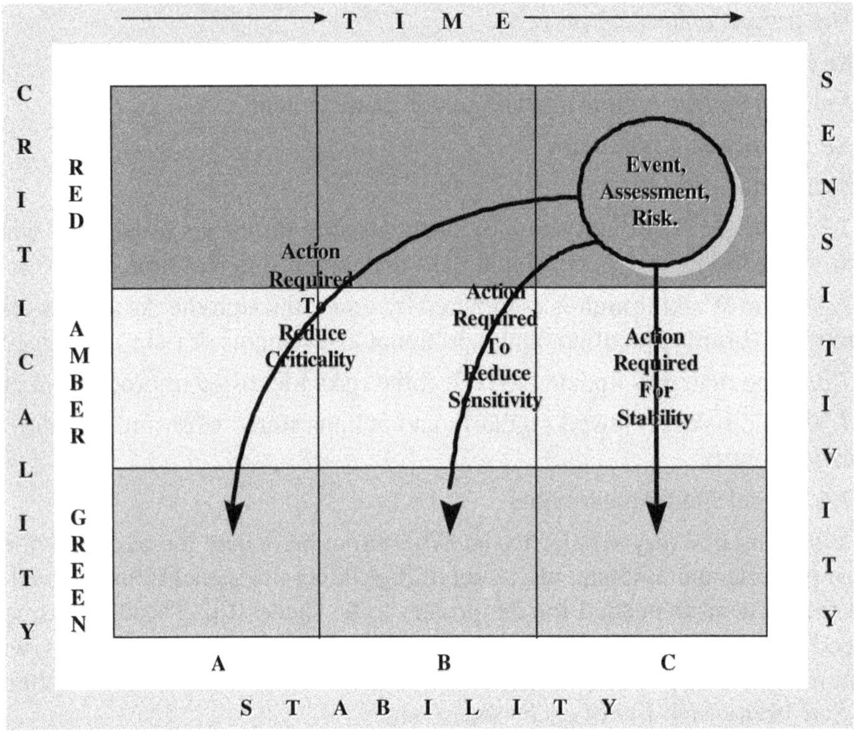

Project Criticality, Stability and Sensitivity: Measures To Be Taken To Reduce The Risk Impact

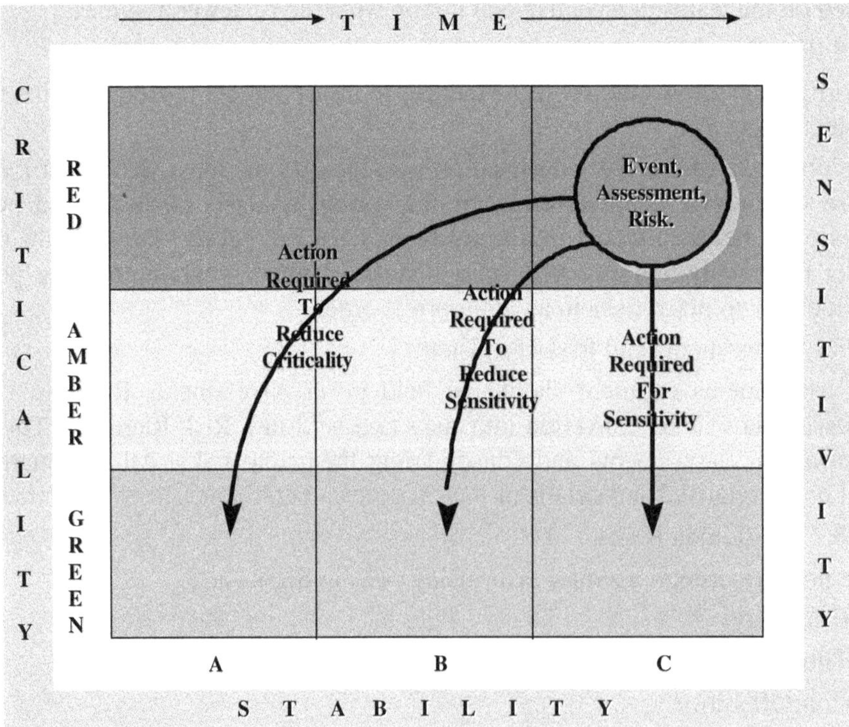

Project Criticality, Stability and Sensitivity: Measures To Be Taken To Reduce The Risk Impact

Criticality

In certain instances the risk may undermine the basic objectives of the project and no amount of money will save the project if such a risk impacts. If not resolved, the uncertainty may halt the progress of the project. Such a risk may be related to the overall programme, a part of the programme, an individual part of the design, or even a particular module of software. This, also, provides a way of representing the effect of such risks on the overall project, where cost impact is small or meaningless.

To satisfy this need a Criticality index is defined. Criticality is in effect a multi-dimensional risk impact rating. Once again, we use the assessment A, B, C. C being dangerous, while A impacts the edge of the system design or the programme. Something which may be important in itself or to one group of users or designers but will not stop progress on the rest of the project.

In most applications of Sigma, Criticality has been the primary means of prioritising risks and has been described in terms of traffic-light ratings of Red, Amber or Green. This can be very effective at concentrating on the project impacts and/or avoiding confusion with ratings of assessment Sensitivity.

Positioning in time

One of the most important things we need to know is *when* we have to do something about an event, assessment, or risk. In the case of a project we need to know when the risk will start to impact the work. Then we must determine when we have to take action to prevent it happening or to reduce its impact. The timing of a risk should always equate to the latest time to start the first necessary action. In this respect, it is analogous with trying to stop a cancer. This must be done at the point that it starts to grow, not when it can be first be seen.

Controllability

Controllability is a measure of confidence that the risk will be managed. It should not be confused with the probability of the risk occurring, which is a measure of how likely the risk is to occur if nothing is done. The controllability grade cannot normally be assigned until the risk has been reviewed and discussed by senior management, whereby an agreement is reached as to their confidence that the risk can ultimately be managed. A 'C' grade means that no risk plans are in place and no action has been taken, whereas an 'A' grade indicates that risk plans or actions are well under way with a very high confidence of success.

10.8.3 Risk Register Reports

Impact Diagrams provide an overview or risk profile of the project. However, the detail of the risks is required for the risk review meeting in order that the detail of the risks can be seen, discussed and actions taken.

The order of the risks in the report is important so that senior management can focus on the key risks first.

If the impact diagram is used to prioritise the risk register the time element can be easily included. For instance there may be an urgent AMBER criticality, C controllability risk that needs attention that is not an obvious priority if the Risk Report is prioritised by Criticality and Controllability alone.

In essence the easiest way to prioritise is to use the Impact Diagram and to treat the highest priority risk as the one nearest to the origin, the next nearest being number two and so on. The intention is to order the risks so that they are roughly in the right order.

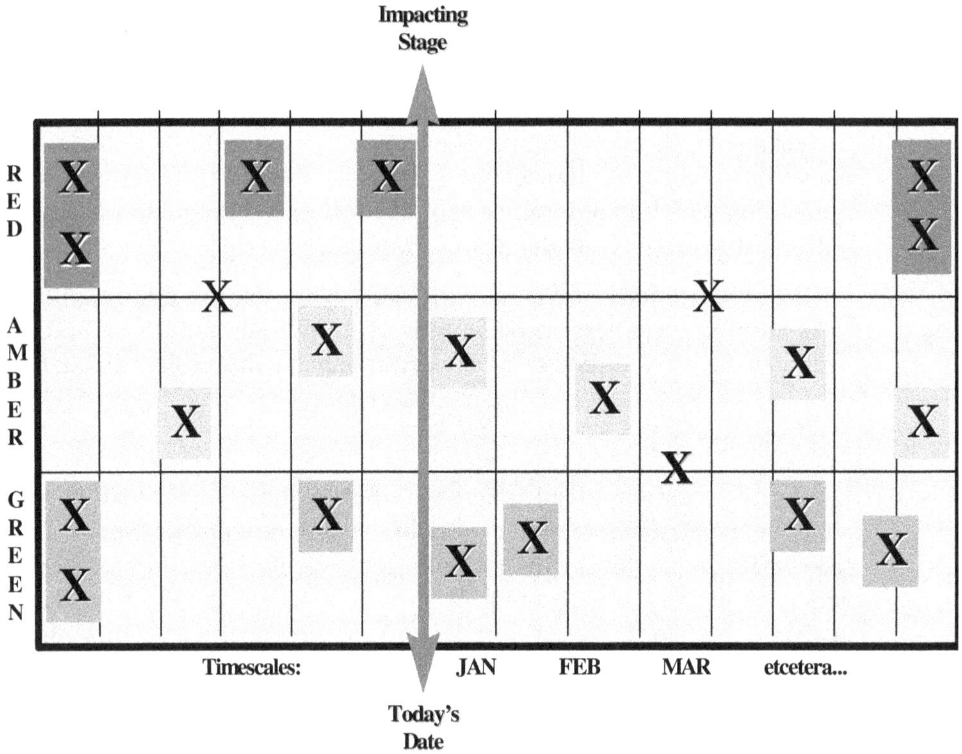

ImpactIng RIsks

10.9 Risk Control

Risks may be attacked at both the strategic and tactical levels. Strategic approaches look for trends and underlying causes for groups of risks. Tactical approaches take each risk at face value.

10.9.1 Strategic Approaches

A strategic viewpoint is achieved by using the Risk Driver approach. Each assessment and subsequent risk is categorised into Technical, Milestone, Decision or Resource to reflect what is driving the poor quality ratings:

- Technical relates to assessments of a technical or complexity nature (e.g. the pure complexity of providing an interface)

- Milestone which applies to assessments regarding timescale dependencies on other projects, or external suppliers, and can be used to identify linkages to project milestones (e.g. an activity which is not inherently complex but may not be feasible due to timescale constraints).
- Decision which is used to describe assessments which require business decisions, business policies or standards (e.g. organisational announcements).
- Resources which relate to resource deficiencies or priorities (e.g. insufficient training resources).

Note that with this categorisation, Policy has been split into Decision and Resource categories. This is necessary when the resource constraints are external to the programme/organisation. When the resource constraints are internal, a simple Policy Driver will cover this.

Categorising assessments and risks in this way identifies the main risk drivers, can simplify the identification of trends and assist in the development of appropriate risk plans.

For example, Red Decision and Resource risks are "show-stoppers" which generally require senior management action. Red Milestone risks are an indication of how tightly the programme is being "squeezed" and Red Technical risks indicate the complexity of the planned activities.

The Risk Driver chart indicates where particular effort is required. In the example below the relatively high number of Decision based risks suggests that the project is being put at risk by having to wait for decisions, probably from within the organisation. A steering committee meeting could potentially resolve most of these risks. If the project is in the early stages, it is already	Technical	Milestone	Resource	Decision	Total

showing signs that the time scales are too ambitious by the high number of milestone risks.					
Red	7	15	4	19	*45*
Amber	12	19	15	26	*72*
Green	10	6	12	12	*40*
Total	29	40	31	57	157

It is important to note that noting that the "normal" Risk Driver profile trends with the phase of the project. i.e. "Normal" would be (using relative terms):

Phase	Technical	Milestone	Resource	Decision
Start of project	Rising	Min.	Max.	Max.
Middle of project	Max.	Rising	Falling	Falling
End of project	Falling	Max.	Min.	Min.

10.9.2 Tactical Approaches

Most risks will need to be addressed specifically (i.e. one action plan for each risk) to address the underlying assessment. Assessments that are placed in the C area of the Sensitivity/Stability matrix are unreliable, represent significant risks, and it is dangerous to continue with the project without taking action. We must do at least one of two things:

- Stabilise them by escalating the assessment to senior management and obtaining agreements that increase confidence that the assessment will turn out to be true.
- Make the project less sensitive to the assessment i.e. Reduce sensitivity by redesign, re-planning or having acceptable fall-back plans in place.

The actions taken to attack the problem may be very different, depending on whether we are trying to reduce Sensitivity or Stabilise. It is normal to try to Stabilise the assessment first before trying to handle sensitivity, which is usually more difficult.

10.9.3 Following Through on Actions

Just as it is possible to introduce risk by planning a project badly, it is possible to address many risks by using normal project management methods, as long as the risk has been identified early enough.

Risks generally come from two areas activities which have not been planned adequately or planned activities which are likely to go wrong. Therefore, the first filter to apply to the risks is to identify those which can be tackled by just improving the plans. Obviously, if there is no project plan the risk is unbounded and the first action must be to create a plan.

10.9.4 The Need for Risk Plans

Risks which cannot be resolved by improved planning must be tackled individually through the use of dedicated Risk Plans. Ultimately, the plans for reducing the risks must be incorporated into the main project plans.

Risk Plans may be divided into "Simple" or "Complex", irrespective of the potential impact of the risk. Simple means that it is possible to resolve the risk quickly say by a simple phone call or single task. For such risks, monitoring the status on the Risk Report is sufficient and minimises bureaucracy. Complex risks require significant resources and time to resolve them and for these a formal Risk Plan is required.

10.9.5 Essential Components of a Formal Risk Plan

For Complex risks, it is essential that a structured plan is formulated. This will clarify thinking, provide the necessary visibility and feed directly into the main planning process:

The basic components of a Risk Plan are:

- The risk statement and its ratings,
- Risk Owner and Risk Action Manager,
- The driving statement and its ratings,
- Assessment Originator,
- Objectives of the Risk Plan i.e. Stabilise the assessment,
- Criteria i.e. how will we know when the objectives have been met,
- Risk Plan summary i.e. what are the steps to meet the objectives,
- Reference to project plans,
- Additional resources required,
- Monitoring process i.e. how often and by whom,
- Re-assessment of the driving assessment (completed after execution of the Risk Plan)
- Fall-back plans i.e. what we do if the Risk Plan fails.

10.9.6 Devising Risk Plans to Attack Risks

10.9.6.1 Developing Risk Plans

It is preferable to develop a number of alternative Risk Plans before a decision is made to implement any one of them. The analysis technique used to identify risks can be used to help understand what type of plans may be appropriate. There are no firm rules that govern the way we approach Risk Plans but, if a simple logic is followed, it becomes easier to be sure all the possible strategies have been considered.

10.9.6.2 Plans for Attacking Assessment Based Risks

Two approaches should be considered for each critical assessment:

- Stabilise the assessment to ensure that it will be right,
- Reduce Sensitivity to the assumption, and make it matter less.

It can, also, be useful to analyse the Risk Driver to understand what sort of assessment is being considered:

- Technical assessments which may relate to the complexity of the design, implementation and the technical interfaces with other systems and projects.
- Milestone assessments which are based on timing constraints and co-ordination with other projects. Appropriate Risk Plans normally result in re-planning and the addition of new milestones to the project plans to check that external deliveries will be met.
- Policy based assessments (including Decision and Resource Drivers) which are caused by the business environment, its policies and the decisions or lack of decisions. Risk Plans aimed at stabilising the a assessment are normally appropriate (e.g. gaining high-level commitment to a policy or standard).

10.9.6.3 Plans for Attacking Planning-Type Risks

A Work Plan Analysis of the project plans may reveal risks that are related to:

- Areas where the plans are of poor quality (C), where we should expect good quality,
- Areas where high probabilities that the contingencies will be used have been identified,
- Areas where large contingencies have been added.

Risk Plans addressing risks that have been identified by an analysis of the project plans often involve the same type of process as that used in main project planning:

- Detailed (re)planning of sensitive areas,
- Re-timing modules and activities,
- Re-structuring the work breakdown,
- Re-allocation of responsibilities for elements of the work within the project,
- Exporting certain elements to other agencies,
- Forming sub-projects,
- Constructing models and prototypes,
- Resolving resources,

- Special programme control procedures,
- Planning parallel activities,
- Identification of linked milestones in other projects,
- Monitoring external dependencies.

10.9.6.4 Selecting Particular Risk Plans

The selection of a particular Risk Plan is normally a simple process; as the plan which is most likely to succeed is often obvious. Occasionally it is necessary to analyse the Return On Investment (ROI) of each plan in order to make a decision.

Having generated a number of alternative Risk Plans for each important Risk, we now have the task of deciding which plan to put into operation. It will normally be obvious which of these plans should be employed first. Our own experience and judgement will be enough, in most circumstances, to choose the plan on the basis of simplicity, cost, time to implement or chance of success.

Often, some selection criteria for Risk Plans will be used before the plans are prepared and this will obviously have a bearing on the plans proposed (e.g. on a tight time scale, only plans which can be implemented quickly will be considered).

Circumstances may change, however, and it is a good idea not to limit plans to those that may be appropriate at the time of initial selection. After all, the first plan that is tried may fail.

When we consider the merits of various Risk Plans, there are a number of factors that must be assessed:

- The time available before the last action date by which the risk must be reduced to an acceptable level,
- The duration of the proposed plan,
- The cost impact of the risk, which may limit the allowable cost of the Risk Plan to produce an acceptable rate of return,
- The remoteness of the risk, which also affects the minimum acceptable rate of return required of the plan,
- The collective judgement in the project team will have to be used to assess many of these factors. However, cost and time scales factors can be approached in a more structured manner, if the choice of plan is not immediately obvious,
- When considering how much to invest in a Risk Plan it is important to know how much time is available before the risk may impact the project. If the risk is a long way away, and remote from the heart of the project, we should think very carefully before immediately implementing a Risk Plan which will expend a lot of effort.

The expected Return On Investment which may be required before the project manager sanctions a Risk Plan, tends to vary with time. Experienced project managers expect returns as high as 50 to 1 if the risk is beyond the planning horizon.

The reason for this is that:

- Any Risk Plan contains its own risk that it may fail,
- Remote risks may disappear of their own accord,
- The fact that we are aware of a remote risk may allow us time to modify our plans to avoid them, without taking any special measures,
- The risk may not be as big as it looks at long range,
- It may be wise to find out more about a risk with a modest plan before we launch the full attack,
- If a modest plan succeeds we have saved resources,
- If a modest plan fails we still have time to launch another, more aggressive, attack,
- If an expensive plan is launched and fails we may not have the time or resources to carry out a further plan,

Error! Reference source not found. Also, as a risk moves through the planning horizon - i.e. when the risk is still there after detailed plans have been developed, it is essential that suitable Risk Plans are prepared quickly to maximise the Return on Investment. Time becomes the essential decision driver.

As the risk approaches, the acceptable rate of return drops rapidly, until plans with very low Returns on Investment may have to be implemented in order to save the project. If the risk is not high Criticality, it may become more cost effective to accept the impact in terms of cost or loss of functionality, and perhaps launch a sub-project later.

However, in these circumstances, we either failed to identify the risk in time to act, or we finalised the Risk Plan too late for it to be effective.

10.9.7 Project Risk Organisation And Responsibilities

The definition of Risk Management roles and responsibilities is crucial to the success of the Risk Management process.

Each risk needs a Risk Owner and every Risk Plan must have a dedicated Risk Action Manager, to ensure that the risk is properly attacked. Each of these roles should have published responsibilities. The roles may be full or part time, as appropriate to the size complexity and criticality of the project. The individuals may be drawn from within the project team, from either the supplier or client personnel, or from an outside source, if this is appropriate or the resources are not available within the project.

10.9.7.1 Risk Ownership and Risk Action Managers

It is common practice in traditional risk management methods to assign a single Risk Action Manager/Owner for each risk. This is normally the person who knows most about the area in which the risk would impact and also actions the risk.

The main problem with this approach is that, particularly on large projects, risks stop being identified effectively as the risk Owner/Manager of a risky area becomes overloaded with Risk Plans.

To avoid this situation, it is recommended that, on all but the smallest of projects (i.e. less than 10 people in the combined supplier/client project team), separate Risk Owners and Risk Action Managers should be assigned for each risk.

The allocation of separate tasks to Risk Action Managers and Owners, whenever possible, produces a system of checks and balances.

The Risk Owner:

- Sets the overall objectives for the plan,
- Certifies that the Risk Plan selected will work,
- Certifies that progress is on schedule and that the plan has succeeded in reducing the risk.

The Risk Action Manager:

- Plans the detail,
- Applies for any necessary resources,
- Carries out the plan and ensures that time and effort is not wasted on activities not strictly associated with the specified Risk Plan.

The Risk Action Manager will tend to be, naturally, efficient at such tasks as they will be busy with their own part of the project.

Separating the Owner of the risk from the Risk Management task is thus very desirable on large projects and ensures that Risk Plans do just enough to effectively attack the risks. It relieves the Project Manager of much of the monitoring effort associated with controlling a large number of different plans and permits him or her an overview of the risks to the project and the Risk Management process.

10.9.7.2 Selecting Risk Action Managers

The choice of Risk Action Manager depends upon the task in hand. Many risks can be managed by quite junior staff. Motivated systems engineers and administrative staff can be empowered to carry out a simple plan which may have very significant effects on the project (e.g. Collecting the latest information from Policy making bodies).

Using junior staff is very cost effective, it is very good training and it can be a very effective motivator. Allocating junior staff tends to prevent the Risk Plans dominating other routine activities, and thus disrupting the rest of the project.

Risk Action Managers should be drawn from outside the project for external risks. In this case the Project Manager identifies suitable candidates, but the project Steering Committee or advisory board appoints them. One of these groups is also responsible for ensuring that any external Risk Action Managers are correctly empowered and controlled by their own line management.

10.9.7.3 Selecting Risk Owners

The choice of Risk Owner is critical to the success of a plan. A person must be chosen who is:

- Knowledgeable about the project area that the risk will impact,
- Informed about the nature of the risk,
- Motivated to see the problem solved,

- Able to see when the plan has been successful,
- Able to recommend that the plan should be stopped.

Care is required to ensure that the Risk Owner is suitably senior and first-line reports to the Project Manager are normally appropriate. This is because risks will normally be reviewed by the senior members of the project team and it is essential that all key risks can be discussed in such a forum.

It is perfectly possible to have an external Risk Owner. The only problem with this external arrangement is ensuring that there is sufficient motivation in supporting the project which will be affected by the risk.

10.9.7.4 The Risk Review Board

The focal point of the Risk Control process is the Risk Review Board. This body ensures that the roles and responsibilities are set, the risks are understood at the appropriate level in the organisation, action plans are set and followed through and the communication flows at the senior level in the organisation.

The basic terms of reference of a Risk Review Board are:

Representation

The senior managers (e.g. Project Managers in a Programme) normally form the core of this meeting. In addition any (senior) Risk Owners will be required to attend. The meeting should be chaired by the Programme/Business Director and facilitated by a Sigma Risk Management expert.

Before the meeting

The Sigma Risk Team will undertake interviews of all agreed key players to capture important and risky assessments. All data will be captured in the Risk as database from which the Risk Register and report will be produced.

The Risk Register will be circulated to all Risk Owners one day prior to the meeting. It is the responsibility of each Risk Owner to review their risks before the meeting and to make sure that they fully understand the risk, agree with the ratings and are clear about any actions underway. To achieve this it may be necessary for the Risk Owner to communicate with the Assessment Originator and/or the Risk Action Manager.

In addition, each Risk Owner should review the Assumption Register (or relevant part of it) to check agreement with other people's assessments and ratings. Any major disagreements should be raised in the Risk Review Board. Minor queries should be fed back to the Risk Team.

During the meeting

The risks will be discussed in priority order as indicated by the Impact Diagram. The process for each risk will be:

- The Risk Owner will clarify the risk briefly (if necessary),
- The meeting will endorse or change the ratings for Criticality, Controllability and Impact Timing.

- For new risks, suitable action/s will be agreed and a Risk Action Manager will be assigned to undertake the action plan.
- For existing risks, the Risk Action Manager will report on mitigation progress and when the risk is considered as resolved, the Risk Owner will agree the closure proposal. Note that the risk is not formally closed until the Assessment Originator agrees to down-rate or close the associated assessment.

At the end of the meeting there will be time to raise any urgent assessment queries and discuss them as risks, if appropriate.

After the meeting

The Risk Register and Impact Diagram will be updated from the meeting and re-issued, within one week, to all Risk Owners as a formal record of the meeting and actions agreed. Risk Action Managers are then responsible to undertake the actions agreed in the Action Status section of the Risk Register, while Risk Owners are responsible for making sure that actions are followed through in a timely fashion.

Immediately following the meeting, the Risk Team will commence the next cycle of interviews.

10.9.7.5 Running Risk Plans

Once the Risk Plan has been agreed and approved, the running of the Risk Plan should be straightforward. The plan should be followed and progress reported to the Risk Owner and Project Manager against time and the resources expended.

Simple action plans (e.g.: phone calls, one day investigations etc.) should be noted quickly and tracked in the Action/Status field of the Risk Report. Complex Risk Plans which extend over a longer period (say more than 5 man-days) should be detailed in the Risk Plan section of the database and ultimately incorporated into the main project plan.

The decision on whether to incorporate a Risk Plan into the main project plans is a judgement based on the relative duration of the Risk Plan relative to the main plans. For example, there is little point in including a 3 man day Risk Plan in the project plans if the planning has only been carried out down to 20 man day activities.

10.9.7.6 Closing Risk Plans

There is a significant difference between closing a plan and just stopping it. Risk Plans should be stopped if they are not succeeding. Closure is only authorised when the objectives have been met. It is critical that Risk Plans are closed or stopped at the appropriate time in order to avoid wasting effort.

Further on, there is no point in expending effort on identifying risks, deciding which to attack, formulating alternative Risk Plans, and then conducting them, if the plan is not properly closed when it is complete or has failed.

10.9.7.7 Stopping a Risk Plan

A Risk Plan must be stopped when:

- Either it is seen to be failing,

- Or it is no longer necessary.

It is essential that money is not wasted on ineffective Risk Plans or the value of the entire process may be questioned.

10.9.7.8 Closing a Risk Plan

It is always best to err on the side of caution when closing a Risk Plan i.e. if in doubt, leave it open. When the Risk Plan is thought to have met its objectives:

- Obtain agreement from the Risk Owner to close the plan,
- Trust a statement or promise only when it is fully endorsed and recorded at the right level in the enterprise,
- Ensure that all the necessary changes resulting from the Risk Plan are incorporated into the main project plans, documentation and specifications,
- Check that any revised practices are reflected in the business area,
- Evaluate if there is any remaining (residual) risk which may still need to be addressed.

Then document the closure in the Risk Administration System.

10.9.7.9 Configuration Control

To allow the Project Management process to be effective, the main projects and management concerned must have an effective change and configuration control system in place. To support the Risk Management element, some form of Risk Administration System will be required, in either a manual format for small projects, or a software based tool (such as Risk) for larger projects.

10.10 Applying The Sigma Process - Practical Considerations

10.10.1 Project Prioritisation Considerations

It is important that the project inventory is updated regularly. Ensure it relies on high quality information, otherwise the risk management exercise will quickly become meaningless (i.e. projects currently being assessed for risks may meet their objectives whilst a new, more critical project flounders because it has not been identified for risk assessment.)

It is, also, important that all relevant contacts are involved in the process (i.e. technical and business). The projects should be prioritised from the overall business perspective, not that of a single department.

10.10.1.1 Using software tools to maintain the project inventory

A sophisticated system is not always necessary for maintaining the project inventory. A simple Word document or spreadsheet can do the job adequately. The main questions to ask when deciding how to record project information, including data for the Criticality/Complexity matrices, are:

- What is the inventory going to be used for?

The inventory is useful for deciding on resource allocation, as well as which projects are approved to go ahead and which should be assessed for risk. The inventory may need to be sorted by various criteria, for example by business criticality, start date, department, even by project manager. If the inventory is going to be used in this complex manner, it may be worth using Microsoft Project or Access database, or something similar.

- How large is the inventory going to be?

  A documented list of projects and their attributes has been used for an inventory of up to 50 projects, without recourse to more complex software.

- Is there a system for prioritising projects already in place at the client? Can this easily be adapted?

  Some clients have been found to have sophisticated yet disparate and unconnected lists of projects, prioritised through departmental influence and politics, rather than by a sensible business level view.

Overall, the purpose of the project prioritisation process is to ensure that there is a sensible, business-level view of which projects contribute most to the business strategy and which need a formal risk management process to increase their chance of successfully meeting their objectives.

Further value can be added through improving resource allocation and the client's general management of projects.

It is not always necessary to visually represent projects using the CC Diagram. Some clients prefer to prioritise projects based solely on the business criticality, and use the other parameters for deciding which projects require formal risk management.

Even then, other management systems can lead senior management to highlight particular projects for formal risk management. For example, through their own discussions with the project managers. Even in these circumstances, plotting the projects on a CC Diagram can help to focus priorities and ensure consistency across the business.

10.10.1.2 Assessment Analysis Considerations

It is important to identify the right people to interview in order to capture assessments. You will need to interview people from the project organisation and the customer/users departments.

These people tend to be:

- Project managers (smaller projects):

  If the project organisation is relatively small, the project manager is likely to be a rich source of information. The project manager should have a good understanding of the project plans and the activities taking place within the project. He should be able to speak on behalf of his direct reports on the project.

- Project managers (larger projects):

In larger projects, the Project Manager will tend to identify his Team Leaders for interview. The Project Manager will be able to provide assessmens relating to the project as a whole and the events it faces relative to overall business objectives whilst the Team Leaders will tend to concentrate on their own area.

A project manager looking at assessments raised by the project team will be able to provide feedback and further assessments.

- Team members:

  Down to a certain level, team members should be interviewed to capture a assessments. They have the front line view and more detailed knowledge of the events and potential problems they could face in delivering the project.

  Clearly it is not necessary to interview everyone including the student on work experience. There is a pragmatic cut-off point where you have to rely on the communication mechanisms within the team ensuring the more senior members have a good idea of what is going on.

  Having said that, if you are getting assessments that are clearly lacking in detail and specifics, it may indicate that you do need to interview more people further down the project organisation.

- Customers/Users:

  Interview those who would suffer most from the failure of the project to deliver, and those who will need to provide resources to the project in the form of finance or future users

10.10.1.3 Getting To The Right Assessment

The Sigma process is designed to capture and analyse a substantially complete set of critical project assessments.

To achieve this the following criteria must be met:

- The key contacts in the organisation are interviewed to capture the assessments,
- The interviews are conducted by a team trained in the Sigmqa methodology,
- Someone with experience of the business and project management is involved, to help capture assessments that are not implicit from the plans,
- The assessments captured are disseminated around the key players to gather counter/multiple viewpoints on the ratings,
- The key players are re-interviewed on a regular basis to review the assessments and to capture new assessments.

In practice, interviewing is the most efficient and successful method of capturing high quality assumptions. Other methods have been tried. However, it is far more difficult to ensure that high quality data is captured.

For example:

- Self-analysis:

Every Key Player needs to be fully conversant in Sigma and its underlying principles, be knowledgeable about project management, and apply a degree of objectivity to their own thinking.

Furthermore, people tend to need prompting to perform this exercise, even if they think it's a great idea, a separate facilitator ensuring regular review would be required. Great caution is required with this approach if quality problems are not to negate all benefits.

- Forms:

  A structured form, which allows project team members to fill in their assessments and rate them is clearly a form of self-analysis and, in practice, a very ineffective means of identifying risks. The form will be seen as an administrative burden and will not receive the attention it deserves.

  The information will inevitably be brief incomplete and unclear and the ratings will be meaningless without the challenge of a facilitator to ensure that the assessment is the right one and the ratings are fully understood and allocated relative to the project and business objectives.

- Workshops:

  If led by a Sigma expert, workshops can produce a lot of data in a short space of time. The data quality however tends to be low, unless significant extra time is spent improving it. People may become more reticent in divulging potentially sensitive information, and assessments tend to be generic, embodying the group point of view and losing much of their specific value.

  One effective way to run a risk assessment workshop is to use a Project Readiness Assessment Walkthrough.

Compared with other approaches, the primary benefits of the interviewing approach are:

- Only a small number of interviewers need to be Sigma experts and have experience of project management to generate high quality output,
- Key contacts do not need to be highly trained in Sigma. They only need to understand how information is graded and how the process works (at a high level),
- Key contacts will talk more openly and provide higher quality information in a one-on-one situation, and differences of opinion are made visible to the interviewer,
- The interviewer is not a stakeholder and can be completely objective,
- The interviewer can judge that the right contacts are regularly interviewed to maintain a complete assessments register.

10.10.1.4 Preparation For The Interview

Key contacts are interviewed not only to capture their assessments and risks, but also to communicate relevant information captured from other key contacts. This can actually lead to further assessments and risks being captured as the interviewee reacts to the new information. Thus, a decision has to be made as to what other assessments should be shown to the Key Player being interviewed.

Ideally each key contact should be aware of assessments and risks raised by all key contacts for the project, and would benefit from the latest report of these on each visit. Should the project prove too large for this to be practical, assessments and risks can be categorised and a sub-group of these reported to each key contact. The risks database facilitates this process.

10.10.1.5 During The Interview

If this is the first time the interviewer has seen the person, they should talk through the Assessment Analysis approach, and determine the correct role of this person in the process.

It is also important for the interviewer to understand the person's role in each project they are a key contact for, so that questions can be directed effectively.

There are a number of key activities that should take place during the interview:

- Check that plans exist for the project and at least for the current phase. Work from a high level milestone plan if it is available or the plan that they are carrying around in their head at the very least.
- Walk them through the plan asking the question "what is your next milestone and do you have any concerns in achieving it?"
- Ask questions based on what planned activities need to take place, focusing on weak areas, activities that are not in the plans and suggest potential problems the interviewee may not have thought of.
- Capture important assessments that have been made explicitly in the plans, or that the interviewee has revealed as a result of your questions.
- Should an assessment be graded as C,C or higher it will be necessary to capture the risk statement straight away. Ask the interviewee what the consequences will be if the assessment does not happen, and capture all other details required to describe the risk.
- Existing assessments and risks should be reviewed with the interviewee. This may lead to a change in grading, wording, timing, or any other attributes of an assumption or risk. The assessment and risk wording and ratings must be the Key Player's and not the interviewer's if ownership and buy-in are to be encouraged.

10.10.1.6 At The End Of The Interview

There are a number of steps to take in completing an interview:

- Review the assessments and risks to ensure the interviewee is happy with the wording and ratings,
- Make sure they represent what they believe to be their major risks/concerns,
- Explain that you will revisit these assessments the next time you visit, and that meantime their risks will be reviewed and action taken by senior management.

10.10.1.7 Review Assessments And Risks Regularly

It is important to review assessments and risks on a regular basis because:

- There should be a constant communication of this information between key contacts and senior management,
- The quality of the assessments changes over time; they may become more or less stable as further information is made available, or the project may become more or less sensitive to it as planning decisions are made,
- Action to control risks and assessments needs to be communicated back to the originators and any resulting changes to the list made according to the originator's feedback.

There are a number of tools that can be used to manage this:

- The Assessments and Risks Register,
- A matrix of key contacts against projects being tracked for risk,
- An interview schedule for all key contacts,
- An interviewing template to provide structure during the interview.

These must be maintained on a regular basis in order that the risk management process remains focused.

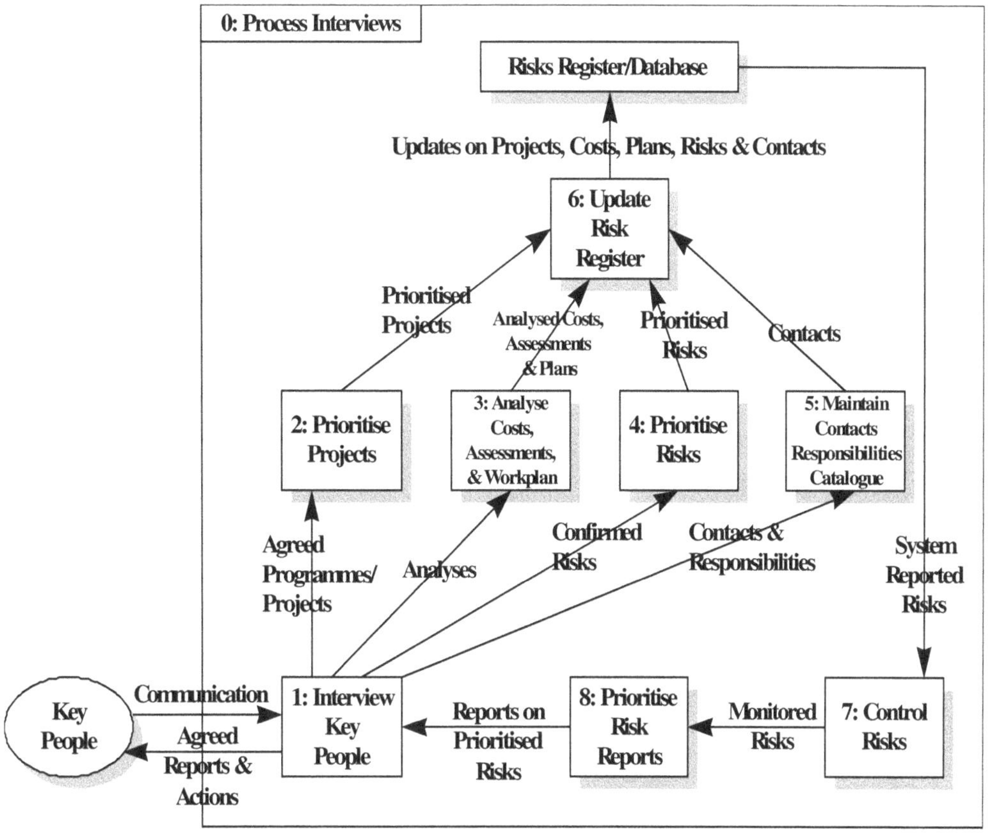

The Interviewing Process

11. Transferring Ownership of The Sigma Process

11.1 Sponsorship And Ownership

The Sigma process can only be effectively handed over to the client organisation, or users when two primary criteria are met:

- A clear sponsor (champion) and new process owners are identified,
- The process is fully up and running and is stable.

11.1.1 Identifying The Process Champions

It is important to ensure that the future sponsor and key people who will be using the process have been involved in it and can testify to the value that it adds. It may still be necessary to continue selling the benefits of the process throughout the hand over period.

The choice of sponsor is critical, since they will have to be able to keep the process on track, reinforcing it where necessary and ensuring it remains focused on what is important to the business.

Their main responsibilities would be:

- Enable the necessary interviews and break down any local resistance,
- Ensuring the senior management risk review process is kept focused, action-oriented and timely,
- Managing any conflict between senior management in the process,
- Applying pressure on those who try to subvert or hijack the process..

11.1.2 Identifying The Process Owners

Equally important as the choice of sponsor is the choice of client process owners. No matter how strongly the sponsor champions the process, ineffective process owners can allow the quality of information from the Sigma method to slip, rendering the functions almost valueless in a matter of weeks following hand over.

There are several critical success factors for ensuring the effective management of the Sigma process:

- Affording time and resources for the process,
- Enthusiasm and attention to detail,
- Access to key players in the organisation.

11.1.2.1 Affording Time For The Process

The amount of effort associated with the process will be far greater than the new process owner will expect.

There may be a tendency to treat the process as a low priority activity to be done in the process owner's spare time. If care is not taken the process will not receive the necessary attention and will quickly fall down the priority list when compared with other direct business responsibilities.

Sometimes the new process owner will see this new responsibility as a poor career move. Under these circumstances there are a number of benefits that should be emphasised:

- Personal exposure to senior management on a regular (trusting) basis,
- Access to all relevant areas of the organisation, affording a much improved cross-functional view of the organisation and a larger network of contacts,
- Greater understanding of the projects being undertaken and the business problems they face,
- Greater appreciation of project management principles and the business as a whole.

11.1.2.2 Enthusiasm And Attention To Detail

An essential ingredient of a successful implementation of the Sigma process is high quality data. The process owner should be able to demonstrate a meticulous attention to detail. If senior management cannot understand the risks or the risks are not presented to them in a consistent manner, they will quickly lose interest and question the value of the process.

Typical groups within an organisation which could provide suitable process owners are:

- Internal consulting groups,
- Programme Offices,
- Quality management groups,
- Audit departments,
- Organisation-wide project/programme management groups.

However, care must be taken with how positively these groups are perceived within each organisation.

11.1.2.3 Access To Key Players In The Organisation

The process owners have to be in such a position as to be able to access:

- Key Players: project sponsors, project managers and key project contacts,
- Senior Management contacts: Sigma process sponsor, senior managers involved in risk review and control,

The process champion will need to intervene quickly in any access problems.

11.1.2.4 Avoiding The Split-up Approach

There may be a temptation to split up the process across the organisation to spread the load and allow part time involvement of the new process owners. Great care is required here as one the key benefits of Sigma, that of providing a cross-organisational communication mechanism, may be undermined.

11.2 Hand Over Process

11.2.1 Training

The training must cover both the theory and practical application of Sigma. Theory without practice inevitably leads to poor quality data and practice without theory extends the learning curve considerably.

11.2.2 Parallel Interviews

One of the most important parts of the hand over programme is the parallel interview sessions. After the training course, a series of parallel interviews are held where the consultant and new process owner conduct a number of interviews together.

This achieves the following:

- The new process owner can learn first hand how the interviews are conducted and how the different interviewees behave,
- The new process owner can practice the interviewing process with a degree of comfort that they can make mistakes,
- The interviewees can visibly see the handover process at work and meet their future interviewers.

Past experience has shown that approximately 15-20 parallel interviews are required to get the average candidate up to speed.

It is useful to arrange for the new process owner to conduct an interview with each of the Key Players during the parallel interviewing process. This allows them to establish a dialogue with each of their contacts by the time the hand over is complete.

It is also useful to interview some new Key Players, so the new process owner can learn how to explain the process and its benefits to the individual.

Parallel interviews should be conducted with the consultant leading for the first few interviews, and then with the new process owner leading in later interviews. Prior to each interview, the consultant should review with the client the documentation required for the interview. This avoids the client losing valuable learning time in the interview being unable to understand the language used or the relevant project background.

11.2.2.1 Consultant Leading Interviews

The main skill learnt by the client through this activity is how to capture high quality assumptions and risks.

The new process owner should have a copy of all the materials that the consultant has to conduct the interview. The consultant conducts the interview as normal. The new process owner will learn how interviews are conducted, and practice capturing assumptions and risks as the consultant asks the questions. When the captured data is recorded in a risk register, the consultant can correct the client's notes after the interview. About 5 to 10 interviews should be sufficient.

11.2.2.2 Client Leading Interviews

One of the most difficult aspects of the interviewing process is asking the right questions and maintaining a dialogue with the interviewee whilst at the same time following a strict code in documenting the assessments and risks and their associated grading. The client will have acquired skills in the mechanics of capturing assessments and risks, and will now have the opportunity to practice asking the right questions to obtain that information.

The consultant should allow the client to run the interview by themselves as much as possible, intervening only where quality is compromised to ensure the best results from the interview are obtained. The consultant should concentrate on asking any questions at the end that may have been missed due to lack of experience.

The consultant should spend time with the new process owner after the interview to discuss what went well (so the client knows they are progressing) and what could be improved.

More time should be spent on this stage of the hand over with the client leading the interviews since they have more to learn at this stage. About 10 to 15 interviews should be sufficient.

11.2.3 Procedures And Supporting Documentation

The client process owners have a lot to learn in a short hand over time i.e.: a complete methodology, the current process, the interviewing technique and using the software support tools. All this needs to be supported by some form of procedures, to provide a reference point during the hand over and to act as supplementary training material should the process owners need to train further people in their organisation.

11.2.4 Software Tool Support

Not only do the new process owners have to learn to use the risks software, but someone will have to be trained in maintaining the software, as it is likely at some stage that they will need to add new fields or categories, or modify the report formats.

The ideal way to achieve this is to provide good documentation of the system, combined with at least half a day's worth hands-on demonstration with the chosen system maintainer. This person should be able to 'play' with the database by themselves (trying to add fields/modify reports etc.) and be able to come back and ask questions before the hand over is complete.

11.3 Ongoing Quality Management

11.3.1 Can they Continue To Do It Themselves?

No matter how well the hand over has been managed the process can still start to fail quickly when the consultants depart if the new process owners do not fully understand all the subtleties of the application of Sigma. A way of minimising this risk is to consciously involve the new process owner in all decisions, discussions, changes etc. during the hand over period.

When adjustments need to be made to the process, involve the new process owners - ask how they would deal with it first. Such adjustments may include:

- Reassessing the list of key contacts where necessary,
- Changing the format of risk reporting to senior management,

- Adjusting interviewing approach or timing,
- Changing the format of the risk review meetings,
- Managing political hiccups that can disrupt the process,
- Seizing opportunities that can enhance the process,
- Provide them with a 'troubleshooting guide' which highlights typical symptoms, what it is that may be going wrong, and ways to correct the problem.

  For example:

  - Not identifying many risks,
  - Senior management do not understand the risks,
  - Key Players start to lose interest in the process,
  - The Risk Review meetings become irregular.

11.3.2 Applying Sigma To The Hand Over Phase

A highly effective way of ensuring a successful hand over within agreed time scales is to apply the Sigma process to the hand over activities. This means treating the hand over as a project and forming a simple Risk Register which is communicated to the client at regular intervals.

If the Process Sponsor is regularly updated with risks to achieving successful hand over, he will be able to take actions to support the consultants. Furthermore, if the hand over is impeded by factors outside the consultants' control, for example late sign-off, problems accessing the right people, and so on, the risk register can provide a valuable audit trail backing up promises to deliver, or supporting any explanations as to why there were delays.

11.4 Integrating Methodologies

In handing over and in applying any Risk Management method, as in any other Management tool, the integration of all existing methodologies is of primary importance.

In choosing the new owner of the Sigma methodology, consideration must be given regarding the experience possessed by the new proprietor. Preference should be given to the people with systems methodology and management procedures training and experience.

The diagram below will serve as a guide on what the knowledge should include.

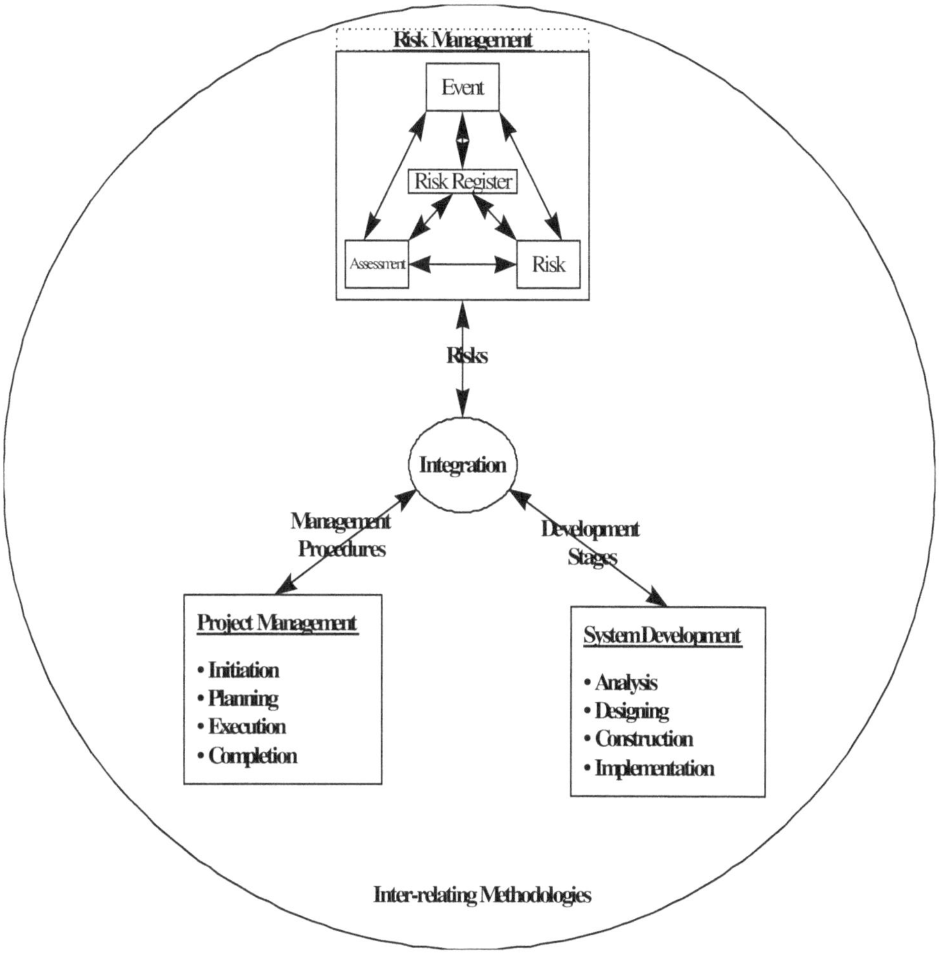
Risk Management
Event
Risk Register
Assessment
Risk
Risks
Integration
Management Procedures
Development Stages
Project Management
• Initiation
• Planning
• Execution
• Completion
System Development
• Analysis
• Designing
• Construction
• Implementation
Inter-relating Methodologies

12. Interfacing

12.1 The Diagrammatic Representation Of The Desired Integration

The diagrammatic flow shown below is the desired overall integration of related top-level processes:

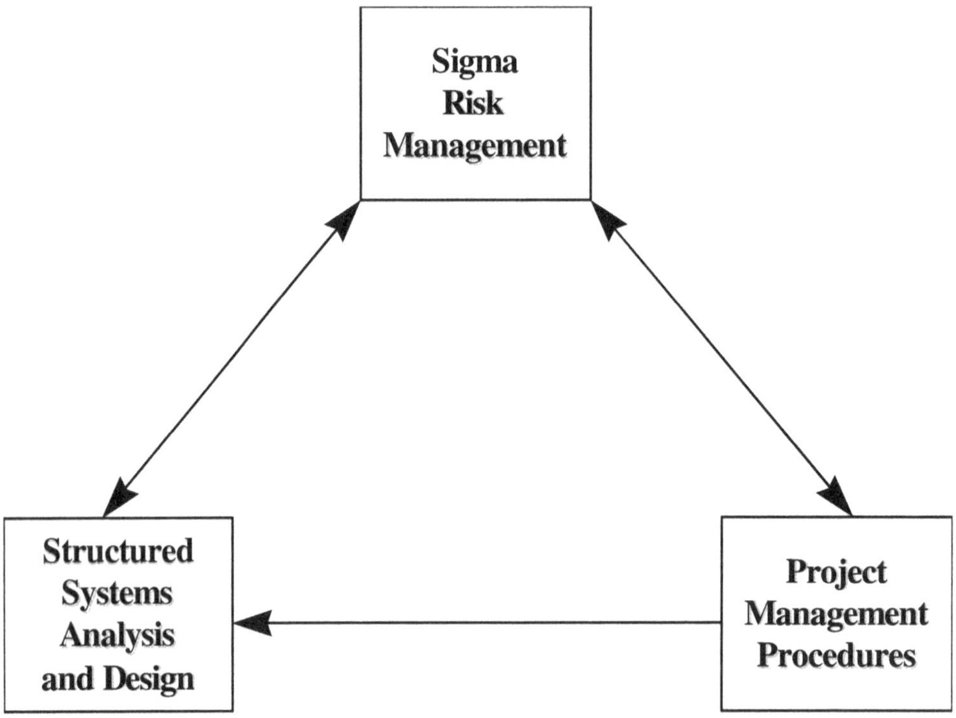

Integration Of Methodologies

12.2 Suggested Interfacing

The suggested interfacing of the Structured Systems Analysis and Design methodology and the Project Management procedures to the Risk Management processes may be done separately as shown in the diagram below:

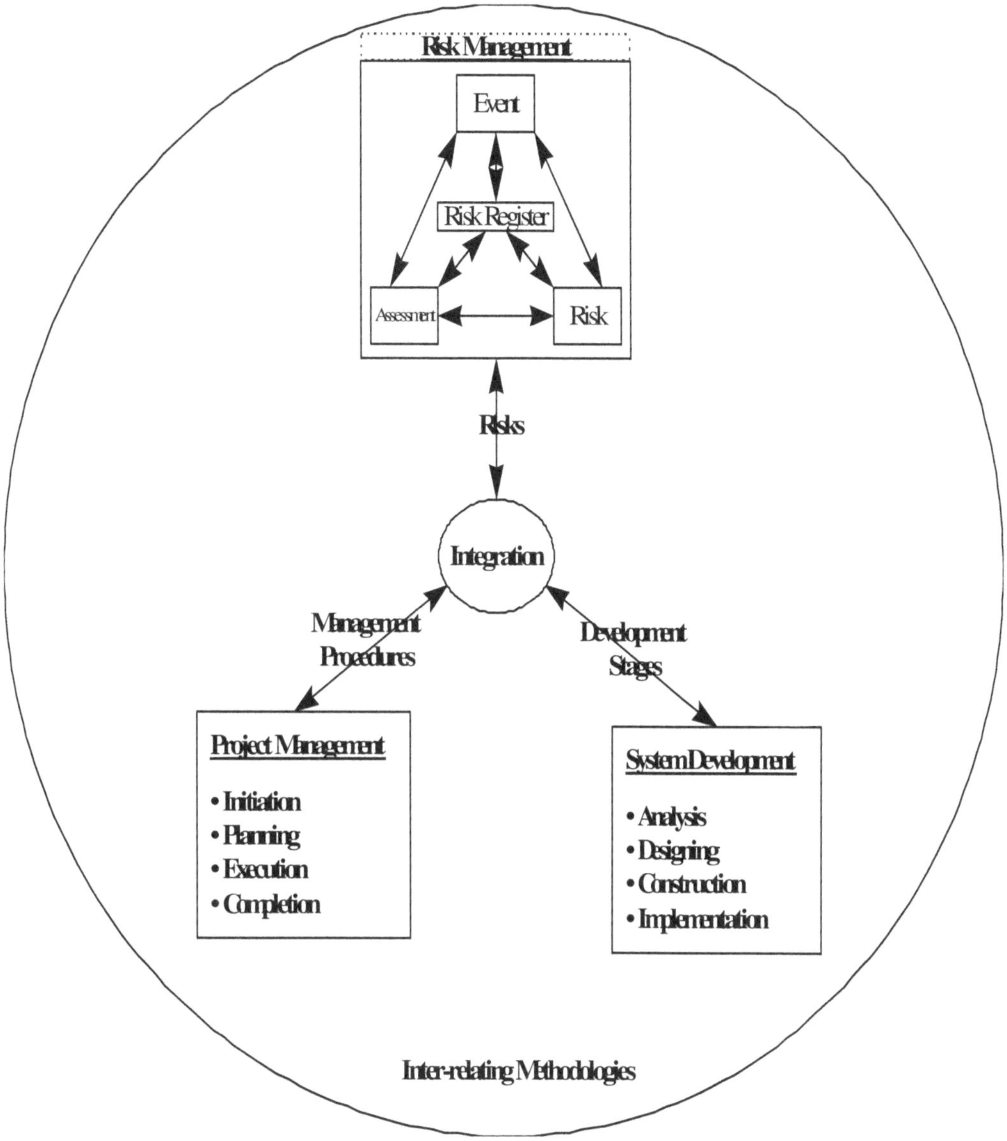
Risk Management
Event
Risk Register
Assessment
Risk
Risks
Integration
Management Procedures
Development Stages
Project Management
• Initiation
• Planning
• Execution
• Completion
System Development
• Analysis
• Designing
• Construction
• Implementation
Inter-relating Methodologies

12.3 Using The Existing Methods

In interfacing the various processes from the different existing organisational methodologies, the main steps of Project Management and the Structures Systems Analysis and Designing methodology, will be incorporated in this exercise.
Namely, the six main stages of system development:

- Analyse,
- Design,
- Construct,
- Implement.

The identified processes of Project Management procedures and Structured Systems Analysis and Designing to be linked to the Sigma Risk Management processes of:

- Events,
- Assessments,
- Risks,
- Plans.

The actual points of interfacing the stages of development, the procedures of managing projects and the assessments analysis of the Sigma methodology, are explored in this book.

12.4 Connection Of Project Management To Sigma

Regarding the connections of the project management procedures to risk management, it is suggested that the link be from the higher level of project management work elements, such as:

- Initiate Risk Management,
- Adjust Project Approach to Risk,
- Control Risk,
- Complete Risk Management.

This is as far as most users drill into the process and generally as far as they are required to by structured analysis and designing methodologies guidelines.

13. Managing The Sigma Risk Programme

13.1 The Diagrammatic Representation Shown.

- O: Sigma Risk Management Decomposition,
- O: Management of the Risk Programme,
- 1: Managing of the Sigma Process,
- 2: Facilitation of the Sigma Programme,
- 3. Practising the Sigma Methodology.

13.2 O: Sigma Risk Management Decomposition

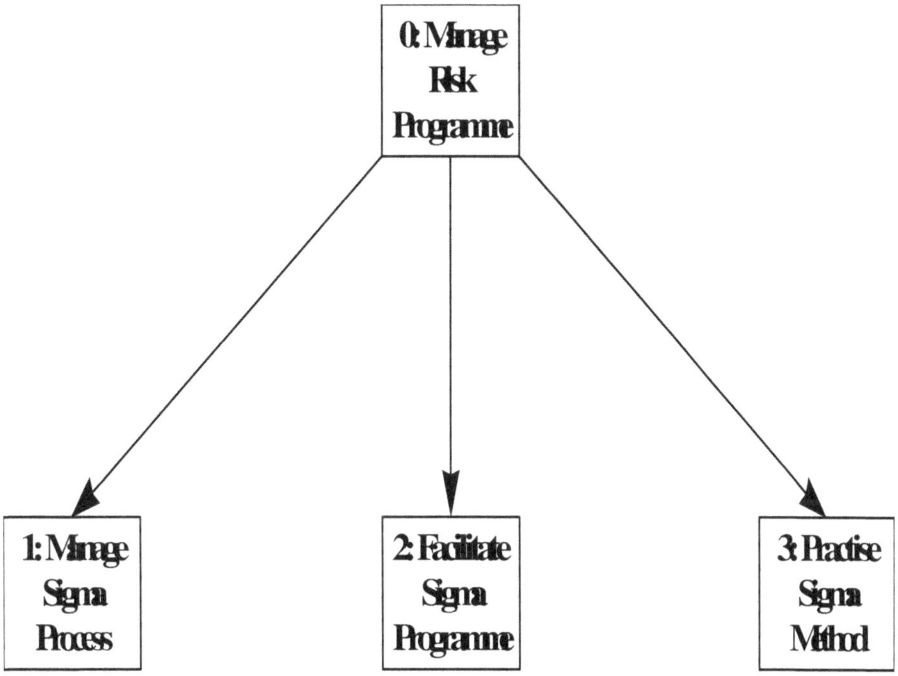

The Sigma Risk Management Decomposition

13.3 O: Management of the Risk Programme

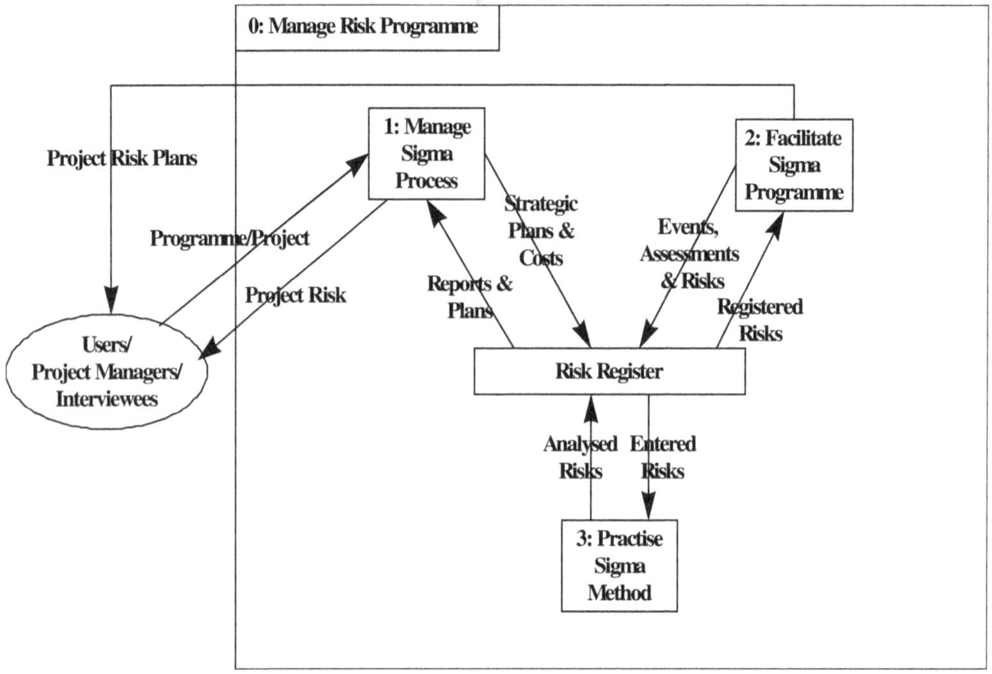

13.4 1: Managing of the Sigma Process

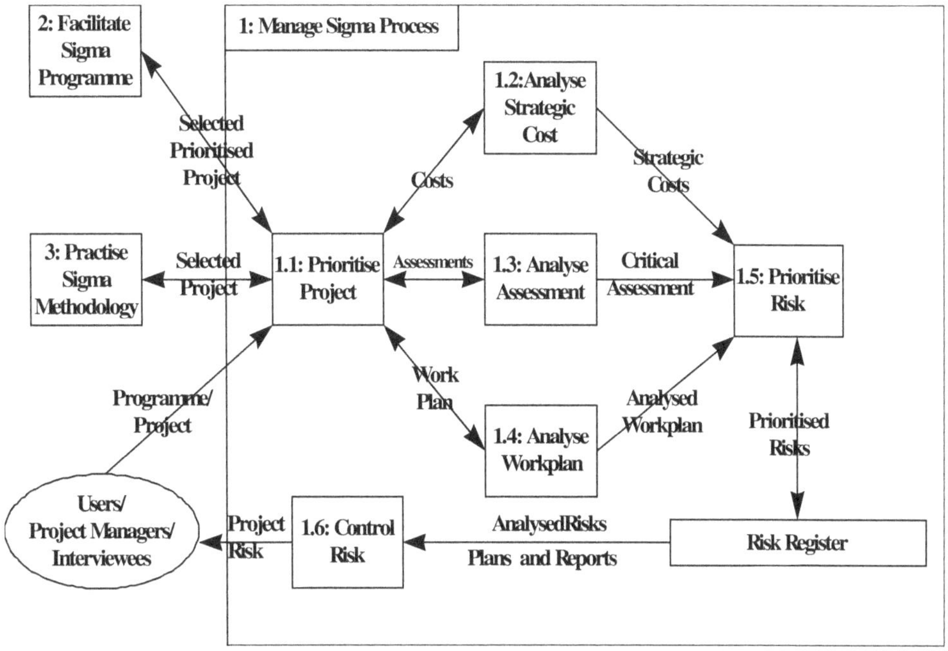

13.5 2: Facilitation of the Sigma Programme

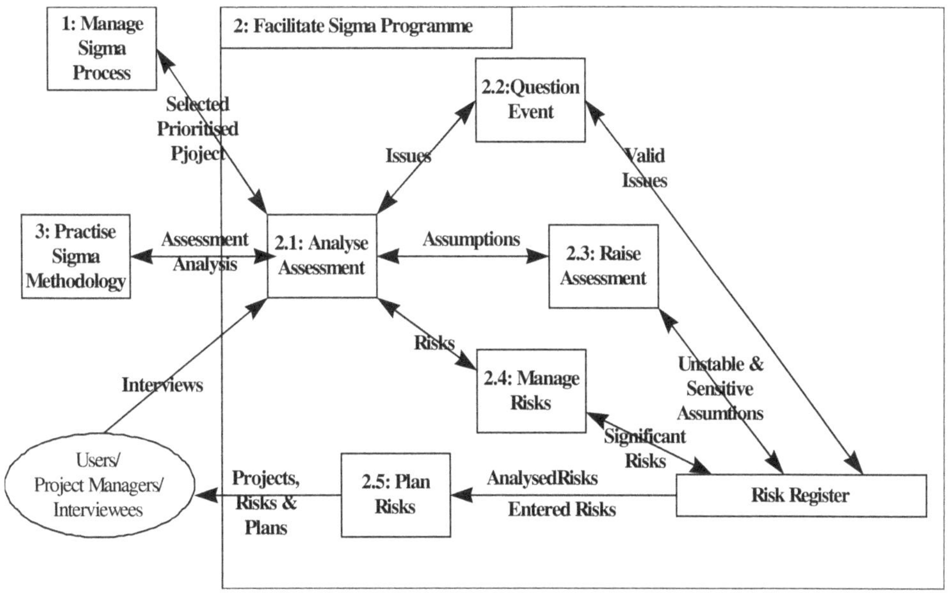

13.6 3: Practising the Sigma Methodology

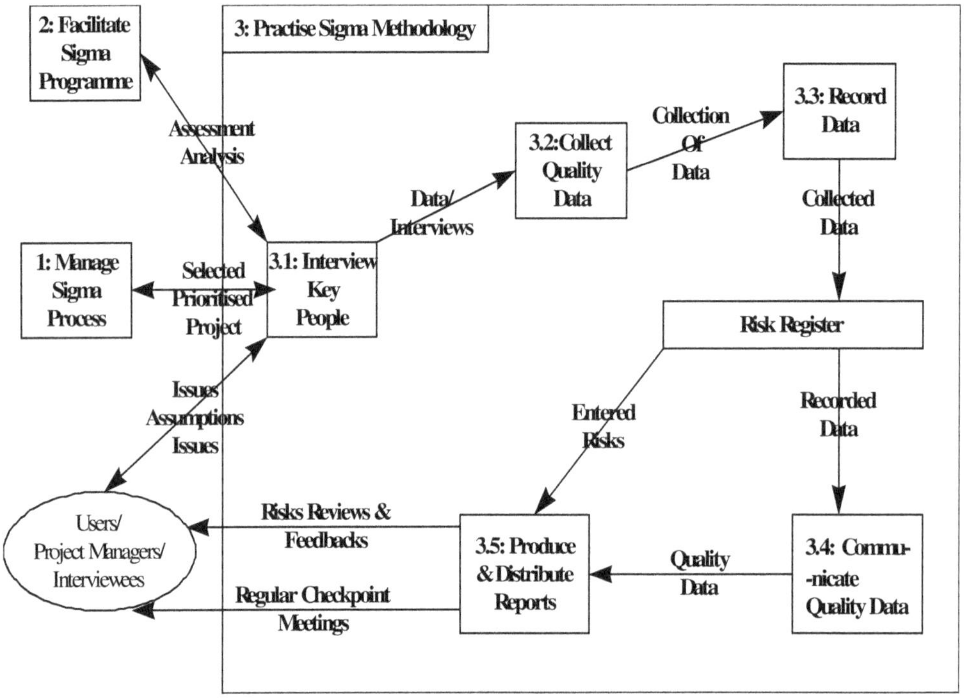
2: Facilitate Sigma Programme
3: Practise Sigma Methodology
Assessment Analysis
3.2:Collect Quality Data
Collection Of Data
3.3: Record Data
Data/ Interviews
Collected Data
1: Manage Sigma Process
Selected Prioritised Project
3.1: Interview Key People
Risk Register
Issues Assumptions Issues
Entered Risks
Recorded Data
Users/ Project Managers/ Interviewees
Risks Reviews & Feedbacks
3.5: Produce & Distribute Reports
Quality Data
3.4: Commu- -nicate Quality Data
Regular Checkpoint Meetings

13.7 Relationship Of Dataflow Diagrams and SIGMA

All dataflow diagrams shown in above pages are based on the PsySys Limited manuals and handouts as used for the Sigma training.

13.7.1 DATAFLOW DIAGRAMS: NUMBERS AND TITLES.	*DESCRIPTION OF DIAGRAMS AND THEIR PROCESSES.*
0: Manage Risk]	Project: something complex that you want (plan) to happen. Risk: Something that you don't want to happen. Project management: Planning and making things happen. Risk management: Attacking anything that might disturb the plan
1: Manage Sigm	The Sigma process consists of an integrated closed loop method v A. Project Prioritisation, B. Strategic Cost Analysis, C. Assessment Analysis, D. Work Plan Analysis, E. Risk Prioritisation, F. Risk Control.
1.1 Prioritise Pro	Only complex and critical projects need to have a fully structured
1.2 Analyse Strategic Cost	Strategic Cost Analysis provides a means of assessing the cost ris

1.3 Analyse Ass	Fundamentally, projects only fail due to two reasons either the wr
1.4 Analyse Work plan	Work Plan Analysis may be used to focus on the risky areas of detailed, multi-level project plans when time is of the essence.
1.5 Prioritise Risk	Prioritisation allows the Project Manager to divert limited resour
1.6 Control Risk	Risks may be attacked at both the strategic and tactical levels. Str
2: Facilitate Sig	The Sigma Programme is essentially a framework process that all
2.1: Analyse Ass	The core of Sigma is Assessment Analysis. This uses structured t
2.2: Question E	Events are open questions which are holding up plans/implemen An Event is any open question which has been asked at the right
2.3: Raise Asses	Many Events are closed by making Assessments in plans. An Assessment is a single, simple, positive or negative statement
2.4: Manage Ris	Unstable/sensitive assumptions create risks.

	Significant risks need to be managed formally. Definition: A Risk is a simple statement of the form: "IF" Assumption proves incorrect, "THEN" Describe the impact.
2.5: Plan Risks	Risk Plans impact project plans. Events, Assessments and risks are inherent in the project plans. Population of assessment and risks registers by progressing Risk
3: Practise Sigm	The Role of a Sigma Risk Management Practitioner includes: Interview 'Key People' within the project, To collect 'Quality' data, Ensure the data collected is recorded in the Risk Regis Communicate the 'Quality' data to Project staff, Produces accurate and timely reports for meetings: Weekly Check Point Meetings, Risk Review Boards.
3.1: Interview K	Identifying the right people to interview is critical to producing a
3.2: Collect Qual	This function requires to: Interview 'Key People' within the project, Collect 'Quality' data.

3.3: Record Data	Having Interviewed the 'Key People' within the project and colle Ensure the data collected is recorded in the Risk Regis
3.4: Communica	The interviews of 'Key People' within the project have been com Facilitate and ensure the Risk Management process st
3.5: Produce Rep	After the initial round of interviews, a suitable forum must be est The best method is to establish a specific Risk Review Meeting w The main function is to: Produce accurate and timely reports for meetings: Weekly Check Point Meetings, Risk Review Boards.
Detester/Database Of Events, Assessments and Risks Register Description.	
Data Store: *Risk Register*	All events, assessments and risks captured should be held in a Ris Remember, only critical assessments will be converted into risks Thus, by filtering the assessments and consolidating them into ris

14 Project Management Improvement

14.1 Weakness In Project Management

In the process of using Sigma, it will soon become apparent that probably the main cause for the threatening risks is project management, or perhaps the weakness of individual/s to manage the growth of a system.

Even if you used Sigma in its fullest, your experience will soon enable you to identify the real cause for the failure in implementing your system. In such cases, your programme/project management may need further support, assistance, training, better communicational ability and proper delegating, or even some listening to other people involved in the on-going project. Employing the expertise of a consultancy may help.

The main point is to try to reduce potential project caused loss by providing efficient *Event* driven project reviews for the critical project/s. Such project consulting steps will create and utilise virtual group of experienced project managers. As a panel of experts they will assess critical projects and provide consulting being perceived as helpful by the project team, the management and the users/clients.

14.2 Process Steps Required

For such a project consulting programme implementation, various process steps are needed:

1. Select critical project,
2. Understand project status,
3. Plan project review,
4. Create reviews agenda
5. Execute project review,
6. Implement change plan,
7. Conclude the project review.

14.3 Collection Of Information

The project manager of the project pending the review should gather the requested information from the existing project documentation. If such documentation is not available, the project manager should collect as much a as possible from verbal discussions.

Such a preparation should include details of:

1. Communication plans,
2. Project organisation plan,
3. Contacts and scopes,
4. Background and status of finances,
5. Schedules,
6. Status and history of resources plans,

7. Quality plan,
8. System documentation,
9. Brief description of the project environment,
10. Risk register prioritisation/s and other reports,
11. Last project review minutes.

A. Agreement On Resources

The final outcome of all communications, discussions and reviews should enable the team members to produce an agreed score on the various project management resources.

The list for such a scoring agreement should include:

1. Quality management,
2. User participation,
3. Requirements management,
4. Communications,
5. Business orientation,
6. Project team,
7. Project planning,
8. Risk management,
9. Technical environment.

14.5 The Score Graph

A scoring card graph can easily be produced on a spreadsheet and it ought to look something like this:

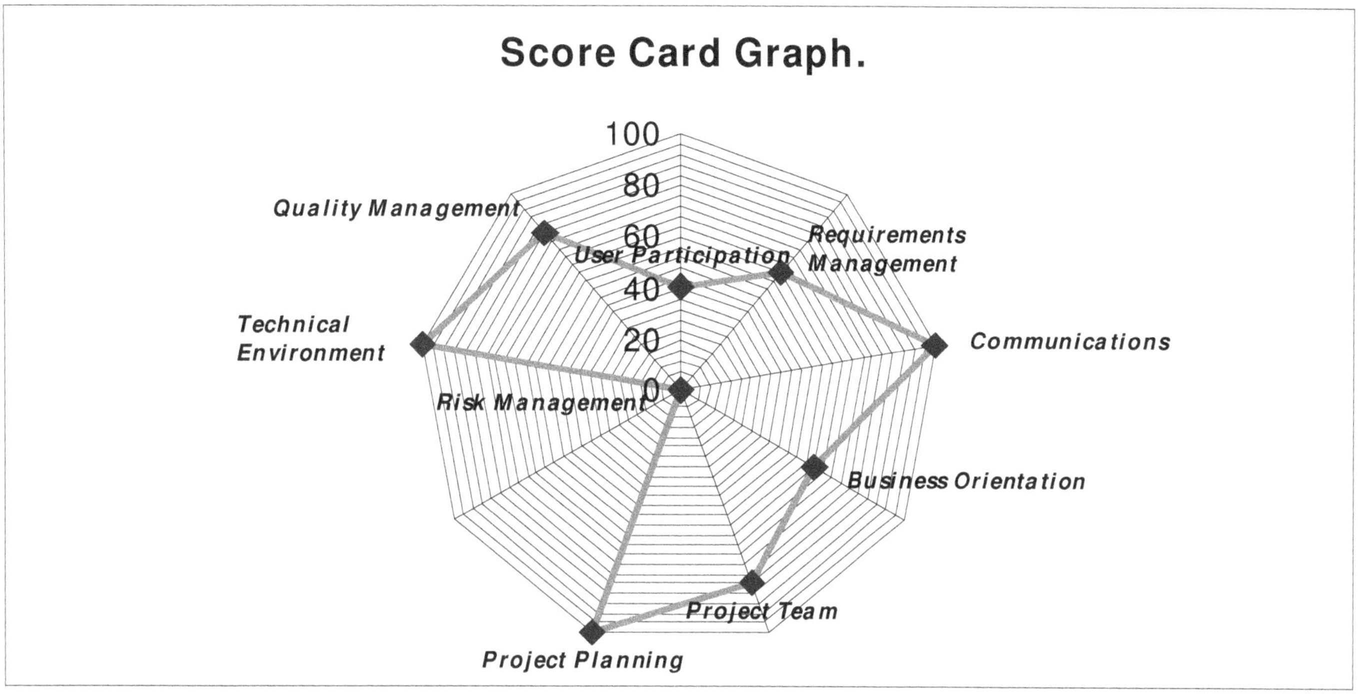

15. Remembering The Main Risk Management Points

A risk is an uncertain event which may have an adverse effect on the project's objectives. Sigma is a proven risk management methodology, which should be very effective in the quest for identifying risks throughout the project life-cycle.

Remember, risk management is:

1. Forward looking, investigating problems and how to deal with threats,

2. A tool enabling communication, getting people at all levels to talk to each other and to interact,

3. A no blame team culture, bringing concerns into the open where actions can be taken and plans put in place, in order to stop a risk occurring.

The Sigma process commences by identifying the enterprises most important and risky projects, as these must be given priority. Sigma is essentially a method that permits the collection of knowledge and experience from those involved, in a form that facilitates the Systematic Interaction and Generic Methodology for Applications:

□ystematic: The varied events, their assessments and the consequential risks relating to or consisting of a system. Methodical in procedures and plans, these are addressed to those involved and deliberating within the parameters of their systems development responsibilities. The results being dependable on:

Interaction: The mutual or reciprocal action which encourages those involved in the programmes and projects to communicate with each other and to work closely with a view to solving the threatening events before they impact on the development of the system. The individuals involved maintain a -

Generic approach, which relates and characterises the whole group of those involved in assessing the events and attacking the threatening ones before they become risks to the development of the system. The end result being the avoidance of apparent problems within the pre-defined users systems requirements. This is enabled by following the -

Methodology: The system architects and the risk management practitioners simply follow the approved body of systems development methods, rules and management procedures employed by their organisation. For practical or even ethical reasons, it must be noted that with such a philosophy, it is seldom possible to fulfil all requirements of very large organisational systems. As such, the *Sigma* methodology is administered in -

Applications: Putting to use such techniques and in applying the risk management principles in the development of various *applications* will involve numerous and varied activities. A concrete issue in developing new applications is the problem of communication among the people involved, the motivation constantly needed for *generic* work, the ability to *interact systematically* and in using a structured systems *methodology*.

RISK MANAGEMENT IN SYSTEMS DEVELOPMENT

The Sigma methodology allows the capture of collective knowledge and expertise from those involved on the project, in a form that facilitates the communication of Events, Assessments and the pro-active management of Risks. Sigma can be applied to any type of project, or programme. In essence, this is the mechanism by which the functions of programmes and projects are held together as a result of the principles operating within the *Sigma* methodology.

Born in Morphou, Cyprus, Andreas holds the degrees of Doctor of Psychology and Doctor of Philosophy. Also, qualifications as a chartered member and fellow of eighteen British professional institutions, including Engineering, Systems, Computing, Directing, Complementary Medicine, Management, Production, Programming, Marketing, Petroleum, Data Processing, Psychotherapy and Counselling. A Research Fellow and Professor (Life) of American Institutes. A member of working parties in Europe on systems and therapy.

During his varied career, Andreas held the positions of Overseas Marketing Executive, Production and Inventory Manager, Group Senior Systems Consultant, European Systems Manager, Principal Technical Adviser, Managing Director and Global Programme Manager with the multi-national organisations of International Computers Limited, Pitney Bowes, Plessey (GEC) Raychem, Engineering Industry Training Board (EITB), PsySys and EDS (Electronic Data Systems).

Participated as an information technology expert to European Union Commissions and as a therapeutic psychologist to the Institute of Psychology and Parapsychology and the Harley Street Centre, London. A published writer, poet and trainer, the subjects include Computing, Systems Methodology, Management and Psychotherapy. For achievements in Systems Engineering, Psychology and Directing, his biographical records are included in the directory of 'Who's Who In The World', published by Marquis of America and other international biographical publications.

Title:THE *SIGMA* METHODOLOGY FOR RISK MANAGEMENT IN SYSTEMS DEVELOPMENT
Author: Andreas Sofroniou

ISBN: 978-1-84753-147-6

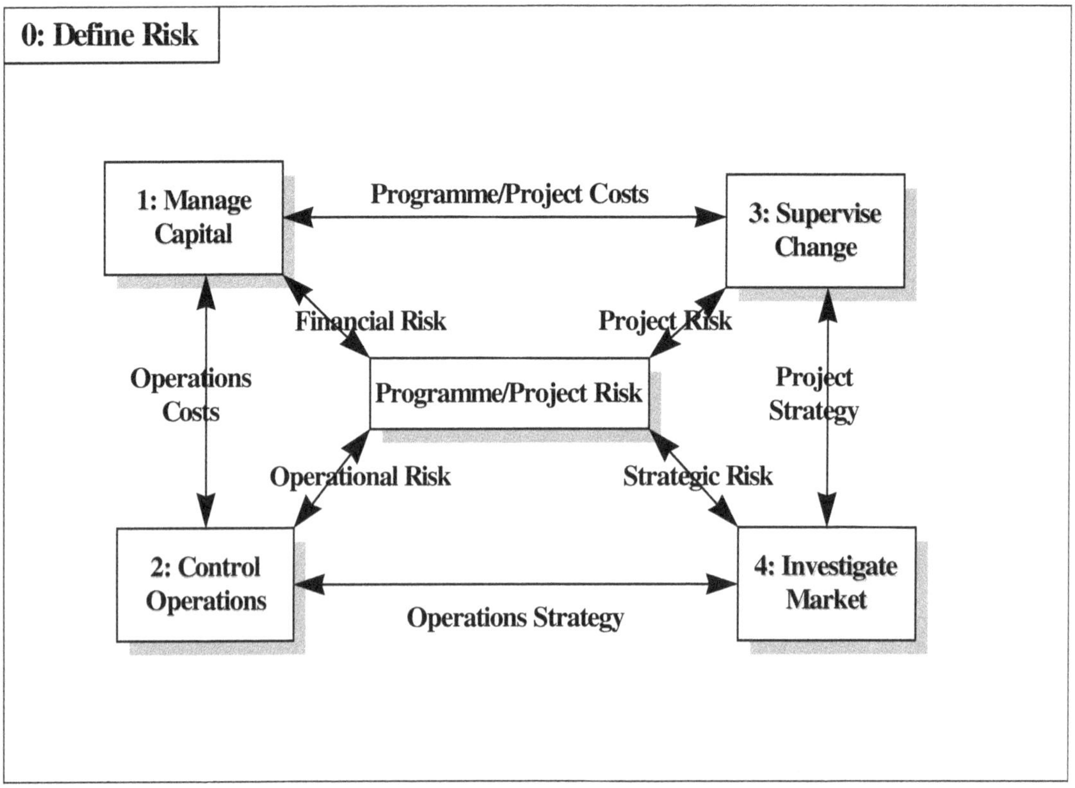
0: Define Risk
1: Manage Capital
Programme/Project Costs
3: Supervise Change
Financial Risk
Project Risk
Operations Costs
Programme/Project Risk
Project Strategy
Operational Risk
Strategic Risk
2: Control Operations
4: Investigate Market
Operations Strategy

Programme Management Workshop

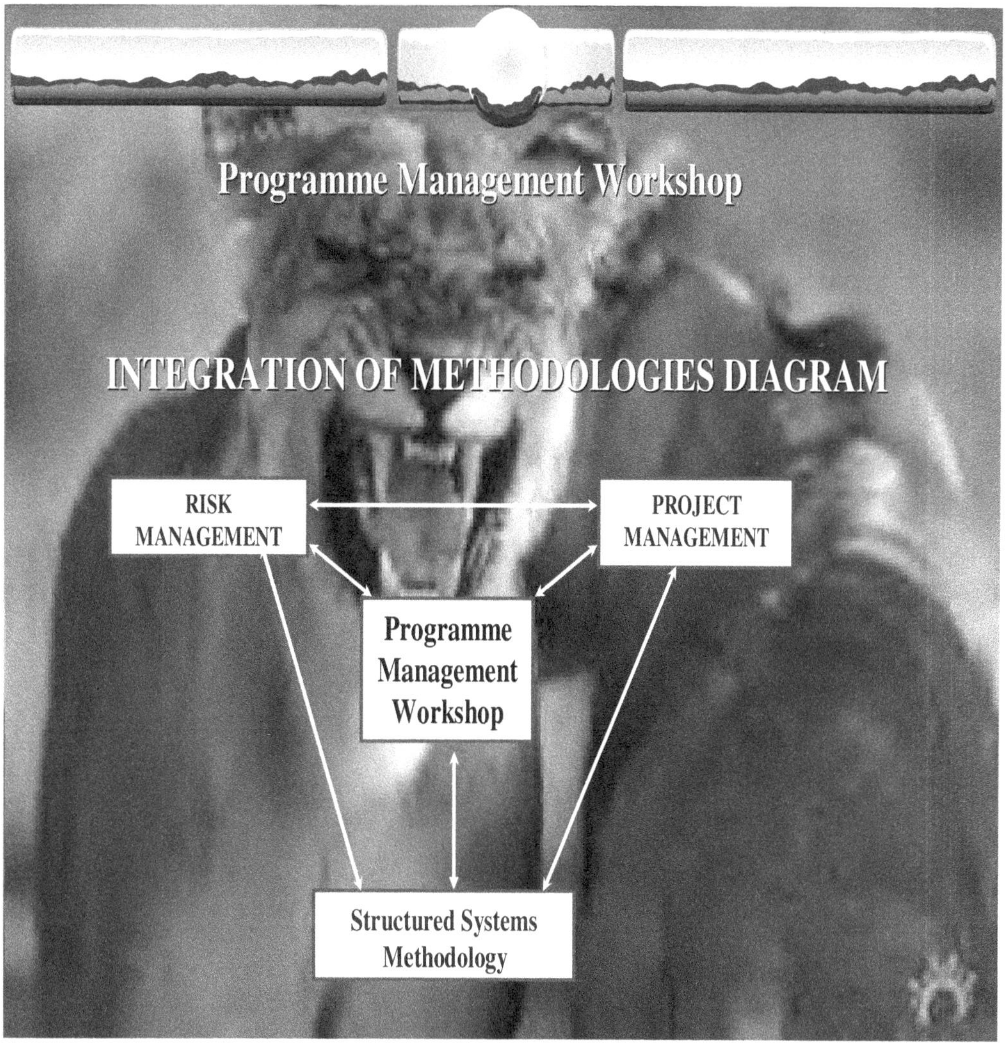

ISBN: 978-1-84753-147-6

Contents

1. MANAGEMENT SUMMARY
1.1 Purpose Of This Book
1.2 The Use of the Book as a Manual
2. THE WORKSHOP
2.1 Workshop Concepts and Measures (Picture)
2.2 Workshop Structure (Picture)
3. INTERFACING
3.1 The Diagrammatic Representation
3.2 Using the Existing Methods
3.2.1 STRUCTURED SYSTEMS METHODOLOGY
3.2.2 PROGRAMME MANAGEMMENT
3.2.3 Risk Management
3.3 TOOLS INTERFACES
4. FUNCTIONAL SKILLS
4.1 Filling the Gap
4.2 Programme Management Overview
4.3 The Fundamentals
4.4 Standards
5. MANAGEMENT FUNCTIONS
5.1 Introduction to Management Functions
5.2 Information Systems Enhancement
5.3 Project Management and Planning Techniques
6. THE POST-WORKSHOP COACHING AND MENTORING
6.1 Programme Management, a Profession
6.2 Post-workshop Coaching and Mentoring
6.3 The Interpersonal Skills of the Coach
7. THE BENEFITS OF PROGRAMME MANAGEMENT
8. PRE-WORKSHOP ACTIVITIES
8.1 Workshop Abstract
8.2. Workshop Abstract

8.3. PMI KEY AREAS AND SELF-ASSESSMENT FORM
9. Case Study: A CURRENT Project
9.1. Abstract
9.2 How CLIENT commissioned the work
9.2.1 Outline project schedule
9.2.2 Business Partners Involved in the project
9.3. Process for Requirements Determination
9.4 Other key soft skills and behavioural traits:
9.5 Outputs from the Facilitated Workshops
9.6 Team Empowerment
9.7 Communication Strategy
9.8. Project Management Style
9.9 Reviews
9.10 Conclusions and Summary
10. THE WORKSHOP AGENDA
11. PROJECT SCORING
11.1 SCORING POINTS
11.2. SCORING EXPLANATION
12. WORKSHOP SLIDES
13. INTEGRATION OF RISKS, PROJECTS AND SYSTEMS

1. MANAGEMENT SUMMARY

1.1 Purpose Of This Book

This book is intended to provide details and guidance as a Programme Management Workshop. The initiation of this book is based on readers' requests for an objective tutorial and workshop for the Programme/Project Management community. A workshop for training that includes a methodology for learning, practising and interfacing with other courses. The workshop material documented herein will include the:

- Pre-workshop activities,
- Project Management principles,
- Integration of major methodologies,
- Case study details,
- Aid to participants' presentation,
- Established Project Management requirements,
- Interfaces of various tools,
- Referencing workshop material,
- Post-workshop coaching.

1.2 The Use of the Book as a Manual

It is intended that this workshop manual will also assist those Programme/Project Managers who wish to use this document as a reference to other training packages.

The objective would be that, if a new, or existing reader wanted to roll out the workshop principles with minimal assistance, could just obtain the details from this Programme Management Workshop package, point the candidates to the contents and guide them to the facilitators for any further training required.

The post-workshop idea of coaching, support and mentoring for the Programme/Project Managers will be continued. Thus, the reader will be able to call as and when help is needed.

2. THE WORKSHOP

2.1 Workshop Concepts and Measures (Picture)

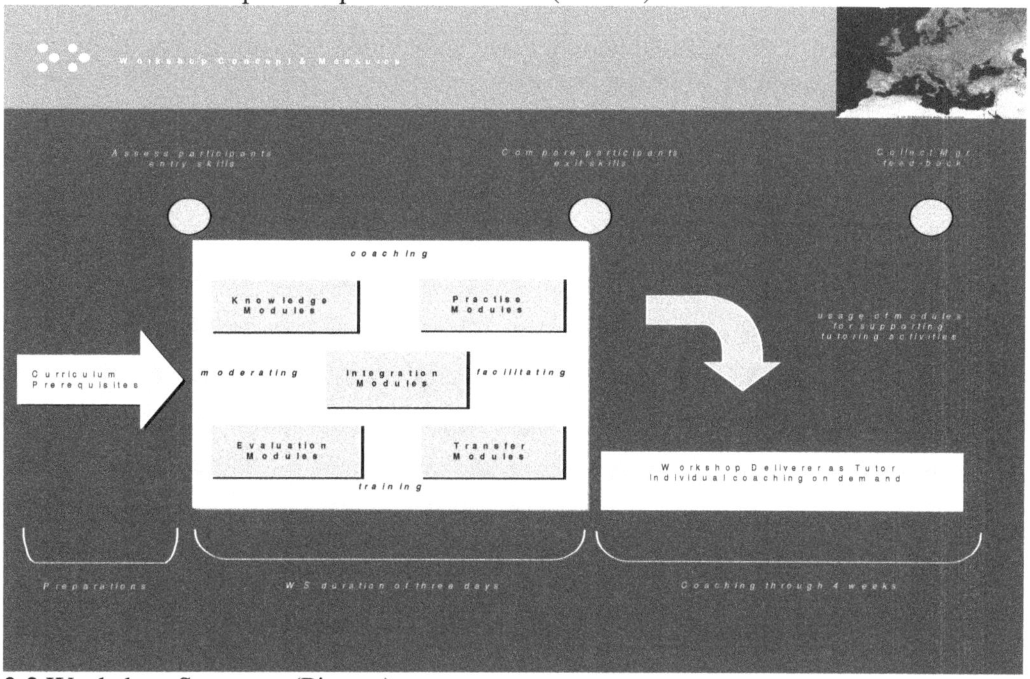

2.2 Workshop Structure (Picture)

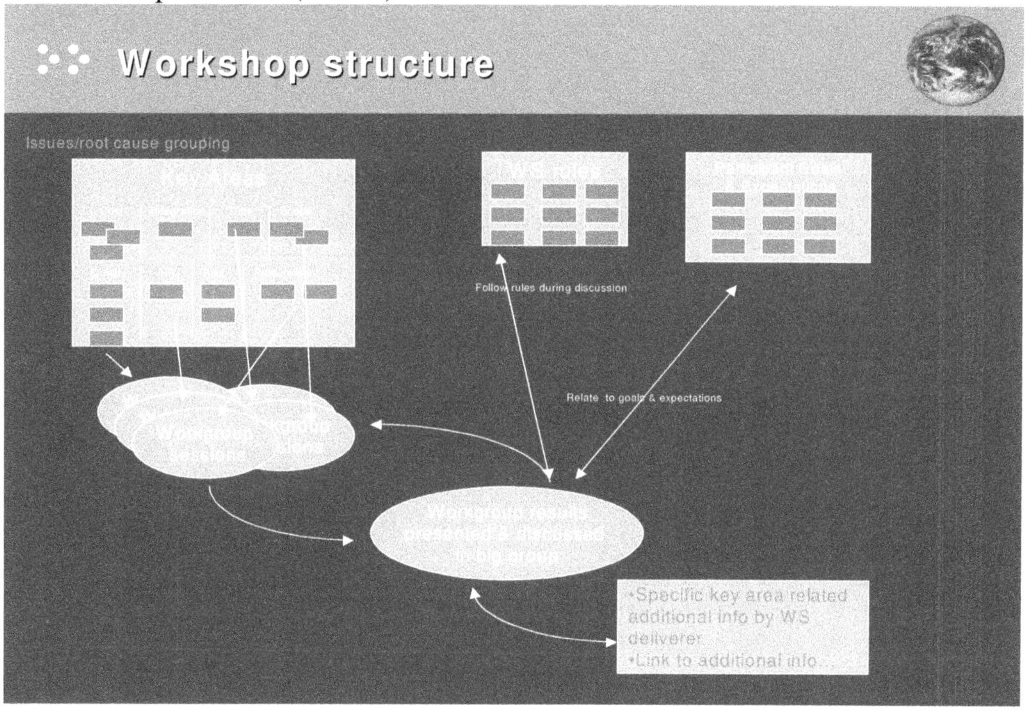

3. INTERFACING

3.1 The Diagrammatic Representation of the Desired Integration

The diagrammatic flow shown below is the desired overall integration of related top-level processes:

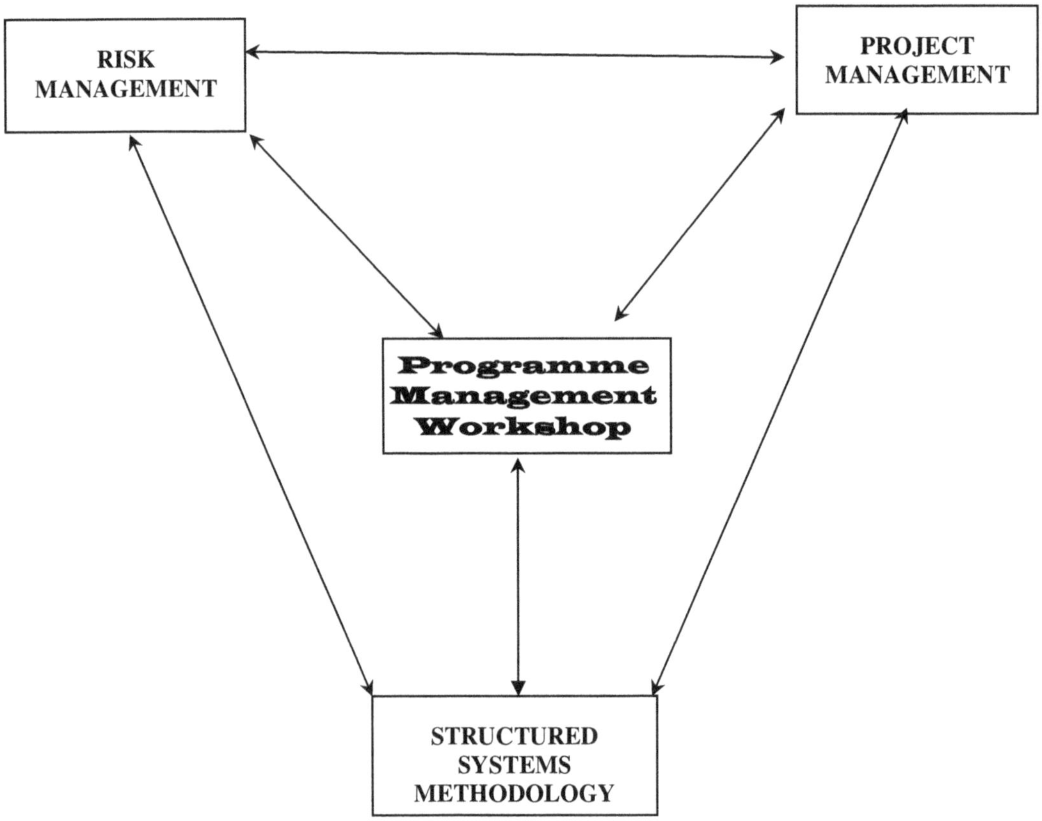

Details of the interfaces of these tools and their processes are shown below.

3.2 Using the Existing Methods

In interfacing the various processes from the different existing methodologies, the main steps of Project Management, Structured Systems Methodology and Risk Management, will be incorporated in this exercise.

3.2.1 STRUCTURED SYSTEMS METHODOLOGY: The main six stages of system development:

- Define,
- Analyse,
- Design,
- Construct,
- Optimise,
- Implement.

3.2.2 PROGRAMME MANAGEMMENT: The four main stages of:

- Start-up,
- Planning,
- Execution,
- Close-down.

3.2.3 Risk Management: The four main processes of:

- Issues,
- Assumptions,
- Risks,
- Plans.

3.3 TOOLS INTERFACES

THE TOOLS SHOWN ABOVE AND THEIR FUNCTIONAL LISTING HAVE A DUAL PURPOSE:

- ENABLE THE WORKSHOP PARTICIPANT/READER TO OBTAIN THE NECESSARY REFERENCES/MATERIAL FOR THEIR WORKSHOP PRESENTATIONS.
- SHOW THE VARIOUS PROCESSES AND FUNCTIONS WITHIN RISKS, SYSTEMS METHODOLOGY AND PROJECT MANAGEMENT.

The actual points of interfacing the various stages of development under the Structured Systems Methodology, the procedures of managing projects (Programme Management) and the assumptions analysis of the Risks methodology are explored in the workshop and in this document.

As such, the Workshop functional skills incorporate a Case study and presentations by the participants, which will include the principles of Programme Management.

Subsequent to the three-day workshop, the 'coaching/mentoring' period will include a pilot practice of the courseware. Further on, it is suggested that the participants evaluate the success of the rollout. Should the rollout be successful, then gain approval for widespread adoption. Thereafter, adjust the practice and courseware for global use and make the practice and courseware available.

4. FUNCTIONAL SKILLS

4.1 Filling the Gap

There can be little doubt that Programme Management will become increasingly important in the years ahead. This workshop is, therefore, aiming to fill a gap in the current business and tutorial literature.

4.2 Programme Management Overview

This Programme Management Workshop has been designed for the Programme/Project Manager and the computer professional who needs an overview of Project Management.

The Programme Management Workshop, as a courseware manual and book, deals with the Management of Projects, where established management procedures and various development methods are explained. This Workshop is intended to give Programme Management staff an overview of the Project Development Methods and some indication of how these relate to the various Project Management Techniques.

4.3 The Fundamentals

The Workshop explores the fundamental aspects of operational computing and the development of new information systems. Projects are conceived and grow from a business need, but what seems clear at the beginning often becomes blurred and confused. In the end projects may not deliver what was expected and costly investment produces few benefits.

4.4 Standards

Just as architects need sets of standards to help them with their plans, so do Systems Analysts, Designers and Programmers. The Project Management and Development Methods described in this book are such, a set of standards. The book contains certain rules, which can be used to develop systems. They are not a substitute for training and experience but a support for these. The methods must be applied with experience and common sense in different ways to different projects. Well trained professionals can do this. In preparing this workshop, the facilitator is mostly concerned with the development and the managing of systems and people in a multi-national corporation as well as the smaller sizes of companies.

5. MANAGEMENT FUNCTIONS

5.1 Introduction to Management Functions

The most important functions that top executives perform include setting policies, planning, and preparing budgets. At the strategic level, these decision-making functions are supported by executive information systems. The objective of these systems is to gather, analyse, and integrate internal (corporate) and external (public) data into dynamic profiles of key corporate indicators.

Depending on the nature of the business, such indicators may relate to the status of high-priority programmes, health of the economy, inventory and cash levels, performance of financial markets, relevant efforts of competitors, utilisation of manpower, legislative events, and so forth.

The indicators are displayed as text, tables, graphics, or time series, and optional access is provided to more detailed data. The data emanate not only from within an organisation's production and administrative departments but also from global information sources.

5.2 Information Systems Enhancement

The present-day efforts are to enhance Programme Management and information systems with adaptive and self-organising abilities by means of learning from the Project Managers' changing information needs and uses.

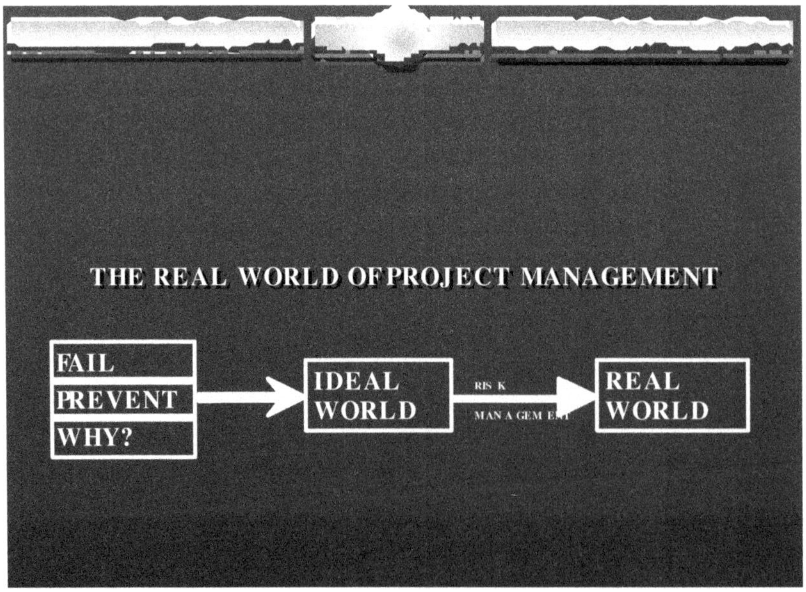

The Project Management systems make use of computational aids for data classification, modelling, and simulation.

Because of the enormous complexity of typical Programme/Project Management responsibilities, the number of changes that can be made and the alternatives that can be pursued, a productive body of quantitative methods has been developed to solve project management problems.

Administrative functions in organisations have as their objective the husbanding and optimisation of corporate resources - namely, employees and their activities, inventories of materials and equipment, facilities, and finances.

The global company's administrative information systems support this objective. They focus primarily on resource administration and provide project management with reports of aggregate data. Executive information systems may be viewed as an evolution of administrative information systems in the direction of strategic tracking, modelling, and decision-making.

Functionally close to payroll systems are personnel information systems, which support the administration of the organisation's human resources. Job and salary histories, inventory of skills, performance reviews, and other types of personnel data are combined in the database to assist personnel administration, explore potential effects of reorganisation or new salary scales (or changes in benefits), and match job requirements with skills.

Project management information systems concentrate on resource allocation and task completion of organised activities.

5.3 Project Management and Planning Techniques

Project Managers frequently face the task of controlling projects that contain unknown and unpredictable factors. When the projects are not complex, bar charts can be used to plan and control project activities. These charts divide the project into discrete activities or tasks and analyse each task individually to indicate weekly manpower requirements. As the work goes forward, progress is charted and estimates are made on the effects of any delays or difficulties encountered during the completion of the project.

Organisations are introducing more sophisticated methods of project planning and control on an ongoing basis. Variations and extensions of techniques are now in use, and they have proven particularly valuable for projects requiring the co-ordinated work of employees and contractors. Project planning and control techniques are now common in many client environments.

In actual projects the relationships among the required tasks are often complex. In many organisations efforts to improve existing products and processes have been formalised.

6. THE POST-WORKSHOP COACHING AND MENTORING

6.1 Programme Management, a Profession

Programme Management is actually a profession rather than an industry. For each project that the Programme Manager is responsible for, he or she will be involved in a range of tasks that tend to start with the initial clarification of the project's objectives, scope, constraints and reporting rules. Through initiation activities, identifying all the actions that are involved in the project, estimating the duration of individual tasks, looking at the dependency one activity has on another and calculating the critical path/s in the project where any slippage will cause delays to the end date.

It is, therefore, vital that Programme Managers undertake a level of training that will introduce them to the skills and attributes that are needed in the role. Further on, companies demand high quality, suitably qualified Programme Managers in most projects.

6.2 Post-workshop Coaching and Mentoring

Because of such demands, the Workshop has been designed with emphasis on the post-workshop coaching and mentoring.

Coaching is about transforming the Programme Manager's possibilities for the future. It is about how a Programme Manager can significantly speed up his/her professional and personal continuous development, to get the results he/she wants in all areas of the programme/project/s.

So coaching gives the Programme Manager the opportunity to focus on her/his needs, which in turn enable the Programme Manager to concentrate on the business at hand. Working with a coach/mentor, after the actual workshop, gives the Programme Manager the opportunity to be exceptional at what she/he does.

The Programme Manager wants results quickly. The post-workshop coaching can speedily get focused and identify the participant's own individual needs. This relationship between the participating Programme Manager and the facilitating coach/mentor has to be built on trust, confidentiality and mutual respect.

6.3 The Interpersonal Skills of the Coach

The participating Programme Manager should expect the coach/mentor to have excellent interpersonal skills so that the Programme Manager feels relaxed, comfortable and prepared to trust the feedback. Of paramount importance is the ability of the coach/mentor to be an empathetic listener.

The Programme Manager is, also, looking for someone who has a sound background in general business and management. A coach, who will be able to understand the kind of issues that a Programme Manager may be facing, Whilst the mentor may not already be familiar with the project, he/she needs to quickly get to know the Programme Manager's business and project/s.

The Programme Manager participating in the workshop must meet the potential coach and then decide how well they relate to each other. The Programme Manager can then decide whether she/he wants a single coaching session or an ongoing month-long relationship. The Programme Manager can use the mentor/coach to help him/her deal with specific business or personal issue, to develop particular interpersonal skills, or simply as a sounding board.

The candidate of the Workshop may discover that the post-workshop mentoring is such a rewarding experience, that the Programme Manager may wonder how he/she ever did without it!

7. THE BENEFITS OF PROGRAMME MANAGEMENT

Actual users have attributed the summarised main benefits listed below to Programme Management.

- Provides the basis for controlling the implementation of strategic business plans.
- Promotes the business view for the justification of projects and provides mechanisms for ensuring their ongoing viability and business integrity.
- The organisation structure encourages user and business participation at all levels and can be tailored to any type, size and complexity of project.
- Separates and clearly identifies and defines the roles and responsibilities in project management.
- The stage concept provides the basis for conscious and continuous management control.
- Concentrates on the real goals of the project, through the products, to ensure a common understanding about what is being produced. This product orientation also enables better estimating, planning and control.
- The planning and control mechanisms are tailored and structured to one another.
- Quality is planned, controlled and assured from the outset of the project.
- Provides an excellent vehicle for encouraging the right people to make the right decision at the right time.
- Confronts the management of risk and uncertainty by asking questions and forcing issues into the open. Dealing with issues can reduce project costs before they become problems.
- Simplifies paperwork by concentrating on essential documentation and the provision of simple but effective reporting procedures.

8. PRE-WORKSHOP ACTIVITIES

8.1 Workshop Abstract

1. PMI KEY AREAS AND SELF-ASSESSMENT FORM
   - READ KEY AREAS, THE SUB-MODULES AND THE SKILLS IDENTIFIED.
   - ENTER OWN SELF-ASSESSMENT GRADES. (THESE ARE CONFIDENTIAL, BETWEEN PARTICIPANT AND FACILITATOR).
2. THE PROJECT Score Card Questionnaire
   - TO BE USED IN ASSESSING THE CASE STUDY SUPPLIED BEFORE THE ACTUAL WORKSHOP.
   - THIS IS ONLY A GUIDE TO PREPARE THE CANDIDATE FOR THE WORKSHOP.
3. CASE STUDY: a current project

   A Collaborative Approach:
   - Business,
   - Government,
   - Changes,
   - Implementation.

   COLLABORATION IS THE KEY:MANUFACTURERS,
   - BUYERS,
   - SELLERS
   - DEALERS,
   - SYSTEM,
   - COMPUTER CHANGES,
   - OTHER INITIATIVES.

8.2. Workshop Abstract

Goals:	1. Train and intensify Programme Management disciplines based on requirements of target audience. 2. Compile and review of Programme Management deliverables, based on a Case Study using processes and templates. 3. Knowledge assimilation of standards: Programme Management, Risks and Structured Methods, and their links to industry standards. 4. Facilitated exchange of participants' experiences. 5. Counselling and coaching of participants on project related and related activities through (a max 4 week) tutoring phase.
Prerequisites:	1. Individual Development Plan (IDP) must be in place. 2. Knowledge and experience about Programme Management methods. 3. Knowledge and experience about Systems Development (overview & navigation). 4. Participants should be engaged in leading project/s most of their time.
Content:	1. Pre-workshop Arrangements for Participants: • Reading and understanding the Abstract of the Case Study supplied, • Comprehension of the PMI Key Areas, their modules and narrative, • Filling in of the PMI Key Areas self-assessment form, • Understanding the Case Study Score Card and its components, • Reading the Workshop Agenda and drafting additional needs, if necessary. 2. Subjects included in the Workshop: • Discussion based on the Pre-workshop activities, • Benefits of Programme Management,

	• Programme Management functions and their interfaces, • Functional skills Programme/Project Managers, • The impact of Programme Management, • Processes, templates usage and PM best practices, • Group exercise based on Case Study, • Discussion on Post-workshop coaching. 3. Focus on Programme Management disciplines (workshop modules) according to the Case Study work: For every workshop module there will be: • Brief discussion of theory. • Practical (case study based) exercises in groups. • Facilitated discussion of deliverables and exchange of experience 4. Organising the coaching phase, which follows the workshop: • Define the participant's individual goals. • Agree individual development activities for the four weeks of coaching.
Methods:	1. Pre-workshop: Abstract of Case Study, PMI Key Areas self-assessment form, Case Study Score Card and workshop agenda. 2. Interactive workshop: Consisting of different interfacing modules and based on a generic Case Study with integrated exercises, followed by tutoring. PMI Key Areas self-assessment form for workshop, Score Card for Case Study assessment. 3. Post-workshop: PMI Key Areas self-assessment form, coaching agreement for main points raised and overall schedule for mentoring.
Duration:	Three days workshop, followed by four weeks of tutoring phase.

8.3 HEADINGS FOR THE PMI KEY AREAS AND SELF-ASSESSMENT FORM

PMI Key Area	Workshop Module	Functional Skills Workshop	Self-assessment Pre-Workshop ABCD (A=Excellent D=Poor)	Self-assessment During Workshop ABCD (A=Excellent D=Poor)	Self-assessment End of Coaching ABCD (A=Excellent D=Poor)

Blank form in the next few pages will assist in determining the various points, as shown below:

- The candidate's own assessment form to be submitted to the workshop coach during the pre-workshop consultation.
- The filled in self-assessment form will be used as a discussion document, on which the training candidate and the workshop coach will agree on the areas and weak points. These will be included as part of the workshop training.
- The discussed self-assessment form will, therefore, influence the contents of the training and the course agenda itself.
- At the end of the workshop training, the candidate will use the same form to assess the score. This will enable him/her to see the difference between the pre-workshop and completed course scores.
- This same form will be used as a guide during the post-workshop one-to-one counselling between the workshop candidate and the coach.

.

8.3. PMI KEY AREAS AND SELF-ASSESSMENT FORM

PMI Key Area	Workshop Module	Functional Skills Workshop	Self-assessment Pre-Workshop ABCD (A=Excellent D=Poor)	Self-assessment During Workshop ABCD (A=Excellent D=Poor)	Self-assessment End of Coaching ABCD (A=Excellent D=Poor)
1. Integration Management	1.1 PWB Components	Goals/performance measurements Project variances (Earned Value, Service Performance Indicators)			
	1.2 Integrated Change Management	Change control plan Assess ongoing project status Interpret and handle variances as part of project control (EV analysis)			
2. Scope Management	2.1 Scope Control	Analyze impact on project scope, time, budget, staff etc. Analyze scope change within existing contract or contract addendum Facilitate change control board where applicable Assess alternatives of scope change outcomes Decide how to escalate involve (DM, CDE, CE)			

PMI Key Area	Workshop Module	Functional Skills Workshop	Self-assessment Pre-Workshop ABCD (A=Excellent D=Poor)	Self-assessment During Workshop ABCD (A=Excellent D=Poor)	Self-assessment End of Coaching ABCD (A=Excellent D=Poor)
	2.2 Estimating	Define and manage the appropriate estimating process usage			
	2.3 Requirements & project scope	Agree & manage requirements, expectations, opportunities (acceptance criteria and sign-offs)			
3. Time Management	3.1 Schedule	Create and maintain appropriate multiple schedules Define appropriate measurements (SPI / EV) Identify and consider stakeholder needs Balance the need for details against comprehensiveness (detailed vs. summarized schedule) How to handle the dynamics of changing baselines also according to performance measurement			

PMI Key Area	Workshop Module	Functional Skills Workshop	Self-assessment Pre-Workshop ABCD (A=Excellent D=Poor)	Self-assessment During Workshop ABCD (A=Excellent D=Poor)	Self-assessment End of Coaching ABCD (A=Excellent D=Poor)
	3.2 Time Recording / CATS	Establish time tracking as an element of the project outlook Perceive time recording as part of an overall reporting process Manage planned effort vs. actual effort, Define and control appropriate thresholds Create and interpret CATS reports Define required project (administrative) profiles			
	3.3 WBS (ES)	Define WBS (ES) within business model constraints (CDE). Balance Schedule WBS against ES-WBS with regard to project schedule control and project time/financial control			
4. Cost Manage	4.1 Cost Model	Create appropriate project cost			

PMI Key Area	Workshop Module	Functional Skills Workshop	Self-assessment Pre-Workshop ABCD (A=Excellent D=Poor)	Self-assessment During Workshop ABCD (A=Excellent D=Poor)	Self-assessment End of Coaching ABCD (A=Excellent D=Poor)
ment		model.(considering inventory costing) Manage Cost Centres (cross charging) Handle purchasing and billing procedures			
	4.2 P&L Outlook	Manage cost variances and adapt outlooks Define performance measures (CPI / EV) Handle expense reporting			
	4.3 Budget	Define/manage project budgets within the business model context			
5. Quality Management	5.1 Quality Plan	Manage the Quality Plan(s) and the QA processes Define/implement actions for optimizing project performance			
	5.2 Configuration Management. Plan	Manage CM Plan(s); usage of results to optimize project and/or perform corrective actions of the			

PMI Key Area	Workshop Module	Functional Skills Workshop	Self-assessment Pre-Workshop ABCD (A=Excellent D=Poor)	Self-assessment During Workshop ABCD (A=Excellent D=Poor)	Self-assessment End of Coaching ABCD (A=Excellent D=Poor)
		overall project change control			
	5.3 Project Standards and Procedures	Control effectiveness of project standards and procedures			
6. Human Resource Management	6.1 Managing Resources	Assess required skills and compile resource estimates Utilize the RTF Process for staffing the project Utilize PPM community & individual networks to identify required skills Create skills inventory and resource estimates Maintain Resource Plans			
	6.2 Project team Development	Create & maintain project team Development Plans Organize appropriate team building activities			
7. Communications	7.1 Communication Plan	Define overall communication plan and strategy Oversee relevant			

PMI Key Area	Workshop Module	Functional Skills Workshop	Self-assessment Pre-Workshop ABCD (A=Excellent D=Poor)	Self-assessment During Workshop ABCD (A=Excellent D=Poor)	Self-assessment End of Coaching ABCD (A=Excellent D=Poor)
Management		project internal & external communication Decide about on 'marketing" activities			
	7.2 Inter-group Coordination, Affected Groups	Co-ordinate deliverables from external groups Manage and escalate issues and risks Push/pull necessary information on time Manage virtual teams (what works / what does not work) Differentiate between appropriate working practices in a multi-vendor environment			
	7.3 Reporting (Status, Dashboard, Variance Analysis, Trend Analysis, Earned	Manage project status for overall project (understand that project control does not simply equal project reporting) Establish guidelines,			

PMI Key Area	Workshop Module	Functional Skills Workshop	Self-assessment Pre-Workshop ABCD (A=Excellent D=Poor)	Self-assessment During Workshop ABCD (A=Excellent D=Poor)	Self-assessment End of Coaching ABCD (A=Excellent D=Poor)
	Value)	summaries / filters or sub-reports when appropriate Understands the effects of reporting outside of EMEA SC (e.g. CE, CI, Dashboard etc.)			
	7.4 Project Public Relations	Market outside immediate area (comfort zone)			
8. Risk Management	8.1 Risk Management	Define appropriate risk process (prompting of management action) Decide on the level of customer involvement on project processes Decide about on central vs. de-central maintenance of risks			
9. Procurement Management	9.1 Contract	Structure and manage contract deliverables Issue and manage contracts within matrix organizations and with suppliers Consider impact of contract type for			

PMI Key Area	Workshop Module	Functional Skills Workshop	Self-assessment Pre-Workshop ABCD (A=Excellent D=Poor)	Self-assessment During Workshop ABCD (A=Excellent D=Poor)	Self-assessment End of Coaching ABCD (A=Excellent D=Poor)
		projects (DU vs. Fixed Price contracts) Negotiate contracts with third party supplier/contractor			
	9.2 Purchase Scenario	Manage purchase orders with third party			
10. Other	10.1 Strategic Value Selling	Assess the VRB process deliverables relative to project (input, deliverables, case scenario)			
	10.2 Organizational Model and PPM Community	Consider shared practices from the PPM Community			
	10.3 Business Context	Consider existing business plan impact on project			

Case Study: A CURRENT Project

[THE FOLLOWING STUDY IS AN EXAMPLE OF A COLLABORATIVE APPROACH TO MANAGING A TIME CRITICAL PROJECT]

9.1. Abstract

The implementation of a time critical project requires a large number of soft skills in addition to the standard set of project management hard skills and supporting toolsets to ensure successful delivery on time and within budget. This paper will provide a case study of how a successful collaboration was achieved between two distinct organisations, the COMPANY and THE CLIENT, in order to deliver a time critical project to implement a major change to the format of the I.T. system.

The following topics of interest to project managers will be covered in this paper:

1. Establishment of ground rules for the engagement and the 'modus operandi'
2. Determination of requirements process – soft skills required
3. Team empowerment and skill sets and how this fits into a structured project management environment
4. How the project managers of each organisation adopted an empowering and collaborative management style
5. Internal and external issues that had to be overcome in adopting this collaborative approach
6. How the project managers knew if they had been successful in meeting the objectives of both organizations – the mechanisms that existed for formal and informal reviews

9.2 How CLIENT commissioned the work

A consultation exercise in 2005 invited the users' views on the format of a replacement scheme of THE LEGACY SYSTEMS, ETC.

9.2.1 Outline project schedule

The following table represents the key milestones of the project agreed between THE COMPANY and THE CLIENT, in order to meet the legislative deadlines:

Requirements gathering	May - July 2005
Project start up commences	July 2005
Business Requirements	July 2005
New System Development (phased)	September 2005 - August 2006
Approved	April 2006
[Include all other stages of System Development and their timescales]	
Post Implementation Review	February-March 2007

9.2.2 Business Partners Involved in the project

The following table shows the full range of business partners involved in this project. All these business relationships required the attributes of working in a partnership with Client Users.

Summary of Soft Skills displayed in the Project

i. The project involved changes of approximately 4500 function points. This was a mixture of new development and changes to existing functionality, all of which had to be thoroughly tested involving most of the partners listed above.

ii. The program of work was set up using structured methodologies. The key message from this project is that to make a collaboration work, a number of key soft skills and behavioural styles must be present in addition to the standard hard skills of planning, scheduling, monitoring and controlling.

iii. The following is a summary of those skills with a number of practical examples given later:

iv. Right People with Ability to Communicate and Resolve Conflict

v. The right people had to be in place and had to be able to specify requirements that could be understood by the system designers and then translated into executable code. It was important for staff working on the project to have communications skills as well as technical skills. [*Soft skill – communication lines had to be open between all relevant parties and many questions asked to seek clarifications. The resolution of conflict was the key in the requirements gathering phase.*]

vi. Establish Trust: Trust had to be established [Soft skill – the project managers had to be able to trust each other and be able to communicate good and bad news in an environment of 'no blame'. The focus was on speedy resolution of issues taking whatever steps were needed.]

vii. Establishing the right climate for collaboration: The project managers in setting up the framework for the project established a mechanism to have a single integrated high-level project plan with shared success criteria, a single integrated team spanning the two organizations. [*Soft skill – the project managers had to use negotiation and persuasion to convince management on both sides that the successful outcome was more important than a rigid process-driven ideology. Both, Project Management standards and Structured Systems Analysis and Designing Methodology allow tailoring which resulted in the flexibility needed*]

viii. Pro-activity when dealing with external communications: Pro-activity had to be displayed when dealing with the Client's many customers who were involved in the project as testers of changed functionality and also when dealing with the media [*Soft skill – the project managers had to adopt different roles during the life of the project. These roles frequently required the ability to 'think outside the box' and to be creative in thinking to overcome obstacles.*]

ix. Culture Change: Culture changes had to be made. The relationship between THE CLIENT and THE COMPANY is governed by a traditional contract between a customer and a supplier for IT services. Both organisations were keen to move to a culture where partnership was the mechanism for achieving change. This project was one of the pioneers of this way of working [*Soft skill – coaching and mentoring of all staff had to take place to examine and change some of the traditional behaviours that existed in both, THE CLIENT and THE COMPANY. This involved appreciation of the different styles of negotiating and the move to a less confrontational way of working. The achievement of win-win for all parties was seen as desirable but achieved in a democratic manner, with some humour displayed in the process.*]

The following sections will illustrate how some of the attitudes and soft skills summarized above were used during the life cycle of the project at different phases and activities.

9.3. Process for Requirements Determination

The starting point for the delivery of the technical part of the project involved the establishment of a detailed requirement and the process and soft skills involved are described below.

The soft skills involved in this process are an illustration of the second habit described by Stephen Covey in his book '*The Seven Habits of Highly Effective People*'. '"Begin with the end in Mind" is based on the principle that *all things are created twice*. There's a mental or first creation, and a physical or second creation to all things.' As Covey goes on to say 'Effectiveness - often even survival - does not depend solely on how much effort we expend, but on whether or not the effort we expend is in the right jungle.' In the case of this time-critical project delivery, it was important to establish from the outset that we were all 'in the right jungle' as it was seen by both parties in the shared risk analysis that the project could not afford to have an incomplete or ambiguous scope.

THE COMPANY and THE CLIENT worked jointly to establish an approach to gathering the requirements using Joint Application Design (JAD) techniques. Workshops were arranged and jointly facilitated by staff. The participants or stakeholders in the JAD sessions were all SELECTED BY THE Client. Those who had an interest in any aspect of the change of formats and those experienced designers/developers who needed to understand the requirements specified. Project managers attended the JAD sessions.

It was agreed with the Client from the outset that a collaborative style of working would best ensure a win-win outcome. The goals of both had to be taken into account in discussions and alignment of these would result in a successful win-win outcome.

An open and honest style of project management was adopted from the outset with regular informal discussions being just as important as the more formal meetings that were put in place as part of the mechanism to run the project in accordance with the Project Management Methodology.

The key soft skill that was important in the facilitated workshops and contributed to a successful outcome was the active management of conflict. Conflict results in an unclear or ambiguous requirement and it was important with the tight timescales that the requirement was not only detailed but was unambiguous and was seen as feasible to implement.

9.4 Other key soft skills and behavioural traits:

- Ask the searching question even if it might appear to be 'dumb'.
- Negotiate for a win-win outcome (it was important to see the points of view from all sides)
- Obtain the strong support of the project sponsor
- Project manager had been trained in facilitation techniques and had successfully applied JAD techniques for other clients. The facilitator has to ensure that there is no ambiguity in the outcome.
- Project manager had the authority to make decisions based on the sound advice given by experienced colleagues and had to have the strength to escalate internally to ensure that all relevant business areas were represented.
- Stakeholders were empowered to make decisions on behalf of their business area and had the business knowledge to do so.
- Stakeholders were experienced designers; with relevant business knowledge and who had the ability to ask searching questions.
- Willingness of all the stakeholders to have a debate but then to accept that the outcome is a jointly agreed outcome for the whole team.

9.5 Outputs from the Facilitated Workshops

The following were the outputs of the facilitated workshops:

1. A draft detailed requirements document. All parties reviewed the detailed requirements document several times before a final version was agreed. This kept changes to requirement throughout the project to a minimum.
2. A request by the client for a fixed-price quotation based on the detailed requirement.
3. Identification and quantification of project risks and issues. These were quantified by in joint review sessions and included in the fixed price quotation. A partnership approach was adopted right from the start.

9.6 Team Empowerment

An empowered team is an efficient working unit that is able to work together and make decisions. The project managers had to display a number of soft skills and attributes to manage the projects in this collaborative way with empowered teams:

- Progress was monitored in regular checkpoint meetings. Issues, risks and project size were also tracked via these meetings. Informal meetings were held as needed.
- The project managers adopted a leadership style that encouraged people to try and work on their own initiative but not be afraid to ask questions of anyone else in the team regardless of what part of the two organizations they sat in. Roles were clearly identified and responsibilities clearly defined.
- Set clear and measurable objectives for everyone in the team based on the understanding of the detailed requirements document. The project managers were looking for end results based on optimization of individual skill sets but playing as a team.
- Ensure that all ideas and information are considered. If a project manager has made a previously incorrect decision or a decision based on an incomplete assessment of all the relevant facts, they had to act decisively to take corrective action. Sometimes a project manager can be wrong!
- Active listening - use of play-back techniques to ensure a correct understanding of what had been said in a particular dialogue
- Senior management was by exception only as characterized in Project Management standards.

9.7 Communication Strategy

A communication plan was produced which detailed all communications between the Client and its external customers and with the Systems Delivery Company at different levels.

Steering Group

	Project Board	
	Project Team (full time)	
	Project Team (part time)	
Technical assurance	Business assurance	User assurance
External partners	Public	Staff

The project board was the vehicle for making all the major decisions on the project strategy. The project manager was a member of this board. The Steering Group oversaw the project but only became involved in major exceptions as reported by the Project Board Chairman.

Publicity took the form of the following:

- Client's website
- Publicity leaflets
- Inserts and dispatch of documents
- Posters
- Bookmarks given away to members of the public
- Shows
- Interviews and articles in the following media:
- Public press
- Trade press
- Radio
- Television

9.8. Project Management Style

A collaborative approach to this project was adopted from the outset. It was essential to have all the staff working effectively as 'one team' from the outset. The project management style was one of openness and honesty. The aim was to create a working environment where issues and problems were detected at the earliest possible opportunity. This meant all staff from whichever organization working together and participating in activities that traditionally they may not have been involved with in a customer-IT supplier relationship.

The open approach and partnering approach is illustrated by the following:

- Matrix-ed organizations were used to advantage to obtain the right project staff
- Independent risk manager displayed listening qualities and as a result more openness in discussing and managing risk was evident
- Sharing of estimates for work to be performed
- Sharing of metrics information at the end of the project
- Sharing of relevant business information during the life of the project

Issues to overcome in adopting a collaborative approach

Internal issues

- Both, Client and Company have methodologies and procedures. These have to be synchronized with each other to ensure consistency.
- Both have particular organizational cultures. Both organizations needed to display a willingness to adapt. Some examples from this case study include the format and style of certain meetings,

involving Client staff in activities that were traditionally the domain of the IT supplier (e.g. system testing).

- Both had to work within existing matrix management structures but could not let decision-making be delayed because of these structures.
- Conflicts of business priorities had to be handled by the Client Project Manager to ensure that the key work was not impacted
- The Company Project Manager had to make sure that all relevant groups in were involved in the planning phases and not at the last minute.

External issues

- Politics - caused a number of key decisions to be delayed from their original planned times.
- High profile nature of the project – Client had to handle significant interest from the media during the later phases of implementation
- Public reaction - Client had to handle communications from the public about the new format of the system. They were able to do this because internal issues had been resolved and a high degree of confidence in delivery was felt.
- Trade reaction - Client had to handle external communications.
- External interfaces - Client had to ensure that external organizations had completed compliance testing of their own systems to accept the new system.

How project success was quantified for both organizations

The criteria for a successful project delivery were established in the Project Initiation document. Both shared the risks and reward of this project in the manner of partners. Neither partner would be successful on their own as the project was so high profile that any failure of one party would have been highly visible. In the case of this project, the fact that new system modifications were seen by suppliers and customers was the main public indicator that the project had been a success.

9.9 Reviews

Informal Reviews

- Conversations between team members, work coordinators and the project managers to check and clarify understanding of requirements, design and test results
- Telephone conversations between project managers to deal with issues, questions with the aim of communicating information as quickly as possible

 Project managers using informal conversations in the office to pick up information, if relevant to project activities

Formal reviews

The formal project measurement of success within this process was the reporting against an agreed baseline using the formal measurement procedures detailed below

Baseline

Project Objectives - time quality cost performance

Business Benefits Delivery Plan

User Requirement

Business Case

Measure

Project Evaluation/ Lessons Learned Review

Close Project

Benefits delivery Report

Exit business Steering Group control

Post Implementation Review

9.10 Conclusions and Summary

The methodology adopted by both organizations has a formal project closedown phase. The review of the new system/project noted the following conclusions in respect of the desirable soft skills and actions required for a collaborative approach to project management:

1. Set clear objectives and stay focused on them

2. The project managers must actively manage conflict and obtain a resolution

3. Set the boundaries for the playing field and allow people the creative freedom to work as a team within the boundaries but don’t let ideology take precedence over the success of the project

4. Establish an open and honest relationship between both parties and communicate the risks involved to both parties

5. Have frequent direct communications both informal and formal. Start out with and maintain a non-confrontational behavioural style

6. Build on mutual trust and respect and create an environment of healthy questioning

7. Have joint plans and ensure that risks are actively managed. Allow appropriate notice and lead time for critical tasks

8. Allow mistakes to happen - learn from them and move on. The motto ‘from a few small failures come greater successes’ applies

9. Use ‘active listening’ techniques as part of project management style.

10. The Workshop Agenda

Time Table	Topics	Method and Goals	Material/s	Who
DAY ONE Session starts at 10.30 5 minutes	*Opening of WS and welcoming of participants.*	*Introduction by WS deliverer*	*None*	*WS deliverer*
12 participants x 2 minutes each = 24 minutes 10.30 – 11.00	Participants getting acquainted.	Salutations and introductory activities	None	Participants
60 minutes 11.00 – 12.00	• Objectives of WS and the Curriculum • WS ground rules • Agenda and WS structure • Scope of WS	Presentation of topics to group, Consensus on WS rules, Presentation of agenda, Presentation of topics which can be addressed in WS, Address problems. (Individual problems will be discussed in depth during coaching session), Mapping of individual issues	Presentation displayed via beamer Pin-boards, pins, pens, cards and labels Usual facilitation material & accessories Confidentiality	WS deliverer

Time Table	Topics	Method and Goals	Material/s	Who
		to WS issues, Placement. Charts displayed in room during WS, Agenda displayed in room to mark progress. Verbal explanation of WS		
45 minutes *12.00 – 12.45*	*BREAK for LUNCH*			
60 minutes 12.45 - 13.45	Participants' expectations & goals. Facilitated discussion of completed pre-activities.	Facilitate discussion of WS group. ing questions and points are used as a guidance for the participants: What do you want to get out of this WS? List your 3 main goals. In which area would you like to enhance you knowledge? List areas where you would like to be	Have the points listed on flipchart, whiteboard, or displayed via beamer Make use of the PMI Key Ares, as an auxiliary aid to the discussion Utilise the EMEA Score Card, as an example on how to review the WS case study and projects in general	WS deliverer steering the discussion. WS participants to discuss.

Time Table	Topics	Method and Goals	Material/s	Who
		supported during coaching period. List most critical issue in a current project. What prevents your project from being successful? What will make your project successful?		
15 minutes 13.45 – 14.00	Sum up of major points requiring further attention	List the most important thing/s, lesson/s learned and tool/s to be shared among candidates.	Flipcharts/whiteboard	Candidates
60 minutes 14.00 – 15.00	Integrated Methodologies. Introduction to Project Management	Top level of Project Management, Risk Management Integration of Methodologies. Project Management principles.	Displayed via beamer.	WS Deliverer.
15 minutes 15.00 – 15.15	*Mid-afternoon break*			

Time Table	Topics	Method and Goals	Material/s	Who
60 minutes 15.15 – 16.15	Mapping of participants' individual expectations (pre-activities) to WS issues (matrix).	Grouping of top 3 expectations and/or issues on Pin-board. Participants to write issues, problems, observations down on cards and pin them on pin-board in the respective area of matrix: Identification of Issues, Writing issues and problems on cards. Grouping of cards into predefined headings, based on the PMI key areas. Reviewing of cards with group, Clarification where applicable, Identification of duplicated points and re-group were	Group activity. Pin-board with prepared matrix.	Participants' classificatio n

Time Table	Topics	Method and Goals	Material/s	Who
		applicable.		
60 minutes 16.15 – 17.15	Case Study Review Part 1 Create collection of the issues and problems, which the participants identified in the case study during the pre-WS preparation. State what individual issues/problems will be addressed Create Case Study Plans, Group candidates into teams, Identify Leader, Analysts, User/s and other roles,	Case Study Requirements Participants to write issues, problems, observations down on cards and pin them on pin-board under the respective heading: Identification of Issue. Writing issues & problems on cards. Teams to Plan the Case Study and the expected development. Discuss and agree Plans. Grouping of cards into predefined headings based on the PMI key areas.	Top level Requirements Catalogue, based on an existing operational system. Pin board Defined headings to group issues.	WS deliver/ facilitator WS participants' input of findings

Time Table	Topics	Method and Goals	Material/s	Who
	within each team.	Review of cards with group: Clarify where applicable, Eliminate doubles, Re-group were applicable.		
DAY TWO 15 minutes 09:00–09:15	*Recap of day 1*	*Presentation*	*Displayed via beamer with reference to wall material*	*WS Deliverer*
60 minutes 09.15 – 10.15	The PMI Key Areas of PMI Key Areas and the Case Study Case Study Review Part 2 Add individual project issues etc. to collection of case study issues.	Review the personal issues and problems the participants provided during 'Participants expectations & goals' topic. Add them to the collection of issues & problems identified in the case study where applicable. Doing so, will address some of the identified issues and problems. Solutions and recommendations will follow,	Pin board Defined headings to group issues.	WS deliverer

Time Table	Topics	Method and Goals	Material/s	Who
		during the workgroup session.		
15 minutes *<u>10.15 – 10.30</u>*	*Mid-morning Break*			
60 minutes <u>10.30 – 11.30</u>	Case Study Review Re-group candidates into workgroups of Leader, Analysts, User/s and other roles.	At beginning of WS each participant is provided with a role, which states a problem or activity, based on WS module, functional skills and any other PMI key area. The content of the envelope to be grouped with the person/s, those who have the same area stated on their cards.	Number of areas are distributed equally to the number of participants	WS deliverer to ask every participant at beginning of WS to agree on roles and activities.
60 minutes <u>11.30 – 12.30</u>	Case Study Review Plan session Each workgroup to be presented with one problem area, the associated	Each Workgroup to identify: Root cause/underlyin g problem, Recommen dation on how to fix it, Define solution.	Define time allowed for exercise Separate groups within meeting room Flipchart paper, pens Allocate timescales for	Individual workgroups WS deliverer to interact with groups to track progress and help where

Time Table	Topics	Method and Goals	Material/s	Who
	issues and problems	Input: issues collection Process: Participants use flipchart of slides to collect their findings. Media is used to present findings and recommendation s to large groups Output: recommendation s to solve issues – of case study, and for the raised issues of the individuals	presentations, for each group Define template of points to be addressed during presentation, based on root cause, alternative way to resolve issue and recommendation.	appropriate
45 minutes *12:30 – 13.15*	*BREAK for LUNCH*			
60 minutes 13.15 – 14.15	Case Study Review Presentations of Workgroup results	Root causes and resolutions proposal to be presented by workgroups, Discussion of proposed solutions, Group feedback. WS deliver provides additional	Charts / slides as prepared by	Workgroups

Time Table	Topics	Method and Goals	Material/s	Who
		feedback on group findings after the initial discussion. Add personal experience/best practice advice.		
60 minutes <u>14.15-15.15</u>	Results of workgroups	Presentation and discussion	Group activity	Participants
15 minutes <u>15.15 – 15.30</u>	*Mid-afternoon Break*			
60 minutes <u>15.30 – 16.30</u>	Managers' Pre-selected Exercise Goal setting	Points pre-selected by participants, based on the Project Score Card and as summarised on Cobb's Paradox diagram. Participants to team up Participants to display principles of teamwork Participants' listing of individual goals for the next 4 weeks. Participants to	Participants to write their goals and objectives. Should be copied to team member/s, as a reference. One copy to WS deliverer/coach, listing the goals the participant would like to achieve.	Teams

Time Table	Topics	Method and Goals	Material/s	Who
		list the top 3 things they want to achieve within the next 4 weeks. Participants to define the support they will require. Goals identified for the coaching period.		
60 minutes 16.30 – 17.30	Goal setting discussion. Share goals, if possible. Progress Review	Participants should be encouraged to share goals. Statement as to whether the WS assisted in achieving the goals.	Goal documentation of the participants	Participants
DAY THREE 15 minutes 09:00 – 09:15	*Recap of day 2*	*Presentation*	*Displayed via beamer with reference to wall material*	*WS Deliverer*

Time Table	Topics	Method and Goals	Material/s	Who
60 minutes 09.15 – 10.15	Summing up of results Tutoring Process and future activities organising. Agree on individual schedules.	WS Deliverer to sum up exercise findings. Groups of participants to select Speaker to represent their findings. Presentation by group leaders to those present Explain what happens after the WS Naming of coach and subsequent steps for mentoring. Explain confidentiality of conversations between coach and participants.	Presentation	Participants/ group leaders Facilitator
15 minutes 10.15 – 10.30	*Mid-morning Break*			
60 minutes 10.30 – 11.30	Tutoring Process and future activities organising.	Explain what happens after the WS	Talk	WS deliverer
60 minutes 11.30 – 12.30	Agree on individual schedules.	Naming of coach and subsequent steps for mentoring.	Talk One to One	Participants WS

Time Table	Topics	Method and Goals	Material/s	Who
		Explain confidentiality of conversations between coach and participants.	discussion	deliverer
45 minutes *12:30 – 13.15*	*BREAK for LUNCH*			
60 minutes 13.15 – 14.15	Case Study, ENTITY MODEL/S Assessment of Entity Model/s, Check that Plans have been met, Skills Evaluation	Participants' Presentations of Entity Model/s. Ascertain that PLANNED objectives have been met. Offer additional support, if any specific topics were not fulfilled.	Participants' presentations of Entity Models. Discussion Counselling	Participants Participants Participants and Facilitator.
15 minutes *14.15 – 14.30*	*Mid-afternoon Break*			
60 minutes 14.30 – 15.30	Course Evaluation by Participants. Conclusion of Workshop.	Participants' feedback and comments regarding the WS.	Written Individual and Personal method of Participant's own overall Workshop Evaluation. (No standard forms will be provided.) Round table discussion	Participants

11. project scoring

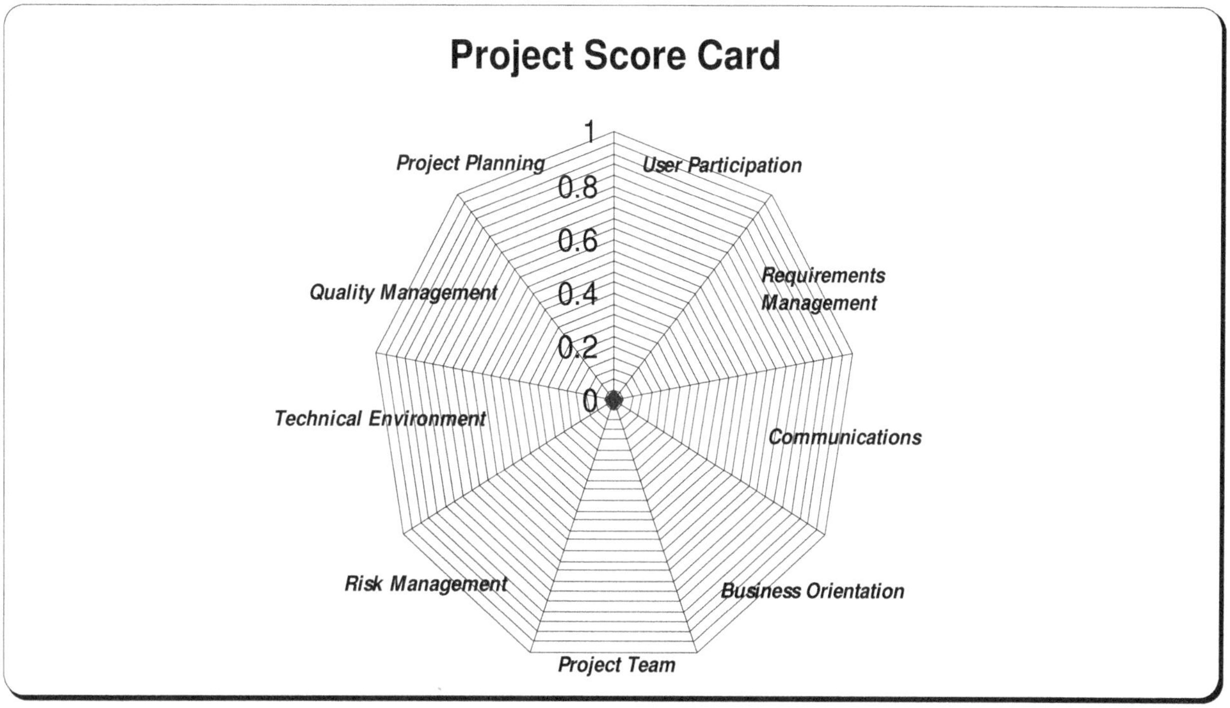

11 SCORING POINTS

1 USER PARTICIPATION	17.5		
Is there a clear focus on user involvement throughout project?			0
Does the project have representative users?			0
Is there a strong working relationship with the user?			0
Have all potential stakeholders been identified and engaged?			0
Project team & customer have agreed expectations for project?			0
2 REQUIREMENTS MANAGEMENT	17.5		
Is the project scope clearly defined, agreed and reviewed regularly?			0
Clear, prioritized & agreed written document of project requirements reviewed regularly?			0
Can prototypes be used to verify project requirements?			0
Mechanism for changes to requirements in place and actively being used?			0
Traceability of requirements against project deliverables?			0
3 COMMUNICATION	15		
Are regular status reviews held for whole project team?			0
Customer relationship maintained through regular communication?			0
Documented communication plan exists and is lived?			0
Effective internal & external reporting procedures?			0
Policy for team members to provide feedback?			0
4 BUSINESS ORIENTATION	12.5		
Do the project objectives align with the business strategy?			0
Does project have business case that details business benefits?			0
Can the business benefit be measured?			0
Does project team understand business domain?			0
Representation from all key areas of business impacted?			0
5 PROJECT TEAM	10		
Committed executive sponsor with necessary authority?			0
Shared common vision and common objectives?			0
Is there a sense of joint responsibility for ownership?			0
Does the project team have defined roles?			0
Does everyone in the team understand and perform their roles?			0
6 PROJECT PLANNING	10		
Detailed plans exist for project with clear visibility to user?			0
Project has schedule of small, regular and attainable milestones?			0
Monitoring carried out against plan & communicated to users			0

regularly?			
Are timely actions being taken against deviations from the plan?			0
Is project management data being collected and used effectively?			0
7 RISK MANAGEMENT	7.5		
Up to date risk register logging all issues, assumptions, risks reviewed regularly?			0
Prioritized risks according to potential timeliness and impact?			0
Regular reviews of risk register involving whole project team and user?			0
Project has escalation pathway for dealing with potential risks?			0
Project has written plans for acting on potential & actual risks?			0
8 TECHNICAL ENVIRONMENT	5		
Project team has technical knowledge required to complete project?			0
Project manager has ability and time to manage project?			0
Project has access to correct development tools & tool knowledge?			0
Is training program in place to ensure required skills provided?			0
Supporting resources provided to ensure successful completion?			0
9 QUALITY MANAGEMENT	5		
Does agreed and documented quality plan exist and being lived?			0
Do practices & standards followed adhere to quality plan?			0
Are non-functional quality attributes required covered in quality plan?			0
Are deviations from standards & concessions documented?			0
Are internal work product reviews taking place?			0
OVERALL PROJECT STATUS:	Green: 80-100		
	Amber:61-79.5		
	Red: 0-60.5		

11.2. SCORING EXPLANATION

1. User Participation
The project has a responsibility to involve the user from conception through to delivery and beyond. This helps reduce the opportunity for misunderstandings, assists in the management of expectations and promotes a collaborative approach to development.
Not only must the project involve users, but it must ensure that the users are representative of the whole user population. Different departments have different needs as do different job functions within those departments.
There must be a healthy and co-operative relationship between the user and the development team. This can be encouraged through two way communications on a regular basis, both formally and informally.
Whilst user involvement is critical, there will be other parties with a vested interest in the outcome of a project. These parties need to be identified and kept in touch with project progress.
By maintaining open lines of communication with the user the project can be spared the shock of unpleasant surprises when milestones are missed, and expensive and unnecessary rework can be avoided early on.

2. Requirements Management
One of the quickest ways for a project to spiral out of control is failure to agree and document the scope of the project and its business objectives.
Requirements must be documented and prioritized with the agreement of the user and the development team. Requirements must be accurate, realistic, and unambiguous. Also, stated at the right level of detail as demanded by the stage of the project.
Functional or usability prototypes are an ideal method for verifying requirements and are relatively inexpensive to build. If prototypes are used, their use must be carefully managed along with user expectations. A prototype is not a complete system.
Change Control mechanisms and a Change Control Board with both user and project representatives must be in place before requirements changes can be made.
All requirements should be traceable from the original objectives through to the project deliverables. Traceability must be bi-directional. This ensures that all customer requirements have been met.

3. Communication
The whole project team should be kept informed about the progress and status of the whole project throughout the development lifecycle. This encourages teamwork and ownership in the project as a whole.
Unless the communication line between the user and the project team remains open it is impossible for the team to manage the expectations of the user, and the team will lose valuable feedback from the user.
A clear communications plan assures both user and project team of their

commitment to communicate with each other in a timely and regular manner.
Project managers need to ensure that correct and accurate information is flowing through to all affected parties in a timely fashion. Informed team members are more effective than uninformed ones.
There must be an active policy to allow any member of the project team to escalate project issues and concerns either in person or anonymously to the appropriate level of management.
4. Business Orientation
Projects are started to fulfill specific business needs which address the overall strategic aims of the business. Embarking on projects which are beyond the organization's experience is likely to be inherently risky.
IT projects are there to serve specific business needs and a documented business case within a value proposition is essential elements for project success.
Appropriate measures must be in place to monitor the commercial benefit to the business. The metrics must be defined and a baseline set down to monitor against.
It is essential that at least some members of the IT project team have exposure to the problem domain to ensure that project staff and customers understand a common language
IT projects often have to serve diverse business needs simultaneously and all impacted business areas must be represented as stakeholders in the project.
5. Project Team
Projects need an individual, who has recognized standing within the organization, to act as the project champion and to assist in removing obstacles that impact on the project's chance of success.
There must be a common vision and understanding of the project objectives. Hidden agendas lead to conflict between members of the team and jeopardize the project as a whole
All members of the team need to feel that they have shared ownership of the project. This instills a sense of responsibility and commitment, and an inherent desire to perform at the highest level.
The project team needs clear definitions of roles and responsibilities ; e.g. Risk Manager, Configuration Manager etc.
Team members must have clear understanding of their own responsibilities but also other team member's responsibilities and the interfaces through which they must communicate.
6. Project Planning
Projects need clear and visible schedules for their delivery commitments which are agreed with the customer, senior management and the project team. Regular and early delivery reduces the risk of misunderstandings.
A project that commits to unrealistic and unattainable schedules will fail. Small and regular milestones help to keep a project on track and maintain customer confidence.

It is not in the interest of the customer or the project to conceal problems and regular customer facing progress reports must be produced.
If a project is facing problems in keeping to its plans, actions must be assigned to individuals on the project team and escalated to the appropriate level of management at the earliest opportunity.
The project must ensure that project metrics are maintained to assist in planning and estimation both for the project itself and future projects.
7. Risk Management
A risk register is a dynamic tool used to document everything that has a potential negative effect on the project. The account recommends the used of the ABCD method of risk analysis.
All items recorded in the risk register must be prioritized and estimates made of size, likelihood and timing of their impact on the project.
The risk register must be maintained throughout the life of the project and must be visible to all members of the project team. Ownership of the risk register will usually reside with the project manager or a nominated risk manager.
The project must ensure that plans are in place to prevent risks happening or to reduce their effect if they cannot be prevented. Risk plans must be regularly reviewed and executed in a timely manner if necessary.
It is understood that project teams will not always have the authority to execute their risk plans, and must ensure that appropriate lines of escalation are in place to take action. It is not usually good policy to transfer risk to other parties.
8. Technical Environment
A certain amount of project work can be learnt "on the job", but a project team must have a core number of people with the requisite technical knowledge to ensure that the team functions efficiently at the outset.
A project is likely to fail unless it has committed IT and User project manager's adequate time and ability to fulfill their roles.
Project team members must be provided with the appropriate development environment and the right tools to enable them to function at an optimum level, e.g. Configuration Management tools,
Training requirements must be identified early and incorporated into the project schedule. Training plans should be timed so that skills can be deployed as soon as possible after they are learnt.
Projects need supporting facilities to function correctly, e.g. real estate, administrative functions, hardware, etc. Resource acquisition must be executed as the project requirements demands.
9. Quality Management
The "Quality Plan" is a single document or set of documents that describes the measures that the project team will undertake to ensure that a satisfactory level of quality is maintained.

The project team must document its standards and practices in the Quality plan, and must ensure that these are being adhered to. Failure to observe documented practice may lead to withdrawal of ISO 9000 certification.
For software development projects it is vital to ensure that service oriented (non-functional) quality attributes such as performance, reliability are documented in the quality plan
It is recognized that projects may have to deviate from the QMS for specific reasons, but it is important that any deviations and their associated concessions are documented in the quality plan.
The Account is mandated to put all deliverable work products through peer review to maximize their value to the customer and to provide a learning experience for members of the project team.

WORKSHOP SLIDES:

THE TRANSPARENCIES/SLIDES SHOWN IN THE NEXT FEW PAGES ARE A SMALL SELECTION, AND ARE ONLY A GUIDE FOR THE WORKSHOP PRESENTATION.

Programme Management Workshop
❖ THE WORKSHOP
❖ PRE-WORKSHOP ACTIVITIES
❖ THE BUSINESS MODEL
❖ INTERFACING OF METHODOLOGIES
❖ WORKSHOP FUNCTIONAL SKILLS
❖ PROJECT MANAGEMENT FUNCTIONS
❖ BENEFITS OF PROJECT MANAGEMENT
❖ THE WORKSHOP CASE STUDY
❖ POST-WORKSHOP COACHING

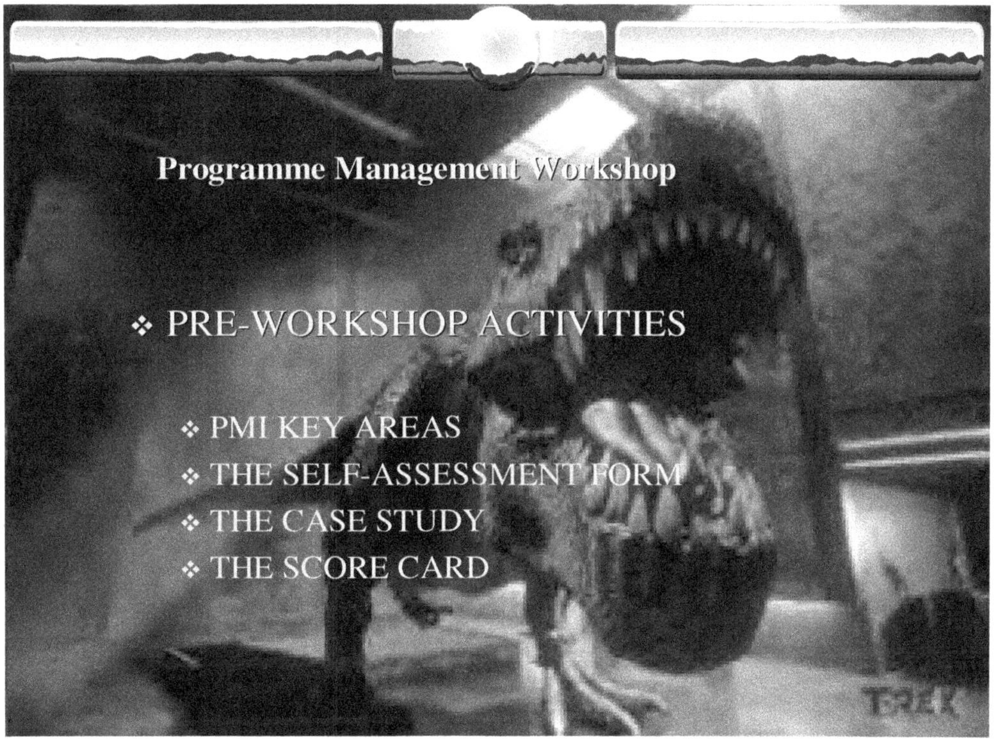
Programme Management Workshop
❖ PRE-WORKSHOP ACTIVITIES
❖ PMI KEY AREAS
❖ THE SELF-ASSESSMENT FORM
❖ THE CASE STUDY
❖ THE SCORE CARD

Programme Management Workshop
❖THE WORKSHOP
❖CONCEPTS AND MEASURES
❖WORKSHOP STRUCTURE
❖THE AGENDA

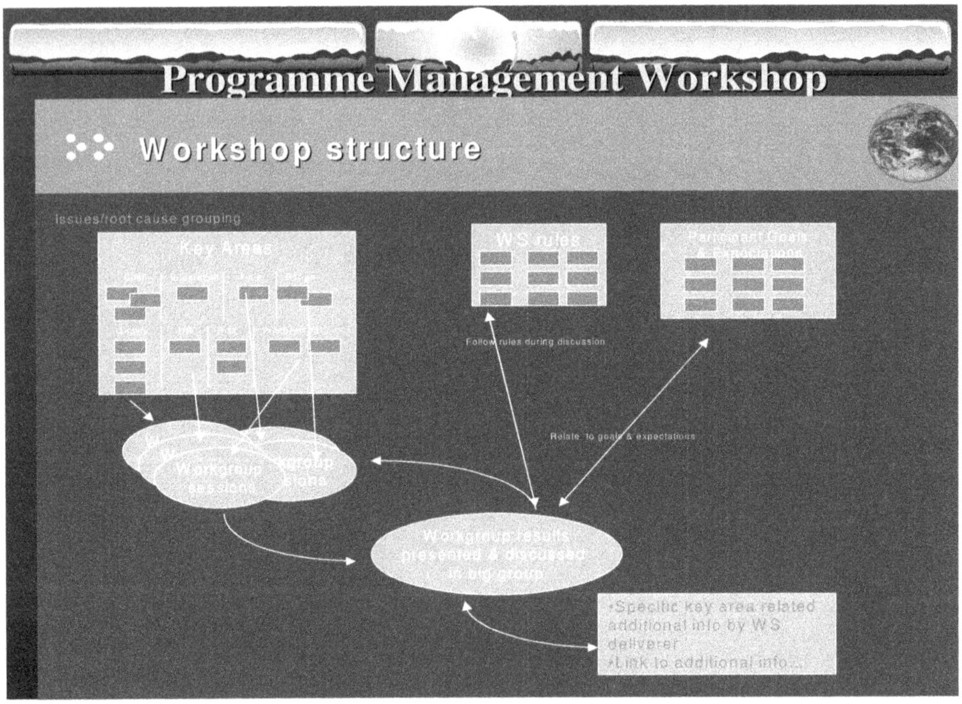
Programme Management Workshop
Workshop structure
Issues/root cause grouping
Key Areas
WS rules
Participant Goals
Follow rules during discussion
Relate to goals & expectations
Workgroup sessions
Workgroup results presented & discussed in big group
•Specific key area related additional info by WS deliverer
•Link to additional info…

Programme Management Workshop
The Score Card:
1. User Participation
2. Requirements Management
3. Communication
4. Business Orientation
5. Project Team
6. Project Planning
7. Risk Management
8. Technical Environment
9. Quality Management

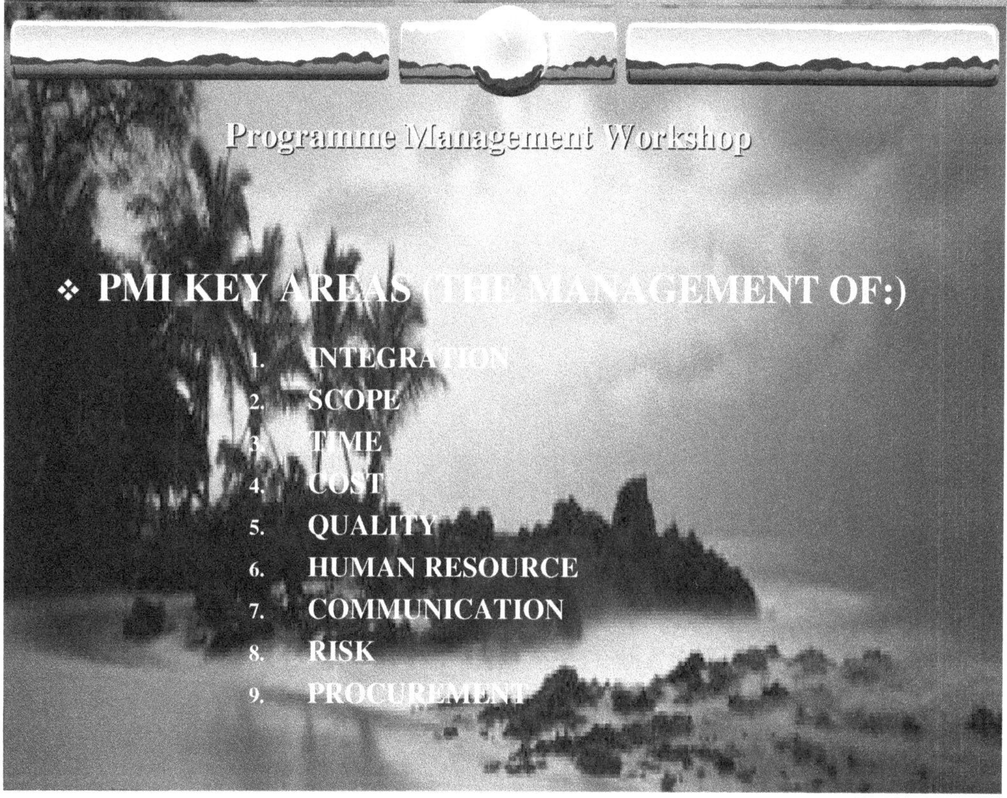
Programme Management Workshop
❖ PMI KEY AREAS (THE MANAGEMENT OF:)
1. INTEGRATION
2. SCOPE
3. TIME
4. COST
5. QUALITY
6. HUMAN RESOURCE
7. COMMUNICATION
8. RISK
9. PROCUREMENT

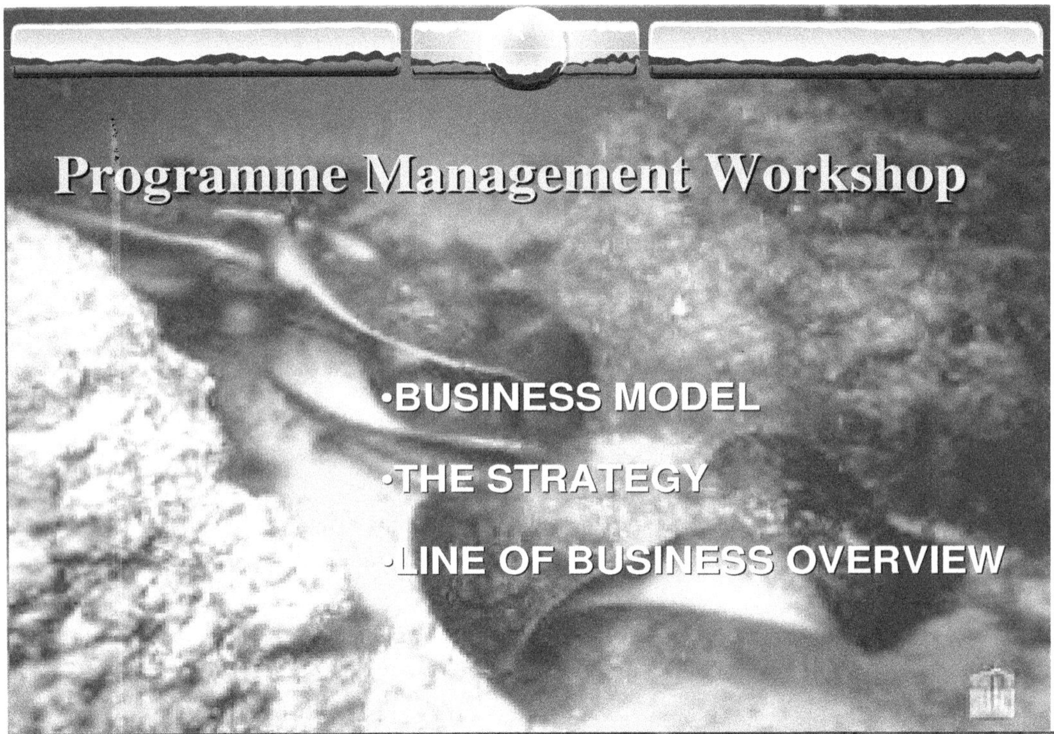
Programme Management Workshop
•BUSINESS MODEL
•THE STRATEGY
•LINE OF BUSINESS OVERVIEW

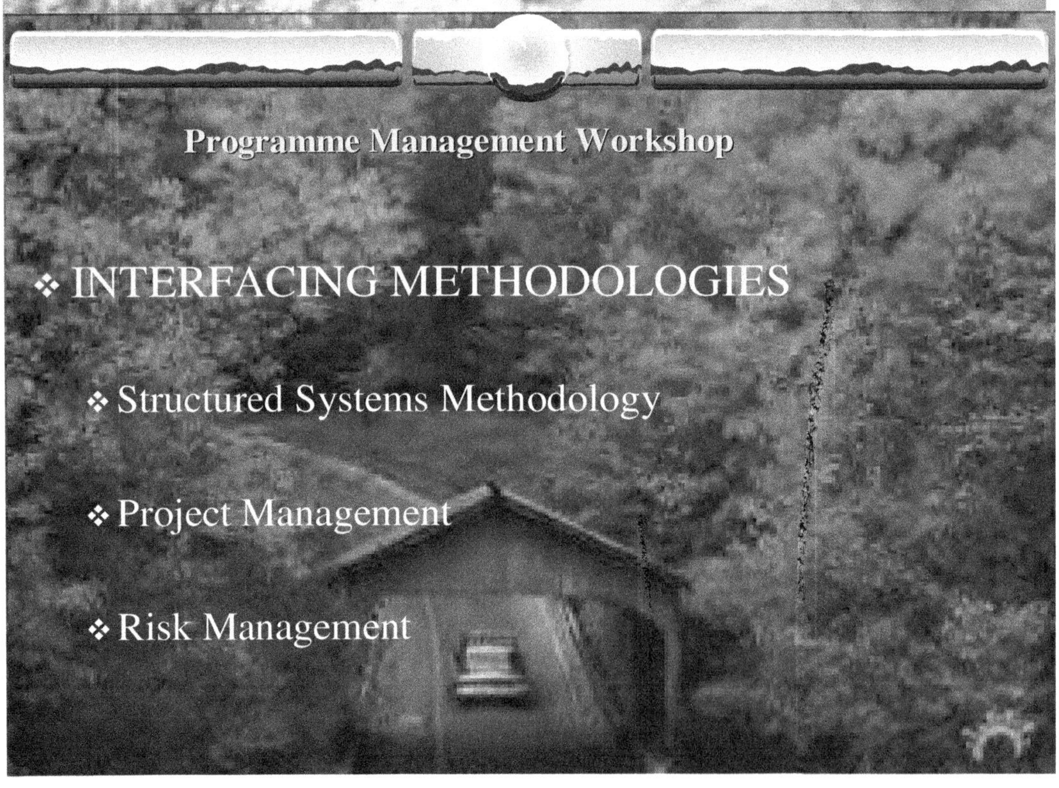
Programme Management Workshop
❖ INTERFACING METHODOLOGIES
❖ Structured Systems Methodology
❖ Project Management
❖ Risk Management

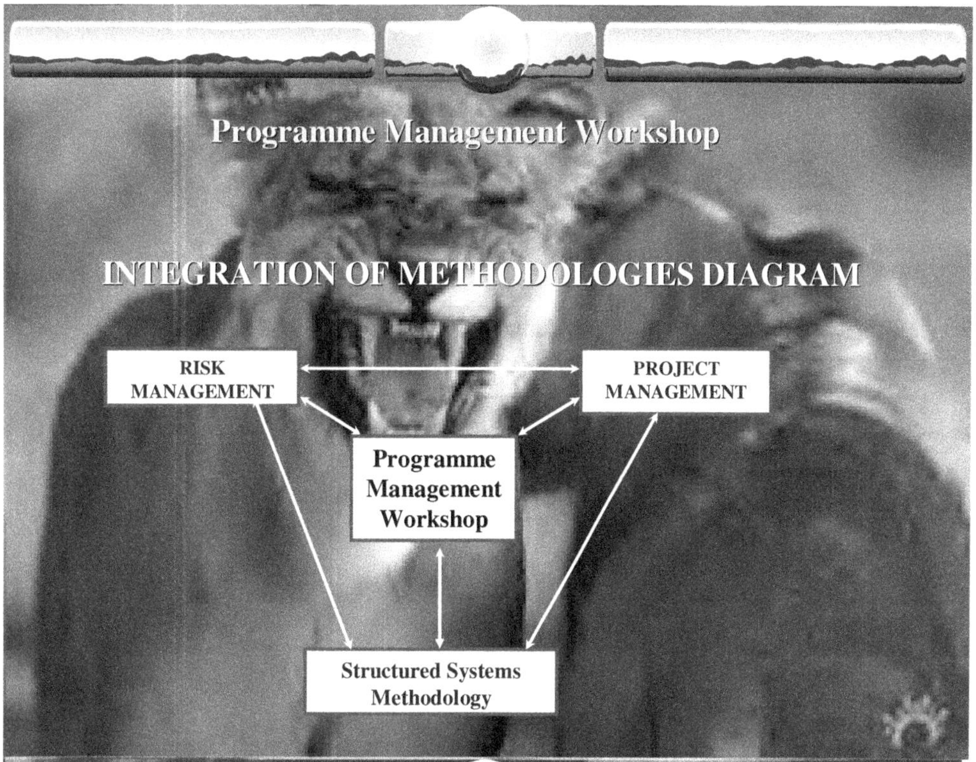
Programme Management Workshop
INTEGRATION OF METHODOLOGIES DIAGRAM
RISK MANAGEMENT
PROJECT MANAGEMENT
Programme Management Workshop
Structured Systems Methodology

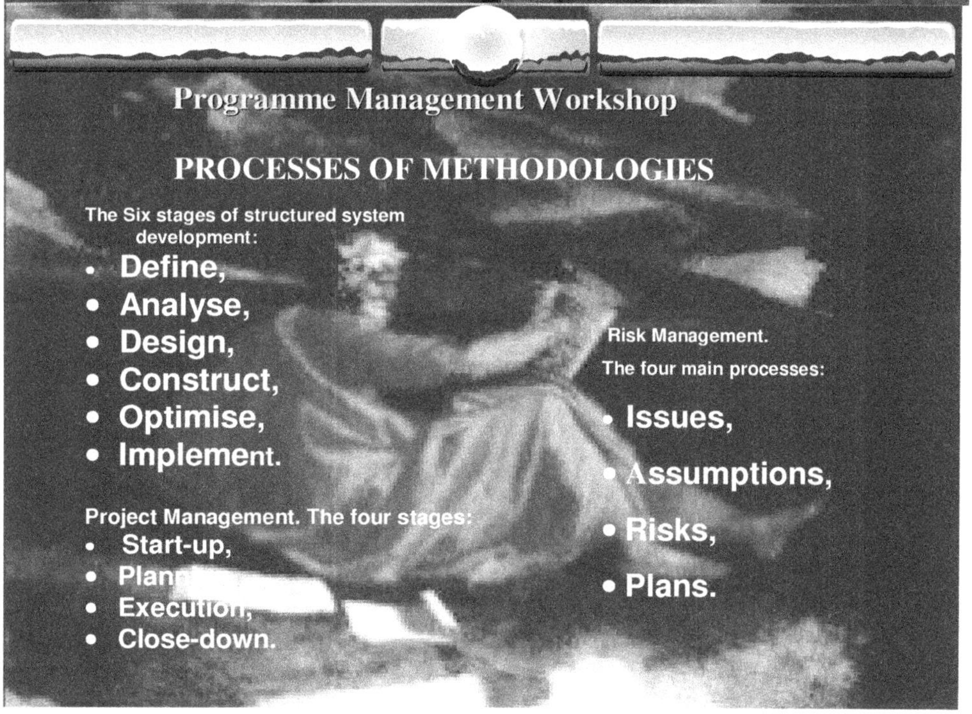
Programme Management Workshop
PROCESSES OF METHODOLOGIES
The Six stages of structured system development:
• Define,
• Analyse,
• Design,
• Construct,
• Optimise,
• Implement.
Project Management. The four stages:
• Start-up,
• Plan
• Executio
• Close-down.
Risk Management.
The four main processes:
• Issues,
• Assumptions,
• Risks,
• Plans.

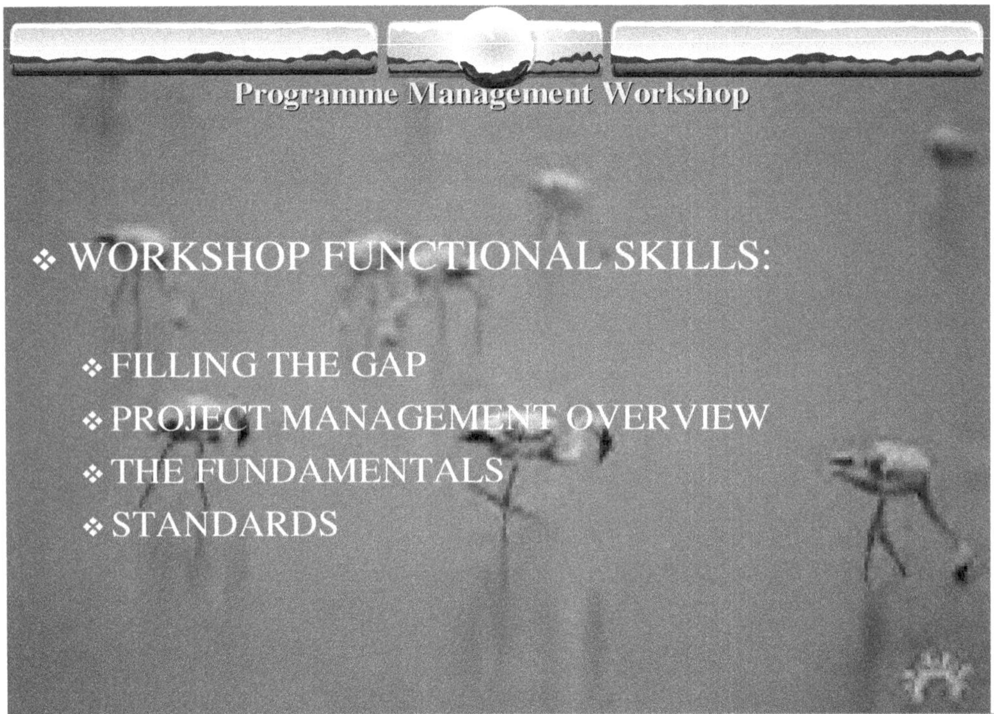
Programme Management Workshop
❖ WORKSHOP FUNCTIONAL SKILLS:
❖ FILLING THE GAP
❖ PROJECT MANAGEMENT OVERVIEW
❖ THE FUNDAMENTALS
❖ STANDARDS

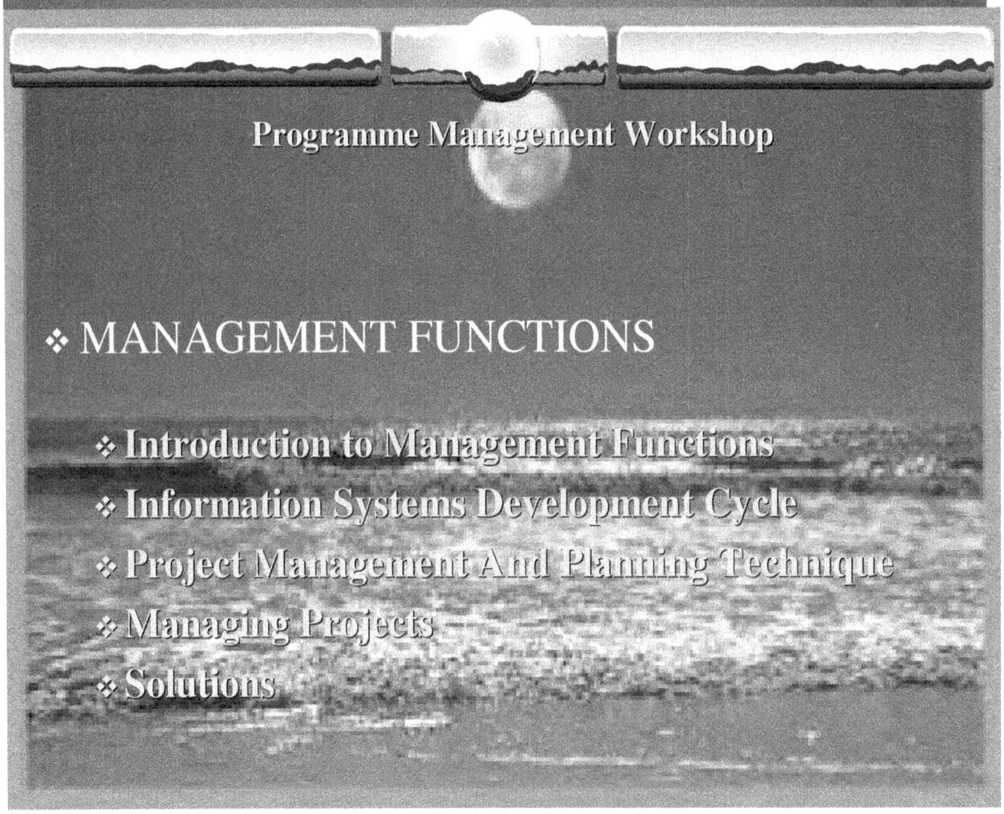
Programme Management Workshop
❖ MANAGEMENT FUNCTIONS
❖ Introduction to Management Functions
❖ Information Systems Development Cycle
❖ Project Management And Planning Technique
❖ Managing Projects
❖ Solutions

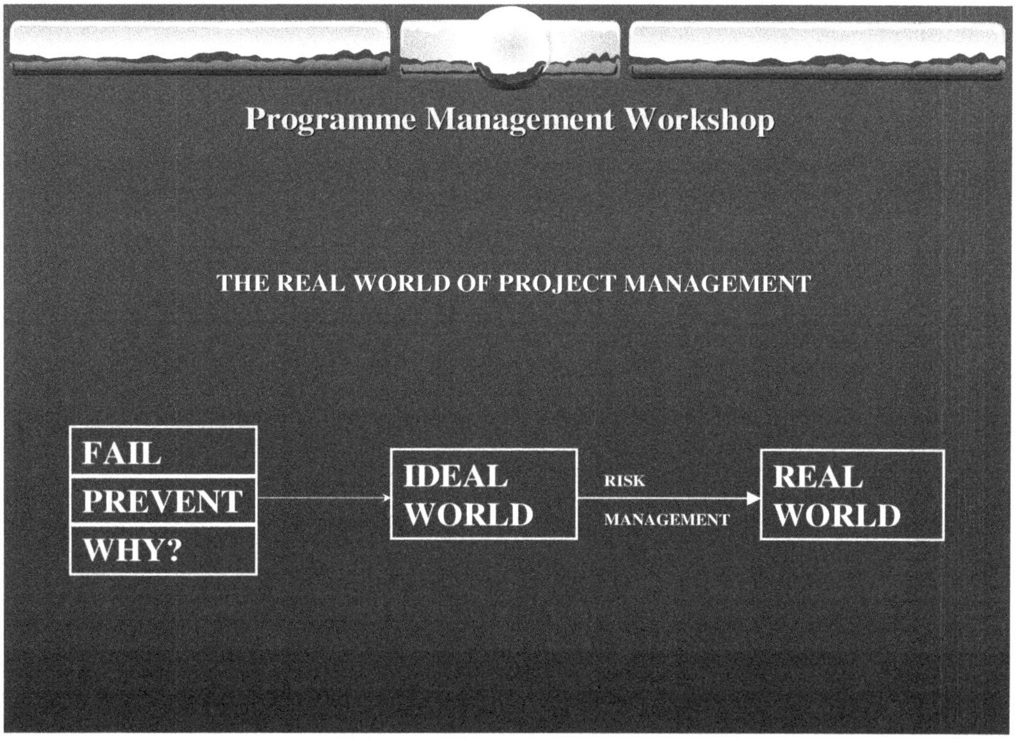
Programme Management Workshop
THE REAL WORLD OF PROJECT MANAGEMENT
FAIL
PREVENT
WHY?
IDEAL WORLD
RISK
MANAGEMENT
REAL WORLD

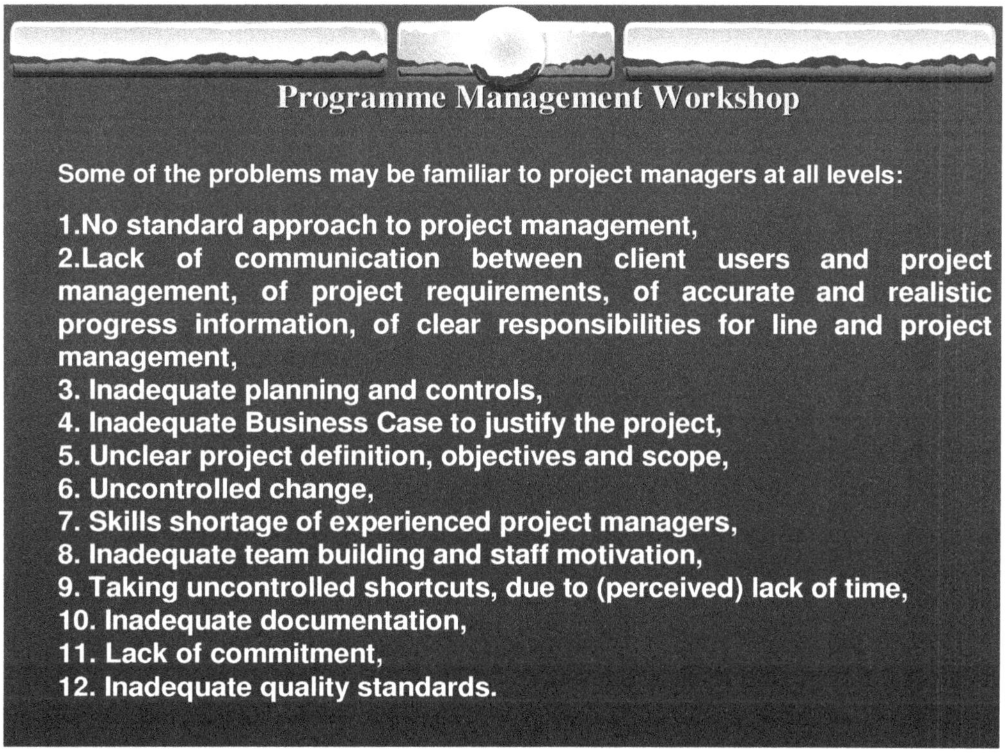
Programme Management Workshop
Some of the problems may be familiar to project managers at all levels:
1.No standard approach to project management,
2.Lack of communication between client users and project management, of project requirements, of accurate and realistic progress information, of clear responsibilities for line and project management,
3. Inadequate planning and controls,
4. Inadequate Business Case to justify the project,
5. Unclear project definition, objectives and scope,
6. Uncontrolled change,
7. Skills shortage of experienced project managers,
8. Inadequate team building and staff motivation,
9. Taking uncontrolled shortcuts, due to (perceived) lack of time,
10. Inadequate documentation,
11. Lack of commitment,
12. Inadequate quality standards.

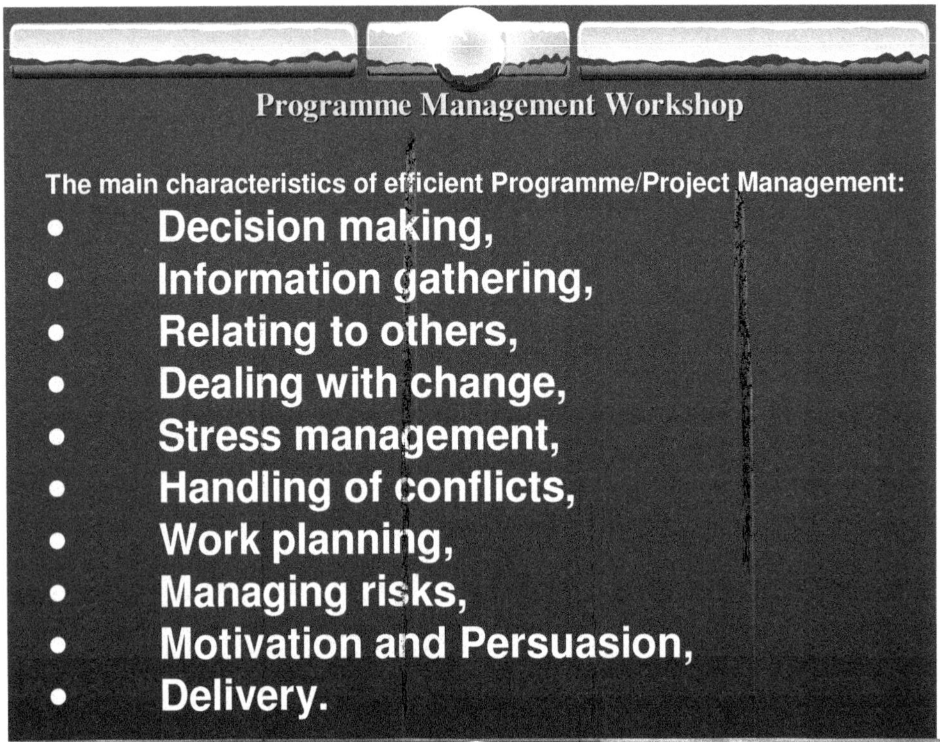
Programme Management Workshop
The main characteristics of efficient Programme/Project Management:
• Decision making,
• Information gathering,
• Relating to others,
• Dealing with change,
• Stress management,
• Handling of conflicts,
• Work planning,
• Managing risks,
• Motivation and Persuasion,
• Delivery.

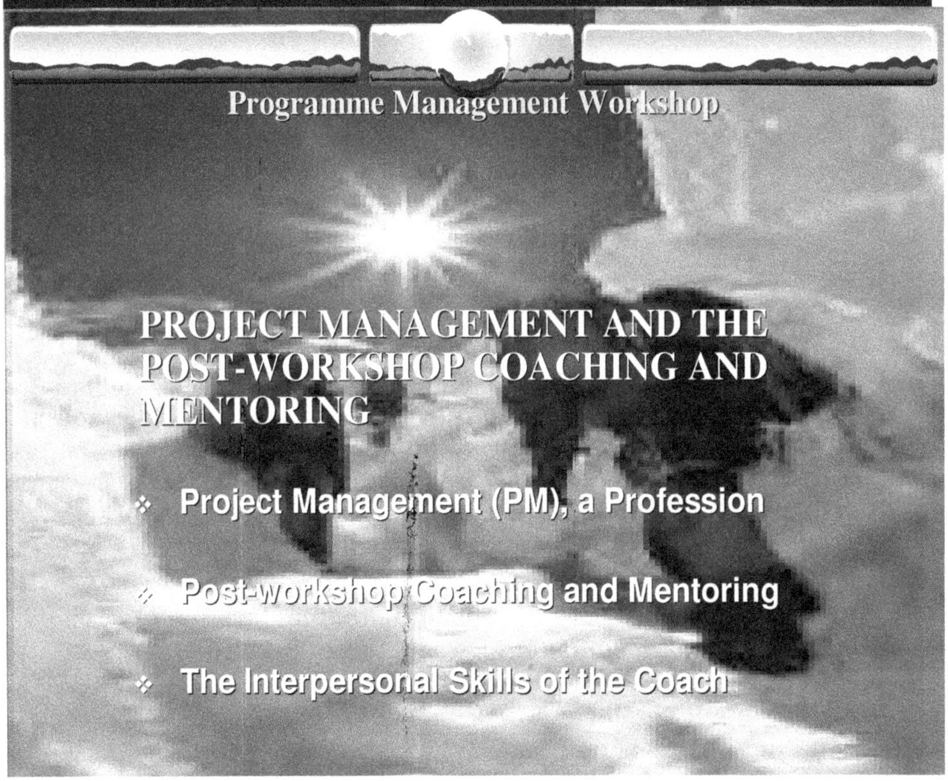
Programme Management Workshop
PROJECT MANAGEMENT AND THE POST-WORKSHOP COACHING AND MENTORING
❖ Project Management (PM), a Profession
❖ Post-workshop Coaching and Mentoring
❖ The Interpersonal Skills of the Coach

Programme Management Workshop

THE BENEFITS OF PROGRAMME MANAGEMENT

Actual users have attributed the summarised main benefits listed below to Programme Management.

1. Provides the basis for controlling the implementation of strategic business plans.

2. Promotes the business view for the justification of projects and provides mechanisms for ensuring their ongoing viability and business integrity.

3. The organisation structure encourages user and business participation at all levels and can be tailored to any type, size and complexity of project.

4. Separates and clearly identifies and defines, the roles and responsibilities in project management.

5. The stage concept provides the basis for conscious and continuous management control.

6. Concentrates on the real goals of the project, through the products, to ensure a common understanding about what is being produced. This product orientation also enables better estimating, planning and control.

7. The planning and control mechanisms are tailored and structured to one another.

8. Quality is planned, controlled and assured from the outset of the project.

9. Provides an excellent vehicle for encouraging the right people to make the right decision at the right time.

10. Confronts the management of risk and uncertainty by asking questions and forcing issues into the open. Dealing with issues can reduce project costs before they become problems.

11. Simplifies paperwork by concentrating on essential documentation and the provision of simple but effective reporting procedures.

13. INTEGRATION OF RISKS, PROJECTS AND SYSTEMS MANAGEMENT
FOR THIS WORKSHOP TO BE SUCCESSFUL, PROGRAM MANAGEMENT AND ITS DIRECTION MUST BE INTEGRATED WITH THE OTHER THREE MANAGEMENT TOOLS. NAMELY:

1. RISK MANAGEMENT,
2. PROJECT MANAGEMENT AND
3. STRUCTURED SYSTEMS METHODOLOGY.

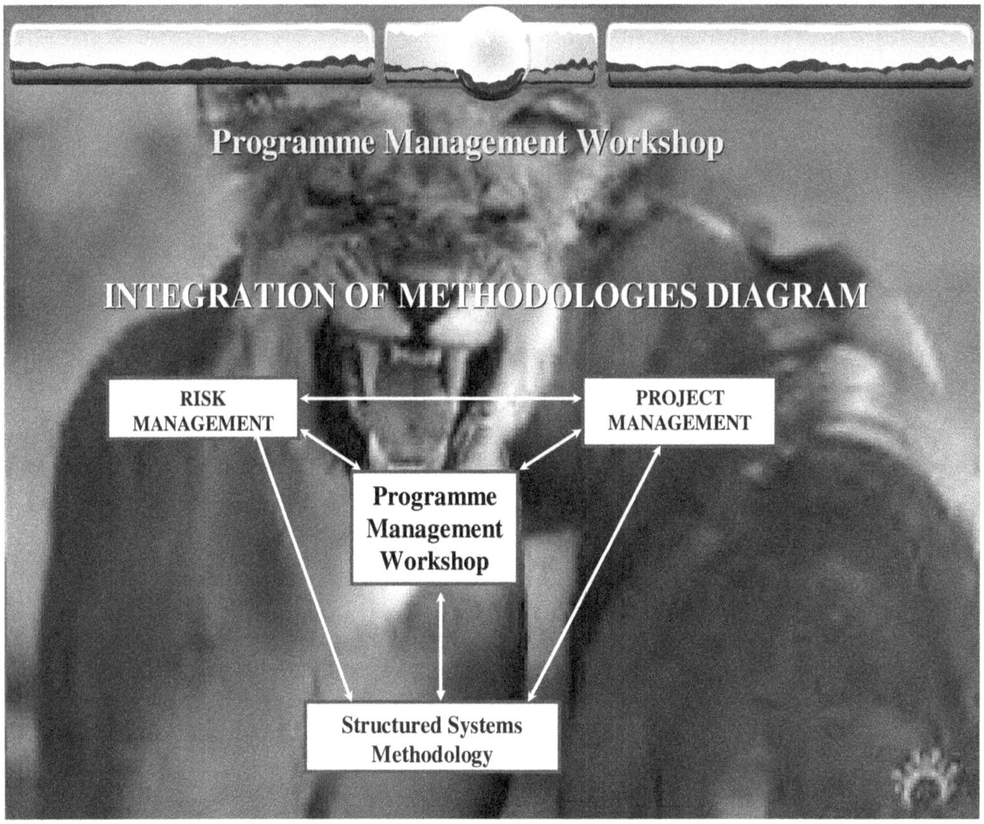

END

THE PROGRAMME MANAGEMENT WORKSHOP, AS A MANUAL AND BOOK, DEALS WITH THE MANAGEMENT OF PROJECTS, WHERE ESTABLISHED MANAGEMENT PROCEDURES AND VARIOUS DEVELOPMENT METHODS ARE EXPLAINED. THIS WORKSHOP IS INTENDED TO GIVE I.T. AND PROGRAMME MANAGEMENT STAFF AN OVERVIEW OF THE PROJECT DEVELOPMENT METHODS AND AN INDICATION OF HOW THESE RELATE TO THE VARIOUS PROJECT MANAGEMENT TECHNIQUES. THE WORKSHOP EXPLORES THE FUNDAMENTAL ASPECTS OF THE MANAGEMENT OF RISKS, PROGRAMMES, STRUCTURED SYSTEMS DEVELOPMENT, OPERATIONAL COMPUTING AND THE CONSTRUCTION OF NEW INFORMATION SYSTEMS.

THE DIAGRAMMATIC REPRESENTATION BELOW SHOWS THE DESIRED OVERALL INTEGRATION OF RELATED TOP-LEVEL PROCESSES:

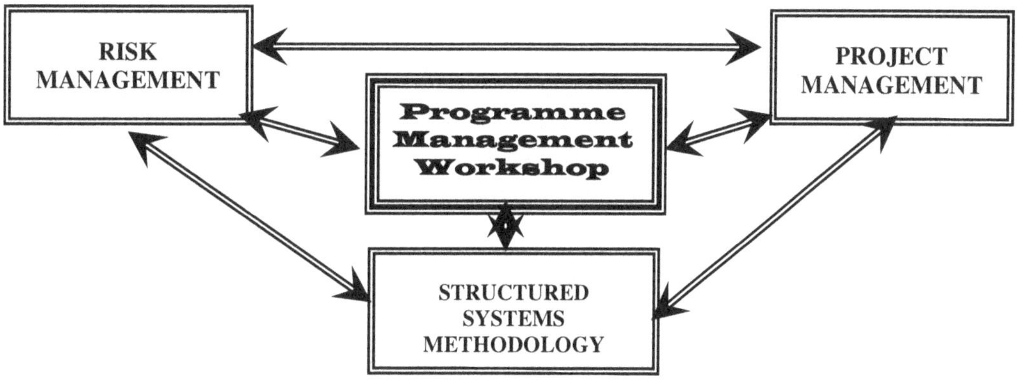

THE PHILOSOPHICAL CONCEPTS OF MANAGEMENT THROUGH THE AGES

ISBN: 978-1-84753-147-6

ANDREAS SOFRONIOU

CONTENTS

1. INTRODUCTION TO MANAGEMENT
2. MANAGEMENT AS A DISCIPLINE
2.1 ETHICS - RAISED QUESTIONS
2.2 CONCEPTS OF MANAGEMENT
2.3 TWENTY-FIRST CENTURY WESTERN LEADERSHIP
2.4 THE ORIGINS OF MANAGEMENT ETHICS
2.5 PRE-HUMAN ETHICS AND NON-HUMAN BEHAVIOUR
2.6 ZOROASTRIANISM ETHICS
2.7 ANCIENT MANAGERIAL ETHICS AND THE MIDDLE EAST
2.8 MANAGEMENT BASED ON RELIGIOUS THOUGHTS
2.9 APPLIED MANAGEMENT ETHICS
2.10 RELATIONSHIP OF LAW AND MANAGEMENT
2.11 A GREAT OPPORTUNITY
3. MANAGEMENT ETHICS THROUGH THE AGES
3.1 THE SEARCH OF TRUTH
3.2 HELLENISTIC AGE PHILOSOPHY
3.3 MORAL THOUGHT AND ACTION
3.4 CONCEPTUAL COMPREHENSION
3.5 THE PHILOSOPHY OF MANAGEMENT
3.6 MANAGEMENT VALUES
3.7 THE EARLY TEACHERS OF BUSINESS STANDARDS
3.8 NOMOS
3.9 POOR LAW
3.10 PLATO (C429-347 BC),
4. THE NATURE AND PURPOSE OF MANAGEMENT
4.1 THE SOURCE OF KNOWLEDGE
4.2 EMPIRICISM IN MANAGEMENT
4.3 AN ATTEMPT IN DEFINING MANAGEMENT
4.4 THE MORAL THEORIES OF THE SOPHISTS
4.5 MANAGEMENT IN ANCIENT GREECE

4.6 THE EARLY SOPHISTS
4.7 THE DOCTRINES OF PROTAGORAS
5. THE EARLIER CONTRIBUTIONS TO MANAGEMENT
5.1 PLATO'S IDEALISM
5.2 SOCRATES AND PLATO
5.3 THE 'REPUBLIC'
6. ARISTOTLE'S CONTRIBUTIONS
6.1 ARISTOTLE'S BEST STATE
6.2 ARISTOTLE'S WORKS ON ETHICS AND POLITICS
6.3 ARISTOTLE'S CONCEPTION OF NATURE
6.4 THE RELATIVITY OF MORAL STANDARDS
6.5 GOOD AND BAD FORMS OF GOVERNMENT
6.6 ARISTOTLE'S ANALYSIS OF STATES
6.7 DEFENCE OF SLAVERY
6.8 THE IDEAL LIFE
6.9 THE IDEAL STATE
6.10 THEORY OF EDUCATION
6.11 ASSESSMENT OF ARISTOTLE'S CONTRIBUTION TO MORAL PHILOSOPHY
6.12 TABLE OF OPPOSITES
7. RELIGION AND MANAGEMENT
7.1 SKEPTICISM IN MANAGEMENT
7.2 THE APPLICATION OF STOICISM IN MODERN MANAGEMENT
7.3 ROMAN STOICISM
7.4 RELIGIOUS CONVICTIONS IN MANAGEMENT
7.5 JESUS CHRIST, THE WILL OF GOD
7.6 THE FIRST PROTESTANTS AND MANAGEMENT
7.7 HISTORY OF NEW ISSUES FACING PROTESTANTISM
7.8 EFFECTS OF RELIGIOUS BELIEFS AND PRACTICES ON MANAGEMENT
7.9 PRESENT SITUATION IN THE PHILOSOPHY OF RELIGION
7.10 STOICISM IN MODERN MANAGEMENT
7.11 THE INFLUENCE OF CHRISTIANITY
7.12 RELIGION, A VALID TRADITIONAL JUSTIFICATION
7.13 PARTICIPATION IN A SOCIAL INSTITUTION

7.14 BEHAVIOURAL DISCIPLINE WITH PRESCRIBED PRACTICES
7.15 MORAL THEOLOGY (CHRISTIAN ETHICS)
7.16 HUXLEY'S NON-RELIGIOUS AGNOSTICISM
7.17 ST THOMAS AQUINAS
7.18 RISE OF THE NATIONAL STATE
7.19 REASON AND REVELATION
7.20 COMPARATIVE ETHICS IN MODERN MANAGEMENT
7.21 NATURALISM
7.23 THE CONCEPTS OF MIDDLE AGES IN MANAGEMENT
7.24 AQUINAS AND THE SCHOLASTICS
7.25 DETERMINISM IN MANAGEMENT
7.26 SELF-IDENTIRY AND IMMORTALITY
7.27 THE FINDINGS OF PSYCHOLOGY
7.28 EGOISM
7.29 SOCIOLOGY
7.30 PROFESSIONAL STATUS
7.31 PHILOSOPHICAL ANTHROPOLOGY
7.32 HISTORY OF PROFESSIONALISATION
7.33 HISTORY OF LINGUISTIC ANALYSIS
7.34 HISTORY OF LITERARY FORMS AND SOCIOLOGICAL CONDITIONS
7.35 OXFORD PHILOSOPHERS
8. MACHIAVELLI AND HIS INFLUENCE ON MANAGEMENT
8.1 MACHIAVELLI ON SCIENCE
8.2 THE SCIENCE OF GOVERNMENT
8.3 SOVEREIGNTY OF THE PEOPLE
8.4 ARGUMENT OF 'THE PRINCE'
8.5 MACHIAVELLI'S POLITICAL BACKGROUND
8.7 MACHIAVELLI'S PRINCIPLES IN CONTEMPORARY POLITICS AND MANAGEMENT
9. KANT
9.1 THE CRITIQUE OF PRACTICAL REASON
9.2 PHILOSOPHY OF "IDEALISM" AND JUSTICE
10. HOBBES
10.1 THEORY OF RATIONALITY

10.2 HOBBES'S ANALYSIS OF HUMAN NATURE
10.3 ANALYSIS OF MORAL EXPERIENCE
10.4 THE STATE OF NATURE
10.5 THE LAWS OF NATURE
10.6 THE SOCIAL CONTRACT
10.7 THE TRUTH IN HOBBES'S THEORY
10.8 THE APPLICATION OF HOBBES'S THEORY TO INDIVIDUAL INTERESTS
10.9 THE RATIONAL STATE
11. LOCKE
11.1 THEORY ON MORALITY
11.2 THE LAW OF NATURE
11.3 THE STATE OF NATURE
11.4 THE ORIGIN OF GOVERNMENT
11.5 THE MORAL LIMITATIONS OF STATE AUTHORITY
11.6 FORCE AND MORALITY
11.7 THE RIGHT TO REVOLT
11.8 ASSESSMENT OF LOCKE'S THEORY
12. ROUSSEAU
12.1 GENERAL WILL
12.2 THE ENLIGHTENMENT AND THE ROMANTIC REACTION
12.3 ROUSSEAU'S MORAL THEORY
12.4 ROUSSEAU'S THEORY IN PRACTICE
12.5 THE FUNCTION OF GOVERNMENT
13. HUME AND BURKE
13.1 CONSERVATISM
13.2 HUME'S MORAL THEORY
13.3 HUME'S POLITICAL THEORY
13.4 BURKE'S CONTRIBUTION TO POLITICAL THOUGHT
13.5 EMPIRICISM AND CONSERVATISM
14. HEGEL
14.1 IDEALISM
14.2 HEGEL'S IDEALISM AND KANT
14.3 IDENTITY OF KNOWLEDGE AND REALITY

14.4 FALLACIES IN HEGEL'S THEORY OF KNOWLEDGE
14.5 HEGEL'S MORAL AND STATE PHILOSOPHY
14.6 THE RATIONAL WILL
15. UTILITARIANISM IN MANAGEMENT
15.1 BENTHAM AND MILL
15.2 JURISPRUDENCE, THE PHILOSOPHY OR SCIENCE OF LAW
15.3 RATIONALISM IN MANAGEMENT
15.4 KIERKEGAARD, SOREN AABYE (1813-55), DANISH PHILOSOPHER.
15.5 THEORIES OF BENTHAM AND MILL
15.6 THE INDIVIDUAL AND UTILITARIANISM
15.7 BENTHAM'S UTILITARIANISM
15.8 PLEASURE AND PAIN
15.9 THEORY OF PUNISHMENT
15.10 ASSESSMENT OF BENTHAM'S THEORY
15.11 MILL'S UTILITARIAN PRINCIPLE
15.12 MILL'S WORK 'ON LIBERTY'
15.13 UTILITARIANISM AND DEMOCRACY
16. KARL MARX
16.1 MARXISM, AN APPROACH TO SOCIAL PHILOSOPHY
16.2 DIALECTICAL MATERIALISM
16.3 MARX'S ECONOMIC THEORY
16.4 THE SOCIALIST REVOLUTION
16.5 THE CLASSLESS SOCIETY
16.6 THE PLANNED SOCIETY
16.7 THE MORAL ASSUMPTIONS OF MARXISM
16.8 THE LOGICAL BASIS OF MARXISM
16.9 SOCIALISM
16.10 MARXISM, COMMUNISM AND SOCIALISM
16.11 THE INFLUENCE OF MARXISM
17. THE MORAL PHILOSOPHY JUSTIFICATION
17.1 HUMAN RELATIONS
17.2 IMPLICATIONS OF EMPIRICISM
17.3 IMPLICATIONS OF RATIONALISM

17.4 HUME'S EMPIRICISM
17.5 MEANING OF JUSTIFICATION
17.6 JUSTIFICATION OF DIFFERENT FORMS OF STATES
17.7 THE THEORY AND PRACTICE IN A STATE
18. MODERN MORAL CONCEPTS
18.1 THE NEW MILLENNIUM
18.2 SOCIAL PRACTICES
18.3 LINGUISTIC EXPRESSIONS
18.4 WORK RELATED PHILOSOPHY
18.5 THE PUBLIC AND THE STOCK MARKET
18.6 CAPITALISM FOR THE INDIVIDUAL
18.7 CAPITALISM FOR THE INDIVIDUAL
18.8 PHILOSOPHICAL CONTRIBUTIONS
18.9 INFLUENCES OF PHILOSOPHY THROUGH THE AGES
18.10 THE EMPIRES AND THEIR IMPACT
18.11 RECENT DEVELOPMENTS
18.12 THE INTERNATIONAL SCENE
18.13 MODERN PHILOSOPHICAL IMPACT
18.14 CAPITALISM
18.15 POLITICAL PHILOSOPHY
18.16 HUMANISTIC SOURCES
18.17 BIOETHICS
18.18 DEONTOLOGICAL ETHICS
18.19 PHILOSOPHY OF PERSONAL IMMORTALITY
18.20 CIVIL DISOBEDIENCE
18.21 DIFFERENCES AMONG COUNTRIES
18.22 LEGAL ETHICS, CRIMINAL CASES
18.23 THE ETHICS OF INTEREST
18.24 LEGAL ETHICS
19. MODERN MANAGEMENT: - THE PHILOSOPHICAL CONCEPTS

1. INTRODUCTION TO MANAGEMENT

The process of managing a team involves the interaction of people where individuals contribute to the running or completion of a task. As in any State or country, under any government, people live together under various laws, rules, regulations and religions. The people elect or they follow a leader, be it a democratic or tyrannical leadership. People under such regimes follow a type of management. In a business environment such methods of management prevail. A Manager will delegate and lead one or more individuals within the organization by running the business or a system.

As in any government, the President or the Prime Minister will maintain the best possible methods for the running of the country and for improving the standards of living. A similar case prevails in the business world. Keeping your staff happy and motivated is an important part of leadership. Especially where a company is undergoing the technological change demanded by modern computing and the Information Technology systems involved. Think of the upheaval that can accompany the demands of a technological change.

Technology of the 21st century is and will be 'electronic mobility'. This will give us the complementary opportunity of being able to work or play as we choose, at any time and anywhere. The 19th and 20th centuries gave us increasing 'physical mobility' through the ship, train, car and the aircraft. Those new freedoms transformed business, personal life and a new style of management. As well as facilitating very large scale economic development, which in turn caused further adaptations of the philosophical concepts as perceived through the ages.

Such technological advance and power brings responsibility. Not everyone responds well to a change or the challenge. While one person may find change exciting, another may be scared rigid. Politically speaking, what is happening outside the country may also affect how an individual views change in politics. Keeping thoroughly abreast of how citizens are feeling is very important. The same exactly viewpoint will exist in an office. Far more important, however, is ensuring that staff know what is happening.

Management styles can, therefore, be considered as political systems where people participate in the smooth running of a country or a company, whether this is a global organization or a fruit stall in the back streets of London. Getting the people to work together, to manage or be managed is vital to the success of a business. Leadership is the key to success, yet not enough effort is being spent on helping to create effective leaders, whether political or business leaders, especially in addressing global issues.

Whole libraries have been devoted to analysing what makes a good leader and yet, although Political Philosophy has a lot to contribute to modern ways of managing, those in the forefront are unaware of the benefits that can be obtained from ancient and modern political philosophers. Ignoring the philosophical thinkers of al ages can be detrimental to the contribution to successful business running.

Traditional management takes into consideration technology. In modern times, getting Information Technology right is only half the battle. Getting the employees to use it is vital to the success of a business. But to enable the correct and efficient use of such technological marvels, people need to learn the new concepts, to train in implementing and using technology. To do this, people need leaders with comprehension of what is involved. Not only the technological aspects, but also the individuals needs. The psychological factors involved, the sociological demands placed upon staff and what makes people tick.

As an example, the training should include methods and procedures governing the way that information is exchanged between the user and the computer system. It ought to involve the consistent formatting of prompts, check boxes, list of options, sliders, messages, and other constructs. Again, as an example, in managing, a leader is responsible for the management of the firm administration, running, managing, of change, care, direction, control and governance. The main emphases are on: an understanding of the processes involved in the exploitation of resources, the analysis of the allocation of resources, and the development and evaluation of management strategies in resource allocation

Within organizations that employ people, managing is the function with policy responsibility for the selection and recruitment of staff, training, performance assessment, career development, disciplinary proceedings, pre-retirement advisory work, equal opportunities policies, pay bargaining, and industrial relations. In small organizations these functions may be combined with other management responsibilities; in large organizations a substantial separate department may be involved in setting policy, its implementation, and in keeping up to date with developments in labour law. In recent years the newer alternative term 'human resource management' has come into use, reflecting the increased importance of this function in labour-intensive service-sector industries.

The responsibilities of a Manager can be summed up:

1. Be in charge.
2. Supervise staff.
3. Adopt team leadership styles
4. Administer and regulate resources.
5. Maintain control or influence members of the team.
6. Deploy the use or know-how.
7. Succeed in surviving or in attaining one's aims.

Such responsibilities are always accompanied by problems. Problems solving can, therefore, be a time consuming function.

Same problems existed through the ages and leaders turned to their learned philosophers to bring forward solutions for the harmonious running of a state or their businesses. Strategic planning, production methods, high outputs for profitability and exporting is nothing new. The Athenians introduced management styles in building Parthenon and many other buildings which are still admired. The shipping docks were as busy then as modern shipping building sites. The training camps for the defence of the state were just as well managed as the Sandhurst and West Point Academies. The Athenian Ergasteria (factories) were employing masses of people. If people were not satisfied with the running of their businesses and their Leaders failed them, they would organize strikes and they would refuse to work until the working conditions improved.

Such political and working circumstances prevailed through the ages, even during the middle ages. The management styles might have been different, but whenever a leader employed the learned thinkers, success always became the forte of the employers. Even the Prince of a state would employee a philosopher to tell him how to run his business. Machiavelli did just that. He wrote his rules of how the Leader would make his people happy. This book takes into consideration Machiavelli's contribution to management. The philosophical details of Machiavelli's writings take a whole chapter in this book.

As such, business improvement through people has long been acknowledged as a management tool, helping organisations of every size, type and location to gain more from their people in support of business goals. This 'tool' is flexible enough to apply to any organisation and sets a standard for good practice in matching what people can do and are motivated to do with what the organisation needs them to fulfil. Benefits include increased productivity, increased motivation, reduction in staff turnover and higher customer and shareholder satisfaction. In fact, such companies consistently outperform competitors in terms of productivity and profitability.

The book is mainly concerned with modern business management and its idealistic concepts. For the profession of management to reach such a functional stage, it had to endure continuous changes in styles and methods of working. The technological changes throughout the centuries have left their mark on the adoption of ways of operating. Especially the current form of Information Technology and Communication, and their availability of details, instantly, has enabled decision making to become a global output on the touch of a button.

Mobile technology is transforming the working environment. Already, much of the workforce spends some time working outside the office. Mobile data technologies are enabling workers on the move to substitute trains, plains and hotel bedrooms for the office. It is increasingly easy to communicate with head office, to exchange information, plan workloads and transact business.

Within five years, the technology will have moved on again to the point where networks will be wireless, laptops will have superseded the humble desktop and smart phones and personal digital assistants will have combined to offer both data and voice in a single device.

The growing capabilities of the wireless technologies, together with major advances such as micro-fuel cells for powering devices, will lead to there being no need to be physically tethered to communications or worried about batteries running down, whether in the office, at home, or on the move.

Such technical power represents a double-edged sword. Used well it can facilitate more fulfilling and productive business and personal lives. In ten years' time we may well look back and wonder how we managed without extensive mobile working.

But used badly, it could be a nightmare of poor practice, increased stress and uncontrolled costs. In particular, failing to follow good philosophical management practice, could quite possibly snatch business and management defeat from the jaws of victory

Such is the impact of technology that people's business historical facts are clouded so much as to ignore the all important contribution of the evolutionary philosophical concepts of Politics, Morality and Religion. As an example, the ethics involved in performing various jobs have undergone changes throughout the ages. Human rights in the working environment, the right of people to dispute, strike and demand better ways of working and living in general, is nothing new.

The reader must remember the strike of workers in ancient Athens, which was the beginning of the democratic approach of running the State and the working places. Or on a lighter mode of thinking, the warning of the ancient Greek women who emphatically told their warring husbands: stop fighting or else you are not having it. That was enough to make the Spartan and Athenian soldiers to stop fighting and seek the warmth of their better halves and families.

When reading the chapters on some of the great thinkers, the reader must remember to translate their writings of Ethics and Morality, the thoughts on Political Philosophy and their interpretation of the various beliefs into how much can be applied to management through the ages. This is the evolutionary and progressive way that Philosophy has given us. Philosophers such as Socrates, Plato, Aristotle, Marx, Hegel, Machiavelli, Hobbs, Adam Smith, Rousseau, Hume, Burke, Bentham and so many more from around the globe.

There is nothing new in the application of styles of management, from democratic to tyrannical and from tolerance to motivation, delegating and selecting of employees. Or the welfare, counselling and stress management of staff. It is hoped that the selection in this book of Philosophers and their ideals will not only help in understanding business and leadership through the aeons, but that it will also assist in moving on with the chosen concepts hand in hand with the future of international management.

Throughout this book the author is mostly concerned with the development and the management of people, the employees who work on their own and individuals who interact in teams. This may include Managers, Leaders and Executives who may be employed by multi-national corporations, software houses, government departments, European Union Commissions, or academia.

Management as a service is given to all types of businesses, in any environment. As a tool at work, managers deal with individual problems, ranging from difficulties within job responsibilities, rifts and business inadequacies, including systems, operational problems and the people involved in such activities.

The moral, ethical, religious, political, cultural and all other philosophical concepts as explained in this book will assist operational groups of people, in various sections of the small and the global business. The modern Executive attempts to merge the latest developments in human sciences and advanced technology. The combination of these concepts, gives a service applicable to any employee, the systems user and the Executive in any of his/her favoured working surroundings.

The Manager's role is to provide a service which will assist in developing skills, diagnose and treat discontinuities which affect the performance of the organization as a whole. The commercial, industrial and human expertise, embrace the whole range of services.

Themes extending to:

- Technology in business environments,
- Directing and management techniques,
- Systems designing,
- Personnel selection,
- Counselling, training and individual development,
- Production methods and artificial intelligence.

Many organisational and personnel problems may be solved. The Manager offers advice and undertakes assignments relating to all aspects of business strategy.

This book will prove very useful to the Executive who wishes to use modern skills, such as the human aspects of system management and directing, setting of tasks, project management and the state-of-the-art in computing, as a tool. The responsibilities within management include the understanding of user personality, human-computer interaction and comparative methods within structured systems designing.

This book will assist in choosing the options, logically – philosophically and will give clear guidance on taking the critical first steps in establishing good corporate policies. Not least, it details how to stay on the right side of the complexities of morality, health, ethics, law and professionalism. Of particular importance is the recommendation to carefully review existing business management practices and processes. These can often be simplified and transformed to extract even more service improvements, just by reading and comprehending the philosophical concepts as explained in the following chapters.

On the academic, educational and training aspect, the importance of a person as a whole must be emphasized. This must be considered as a major factor in dealing with organisational, system and personal problems. In the last few years, modern universities prepare their courses to suit the business environment and towards the professional accreditation of the appropriate professional institution and the various councils. The whole venture of academia and the institutions is seen by businesses as a pro for a continuous human development policy. This ensures high quality employment opportunities, secured in growth industries at the forefront of technological changes.

Whatever the source of knowledge for the reader, it must be remembered that the moral, ethical, religious, political, cultural and all other philosophical concepts are of uppermost importance in succeeding in modern business management.

2. MANAGEMENT AS A DISCIPLINE

2.1 ETHICS - RAISED QUESTIONS

The Management of a group of people in a business environment is the discipline concerned with what is ethically good and bad, or right and wrong.

As this is a subject for leadership, questions are asked and answers are sought:

- How should we lead?
- Shall we aim at happiness or at knowledge, virtue, or the creation of beautiful objects?
- If happiness is chosen, will it be our own or for all?

Management deals with such questions at all levels. Its subject consists of the fundamental issues of practical decision-making, and its major concerns include the nature of ultimate value and the standards by which human actions can be judged right or wrong.

The terms management and leadership are closely related. Strictly speaking, however, the term refers not to managing itself but to the field of study, or branch of inquiry, that has business as its subject matter. In this sense, management as a subject is equivalent to political philosophy. Although management has always been viewed as a branch of business, its all-embracing practical nature links it with many other areas of study, including anthropology, economics, history, political philosophy, psychology, sociology, and theology.

Yet, management remains distinct from such disciplines because it is not a matter of factual knowledge in the way that the sciences and other branches of inquiry are. Rather, it has to do with determining the nature of normative theories and applying these sets of principles to practical use.

The 21st century has seen new twists to these old themes and an increased attention to the application of leadership to practical problems..

2.2 CONCEPTS OF MANAGEMENT

Management consists of a set of human rules, which morally allow an individual to interact in, or live freely within a group of people. This may be in society at large, a team, a professional body, or a group of people with similar interests.

Historically, management is as old as human comprehension. Management and leadership can be traced back to the pre-historic prohibited and accepted patterns of attitudes. Through the ages, attempts were made by thinkers to clarify the way people behave under leadership, share things, mix in numbers, and maintain standards.

In modern times, the catalogue of such values and rules become part of all professions. Management concepts change with the advent of a new belief, codes of practice, reliance on each other, suitability foe spinning and what is politically correct. People live in societies for what they can get out of it and they do same with in a team. What exactly and how much one can get out of a business will depend on the ethical standards set in the respective job. Management as such, will include the religious beliefs, the laws, and social norms.

2.3 TWENTY-FIRST CENTURY WESTERN LEADERSHIP

The brief historical survey of Western management styles and the ethical approach within any type of leadership from Socrates to the 21st century has shown three constant themes.

Since the Sophists, there have been:

- Disagreements over whether ethical judgments in trading are truths about the world or only reflections of the wishes of those who make them,
- Frequent attempts to show, in the face of considerable scepticism, either that it is in one's own interests to do what is good or that, even though this is not necessarily in one's own interests, it is the rational thing to do,
- Repeated debates over just what goodness and the business standard of right and wrong might be.

The 21st century has seen new twists to these old themes and an increased attention to the application of business ethics to the practical problems of managing. Each of these major questions is considered in the following chapters.

2.4 The Origins Of Management Ethics

When did management morality begin and how did it originate? If we are referring to ethics proper, i.e. the systematic study of what we ought to do, it is clear that ethics can only have come into existence when human beings started to reflect on the best way to live. This reflective stage emerged long after human societies had developed some kind of morality, usually in the form of customary standards of right and wrong conduct. The process of reflection tended to arise from such customs, even if in the end it may have found them wanting.

Accordingly, leadership ethics began with the introduction of the first moral codes. Virtually, every human society has some form of myth to explain the origin of morality and leadership. In the Louvre in Paris there is a black Babylonian column with a relief showing the sun god Shamash presenting the code of laws to Hammurabi. The Old Testament account of God giving the Ten Commandments to Moses on Mt. Sinai might be considered another example.

In Plato's Protagoras there is an avowedly mythical account of how Zeus took pity on the hapless humans, who, living in small groups and with inadequate teeth, weak claws, and lack of speed, were no match for the other beasts. To make up for these deficiencies, Zeus gave humans a moral sense and the capacity for law and justice, so that they could live in larger communities and cooperate with one another.

That management morality should be invested with all the mystery and power of divine origin is not surprising. Nothing else could provide such strong reasons for accepting the moral law. By attributing a divine origin to morality, the priesthood became its leader, interpreter and guardian, and thereby secured for itself a power that it would not readily relinquish. This link between morality and religion has been so firmly forged that it is still sometimes asserted that there can be no management without religion. According to this view, ethics ceases to be an independent field of study. It becomes, instead, moral management and leadership.

There is some difficulty, already known to Plato, with the view that morality was created by a divine power. In his dialogue Euthyphro, Plato considered the suggestion that it is divine approval that makes an action good.

Plato pointed out that if this were the case, we could not say that the gods approve of the actions because the actions are good. Why then do the gods approve of these actions rather than others? Is their approval entirely arbitrary? Plato considered this impossible and so held that there must be some standards of right or wrong that are independent of the likes and dislikes of the gods.

Modern philosophers have generally accepted Plato's argument because the alternative implies that if the gods had happened to approve of torturing children and to disapprove of helping one's neighbours, then torture would have been good and neighbourliness bad.

2.5 PRE-HUMAN ETHICS AND NON-HUMAN BEHAVIOUR

Can we do better than the religious accounts of the origin of morality? Because, for obvious reasons, we have no historical record of a human society in the period before it had any standards of right and wrong, history cannot tell us the origins of managing. Nor is anthropology able to assist because all human societies studied have already had, except perhaps during the most extreme circumstances, their own form of leadership.

Fortunately there is another mode of inquiry open to us. Human beings are social animals. Living in a social group is a characteristic we share with many other animal species, including our closest relatives, the apes. Presumably, the common ancestor of humans and apes also lived in a social group, so that we were social beings before we were human beings.

Here, then, in the social behaviour of nonhuman animals and in the evolutionary theory that explains such behaviour, we may find the origins of human leadership. Social life, even for nonhuman animals, requires constraints on behaviour. No group can stay together if its members make frequent, no-holds-barred attacks on one another. Social animals either refrain altogether from attacking other members of the social group, or, if an attack does take place, the ensuing struggle does not become a fight to the death--it is over when the weaker animal shows submissive behaviour toward the Leader/Manager.

It is not difficult to see analogies here with human moral codes. The parallels, however, go much further than this. Like humans, social animals may behave in ways that benefit other members of the group at some cost or risk to themselves. Male baboons threaten predators and cover the rear as the troop retreats.

Leader Wolves and wild dogs bring meat back to members of the pack not present at the kill. Gibbons and chimpanzees with food will, in response to a gesture, share their food with others of the group. Dolphins support sick or injured animals, swimming under them for hours at a time and pushing them to the surface so they can breathe.

It may be thought that the existence of such apparently altruistic behaviour is odd, for evolutionary theory states that those who do not struggle to survive and reproduce will be wiped out in the ruthless competition known as natural selection. Research in evolutionary theory applied to social behaviour, however, has shown that evolution need not be quite so ruthless after all. Some of this altruistic behaviour in leaders is explained by kin selection.

The most obvious examples are those in which parents make sacrifices for their offspring. If wolves help their cubs to survive, it is more likely that genetic characteristics, including the characteristic of helping their own cubs, will spread through further generations of wolves.

2.6 ZOROASTRIANISM ETHICS

The precepts of Mazdean ethics focus upon the maintenance of life and the fight against evil. To avoid such conflict and in order to maintain life one must earn one's living by means of cattle breeding and agriculture and one must procreate.

To fight against evil is to combat the demons and whatever beings, men or animals, belong to them. The two points of view seem to coincide, considering that the forces of evil are the forces of death: good is opposed to evil as light is to darkness, as life is to non-life.

The life precepts can be transposed into fight precepts; for instance, Zatspram as a struggle against the she-demon AZ, “Concupiscence”, interprets eating and drinking.

The two points of view, however, are also contradictory: how can man fight the forces of evil without suppressing certain lives, such as baleful animals? The second viewpoint prevails: Iran ignores, even in theory, the universal respect of life. Buddhism preaches that, or that justifies the vegetarian diet of Brahmanic India. Social reasons (e.g., the desire to maintain family privileges) apparently explain the development of consanguineous marriage, an acute form of endogamy.

The balance of the good and evil deeds, words, and thoughts of the whole life should determine life in the future. This principle, however, is tempered to allow for human weakness. All faults do not have to be registered or weighed forever on the scales. There are two means of effacing them: confession and the transfer of supererogatory merits (the equivalent of the Roman Catholic "Treasury of Merits" of Christ and the saints). The latter is the justification for the prayers and ceremonies for the departed.

2.7 ANCIENT MANAGERIAL ETHICS AND THE MIDDLE EAST

The first management and leadership ethical precepts were certainly passed down by word of mouth by parents and elders, but as societies learned to use the written word, they began to set down their ethical beliefs. These records constitute the first historical evidence of the origins of management and leadership.

The earliest surviving writings that might be taken as management textbooks are a series of lists of precepts to be learned by boys of the ruling class of Egypt, prepared some 3,000 years before the Christian era. In most cases, they consist of shrewd advice on how to live happily, avoid unnecessary troubles, and advance one's career by cultivating the favour of superiors. There are, however, several passages that recommend more broadly based ideals of conduct, such as the following:

- Rulers should treat their people justly and judge impartially between their subjects.
- They should aim to make their people prosperous.
- Those who have bread are urged to share it with the hungry.
- Humble and lowly people must be treated with kindness.
- One should not laugh at the blind or at dwarfs.

Why then should one follow these precepts? Did the ancient Egyptians believe that one should do what is good for its own sake? The precepts frequently state that it will profit a man to act justly, much as we say, "honesty is the best policy”. They also emphasize the importance of having a good name.

Since these precepts are intended for the instruction of the ruling classes, however, we have to ask why helping the destitute should have contributed to an individual's good reputation among this class. To some degree the authors of the precepts must have thought that to make people prosperous and happy and to be kind to those who have least is not merely personally advantageous but good in itself. If nothing else good for the building of the Pyramids

The precepts are not works of management ethics in the philosophical sense. No attempt is made to find any underlying principles of conduct that might provide a more systematic understanding of business. Justice, for example, is given a prominent place, but there is no elaboration of the notion of justice nor any discussion of how disagreements about what is just and unjust in business might be resolved.

Furthermore, there is no probing of leadership ethical dilemmas that may occur if the precepts should conflict with one another. The precepts are full of sound observations and practical wisdom, but they do not encourage theoretical speculation.

The same practical bent can be found in other early codes or lists of ethical injunctions. The great codification of Babylonian law by Hammurabi is often said to have been based on the principle of "an eye for an eye, a tooth for a tooth", as if this were some fundamental principle of managing, elaborated, and applied to all cases. In fact, the code reflects no such consistent principle. It frequently prescribes the death penalty for offences that do not themselves cause death e.g. for robbery or for accepting bribes. Moreover, even the eye-for-an-eye rule applies only if the eye of the original victim is that of a member of the patrician class, if it is the eye of a commoner the punishment is a fine of a quantity of silver.

Apparently such differences in punishment were not thought to require justification. At any rate, there are no surviving attempts to defend the principles of managing justice on which the code was based.

The Hebrew people were at different eras captives of both the Egyptians and the Babylonians. It is therefore not surprising that the law of ancient Israel, which was put into its definitive form during the Babylonian Exile, shows the influence both of the ancient Egyptian precepts and of the Code of Hammurabi.

The book of Exodus refers, for example, to the principle of "life for life, eye for eye, and tooth for tooth". Hebrew law does not differentiate, as the Babylonian law does, between patricians and commoners, but it does stipulate that in several respects foreigners may be treated in ways that it is not permissible to treat fellow Hebrews; for instance, Hebrew slaves, but not others, had to be freed without ransom in the seventh year.

Yet, in other respects Israeli law and morality developed the humane concern shown in the Egyptian precepts for the poor and unfortunate:

- Hired servants must be paid promptly, because they rely on their wages to satisfy their pressing needs.
- Slaves must be allowed to rest on the seventh day.
- Widows, orphans, and the blind and deaf must not be wronged.
- The poor man should not be refused a loan.

There was even a tithe providing for an incipient welfare state. The spirit of this humane concern was summed up by the injunction to "love thy neighbour as thyself," a sweepingly generous form of the rule of reciprocity. Such were the concepts of leadership and the management of such rules.

The famed Ten Commandments are thought to be a legacy of Semitic tribal law when important commands were taught, one for each finger, so that they could more easily be remembered. (Sets of five or 10 laws are common among preliterate civilizations.)

The content of the Hebrew commandments differed from other laws of the region mainly in its emphasis on duties to God. In the more detailed laws laid down elsewhere, this emphasis continued with as much as half the legislation concerned with crimes against God and ceremonial and ritualistic matters, though there may be other explanations for some of these ostensibly religious requirements concerning the avoidance of certain foods and the need for ceremonial cleansings.

In addition to lengthy statements of the law, the surviving literature of ancient Israel includes both proverbs and the books of the prophets. The proverbs, like the precepts of the Egyptians, are brief statements without much concern for systematic presentation or overall coherence. They go further than the Egyptian precepts, however, in urging conduct that is just, upright, and pleasing to God.

There are correspondingly fewer references to what is needed for a successful career, although it is frequently stated that God rewards the just. In this connection the Book of Job is notable as an exploration of the problem raised for those who accept this motive for obeying the moral law:

2.8 MANAGEMENT BASED ON RELIGIOUS THOUGHTS

The subject of religion and its influence on modern management is treated in a number of articles. For treatment of particular religious systems, as well as founders, reformers, and other religious personages, the reader can refer to other writings. Such scripts and literature often cover the following religious subjects:

Buddhism, Calvin, Christianity, Confucianism, Eastern Orthodoxy, European Religions, Hinduism, Islam, Christ and Christology, Judaism, Luther, Middle Eastern Religions, Moses, Mystery Religions, Protestantism, Roman Catholicism, Shinto, Sikhism, Taoism, Zoroastrianism and Parsiism.

The various beliefs by human beings in relation to what they regard as holy, sacred, spiritual, or divine. Religion is commonly regarded as consisting of a person's relation to God or to gods or spirits. Worship is probably the most basic element of religion, but moral conduct, right belief, and participation in religious institutions are generally also constituent elements of the religious life as practiced by believers and worshipers and as commanded by religious sages and scriptures.

The Hebrew tradition had a tendency to place great emphasis on compliance with the letter of the law; the Gospel accounts of Jesus portray him as preaching against this "righteousness of the scribes and Pharisees," championing the spirit rather than the letter of the law. This spirit he characterised as one of love, for God and for one's neighbour.

But since He was not proposing that the old teachings be discarded, He saw no need to develop a comprehensive ethical system. Christianity thus never really broke with the Jewish conception of morality as a matter of divine law to be discovered by reading and interpreting the word of God as revealed in the Scriptures.

This conception of morality in management had important consequences for the future development of Western business ethics. The Greeks and Romans, and indeed thinkers such as Confucius too, did not have the Western conception of a distinctively moral realm of conduct. For them, everything that one did was a matter of practical reasoning, in which one could do well or poorly.

In the more legalistic Judeo-Christian view, however, it is one thing to lack practical wisdom in, say, household budgeting, and a quite different and much more serious matter to fall short of what the moral law requires. This distinction between the moral and the non-moral realms in managing now affects every question in Western business ethics, including the very way the questions themselves are framed.

The new Christian ethical standards did lead to some changes in Roman morality. Perhaps the most vital was a new sense of the equal moral status of all human beings.

The Stoics had been the first to elaborate this conception, grounding equality on the common capacity to reason. For Christians, humans are equal because they are all potentially immortal and equally precious in the sight of God. This caused Christians to condemn a wide variety of practices that had been accepted by both Greek and Roman business moralists.

Once the Roman Empire became Christian, however, this was one of the inconvenient ideas that had to yield. In spite of what Jesus had said about turning the other cheek, the church leaders declared that killing in a "just war" was not a sin. The Christian condemnation of killing in gladiatorial games, on the other hand, had a more permanent effect.

Finally, but perhaps most importantly, while Christian emperors continued to uphold the legality of slavery, the Christian church accepted slaves as equals, admitted them to its ceremonies, and regarded the granting of freedom to slaves as a virtuous, if not obligatory, act. This moral pressure led over several hundred years to the gradual disappearance of slavery in Europe. Instead in modern principles of management we have employers and employees.

The Christian contribution to improving the position of employees can also be linked with the distinctively Christian list of virtues. Some of the virtues described by Aristotle, as, for example, greatness of soul, are quite contrary in spirit to Christian virtues such as humility. In general, it can be said that the Greeks and Romans prized independence, self-reliance, magnanimity, and worldly success.

By contrast, Christians saw virtue in meekness, obedience, patience, and resignation. As the Greeks and Romans conceived virtue, a virtuous slave (or modern terms – an employee) was almost a contradiction in terms, but for Christians there was nothing in the state of slavery (employment) that was incompatible with the highest moral character of management.

2.9 APPLIED MANAGEMENT ETHICS

The most striking development in the study of management ethics since the mid-1960s has been the growth of interest among philosophers in practical, or applied, ethics; i.e., the application of normative theories to practical moral problems. This is not, admittedly, a totally new departure. From Plato onward moral philosophers have concerned themselves with practical questions, including suicide, the exposure of infants, the treatment of women, and the proper behaviour of public officials.

Nevertheless, during the first six decades of the 20th century moral philosophers largely isolated themselves from practical ethics - something that now seems all but incredible, considering the traumatic events through which most of them lived. There were one or two notable exceptions.

The philosopher Bertrand Russell was very much involved in practical issues, but his stature among his colleagues was based on his work in logic and metaphysics and had nothing to do with his writings on topics such as disarmament and sexual morality. Russell himself seems to have regarded his practical contributions as largely separate from his philosophical work and did not develop his ethical views in any systematic or rigorous fashion.

The prevailing view of the period was that moral philosophy is quite separate from 'moralising', a task best left to teachers of management. What was not generally considered was whether moral philosophers could, without merely preaching, make an effective contribution to discussions of practical issues involving difficult business, leadership and management questions.

Applied management ethics soon became part of the teaching of most philosophy departments of universities in English-speaking countries. Here it is not possible to do more than briefly mention some of the major areas of applied business ethics and point to the issues that they raise.

2.10 RELATIONSHIP OF LAW AND MANAGEMENT

The legal philosopher Lon Fuller has distinguished between 'the morality of aspiration' and 'the morality of duty'. The former may be denoted ethics, the latter law. Ethics tells people what they should do and embodies the ideals they should strive to attain. Unethical behaviour leads to punishments that are related to how an individual is perceived, both by himself and by his fellow man. Law, on the other hand, provides boundaries of actions, set by society, beyond which a person may go only by risking external sanctions, such as incarceration or loss of a medical license.

This may explain why ethical codes usually involve generalities, while laws tend to be more specific. For example, the Hippocratic Oath, formulated in the 5th century BC, is concerned with the physician's doing no harm, refraining from performing abortions and giving deadly drugs, and maintaining strict confidentiality. Law, on the other hand, may permit abortions under certain circumstances, permit the giving of potentially lethal drugs in extreme situations, and sanction the violation of confidentiality when the interests of society demand it.

At this point of writing the author would like to introduce his own thoughts of a kind of International Code of Management.

- A Manager must always maintain the highest standards of professional conduct.
- A Manager must practice his profession uninfluenced by motives of profits only.
- A Manager must always bear in mind the obligation of protecting his employees' rights.
- A Manager shall preserve absolute secrecy on all he knows about his company because of the confidence entrusted in him.

Modern managers now worry about the law as well as ethics, and they fear criminal lawsuits that allege malpractice. In fact, managers are rarely taken to court on criminal charges for actions concerning decisions that are made in good faith

While ethics and law are concerned with different concepts of right and wrong, in management they find common ground in their fundamental principles. Both law and ethics in business rest on the principle of self-determination by competent individuals.

2.11 A GREAT OPPORTUNITY

Mobile technology has changed the ways we live and work. But its real potential has not yet been achieved. Harnessing technology is vital for businesses who want to perform better. Among the new trends emerging are that businesses are increasingly selective in their applications of management and are much more astute in measuring its benefits.

Within 20m years mobile and wireless technologies have become rapidly maturing and pervasive methods of applications. The necessity to improve in various areas is constantly demanded. Improving mobile working and the management practices of this can have a fundamental effect on the attractiveness of a company. Becoming more flexible can help reduce staff turnover and create a happier workforce. One of the major points raised in many of the philosophical concepts explained in this book.

The message to business, leaders, directors, managers and executives is clear; the trend towards flexible working practices is strong and irreversible – and for a good business management and lifestyle reasons. The key for businesses is to understand this trend and to protect their future competitiveness by blending the innovative and evolving technologies with new ways of working.

3. MANAGEMENT ETHICS THROUGH THE AGES

3.1 THE SEARCH OF TRUTH

To be a philosopher (lover of wisdom) means that one uses reason and argument in the search for truth and the nature of reality, especially of the causes and nature of things and of the principles governing existence, perception, human behaviour, and the material universe.

Philosophical activities can also be directed at understanding and clarifying the concepts, methods, and doctrines of other disciplines, or at reasoning itself and the concepts, methods, and doctrines of such general notions as truth, possibility, knowledge (epistemology), necessity, existence (ontology and metaphysics), and proof.

Philosophy has many different areas, classified according to the subject-matter of the problems being addressed thus:

- Philosophy of mind is concerned with questions such as 'how does the mental interact with the physical'?
- Philosophy of mathematics with questions such as 'what constitutes a proof?'
- Of religion ('does God exist?');
- Of science ('what constitutes good evidence for a hypothesis?');

The first philosophers were also the first scientists, people who asked questions about the physical world and who attempted to answer them by observation (empiricism) and reasoning (rationalism) rather than by appealing to magic or to a God of some kind. These people, known as the pre-Socratics, were the precursors of Socrates, Plato, and Aristotle, the three great philosophers who set the agenda for many of the philosophical questions debated today.

Philosophy regularly gives birth to new disciplines as one group of the questions it is trying to answer become amenable to study by the physical sciences. Psychology, for example, is a discipline that is still in the process of separating itself from philosophy. Great advances in philosophical thinking have usually accompanied great advances in scientific thinking.

For example, Galileo's work on the mechanics of planetary motion in the late 16th century was a motivating force in Descartes' work on knowledge and justification, while the physicist Albert Einstein (1879-1955) paid tribute to Hume as one of the philosophers whose work inspired his theory of relativity. In the 20th century, the principal schools of philosophy are continental philosophy and logico-analytic philosophy. Within these principal schools, however, there are major divisions according to sides taken in the various great disputes of philosophy.

For example, until fairly recently it was a matter of great concern whether someone was a dualist or a monist - whether they believed that there are two different sorts of substance (the physical and the mental), or only one sort - either the physical (materialism) or the mental.

There are also major disputes about whether or not there are such things as 'innate ideas', concepts that are inborn rather than acquired through experience, and whether we can make sense of a world that is independent of us and our minds (realism) or whether the mind is in fact more fundamental than some extra-mental reality (idealism).

Rather than being empirical scientists, philosophers try to discern the logical form of the problems in which they are interested and to discover hidden fallacies or habits of mind, which might be obscuring understanding. The only experiments indulged in by philosophers are thought experiments.

The interpretation of various doctrines in modern physics is currently of great interest to philosophers: at least one interpretation of the laws of quantum physics would invalidate some of the rules of classical logic. Moreover, advances in engineering, computing, management and psychology have brought us close to the production of an artificial intelligence, a fact of interest not only to philosophers of mind, but one that introduces ethical questions of great importance.

Major areas in which philosophy can be applied to the problems of everyday life are business management, moral and political philosophy, especially in medical ethics such as the prevention of conception and the enhancement of fertility.

In such cases very deep moral problems arise, the solutions to which require sustained and critical examination of what is right and what is wrong. Interdisciplinary committees in which philosophers play a major part usually carry out these investigations.

3.2 HELLENISTIC AGE PHILOSOPHY

The philosophers of the period pursued autarheia: self-sufficiency, or nonattachment. The cynics, whose founder was Diogenes of Sinope, took the most extreme position. (c. 400-325 BC) Behind his rejection of traditional allegiances lay a profound concern with moral values. What matters to human beings, he taught, was not social status or nationality but individual well being, achieved by a reliance on one's natural endowments. He was followed by the attractive couple Crates (c. 365-285 BC) and Hipparchia. Zeno (335-263 BC), founder of the stoics, began from here. To the stoics nothing is good but virtue, nothing bad but vice; all else is indifferent.

The stoics were pantheists. They believed that all is in the hands of God; indeed, God is all. Moreover, all is for the best in the best of all possible worlds, and human beings only have to accept and give praise. Zeno was succeeded by a religious genius named Cleanthes (331-232 BC) and he by the great systematiser Chrysippus (c. 280-207 BC). The 2nd century produced Panaetius (c. 185-109 BC). He smoothed away some of the sharper stoic paradoxes for the Romans, and the first brought Poseidonius (c. 135-50 BC), another mediator between east and west.

Epicurus (341-270 BC), an Athenian contemporary of Zeno, stood poles apart in thought from the stoics. In opposition to their moralism he taught that the goal of life is pleasure, a position for which he has been much maligned. In fact, he advocated the simple life as being the most pleasurable and said that it was impossible to live pleasurably without being wise, just, and honest.

3.3 MORAL THOUGHT AND ACTION

Ethics is the philosophical study of the nature and grounds of moral thought and action. Ethical theories in this pure sense are sharply distinguished from moral systems, which are directed towards drawing up particular sets of rules by which to live (such as Christian morality), and from practical or applied ethics, the analysis of arguments advanced for particular moral conclusions (such as the rightness or wrongness of abortion).

The most fundamental question in ethics is usually taken to be the justification of morality that is whether or not it can be demonstrated that moral action is rational. Schools of ethics can be divided, very roughly, into three sorts.

The first, which derives from Aristotle's *Ethics*, gives pride of place to the virtues, such as justice, charity, and generosity, which are thought of as dispositions to act in ways that both tend to the fulfillment of the person who has them and to benefit the society of which he or she is a member. Aristotle's ethics are also often described as naturalistic, in that he seeks to exhibit a harmony between morality and human nature.

The second, which is defended in most depth by Kant, is the school, which makes the concept of duty central to morality (called 'deontology'). Kant argued that the only thing, which is 'good in itself' (as opposed to merely 'good' as a means), is a 'good will', one that is freely in accordance with duty.

Knowledge of one's duty, for Kant, follows from a realization that one is a rational being, and thus bound to obey what he called the 'categorical imperative', the requirement to respect all rational beings as autonomous 'ends in themselves'. Kant's views of morality are intimately connected with his view of free will.

The third school of ethics is utilitarianism whose goal is the 'greatest happiness of the greatest number'. Ethical theories may also be divided in another way, according to whether or not they allow that there is such a thing as objective moral truth; Hume, as a subjectivist, held that morality is profoundly rooted in our 'sentiments'. Ethics in the last century has been largely preoccupied with analysing the meaning of moral language, as in Ayer's theory of emotivism, whereby the meaning of a moral statement consists in its expressing an emotional attitude

3.4 CONCEPTUAL COMPREHENSION

It is believed that the subject of ethics in modern times has become very important to the many professions. With this in mind, this book hopes to address an important subject regarding the way people live as individuals and in business groups, whatever the choice may be.

The content of this book will still be of importance to the reader and without any compromising, a training tool for the practitioners of the various modern professions, especially management. There is no doubt that this subject is deep and vast. Backed by recent social events and political debating, business management can only be helpful in preparing people to obtain an acceptable style of living and a harmonious mode of interacting with society.

The book concentrates on the historical established concepts and didactics of philosophers through the ages. This starts from the classical Hellenic rhetorics to the modern European philosophical thoughts and ideas. All the teachings of philosophers and sophists explain the right of a person to live as a politis (citizen) in a near enough democratic state. As an entity (with his/her own attributes and behaviour) the right to work, integrate and to live in a society, Philosophers have debated the morals, norms, laws, beliefs, and religions and logically enough what can be an acceptable pattern of attitudes within the parameters of social tolerance in a business world.

Philosophers through the aeons have advised and counselled on the upbringing of children and offered guidance in establishing the right relationship between the child, the parents, and the state. More recently, analytical philosophies such as the neo-Freudian and Jungian schools established the methods of treating people, based on the classical idealism.

Socrates being the protagonist where he developed the method of asking questions and seeking answers. Sophocles, through his surviving tragedies, is certainly the major contributor to the psychoanalytical Oedipus and Electra complexes and perhaps the biggest influence on Freud and his successors.

Various branches of psychology deal with the pre-natal and post-natal influences and expand into the realms of continuous development of the human personality. Remember that the personality and its complex characteristics never stop developing, from the foetus stage to birth right through to old age.

Moral Philosophy (just as much as Social Philosophy and Political Philosophy) maintains closer links with the constitution of the individual, his working environment and the groups living together, simply because a human being all along bears with himself/herself the philosophy of the environment they live in and work; the beliefs and the philosophy established through the ages.

What a better way to accept a human being, other than the use of the logic as taught by the traditional philosopher and as followed by the individual seeking assistance with the understanding of his/her nature?

Political and Moral philosophy has been with us since the times of the olden. As such, this book includes the ideas of Plato, Aristotle, Machiavelli, Hobbes, Locke, Rousseau, Hume, Burke, Hegel, Bentham, Mill, Marx, and the other philosophers in contemporary thoughts. The logic expressed by these and other philosophers can only assist in the understanding of business, management, directing and leadership.

Put in an alternative way. Management must incorporate all that a person carries in his complex nature. His/her own philosophical ideals, own beliefs, rights, religion, norms, political philosophy. It can, therefore, be maintained that in such circumstances an individual can be assisted by management incorporating philosophical concepts.

3.5 THE PHILOSOPHY OF MANAGEMENT

If this book is to accomplish its purpose and be of real service to management, the citizen, mothers, fathers and the society of the future generation, it must be applicable and adaptable to people in all walks of life, simple and direct in its contents.

The present book is intended to be, not primarily a history of ethics, but a critical examination of the philosophy of management with a view to defining the basic assumptions, which have been made by the great philosophical thinkers of the past and the fundamental issues about which controversy still continues.

There are various ideas and beliefs, which a manager must determine as to whether they are suitable for any application to any businesses around the globe. For instance, the thoughts of Descartes on Determinism, that body and mind must be separated - the mind is free but the body is determined in every aspect. Although at the end Descartes had to accept that the mind can influence the body.

Another method that can be used by the manager (at his/her own discretion) is the dialectical materialism, which is the philosophical basis of Marxism. Although this concept centres on the universal reason behind social events, the basic idea of reason behind human events works through the ideas held by an individual, until they are challenged by ideas, which replace them and are challenged usually by conflict. So conflict (war), reasoned Hegel, is an instrument of progress.

Further on, Voltaire's critique on organised religion, oppression and civil injustices, can be considered as an analytical instrument.

There are many more philosophical concepts, which can be adopted, as suitable for the study of cultures and their ethical beliefs. Probably, the most famous of all sayings being the Aristotelian 'know-thyself', followed by 'moderation in everything'. 'Knowing yourself' is a good guide towards the 'moderating factors' can be very useful to the manager, in monitoring his/her own beliefs and rejections. Aristotle also believed that happiness stems from human reason; ideal political state an enlightened monarchy. All his works have had a profound effect on thinkers throughout the ages.

About the same time, 'moderation in all things' was also urged by Epicurus. Epicurus was the founder of the term of 'hedonism'. He taught that pleasure is the chief aim of happy life.

In many philosophical studies subjectivity dominates the reader's catharsis, thus posing the questions 'who am I'? What is man? Those familiar with Jean-Paul Sartre and Albert Camus' works will recognise the concept of Existentialism. The reader seeks to distinguish between essence and existence. Answers to such questions are many and can even conclude with the short comment of 'become committed to something, even yourself'. Sartre, as a leader of Existentialist movement, claimed that man creates a meaning for his existence by taking responsibility for own destiny.

Platonism can certainly hold its own in management. Plato held that mankind often defeats the purpose of the Universe and its Creator. Further on, he maintained that it is man's duty to live a good life, but he may choose to live a wicked one. A student of Socrates and teacher of Aristotle, his teachings were contained in written Dialogues. Plato, stressing the idea of the good rather than material appearances, has influenced the thought on moral philosophy.

Certain moral philosophical concepts, such as stoicism appear to be suitable to the modern one to one sessions. Stoics, the followers of Zeno, maintain that man should guide his life by reason and not by passion. Thus virtue was the greatest good. Stoics have also made a fundamental distinction between goals, which are under human control and those, which are not. In the second case, man must endure what cannot be altered while he cultivates the self-sufficient life of reason.

The concept of Utilitarianism by Bentham and Mill will be discussed further in this book. Basically, both thinkers maintained that the greatest good of the greatest number is the criterion of morality, insisting that the real test of goodness was the social consequence.

Although Mysticism is not included in this book, the reader may want to discuss and bring forward the beliefs of religion, the experience of direct contact and unity with ultimate reality through prayer, meditation, trance, relaxation, or other means.

The next chapter of this book attempts to define the nature and scope of management generally and its application to the field of business ethics. The study of this chapter is essential at some stage if the logical foundations of management are to be appreciated. Only so can management in the proper sense be understood.

Some chapters deal with the main issues of ethics and management defined in simple terms and based on the teachings of the early thinkers of Classical Greece. The final chapter attempts to define the basic issues, which have emerged in the historical chapters and to relate them to the logical alternatives set forth in the first few chapters.

As the book is based on the experience gained in practising various professions for the last forty years, it is hoped that it will prove of value to other people interested in management and of special assistance to students everywhere.

Whatever the philosophical concepts chosen for the acceptance of the individual, the reader must bear in mind that Utopia is only in fiction. The Greeks used the word Utopia for 'Nowhere'. In modern times, Utopia came to mean the perfect society, or in this case of our discussion, the perfect person. As in modern journalism Utopia is used to ridicule a fanciful idea of a better society, so must the reader be careful that Utopia is not fancifully used to ridicule the ethics of a society and their philosophical aspirations.

3.6 MANAGEMENT VALUES

Management is the discipline concerned with the process of managing a team and the interaction of people, where individuals contribute to the running or completion of a task.

As in any State, central government or country, under any form of governing, people live together under various laws, rules, regulations and religions. The people elect or they follow a leader, be it a democratic or tyrannical leadership. People under such regimes follow a type of management. In a business environment such methods of management prevail.

A Manager will delegate and lead one or more individuals within the organization by running the business or a system what is morally good and bad, right and wrong.

The term is also applied to any system or theory of moral values or principles, such as:

- How should we live?
- Under what employment rules and standards should we work?
- Shall we aim at happiness or at knowledge, virtue, or the creation of beautiful objects?
- If we choose happiness, will it be for our own, or the happiness of all?
- And what of the more particular questions that face us: Is it right to be dishonest in a good cause?
- Can we justify living in opulence while elsewhere in the world people are starving?
- If conscripted to fight in a war we do not support, should we disobey the law?
- What are our obligations to the other creatures with whom we share this planet and to the generations of humans who will come after us?

Management ethics deal with such questions at all levels. Its subject consists of the fundamental issues of practical decision-making, and its major concerns include the nature of ultimate value and the standards by which human actions can be judged right or wrong.

The terms ethics and morality are closely related. We now often refer to ethical judgments or ethical principles where it once would have been more common to speak of moral judgments or moral principles. These applications are an extension of the meaning of ethical management.

Although ethics has always been viewed as a branch of philosophy, its all-embracing practical nature links it with many other areas of study, including anthropology, biology, economics, history, politics, sociology, and theology.

Yet, ethics as a subject remains distinct from such disciplines because it is not a matter of factual knowledge in the way that the sciences and other branches of inquiry are. Rather, it has to do with determining the nature of normative theories and applying these sets of principles to practical moral problems.

3.7 The Early Teachers Of Business Standards

Ironically, an important stimulus for the development of management came from a group of teachers to whom the later Greek philosophers - Socrates, Plato, and Aristotle - were consistently hostile: the Sophists. This term was used in the 5th century to refer to a class of professional teachers of rhetoric and argument. The Sophists promised their pupils success in political debate and increased influence in the affairs of the city. They were accused of being mercenaries who taught their students to win arguments by fair means or foul. Aristotle said that Protagoras, perhaps the most famous of them, claimed to teach how to make the weaker argument the stronger.

The Sophists, however, were more than mere teachers of rhetorical tricks. They saw their role as imparting the cultural and intellectual qualities necessary for success, and their involvement with argument about practical affairs led them to develop views about management ethics.

The recurrent theme in the views of the better known Sophists, such as Protagoras, Antiphon, and Thrasymachus, is that what is commonly called good and bad or just and unjust does not reflect any objective fact of nature, but is rather a matter of social convention.

It is to Protagoras that we owe the celebrated epigram summing up this theme, "Man is the measure of all things”. Plato represents him as saying, "Whatever things seem just and fine to each city, are just and fine for that city, so long as it thinks them so”. Protagoras, like Herodotus, was an early social relativist, but he drew a moderate conclusion from his relativism. He argued that while the particular content of the moral rules may vary, there must be rules of some kind if life is to be tolerable. Thus Protagoras stated that the foundations of an ethical system needed nothing from the gods or from any special metaphysical realm beyond the ordinary world of the senses.

The Sophist Thrasymachus appears to have taken a more radical approach - if Plato's portrayal of his views is historically accurate. He explained that the concept of justice means nothing more than obedience to the laws of society and, since the strongest political group in their own interests makes these laws, justice represents nothing but the interests of the stronger. This position is often represented by the slogan ‘Might is right’. Thrasymachus was probably not saying, however, that whatever the mightiest do really is right; he is more likely to have been denying that the distinction between right and wrong has any objective basis.

Presumably he would then encourage his pupils to follow their own interests as best they could. He is thus an early representative of Scepticism about morals and perhaps of a form of egoism, the view that the rational thing to do is follow one's own interests. It is not surprising that with ideas of this sort in circulation other thinkers should react by probing more deeply into ethics to see if the potentially destructive conclusions of some of the

Sophists could be resisted. This reaction produced works that have served ever since as the cornerstone for the entire edifice of Western ethics.

3.8 NOMOS

Greek: "law," or "custom", plural NOMOI, in law, the concept of law in ancient Greek philosophy.

The problems of political authority and the rights and obligations of citizens were a major concern in the thought of the leading Greek Sophists of the late fifth and early 4th centuries BC. They distinguished between nature (physis) and convention (nomos), putting laws in the latter category.

Law generally was thought to be a human invention arrived at by consensus for the purpose of restricting natural freedoms for the sake of expediency and self-interest. This view of law as arbitrary and coercive was not conducive to social stability, however, and thus was amended by Plato and other philosophers, who asserted that nomos was, or at least could be, based upon a process of reasoning whereby immutable standards of moral conduct could be discovered, which could then be expressed in specific laws. The dichotomy between the negative and positive views of law was never actually resolved.

3.9 POOR LAW

In British history, body of laws undertaking to provide relief for the poor, developed in 16th-century England and maintained, with various changes, until after World War II. The Elizabethan Poor Laws, as codified in 1597-98, were administered through parish overseers, who provided relief for the aged, sick, and infant poor, as well as work for the able-bodied in workhouses. Late in the 18th century, this was supplemented by the so-called Speenhamland system of providing allowances to workers who received wages below what was considered a subsistence level.

The resulting increase in expenditures on public relief was so great that a new Poor Law was enacted in 1834, based on a harsher philosophy that regarded pauperism among able-bodied workers as a moral failing.

The new law provided no relief for the able-bodied poor except employment in the workhouse, with the object of stimulating workers to seek regular employment rather than charity. The growth of humanitarian feeling in the 19th century helped to mitigate the harshness of the law in practice, and the phenomenon of industrial unemployment in the 20th century showed that poverty was more than a moral problem. The social legislation of the 1930s and '40s replaced the Poor Laws with a comprehensive system of public welfare services.

3.10 PLATO (*C*429-347 BC),

Plato is the Greek philosopher much influenced by Socrates. After the latter's death in 399, Plato travelled widely before returning to Athens in *c*.387 and founding the Academy. Here he spent the last forty years of his life, devoting himself to teaching and writing. His *Dialogues* are the first unfragmentary body of Greek philosophical writing to have survived, and they had a powerful influence on later philosophers, notably Plotinus. His *Apology* provided a re-creation of the unsuccessful defence, which Socrates offered at his trial in 399 BC.

The early *Dialogues*, for example Gorgias and *Protagoras* examine the question of the essence of virtue (see ethics) and represent a serious questioning of current philosophical thought. These works adopted Socrates' renowned method of argument, whereby a protagonist's definition was demonstrated to be untrue by a logical series of questions and answers. In the later Dialogues, however, the figure of Socrates served more as a mouthpiece for Plato's developing ideas. Thus in the *Republic* he tackled the question of the perfect constitution, arguing that perfect unity would come not through democracy, but through the rule of the enlightened despot. In the *Laws* he rejected the excesses of Athenian democracy and argued that extremes of government were to be avoided.

In metaphysics, Plato's Theory of Forms, introduced in the *Phaedo*, postulated the existence of unchanging and eternal objects; each Form Plato regarded as the indivisible essence of a particular thing or concept. For example, particular objects are tables, are called ‘tables’, and can be recognized as such because they are related to the essential Form of the Table.

Plato's teachings had a profound influence both on Aristotle and on several Roman authors, notably Cicero, shaping the development of Christian theology and Western philosophy. His works were translated into Latin in the late 15th century and became central to Renaissance scholarship and ideas.

4. THE NATURE AND PURPOSE OF MANAGEMENT

4.1 THE SOURCE OF KNOWLEDGE

By the end of the twentieth century, the management of Information Technology was regarded as a source of knowledge, which transcended the discoveries of natural sciences. Science marked an advance on the uncritical and often unrelated beliefs of ordinary life, yet it was itself based on the observations of the senses and consisted of the uncertain generalisations based upon them.

On such subjects, it was believed, reason was alone competent to pronounce and, when it did so, its conclusions were characterised by a logical and global certainty, which the generalisations natural science could never claim.

The different conceptions of management ultimately depend upon the nature of knowledge.

There are numerous propositions of which the falsity is perfectly conceivable. It may be true that 'a depressed person is withdrawn' or that neurosis is caused by bad early childhood experiences', but these propositions are not entirely true. On the contrary, there falsity is perfectly conceivable, even if observations appear to confirm their truth.

The discussion just illustrated is variably referred to as the distinction between rational and empirical knowledge, or between a priori and a posteriori knowledge, or between truths of reason and truths of fact. It is true to say that philosophers claim, or at least imply that their theories are rational and a priori.

Where one cannot differ is the view of the scope of such knowledge in management. The main difference has been where the view is held that rational knowledge is always analytic, while some have held the opinion that it is sometimes synthetic.

Any managers, who wish to expand on the knowledge of analytic and synthetic propositions, will find Kant's definition very useful. Immanuel Kant's definition is as follows: Analytic propositions 'add nothing through the predicate to the concept of the subject, but merely break it up into those constituent concepts that have all along been thought in it, although confusedly', while synthetic judgements 'add to the concept of the subject a predicate which has not been in any wise thought in it, and which no analysis could possibly extract from it'.

Modern managers have devoted much attention to the study of analytic propositions and have concluded that they do not make any assertion about the empirical world. They simply record our determination to use words in a certain fashion. They are, in other words, tautologies; and the reason why we think it worth while to assert them and sometimes, as in mathematics, to draw elaborate deductions from them, are that our reason is too limited to recognise their full significance without going through these complex verbal processes.

These considerations may appear to be extremely abstract and their connection with what is commonly understood as 'management' far from obvious; but in fact this connection is both simple and fundamental. For management is the quest for certainty and if certainty is a characteristic of propositions, then an enquiry into the nature and scope of certain (priori) propositions must be the essential task of management. If the general object of management is to discover the nature and implications of rational thinking, then an enquiry into the nature of the propositions by which rational thinking is expressed is necessarily one of the most important tasks of management so understood.

All managers who have recognised the distinction between analytic and synthetic propositions agree that analytic propositions are necessary. Controversy has centred on the question whether synthetic propositions may also sometimes be priori.

Until recently, it was widely believed that management could establish facts about the existing world quite independently of experience. Management was, indeed, often looked to for rational justification of beliefs, such as religious and moral beliefs, already held on non-rational grounds and it was assumed that this justification could be given independently of experience.

During the present era, there has been a strong reaction from these methods and a growing acceptance of the alternative view that the function of management is to clarify rather than to extend the content of knowledge.

4.2 EMPIRICISM IN MANAGEMENT

Before the present century, when the doctrine has received wide support, the most celebrated exponent of Empiricism was the Scottish philosopher David Hume (17II-1776), now generally recognised to have been one of the greatest philosophers of all time. Hume held that the only propositions which are certainly true are those which describe 'relations of ideas', by which he meant analytic relationships in the sense defined above.

Hume's revolutionary account of the function of reason naturally evoked a reaction, and the philosophies of the great thinkers Immanuel Kant (1724-1804) and Georg Wilhehn Friedrich Hegel (1770-183I) were attempts to restore to reason the positive functions which Hume had denied to it.

Kant and Hegel sought to do this by stressing the active function of the mind in knowledge and, in particular, by arguing that, while synthetic propositions may by themselves be devoid of logical necessity, they are characterised by another kind of necessity (which Kant called 'transcendental necessity') derived from the mind in which they originate. They are necessary, not in the logical sense that their falsity is inconceivable, but in the transcendental sense that experience could not take the form which it does take unless they were assumed to be universally true.

Many philosophers would question whether a theory of this sort constitutes any real answer to Hume's empiricism. They would question whether 'transcendental' necessity is more than the empirical regularity admitted by Hume - whether, for example, the fact that we always interpret our experience in regularities justifies the conclusion that we accept it in this way. It must, at least be admitted, that other philosophers who think like him have their experience in this way.

Apart from this general objection to Kant's theory, Hegel thought that it was vitiated by the fundamental contradiction of asserting, on the one hand, that all knowing takes the form of judging and yet claiming that experience cannot be explained except on the assumption that there are things-in-themselves. As Hegel was quick to observe, these propositions are essentially contradictory; if it is impossible for us to have cognitive experience which does not take the form of judging, it is impossible for us to know or conceive of or make any consistent assertion about things-in-themselves, for in so doing we are interpreting them in accordance with the way in which our minds are bound to think.

Things-in-themselves which are thought about and talked about cannot be things-in-themselves; they must be things as they appear to the thinker. Hegel, therefore, arrived at the conclusion that Kant did not carry his argument far enough and that its logical implication is that cognitive experience consists exclusively of judgements.

4.3 AN ATTEMPT IN DEFINING MANAGEMENT

The naive conception of management as a set of dogmatic axioms defining the rights and duties of the individual conceals the basic purpose of management. For management consists essentially in directing the process of thinking upon itself with a view to ascertaining what thought consists in, and what it can establish.

In the light of the foregoing considerations, management may be briefly defined as the study of the nature and implications of *rational thought.* From this general study conclusions may be drawn about the implications of rational thought in specific fields, such as the moral and political, and these implications constitute management. If, as the empiricist believes, management leads to the conclusion that the rational part of experience is much smaller than is commonly supposed, this is itself a rational proposition of the first importance.

The purpose of the present chapter has been to indicate, in the most general and summary fashion, the logical background of management. Issues have been touched on which could not be adequately discussed in less than a volume devoted to their special consideration. But, enough will have been said for the purpose of the present book if it has been made clear that Management is not an independent subject but is intimately bound up with the great issues of logic, psychology, sociology and all other social subjects.

4.4 THE MORAL THEORIES OF THE SOPHISTS

Managers and Directors are often surprised when they hear of the problems and concerns, which clients present. In most cases, clients express their difficulties in obtain9ing a service. It would seem that many members of society are at any given time a prey to despair and anxiety engendered by disappointment, disillusionment, anger, and powerlessness in the face of disintegrating client and managers relationships.

Such people are often workers who can no longer bring to their jobs the enthusiasm, commitment and energy which they displayed before their relationships with management began to founder. Others manage to maintain a high level of work performance and seem to have lives which are based on a strict, almost hermetically sealed, division between the personal and the professional, the home and the work-place. Frequently, they share in common a sense of anguished bewilderment which comes from an alarming lack of awareness of themselves as beings of worth and complexity, which are by definition relational and part of the created order.

Their way of viewing themselves and the world is so closed and narrow that they are philosophically ill equipped to live at the depth which a crisis of social interaction inevitably demands and will often resort to prescribed medication, alcohol and narcotics in order to numb the pain.

In an age where the power and influence of institutional values are of lesser importance, there is a sense in which for many people their philosophical beliefs in management become the arena for their deepest yearnings and aspirations. Philosophy has relevance because it concerns the nature of self and the relationship between human beings, their environments, and their political state at large.

Sometimes, the client brings with him, or her, the raw material for new learning. This can be reached if client and manager can together discover the way forward to new paradigm, based on a mutual recognition of their philosophical beliefs. Affirm the client's infinite value as persons and restore their philosophical conceptions. To come to some realisation that people embody a value system and that managers are essentially redemptive; that they can restore hope and bring a meaning to someone's existence. The modern manager's concern should be with persons.

4.5 MANAGEMENT IN ANCIENT GREECE

Socrates, the ancient Athenian philosopher, was the first of the great trio of ancient Greeks--Socrates, Plato, and Aristotle--who laid the philosophical foundations of Western culture. As Cicero said, Socrates "brought down philosophy from heaven to earth"--i.e., from the nature speculation of the Ionian and Italian cosmologists to analyses of the character and conduct of human life, which he assessed in terms of an original theory of the soul. Living during the chaos of the Peloponnesian War, with its erosion of moral values, Socrates felt called to shore up the ethical dimensions of life by the admonition to "know thyself" and by the effort to explore the connotations of moral and humanistic terms.

The major contribution of Greece was a body of philosophical and cosmological ideals about justice, more apt for orators' appeals to popular assemblies than for perceptual application to day-to-day life situations. Early Greek cosmologies, embedded in some of the earliest myths, had seen the individual as held within a kind of transcending harmony of the universe, emanating from the divine law (logos) and expressed in relation to human life in the law (nomos) of the polis, the city-state.

The later Sophists, however, who examined critically all assumptions relating to life in the city-state, pointed to the wide disparities in human law and morals and rejected the claim that this human law (nomos) necessarily reflected any universal law (logos). Taking man as "the measure of all things", they rejected any claims of his law (nomos) to absolute value and saw law and justice and values generally as created by men's reasons, in their multitudes and generations, in all their individuated, relativistic, and historically changing dimensions.

In the restless intellectual and political climate of 5th-century Athens, Plato was concerned to redefine the nature of justice by relating it to something far more permanent and absolute than the nomos of the city-state. He assigned "reality" to the unchanging archetypal forms--i.e. The ideas of things, rather than the ephemeral phenomena, as superficially and confusedly are perceived by individual men who are not enlightened by philosophy. In the utopia described in the Republic, Plato defines justice in an architectonic sense: justice prevails when the state is ordered in accordance with the ideal forms ascertained by its philosopher-kings and is thus unrelated to the nomos of the city-state.

There is no need for human law, since transcendental knowledge rules. In his later thought, however, as revealed in Politicus (the "Statesman") and the Laws, when he is concerned to describe a more practicable but nevertheless "second best" state, Plato assigns to law a role almost as important as that of knowledge in the Republic. A famous classification of states given in Politicus is indeed based on the criterion of whether or not they are ruled by law. The law as Plato here conceived it, however, was not mere convention or the imperfect individual judgments of men but a reflection of the common human reason in its full development.

To this extent the rule of law might approximate the ideal rule of knowledge envisaged in the Republic, for in the inherited law of men is crystallized that much wisdom of which they are capable. And yet it was difficult for Plato to find justification for such an argument in his basic philosophical position, with its emphasis on the contrast between the mere opinion of ordinary men and the transcendental knowledge of the philosopher.

Aristotle, who in common with Plato held a view of nature or reality that transcended the variability of things as perceived by the senses, was, however, able more successfully to defend the validity of a law resulting from the practice of ordinary men. For Aristotle's transcendental reality is more firmly related to things as they are: it comprises that, which they will become as their potentialities unfold in nature toward the end that is theirs in nature.

Man, in his nature, is moral, rational, and social, and his law may be judged by the extent to which it facilitates the development of these innate qualities. The Greek conception of natural law underwent further refinement by the Stoic school of philosophy, which became active toward the end of the 4th century BC.

The Stoics posited the existence of a natural law, the just naturale, which was an emanation of the lex aeterna, the law of reason of the cosmos. The existence of an innate reason in men linked everyone with the cosmic order and subjected all to a universally valid moral law. This latter concept thoroughly infused Roman thinking, largely as a result of the influence of Stoic philosophy on Rome.

If management is understood in the sense defined in the previous chapter, the first managerial thinking of any consequence took place in Ancient Greece in the sixth century B.C. There had, it is true, been considerable speculation before this time about many of the questions with which the philosophy of management is concerned, but the basis of belief was generally found in religion or mythology or tradition, and little or no attempt was made to subject this basis to rational scrutiny. It was the Greeks of the sixth century B.C. who first sought, in a determined and systematic fashion, to arrive at a conception of reality based on genuinely rational foundations.

During the sixth century B.C. these early philosophers generally concentrated their efforts on reaching some simple and comprehensive conception of reality as a whole and took little interest in the problems of management. But it is necessary to understand the nature of their achievement in this broader field if the origin and purpose of their theories are to be properly appreciated. It may be said that, in general, their early enquiries were directed to answering the question 'What is reality?'.

In the fifth century B.C. acceptance of tradition began to crumble because in that century the Greeks began to travel and establish colonies, and these adventures brought them into contact with communities who observed customs and laws very different from their own. For the first time they had to recognise that their own customs and laws were not universal and to consider whether there was any reason for believing them to be better than others.

Their first reaction was to conclude that one set of laws was as good as another for the purpose of the community which accepted them. Hence they drew a distinction between the unchanging rules of physical Nature and the variable forms of manmade Law. The former they regarded as essentially objective, and the latter as essentially subjective.

4.6 The Early Sophists

These early social philosophers are commonly known as the 'Sophists' or 'wise men'. 'Wise man' was the original meaning of the word 'sophist', although it now usually indicates someone who is clever and plausible rather than wise and honest. Indeed, the modem meaning of the word is substantially the meaning which the Sophists, by their practices, gave to it. For many of them concentrated on the teaching of rhetoric, and by this was meant the art of arguing persuasively irrespective of the real merits of the case. The importance of this art arose from the fact that during the greater part of the fifth Century B.C. Athens had a democratic constitution, and it was important for those who administered policy to be able to justify their actions before the popular assembly.

The Sophists were the first professional teachers of Ancient Greece and, one could argue, the first lecturers on management. In most cases they either demanded, or received fees for teaching and for advising their pupils; generally those (pupils) who hoped to succeed in public life. But they did not belong to any central establishment, and they did not share any common outlook which automatically made them members of a 'school'. Many were engaged in the day-to-day business of teaching, but a few tried to work out a consistent social philosophy, and a short account of the principal doctrines which they advocated will now be given.

4.7 THE DOCTRINES OF PROTAGORAS

Protagoras of Abdera (500-430 B.C.), whose doctrines are described in Plato's dialogue. *Protagoras,* put forward an interesting theory which attempted to combine recognition of the essential subjectivity of moral laws with a practical method of achieving that acceptance of a common code of law and convention upon which the cohesion and survival of a society depend. His view of the subjectivity of law was expressed in the dictum that 'Man is the measure of all things, of things that are and of things are not.' Plato explains this doctrine as meaning that 'things are to me as they appear to me and to you as they appear to you'.'.

Protagoras recognised that general acceptance of this doctrine might have serious practical consequences. If people became generally aware that one moral belief was as true as another they might well come to discard all moral beliefs whatsoever, and their individual desires in complete disregard of their duties. Protagoras therefore argued that, although all are equally true, some are *better* than others, namely the of the average and representative, and that it is the duty of the Sophist to persuade everyone to accept those different beliefs which are likely to be held. Persons are, in Protagoras's view, just as true, so good in the sense that they differ from the majority, and thus tend to cause dissension.

Protagoras claimed that the Sophists performed a useful function in persuading people to accept 'better' moral beliefs, even if they were not in an objective sense 'truer' than other moral beliefs, for he thought that civilised society depended upon the general acceptance of such beliefs. Without them, Protagoras thought, men would live what Hobbes was later to call a 'state of nature', and their condition would then be no better than that of animals.

Expressed in modern terms, the theory of Protagoras is that moral beliefs are purely subjective, but that they discharge a useful function in upholding the law and order which are the basis of a civilised society. These will be assured if a coherent set of beliefs is generally accepted throughout a given society, and if that acceptance is maintained and strengthened by effective 'propaganda'. There is, of course, no strictly moral reason why that acceptance 'ought' to be promoted, but there is a *logical* reason if such acceptance of a coherent set of beliefs is a necessary condition of social stability, and the members of the society in question desire social stability.

Thus Protagoras accepted the general view of the Sophist that Law, in contrast to Nature, was subjective and man-made, but he claimed that it was justified (in a utilitarian sense) by the function, which it performed in maintaining a condition, which the great majority of men desired.

5. THE EARLIER CONTRIBUTIONS TO MANAGEMENT

5.1 PLATO'S IDEALISM

There are certain societies where the thoughts of the wise elders are handed down from generation to generation. Unknowingly to the young listeners, the mode of thinking is a gift. The day comes when the young citizen realises that reasoning is as natural as any other tool used to perform chores. From a very early stage of development, the philosophical rationale of 'if, then' becomes a method of thinking.

With logic, plus the story telling of the myths, knowledge becomes enriched, which indeed justifies the saying 'knowledge itself is power'. Using such learning to 'know thyself' leads to the wide and deep understanding of human life, the world at large and the citizens' strives. Some managers will still wonder whether such 'undisciplined' learning can benefit the structured western societies and whether this is just a fashionable sophism, which will never fit the universities-taught management studies.

Philosophy and its logical thinking do not only apply to the arts and sciences. In the mid-eighties experts in systems, artificial intelligence and information technology adopted the 'if, then', also other cognitive concepts to the benefit of human-computer interaction and technology in general. Even earlier in the sixties, structured analysis and the designing of systems benefited from philosophy and to some extend from psychology.

The new trend in using counselling and in some management styles is failing in re-adapting the individual. The same failure applies to psychiatry, because as a service to human beings, became too dependent on the prescriptions of sedatives and tranquillisers, thus failing the very essence of diagnosing the cause and finding where the problem is residing.

If modern individual ails and social problems are the effect of various causes, then managers must pay more attention to the philosophical process of 'cause and effect'. This classical and Aristotelian concept will be found to be very useful in treating today's complex employees' demands. To satisfy such paramount demands placed on counselling, psychotherapy, psychiatry, and psychology in general, it means that more reading and learning of philosophical schools of ideas and their applications is required by modern management students and managers in general. Academic and training courses need to broaden the psychotherapist's knowledge by introducing principles of philosophy, before one becomes a qualified manager or director.

5.2 SOCRATES AND PLATO

It is generally agreed that Plato (427-347 B.C.) was one of the greatest and most influential thinkers of antiquity. His thoughts have come down to us for the most part in a series of twenty-six dialogues, in the majority of which his teacher Socrates (469-399 B.C.) is the principal speaker. It is true that some scholars (notably the late Professors John Burnet and A. E. Taylor) held that the dialogues in which Socrates is the principal speaker are substantially accurate records of the theories and arguments of Socrates himself, and that only the last dialogues, such as the *Statesman, Timeus, and Laws,* in which Socrates does not appear, describe the theories of Plato.

On the whole, however, this interpretation has not been generally accepted, and in this chapter the theories expounded by Socrates in the *Republic* will, in accordance with the usual practice, be referred to as Plato's theories. Even if some of these theories were originally advanced by Socrates, it seems reasonable to assume that Plato would not have expounded them in such detail unless he had accepted them as being, in the main, both true and important; and it is hardly likely that, when expounding these theories, Plato would not modify them in the light of his own critical reflections.

Unlike Plato, Socrates left no writings of his own, but Plato's dialogues provide us with a vivid impression of his personality and outlook. There is no exact parallel in modern times to the position which he occupied in Athenian society. A man of similar interests and aptitudes would today probably be a university teacher of philosophy, but when Socrates lived there was nothing corresponding to a university. Higher education, as we should call it, was carried on by the professional teachers known as the Sophists, who offered instruction to anyone who was willing to pay for it. Socrates thought the receipt of such payment degrading, but his method of teaching was in many ways similar to that of the Sophists, although the doctrines which he taught were different.

Socrates taught by the method of question and answer, which was known as 'dialectic'. He was ruthless in exposing uncritical assumptions and pretentious dogmas of all sorts, and his criticism of the democratic constitution of Athens appears to have been the real reason for his trial and condemnation to death, although the alleged offence was that of not worshipping the recognised gods of the state and corrupting the young by teaching them to follow his example. Yet, combined with this tendency to question and challenge existing beliefs, he had a firm faith in certain fundamental principles - the immortality of the soul, the objectivity of moral standards, and the reality of an unchanging world behind the world of sense and time. Nor did he ever question the guidance he received from an inner 'voice' which, he claimed, spoke to him from time to time, and which he regarded as a 'divine sign' that should always be respected.

Plato was a pupil of Socrates and, apart from two short interludes when he participated in active politics, he devoted his life to the teaching of philosophy. His teaching was of a more formal character than Socrates', and it was conducted in an institution called the *Academy,* which Plato founded, probably about the year 387 B.C., when he was forty years of age. The Academy was set up by Plato primarily for the disinterested pursuit of knowledge and this distinguished it from other contemporary teaching institutions, which aimed at preparing their students for the practical business of life. The Academy was, in fact, one of the earliest universities in the modem sense of the word, and its activity continued without interruption for nearly a thousand years.

5.3 THE 'REPUBLIC'

The theory which will be discussed in the present chapter is the Theory of the Ideal State expounded in Plato's dialogue the *Republic.* While, as in all the earlier dialogues, the exposition of the theory is made by Socrates, it will be referred to, for the reasons previously mentioned, as Plato's theory, although Socrates may even have inspired some of its basic ideas. The theory is presented as a constructive alternative to what Plato regarded as the false and dangerous teaching of the Sophists, and it is inspired throughout by acceptance of the Socratic axiom that 'virtue is knowledge'.

As already observed, Socrates lived from 469 to 399 B.C. and Plato from 427 to 347 B.C. A. E. Taylor has shown that the available evidence indicates that the action of the *Republic* must be supposed to have taken place about the time of the Peace of Nicias in the spring of 421 B.C. This makes it probable that, in so far as the dialogue is historically accurate, it records what Socrates was saying about the age of forty-eight.

It is difficult to place the *Republic* in any one category of philosophical discussion. It examines problems of ethics and political philosophy as well as those of logic, metaphysics and psychology. This is indeed one of the great merits of the work, for it draws attention to the important fact that the different branches of philosophy are intimately connected and that ethical and political doctrines cannot be finally assessed without consideration of their logical and metaphysical assumptions.

The main object of the dialogue was to refute the Sophists' theory that moral principles have a subjective foundation and to show that they have, on the contrary, a rational and objective basis. Plato thinks that the essence of morality is *justice,* but it is important to recognise that he is using the word in a much wider sense than would now be customary. The English word 'justice' is derived from the Latin word *ius,* which means 'what is enforced by human authority'. That is an essentially legal conception, but for Plato the word had a moral significance, and is probably best translated simply as 'goodness'.

The object of the *Republic* is, then, to enquire into the nature of goodness and the way in which it may be known. As already observed, this enquiry is conducted through the medium of a dialogue. The speakers are: Socrates; Cephalous, a retired merchant living at Piraeus; Polemarchus, Lysias, and Euthydemus - sons of Cephalous; Thrasymachus, the Sophist; and Plato's elder brothers, Glaucon and Adeimantus.

6. ARISTOTLE'S CONTRIBUTIONS

6.1 ARISTOTLE'S BEST STATE

ARISTOTLE (384-322 BC) is one of the most celebrated Greek philosophers. At the age of 17 he joined Plato's Academy, where he stayed until shortly after Plato's death in 347. He was later (343-2) appointed tutor to Alexander the Great. In 335 he returned to Athens, where he established a school and a collection of manuscripts, which was the model for later libraries. He organized research projects, the fruit of one being a comparative study of 158 Greek constitutions. Following the death of Alexander in 323, he was charged with impiety and left Athens, dying soon afterwards in Chalcis.

His output was enormous and survives largely in the form of notes for lectures delivered at the Lyceum, successor to Plato's Academy. Aristotle's work encompasses dialogues, which exist only in fragments; collections of historical information; the extant *Constitution of the Athenians* (though the authorship of this is now doubted); and scientific and philosophical works which are mostly extant, such as the *Nicomachaean Ethics*, the *Politics*, and the *Metaphysics*, some of which reveal the influence of Plato.

These writings reveal the encyclopedic nature of Aristotle's interests and his logical, carefully organized work laid the foundations of many later philosophical enquiries. He introduced the systematic study of logic, developing a system for describing and assessing reasoning that remained the core of the discipline until the 19th century. Contemporary categorical grammar can be traced to Aristotle's interest in the functioning of words, giving him a special place in philosophical logic and in linguistics.

The central questions of Aristotle's *Metaphysics* (What is substance?) and his *On Coming to be and Passing Away* (How do things come into existence and cease to exist?) are still hotly debated. In *De Anima* (On the Soul) Aristotle discussed the soul, or psyche; that which makes something alive and capable of the activities characteristic of life. In claiming that the psyche is dependent upon the body, Aristotle anticipated the mind/body debate current in philosophy of mind.

Contemporary ethics also owes a debt to Aristotle's *Ethics*. His claim that all action aims at *eudaimonia*, or happiness, seemingly has much in common with modern-day utilitarianism; however, Aristotle's stress on the several virtues is in tension with utilitarianism's promise of a single (if not simple) principle for deciding all moral questions.

Aristotle's work was rediscovered by Arab scholars, notably Avicenna and Averroes, and, translated into Latin, shaped the development of medieval thought in the arts and sciences. St Thomas Aquinas reconciled the Aristotelian doctrines with those of Christian theology and they remained a key part of higher education in Europe from the 13th to the 17th centuries.

6.2 ARISTOTLE'S WORKS ON ETHICS AND POLITICS

Undoubtedly Aristotle's writings can be applied to the philosophy of modern management. As a very vital point to this claim the reader's attention is drawn to the application of the principles as explained in the very few surviving papers.

In emphasizing the crucial differences in the purposes of the theoretical and practical sciences, Aristotle indicates that the practical disciplines, unlike the theoretical, are for the sake of doing or making something and not for the sake of contemplating, defining, or knowing it.

Thus, at the start of his Nicomachean Ethics he explains how the practical sciences are incapable of the exactness of the theoretical sciences, for their subject matters are not limited to things that are amenable to precise definition, but involve habits and skills, which can be acquired and lost, and associations and institutions, which in their changes affect the accomplishment of political actions and the practicability of moral ends.

However precise biological or psychological definitions may be, man varies as moral agent and as citizen according to environmental determination, educational background, and the influences of family, economic position, social class, means of livelihood, and even the associations of his leisure. Relating ethics to politics, Aristotle set out to demonstrate that problems of morality as they affect the individual could not be separated from each other or from problems of political association.

The Ethics and Politics, therefore, do not develop separate sciences or independent subject matters but rather supplement each other by treating a common field according to different aspects. Although he treated moral problems in terms of the potentialities of individual men, the ability to practice and actualise these potentialities is dependent upon political circumstances. Therefore, in the first chapters of Book 1 of the Ethics, Aristotle begins by introducing moral considerations into the broad context of political philosophy, and he ends by returning, in the concluding Book 10, from the examination of happiness and the contemplative life to a shrewd statement of the contribution of law to moral questions, which forms the transition from ethics to politics.

Aristotle's approach to ethics is teleological; that is, he discusses ethics not in terms of moral absolutes but in terms of what is conducive to man's good. This approach leads him to examine various kinds of good and to arrive at the identification of the highest good with the attainment of happiness. After careful discussion of the problematic concept of happiness, Aristotle arrives at a definition of happiness as activity of the soul in accordance with virtue. Aristotle distinguishes moral virtues and intellectual virtues, which are determined, respectively, by the irrational and the rational powers of the soul.

Man, however, does not possess these virtues at birth but comes endowed with the capacity, or disposition, for developing them in the course of time. For example, a child begins by following his parents' injunction to tell the truth without initially realizing the moral excellence of his action; yet eventually the habit of veracity becomes an ingrained part of his moral character. Aristotle then differentiates virtue from vice, arriving at the definition of virtue as a "mean", or middle disposition, between the vicious extremes of excess and deficiency; courage, a virtue, for example, is the mean between cowardice and rashness.

Aristotle concludes his discussion by defining the highest happiness opened to man. Because happiness is an activity in accordance with virtue, it follows that the highest happiness should be in accordance with man's highest virtue. And that, according to Aristotle, is the activity, which distinguishes man from the other animals, namely the activity of reason or activity in accordance with reason. Thus in its ideal form happiness turns out to consist in a life of intellectual contemplation.

Aristotle, on the other hand, also concedes that the political life (activity in accordance with moral virtue) can bring happiness, albeit 'in a secondary degree'. The Politics takes up the problems of human action and association as they bear on the ends of communal life encompassed in living well. But the choice of political ends requires a complex examination of possible criteria capable of application to the vast diversity of men and human conditions.

Grounding his argument on the premise that man is "naturally" a political animal, Aristotle develops the theory of the state, distinguishes various kinds of constitution, and considers the best state for the particular circumstances, character, and conditions of the citizens. Aristotle also discusses the nature and causes of political instability and revolution. The last two books of the Politics--part of an unfinished description of the ideal state--are largely concerned with education.

Although Aristotle is well known as a philosopher, scientists acknowledge his influence in almost every branch of the sciences. He definitely benefited from Plato (his teacher) on matters of the *politis* and the personality characteristics of the individual. What many modern thinkers forget is the impact that Aristotle made with his research into the specific sciences. In his Athenian *academia,* Aristotle established his unique method of teaching - the *peripatetic*. By this time, he had also become a well-known biologist. It is a fact that specimens sent to him by his ex-pupil Alexander the Macedonian backed many of his biological experiments. It is said that Alexander the Great collected samples from every country he conquered and forwarded them to his tutor.

Aristotle established a scientific methodology, which, even in modern days, influences the academic world. His research in biology, his writings in physics and his afterthoughts (meta - after) his papers and lectures on physics (*metaphysica*) undoubtedly made an impact on the method of treating people. His philosophy has helped therapists through the centuries, more so the modern methodology of therapeutic philosophy. His sayings of 'know thyself' and 'moderation in everything' are mottoes applied in modern therapeutic philosophy. His work and thoughts on education, psychology, politics, law and government, physics, mathematics, medicine, logics, art… are but some of his contributions to humanity.

Aristotle was born in 384 B.C. when Plato was forty-three, and died in 322 B.C. at the age of sixty-two. He was therefore thirty-seven years old when Plato died in 347 B.C. He was sent to Athens at the age of eighteen for higher education, and was a member of Plato's Academy for twenty years. He subsequently spent three years in Asia Minor, where he pursued his scientific interests, particularly marine biology. In 343 B.C. he became tutor to Alexander, Prince of Macedon, and afterwards Alexander the Great, who was then a boy of thirteen. There is no indication, however, that he exercised any influence on Alexander's character.

The *Politics* makes it clear that he disliked all types of dictatorship and, like Plato, thought that the small city-state, which had no political ambitions, provided the most favourable environment for the good life. It is also very noticeable that Aristotle never refers to his pupil's great conquests anywhere in his writings-probably because he had little sympathy with them, and did not regard them as examples of the way in which rulers should use their powers.

When Alexander was called to the Macedonian throne by the murder of his father in 336 B.C., Aristotle returned to Athens. At this time the presidency of the Academy, which had been filled since Plato's death by Speusippus, became vacant, but Aristotle was not selected to succeed him. He may have been offended, for in 335 B.C. he opened a rival school known as the Lyceum, and some members of the Academy followed him there. For the next twelve years he was fully occupied by his work in the Lyceum, and he gradually developed a teaching tradition of his own, departing from the Platonic tradition of the Academy by making bio1ogy and history, instead of mathematics, the primary subjects of study.

The Politics, like Aristotle's other works, takes the form of a treatise, not a dialogue. And its style is quite different from that of Plato's dialogues. This is explained by the fact that, while Plato's lecture notes have been lost, many of his books have come down to us. On the other hand, Aristotle's books have almost all been lost, but many of his lecture notes have survived. Scholars are generally agreed that the 'works' of Aristotle as we know them consist of his lecture manuscripts edited by his pupils after his death.

The argument of the *Politics* is not by any means consistent, and scholars attribute this to the fact that it was probably composed over a period of time during which the influence of Plato's teaching on Aristotle's thinking became weaker. Thus Sabine, following Jaegar, puts forward the hypothesis that Books II, iii, VII, and VIII, which are concerned primarily with theories of the Ideal State, were written soon after Plato's death in 347 B.C.; while Books IV, V, and VI, which are concerned primarily with the study of actual states and the conditions governing their stability. It is true that he assumes that the political ideal varies from state to state and argues that the duty of government is to realise that political ideal as completely as possible whatever form it may take.

Apart from philosophy in the strict sense, Plato was mainly interested in mathematics and Aristotle in biology, and their philosophies in many ways reflect this difference. Thus Plato believed that in politics it was possible to establish principles having the precision and certainty of mathematics, whereas Aristotle believed that in politics, as in biology, careful and patient empirical enquiry was the only way of arriving at reliable generalisations.

Plato believed that the apprehension of the Form of the Good would reveal exactly how a community ought to be organised and governed, whereas Aristotle thought that the right organisation for any given state could only be discovered by careful examination of its other characteristics. This, at any rate, is what he said in the most consistent assessment of the central books already referred to (Books IV, V, and VI). In the Books which are believed to have been written first (Books II, iii, vii, and VIII) he makes some statements which imply a conception of the Ideal State closer to that of Plato; but if it is true that Books IV, V, and VI were written some fifteen years later it is reasonable to suppose that they present us with his more mature and considered thoughts on political theory.

6.3 ARISTOTLE'S CONCEPTION OF NATURE

In Book I (which, as already observed, was probably the last Book of the *Politics t*o be written) Aristotle explains the novel sense in which he understands the word 'nature' and the fundamental part, which the conception plays in his therapeutic philosophy. He understands this word in a very different sense from the Sophists. For them it meant the permanent and objective characteristics of independent reality in contrast to the variable and subjective beliefs and conventions of individuals or communities; but for Aristotle 'nature' is essentially a biological conception. In his own words:

The nature of a thing is its end. For what each thing is when fully developed, we call its nature, whether we are speaking of a man, a horse, or a family.

Thus for Aristotle the nature of a thing is not what the thing is but what it is *capable of becoming.* Its nature is not static but a developing conception. Just as in biology the 'nature' of a seed can only be discovered by the observation of its growth, so in politics the nature of a state can only be discovered by observation of its development and tendencies. In practice, this means the study of its history and the observation of its dominating tendencies, whether these are to autocratic or democratic forms of government, to an expanding or stable economy, and so on.

After defining the nature of a thing as its 'end', Aristotle adds the important proposition that 'the final cause and end of a thing is the best'. This he seems to mean that the destined end of a thing's development is necessarily a good end. It is not clear whether this proposition is intended to be analytic or synthetic. Whether Aristotle is implying that the 'nature' or destined end of a thing is what is *meant* by its 'good', or whether he only means that end is, as a matter of either fact or necessity, always characterised by goodness.

There are many passages in the *Politics,* which suggest that Aristotle recognised a standard of moral value quite distinct from the natural tendencies of the state, and thought of it as external and independent. But in the passages where he speaks of 'the natural' as *ipso facts* 'the good', he seems to imply that the terms are synonymous, that, in *his* sense of the word, 'the natural' is what is meant by 'the good', i.e. that the attainment of an organism's destined end is its supreme good and defines the standard by which its actual evolution must be approved or condemned.

It would, however, be untrue to say that the *Politics* as a whole justifies this interpretation of Aristotle's conception of morality. Most of his references to the subject suggest that he accepted the 'non-naturalistic' theory of morality; although at the same time he recognised the relativity of moral judgements to the actions or situations being judged and the consequent impossibility of making these judgements without knowledge of the characteristics of the actions or situations in question. This means, in modem terminology, that he regarded moral judgements as synthetic, and consequently thought it impossible to discover moral truths without knowledge of the concrete situations, which exemplify them.

Having defined the sense in which he uses the word 'nature', Aristotle claims that 'it is evident that the state is a creation of nature, and that man is by nature a political animal'. For 'the proof that the state is a creation of nature and prior to the individual is that the individual, when isolated, is not self-sufficing; and therefore he is like a part in relation to the whole'.

Aristotle is here stating what has since been designated as the Organic Theory of the State. It has been so called because it conceives of the state as a kind of organism.

According to the theory, the state is not a mere collection of its parts but an organic combination of them, so that none of these parts would be what it is if separated from the rest. The essential features of an organism are most simply illustrated by the human body.

These are that:

(a) Parts (e.g. a heart and a foot) no longer exist in the same form if separated from the body;

(b) The health of the whole depends upon the health of the Parts and *vice versa;*

(c) Some parts (e.g. the heart) have a more essential function to perform than others (e.g. the appendix).

According to the Organic Theory, all these propositions are true of a political society. It is not a mere collection of individuals, but has an organic unity of its own. For this reason, there can be no real conflict between its interest and the true interests of its constituent members.

Finally, different members, or classes of members, have different functions to perform and different levels of importance.

6.4 THE RELATIVITY OF MORAL STANDARDS

One of the most important implications of Aristotle's theory is that the moral standards of a society are relative to its 'nature' and thus liable to variation from state to state. Thus Aristotle says:

Laws, when good, should be supreme. But what are good laws has not yet been clearly explained; the old difficulty remains. The goodness or badness, justice or injustice, of laws varies of necessity with constitutions of states.

Unlike Plato, who set himself to describe an Ideal State, Aristotle believes that the best possible state may take a variety of different forms. He does not think that it would be true to assert as a universal principle that the power of government is always best exercised by a single man, or by a minority, or by the community as a whole. It is possible for any of these alternatives to provide the best form of government for a community, and it is also possible for any of them to provide a bad form of a state for its own selfish purposes.

This principle follows simply from the Organic Theory, for on that theory the interest of the organism is always more important than the interest of any one or any group of its constituent elements. Indeed, since the latter are organic constituents of the whole their true interest must coincide with the interest of the whole.

6.5 GOOD AND BAD FORMS OF GOVERNMENT

Aristotle then classifies the various possible forms of government accordingly as to whether the power of government is exercised by one, or by the few, or by the many, and as to whether the government, however consoled, aims at promoting the common interest (in which case it is a good government) or at promoting the special interest of the governing class (in which case it is a bad government).

The classification based on these two principles is as follows:

Government by:	Good Government	Bad Government
One	*Monarchy*	Tyranny
Few	*Aristocracy*	*Oligarchy*
Many	Polity	*Democracy*

[The author in his many years of management and executive positions maintains that similar principles are applicable to the modern science of management and directing.]

Aristotle sums up the defects of the bad forms of government as follows:

Tyranny is a kind of monarchy, which has in view the interests of the monarch only; oligarchy has in view the interest of the wealthy; democracy, of the needy; none of them the common good of all.

Aristotle points out that, as a matter of fact, government by the few is government by the rich, and government by the many is government by the poor since 'the rich everywhere are few and the poor numerous'. He thinks that the principal difference between oligarchy and democracy lies in the different conceptions of justice. Democrats believe that men are equal by birth and should therefore have equal political rights, whereas oligarchs that these rights should be in proportion to wealth.

Aristotle thinks that these different conceptions of justice reflect the biased judgement of men who are primarily concerned to advance their own interests, and overlook the fundamental principle that 'a state exists for the sake of a good life and not for the sake of life only'. He concludes that political rights should be awarded to people in proportion to the contribution which they make to the moral purposes of the state, one of which is that the general (as distinct from any sectional) interest should be the object of all political action.

Aristotle next considers whether the few or the many are likely to be the better rulers. He recognises that the few are more likely to possess outstanding ability, but observes that there are also advantages in the rule of the many as they bring varied points of view to bear on issues of policy, and are therefore less likely than the few to approve a wrong policy. This does not mean that in a polity there is no place for the expert, but it does mean that in such a constitution he is not the final judge of his work. The expert is necessary to formulate and apply a policy, but the people whom it is intended to benefit are better fitted than he to judge whether it is a good policy. Aristotle illustrates this principle by some simple analogies:

There are some arts whose products are not judged of solely, or best, by the artists themselves. The user or, in other words, the master, of the house will even be a better judge than the builder, just as the pilot will judge better of the rudder than the carpenter, and the guest will judge better of a feast than the cook.

The principle that 'the guest will judge better of a feast than the cook' has, indeed, become a basic principle of modem democracy. Modem communities are not too vast to permit of government by popular assembly, which was the form of democracy that Plato knew and condemned, nor do they claim that, even if some form of referendum could surmount this difficulty, it would be desirable. The need for experts to formulate and execute policy is generally recognised, but democratic peoples claim the ultimate right to approve or condemn that policy, ' and to select other rulers if they are dissatisfied with the achievements of their existing government.

In discussing the differences between good and bad forms of government Aristotle draws attention to another fundamental principle now commonly regarded as essential in a democratic state. This is the principle of *government by consent.* Thus, he says of bad forms of government: 'they are despotic, whereas a state is a community of freemen. By this he means that a good government, which attempts to promote the interest of the community as a whole, will receive the willing consent of the whole people, whereas a government which attempts to promote the interest of only a particular section of the community will find it necessary to govern the rest of the community by despotic measures.

This appears to be true in practice, for modem democracies have generally been most successful where there has been a consciousness of common interests underlying sectional differences, and where the government has sought to achieve an acceptable compromise when the interests of different classes have appeared to conflict. On the other hand, where sectional interests have been in sharp conflict, and the government has clearly identified its policy with the interests of one of the sections, democracy has usually tended to give way to government by force.

Aristotle believes that one of the most important safeguards against the bad forms of government is respect for impersonal law. This law is not, as Plato thought, revealed by immediate insight to a gifted few, but is gradually discovered in and through experience. Such, at least, is Aristotle's view when he expresses his own most mature thought. When he is subject to the influence of Plato's teaching he sometimes writes as though the law were something standing outside and independent of the state.

Thus, the influence of Plato is obvious at the end of Book III, where Aristotle says that if a perfectly virtuous man could be found it would be right to give him supreme power. This is an admission that the theory of Plato's Republic would be justified if only perfectly virtuous men could be found. On the other hand, if political ideals are definable in terms of 'natural' development, the law must necessarily vary with the circumstances of the community to which it applies.

6.6 ARISTOTLE'S ANALYSIS OF STATES

In Book IV Aristotle directs his attention to the nature of actual states since, as he says, the best is often unattainable and the statesman should therefore acquaint himself not only with what is best in the abstract, i.e. theoretically, but with what is best relatively to circumstances, i.e. practically. Books IV, V, and VI are all devoted to an examination of the best practicable states in different sets of circumstances and constitute an empirical study of the kind which is a necessary foundation for sound policy if the assumptions of Aristotle's Organic Theory are true.

For on those assumptions the best constitution for a specified state can be determined only after a study of its history, traditions, economic and geographical circumstances, and so on. In these Books Aristotle accepts the implications of his doctrine that the natural end of a state is its ideal, and he seems to regard its natural end as a stable and harmonious condition in which all individuals and groups occupy the place for which they ate best fitted.

The general conclusion which Aristotle reaches after considering the various forms which government in practice may take is that for the average city state a compromise between oligarchy and democracy, with the middle class holding the balance of power, will prove most satisfactory. If either the rich or the poor enjoy too much preponderance the one class is almost certain to be oppressed by the other. This is likely to precipitate a revolution.

Indeed, Aristotle wrote that the exploitation of one class by another is the usual cause of revolutions. This danger can be avoided only if general instead of sectional interests are made the determining principles of government. Aristotle thinks that this implies that the weaker classes must not be exploited; that good relations must exist between rulers and ruled; that no individual or class should become too powerful; and that the magistrates should be free from all forms of corruption.

In short, Aristotle reaches the conclusion that a state whose government is a mechanism for exploiting rival forces will be unstable and likely to break down in revolution, while a state in which these forces are evenly balanced, and the government's decisions are determined by moral principles embodied in a legal code which applies to all, will be stable and happy. All this is consistent with, and indeed, follows from, Aristotle's underlying hypothesis of an Organic State. For if the state is an organism it cannot be a healthy one unless its various forces are balanced and harmonised, and only on these conditions will it fulfill its ultimate purpose of providing its members with the conditions for the best possible life.

6.7 DEFENCE OF SLAVERY

Aristotle, like Plato, recognises as a natural implication of the Organic Theory that different classes of citizen have functions of differing value and importance. Thus, he sees nothing inconsistent with his principles in defending the contemporary institution of slavery, which everyone in Ancient Greece accepted as a normal and essential element in social life. He defends slavery on the ground that 'from the hour of their birth, some are marked out for subjection, others for rule'. He admits that sometimes a natural master may be found living in a condition of slavery, but he denies that this is any ground for condemning slavery in general. It only shows that individuals are not always found in their proper classes.

But, he is quite satisfied that men do fall naturally into two classes; those who possess reason, and those who do not possess it and can only respect it. In his view, natural slaves are capable only of an inferior kind of existence, and are not capable of undertaking the responsibilities of citizenship. They are, indeed, nothing more than animate tools.

Aristotle's belief in the inherent inferiority of a large proportion of human beings stands in sharp antithesis to the modern belief in the rights of man, yet it differs in degree rather than in nature from the assumptions of intrinsic inequality which, in one form or another, have been common in the political and social outlook of practically every community. Moreover, even the modem world is not without examples of racial discrimination, which are defended by essentially the same arguments as those employed by Aristotle. There may, conceivably, be some moral justification for such discrimination, but empirical philosophers could readily account for it as the natural effect of social and economic conditions in which such discrimination has proved advantageous to the possessors of power and privilege. Even those who accept objective moral distinctions might well regard this causal explanation of the condoning of political inequality as highly plausible.

6.8 THE IDEAL LIFE

Aristotle's approval of slavery is closely connected with his conception of the ideal life. This he conceives differently from Plato, who thought that the ideal life for anyone was that in which he made his natural and proper contribution to the welfare of the community, whether as producer, auxiliary or guardian. Such, indeed, is the logical implication of an Organic Theory, since it implies that the welfare of the whole transcends, and indeed ensures, the welfare of the parts. But in Book VII of *the Politics* Aristotle advances the view that the highest virtue consists not in action but in contemplation, not in the exercise of power but in the pursuit of truth. For such a mode of life leisure is obviously necessary.

No one absorbed in the exacting business of practical administration can, in Aristotle's view, at the same time engage in the disinterested pursuit of truth, which is both of supreme value in itself and of indirect value if the right principles are to be applied in practical life. Hence, those who are capable of the highest intellectual activities must be given the leisure and freedom to pursue them without distraction, and have their practical needs supplied by those who are inherently incapable of those disinterested pursuits.

Aristotle has a strong case for maintaining that the disinterested activities of life have the highest value. For the practical life consists of activities which are a means to the end of living the securing of food, shelter, clothing, security of person and property, etc., but the attainment of these leaves unanswered the question of the ultimate purpose of life. Aristotle believes that the ultimate purpose of life is the enjoyment of pursuits, which are valuable in them, and not merely as a means to something, which is valuable in it. Such activities as the creation or enjoyment of music and the pursuit of knowledge are, in Aristotle's opinion, intrinsically valuable in this way, whereas the mere attainment of the necessary conditions of living has no value in itself, but derives its value from being a necessary condition of these higher activities.

6.9 THE IDEAL STATE

In Books VII and VIII (which, as already observed, were probably written some fifteen years before Books IV, V, and VI) Aristotle outlines a conception of the Ideal State, which is strikingly similar in some respects to the conception put forward by Plato, particularly in the *Laws.* Aristotle argues that the Ideal State should be as small as is consistent with independence. Independence is of prime importance, since otherwise the state will depend on foreign trade and this will have to be protected by armed forces that will make heavy inroads on the available resources of manpower and wealth.

Aristotle would clearly have regarded the people of modern Britain as very unfavourably placed for the pursuit of the ideal life in view of their dependence upon foreign trade and the extent to which their energies and resources must therefore be directed to industrial production and national defence. He would have regarded a sparsely populated and relatively self-sufficient country such as Eire as a far more favourable environment for the pursuit of the disinterested values of life.

Although Aristotle was writing with reference to conditions in Ancient Greece he raises a fundamental question, which has a direct relevance to modem conditions, namely the question whether the complex organisation of a modem industrial community is compatible with the survival of the disinterested activities to which he attached supreme value. It is already clear that the close dependence of such a community upon trade with its neighbours makes it peculiarly vulnerable to economic and political disturbances elsewhere, and that when war comes to it the normal activities of every section of the community are likely to be disturbed.

6.10 THEORY OF EDUCATION

Aristotle's theory of education is set forth in Book VII, chapters 13-17, and Book VIII of the *Politics.* Like Plato, he believes that education has primarily a civic function: 'the citizen should be moulded to suit the form of government under which he lives. Moreover, 'the training in things which are of common interest should be the same for all. Hence the education of the young should be the responsibility of the state and should not be left in private hands.

Aristotle's discussion of the purposes of education is dominated throughout by the distinction already drawn between the means and the end between action and that which action seeks to achieve. As the end of all action is leisure, Aristotle thinks that the right use of leisure should be the ultimate end of education, although it must naturally also cover pursuits, which are essential means to attaining this end. As he says:

There are branches of learning and education which we must study merely with a view to leisure spent in intellectual activity, and these are to be valued for their own sake; whereas those kinds of knowledge which are useful in business are to be deemed necessary, and exist for the sake of other things.

In modem language, Aristotle is saying that education should not be confined to vocational training, but should cover those activities, such as the composition and enjoyment of music and the disinterested pursuit of knowledge, which are valuable in them and not merely as a means to some further end. He specifically states that mere 'amusement' is not a proper occupation for leisure since it has no value in itself but merely acquires value by serving as a relaxation from work.

Aristotle does not fulfil his promise to consider in detail the form, which education in the right use of leisure should take, but it is clear that he considers the composition and enjoyment of music and scientific and philosophical research to be appropriate methods of enjoying it. His conception of the earlier stages of education is very similar to Plato's. He stresses the importance of influencing children by the right kind of stories, pictures, and plays. He believes that education should first be directed to the cultivation of the body, secondly to the control of the appetites, i.e. character training, and finally to the development of the mind. The latter is the ultimate end to which the earlier stages of education are means:

The care of the body ought to precede that of the soul, and the training of the appetitive part should follow: none the less our care of it must be for the sake of the reason, and our care of the body for the sake of the soul.

The difference between the educational theories of Plato and Aristotle is thus subtle but important, and originates in Aristotle's belief that 'to be always seeking after the useful does not become free and exalted souls'. For Plato the purpose of education is to fit the individual to make his appropriate contribution to the life of the community, whether he is producer, auxiliary, or guardian.

Thus even the higher studies, which the guardians pursue in the intervals of administrative activity, are undertaken essentially for the purpose of acquiring a more accurate vision of the moral principles by which such activity should be directed. But Aristotle conceives of the ultimate purpose of education in more individualist terms. He recognises that it is essential, in the first place, to produce citizens who will contribute to the formation of a stable and harmonious society; but he regards this as a mere means to making possible the higher and disinterested activities which have a value in themselves.

6.11 ASSESSMENT OF ARISTOTLE'S CONTRIBUTION TO MORAL PHILOSOPHY

The argument of Aristotle's *Politics* is not based on any simple and central idea like that which runs through Plato's *Republic,* and it is impossible to identify the principles of his philosophy with a single and consistent theme. In part this is due to the fact that the *Politics* was composed over a period of some fifteen years during which Aristotle's thinking gradually became more independent of his teacher's. But the more important point to notice is that, when Aristotle achieved this independence of Plato, he found himself impelled to reject the rationalist in favour of an empirical conception of political ideals. In the *Republic* such ideals had been identified with a set of principles, while in Book 1 of the *Politics* they are identified with the laws governing the natural development of a society.

As already observed, Aristotle appears generally to adopt a point of view, which is something of a compromise between these two extremes. He regards moral laws as objective yet he lays great stress upon their relativity to the potential development of the individual or society to which they relate. In so far as the *Politics* has a dominating theme it may therefore be described as that of ascertaining and defining the principal forms of the 'best possible state' in the light of the various circumstances which condition it. Aristotle must be given credit for the formulation of a theory, which from many points of view seems to account for widely held convictions regarding the basis of political obligation.

Perhaps the most striking feature of the *Politics* is the extent to which, notwithstanding the very different political and social environment of Ancient Greece, Aristotle succeeded in formulating the principles, which are now generally accepted as the moral basis of democratic government. In so doing he demonstrated his greatness as a philosopher, for it required insight of a high order to recognise, within the narrow confines of the city state, the operation of the principles which, many centuries later, have come to be accepted as the essential foundation of the democratic way of life.

Thus forming the basic principles of a philosophy:

- For helping the people of a state,
- Human beings achieving a personal harmonisation within themselves and in their integration with society,
- Acceptance by the community and interaction with other citizens.

6.12 TABLE OF OPPOSITES

In Pythagorean philosophy, is a set of 10 pairs of contrary qualities. The earliest reference is in Aristotle, who said that it was in use among some contemporary Pythagoreans. But Aristotle provided no real information about its function in Pythagorean practice or theory or about its origin. Some scholars have detected possible archaic elements in it, but others have suggested that its originator was in fact Speusippus, Plato's nephew. Because no statements of Pythagoras have survived, and because Aristotle customarily accommodated pre-Socratic philosophy to his own terminology and problems, the problem is difficult to resolve.

Aristotle's table of the Pythagorean opposites is as follows:

- Limited - Unlimited
- Odd - Even
- Unity - Plurality
- Right - Left
- Male - Female
- At Rest - In Motion
- Straight - Curved
- Light - Darkness
- Good - Evil
- Square - Oblong

Aristotle remarked that Alcmaeon of Croton, a medical writer, also had pairs of contraries as the first "principles" of things and also of most human things, but he did not know whether contemporary Pythagoreans influenced Alcmaeon in this regard or vice versa. Aristotle associated moral prestige with the left-hand column, because the "good" things appear in that column. The table had some currency among Aristotle's contemporaries, perhaps in the Academy (Plato's school in Athens), but his references are made merely in the interest of supporting certain views of his own.

Aristotle's formal table has 10 members, because the Pythagoreans considered 10 the perfect number. But the pairs varied in different authors. Possibly no list or set number of opposites became canonical among the Pythagoreans.

7. RELIGION AND MANAGEMENT

7.1 SCEPTICISM IN MANAGEMENT

The term Skepticism is used for any philosophical position that maintains that our beliefs about a certain subject matter cannot be justified. Epistemology, the philosophical theory of knowledge, has often been regarded as the search for an effective answer to skepticism. Skepticism can be either global or local.

Global skepticism is concerned with all our beliefs about the external world, and claims that we can have no knowledge of the way that the world really is.

Local skepticism is more specific, and only claims that beliefs in a certain area, such as ethics, cannot be justified. Local skepticism can be used as a way of showing that commonly accepted beliefs about a subject could not be maintained because they lead to a sceptical conclusion. Hume, for example, used skepticism in this way in his discussion of induction.

7.2 THE APPLICATION OF STOICISM IN MODERN MANAGEMENT

A stoic is considered to be a member of a philosophical school founded by Zeno of Citium (Cyprus) *c*.300 BC. The name derives from the fact that he taught in the *Stoa poikile* ('Painted Colonnade') at Athens. Zeno's followers propounded various metaphysical systems, united chiefly by their ethical implications. All were variants on the pantheistic theme that the world constitutes a single, organically unified and benevolent whole, in which apparent evil results only from our limited view.

Their philosophy had at its core the beliefs that virtue is based on knowledge; reason is the governing principle of nature; individuals should live in harmony with nature. The vicissitudes of life were viewed with equanimity: pleasure, pain, and even death were irrelevant to true happiness. In time, the idea that only the consummately wise man (the philosopher) could attain virtue was challenged, and Stoicism became more relevant to the reality of politics and statesmen.

This, the Stoic belief in the brotherhood of man, helped the philosophy to make a real impact in later republican Rome, upon such men as the young Cato (whose suicide brought him a martyr's fame), Brutus, and Cicero. Later it underlay much aristocratic opposition to the emperors, but even so its disciples included Seneca, tutor and adviser to Nero, and the emperor Marcus Aurelius.

7.3 ROMAN STOICISM

The Middle Stoa, which flourished in the second and early 1st centuries BC, was dominated chiefly by two men of Rhodes: Panaetius, its founder, and his disciple Poseidonius. Panaetius organized a Stoic school in Rome before returning to Athens, and Poseidonius was largely responsible for an emphasis on the religious features of the doctrine. Both were antagonistic to the ethical doctrines of Chrysippus, who, they believed, had strayed too far from the Platonic and Aristotelian roots of Stoicism. It may have been because of the considerable time that Panaetius and Poseidonius lived in Rome that the Stoa there turned so much of its emphasis to the moral and religious themes within the Stoic doctrine.

Panaetius was highly regarded by Cicero, who used him as a model for his own work. Poseidonius, who had been a disciple of Panaetius in Athens, taught Cicero at his school at Rhodes, later went to Rome, and remained there for a time with Cicero. If Poseidonius admired Plato and Aristotle, he was particularly interested--unlike most of his school--in the study of natural and providential phenomena.

In presenting the Stoic system in the second book of De natura deorum (45 BC), Cicero most probably followed Poseidonius. Because his master, Panaetius, was chiefly concerned with concepts of duty and obligation, it was his studies that served as a model for the De officiis (44 BC) of Cicero. Hecaton, another of Panaetius' students and an active Stoic philosopher, also stressed similar ethical themes. If Chrysippus is to be commended for his diligence in defending

Stoic logic and epistemology against the Skepticism of the New Academy (3rd-2nd century BC), it was chiefly Panaetius and Poseidonius who were responsible for the widespread popularity of Stoicism in Rome. It was precisely their turning of doctrine to themes in moral philosophy and natural science that appealed to the intensely practical Romans. The times perhaps demanded such interests, and with them Stoicism was to become predominantly a philosophy for the individual, showing how--given the vicissitudes of life--one might be stoical. Law, world citizenship, nature, and the benevolent workings of Providence and the divine reason were the principal areas of interest of Stoicism at this time.

These tendencies toward practicality are also well illustrated in the later period of the school (in the first two centuries AD) in the writings of Lucius Seneca, a Roman statesman; of Epictetus, a slave freed by Nero; and of Marcus Aurelius, a Roman emperor. Both style and content in the Libri morales (Eng. trans., Moral Essays) and Epistulae morales (Moral Letters) of Seneca reinforce the new direction in Stoic thought.

The Encheiridion (Manual) of Epictetus and the Meditations of Marcus Aurelius furthered the sublime and yet personal consolation of the Stoic message and increasingly showed the strength of its rivalry to the burgeoning power of the new Christianity. The mark of a guide, of the religious teacher, is pre-eminent in these writings.

It is difficult to establish with any precision, however, the extent of Stoic influence by the time of the first half of the 2nd century AD. So popular had these ideas become that many specifically Stoic terms (viz., right reason, comprehension, assent, indifference, logos, natural law, and the notion of the wise man) commonly were used in debate and intellectual disputes.

7.4 RELIGIOUS CONVICTIONS IN MANAGEMENT

Though religious conviction shows itself in moral behaviour, it has been argued that religious people have not shown outstanding moral qualities. An 18th-century English philosopher and churchman, Bishop George Berkeley, when presented with this objection, remarked that nothing evil can be attributed as such to the Christian religion and that the only legitimate comparison is that between a person who is a Christian and what the same person would have been otherwise. Arguing a stark contrast with morality, however, has sometimes supported the distinctiveness of the Christian faith.

The 19th-century Danish philosophical theologian Søren Kierkegaard, for example, by a too literal misreading of the biblical story of Abraham and Isaac (Gen. 22), supposed that religious obedience must be in radical opposition to moral duty. However that may be, religious men often may be only too well aware of their moral lapses, their sins, and for this very reason they seek the grace and power of God.

The good that they would do they do not do, and the evil that they despise they continually do, as St. Paul noted in his letter to the Romans. In this moral predicament, those with a Christian commitment believe that the grace and power of God comes to inspire and release them from the dominion of sin. This does not mean that the Christian never sins, but it does mean that he is assured of ultimate victory over sin. The Christian Church is viewed not as a society of saints but a school for sinners.

Those outside the sects as hardly to the sectarians' credit regard the exclusiveness of religious sects. For Christians, sectarian exclusiveness is viewed as a scandal to the gospel that they preach. On the other hand, the criticisms of Puritanism that hold it as inevitably negative and oppressive sometimes fail to see that it may be neither negative nor oppressive if it is grounded in a spiritual and religious vision.

The doctrine of grace (the view that God grants man abilities that man does not merit by his own efforts) has sometimes appeared to make God himself--interpreted as the spirit dwelling in a man--the actual agent of good behaviour. In this way, some interpretations of the doctrines of grace have compromised man's freedom and come close to denying man responsibility for his actions.

Outside Christianity, critics have pointed to the gap between religious profession and moral action, though within Christianity, with its strong emphasis on moral transformation, the gap has been very wide and the criticism most challenging. In Hinduism for instance, Gandhian reformational and non-violence ideals have not mixed well with social corruption or with the type of neutralism that allowed China to persecute Tibetan Buddhists. Again, the Buddhist who goes to a temple is not necessarily compassionate as his religion dictates, and the Muslim who attends services in a mosque may be less filled with an inner sense of justice and patience than with thoughts of a holy war.

In Sri Lanka (Ceylon) and Vietnam nationalist loyalties have given rise to violence untypical of Buddhism. In the last resort, however, each religion will appeal to its doctrine of salvation when presented with a gap between its moral ideals and the actual actions and behaviour of its adherents.

7.5 JESUS CHRIST, THE WILL OF GOD

In Jesus' teaching, the nearness of God is itself viewed as a moving force. It creates, as it were, a field of force and challenges the whole person to obey the will of God unconditionally ("Let your loins be girded and your lamps burning"; Luke 12:35). As little as Jesus tolerated attempts at calculating the time when the Kingdom of God should come, so much the more did he demand that men reckon with its coming.

The relation between eschatology and ethics in Jesus' teaching, however, needs to be further clarified. His commandments nowhere have the character of prophetic sayings, and their content is not given an eschatological basis even where Jesus linked them with the promise of heavenly reward and, correspondingly, with the threat of damnation in the Last Judgment (e.g., Matt. 24:24ff. Luke 19: 11ff) God's will is valid in itself, always and everywhere.

For this reason, it is incorrect to characterize Jesus' demands as "interim ethics"; i.e., as exceptional emergency laws in the situation of the world that lies in the blaze of the cosmic catastrophes accompanying the shift of the aeons and the speedy dawn of the Kingdom of God (as did Albert Schweitzer, a great Alsatian theologian, medical missionary, and Nobel laureate). Jesus did not draw arguments for his ethical demands from the perishing order but, rather, from the existing world, the Old Testament commandments, the creation, and experiences known to everyone.

Thus, he did not aim at forming a "holy remnant", which would escape the rejection awaiting others in the Last Judgment, on the basis of some kind of select monastic rule.

The certainty of God's nearness is, nevertheless, the open or concealed point of reference for Jesus' exposition of the will of God and explains his attitude to the Old Testament Law. Corresponding to the character of the Old Testament legal tradition, he refers to the will of God in single sayings and in comments in relation to individual commandments, and, it should be noted, he did not develop these into coherent "moral teaching". Rather, he took up quite different kinds of commandments as concrete examples, above all from the Decalogue and related texts, concerning one's behaviour toward one's fellow human beings (on murder and anger, adultery and divorce, oaths, retaliation, love for others; see Matt. 5:21ff.) and also ceremonial commandments (concerning the Sabbath, prayer, fasting, and defilement) and other cultic duties.

Jesus always went to the root of these commandments, and he did not content himself with the mere letter of the Law but disclosed within the Law - sometimes even against the letter of the Law (Mark 10:1ff.) - The genuine will of God. Though Jesus respected the Law, it was no longer for him the only source of the knowledge of God's will and no longer the absolute intermediate authority that exclusively mediates people's relation to God. From this basis are to be understood both Jesus' exposition of the Law and also his criticism of all formalistic casuistry, which is for him only "human tradition". Jesus thus brings about a confrontation between the reality of God, which is no longer disguised by holy letter and tradition, and the similarly undisguised reality of man.

People also can no longer delude themselves into believing that their pious works would represent them before God and thus keep on piling them up, as it were, like the Pharisee (Luke 18:11ff.). What God wants from humanity is not something but humanity itself, unconditionally and undividedly. The classic passages for these thoughts are the antitheses of the Sermon on the Mount (Matt. 5:21-48). They sharpen God's demands to the utmost extreme and leave no room for merely legalistic behaviour. Their leitmotiv is: "Not only, but even."Even anger, the lustful look, the "legal" divorce, retaliation that keeps within the limits prescribed, and love that excludes the enemy are against God's will.

These extreme demands are meant not so much to be paradoxically over demanding as, rather, liberating:

- Firstly, they are formulated in a way that everyone can understand. They include numerous references to the natural, un-perverted practices of people in their daily lives.
- Secondly, the demands do not describe an unattainable distant goal, which all human action must of necessity fail to meet.

Rather, Jesus pointed again and again to what the heavenly Father has done, does, and will do with his children and to God's possibilities, which are unlimited, whereas a person might despair of his or her own limited possibilities and impotence (Mark 10:27). Jesus' sayings about faith (Mark 9:23ff.), prayer (Luke 11:1ff. Matt. 6:1ff.), or worry (Matt. 6:25ff.) are examples of this. Wherever Jesus calls on people to decide "for themselves" for God, he bases the argument on the fact that God has already decided for humanity.

The unlimited readiness to forgive that he calls for also has its motivation in the limitless mercy of God, which he demonstrates toward the guilty in unfathomable measure (Matt. 18:23ff.). Jesus draws his hearers into this relation to God and, therefore, does not engage in abstract reflections about whether his demands are capable of fulfillment. In this way, what a person loses is the characteristic of being able to attain meritorious achievements (Matt. 20:1ff.). On the other hand, Jesus certainly did not give up the thought of "reward".

The reward, however, is not a material prize, although images of this kind are not lacking, but the confirmation and perfection of the relation to God (Matt. 25:14ff.). The idea that human beings can claim and charge payment from God is for Jesus completely excluded (Luke 17:10) The nearness of God, the real God, also brings humanity, no longer graded and classified in traditional categories, into urgent and imperious proximity. How much Jesus was concerned with human beings is shown especially by his commandment of love, which he not only taught but also practiced to the point of offensiveness. In it is concentrated the "better righteousness" that "He demands" of his disciples (Matt. 5:20).

Jesus has taken over the Old Testament dual commandment of love of God and one's neighbour (Deut. 6:5; Lev. 19:18), which is also in Judaism a summary of the whole Law.

But it is characteristic of Jesus' preaching that:

(1) He consistently subordinated all other laws--e.g. The Sabbath commandment--to this highest critical standard (e.g., Mark 2:27; 3:4),

(2) He extended and heightened love of one's neighbour to love of one's enemies (Luke 6:27ff.),

(3) His commandment does not have the abstract ideal of a general philanthropy at its root. Rather, he directed his hearers into the situations--always eventful and concrete--where they encounter their enemy (Matt. 5:38ff.) and their fellows in need (Luke 10:25ff.).

Behaviour toward one's fellow is so important for Jesus that it is all that is spoken of in many of his utterances, without any mention of the first commandments of the Decalogue concerning behaviour toward God (e.g., Matt. 5:25ff. 7:12; 19:16ff.).

The distinction, which modern moral philosophy makes between individual and social ethics has, in respect to Jesus' teaching, only limited application. To be sure, Jesus did not draw up a program for a new order for the world and the nations, he did not demand a more just distribution of property, did not fight against the differences existing between masters, slaves, and hired workers, and did not give any directives for a better administration of justice.

The world he had before his eyes was the world as it was, within the horizon of Palestinian Jewish rural conditions, and not the world, as it ought to be. His sayings, parables, and illustrations show how keenly he assessed everyday life and how clearly he described it in his graphic, vigorous way--not glorifying this world as an eternally valid, divinely willed order, and also not getting morally indignant about it.

Rather, he calls on people to behave in this given world in conformity to the original will of God and his dawning Kingdom; e.g., to renounce the reign of mammon (Matt. 6:24; Luke 16:9ff.). Jesus did not, however, require a complete surrender of property from everyone. His followers were not to avail themselves of the legally regulated facilities for asserting one's own rights and were not to conform to the ways of customary behaviour in the world.

The assertion that the world cannot be governed with the Sermon on the Mount is thus not to be denied. Jesus' sayings about retaliation and his commandment of love are not juristically practicable as they stand, because they can only serve as a guide for the one who has been wronged by someone else or who is required to divide his possessions with another person.

Legislators and judges have to decide exclusively about the rights of others and must restrain evil for the sake of the general social order. But the truism about the impracticability of the Sermon on the Mount conceals the fact that Jesus' teaching contains strong impulses toward social criticism. Jesus unmasks as hollow conventions many ostensibly valid standards, explaining the Law according to the norm of the commandment of love and applying it to concrete situations.

For this reason he also resists egocentricity, not only of individuals but of entire religiously and socially privileged groups, and joins with discriminated-against people (e.g., heathens, Samaritans, tax collectors, and harlots). Thus, Jesus calls on people to live a life that corresponds to the proximity of God's Kingdom, although the validity and urgency of his commandments require no apocalyptic basis. The act of their proclamation, however, stands nonetheless close to Jesus' own mission (Luke 11:32ff.). Whether, and in what way, he expressed the fact of his mission by the use of Christological titles is not thereby decided. Jesus knew that he had been sent to the "lost sheep of the house of Israel" (Matt. 15:24; 9:36). His ministry, seen as a whole, was confined to the sphere of his own people.

Only a few significant words and scenes point forward to the inclusion of non-Jews, in a new, eschatological people of God (Matt. 8:11ff.). Jesus, however, did not organize a mission to the heathen (Matt. 10:5ff.) nor a worldwide "church". The only saying of this kind, spoken to Peter (Matt. 16:17ff.), has been placed in the mouth of the earthly Jesus by the later church and clearly reflects its situation, doctrine, and discipline. But Jesus certainly did call into existence a movement in Galilee and allowed at least the narrower circle of his disciples, if not all of his followers, to share in his wanderings and ministry.

Later tradition first identified the latter group alone with the Apostles (authorized emissaries), the circle of whom was, however, not originally restricted to that group (cf. I Corinthians. 15:5ff.). The number 12 symbolizes the 12 tribes of Israel. If Jesus appointed these disciples himself, he thereby demonstrated his eschatological claim on the whole of Israel. According to the saying in Matt. 19:28 and Luke 22:30, which were probably not formulated until later, he conferred on them the office of ruling and judging the perfected Israel of the new aeon.

7.6 THE FIRST PROTESTANTS AND MANAGEMENT

It was left to the 17th-century English philosopher and political theorist Thomas Hobbes to take up the challenge of constructing an ethical system on the basis of so unflattering a view of human nature (see below). Between Machiavelli and Hobbes, however, there occurred the traumatic break-up of Western Christianity known as the Reformation. Reacting against the worldly immorality apparent in the Renaissance church, Martin Luther, John Calvin, and other leaders of the new Protestantism sought to return to the pure early Christianity of the Scriptures, especially the teachings of Paul, and of the Church Fathers, with Augustine foremost among them.

They were contemptuous of Aristotle (Luther called him a "buffoon") and of non-Christian philosophers in general. Luther's standard of right and wrong was what God commands. Like William of Ockham, Luther insisted that the commands of God cannot be justified by any independent standard of goodness: good simply means what God commands. Luther did not believe these commands would be designed to satisfy human desires because he was convinced that desires are totally corrupt. In fact, he thought that human nature was totally corrupt. In any case, Luther insisted that one does not earn salvation by good works: one is justified by faith in Christ and receives salvation through divine grace.

It is apparent that if these premises are accepted, there is little scope for human reason in ethics. As a result, no moral philosophy has ever had the kind of close association with any Protestant church that, say; the philosophy of Aquinas has had with Roman Catholicism. Yet, because Protestants emphasized the capacity of the individual to read and understand the Gospels without obtaining the authoritative interpretation of the church, the ultimate outcome of the Reformation was a greater freedom to read and write independently of the church hierarchy.

This made possible a new era of ethical thought. From this time, too, distinctively national traditions of moral philosophy began to emerge; the British tradition, in particular, developed largely independently of ethics on the Continent. Accordingly, the present discussion will follow this tradition through the 19th century before returning to consider the different line of development in continental Europe.

7.7 History Of New Issues Facing Protestantism

Attacks on the churches during the 19th century (and after) were twofold: social and intellectual. Rapidly growing cities and industry created a proletariat estranged from religious life. Many of the political leaders, especially in Europe, claimed that the churches were bulwarks of that order of society, which must be overthrown if justice was to be secured for the working class. Some of the earlier forms of socialism were atheistic or at least deistic and suspected free churches as fiercely as they suspected an alliance between altar and throne.

Social and economic thinkers, such as Karl Marx (1818-83), argued that religion was the opium of the people that it bade human beings to be content with their lot when they ought to be discontented. In response to such views, in nearly every European country, Catholic or Protestant, there came into existence groups of "Christian Socialists," who believed (at least) in the doctrine that workers had a right to social and economic justice and that a Christian ought in conscience to work toward those political conditions that would achieve more social justice for them.

Except for these basic views the Christian Socialists varied greatly in their outlook and ideas, whether political or theological. Adolf Stöcker (1835-1909), a court preacher in Berlin, was an anti-Semitic radical politician; and Charles Kingsley (1819-75), a clergyman novelist in England, was a warm-hearted conservative who deeply sympathized with and understood the working class.

The most profound of all the Christian Socialists was Frederick Denison Maurice (1805-72), a theologian of King's College in London until he was ejected in 1853, then a London pastor, and finally a professor of moral philosophy at Cambridge.

But in England and America the radical wing of Protestants - especially Baptists and primitive Methodists - did as much for the workers' religion as the intellectual leadership of a few Anglican theologians. In some cases the endeavours made Socialist parties possible for the Christian voter; in others they persuaded Christian voters or politicians - without actually voting for a Socialist party - to adopt policies that led toward a welfare state.

Nevertheless, they made Christians more conscious of a social responsibility. In America the Social Gospel excited much influence in the churches at the end of the 19th century, and its most influential leader was a Baptist, Walter Rauschenbusch (1861-1918). Whereas in Catholic countries political parties arose that especially appealed to Christian voters and often used the word Christian in their name, in all the Protestant countries all political parties needed to appeal to Christian voters, and few avowedly secular parties had political success.

7.8 Effects Of Religious Beliefs And Practices On Management

One of the effects of religious beliefs and practices is sacralisation, a process in which certain persons, days, or objects become regarded as sacred. If such objects are granted more than the status of symbols, they may become objects of idolatry or superstition. Belief in salvation, which often accompanies religious commitment, can have various practical results.

If salvation is viewed as something that inspires progress and may be accomplished in the realm of time, such doctrines of salvation encourage social reforms and projects that envision an abundant life for humanity. If, on the other hand, salvation is viewed as something that is beyond the realm of time and set entirely apart from this world--something for which at best this world is a probation and at worst a sink of misery and iniquity from which the sooner man is released the better--such doctrines of salvation can be excessively individualistic and may even encourage oppression and tyranny.

Religious belief has sometimes led men to detailed conclusions about nature and history. Good harvests have been interpreted as due rewards for appropriate worship or good behaviour, or both; calamities have been viewed as the results of sin, either ceremonial or moral. If God is believed to be in control of history, a nation that does what is right and follows his guidance, as expressed through its prophets and other religious personages, is expected to experience national prosperity and success. In previous periods, when this did not occur, the ensuing calamities were attributed to the backslidings of earlier generations.

Many observers of religion claim that in the modern world few would suppose that God intervenes in this direct and predictable way. According to this view, God's activity in the world, apart from being expressed in its constant creativity and conservation, is effective through man's own intellectual and physical activity. Insofar as 'man's own creativity' is exercised, however, within the framework of the order that the world displays, and in no way violates it, one cannot exclude a similar creativity on the part of God.

Admittedly, the fact that man expresses his activity through an intermediate organism (his body) indicates that there is no exact parallel between God and man; nevertheless, because God's activity terminates with the universe, the analogy with God's activity might very well be expressed in the number of ways in which man can effect creative development in his own body.

7.9 Present Situation In The Philosophy Of Religion

In the latter part of the 20th century in Western Europe and the United States there has been an Empirical philosophy of religion, the interest of which has been in religious language and the kind of Empirical basis there can be for religious discourse. The definitive question has been concerned with what are the patterns of religious reasoning and what is the character of religious language if such discourse points back to and articulates situations of the particular kind that have been discussed above.

The approach originated in what has been called Logical Positivism. According to the verification principle, which gave what the Positivists considered to be the touchstone of meaning, an assertion had meaning if and only if it was verifiable at least in principle by sense experience. Logical Positivists were not at all daunted when this seemed to exclude the whole of theology and a good deal of ethics from meaningful discourse.

Since the 1950s, however, there has been a reaction against the Positivist's veto, and the works of the Austrian British philosopher Ludwig Wittgenstein are symptomatic of those who broadened Empiricism so that it has become interested in displaying and elucidating the variegation of language, in setting language in actual contexts, and in relating it to specific situations.

Significantly, this mellowing of Empiricism has been accompanied by a growing interest in personality and the self. This newer emphasis of Empiricism unites with Existentialism in suggesting that personal situations may very well provide helpful parallels to religious situations. There has been introduced into the philosophy of religion a renewed sense of the significance of mystery and a new emphasis on theological reticence.

With this has come a renewed awareness of the significance of metaphor, myth, and symbol, and there has also emerged a significant use of the concept of the model. The uses of terms like myth and mythological, it is important to recognize, does not mean that the assertions so called are false. Myth includes stories that try to articulate what is objectively given in a certain religious situation. Myths also relate to historical events--though the myth may be selective in its choice of such events--when speech about these events is used to articulate a claim of a transcendent kind. In other words, myth, metaphor, symbol, and model are all ways of expressing in ordinary language an extraordinary point.

The present stress on metaphors and models in religious language, however, inevitably raises two far-reaching questions: the question of reference and the question of criteria. The former concerns the possibility of the assurance that one is talking about anything at all. The latter concerns what the criteria are for better and worse ways of talking. The question of criteria has been answered in terms of the logical character and the empirical pattern of the multi-model discourse to which the different strands arising from the different metaphors or models give rise. That this discourse talks about something, must in the end rest on the claim that, in a disclosure situation, a subject is relatively passive i.e. aware of an activity bearing on his himself and thus aware of something other than himself about which he is talking.

In this context the significance of the Existentialist approach is to underline, as does recent Empiricism, the importance of a wider view of human experience than ordinary scientific experience might allow and to point one to highly significant personal situations that cannot be netted in scientific terms. The phenomenological approach, as developed by the Moravian philosopher Edmund Husserl, represents an attempt to be objective and scientific about experience, an endeavour to set out facts un-compromised and unprejudiced by metaphysical frameworks.

As an endeavour to reach agreement on what is being talked about and as an attempt to seek the simplest and clearest interpretations, many philosophers of religion and theologians have applauded the phenomenological approach. There can be no question, however, about a purely scientific account of a religious situation--that would be a contradiction in terms, and, though there can be a phenomenological approach to religious situations, there can be no phenomenological explanation of them that claims to be adequate.

The main contribution of Phenomenology is that of encouraging scholars to describe situations with as much critical analysis as possible. Logical Empiricism, it might be said, has absorbed something of the Phenomenologists' concern. It has certainly raised questions about and directed interest toward the way situations are talked about and interpreted, the possibility of there being different interpretations of the same situation, and so on. In this way it has provided the tools for and greatly stimulated contemporary interest in hermeneutics (critical interpretations)--a second order appraisal of interpretations together with an interest in their empirical bases.

As to the future of the philosophy of religion, a merging of the Empirical and Existential strands may well be expected. Metaphysical and religious views of the future most likely will combine conviction with tolerance and commitment with openness. The commitment and the conviction will probably come from moments of vision. Claims to finality, fanaticism, and bigotry will disappear, it is hoped, when it is made obvious that no self-guaranteed translations of what disclosure is are given, and tolerance and openness will arise from the acknowledgment that all understanding of these moments of vision is a multiple exploration, an exploration yielding different strands of discourse.

Solutions to contemporary problems, social and intellectual, demand a multiple consideration by scholars from many disciplines of all the issues involved in the problem, a consideration set within a framework of faith and morality in which man is interpreted as distinctively human, characteristically a person.

From such inter-professional, inter-disciplinary groups may emerge a new metaphysics and a new theology linked with, but by no means prescriptive of, assertions in other subjects. In this way there may be created a new culture--scientific, moral, religious, and technological at the same time. To be involved in such groups would seem to be the main task of the philosopher of religion, as of the metaphysician, today. If he is successful and if these interdisciplinary groups are creative, the modern period will then take its place among those that have marked crucial turning points in the history of mankind and its culture.

7.10 STOICISM IN MODERN MANAGEMENT

If the influence of Stoic doctrines during the Middle Ages was largely restricted to the resolution of problems of social and political significance, it remained for the Renaissance, in its passion for the rediscovery of Greek and Roman antiquity, to provide a basis for the rebirth of Stoic views in logic, epistemology, and metaphysics, as well as the documentation of the more familiar Stoic doctrines in ethics and politics.

Late in the 16th century, Justus Lipsius, a Flemish scholar and Latin Humanist, was responsible for the first restatement of Stoicism as a defensible and thoroughgoing (Christian) philosophy of man. His treatises De constantia (1584) and Politicorum sive civilis doctrinae libri V (1589) were widely known in many editions and translations. His defence of Stoic doctrine in Manuductio ad Stoicam Philosophiam (1604) and Physiologia Stoicorum (1604) provided the basis for the considerable Stoic influence during the Renaissance.

Around the turn of the 17th century, Guillaume du Vair, a French lawyer and Christian philosopher, made Stoic moral philosophy popular, while Pierre Charron, a French theologian and Skeptic, utilized Stoic themes in De la sagesse (1601; Eng. trans., Of Wisdome, 1608), as did the Skeptic Michel de Montaigne in his Essais (1580; Eng. trans. 1603). Through the work of Lipsius, Stoic doctrines were to influence the thought of Francis Bacon, a precursor of modern philosophy of science, and, later, the De l'esprit des Lois (1748; Eng. trans., The Spirit of Laws, 1750), by the political theorist Charles-Louis, baron de Montesquieu.

In the continuing and relentless war against the Aristotelianism of the later middle ages, the doctrines of Stoicism influenced many prominent figures of the Renaissance and Reformation periods. Pietro Pomponazzi, an Aristotelian of early 16th-century Italy, in defending an anti-Scholastic Aristotelianism against the Averroists, who viewed the world as a strictly necessitarian and fated order, adopted the Stoic view of Providence and human liberty.

The 15th-century Humanist Leonardo Bruni absorbed Stoic views on reason, fate, and free will. Pantheism, the view that God and nature are unitary in the sense that God is an impersonal being, and naturalism, the view that nothing is supernatural, both of which identify God with the cosmos and ascribe to it a life process of which the world soul is the principle, were widely held

Renaissance notions. Such a pantheistic naturalism was advocated--though from diverse standpoints--by Francesco Patrizi, a versatile Platonist, and by Giordano Bruno, defender of an infinite cosmos; and in both authors the inspiration and source were fundamentally Stoic.

In the development of a philosophy of public law, based upon a study of man, Stoic elements are found in the Utopia (1516; Eng. trans. 1551), by Thomas More and the De Jure Belli ac Pacis (1625; Eng. trans. 1682), by Hugo Grotius. This latter work is one of the most famous Renaissance treatises on the theory of natural and social rights.

The foremost Swiss reformer of the early 16th century, Huldrych Zwingli, who regarded justification by subjective belief as the foundation of the new Christianity, utilized Stoic views on the autonomy of the will, on the absolute predestination of the good and evil man, and on moral determinism. Another Stoic influence of considerable importance in the tradition of Christian Humanism was the view that all religions have a common basis of truths concerning God--a universal Deism.

Among those who favoured such a view were Zwingli and Desiderius Erasmus, the great Renaissance Humanist and scholar. More and Grotius also laid special stress on this view, and its influence was felt in the moral, social, and even the artistic life of the 16th century. Later, Herbert of Cherbury, often called the father of Deism, further developed the idea of religious peace and the reduction of opposing religious views to common elements. This view became one of the most popular ideas of the 17th century.

Philipp Melanchthon also cultivated Humanism and the philosophy of antiquity as a basis for a 'Reborn Christian'. Although Aristotle was his chief inspiration, Melanchthon made telling use of the Stoic theory of knowledge, with its notions of innate principles and the natural light of reason, which teach man the great truths of metaphysical and moral order. Stoicism thus became the basis for the natural-law theory, which holds that the state is of immediately divine origin and independent of the church--a Protestant view opposed by Catholic writers.

The Cartesian revolution in thought in the 17th century brought forward several Stoic notions: that morality consists of obedience to the law of reason, which God has deposited within man; that ethics presupposes a knowledge of nature, because man must learn to know his place in the world, for only then may he act rightly; that self-examination is the foundation of ethics; and that the innateness and commonality of truths bespeak the view that only thoughts and the will belong properly to man, for the body is a part of the material world.

René Descartes particularly developed such views. He was often hailed as the father of modern philosophy, in his dualism of mind (or soul) and body.

Benedict de Spinoza, a freethinking Jewish Rationalist, made similar use of Stoic views on the nature of man and the world. That aspect of Spinoza's thought that is debatably labelled pantheist is essentially Stoic in character. Together with the Cartesians, Spinoza insisted upon the importance of internal and right reason as the sole means by which to attain to indubitable truths and to the possibility of human freedom.

Blaise Pascal, a French scientist and religious writer, also was sympathetic to Cartesian conceptions of man and nature. Though he turned his back on philosophy, his religious thought retained the Cartesian and Stoic insistence on the independence of human reason, holding that man is fundamentally a thinking being, innately capable of making right decisions. There is an important and crucial difference and conflict between Pascal's views and those of Spinoza and the Cartesians: for Pascal, though the use of (the Stoic) right reason might result in proofs and demonstrations that lead to the God of truth, it would never lead to the God of love, the one true God.

Thus, the Stoic exaltation of reason to an entity in its own right--indeed, to a divine entity--as exemplified among the Cartesians and in the thought of Spinoza, was rejected by Pascal in the Jansenist Christianity that he finally adopted--a rejection that, because it also repudiated free will, distinguishes Pascal from those who held Stoic as well as alternative conceptions of human freedom and responsibility. Christianity in general, in spite of striking contrasts with Stoicism, has found elements within it that parallel its own position.

As the Stoic, for example, feels safe and protected in the rational care of some immanent Providence, so the Christian senses that a transcendent though incarnate and loving God is looking after him. And in general, Stoicism has played a great part throughout the ages in the theological formulation of Christian thought as well as in the actual realization of the Christian ideals. Contemporary philosophy has borrowed from Stoicism, at least in part; its conviction that man must be conceived as being closely and essentially connected with the whole universe.

Contemporary Humanism still contains some obviously Stoic elements, such as its belief in the solidarity of all peoples based upon their common nature, and in the primacy of reason. It is perhaps just because Stoicism has never become a full-fledged philosophic system that, many centuries after the dissolution of the Stoic school, fundamental themes of its philosophy have emerged again and again, and many have become incorporated into modern thinking.

7.11 THE INFLUENCE OF CHRISTIANITY

Evidences of religious attitudes and loyalties exist in every sector of human life--in human experience in general; in "culture," the complex interweaving of attitudes, concerns, and views; and in history, the record of social and personal behaviour.

Others point to examples of the wholesome moral and spiritual effects that religion has had on business. They mention that society has ceased to practice child exposure and there has been a notable development in the status of women in society. Religion, where it is not parodied, misrepresented, or misunderstood, broadens rather than narrows vision. Insofar as human nature is inadequately understood, if no place is granted to the spirit of man, human nature, it is argued, will never find satisfaction except through the self-realization and self-fulfillment that come from responding to the inspiring ideal.

7.12 RELIGION, A VALID TRADITIONAL JUSTIFICATION

Religion as pointing to an ultimate power, being, or value more generally, persons who are outside the particular religions and who have nevertheless acknowledged religion as significant often seem to base their views on a fundamental feeling of absolute dependence.

The grandeur of the universe, the character of the moral struggle, reflections on human nature, and an awareness of moral values inspiring men to reform society have all joined together to point men to an ultimate power or being--a "power, not ourselves, which makes for righteousness," according to the 19th-century English poet Matthew Arnold.

The fundamental difference in the latter part of the 20th century between the secularist and the religious person most likely has been between someone who takes a narrower and someone who takes a wider view of humanity. That there is an acknowledged need in modern times to give a moral direction to technology seems too many to bring with it the need for a religious view of the universe.

7.13 PARTICIPATION IN A SOCIAL INSTITUTION

Whatever the diversities, religious faith is not only self-involving, but it has a social dimension as well. Hermits apart, religion brings people together as children of one family having a common father. For Christians, the significance of the universal religious community, the church, has been variously interpreted.

Some, with a Protestant emphasis, have viewed the church as a voluntary institution created ad hoc for the convenience of its members to enable them to gather together to worship, to sing hymns, and to share common interests and beliefs.

The Catholic view is that the church is a social institution that is derived from God and whose structure expresses the givenness of God himself. To be of religious significance, however, social practices and moral codes, like inner experiences must have depth, a transcendent dimension, or they become superficial and dangerous parodies of religion, all the more dangerous for being in their outward features so similar.

7.14 BEHAVIOURAL DISCIPLINE WITH PRESCRIBED PRACTICES

Many religions bind their adherents to specific practices and particular moral codes. Thus, conversion has often shown itself in radical changes of behaviour; e.g., an alcoholic becoming a total abstainer. Such behaviour as murder, lying, breaking promises, stealing, and committing adultery has been condemned by the world religions.

So strong is the ethical element in Confucianism that some regard it more as an ethical system than a religion. Yet, ethical (and ceremonial) codes can be transformed imperceptibly into no more than current social conventions and mere customs. Whether such codes have changed or not, their range and detail vary widely.

Pork is eaten by Christians but is considered to be unclean by Jews and Muslims. Muslims and Buddhists abstain totally from alcohol; Christians and Jews need not. A Sikh will not shave his beard; but Hindus, Christians, and Muslims are free to do so if they wish. In contrast with Christians, Buddhists will not kill animals, and Muslims may practice polygamy.

7.15 MORAL THEOLOGY (CHRISTIAN ETHICS)

Christian theological discipline concerned with identifying and elucidating the principles that determine the quality of human behaviour in the light of Christian revelation. It is distinguished from the philosophical discipline of ethics, which relies upon the authority of reason and which can only call upon rational sanctions for moral failure.

Moral theology appeals to the authority of revelation, specifically as found in the preaching and activity of Jesus Christ. The moral teaching in Christian communities has varied in the different eras, regions, and confessional traditions in which Christianity has been professed.

The Roman Catholic tradition has been inclined to emphasize the mediating role of ecclesiastical institutions in its approach to the moral authority of revelation. Protestant churches have often put great emphasis on the direct, or immediate, moral responsibility of the individual before God. The influence of the spiritual director for the moral welfare of the individual Christian has been a significant aspect of Eastern Christianity. Moral theology has at times seemed to be restricted in its scope to a consideration of those thoughts, works, and actions that are viewed as offensive to God and spiritually harmful to human beings--that is, an enumeration of sins.

It was thus seen as a negative complement of ascetical and mystical theology, which presupposes a more positive orientation of the individual toward God. Many moral theologians, however, have believed that it is more faithful to the spirit of the New Testament and of early theology not to separate moral teaching from the religious anthropology that is implicit in the message of the Gospels.

This approach has been reflected in the traditional Eastern Christian emphasis on the divinization of man through his association with Jesus Christ and in the Protestant concern with the moral power of justification. Medieval and post-Reformation Roman Catholic moral theology tended to separate moral teaching from dogmatic theology.

The significance of the relation of moral teaching to divine revelation lies in the problem of determining the nature of the particular "highest good" that characterizes any ethical system. Without such a determination of the nature of this good, one could easily have the impression that morality is simply obedience to a set of rules or laws the observance of which has been labelled, more or less arbitrarily, good. In the light of revelation, sin is seen as a deterioration of the fundamental disposition of a person toward God, rather than as a breaking of rules or laws.

Virtue is viewed as the habitual capacity of a person to respond freely and consciously to situations in a manner that reflects and intensifies his conformity to Jesus Christ. The diverse approaches to moral theology through the centuries have varied greatly in their recourse to logical reasoning and in the degree of their acceptance of general moral principles that are considered universally applicable. A recent tendency challenging the validity of such general principles is called situation ethics.

Contemporary moral theology must confront problems resulting from modern technology, such as the moral issues related to the use of sophisticated instruments of warfare, individual responsibility in large corporate institutions, the demands of social justice, and developments in the biological sciences.

7.16 HUXLEY'S NON-RELIGIOUS AGNOSTICISM

The essence of Huxley's agnosticism--and his statement, as the inventor of the term, must be peculiarly authoritative--was not a profession of total ignorance, nor even of total ignorance within one special but very large sphere; rather, he insisted, it was "not a creed but a method, the essence of which lies in the rigorous application of a single principle," viz., to follow reason "as far as it can take you"; but then, when you have established as much as you can, frankly and honestly to recognize the limits of your knowledge.

It is the same principle as that later proclaimed in an essay on "The Ethics of Belief" (1876) by the British mathematician and philosopher of science W.K. Clifford: "It is wrong always, everywhere and for everyone to believe anything upon insufficient evidence." Applied by Huxley to fundamental Christian claims, this principle yields characteristically sceptical conclusions: speaking, for example, of the Apocrypha (ancient scriptural writings excluded from the biblical canon), he wrote: "One may suspect that a little more critical discrimination would have enlarged the Apocrypha not inconsiderably."

In the same spirit, Sir Leslie Stephen, 19th-century literary critic and historian of thought, in An Agnostic's Apology, and Other Essays (1893), reproached those who pretended to delineate "the nature of God Almighty with an accuracy from which modest naturalists would shrink in describing the genesis of a black beetle". Agnosticism in its primary reference is commonly contrasted with atheism thus: "The Atheist asserts that there is no God, whereas the Agnostic maintains only that he does not know."

This distinction, however, is in two respects misleading: first, Huxley himself certainly rejected as outright false--rather than as not known to be true or false--many widely popular views about God, his providence, and man's posthumous destiny; and second, if this were the crucial distinction, agnosticism would for almost all practical purposes be the same as atheism.

It was indeed on this misunderstanding that Friedrich Engels, the co-worker of Karl Marx, attacked both by enthusiastic Christian polemicists and Huxley and his associates as "shame-faced atheists," a description that is perfectly applicable to many of those who nowadays adopt the more comfortable label. Agnosticism, moreover, is not the same as Skepticism, which, in the comprehensive and classical form epitomized by the ancient Greek Skeptic Sextus Empiricus (2nd and 3rd centuries AD), confidently challenges not merely religious or metaphysical knowledge but all knowledge claims that venture beyond immediate experience.

Agnosticism is, as Skepticism surely could not be, compatible with the approach of Positivism, which emphasizes the achievements and possibilities of natural and social science--though most agnostics, including Huxley, have nonetheless harboured reserves about the more authoritarian and eccentric features of the system of Auguste Comte, the 19th-century founder of Positivism.

7.17 ST THOMAS AQUINAS

It would be out of place in a general survey of this period to trace in detail the complex controversies about the relative authority of Church and State, which continued during the following centuries. The only figure of real philosophical significance who emerged during the period in question was St Thomas Aquinas (1227-1274), who sought to combine and harmonise the teaching of divine revelation on the one hand and that of philosophical and scientific enquiry on the other.

The need for such an enquiry was directly occasioned by the rediscovery of Aristotle's works in the early thirteenth century and the translation of the *Politics* from the Greek text about the year 1260. Aristotle had proceeded on the assumption that human reason is the final arbiter of truth and that the discoveries of the special sciences are coordinated and harmonised, in the final synthesis provided by philosophy. St Thomas did not dispute the validity of these scientific and philosophical principles, but he argued that they have to be supplemented by divine revelation if the universe is not to remain an ultimate mystery. The findings of revelation do not, however, conflict with the principles of science and philosophy. All three sources of knowledge are necessary for a complete and synoptic understanding of the universe and man's place in it.

Like knowledge, the universe itself constitutes a hierarchy reaching from God at the top to the lowest of living creatures. All have their natural end or function, and each living creature in striving to achieve its natural end contributes, in a greater or less degree, to fulfilling the purpose of the universe. Men own position is of special importance since he is at once akin to the lower animals in virtue of his body and to God in virtue of his soul. It is this dual status, which creates the conditions of the moral fife, and gives rise to the laws and institutions through which the moral law is expressed.

Finally, that part of the universe constituted by human society is also a hierarchy, for it consists of different classes having ends and functions arranged in such a way that the lower serves the higher and the higher direct the lower. The common good is what defines and determines the rights and duties of both. In particular, the authority of a ruler over his subjects is not arbitrary but exists only in so far as it promotes the good of the community as a whole. It is, in fact, a ministry derived from God.

Lawful authority is quite different from the arbitrary exercise of power and there may be occasions when it is justifiable for a people to resist their rulers. It is, in fact, justifiable to do so whenever resistance is less harmful to the common good than the tyranny, which it seeks to remove.

St Thomas devoted much thought to analysing the conception of law, and the fourfold classification, which he arrived at, throws further light on his theory of 'lawful authority'.

He distinguished the following senses of the word:

(1) *Eternal Law* is the expression of the reason of God and embodies the laws, which determine the nature of the universe as a whole.

(2) *Natural Law* is that part of Eternal Law which determines the nature of living creatures. It is illustrated by the natural tendencies to avoid death and to reproduce the species, to seek 'good and avoid evil', and to achieve the destiny natural to the species in question. In human beings Natural Law is specially manifested in the desire for a virtuous and rational life.

(3) *Divine Law* consists of those moral principles brought to man's consciousness through Revelation (such as the Decalogue or the rules of Christian morality).

(4) *Human Law* consists of the laws enacted by human authorities for the direction of human beings.

It is the relationship between Natural Law and Human Law, which determines whether a political authority is lawful or not. For Human Law is justified only in so far as it is a faithful expression of the underlying Natural Law, which is in turn an expression of the reason of God. Since Natural Law applies to all rational creatures, rulers as well as subjects must obey it.

St Thomas believed that God had implanted in the human mind the knowledge of Natural Law and a disposition to obey it. It is from this knowledge and disposition that virtuous acts result, but man's fallible judgement is liable to error, and it is therefore important to give Natural Law an authoritative expression in Human Law, such as the civil laws of a state, to ensure that it is recognised and that imperfect men are restrained from evil acts. What St Thomas never does is to define an objective criterion for distinguishing those human laws, which faithfully express Natural Law from those, which do not; but this, of course, is something which philosophers have yet to do. His theory offered a justification for the belief (universal in his day and still accepted by the vast majority of people) that the moral law, whether clearly recognised or not, is objectively grounded in the structure of the universe.

But, however important and illuminating St Thomas's theory of law may have been, he was only restating the doctrine of Natural Law, which had been conceived of in all essentials by the Stoics many centuries before. His more original and lasting claim to fame were his attempted reconciliation of philosophy and religion, and his rejection of the reactionary doctrine that the authority of the Church should extend to matters of scientific research. St Thomas taught that the Church stood in no danger from scientists and philosophers, as the truths, which the latter discover belong to a different sphere.

Where the literal interpretation of scripture is contradicted by the discoveries of science that literal interpretation must be rejected as false, but this leaves unimpaired the essentially religious message which science can neither refute nor demonstrate. Such has become the official attitude of the Roman Church to the discoveries of science, and its members have in consequence avoided the necessity for an embarrassing adjustment of beliefs of the sort, which the Protestant Churches have had to make from time to time. In particular, the Roman Catholic Church found it relatively easy to adjust its theology to the teaching of the Darwinists although the latter caused widespread consternation among Protestants.

One result of the writings of St Thomas was that Roman Catholics gradually abandoned the theory that religion, acting through the machinery of the state, should dominate science and philosophy. In the political sphere the same tendency was manifested by the gradual weakening of papal claims to appoint and depose kings, and by the substitution of nationalist sentiment for ecclesiastical authority as the dominating force behind government. Thus it is true to say that St Thomas contributed in no small measure to the evolution of the modem nation-state built on a secular foundation.

The followers of Martin Luther (1483-1546) and John Calvin (1509-1564) were, by contrast, strongly inclined towards theocratic systems of government, and Calvin actually established a theocratic state in Geneva. Several of the Protestant states of Northern Europe have created 'established' religions which have helped to maintain a close harmony between Church and State, and to ensure that no really independent criticism of political rulers is made by the ecclesiastical authorities, and that the aims of government do not conflict in any essential respect with the principles of the established faith.

But today, under the powerful influence of the popular franchise, the policy of democratic governments is gradually becoming less subject even to the 'established' faith; and the modern version of the theocratic state is rather to be found in the totalitarian countries where, although religion in the traditional sense may count for little, the policy of government is subordinated to what is, in all essentials, a religious creed.

7.18 RISE OF THE NATIONAL STATE

It was in the fourteenth century that the national state was firmly established, and that national kings began to claim a sovereignty, which inevitably led to conflict with the Papacy. Pope Boniface VIII, most forcibly expressed the claims of the latter, in his famous Bull *Unam Sanctam* (A.D. 1302). The counter-claims of the national kings were advanced by John of Paris and others, but most notably, by Marsiglio of Padua (1278-1343).

Counterclaims from many points of view Marsiglio were the most revolutionary thinker of his time. Not only did he advocate that the Church should be subservient to the State, but he advanced what was then the highly original theory that neither Popes nor kings held their authority by divine right but received it from the sovereign people. This suggestion was too far in advance of contemporary thought to be accepted by either Church or monarchy during eagerly welcomed two centuries the Renaissance.

Marsiglio maintained that the chief end of government is peace and that a monarchy in general is more effective for achieving this than a republic; but he insisted that monarchs do not possess any superhuman or divine authority. Their authority is derived solely from the people over whom they rule, and is exercised subject to popular control and to any legal limitations, which the people may decide to impose.

Marsiglio advanced a similar theory of ecclesiastical authority. To him the Church consisted not of the clergy alone but of the whole body of Christian men and women, and the supreme authority therefore resided neither in clerical synods nor in the Papal Curia but in a general council consisting of both clergy and laity. In short, Marsiglio argued that both in Church and State, which are simply different associations of the same people, sovereignty ultimately resides in the people, although responsibility for its actual exercise may be delegated to others.

Marsiglio's views were, as already remarked, revolutionary and had little immediate influence. The assessment of the influence, which they subsequently exercised, belongs properly to the next chapter, where the conception of the national state, as expounded by Machiavelli, will be examined. But it is interesting to observe at this point that a thinker who was born only four years after St Thomas Aquinas died made the first serious challenge to the doctrine of universal law.

7.19 REASON AND REVELATION

It is clear that the lengthy period of human history which has been briefly reviewed in this chapter was mainly dominated by the powerful influence of the Christian faith and the general acceptance of it as the ultimate authority defining man's place in the universe and his moral duties. The Greek conception of human reason as an adequate and final key to the understanding of the universe was abandoned and the need to supplement it by an entirely different mode of insight accepted. Reason and revelation were, in short, set forth as different but complementary sources of human understanding which could not contradict each other.

While the acceptance of such a dual authority raises many difficulties, there is much in the most recent philosophical developments, which tends to justify it. For if the conception of reason which was put forward by David Hume, and has more recently been accepted by the Logical Positivists of the twentieth century, is accepted then reason, as shown in Chapter I, is incapable by itself of establishing any matter of fact or ideal of real world is hypothetical and sought elsewhere.

If religion can provide such directives then it must be accepted as an alternative source of guidance which reason, from its very nature, cannot challenge. That may not be regarded as a wholly satisfying conception of the status of religion, but it is the conception which was defended by St Thomas Aquinas and which seems to be implied by much in current philosophical thought.

If such a view of the role of religion is accepted it follows that religion has not, strictly speaking, made any contribution to moral philosophy, although it has greatly influenced and has been largely responsible for moral assumptions upon which political theories have been based and for the political institutions which have consequently evolved. In particular,

Christianity has given a new meaning and greater strength to the Stoic conceptions of universal law and universal citizenship, which are inherent in the political and legal framework of all liberal democracies. But it has stopped short at the essentially philosophical questions of what these moral assumptions imply and what their status is in the hierarchy of knowledge.

7.20 COMPARATIVE ETHICS IN MODERN MANAGEMENT

Sometimes called Descriptive Ethics, this is the empirical (observational) study of the moral beliefs and practices of different peoples and cultures in various places and times. It aims not only to elaborate such beliefs and practices but also to understand them insofar as they are causally conditioned by social, economic, and geographic circumstances. Comparative ethics, in contrast to normative ethics, is thus the proper subject matter of the social sciences (e.g., anthropology, history, sociology, and psychology).

Empirical studies show that all societies have moral rules that prescribe or forbid certain classes of action and that these rules are accompanied by sanctions to ensure their enforcement. Of particular interest in comparative ethics are the similarities and differences between the moral practices and beliefs of different people, as explained by physical and economic conditions, opportunities for cross-cultural contacts, and the force of inherited traditions facing new social or technological challenges.

It has been observed, for example, that virtually every society has well-established norms dealing with such matters as family organization and individual duties, sexual activity, property rights, personal welfare, truth telling, and promise keeping, but not all societies have evolved the same norms for these various aspects of human conduct. Some social scientists concentrate their attention on the universality of basic moral rules, such as those forbidding murder, theft, infidelity, and incest.

Others are more concerned with the diversity of moral practices e.g. monogamy versus polygamy; caring for the aged versus parricide; the forbidding of abortion versus voluntary feticide. The question then arises whether similarity or diversity is more fundamental, whether similarity supports the validity of the practice, and whether diversity supports a relativism and skepticism. Clearly a consensus of all peoples in a moral opinion does not of itself establish validity.

On the other hand, widespread agreement may support the argument that morality is rooted in human nature, and, if human nature is fundamentally everywhere the same, it will also manifest this similarity in significant ways, including morality. Such questions are philosophical and lie beyond the scope of the social sciences, which are restricted to empirically verifiable generalizations.

Another question concerns the development of morals. Insofar as this is an empirical issue, it must be distinguished from the question whether there is progress in morality. For progress is an evaluative term--whether the moral ideals, for example, or the practices of civilized peoples, or both, are higher than those of primitive peoples is itself a question of moral judgment rather than of social science. Still, social scientists and moral philosophers alike have noted important changes that have taken place in the historical development of various peoples.

7.21 NATURALISM

An outlook which stresses the role of facts about human nature in explaining human thought, and, more generally, sees human beings firmly as parts of the natural order. Naturalism is broadly opposed to religious and metaphysical outlooks. Thus naturalism is frequently (although not necessarily) associated with materialism and a high estimation of the physical sciences. Naturalist theories have both an explanatory and a justificatory aspect.

They seek in the first instance to show that it is possible to explain why we think the way we do in terms of facts about our natural constitution; and they then seek to show that by appealing to those facts it is possible to provide as much of a justification for our ways of thinking as can reasonably be demanded. There are important strains of naturalism in the philosophies of Hume and Wittgenstein. Ethical naturalism regards moral judgements as grounded in, and perhaps even as deducible from, facts about human nature.

7.22 CAUSATION IN BUSINESS MANAGEMENT

This refers to the seemingly necessary connection between one event (the cause) and another (the effect). Philosophical discussions of the concept are mainly concerned with analysing what the causal relation actually is, what sort of things are linked by causation (is it objects, events, states, or processes?), and how we can know when one thing causes another (what distinguishes a genuine causal connection from an accidental correlation?).

Other questions raised are whether causation is a necessary relation (could a cause operate but its effect fail to occur?), and whether causal relations have a unique temporal direction (can an effect precede its cause? Can a cause be instantaneous with its effect?). Much of the modern debate begins with Hume, who analysed causation as the 'regular succession' of spatio-temporally proximate objects. He used sceptical conclusions about the inability of both reason and experience to account for our knowledge of causal relations to support his view that it is based on the psychological phenomenon of custom, or habit.

This view enabled Hume to reconcile the view that man is part of the natural causal nexus, with the appearance of free will. Hume's account awoke Kant 'from his dogmatic slumbers' to produce his own position in which causal relations are imposed by the mind on to the world. Recent developments in theoretical physics have somewhat diminished the importance of causation, though they seem to support a non-necessary, probabilistic interpretation. For example, in microphysics it is not possible to determine with unlimited accuracy, but only in probabilistic terms, both the position and momentum of a particle (according to the uncertainty principle of the physicist Werner Heisenberg, 1901-76).

7.23 THE CONCEPTS OF MIDDLE AGES IN MANAGEMENT

The decline of ancient civilization in the West was severe; not, indeed, in technology, for the horse collar, the stirrup, and the heavy plough now came in; but political philosophy, like other intellectual interests, became elementary. In the Byzantine Empire, on the other hand, Justinian's lawyers in 529-533 produced the Codex Constitutionum, the Digest, the Institutes, which defined and condensed Roman law, and the Novels.

The Byzantine basileus, or autocrat, had moral responsibility for guarding and harmonizing an elaborate state, a "colony" of heaven in which reason and not mere will ought to rule. And this autocracy and the orthodox form of Christianity were inherited by the Christianised rulers of the Balkans, of Kievan Russia, and of Muscovy. In the West, two essential principles of Hellenic and Christian political philosophy were transmitted, if only in elementary definitions, in rudimentary encyclopaedias. Isidore of Seville in his 7th-century Etymologiae, for example, asserts that kings rule only on condition of doing right and that the rule reflects a Ciceronic law of nature "common to all people and mankind everywhere by natural instinct."

Further, the barbarians respected the civilization they took over and exploited. When converted, they revered the papacy, and in 800 the Frankish Charlemagne even revived the Western Empire as holy and Roman. The idea of Christian empire coterminous with civilization thus survived in Western as well as Eastern Christendom.

7.24 AQUINAS AND THE SCHOLASTICS

At this point we may pass over more than 800 years in silence, for there were no major developments in ethics in the West until the rise of Scholasticism in the 12th and 13th centuries. Among the first of the significant works written during this time was a treatise on ethics by the French philosopher and theologian Peter Abelard (1079-1142). His importance in ethical theory lies in his emphasis on intentions.

Abelard maintained, for example, that the sin of sexual wrongdoing consists neither in the act of illicit sexual intercourse nor even in the desire for it, but in mentally consenting to that desire. In this he was far more modern than Augustine, with his doctrine of grace, and also more thoughtful than those who even today assert that the mere desire for what is wrong is as wrong as the act itself.

Abelard saw that there is a problem in holding anyone morally responsible for the existence of mere physical desires. Later medieval writers took up his ingenious solution, and traces of it can still be found in modern discussions of moral responsibility. Scholars in Western Europe did not know Aristotle's ethical writings during Abelard's time. Latin translations became available only in the first half of the 13th century, and the rediscovery of Aristotle dominated later medieval philosophy.

Nowhere is his influence more marked than in the thought of St. Thomas Aquinas (1225-74), often regarded as the greatest of the Scholastic philosophers and undoubtedly the most influential, since his teachings became the semi-official philosophy of the Roman Catholic Church. Such is the respect in which Aquinas held Aristotle that he referred to him simply as The Philosopher, and it is not too far from the truth to say that the chief aim of Aquinas' work was to reconcile Aristotle's views with Christian doctrine. Aquinas took from Aristotle the notion of a final end, or summum bonum, at which all action is ultimately directed; and, like Aristotle, he saw this end as necessarily linked with happiness.

This conception was Christianised, however, by the idea that happiness is to be found in the love of God. Thus a person seeks to know God but cannot fully succeed in this in life on earth. The reward of heaven, where one can know God, is available only to those who merit it, though even then it is given by God's grace rather than obtained by right. Short of heaven, a person can experience only a more limited form of happiness to be gained through a life of virtue and friendship, much as Aristotle had recommended.

The blend of Aristotle's teachings and Christianity is also evident in Aquinas' views about right and wrong, and how we come to know the difference between them. Aquinas is often described as advocating a "natural law" ethic, but this term is easily misunderstood. The natural law to which Aquinas referred does not require a legislator any more than do the laws of nature that govern the motions of the planets. An even more common mistake is to imagine that this conception of natural law relies on contrasting what is natural with what is artificial.

Aquinas' theory of the basis of right and wrong developed rather as an alternative to the view that morality is determined simply by the arbitrary will of God. Instead of conceiving of right and wrong in this manner as something fundamentally unrelated to human goals and purposes, Aquinas saw morality as deriving from human nature and the activities that are objectively suited to it. It is a consequence of this natural law ethic that the difference between right and wrong can be appreciated by the use of reason and reflection on experience.

Christian revelation may supplement this knowledge in some respects, but even such pagan philosophers as Aristotle could understand the essentials of virtuous living. We are, however, likely to err when we apply these general principles to the particular cases that confront us in everyday life. Corrupt customs and poor moral education may obscure the messages of natural reason.

Hence, societies must enact laws of their own to supplement natural law and, where necessary, to coerce those who, because of their own imperfections, are liable to do what is wrong and socially destructive. It follows, too, that virtue and human flourishing are linked. When we do what is right, we do what is objectively suited to our true nature. Thus the promise of heaven is no mere external sanction, rewarding actions that would otherwise be indifferent to us or even against our best interests.

On the contrary, Aquinas wrote "God is not offended by us except by what we do against our own good." Reward and punishment in the afterlife reinforce a moral law that all humans, Christian or pagan, have adequate prior reasons for following. In arguing for his views, Aquinas was always concerned to show that he had the authority of the Scriptures or the Church Fathers on his side, but the substance of his ethical system is to a remarkable degree based on reason rather than revelation. This is strong testimony to the power of Aristotle's example. Nonetheless,

Aquinas absorbed the weaknesses as well as the strengths of the Aristotelian system. His attempt to base right and wrong on human nature, in particular, invites the objection that we cannot presuppose our nature to be good. Aquinas might reply that it is good because God made it so, but this merely shifts back one step the issue of the basis of good and bad:

Did God make it good in accordance with some independent standard of goodness, or would any human nature made by God be good? If we give the former answer, we need an account of the independent standard of goodness. Because this cannot--if we are to avoid circular argument--be based on human nature, it is not clear what account Aquinas could offer. If we maintain, however, that any human nature made by God would be good, we must accept that if God had made our nature such that we flourish and achieve happiness by torturing the weak and helpless among us that would have been what we should do in order to live virtuously.

Something resembling this second option--but without the intermediate step of an appeal to human nature--was the position taken by the last of the great Scholastic philosophers, William of Ockham (c. 1285-1349?). Ockham boldly broke with much that had been taken for granted by his immediate predecessors.

Fundamental to this was his rejection of the central Aristotelian idea that all things have a final end, or goal, toward which they naturally tend. He, therefore, also spurned Aquinas' attempt to base morality on human nature and with it the idea that happiness is man's goal and closely linked with goodness. This led him to a position in stark contrast to almost all previous Western ethics. Ockham denied all standards of good and evil that are independent of God's will. What God wills is good; what God condemns is evil. That is all there is to say about the matter.

This position is sometimes called a divine approbation theory, because it defines "good" as whatever is approved by God. As indicated earlier, when discussing attempts to link morality with religion, it follows from such a position that it is meaningless to describe God himself as good. It also follows that if God had willed us to torture children, it would be good to do so.

As for the actual content of God's will, according to Ockham, that is not a subject for philosophy but rather a matter for revelation and faith. The rigour and consistency of Ockham's philosophy made it for a time one of the leading schools of Scholastic thought, but eventually it was the philosophy of Aquinas that prevailed in the Roman Catholic Church.

After the Reformation, however, Ockham's view exerted influence on Protestant theologians. Meanwhile, it hastened the decline of Scholastic moral philosophy because it effectively removed ethics from the sphere of reason.

7.25 DETERMINISM IN MANAGEMENT

In philosophy, the theory that all events, including moral choices, are completely determined by previously existing causes that preclude free will and the possibility that a human could have acted otherwise. The theory holds that the universe is utterly rational because complete knowledge of any given situation assures that unerring knowledge of its future is also possible.

Pierre-Simon, Marquis de Laplace, in the 18th century framed the classical formulation of this thesis. For him, the present state of the universe is the effect of its previous state and the cause of the state that follows it. If a mind, at any given moment, could know all of the forces operating in nature and the respective positions of all its components, it would thereby know with certainty the future and the past of every entity, large or small.

The Persian poet Omar Khayyam expressed a similar deterministic view of the world in the concluding half of one of his quatrains: "And the first Morning of Creation wrote / What the Last Dawn of Reckoning shall read." Indeterminism, on the other hand, though not denying the influence of behavioural patterns and certain extrinsic forces on human actions, insists on the reality of free choice. Exponents of determinism strive to defend their theory as compatible with moral responsibility by saying, for example, that evil results of certain actions can be foreseen, and this in itself imposes moral responsibility and creates a deterrent external cause that can influence actions.

7.26 SELF-IDENTITY AND IMMORTALITY

When there has been a self-disclosure of transcendence, of what cannot be characterized in space and time, one cannot say that any self so disclosed entirely comes to an end. In this sense, there is an argument for personal immortality, though one can only talk sensibly about it by expressing immortality in terms of continuing personal life.

In Christianity this becomes speech about the resurrection of the body, and in Hinduism it becomes speech about reincarnation in this world or in the universe at large. All detailed talk about a future life, whether in Christianity or other religions, is only a way of spelling out and pointing back to that experience of man's transcendence here and now, in terms of language that expresses the claim that such a transcendent element is not annihilated by death.

To be articulate about immortality, emphasis is placed on features of life that, at first view, has high significance and point here and now to experiences in which man's self-disclosure is most often found e.g. Inspiring music or the intimate and deep fellowship of a particularly significant meal. General claims for immortality in relation to an objective disclosure (whether it is spoken of in terms of God or moral ideals) have to be distinguished from, though they have evident similarities to, the Christian claim for eternal life.

Eternal life is, according to the Christian view, a subjective self-disclosure alongside the objective disclosure of God's activity in Jesus Christ, and it is as unique as the uniqueness of God in Christ, a uniqueness that is, however, an inclusive, and not exclusive, uniqueness.

7.27 THE FINDINGS OF PSYCHOLOGY

Religion incorporates certain characteristic feelings and emotions such as wonder, awe, and reverence. The religious person tends to show a concern for values, moral and aesthetic, and to seek appropriate action to embody these values. He is likely to characterize behaviour not only as good or evil but also as holy or unholy and people as not only virtuous or unvirtuous but also as godly or ungodly.

As a feature of human existence, religious life can be studied, for example, in terms of psychology, sociology, and history. Among the first books in the psychology of religion were two by Jonathan Edwards, an 18th-century American theologian: A Faithful Narrative of the Surprising Work of God (1737) and A Treatise Concerning Religious Affections (1746). About a century later, during a period of religious "revivals," interest developed concerning the age at which conversions most often took place--the period of adolescence.

Reflections on such facts, and in this sense the psychology of religion, only came, however, with the works of two American psychologists: Edwin Diller Starbuck's Psychology of Religion (1889) and the classical treatment by William James's Varieties of Religious Experience (1902).

Generally, the psychology of religion has shown that though religion for some is a crisis experience, for others it is a natural growth. As psychology became more analytical it became more interested in the abnormal, in neuroses and dreams, in the techniques of hypnosis, and in the kinds of experience induced by drugs. When Freud spoke of religion as an illusion, he maintained that it is a fantasy structure from which a man must be set free if he is to grow to maturity; and in his treatment of the unconscious he moved toward atheism.

The study of the unconscious by the Swiss psychiatrist Jung, however, suggested that dominant archetypes (implying innate tendencies to form symbolic images) are supplied by a racial unconscious, thus providing a psychological approach to belief in God. In classifying individuals into different types, psychology has distinguished between religious people who are: "extrovert" or "introvert" (Jung), "healthy minded" or "sick" (William James), and "objective" or "subjective" worshippers (J.B. Pratt).

There is always the danger, however, that psychological distinctions may beg too many philosophical questions. The modern German Protestant theologian Rudolf Otto wrote one of the most widely accepted studies of religious experience in regard to feelings. In his Idea of the Holy, Otto analysed what is distinctively religious in terms of the unique concept of the "numinous"; i.e., something both awesome and appealing, both fearful and attractive.

Psychology, however, is concerned not only with individuals but also with what is known about group behaviour, which can also be of importance in any study of the Christian Church or other religious institutions regarded as communities of religious people. The authority of a religious leader, like that of all leaders, is derived from his symbolic character and the extent to which the leader and his followers share a common ideal.

7.28 EGOISM

(From Greek ego, 'I'). In philosophy, an ethical theory holding that the good is based on the pursuit of self-interest. The word is sometimes misused for egotism, the overstressing of one's own worth. Egoist doctrines are less concerned with the philosophic problem of what is the self than with the common notions of a person and his concerns. They see perfection sought through the furthering of a man's own welfare and profit--allowing, however, that sometimes he may not know where these lie and must be brought to recognize them. Many ethical theories have an egoist bias.

The hedonism of the ancient Greeks bids each man to seek his own greatest happiness; in the 17th century, Thomas Hobbes, a Materialist, and Benedict de Spinoza, a Rationalist, held in different ways that self-preservation is the good; and those who stress the tending of one's own conscience and moral growth are likewise egoists in this sense. In contrast with such views is an ethics that is governed more by man's social aspects, which stresses the importance of the community rather than that of the individual. Under this heading come such theories as Stoic cosmopolitanism, tribal solidarity, and utilitarianism, which are all forms of what the positivist Auguste Comte called altruism. The distinction, however, cannot always be neatly drawn.

7.29 SOCIOLOGY

Branches of the science of human behaviour that seeks to discover the causes and effects that arise in social relations among persons and in the intercommunication and interaction among persons and groups. It includes the study of the customs, structures, and institutions that emerge from interaction, of the forces that hold together and weaken them, and of the effects that participation in groups and organizations have on the behaviour and character of persons.

Sociology is also concerned with the basic nature of human society, locally and universally, and with the various processes that preserve continuity and produce change. It is social life that is distinctive in the regulation of behaviour in human beings; the human animal does not have such instincts as serve to guide the behaviour of lower animals, and he is therefore more dependent on social organization than is any other species. Institutionalised social forms therefore are assumed to play the major part in influencing human actions, and it is the task of sociology to discover how these forms operate on the person, as well as how they are established, develop, elaborate, interact with one another, and decay and disappear.

Among the most important of such structures is the family, the subject of an important field of sociology. The peer group, the community, the economic and political orders, various voluntary associations, and special organizations such as the church and the military are of particular importance in this inquiry.

Though sociology can be considered as a part of the Western tradition of rational inquiry inaugurated by the ancient Greeks, it is specifically the offspring of 18th- and 19th-century philosophy and has been viewed as a reaction against the frequently non-scientific approaches of classical philosophy and folklore to social phenomena.

It was for a time presented as a part of moral philosophy, which covered the subject matter that eventually, also became the concern of the various social sciences that are now separate from moral philosophy. Some aspects of other fields remain of interest to the sociologist. Although psychology has traditionally centred its interest on the individual and his internal mental mechanisms, and although sociology has given its major attention to collective aspects of human behaviour, the two disciplines share the subfield of social psychology.

The relation of sociology to social anthropology is even closer, and until about the first quarter of the 20th century the two subjects were usually combined in one department, differentiated mainly by the emphasis of the anthropologists on the sociology of preliterate peoples.

Recently even this distinction has been fading, as social anthropologists have increasingly added studies of various aspects of modern society to their field of interest. Political science and economics had much of their early development in the practical interests of nations and for a time evolved separately from basic sociology; but recently in both fields an awareness of the potential utility of some infusion of sociological concepts and methods has brought relations closer.

A somewhat similar situation has also been developing in respect to law, education, and religion and to a lesser extent in such contrasting fields as engineering and architecture. Nineteenth-century sociology, influenced by the successes of biology and evolutionary theory, took an interest in resemblances between men and lower animals--in their having, for example, similar instincts--and also in the parallels between biological and social evolution.

These interests have declined, but sociology continues to share with the other sciences some interest in ecology, behavioural genetics, and questions of fertility and mortality as they relate to population studies. There is also a conviction among sociologists that contact between physiology and sociology is necessary to avoid errors of ignorance in both fields.

7.30 PROFESSIONAL STATUS

The Greek philosophers and the line of European philosophers in the succeeding centuries throughout Western civilization discussed much of the subject matter of sociology without thinking of it as a distinct subject. In the early 19th century all the subject matter of the social sciences was discussed under the heading of moral philosophy.

Even after Auguste Comte introduced the word sociologie in 1838, the matter was combined with other subjects for some sixty years. Not until the universities undertook a commitment to the subject could a person make a living as a full-time sociologist. This commitment had first to be made by scholars of other fields, of which history was a principal early sponsor.

As early as 1876, at the new Johns Hopkins University, some of the content of sociology was taught in the department of history and politics. In 1889 at the University of Kansas, the word appeared in the title of the department of history and sociology. In 1890 at Colby College, a historian, Albion Small, taught a course called sociology, as did Franklin H. Giddings in the same year at Bryn Mawr College.

But the first real commitment to the creation of a field of sociology took place in 1892 at the new University of Chicago, where newly arrived Albion Small asked for and received permission to create a department called sociology--the first such in the world. In the following year or two, departments in the subject were founded at Columbia, Kansas, and Michigan and very soon afterward at Yale, Brown, and many other universities.

By the late 1890s nearly all of the educational institutions in the United States either had departments of sociology or offered courses in the subject. In 1895 the American Journal of Sociology began publication at the University of Chicago, in time to be followed by a large number of journals in many other countries. Ten years later the American Sociological Society was organized. Also to be followed in time by a large number of national, regional, international, and special sociological organizations. These quickly institutionalised the subject and have continuously served to guide its directions and to establish, very roughly, its boundaries. Eventually in 1949 the International Sociological Association was established under the sponsorship of UNESCO, and Louis Wirth (1897-1952) of the University of Chicago was elected its first president.

The rapid growth in numbers of full-time sociologists, along with growth of publications, allowed the content of the discipline to expand rapidly. By 1970 there were more than a dozen important sociological journals and an indefinite number of minor journals in the U.S., as well as a considerable number in other nations. Research grew throughout the 20th century at an accelerated pace, especially since the 1920s, partly because of strong financial support from foundations, government, commercial sources, and private gifts. Along with this came a flourishing of research institutes, some affiliated with university departments and some independent.

A small but increasing number of sociologists gain their livelihood through full-time research independent of universities. Similar developments have occurred in various other parts of the world, with variations resulting from special conditions in each case. In France, where Auguste Comte and later Émile Durkheim gave early impetus to sociology, there was early development in many fields of the subject.

The two world wars slowed the development, but after 1945 a strong revival of interest in sociology took place, during which the French government established a number of institutes in the social sciences at the level of institutes in the natural sciences, including several in Paris for sociological research--notably the Centre d'Études Sociologiques, the Institut National d'Études Démographiques, and the Maison des Sciences de l'Homme. These institutes receive government funds and employ many full-time sociologists, some of them among the prominent scholars in the nation. French universities have been somewhat more conservative; the Sorbonne, for example, had in 1970 only one chair officially assigned to sociology.

The new University of Nanterre, however, established a department with four professorships. A rich amount of research publication has been produced in France since World War II, particularly in general sociology, theory, methodology, social psychology, industrial sociology, and the sociology of work. German sociology had a strong base in the late 19th century and afterward, and the writings of Ferdinand Tönnies, Max Weber, Georg Simmel, and others were influential in all parts of the world.

By the early 1930s, however, official Nazi hostility had impeded its development and by the time of World War II had destroyed it as an academic subject in Germany. Immediately after the war a new generation of scholars, aided by visiting sociologists, imported the new empirical research methods and began the development of a style of German sociology much different from the earlier theoretical and philosophical traditions.

At the University of Frankfurt, Max Horkheimer's Institut für Sozialforschung (social research), established by private financing before the war, was revived and has stimulated much research production. West German universities remained conservative for a time, but two newly created universities--the Free University of Berlin and the University of Constance--made sociology one of their major subjects.

By 1970 most West German universities had at least one chair in sociology. National needs received special emphasis, including administrative research of use to planning, studies of unemployment, youth problems, and delinquency. A significant amount of research also is published in such fields as rural sociology, political sociology, and the family. In Great Britain, despite the early prominence of Herbert Spencer and L.T. Hobhouse, sociology was little regarded by leading universities until the mid-20th century. Before World War II Britain excelled in anthropology, especially in the study of non-white societies of the empire. Sociology concentrated on studies of the poor, and much of it was undertaken by persons whose affiliation was similar to that of social workers in the United States.

The major pre-war sociology department, at the London School of Economics, had the objective more of social reform than scientific research. In the post-war period, however, a considerable revival of sociology took place; Oxford and Cambridge recognized the subject by creating positions for sociologists, and various new universities established chairs and departments. Significant work in Britain has been done in such fields as population and demography, sociology of organization, and general sociology.

The Tavistock Institute of Human Relations in London has become world famous and concentrates on human relations in the family, the work group, and organizations. A parallel growth took place in Canada, Australia, and New Zealand. Canada, with some apparent reluctance, allowed itself to be much influenced by American sociology and has built many new departments with sociologists trained in the United States. The Scandinavian countries have also to a considerable extent adopted the methods and some of the content of American sociology, and the subject has had rapid development in many of the universities and in research institutes, some of which are connected with universities.

There is also a considerable amount of interchange between sociologists in these countries. Japan has a record of much sociological activity dating back to the 1870s. The Japanese Sociological Society (Nippon Shakai Gakkai), headquartered at the University of Tokyo, was founded in 1923; by 1960 there were about 150 universities and colleges with courses in the subject. In the early period sociology was nearly all imported; Comte and Spencer, and later Giddings and Gabriel Tarde, were their important theorists.

After World War II there were rapid changes in sociology in Japan, with empirical research methods largely replacing the earlier philosophical style. Importations from American sociology became abundant. Popular among these were industrial sociology, educational sociology, public opinion research, and the study of mass communications. Sociology in the former Soviet Union was long held back by the perceived incompatibility of the subject with Marxist theory.

Eventually, however, it was permitted to develop, and sociological institutes and chairs of sociology increased. By 1970 the Soviet Sociological Association had more than a thousand members. Leading research interests included such subjects as labour productivity, education, crime, and alcoholism.

Soviet sociology generally displayed an apparent tendency to avoid issues that might have implied conflict with Marxist thought. Nations under the influence of the Soviet Union were also from time to time inhospitable to sociology, but the strong interest of younger scholars made possible some relaxation of this opposition, and in the second half of the 20th century there was considerable progress of sociology in such countries as Hungary, Poland, the Czech Republic, and Slovakia, with occasional setbacks in some areas. In Israel the dominant department of sociology is at the Hebrew University in Jerusalem, where there are also several research institutes.

Israeli sociology maintains continuous close contacts with American sociology, and many of the leading Israeli sociologists have had training or teaching experience in the United States. Among the specialties in Israel are research in methodology, communication, criminology, and the collective settlements (kibbutzim) in which new forms of custom and social organization are observed while under development.

The passing of the Fascist regime in Italy and the relative liberalization in Spain opened the door to sociology, and academic chairs and research institutes are gradually increasing in these countries. Of particular interest are studies of industrial efficiency and social mobility.

The general conservatism of universities, however, may constitute a retarding influence for some time to come. In Latin America objective sociology has been much resisted, partly because it has been viewed as a threat to the political and social order but also because of meagre financial support of research and the low salary level of professors, many of who must supplement their earnings in the practice of law, in civil service, and in other occupations. In the 1960s, however, the number of full-time chairs increased, and a number of research institutes, some financed by U.S. funds, were established.

Political instability in some countries remains a major hindrance, and in such countries able scholars continue to be forced from their university positions from time to time. Little by little, sociology is penetrating into some of the developing nations. A number of African universities have formed departments, and the subject is gaining in importance in the Philippines, India, Indonesia, and Pakistan.

7.31 PHILOSOPHICAL ANTHROPOLOGY

This is the discipline that seeks to unify the several empirical investigations of human nature in an effort to understand individuals as both creatures of their environment and creators of their own values. The word anthropology was first used in the philosophical faculties of German universities at the end of the 16th century to refer to the systematic study of man as a physical and moral being.

Philosophical anthropology is thus, literally, the systematic study of man conducted within philosophy or by the reflective methods characteristic of philosophy; it might in particular be thought of as being concerned with questions of the status of man in the universe, of the purpose or meaning of human life, and, indeed, with the issues of whether there is any such meaning and of whether man can be made an object of systematic study.

What actually falls under the term philosophical anthropology, however, varies with conceptions of the nature and scope of philosophy. The fact that such disciplines as physics, chemistry, and biology--which are now classified as natural sciences--were until the 19th century all branches of natural philosophy serves as a reminder that conceptions of philosophy have changed.

Twentieth-century readings of philosophical anthropology are much narrower than those of previous centuries.

Four possible meanings are now accepted:

(1) The account of man that is contained in any comprehensive philosophy;

(2) A particular philosophical orientation known as humanism (see humanism), in which the study of man provides the foundation for all else--a position that has been prominent since the Renaissance;

(3) A distinctive, 20th-century form of humanism that on occasion has claimed the label of "philosophical anthropology" for itself and that has taken the human condition, the personal being-in-the-world, as its starting point;

(4) Any study of man that is regarded as unscientific.

Philosophical anthropology has been used in the last sense by 20th-century anti-humanists for whom it has become a term of abuse; anti-humanists have insisted that if anthropology is to be possible at all it is possible only on the condition that it rejects the concept of the individual human subject.

Humanism, in their eyes, yields only a pre-scientific, and hence a philosophical (or ideological), non-scientific anthropology. By tracing the development of the philosophy of man, it will thus be possible to deal, in turn, with the four meanings of philosophical anthropology.

First, however, it is necessary to discuss the concept of human nature, which is central to any anthropology and to philosophical debates about the sense in which and the extent to which man can be made an object of systematic, scientific study.

7.32 HISTORY OF PROFESSIONALISATION

In his Éléments de philosophie (1759; "Elements of Philosophy"), Jean d'Alembert, an 18th-century French mathematician, and Encyclopaedist, wrote: Our century is the century of philosophy par excellence. If one considers without bias the present state of our knowledge, one cannot deny that philosophy among us has shown progress. D'Alembert was calling attention to that reflective self-examination for which the 18th century is famous, and he was undoubtedly referring to the activities of mathematicians like himself, jurists, economists, and amateur moralists rather than to narrow philosophical specialists.

But the 18th century was clearly the "century of philosophy par excellence" in a more technical sense too. For it was the period in which philosophising first began to pass from the hands of gentlemen and amateurs into those of true professionals. The chief sign of this shift was the return of reputable philosophy to the universities.

This transformation first occurred in Germany and is chiefly associated with the University of Halle (founded 1694). In the time of the generation that lies between Leibniz (died 1716) and Kant (born 1724), the philosophical climate changed profoundly.

The chief representative of this change was Christian Wolff, who taught philosophy at Halle and was the intermediary between the ideas of Leibniz and those of Kant and the profoundly different conceptions of philosophising for which they stood. Kant later called Wolff "the real originator of the spirit of thoroughness in Germany"; and Wolff was indeed a pioneer in those techniques that transform philosophy into a professional discipline--the self-conscious adoption of a systematic approach and the creation of a specialized philosophical vocabulary. Wolff carefully distinguished the various fields of philosophy; wrote textbooks in each of them, which were used in the German universities for many years; and created many of the specialized philosophical terms that have survived to the present day.

The German Enlightenment was the first modern period to produce "specialists in philosophy". In England philosophising in the universities did not become serious until well after the time of Hume, but already philosophical fields had been sufficiently distinguished to be represented by distinct professorships. The titles professor of mental or moral or metaphysical philosophy, as they arose at Oxford and Cambridge, was the product of the late 18th and early 19th centuries.

Two additional factors of the German Enlightenment are relevant:

- The founding of the first professional journals;
- The rising concern of philosophy with its own history.

The learned journal, like the scientific society, was an innovation of the 17th century. But what had begun, as a general intellectual endeavour became in 18th-century Germany a specifically philosophical enterprise. Journals were published in great numbers; e.g., Acta Philosophorum (Halle, 1715-26), Der Philosophische Büchersaal (Leipzig, 1741-44; "The Philosophical Book Room"), and the short-lived Neues philosophisches Magazin (Leipzig, 1789-91), devoted exclusively to the philosophy of Kant.

More interesting still is the flowering of voluminous German histories of philosophy after 1740. By the 18th century there was already a vast accumulation of historical materials, and the self-conscious feeling that philosophy constitutes a specific field the past of which is worth examination and careful ordering combined with the German spirit of thoroughness to produce a series of massive histories such as Johann Brucker's Historia Critica Philosophiae, 6 vol. (1742-44;

The History of Philosophy); Johann Buhle's Lehrbuch der Geschichte der Philosophie, 8 vol. (1796-1804; "Textbook on the History of Philosophy"); Dietrich Tiedemann's Geist der spekulativen Philosophie von Thales bis Berkeley, 6 vol. (1791-97; "The Spirit of Speculative Philosophy from Thales to Berkeley"); and Gottlieb Tennemann's Geschichte der Philosophie, 11 vol. (1789-1819; excerpted in A Manual of the History of Philosophy).

7.33 HISTORY OF LINGUISTIC ANALYSIS

Sometimes called "ordinary language" Analysis or even "Oxford philosophy" from its later stronghold, this movement was, in fact, largely the product of two philosophers of the first half of the 20th century who were associated with the University of Cambridge, G.E. Moore (1873-1958) and

Ludwig Wittgenstein (1889-1951). Moore made the examination of the assertions of other men philosophically popular i.e. the practice of directing the philosopher's critical energies to the mistakes of his contemporaries.

The major subjects of his interest were ethics and the theory of knowledge; his thought was always Realistic and commonsensical, and he introduced into philosophy an unbelievably precise and closely applied analytical method. It was Moore's passion for clarity and his infinite pains "to get everything exactly right" that served as moral inspiration to a succeeding generation of younger men who had attended his Cambridge lectures over a span of 30 years. Wittgenstein had begun as a kind of adjunct to the Vienna Circle.

There was a time when his philosophical position was much like that of Russell and Carnap; but as he later became more sceptical of the foundations of mathematics and logic, his interest turned from logic and artificial language systems toward a critical examination of ordinary natural language. This change was principally registered in his Philosophical Investigations, posthumously published in 1953, which has become the true bible of Linguistic Analysis.

For it is here that Wittgenstein showed how a man's entire world is constituted by his linguistic experience and suggested, "All philosophy is critique of language". Wittgenstein thought that to ask "Why do we use this particular word or expression?" was the crucial philosophical question since a focusing of philosophy not upon the world but upon the mechanisms of linguistic use would solve most of the perplexities that have plagued philosophising.

Thus Linguistic philosophy was to perform a therapeutic function. Wittgenstein's example found many followers in the United States and, particularly, in England. There philosophers Gilbert Ryle, J.L. Austin, and P.F. Strawson have examined "category mistakes," "systematically misleading expressions," "mental-conduct concepts" (such as "other minds"), and all of the major "perception words" such as "looking," "seeing," "sensing," "feeling," and the like.

The effect of this concentration not upon things or ideas but upon words has, for members of this school, turned the customary works on ethics, aesthetics, or the philosophy of religion into treatises entitled "The Language of Ethics" or "The Language of Aesthetics" or "The Language of Religion." And these efforts are all, in Wittgenstein's terms, "a battle against the bewitchment of our intelligence by means of language".

7.34 HISTORY OF LITERARY FORMS AND SOCIOLOGICAL CONDITIONS

The literary forms in which philosophical exposition was couched in the early modern period ranged from the scientific aphorisms of Bacon and the autobiographical meditations of Descartes to the systematic prose of Hobbes and the episodic propositional format of Leibniz.

Two basic tendencies, however, can be discerned:

- The early Renaissance commitment to the dialogue form (already noted), inspired by the rediscovery of the Platonic dialogues;
- The later prevalence of the systematically ordered treatise, undoubtedly influenced by the enormous prestige of deductive mathematics.

The concept of serial order stressed by geometry, in which the reasoner passes from more universal axioms to more specific derivative propositions, influenced in turn the style of Hobbes, Descartes, and Spinoza.

The order of presentation in Hobbes's Leviathan and in Descartes's Principia Philosophiae reflects this serial concern, while Spinoza's Ethics utilizes the Euclidean method so formalistically as almost to constitute an impenetrable barrier to the basic lucidity of his thought. Medieval philosophy with its texts, readings, learned authorities, Disputed Questions, Quodlibetal Questions (brief academic discussions), and its Summas was characteristically associated with the medieval university. It is a singular fact, therefore, that from the birth of Bacon in 1561 to the death of Hume in 1776--i.e., for 200 years--not one first-rate philosophical mind in Europe was permanently associated with a university.

The fact is that, as the age of the saint passed into that of the gentleman, philosophers too reflected this profound change in their titles, their social status, and their economic situation. Sir Francis Bacon was a lawyer, judge, and attendant upon the royal court.

Thomas Hobbes was the tutor and companion of young noblemen. René Descartes, son of a noble family, travelled and studied at leisure, retiring to Holland to live out his life on inherited income. Gottfried Wilhelm Leibniz, courtier, diplomat, and scholar, became a privy councillor and baron of the Holy Roman Empire.

Thus philosophers often belonged to the lesser nobility or were closely associated with the nobility, to whom--like poets--they dedicated their works; and they lived not by philosophy but for it--either independently, by pensions, gifts, inherited income, or in the households of the nobility.

Thus, philosophy in the 16th and 17th centuries was clearly the preoccupation of widely scattered elite; and this meant that, despite the printed essay, much philosophical communication took place within a small but at the same time loose and informal circle.

Treatises were circulated in manuscript; comments and objections were solicited; and a vast polemical correspondence was built up. Prior to its publication, Descartes prudently sent his Meditationes to the theologians of the Sorbonne for comment; and, after its publication, his friend Mersenne sent it to Hobbes, Antoine Arnauld, and Pierre Gassendi, among others, who returned formal "objections," to which Descartes in turn replied.

In addition, the 17th century possessed a rich repository of philosophical correspondence, such as the letters that passed between Descartes and the scientist Christiaan Huygens, between Spinoza and Henry Oldenburg (one of the first secretaries of the Royal Society), and between Leibniz and Arnauld.

But philosophers were also familiar with the great monarchs and administrators of the age: Descartes gave philosophical instruction to Queen Christina of Sweden, Leibniz was an intimate of Queen Sophia Charlotte of Prussia, and Spinoza enjoyed the personal friendship of the Dutch politician Johan de Witt. The chief fact, however, remains the sharp separation of creative philosophers from the formal centres of learning:

Hobbes expressed extreme contempt for the decadent Aristotelianism of Oxford; Descartes, despite his prudence, scorned the medievalists of the Sorbonne; and Spinoza refused the offer of a professorship of philosophy at Heidelberg with polite aversion. It was to be another 100 years before philosophy returned to the universities.

7.35 OXFORD PHILOSOPHERS

After World War II, Oxford University was the centre of extraordinary philosophical activity; and, although Wittgenstein's general outlook on philosophy--his turning away, for example, from the notion of formal methods in philosophical analysis--was an important ingredient, many of the Oxford philosophers could not be called Wittgensteinians in the strict sense.

Especially critics--have often characterized the method employed by many of these philosophers--as an "appeal to ordinary language", and they were thus identified as belonging to the school of "ordinary language" philosophy.

Exactly what this form of argument is supposed to be and what exemplifies it in the writings of these philosophers has been by no means clear. Gilbert Ryle, Moore's successor as editor of a leading journal, Mind--and especially in his The Concept of Mind--was among the most prominent of those analysts who were regarded as using ordinary language as a philosophical tool. Ryle, like Wittgenstein, pointed out the mistake of regarding the mind as what he called "a ghost in a machine"--to defeat the radical dualism of mind and body that has characterized much of philosophical thinking--by investigating how people employ a variety of concepts, such as memory, perception, and imagination, that designate "mental" properties.

He tried to show that, when philosophers carry out such investigations, they find that, roughly speaking, it is the way people act and behave that leads to attributing these properties to them, and that there is no involvement of anything internally private. He also attempted to show how philosophers have come to dualistic conclusions--usually from having a wrong model in terms of which to interpret human activities.

A dualistic model may be constructed, for example, by wrongly supposing that an intelligently behaving person must be continually utilizing knowledge of facts--knowledge that something is the case. Ryle contended, on the contrary, that much intelligent behaviour is a matter of knowing how to do something and that, once this fact is acknowledged, there is no temptation to explain the behaviour by looking for a private internal knowledge of facts.

Though Ryle's objectives were similar to those of Wittgenstein, his results have often seemed more behaviouristic than Wittgenstein's. It is true that Ryle did ask, in pursuit of his method, some fairly detailed questions about when a person would say, for example, that someone had been imagining something; but it is by no means clear that he was appealing to ordinary language in the sense that his was an investigation into how, say, speakers of English use certain expressions. In any case, the charge, often voiced by critics, that this style of philosophising trivializes and perverts philosophy from its traditional function would probably also have to be levelled against Aristotle, who frequently appealed to "what we would say."

A powerful philosophical figure among post-war Oxford philosophers was John Austin, who was White's professor of moral philosophy until his death, in 1960. Austin felt that many philosophical theories derive their plausibility from overlooking distinctions--often very fine--between different uses of expressions, and he also thought that philosophers too frequently think that any one of a number of expressions will do just as well for their purposes. (Thus, ignoring the difference between an illusion and a delusion, for example, gives credence to the view that what one immediately perceives are not physical objects, but sense data.) Austin's work was, in many respects, much closer to the ideal of philosophy as comprising the analysis of concepts than was that of Ryle or Wittgenstein.

He was also much more concerned with the nature of language itself and with general theories of how it functions. This novel approach, as exemplified in How to Do Things with Words (1962), set a trend that has been followed out in a growing literature in the philosophy of language.

Austin took the total speech act as the starting point of analysis, which allowed him to make distinctions based not only upon words and their place in a language but also upon such points as the speaker's intentions in making the utterance and its expected effect on the audience. There was also in Austin's approach something of the program of Russell and the early Wittgenstein for laying bare the fundamental structure of language.

8. MACHIAVELLI AND HIS INFLUENCE ON MANAGEMENT

8.1 MACHIAVELLI ON SCIENCE

The time, which elapsed between the death of Marsiglio in 1343 and the birth of Machiavelli in 1469, saw the beginning of the great intellectual and spiritual revolution known as the Renaissance. During this period both the Empire and the Papacy lost much of their power and prestige; the modern type of sovereign state came into being, and strong monarchies were established in France, Spain, and England. It was unlikely that these tremendous changes would take place without important repercussions in political philosophy, and Machiavelli worked out a theory of government which marked a complete break with the theories based upon the principle of Natural or Moral Law which had dominated political thought during the preceding fifteen centuries of the Christian era.

Niccolo Machiavelli was born in Florence, the son of a jurist, and entered public life in 1494, the year in which Charles VIII of France invaded Northern Italy and the Medici were expelled from Florence. His first post was that of Clerk in the Second Chancery of the Commune and in I498 he was promoted to the rank of Second Chancellor and Secretary and continued in this office till the year 15I2. While thus employed he undertook a large number of diplomatic missions both to the petty courts of Italy and to other countries, and it was the experience of these missions which was largely responsible for forming the views which he subsequently expounded in his political writings. His mission to the camp of Cesare Borgia, Duke of Valentinois, specially influenced him in 1502. Although Machiavelli had undertaken this mission unwillingly, he soon conceived an intense admiration for Cesare's resourcefulness in resorting alternatively to diplomacy and force as instruments of government and for his firm administration of conquered provinces. He showed a rare judgement in handling both friends and enemies for the furtherance of his own purposes. His methods of conquest were ruthless, but he governed those whom he had conquered with justice. Although Cesare ultimately fell from power Machiavelli idealised his achievements to the end, and obviously thought that Cesare had attained, more nearly than any other public figure of the time, to the embodiment of the perfect ruler.

Soon after the battle of Ravenna (1512), in which Spanish and Italian forces sought to relieve Ravenna from siege by the French, Giovanni de Medici brought a Spanish army into Tuscany, the government on which Machiavelli depended fell, and the Medici once again assumed control in Florence. In November 1512 Machiavelli lost his post and was exiled from Florence. In 1513 he was imprisoned and tortured for his alleged complicity in a plot, but was soon released and retired to a farm near San Casciano. In the last year of his life he undertook some official missions at the request of Pope Clement VII, but he died after a short illness in June 1527.

Machiavelli's writings belong to the period after his fall from office in November 1512, but their substance is clearly determined by his first-hand experience of political and diplomatic life during the two previous decades. His reflections are set forth in two complementary works, the *Discourses and The Prince,* which was published posthumously in 1531 and 1532. The *Discourses,* of which the full title is *Discourses on the First Decade of Titus Livius,* are ostensibly a commentary on Livy's history of Rome, but really take the form of a fundamental enquiry into the origin and maintenance of states. *The Prince* has the more limited purpose of defining the principles by which the ruler of a state already formed can most effectively cement and strengthen it. The *Discourses* are therefore a study in political science, while *The Prince* is a manual for the guidance of rulers based upon the principles set forth in the *Discourses.*

8.2 THE SCIENCE OF GOVERNMENT

Machiavelli cannot be described as a profound philosopher, but his works have a special interest for the philosopher as an attempt to solve the problems of politics in purely scientific terms. Most political philosophers have tried to find a moral justification for the ideals of government, but Machiavelli is a political thinker who treats moral convictions simply as psychological forces, which play their part, along with other influences in shaping the history of nations. He denies that these moral convictions have any foundation of an objective character, or provide any rational principle by which human conduct can be justified or condemned. As a political scientist Machiavelli is not interested in what men ought to be, for to him this is a question to which no objective or rational answer can be given. He is only interested in what men are, although this of course includes the nature of the moral convictions, which they actually hold.

Thus Machiavelli contemplated the political scene with the detached vision of a scientific investigator. He was not concerned to solicit support for any moral convictions about the proper ends of government, for he had none. He thought that government should aim at doing what it would ultimately be compelled to do -achieve the purposes for the sake of which men accept the obligations and restrictions which it imposes on them; and he thought that the primary object of the political scientist was to discover and define these purposes and then proceed to show, in the light of experience, how they can be most effectively achieved.

Machiavelli's theory of the origin of government is remarkably similar to that which the British philosopher, Thomas Hobbes, was to propound more than a century later. Men, according to Machiavelli, are 'ungrateful, fickle, deceitful, cowardly, and avaricious'. Their social qualities are expressions of self-interest in disguise, and result from a calculation that a socially organised life affords, on balance, more benefits than drawbacks to the individual. That is the only possible justification of the restraints and limitations imposed by government. They have no value in themselves and cannot be justified as the expression of any kind of 'natural law'.

What the individual demands above all things is, according to Machiavelli, security of person and property so as 'to enjoy freely his own without suspicion, not to doubt of his wife's or daughters' honours, not to be in fear for his sons, or for himself '. Once this basic demand has been satisfied, the individual may seek, in addition, wealth and honour. But he seeks these things only for himself and for his family, and he co-operates with other members of his state only because he realises that if everyone were to seek these benefits for himself there would result what Hobbes was later to call the ' war of everyman against everyman', and the attainment of security would be as remote as ever.

Experience, according to Machiavelli, shows that security, wealth, and honour can only be enjoyed by the individual who co-operates with others to realise these ends, and in practice the security of the individual is found to depend on the security of the state to which he belongs. This is the real origin of those moral distinctions between good and bad, or just and unjust, which are so influential in human life. What is good or just is what contributes to the security and prosperity of the state and all its members; what is bad or unjust is what has the contrary effect.

On this principle, and this principle alone, is it rational to praise or blame, reward or punish the individual for his conduct. Occasionally the interest of the state may result in the sacrifice of the individual, but on the whole and in the long run what benefits the state will benefit its individual members too.

8.3 SOVEREIGNTY OF THE PEOPLE

If, as Machiavelli holds, the state is formed in order to satisfy the basic demands of the individual, it follows that the citizens of a state are the ultimate holders of sovereign power. The actual exercise of this power may be largely or wholly delegated to a single individual, or to a small group of individuals, but its ultimate source must necessarily be the people as a whole if their demands constitute the ultimate reason why the state exists at all. Machiavelli accepts this implication of his theory. Indeed, he subscribes with enthusiasm to Aristotle's opinion that on broad issues the judgement of the community is less likely to be in error than the judgement of a single individual or a small group of individuals. As he says:

As touching wisdom, and settled staidness, say that the People is wiser and more staid, and have more exact judgement than a Prince. And therefore not without cause the People's voice is likened to God's voice; for we see that the universal opinions bring to pass rare effects in their presages, so that it seems by their secret virtues they foresee their own good or evil.

Thus, contrary to the impression often formed by those who read *The Prince* alone, Machiavelli is no advocate of absolute monarchy. On the contrary, he believes that only in those states in which government is ultimately based upon a democratic foundation is it safe to assume that the power of government will not be abused. He admits that a limited monarchy may sometimes be necessary for a period, but he insists that a sound basis for government will be achieved only when the people themselves assume the ultimate responsibility.

There is one important respect in which, Machiavelli believes, the state as a whole differs from most of the individuals who constitute it. The majority of citizens are content with the security of person and property and only a small minority will seek power over their fellows. But an insatiable appetite for power dominates states as a whole and those, which do not try to extend their power, are bound in the long run to lose it. There is no stability or contentment in the field of international relations. One state can achieve the predominance, which all desire only at the expense of another, and that other is bound to be dissatisfied with its inferior status. National security, in other words, can only be achieved by national superiority, and the superiority of one nation implies the inferiority, and thus the insecurity, of another. The vicious circle thus created has been a familiar feature of international relations in modem times.

8.4 ARGUMENT OF 'THE PRINCE'

While the *Discourses* set forth Machiavelli's considered conclusions on the motives of human action and the basis of government, *The Prince* is concerned with the more practical question of the methods which a 'Prince' or monarch must employ in order to govern a community effectively. Machiavelli thought that a monarchy or dictatorship could be justified for two purposes only - the making of a state out of smaller units or the reforming of a corrupt state. *The Prince* is therefore essentially a manual of worldly wisdom prepared for the guidance of a ruler faced with one or other of these situations.

It was specially written with a view to showing how Italy could be welded into a strong and unified state out of the five principalities, the territory of the Roman Church, the Kingdom of Naples, the Duchy of Milan, and the Republics of Venice and Florence, into which the country was divided at the beginning of the sixteenth century.

The outstanding characteristic of *The Prince* is the complete absence of moral principle in its argument. It lies down, with scientific detachment, the general principles by which, Machiavelli believes; a state can be most effectively unified and strengthened. Whether the means thus prescribed are, in the usual sense of the word, 'moral' is of no concern to Machiavelli. He is only interested in the question whether they are elective for the end in view, the creation and maintenance of a strong, united and expanding state. For the reasons set forth in the *Discourses this* end is assumed to be the primary object of politics, and to be dictated by men's fundamental demand for personal security. Whether it is a 'good' end or not is to Machiavelli a meaningless question unless 'the good' is equated with 'the desired'.

The successful 'Prince' must, Machiavelli thinks, have a reliable army, composed of native troops rather than foreign mercenaries, for all government ultimately rests on force and would soon collapse without it. He must be feared, but not hated, by his people, and must respect the integrity of their property. While he should resort, whenever it seems likely to be useful, to violence, cruelty and deceit, he should, as far as possible, give the appearance of a noble and exalted character, so that his unscrupulous methods may be all the more effective when they are employed.

The common faith in religion and morality, and the fear, greed, and credulity of human nature, should all be ruthlessly exploited wherever they can contribute to the purposes of government. This cynical attitude to morality is nowhere better illustrated than in the eighteenth chapter of *The Prince,* where Machiavelli extols the deliberate employment of deceit in exploiting the simple credulity of the average man. Thus he writes:

Therefore a wise lord cannot, nor ought he to, keep faith when such observance may be turned against him, and when the reasons that caused him to pledge it exist no longer. If men were entirely good this precept would not hold, but because they are bad, and will not keep faith with you, you too are not bound to observe it with them. But it is necessary to know well how to disguise this characteristic, and to be a great pretender and dissembler; and men are so simple, and so subject to present necessities, that he who seeks to deceive will always find someone who will allow himself to be deceived. Therefore it is necessary for him to have a mind ready to rum itself accordingly as the winds and variations of fortune force it, yet not to diverge from the good if he can avoid doing so, but, if compelled, then to know how to set about it.

8.5 MACHIAVELLI'S POLITICAL BACKGROUND

Machiavelli's disdain for moral principles is largely explained by the circumstances of his time, since with the breakdown of faith in Christian principles men were left without any generally accepted moral creed, and the tangible ideals of security and happiness became the dominating motives of their conduct. In Italy this tendency was strengthened by the weak and divided state of the country, and the danger to which it was exposed by the ambitions of powerful nation-states like France and Spain.

The respect, which the Roman Church had formerly enjoyed, had largely disappeared because of the part, which the Pope had played in opposing the unification of Italy and inviting foreign intervention. Murder and cruelty were gradually coming to be regarded as normal and legitimate agents of effective government. Thus Machiavelli's cynicism was a reflection of the age in which he lived, and his political contemporaries would have generally endorsed the principles, which he advocated. He stands out from them simply because he gave clear and candid expression to those views in writings which have survived the age to which they directly relate.

Yet, although Machiavelli's writings were in large measure a reflection of contemporary conditions, they possess a more permanent significance. The very fact that his name is still the basis of an epithet, which is often applied to methods of organising and directing political power, shows that methods similar to those which he extolled may still be practised despite the moral opprobrium which they may excite. Indeed, since politics both in the national and in the international sphere consists so largely in the organising of power for the achievement of specified ends, the employment of methods, which experience shows to be effective for this purpose, is to a large extent inevitable.

This is most obviously seen in the record of modem dictatorships where violence, deceit, and the exploitation of human credulity have been familiar features of the technique of government. In democracies, where the rule of law is respected, and government policy is exposed to the scrutiny of an educated and critical public, there is much less scope for the exercise of Machiavellian methods. Yet anyone with a direct experience of party politics would probably agree that in the organisation of political power the end often takes precedence over the means, and the means are often assessed primarily by their effectiveness in furthering the end in view.

8.6 MANAGEMENT AND MORALITY

For the modern Executive the main interest of Machiavelli's writings lies in the assumption that a scientific approach to the problems of individuals is alone rational, and is fully adequate. He nowhere justifies this assumption, and it could not be justified without a demonstration, such as has been attempted in more recent times. They maintain that the facts of morality are empirical, and the study of morality is therefore a science.

If, in other words, it can be shown that moral experience consists exclusively of feelings or desires, possibly of a specific character and judgements about those feelings or desires and that a moral fact is therefore never a reason why something ought to be done but at most a cause why it is done, then Machiavelli's purely scientific analysis of social and individual problems can be justified. For moral beliefs will, on such an analysis, simply rank as one of the many influences, which help to determine the conduct of individuals. It is quite clear that Machiavelli did, in fact, regard moral experience in this light.

He reversed the Schoolmen's dictum *quid, quid petitur, petitur, sub specie boni* and argued that ends are called good because they are desired, and not desired because they are judged to be good. On this assumption a scientific approach to Individual problems is the only rational one and those who seek to solve social issues by applying an objective standard of morality are simply complicating the problem by intruding their own subjective prejudices, and thus failing to provide a solution in the scientific manner, which is alone rational.

The scientific solution of human problems, which Machiavelli advocated, consists in the dispassionate determination of the ends which government is created to achieve, and the dispassionate employment of the means, which experience shows to be most effective for this purpose. Whether the ends are 'good' in any other sense than that they are desired is to Machiavelli a meaningless question; and so is the supplementary question whether the means employed to achieve these ends are 'legitimate'.

The business of the rational manager is to determine the nature of the ends desired by a scientific study of human nature, and to select the means by a scientific study of philosophical history. In short, Machiavelli thought that the ideal statesman would be a scientist, unlike Plato, who thought that he would be a philosopher.

Whether this conception of the statesman's nature and functions can be accepted depends, as has been shown, on the nature of moral experience. Machiavelli never sought to deny the reality or influence of that experience, but he thought that its place both in political theory and in practical politics had been generally misconceived. It had been thought of as providing a rational directive by which all practical issues could be solved, whereas to Machiavelli it was itself part of the irrational material which the rational statesman can neither justify nor condemn, but which he must necessarily recognise if his plans and calculations are to be successful.

Religious beliefs have, in Machiavelli's view, the same status and functions as moral principles. They are without objective significance, but may prove valuable allies of the statesman if they can be used to influence people to pursue the ends, which he is seeking to achieve. It is, for example, likely to be of great help to a national leader if a war which is really being fought for purposes of national survival or aggrandisement is generally believed to be a war against the forces of evil and the devil.

Thus Machiavelli's attitude to philosophy was remarkably similar to that subsequently adopted by Karl Marx.

Both believed that political forces are essentially 'material' or irrational forces and that the moral judgements frequently evoked by these forces are themselves the expression of forces, which are equally irrational. Both held that only the detached observer who studies all these forces in a scientific spirit, and directs them in the way best calculated to achieve the end in view achieves rationality. In politics the only end, which can be consistently pursued, is the end which government is created to achieve, for the power of government depends upon the support of those who create and sustain it.

8.7 MACHIAVELLI'S PRINCIPLES IN CONTEMPORARY POLITICS AND MANAGEMENT

Some of Machiavelli's principles have found a ready application in the totalitarian systems of modem times. Yet it is clear from the argument of the *Discourses* that dictatorship was not to Machiavelli the best form of government, and was only justified as an expedient in special circumstances. Indeed, in so far as totalitarian systems have accepted an organic conception of the state, and have subordinated the interests of the individual to the pursuit of an 'ideology', they have not conformed to Machiavelli's conception of good government as set forth in the *Discourses.*

For it is clear from that work that Machiavelli found both the origin and justification of government in its power to promote the security and happiness of the individual? Its power to govern depends upon the willingness of those whom it governs to obey, and this willingness to obey will not continue if government fails to achieve the purposes for which it was established. It is in the democratic rather than in the totalitarian systems of the present day that Machiavelli's theory finds its fullest application, for only in the democracies is the individual's will, expressed collectively in the will of the majority, the real determinant of policy.

It may be said that Machiavelli's psychology was perverse, and that human beings look to their governments for more positive and less selfish benefits than the provision of personal security and happiness. Today this is undoubtedly the case, but it is only because modem governments ensure the personal security of the individual as a matter of course that they are permitted and encouraged to devote a large part of their energies to more positive ideals. If personal security or, as we should now say, the 'rule of law'-were not already firmly established, it is safe to say that the more positive aims of modem governments could not be pursued.

It is clear, therefore, that Machiavelli's theory cannot be dismissed as a mere compendium of maxims for the successful dictator if the *Discourses* as well as *The Prince.* When viewed as a whole his political theory belongs to the distinguished tradition of thought to which Hobbes, Hume, Bentham, and Marx were subsequently to make their contribution. It is the tradition, which finds in science, instead of in morals, the key to a rational understanding of individual forces and the successful achievement of the ends of government. It is a tradition, which has acquired a new importance in the present century with the development of logical doctrines, which claim to prove that moral experience cannot, from its very nature, provide rational directives for human conduct.

9. KANT

9.1 THE CRITIQUE OF PRACTICAL REASON

In the ethics of the 18th-century German philosopher Immanuel Kant, founder of critical philosophy, a moral law that is unconditional or absolute for all agents, the validity or claim of which does not depend on any ulterior motive or end. "Thou shalt not steal", for example, is categorical as distinct from the hypothetical imperatives associated with desire, such as "Do not steal if you want to be popular".

As far as Kant was concerned there was only one such categorical imperative, which he formulated in various ways. "Act only according to that maxim by which you can at the same time will that it should become a universal law" is a purely formal or logical statement and expresses the condition of the rationality of conduct rather than that of its morality, which is expressed in another Kantian formula: "So act as to treat humanity, whether in your own person or in another, always as an end, and never as only a means."

Because of his insistence on the need for an empirical component in knowledge and his antipathy to speculative metaphysics, Kant is sometimes presented as a Positivist before his time; and his attack upon metaphysics was held by many in his own day to bring both religion and morality down with it. Such, however, was certainly far from Kant's intention. Not only did he propose to put metaphysics "on the sure path of science," he was prepared also to say that he "inevitably" believed in the existence of God and in a future life. It is also true that his original conception of his critical philosophy anticipated the preparation of a critique of moral philosophy.

The Kritik der praktischen Vernunft (1788, spelled "Critik" and "practischen"; Critique of Practical Reason), the result of this intention, is the standard source book for his ethical doctrines. The earlier Grundlegung zur Metaphysik der Sitten (1785) is a shorter and, despite its title, more readily comprehensible treatment of the same general topic. Both differ from Die Metaphysik der Sitten (1797) in that they deal with pure ethics and try to elucidate basic principles, whereas the later work is concerned with applying what they establish in the concrete, a process that involved the consideration of virtues and vices and the foundations of law and politics.

There are many points of similarity between Kant's ethics and his epistemology, or theory of knowledge. He used the same scaffolding for both--a "Doctrine of Elements", including an "Analytic" and "Dialectic", followed by a "Methodology"; but the second Critique is far shorter and much less complicated. Just as the distinction between sense and intelligence was fundamental for the former, so is that between the inclinations and moral reason for the latter. And just as the nature of the human cognitive situation was elucidated in the first Critique by reference to the hypothetical notion of an intuitive understanding, so is that of the human moral situation clarified by reference to the notion of a "holy will."

For a will of this kind there would be no distinction between reason and inclination, a being possessed of a holy will would always act, as it ought. It would not, however, have the concepts of duty and moral obligation, which enter only when reason and desire find themselves opposed. In the case of human beings, the opposition is continuous, for man is at the same time both flesh and spirit; it is here that the influence of Kant's religious background is most prominent.

Hence, the moral life is a continuing struggle in which morality appears to the potential delinquent in the form of a law that demands to be obeyed for its own sake--a law, however, the commands of which are not issued by some alien authority but represent the voice of reason, which the moral subject can recognize as his own. In the "Dialectic", Kant took up again the ideas of God, freedom, and immortality. Dismissed in the first Critique as objects that men can never know because they transcend human sense experience, he now argued that they are essential postulates for the moral life.

Though not reachable in metaphysics, they are absolutely essential for moral philosophy. Kant is often described as an ethical Rationalist, and the description is not wholly inappropriate. He never espoused, however, the radical Rationalism of some of his contemporaries nor of more recent philosophers for whom reason is held to have direct insight into a world of values or the power to intuit the rightness of this or that moral principle. Thus, practical, like theoretical, reason was for him formal rather than material, a framework of formative principles rather than a content of actual rules.

This is why he put such stress on his first formulation of the categorical imperative: "Act only on that maxim through which you can at the same time will that it should become a universal law." Lacking any insight into the moral realm, men can only ask themselves whether what they are proposing to do have the formal character of law, the character, namely, of being the same for all persons similarly circumstanced.

9.2 PHILOSOPHY OF "IDEALISM" AND JUSTICE

Another line of thought, which was also divorced from natural-law concepts, was contained in the Idealist philosophy of Immanuel Kant. Fundamental to Kant's ethical and jurisprudential reasoning is the premise that all moral concepts have their basis wholly in a priori thought, which they can be arrived at by reason alone, without reference to experience or recourse to intuition of rules alleged immanent in experience.

Man, furthermore, is a free agent whose actions are determined by aims that he is at liberty to select. From such premises Kant deduced the nature of an ideal law, in which is implicit a theory or criterion of justice. This ideal law comprises the conditions under which all members of society can enjoy the maximum freedom from subjection to the arbitrary will of others. But Kant's supposedly a priori concepts are in fact as transcendental as anything natural lawyers have offered. It is thus not surprising that later thinkers, such as

Johann Fichte, Kant's Idealist successor, had little difficulty in putting the new Kantian wine into natural-law bottles.

The 20th century saw a fresh attempt at the Kantian approach in the work of the German legal philosopher Rudolf Stammler. Adopting the Kantian position that knowledge is independent of sensory experience, Stammler set out to discover pre-experiential categories, or "pure forms", of thinking about law. Stammler arrived at a social ideal of a "community of free-willing men," an ideal that he claimed to have universal validity because of its supposed a priori basis.

Having thus arrived at a "pure" ideal of society, untainted by empirical content deriving from sense perception, he felt able to formulate equally pure principles for just law that would regulate his ideal society. Stammler's pure idea of society comprised the harmony of individual and common purposes: his pure idea of just law thus comprised those principles conducive to such harmony, the mutual respect of individuals for each other's purposes and the participation of all in the achievement of the common purposes. Josef Kohler, Stammler's close predecessor in that subject in the Berlin University, fed the different stream of Idealism flowing from Hegel's philosophy of history into jurisprudence.

His work is still another effort to relate social facts and the norms of justice by exposing the immanence of values in facts--in "civilization" in Kohler's case.

In perspective, these idealisms, despite their formal or philosophical antagonism to "rationalism" and natural-law thinking, seem to have reinforced in the age of the Industrial Revolution the individualist and libertarian trends that natural law had built up successively against medieval church and empire, the shackles of medieval social, political, and economic organization, and 18th-century despotism.

10. HOBBES

10.1 THEORY OF RATIONALITY

Thomas Hobbes was born at Malmesbury in 1588 and died in 1679 at the age of ninety-one years. After completing his school and university education he became tutor to the Cavendish family, with whom he remained until 1628 when his pupil, the second Earl of Devonshire, died. He subsequently became tutor to the Clinton family until 163I, when he returned to the Cavendish family to act as tutor to the third Earl. In 1640 the summoning of the Short Parliament provoked him to circulate a pamphlet defending the absolute rights of the King, but this evoked considerable hostility, and he deemed it prudent to remove to Paris, where he stayed for the next eleven years.

During this period he wrote his principal work, *Leviathan,* which was published in London in 1651. It met with widespread opposition, because his attempt to justify the absolute rights of whatever government happened to be in power was repugnant to the Royalists (who believed in the Divine Right of Kings), his atheism was condemned by the Church of England, and his subordination of ecclesiastical to civil authority was unacceptable to the Roman Church.

The exiled Royalists in Paris particularly disliked a doctrine, which, if true, would have justified their permanent exile, and Hobbes was consequently banished from their Court. In these circumstances he thought it wise to make his peace with the Council of State of the 'Rump Parliament'. After the Restoration of the Monarchy in 1660 Hobbes was pardoned by the King and gradually came into favour at Court. But the *Leviathan con*tinued to evoke hostility in ecclesiastical circles, and a Parliamentary Committee was appointed to receive information about it. No action, however, was taken and Hobbes spent the rest of his life quietly in England.

A recital of the principal political events, which occurred during Hobbes's long life, is sufficient to indicate the troubled and uncertain character of the times. The First Civil War between King and Parliament (1642-1645), the Second Civil War (1648), the execution of Charles I (1649), the rule of the 'Rump Parliament' (1649-1653), Cromwell's Protectorate (1654-1658), and the Restoration (166o) all took place within that period. It is therefore hardly surprising to find that in his political theory great stress is laid upon the advantages of strong and stable government, and the importance of submission to its authority.

10.2 HOBBES'S ANALYSIS OF HUMAN NATURE

Hobbes's theory of the state is no exception to the generalisation that political theories are, as a rule, expositions of the author's conception of the Ideal State. In the case of Hobbes's theory the word 'ideal' has a special and unusual significance; but it is none the less true that he distinguishes between states as they are and states as he thinks they ought to be, and devotes a large part of *the Leviathan* to expounding and defending his conception of the Ideal State. For this reason it is misleading to describe Hobbes's political theory as a 'mechanistic' theory, for that suggests that he believed that the characteristics of actual states could be inferred from the principles of human psychology. Up to a point Hobbes does regard the actions of human beings as determined by their nature and environment, but he also recognises that they have a faculty of *reason* by which they try to calculate the most effective means of realising their desires; and as their calculations may be either valid or fallacious, the use of reason introduces an indeterminate element into what would otherwise be a completely determined system.

Hobbes's analysis of human nature is based on four important empirical generalisations:

(i) In the first place, he thinks that the basic motives of all voluntary action (which he distinguishes from involuntary bodily processes such as breathing) are *desire and aversion.* He thinks that desire and aversion are two opposite forms, by which he means a combination of *feeling and* willing (which he does not distinguish in the manner of modem psychologists). Endeavour takes these opposite forms according as it is directed towards or away from that which causes it. Hobbes uses the word Contempt to signify the attitude of indifference felt towards objects, which excite neither desire nor aversion.

(ii) Secondly, Hobbes thinks that men desire not only immediately attainable objects but also the assurance that they will be able to gratify future desires.

In his own words:

The object of man's desire is not to enjoy once only, and for one instant of time; but to assure forever the way of his future desires. Put more shortly, a fundamental object of human desire is power, which Hobbes defines as 'present means to obtain some future apparent good'.

(iii) In the third place, Hobbes believes that, when physical and mental capacities are both taken into account, men have, in general, the same ability to attain their ends. Lack of physical strength is usually compensated by mental ability and vice versa.

(iv) Finally, Hobbes believes that men have a faculty of reason by which they 'acquire the knowledge of consequences and dependence of one fact upon another'. Such knowledge is acquired by generalisation from experience, and it enables men to calculate the most effective means for attaining the objects of their desires.

If a man had no faculty of reason, his actions would, in theory at least, be predictable in any given circumstances from knowledge of his desires and his environment, since he would react automatically to any given situation. But the operation of reason, which may reach either valid or fallacious conclusions about the best means of realising these desires, introduces indeterminate elements.

Hobbes speaks as though the desire for power (described under (ii) above) is as fundamental as the other basic desires of human nature. But it seems clearly to be a derivative desire following on the use of reason. To desire the power to gratify one's future desires appears to result from the realisation that one always wishes to gratify one's desires, which is in turn a generalisation based upon specific experiences of desire.

Hobbes's four generalisations are clearly of an empirical character, and they must stand or fall by the test of experience. There is no a priori necessity in the proposition that desire (whether or not conditioned by reason) is the universal cause of voluntary action; or that men are in general equal in ability; or that they possess a faculty of reason. And if these generalisations are untrue the deductions, which Hobbes draws from them in working out his Theory of the Ideal State, will be invalid.

10.3 ANALYSIS OF MORAL EXPERIENCE

Hobbes can find no place in his analysis of human nature for specifically moral experience. The words, which appear to describe such experience, can, he thinks, be defined wholly in terms of non-moral concepts. But they must be differently defined at the pre-social and social stages of development.

At the pre-social stage, when men are not members of any organised society, 'good' simply means 'whatsoever is the object of any man's appetite or desire' and 'evil' means 'the object of his hate and aversion'.' Hobbes thus recognises no independent standard of good and evil. A man's desires and aversions determine what is good and bad for him, and this is the only sense in which anything can be good or bad until the individual transfers his natural liberty to do as he pleases to someone else. As Hobbes expresses the point:

These words of good, evil and contemptible are ever used with relation to the person that useth them: there being nothing simply and absolutely so; nor any common rule of good and evil to be taken from the nature of the objects themselves; but from the person of the man (where there is no commonwealth), or (in a commonwealth) from the person that representeth it; or from an arbitrator or judge, whom men disagreeing shall by consent set up, and make his sentence the rule thereof.

By this Hobbes means that, if a man lives outside a political society, his own desires and aversions will determine his conception of what is good and evil; while if he lives within such a society his conception of what is good and evil will be determined by the person or persons constituting the sovereign power. The reason for this distinction will become clear in the following paragraphs.

10.4 THE STATE OF NATURE

From the premises that every individual naturally seeks his own good, and that no individual is decisively superior to any other, Hobbes concludes that, apart from the coercive power of a central government, men would live in a condition of war - 'of every man against every man'. By this he does not mean that they would be continuously engaged in fighting but that they would be constantly exposed to the danger of attack and have no security except that which their own strength and resourcefulness might provide. Under such conditions Hobbes thinks that the pursuits of civilised life would be impossible, and that the life of man would be 'solitary, poor, nasty, brutish, and short'.

This, Hobbes thinks, would be the condition of man in a 'state of nature', i.e. the condition in which he would live if he did not belong to a political organisation. Hobbes believes that this conclusion is strengthened by the observation that, in the absence of such an organisation, the consequences are observed. To illustrate the point, he refers to the life of savages and the conduct of independent sovereign states. The first of these analogies would not now be regarded as a good one. Anthropological research has shown that, even in the most primitive forms of society, there are the elements of a social life and a moral code, and that Aristotle was much nearer the truth in describing man as a 'political animal'.

Hobbes is, however, on stronger ground when he refers to the conduct of sovereign states. Until relatively recent times, when an attempt has been made to have international disputes resolved by international authorities such as the League of Nations and the United Nations Organisation, states usually claimed the right to judge for themselves what they were justified in doing, and this was usually identical with what they believed to be in their interest. It may also be true that the general observance of a moral code of behaviour by individuals is largely explained by habit and the fear of punishment, and that, without this fear, selfish disregard of others' interests might be far more common.

10.5 THE LAWS OF NATURE

Hobbes thinks that man escapes from the state of nature by using *his reason.* Reason does not select the ends of action - these are determined solely by desire or aversion-but it reflects on the consequences of acts and shows man how his desired ends may be most speedily achieved. The general principles, which emerge from these reflections, are called 'Laws of Nature'. Hobbes's own definition of a Law of Nature is as follows:

A law of nature is a precept, or general rule, found out by reason, by which a man is forbidden to do that which is destructive of his life, or taketh away the means of preserving the same, and to omit that by which he thinketh it may best be preserved.'

In this definition Hobbes is using the word 'forbidden' in a metaphorical sense. He does not mean that men are forbidden to do what is destructive of their lives by any authority, human or divine. He simply means that men naturally desire to preserve their lives, and that their reason shows them what they must avoid doing if they wish to preserve their lives. To disobey such a law is not morally wrong but simply irrational, since it involves doing something which reason shows to be inconsistent with the satisfaction of the universal desire to preserve one's life.

Hobbes enunciates several Laws of Nature, of which the first three are especially important. The First Law is the most fundamental of all, since he believes that the others can be deduced from it. It is stated as follows:

Every man ought to endeavour peace as far as he has hope of obtaining it, and when he cannot obtain it, that he may seek, and use, all helps and advantages of war. The first branch of which rule contained the first and fundamental Law of Nature, which is to *seek peace and follow it;* the second, the sum of the right of nature, which is, *by all means we can to defend ourselves.*

By this law, Hobbes simply means that where a man can live at peace with his neighbours it is rational to do so, but that where this proves impossible it is rational to fight with the most effective means available. These alternative courses are rational in the sense that they will most effectively promote the peace and security which all men desire.

The Second Law of Nature is derived from the First and is expressed as follows:

That a man be willing, when others are so too, as far forth for Peace and defence of himself he shall think it necessary, to lay down this right to all things; and be contented with so much liberty against other men, as he would allow other men against himself.

As Hobbes remarks, this Law can be expressed more simply as the Law of the Gospel: 'Whatsoever you require that others should do to you, which do ye to them.' The Law states, in other words, that if a man wishes others to respect his desire for peace and security he must respect their desire for these same things. If he continues in a state of nature and does whatever he thinks most likely to preserve his life he must expect others to do likewise; and one of the things, which every man will then want to do, is to limit the power of others to interfere with his liberty. If everyone is trying to limit the power of others there will result that state of war in which a man's only security will be what his own strength and ingenuity can provide.

Now Hobbes holds that everyone has what he calls a 'right of nature' to use his own power, as he will himself, for the preservation of his own Nature; that is to say, of his own Life'. In accordance with his factual analysis of moral concepts, Hobbes does not mean by this 'right of nature' any moral right to use one's power as one thinks best, but simply the liberty to do so. Liberty, in turn, he defines as 'the absence of external impediments: which impediments may often take away part of a man's power to do what he would; but cannot hinder him from using the power left him according as his judgement and reason shall dictate to him. All this is just a complicated way of saying that a man can do what he is not prevented by external constraints from doing. The novelty of Hobbes's view lies in his denial that a man is ever prevented from doing something by the consideration that the act is, in an objective and moral sense, wrong. He may be prevented from doing something which he wants to do because he *cannot* do it: he is never prevented from doing it-in a state of nature-by the consideration that he *ought not* to do it.

10.6 The Social Contract

But Hobbes believes that a man may voluntarily 'lay down his right to do all things' (as he puts it in the Second Law of Nature). By this he simply means that a man may voluntarily forgo his natural *power* to do all things. Hobbes thinks that a man may do this in either of two ways: he may simply *renounce* it 'when he cares not to whom the benefit thereof redoundeth or he may *transfer* it 'when he intendeth the benefit thereof to some certain person or persons', i.e. when he deliberately authorises some other person or persons to exercise the power which was originally his. Hobbes continues:

When a man hath in either manner abandoned, or granted away his right; then he is said to be *obliged or bound,* not to hinder those to whom such right is granted, or abandoned, from the benefit of it: and he *ought,* and it is his *duty,* not to make void that voluntary act of his own.

To say that a man who has transferred his natural right, or rather liberty, to do something is *obliged or bound* not to prevent its exercise by someone else tends, however, to conceal the real nature of Hobbes's analysis. He is not saying that there is some objective moral sense in which a man ought not to prevent the exercise of the transferred power by someone else, nor is he saying that a man is bound, in the sense of being physically coerced, to allow the exercise of the transferred power by the person to whom it has been transferred. What Hobbes means is that it is *irrational* to prevent the person to whom one has transferred the power from exercising it. As he puts it in the same context, it is 'an absurdity', for it involves the contradiction of attempting, at one and the same time, to transfer and to retain a natural power.

Now if Hobbes is right in assuming that men's actions are determined solely by desire and aversion, a man will transfer one of his natural powers to someone else only if he believes that by so doing his desires are more likely to be satisfied. His dominating desire is for power. Hence, Hobbes concludes, 'the motive and end for which this renouncing and transferring of right is introduced is nothing else but the security of a man's person in his life.

To achieve this result Hobbes thinks that every man must make a covenant of the following sort with every other man:

I authorise and give up my right of governing myself to this Man, or to this Assembly of men, on this condition, that thou give up thy right to him, and authorise all his actions in like manner.

This is what Hobbes calls the *social contract.* It is the origin of the unity, which pervades a state or (as he calls it) a commonwealth. The man or assembly of men to which the right of government is transferred Hobbes calls the 'sovereign'. This he defines as follows:

One person, of whose acts a great multitude, by mutual covenants one with another, have made themselves every one the Author, and to the end he may use the strength and means of them all, as he shall think expedient, for their peace and common defence.

All members of a commonwealth other than the sovereign he *calls subjects.*

Commonwealths by Institution and Commonwealths by Acquisition Hobbes points out that sovereigns, and therefore commonwealths, may be established in either of two ways-by *institutions* or by *acquisition.* The type already described, which is established by a group of men agreeing among themselves to submit themselves to a central sovereign power, is a commonwealth, whereas a commonwealth by acquisition is defined as *follows:*

A commonwealth by acquisition is that where the sovereign power is acquired by force; and it is acquired by force when men singly, or many together by plurality of voices, for fear of death or bonds, do authorise all the actions of that man, or assembly, that bath their lives and liberty in his power.

The obligation of subjects to the sovereign is understood to last as long, and no longer, than the power lasteth by which he is able to protect them. For the right men have by Nature to protect themselves, when none else can protect them, can by no covenant be relinquished?

The latter statement appears to be quite inconsistent with the former, yet it surely represents the position, which is implied by Hobbes's general theory. For in his view men enter into the social contract and transfer their natural powers to their sovereign in order to obtain peace and security, and if the sovereign fails to promote these ends he fails to fulfill the purpose for which power was transferred to him. In these circumstances it seems only rational that his subjects should withdraw the power, which they transferred to him and transfer it to another sovereign who will ensure peace and security more effectively. The emphasis, which Hobbes elsewhere lays on the inconsistency of breaking the social contract, cannot therefore be reconciled with the purposes of that contract, and appears to be a somewhat uncritical expression of his intense anxiety to ensure strong and stable government at almost any price.

If Hobbes's theory really implies that it is rational for people to replace a sovereign who has failed to carry out the purposes for which he was elected, the common interpretation of that theory as a defence of absolute dictatorship must be rejected and it must be recognised, on the contrary, as supporting the principle of government by consent.

The truth seems to be that Hobbes did not distinguish clearly between the *absolute* and the *irrevocable* transfer of power. It is one thing to transfer absolute, i.e. unqualified, power to a sovereign, but it does not follow that such a transfer is irrevocable. The important points which Hobbes stresses are (a) that it is the essence of sovereignty to be absolute and unqualified, and (b) that a government possessing sovereign powers is the foundation of a stable and orderly, community.

10.7 THE TRUTH IN HOBBES'S THEORY

Thus Hobbes's theory lays down two important principles of government. In the first place, it emphasises the important fact, which loose talk about 'self-government' has tended to obscure, that all government *necessarily* involves the exercise of force by the government upon the governed. It is of the essence of government that a relatively large group of people should be controlled by a relatively small group, or even by a single individual, and this relationship is found even where self-government is said to exist. That entire self-government means in practice is that the governed have some measure of control over the selection of those who govern them, and thus, indirectly, over the policy which is pursued.

A more direct influence over policy is exercised by the governed in those communities where major issues of policy are submitted to a referendum. But, even where this is done, there usually remains a large range of issues on which decisions of policy remain the government's responsibility. Moreover, one of the principal objections to the use of the referendum is that it limits the responsibility of the government and gives to those who are not responsible for implementing a policy the power to decide what that policy should be.

Thus except in those countries (e.g. Switzerland) where a referendum is employed as a recognised piece of government machinery, democratic governments have full responsibility for policy so long as they remain in power. They differ from Hobbes's sovereign only in the limitations imposed on the exercise of that power by their limited tenure of office and by the laws or conventions of the constitution under which they are elected.

Hobbes's theory emphasises that in commonwealths by institution the establishment of the government is a voluntary act on the part of the subjects. The government is that which 'men, disagreeing, shall by consent set up'.' As previously observed, it is only in special circumstances that commonwealths appear to originate in this way; but if the 'consent' to which Hobbes refers is understood as a continuing instead of an irrevocable consent it describes exactly the foundation upon which democratic government rests. For it then means that, for a limited time, and on the understanding that the government observes certain limitations, whether of law or convention, upon its freedom of action, it will enjoy real power to govern as it thinks desirable and will be supported by the large majority of people.

Not all that it does will necessarily be acceptable to everyone, but so long as it does not seriously outrage the feelings or principles of a substantial proportion of the people, it will continue to receive general support on the ground that respect for a central government is in the general interest of the whole community, and that this particular government has been elected, and is governing, in accordance with the recognised principles of the constitution.

10.8 THE APPLICATION OF HOBBES'S THEORY TO INDIVIDUAL INTERESTS

Hobbes's analysis of government is particularly plausible when applied to the international field, for the conditions of external security are in principle the same as those of internal security. In both cases the primary need is to eliminate the danger of strife arising from competing interests. In the civil sphere Hobbes believed that this could be done by the transfer to a sovereign body of the individual's natural power to defend his own interests; and in the international sphere it is clear that war would be impossible if all power were transferred to a single and united sovereign body.

Because this has not so far been done and individual nations still retain power for the defence of their interests, Hobbes would have said that these nations still live in a 'state of nature'. The fact that they undertake, in pacts and treaties, not to go to war with one another, it would have seemed to him no guarantee of peace. As he said, 'Covenants without the sword are but words, and of no strength to secure a man at all'; and he would undoubtedly have considered that the two World Wars of the twentieth century had afforded abundant confirmation of this principle.

Important steps have been taken during the present century to establish an international organisation for the prevention of war. But neither the League of Nations, nor the United Nations Organisation has taken over the power of individual nations to defend their interests. It is true that the nations belonging to these organisations have had a so-called 'moral obligation' not to use military power except with the approval of the organisation.

10.9 THE RATIONAL STATE

Hobbes's political theory is, as already observed, no exception to the generalisation made in earlier chapters, that a political theory is an attempt to justify a certain conception of the Ideal State. The novelty of Hobbes's theory lies in his attempt to define the 'ideal' in purely non-moral terms. Whereas the majority of political philosophers have conceived of the ideal as the *moral* ideal,

Hobbes conceives of it as the *rational* ideal, and thus regards the Ideal State as the sort of state, which would result if men correctly judged the most effective means for achieving their desires. The purpose of government, in Hobbes's view, is not to realise and maintain the pattern of a morally ideal state but to achieve the fundamental desires of its citizens.

His primary object in the *Leviathan* is to justify his theory that, human nature being what it is, a strong government, to which absolute power has been transferred in accordance with the terms of the social contract, will afford the best assurance of the peace and security which human beings desire above all else. He recognises that existing states may fall short of this ideal, but he attributes this to the intellectual, as distinct from the moral, frailty of human beings.

Hobbes's political theory is therefore a utilitarian, as distinct from a moral, theory; and it is a utilitarian theory of the basic and non-moral form, which attempts to justify the institution of government on the ground of its utility in promoting the realisation of men's desires. His theory does not recognise any independent standard by which these desires may be approved or condemned.

Hobbes has, of course, to account for the facts of alleged 'moral' experience, and the propositions embodying moral terms, such as 'right', 'ought', and 'good', by which such experience is described. He does not deny that these moral terms have *some* meaning. What he denies is that they have the meaning, which appears to be implied by ordinary speech. It appears to be implied by ordinary speech that they are names for unique conceptions of a special character not definable in terms of desire and interest. Hobbes, on the contrary, believes that they are simply alternative names for conceptions, which could be more clearly and less ambiguously described in these terms. He

Would claim that the facts of politics-both the characteristics of actual states and the ideals pursued by parties and politicians-can be fully accounted for in terms of desire and interest. It is, according to him, interest, not duty, which accounts for the obedience shown by subjects to their sovereign. There is no *moral* sense in which they *ought* to obey their sovereign, but there is a *rational* sense in which they *must* do so if they desire (as he thinks they do) to enjoy peace and security.

Hobbes would undoubtedly have thought that the history of politics during the past three centuries had abundantly vindicated his analysis. He could have pointed to the landowner and the manufacturer proclaiming the moral value of private property and the manual worker proclaiming the moral value of social equality; or to the employer organising for higher profits and the 'worker striking for higher wages; and he would undoubtedly have claimed that his analysis of human society in terms of interest was abundantly justified, and that the good was a euphemism for what the individual or group in question believed to be its interest.

A naturalistic political theory of this sort avoids the main difficulty, which confronts a moral theory, namely, that of establishing the truth of the moral propositions which it accepts. This difficulty arises because there is no agreed basis of moral fact by which the truth or falsity of moral propositions can be ascertained. The only moral propositions which can be verified in a scientific manner are the propositions describing people's moral beliefs-such propositions as that A believes X to be right, or that B believes X to be wrong.

Propositions of this sort can be verified or refuted on the assumption that people do, in general, accurately describe their beliefs on such matters-by such devices as a social survey or a ballot. But it is fallacious to infer from the proposition 'A believes X to be good' the proposition that 'X is good' or, in general, to infer that the belief has an objective significance.

Hobbes's theory, on the other hand, has a purely factual basis. He claims to account for the facts of politics wholly in terms of the facts of human desires, and the means of achieving them, without reference to any independent moral standard.

His theory therefore represents an important alternative to the Moral Theories which most of his predecessors supported. Its potential importance has become all the greater with the general difference in moral faith, which has been witnessed during the present century. Should this decline continue, and moral standards become progressively less adequate as a foundation for political society, the alternative principle enunciated by Hobbes may come to be accepted as the true foundation.

11. LOCKE

11.1 THEORY ON MORALITY

One searches in vain for a consistent moral theory in Locke. His view that morality can be a science, as certain as mathematics, is well known. This might imply rationalism, and there are indeed rationalist trends in his moral philosophy--although sometimes when advocating a science of morals he seems to have in mind simply the possibility of an exact analysis of the terms used in moral discourse and the clarification of moral statements.

At other times, he puts forward a hedonist theory. "That we call good which is apt to cause or increase pleasure or diminish pain in us." But not every good is moral good: "Moral good and evil is only the conformity or disagreement of our voluntary actions to some law, whereby good or evil is drawn on us, from the will and power of the law-maker." In this view law rests on God's will, "the true ground of morality", though in saying this Locke does not appear to be consistent

Hobbes had maintained that the revolutionary overthrow of an established government would lead to immediate anarchy, but the English Revolution of 1688 had no such catastrophic consequence. Far from finding themselves in a 'state of nature', the people of England in 1688 simply witnessed a change of sovereign and a slight strengthening of Parliament at the expense of the Crown.

These changes were of profound importance for the future of government in Britain, but they took place without violence, and were generally welcomed by the majority of citizens. John Locke (1612-1704) set himself to justify this revolution, and to establish the proposition that the authority of government depends upon its conformity to the moral law. His main exposition of this doctrine is found in Book II of his treatise *Of Civil Government,* which is alternatively entitled An *Essay Concerning the True Original Extent and End of Civil Government.* It was published in 1690, just two years after the Revolution.

Locke was educated at Westminster School and Christ Church, Oxford, and subsequently studied medicine. He became personal physician in 1666 to Anthony Ashley Cooper, afterwards the Earl of Shaftesbury, and received important public appointments when Shaftesbury became Lord Chancellor in 1672. Shaftesbury subsequently took part in the plot to place the Duke of Monmouth on the throne and, although Locke did not play any part in it, James II tried to effect his extradition. But he was subsequently pardoned and returned to England after the accession of William of Orange. Apart from the *Letter Toleration the* treatise of *Civil Government* and other political writings, he published an important contribution to the theory of knowledge entitled *An Essay concerning Human Understanding.*

Locke's political theory, like that of Hobbes, reflects the circumstances of his time. just as Hobbes, living in the uncertain and dangerous period of the Civil War, was anxious to justify a strong government with overwhelming power, so Locke, who had suffered persecution under the Stuarts, wished to justify the revolution which deposed them, although it is only fair to add that his views about the morality of revolutions had been arrived at before 1688.

Locke argued that governments could be removed by revolution without the dissolution of society, and that any government could be justifiably displaced in this way under certain conditions. These ideas were eagerly welcomed a century later by the American colonists as a justification of their refusal to recognise the British Parliament, and were thus, in some measure, responsible for all the profound consequences, extending to the present day, which have followed from the political independence of the United Kingdom and the United States.

11.2 THE LAW OF NATURE

Locke's political theory, like Hobbes's, is a theory of the Ideal State, but it differs fundamentally in being a moral theory. While Hobbes thought that the Ideal State is ideal in a *rational* sense, Locke thinks that it is ideal in a *moral* sense. His theory is based on the assumption that there is a Law of Nature, and that this Law is of a specifically moral character. He consequently conceives of the Ideal State as a *morally* ideal state.

Locke, however, makes no attempt to justify the assumption that there is a basic moral law of this sort beyond asserting that it is self-evident: The state of Nature has a law of Nature to govern it, which obliges every one, and reason, which is that law, teaches all mankind who will but consult it, that being all equal and independent, no one ought to harm another in his life, health, liberty, or possessions; for men being all the workmanship of one omnipotent and infinitely Wise Maker; all the servants of one sovereign Master, sent into the world by His order and about His business; they are His property, whose workmanship they are made to last during His, not one another's pleasure.

He subsequently refers to the Law of Nature as the 'will of God'.

From the start, therefore, Locke's approach to political theory differs fundamentally from that of Hobbes. Hobbes regarded man as a being activated by desire and endowed with a rational faculty capable of showing him how his desires can be most fully satisfied. Locke, on the other hand, regards the individual as a being whose reason reveals an independent law prescribing moral standards to which he ought at all times to conform. Hobbes in short regards man as a rational but amoral being, while Locke regards him as essentially moral.

Locke's theory conforms much more closely to the tacit assumptions of the majority of people both in his day and ours, but he does not justify the dogmatic assumptions which he makes about the Law of Nature and what it prescribes. He seems to regard these assumptions as self-evidently true, and to those who agree with him on this point his general theory may appear adequate. But it is unlikely to satisfy those who deny the existence of an independent moral law, or differ from him in their view of what that law prescribes.

11.3 THE STATE OF NATURE

While Locke's conception of the Ideal State thus differs radically from that of Hobbes, his account of the origin of political society has much in common. In the first place, his conception of the state of nature is very similar. The difference between this conception of the state of nature and Hobbes's conception is that Hobbes recognised a Law of Nature only in the *logical* sense of a rational calculation. By the Law of Nature Locke means an independent moral standard. Or, to illustrate the contrast in their own words, Hobbes thinks that the purpose of reason is to 'acquire the knowledge of consequences', whereas Locke thinks that it 'teaches all mankind who will but consult it, that being all equal and independent, no one ought to harm another in his life, Death, liberty, or possessions. Despite these differences, however, both philosophers conceive of the state of nature as the hypothetical state (which may at some time have been an actual state) in which men would live if they were not subject to a government.

11.4 THE ORIGIN OF GOVERNMENT

Again, Locke offers a similar explanation of the origin of government. Like Hobbes, he believes that men agree to establish a government in order to enforce the Law of Nature. While Hobbes regards this law as rational in character and Locke regards it as moral, both think that it is because men disagree about its practical implications and cannot, in any case, be relied on to observe it voluntarily, that they transfer to a central sovereign body the power to enforce it. As Locke says:

Civil government is the proper remedy for the inconveniences of the state of Nature, which must certainly be great where men may be judges in their own case.

So far Locke's account of the nature of government bears a close resemblance to Hobbes's. But because he regards the Law of Nature as a moral law he naturally rejects Hobbes's doctrine of absolute sovereignty. Hobbes thinks that if men were rational they would, in their own interest, transfer unlimited power to a sovereign body. Whether or not this would, in fact, be the rational thing to do, Locke thinks that power should always be subject to the Law of Nature, i.e. to morality. As he says, 'Nobody can transfer to another more power than he has in himself, and nobody has an absolutely arbitrary power over himself, or over any other.' He continues:

A man . ... having, in the state of Nature, no arbitrary over the life, liberty or possession of another, but only so much as the Law of Nature gave him for the preservation of himself and the rest of mankind, this is all he doth, or can, give up to the commonwealth, and by it to the legislative power, so that the legislative can have no more than this. Their power in the utmost bounds of it is limited to the public good of the society.'

11.5 THE MORAL LIMITATIONS OF STATE AUTHORITY

It is clear from these quotations that Locke believes that all governments are subject to the moral standards defined by the Law of Nature, and does wrong if their actions conflict with these standards. No government, in his view, has an absolute right to govern as it pleases, any more than an individual has an absolute right to act as he pleases. Locke's insistence on this principle is primarily directed against the doctrine of the 'Divine Right of Kings' - the doctrine that a king can do no wrong because his authority is derived from God and because his acts express the will of God. Locke thinks that kings are fallible human beings whose acts are subject to the moral law, and who are liable to violate it.

Locke's insistence on the moral limitations to a government's authority is sometimes regarded as standing in sharp contrast to Hobbes's defence of absolute sovereignty. It is certainly true that Hobbes recognises no *moral* limitation to a government's authority in the sense in which Locke understands the word 'moral'; but Hobbes does not, as observed in the previous chapter, regard that authority as irrevocable.

He believes that it is to the interest of individuals to permit absolute power to their government so long as that government fulfils the purpose for which it has been set up-the maintenance of public order and security - but he believes that, if a government should fail to do this, its subjects should, in their own interests, refuse to obey it. Hobbes certainly lays more stress on the advantages of obedience than on the justification of rebellion, but that was no doubt partly due to big natural timidity and his experience of the hazards of civil strife.

Thus, the difference between the views of Hobbes and Locke on the extent of governmental authority was one of emphasis rather than one of principle. They did, however, justify the right of rebellion on very different grounds. Hobbes thought that rebellion would be justified on grounds of individual self-interest.

The fact is that Hobbes and Locke were emphasising two distinct, but complementary, principles in all government. Hobbes saw that it is the essence of a government to govern, and that for this purpose it must be in a position to enforce its decisions on the governed. Locke saw that it is none the less true that this compulsory power can be exercised only so long as the majority of the governed-who far outnumber the government-consent to submit to this compulsory power; and he argued that they are justified in withholding that consent if the government does not conform to the moral principles which they accept.

Hobbes also recognised the voluntary basis of government (except in 'commonwealths by acquisition) when he stressed the voluntary character of the social contract, but he was less concerned than Locke with the circumstances under which this consent should be withdrawn, and he was inclined to think that they would arise only in the most exceptional conditions. These differences of emphasis on the relative importance of consent and authority were doubtless due in large measure to Hobbes's conviction that strong and stable government is the primary interest of all men, and to Locke's anxiety to justify revolt against a monarch who had done him personal injury and whose policy he believed to be inconsistent with the moral law.

Hence., while the principle of popular consent to government is implicit in Hobbes's account of the origin of 'commonwealths by institution', it is consent of a much more passive character than that which Locke thought necessary to ensure observance of the Law of Nature by a government.

Locke recognises, however, that government cannot be based on individual consent, since individuals may disagree in their conceptions of the government's duty. He thinks it obvious that in practice the consent upon which the government's authority depends must be that of the majority since the majority is the decisive political force:

That which acts any community being only the consent of the individuals of it, and it being one body, must move one way, it is necessary the body should move that way whither the greater force carries it, which is the consent of the majority, or else it is impossible it should act or continue one body, one community, which the consent of every individual that united into it agreed that it should; and so everyone is bound by that consent to be concluded by the majority.

In this passage Locke is obviously writing of what we should call a 'democratic' society, for in autocracies a small minority has often dominated the majority by force and fear. But in a democracy, Locke thinks, it is obvious that, if universal support cannot be obtained for a certain course of action, the policy which receives majority support must prevail. He thinks that everyone who belongs to such a society implicitly agrees to accept the principle of majority rule.

Locke does not; however, appear to recognise the potential inconsistency between the principle of majority rule and the Law of Nature as he understands it. The latter, as already observed, is a moral law which teaches that 'no one ought to harm another in his life, health, liberty, or possessions', but it does not seem impossible that the majority may, on occasion, think it right to harm someone in one of these respects. Indeed, Locke would almost certainly have regarded such modem intrusions upon private property as requisitioning and the imposition of death duties, both of which have been endorsed by Parliamentary majorities in modem times-as a violation of the natural rights of the property owner.

The fact is that Locke never squarely faced the dilemma that if the individual's natural rights are indefeasible it is just as wrong for a majority as for an individual tyrant to deprive him of them; while, if the will of the majority is necessarily decisive in determining policy, there can be no assurance that an independent and objective 'Law of Nature' will be upheld.

Yet even if Locke's assumption that there are self-evident and unchanging natural rights cannot be justified, he lays down a fundamental democratic principle when he insists on the importance of a general acceptance by the community of a common conception of natural rights. For this has become a basic principle of modem democracy.

The democratic constitution is distinguished from the totalitarian mainly by the recognition which it accords to a code of individual rights which is accepted by the majority and upheld by their 'greater force' when challenged either by the government or by minorities. Nations in which there is a serious division of opinion regarding the character of individual rights lack the conditions necessary for a stable democracy, for they contain a standing challenge to whichever conception of those rights happens to be upheld by the existing government.

Thus Locke's theory of the state becomes a substantially accurate analysis of a modem democratic constitution once the relativity of 'natural rights' to time and place has been admitted. For the essence of democracy is to accord to the individual certain rights recognised as inviolate, and to defend these rights when they are threatened either by government or faction. Modern democracies may not conceive of natural rights as Locke did, but they agree with him that the first duty of government is to ensure that these rights, however conceived, are never sacrificed to the exercise of arbitrary force.

11.6 FORCE AND MORALITY

The problems raised by Locke's principle of majority rule should not, however, be allowed to obscure the essential foundation of his political theory. Its whole structure is based on the fundamental axiom that there is a moral law to which both individuals and governments are subject and that no individual should be subject to 'the inconstant, uncertain, unknown, arbitrary will of another man'. Thus, in spite of many similarities, Locke's theory of political obligation is really the very antithesis of Hobbes's.

According to Hobbes, law - the law enacted by the sovereign power - is the foundation, and the only foundation, of morality; but according to Locke morality - as embodied in the Law of Nature- is the foundation of the only laws which a citizen has an obligation to obey.

If the majority agrees that a civic law conflicts with the moral law the citizen has, on Locke's theory, no obligation to obey it.

It is because moral motives continue to play a prominent part in politics, as in other spheres of human activity, that Locke's political theory, in spite of its difficulties and inconsistencies, appears so much more adequate than Hobbes's theory as a justification of government. For even in a constitution, such as the British constitution, where Parliament is in theory the holder of absolute power, its actions are judged, both by its members and by the community in general, by a moral standard, and no Parliament which sought to violate that standard in some fundamental way, e.g. by suppressing basic political liberties, would be likely to survive. Parliament enjoys sovereignty only within the limits of a moral code which may vary from generation to generation but which, whatever form it takes, is accepted as an independent standard to which all legislation ought to conform.

The weakness of Locke's theory lies not in the importance which he attaches to an independent moral standard but in his failure to show how that standard is ascertained and defined. As already observed he refers to it both as the Law of Nature and the 'will of God' and appears to regard it as a self-evident *a priori* principle. If it is, indeed, an *a priori* principle which should be self-evident to everyone, then Locke may be justified in his somewhat dogmatic account of its nature.

But there are today so many different conceptions of the nature of human rights that it is difficult to accept Locke's assumption that their nature is *a priori* and self-evident. It seems far more consistent with the facts of comparative morality to admit the essential relativity of the moral standards of different communities, and to define these in terms of what the majority of citizens believe them to be.

An analysis of this sort has at least the advantage of providing a link between the moral law and the principle of majority rule which, on Locke's' own theory, appear plainly inconsistent. For on his theory there is no guarantee that the majority will not sometimes exploit its superior power and violate the natural rights of the individual citizen. On the other hand, if the moral law is defined as what the majority of citizens believe to be the moral law, then a conflict of this sort is impossible, and democracy can be defined as that form of society in which the majority recognises that individuals have indefeasible rights.

But of course such an analysis makes it impossible to condemn, on any moral grounds, a society in which the majority do not recognise such rights.

11.7 THE RIGHT TO REVOLT

Whether the Law of Nature be a relative or an absolute principle, Locke's view that revolution is justified when that law is violated by a government appears to be substantially correct both as an account of the causes and as a justification of the act of revolution. So long as a government operates within the limits defined by the prevailing moral code of a community its moral authority is recognised, and the obligation to obey it is accepted, by the bulk of citizens.

Those who reject the prevailing moral code of the majority may obey the government from other motives, e.g. to avoid punishment or to maintain national unity; but they constitute potential revolutionaries, and if their views are shared by a large minority civil strife is likely to break out. It was, for example, obviously a disagreement on a fundamental moral issue between the government and a large minority of citizens which led to the revolutionary activities of the Suffragettes in 19I3 and 19I4 and to the civil war in Southern Ireland before the creation of the Irish Free State.

The fact that those who differ from their government on a moral issue of this character are potential revolutionaries was felt to justify the imprisonment without trial during the Second World War of a number of citizens who appeared to believe that the war with Germany was morally unjustifiable.

Locke's own statement of the principle justifying revolution is as follows:

'There remains still in the people a supreme power to remove or alter the legislative, when they find the legislative act contrary to the trust reposed in them.'

The 'trust', Locke adds, is for 'attaining an end', and 'whenever that end is manifestly neglected or opposed, the trust must necessarily be forfeited, and the power deprive into the hands of those that gave it, who may place it anew where they shall think best for their safety and security'. The end of government Locke describes as follows:

The great and chief end, therefore, of men uniting into commonwealths, and putting themselves under government, is the preservation of their property; to which in the state of Nature there are many things wanting.

He explains that by 'property' he means 'lives, liberties, and estates'.

In short, Locke thinks that the primary object of government is the preservation of the individual's life, liberty and possessions, and that when it fails, in the opinion of the majority, to fulfill this trust it should be removed and replaced.

11.8 Assessment Of Locke's Theory

Locke's theory, like Hobbes's, has often been criticised as artificial and over-simplified in view of the way in which he accounts for the origin of the state in terms of the rational and calculating choice of individuals. It is said that he greatly underestimated the part played by irrational factors, such as various manifestations of the 'herd instinct, in creating and maintaining political societies and that his theory, in so far as it claims to be an historical account of the origin of such societies, is wholly false. It must be admitted that Locke often writes as though he did believe that his theory was historically valid.

Yet even though this claim must be rejected-and the evidence of history, anthropology, and psychology alike show it to be false - his theory, like Hobbes's, can be alternatively regarded as an attempt to justify political society instead of to account for its historical origin. This, in any case, is its more important aspect as a philosophical theory.

So conceived, Locke's theory, like the majority of theories, is essentially an attempt to justify, on moral grounds, a certain conception of the purpose of government. He claims that its primary purpose is to preserve men's property, by which is meant their lives, their liberties and their possessions. Government is entrusted with that responsibility, and it can justifiably be removed and replaced if it - fails to discharge it. Thus in Locke's view the individual, not the state, is the object of supreme value, and the state is a mechanism established to promote the individual's good.

Locke's exposition of his theory does not make it easy to distinguish what he intended to be factual analysis from what he intended to be the exposition of a moral ideal; and it may well be that he did not always have this distinction clearly before his mind. It is also by no means clear whether he believed that his factual analysis was true of all states whatsoever, or only of contemporary England and states similarly organised. But it is clear that, however the theory is interpreted in detail, an essential part of it is the moral argument that the primary purpose of government ought to be the protection of the individual's life, liberty and possessions-in short, his natural rights-

and that a government which does not seek to promote this end forfeits all claim to moral authority.

The influence of Locke's theory has been great just because it has appeared to clarify and correlate so effectively the implicit assumptions about the rights of government and subjects which have prevailed in the English-speaking world since the Revolution of 1688. Its influence has been even greater in America than in Britain since, in the first place, it was widely cited as a justification of the American Revolution and, in the second place, the principle of a natural law to which even governments are subject is embodied in the Articles of the American Constitution.

The unwritten British Constitution is in theory closer to Hobbes's principle of unlimited sovereignty, but in practice the British Parliament observes numerous unwritten conventions which have, in practice, the force of moral law, and Parliament is regarded by the community at large as subject to moral standards no less than the individual citizen.

Locke's contribution to philosophical theory may therefore be shortly described as that of defining the moral responsibilities of government and modern global business. He sought to revive the belief in an independent moral law which had been almost universally accepted throughout the Middle Ages; and in doing so he defined a principle which has been accepted by all modem democracies and is now being extended to the international sphere in the Charter of Human Rights of the United Nations Organisation.

It was Plato's principle of justice in a new form-a principle which sought to defend the individual against the tyranny of the community; to ensure that the weak are not exploited by the strong; and to insist that the proper function of government is the realisation in human affairs of a moral pattern and not simply the organisation of power.

12. ROUSSEAU

12.1 GENERAL WILL

Jean Jacques Rousseau was born in Geneva, the son of a mad watchmaker, in 1712, and died in 1778. Having, left school at the age of twelve, and failed to settle in any of the trades to which he had been apprenticed, he fled from Geneva to Savoy four years later, and began a life of wandering and exile which, apart from twelve years spent in Paris (1744-1756), continued to his death. For part of these early years he was supported by women who befriended him; for part of them he lived the life of a vagabond and earned a livelihood as best he could.

In 1743 he became secretary to the French Ambassador to Venice, and appears to have served him well, but quarrelled because he received no salary. In I710 he achieved fame through winning a prize offered by the Academy of Dijon for the best essay on the question 'Have the arts and sciences conferred benefits on mankind?' Rousseau answered the question in the negative, contending that the arts and sciences create artificial wants and jeopardise the natural morality of unspoiled man. This theme was elaborated in his *Discourse on Equality (1754),* in which Rousseau argued that 'man is naturally good, and only by institutions is he made bad'.

It was in 1762 that Rousseau's two most important works were published - Emile, his treatise on education, and the *Social Contract or Principles of Political Right.* The first offended both the Catholic and Protestant Churches by its support of natural religion, and the latter offended both the Council of Geneva and the French Government by its implied denial of the Divine Right of Kings. Rousseau left France and was befriended by Frederick the Great, who gave him asylum at Motiers.

After spending three years there, however, he incurred local suspicion, which placed his life in danger, and he fled to England in 1765. George 111 granted him a pension, and he formed friendships with both Burke and Hume. Burke found his vanity intolerable and their association was short-lived. Hume was a faithful friend but in the end Rousseau's delusions convinced him that Hume was engaged in plots against his life. He fled to Paris, where he spent his last years in great poverty, and is believed to have died by his own hand.

12.2 THE ENLIGHTENMENT AND THE ROMANTIC REACTION

Rousseau was one of the leading figures in the so-called 'Romantic Reaction', which followed the 'Age of Enlightenment'. The latter was the name given to the period from about 1650 till late in the eighteenth century when the leading thinkers of both England and France were inspired by a faith in the power of human reason to achieve a final understanding of the universe and to provide a rational guide for human conduct. Other faculties, such as feeling or intuition, were held to be essentially inadequate for this purpose. Hobbes's philosophy was an early expression of this outlook. After the middle of the eighteenth century, however, there was a reaction against this faith in reason, and as this reaction took the form of looking to feeling or intuition instead of to reason for fundamental truth, it came to be known as the 'Romantic Reaction'.

Rousseau was, from certain points of view, a leading representative of this Romantic Reaction, and his works bear all the marks of an intensely emotional faith in the truth of the principles, which he advocates. This characteristic made his writings highly elective as propaganda, although they are without the careful logic of the rationalists. Thus, it is generally agreed that the central theme of Rousseau's *Social Contract-man's* loss of his natural liberties in the modern state played no small part in fanning the flames of discontent, which culminated in the French Revolution.

As observed in earlier chapters, philosophies are essentially attempts to justify a certain conception of the ideal state, and it is of special importance to bear this in mind when reading the *Social Contract* as much of what Rousseau says is obviously untrue if regarded as a description of actual states. For example, his account of the way in which a political society originates, and the emergence of its 'general will', is intended to be an account of the way in which the *ideal society* would develop. Rousseau does not claim that every society has developed in this way, and indeed he thinks that only small and intimate societies like the Greek city states could be expected to do so.

Hence he states the fundamental problem of politics as follows:

The problem is to find a form of association which will defend and protect with the whole common force the person and good of each associate, and in which each, while uniting himself with all, may still obey himself alone, and remain as free as before.'

Rousseau argues that the social contract provides the solution to this fundamental problem. By this he means that a society founded upon a social contract, understood in the sense in which he defines it, will provide its members with both the freedom of the state of nature and the advantages of civil law and order. He defines the individual within the social contract as follows:

Each of us puts his person and all his power in common under the supreme direction of the general will and, in our corporate capacity, we receive each member as an indivisible part of the whole. At once, in place of the individual personality of each contracting party, this act of association creates a moral and collective body, composed of as many members as the assembly contains votes. Thus receiving from this act its unity, common identity, life and will.

This public person, so formed by the union of all other persons, formerly took the name of *city,* and now takes that *of republic or body politic;* it is called by its members *State* when passive, *Sovereign* when active, and *Power* when compared with others like itself.

This quotation embodies the essence of Rousseau's philosophy, but it is stated in a misleading way, as it suggests a description of the way in which political societies do, as a rule, originate and develop. This, however, is not

Rousseau's meaning. He is actually describing the origin and constitution of an ideal state, and he would have been the first to admit that this description seldom, if ever, applies to actual states. In other words, he is telling us how a state would have to originate and be constituted in order to meet the claims of both individual liberty and social order.

The outstanding characteristic of such an ideal state would be *its organic* character; it would, as Rousseau says in the passage just quoted, be a 'collective body', a 'public person', and a 'body politic'. For only if it takes this form will there be no conflict between the natural liberty of the individual and the collective will of the state. If the state is a genuine organism there will be no such conflict, for the true will and interest of the individual will coincide with the will and interest of the state, just as the health of a bodily organ depends on the health of the body as a whole. If there appears to be a conflict between the two this is because 'each individual, as a man, may have a particular will contrary or dissimilar to the general will which he has as a citizen. His particular interest may speak to him quite differently from the common interest.

Rousseau believes that the continuation of this conflict between an individual will and the general will would prove the undoing of the body politics. Accordingly, he thinks that it should be resolved as follows:

Whoever refuses to obey the general will shall be compelled to do so by the whole body. This means nothing less than that he will be forced to be free; for this is the condition which, by giving each citizen to his country, secures him against all personal dependence.

To Rousseau there is nothing paradoxical in this conception of being 'forced to be free', for he believes that the citizen is truly free only when he conforms to the general will. In so far as a citizen opposes the general will, cannot be his 'real' will, for his 'real' will is always identical with the general will of the whole community. This follows, indeed, from the assumption that the state-the ideal state-is an organic whole, for on that assumption there can be no conflict between the purposes of the whole and of the part any more than there can be a conflict between the health of a n aiding body and the health of one of its organs. In both cases the true interests of whole and part are identical.

The practice of 'forcing people to be free' has become familiar during recent decades, and has been frequently illustrated in totalitarian communities. Those who have refused to accept and practise the official 'ideology' as defined by the government have been forced to do so by threat of imprisonment or torture; and the compulsion has been carried out in the name of the people's will'. But such states have all differed in one fundamental respect from the ideal state of Rousseau; namely, they have been without any machinery for discovering the free will of the people as a whole.

On the contrary, they have always resorted to a powerful mechanism of central propaganda for ensuring, as far as possible, that everyone accepts a uniform code of belief and practice, and the 'will of the people' has therefore in fact meant the will of the government. Rousseau would have regarded such states as a complete travesty of his ideal.

Rousseau distinguishes *general will* from both the *will of the majority* and the *will of all.* The latter wills are, in Rousseau's opinion, the wills of groups of individuals who happen to agree. The will of the majority is, of course, the will shared by the majority of the members of a community, while the will of all is the will shared by all the members of a community. But the general will is the will of an *individual-of* the 'collective body', which the act of association creates in an ideal state. Neither the will of the majority nor the will of all can, in Rousseau's view, provide a moral basis for the state, for they represent mere forces, devoid of moral authority, which may, indeed, overwhelm the will of an individual, but which do not thereby make him conform to his 'real' will.

Although this conception of a general will is strange to people with a democratic outlook, and may appear to them quite inapplicable to human society, its general significance is apparent when the analogy with a physiological organism is borne in mind. For such an organism does, to all appearances, exhibit a fundamental urge to survival and reproduction, and the functioning of all its organs is dominated by these primary purposes.

Whether a human society can achieve such a unity is far from certain. That its individual members may have a *common* interest or *common* purpose in certain circumstances does not prove that they have a *single* interest or a *single* purpose. Nor does the fact that, following on initial disagreement among its members, a group of people ultimately comes to accept a common policy prove more than that it feels it more important to agree on some policy than on none. Nor, again, does the undoubted fact that an individual's motives and ideals may be largely fashioned by the social influences, which surround him, prove that his outlook can be explained wholly in terms of these influences.

For these and other reasons the democrat is unconvinced that, however much the individual is conditioned by his social environment, his individuality can be explained away, or that it is necessary for it to be absorbed in the will of society as a whole if that society is to be described as good.

Now it is, as previously remarked, with the latter question the question of the good society-that Rousseau is primarily concerned. Even if no existing society does exhibit a general will Rousseau believes that the ideal society *would* exhibit such a will and that this (will) would be a good will. As he said:

The Sovereign, merely by virtue of what it is, is always what it should be.

Rousseau had previously made the same point in his *Discourse on Political Economy:*

The body politic, therefore, is also a moral being possessed of a will; and this general will, which tends always to the preservation and welfare of the whole and of every part, and is the source of the laws, constitutes for all the members of the State, in their relations to one another and to it, the rule of what is just or unjust.

A general will, in short, is a good will, and defines, through the medium of the law, what a citizen ought to do. But a state itself is not subject to any moral law. For, while the citizen, in his dual capacity as legislator and subject, is subject to the general will which he has assisted to formulate, the Sovereign, i.e. the state in its active capacity, cannot impose on itself a binding law.

It is in the position of an individual who makes a contract with himself; and this makes it clear that there neither is nor can be any kind of fundamental law binding on the body of the people-not even the social contract itself.

The progress of international co-operation during the past thirty years suggests the possibility that, if a general will can develop in a state, it may ultimately develop in humanity as a whole. But, Rousseau explicitly denies this possibility. The general will of a state define the standard of morality for its citizens, but the state itself is a law unto itself and can do no wrongly. There is little doubt that this doctrine, as developed by Hegel and his followers, has been held to justify a theory of 'power politics', which appears quite immoral to supporters of liberal democracy.

Apart from the theoretical objections, which may be made to Rousseau's theory, it is difficult to see how it could be applied. Rousseau seems to assume that in a small and compact society, modelled on the pattern of the Greek city-states, such a will could be achieved, and that the large majority of people would recognise it when it was achieved; but this is a highly speculative assumption.

Nor is the determination of the general will made easier when its alleged end is taken into account. This end is defined by Rousseau as the 'common good', the implication being that a particular will aims at its own selfish good, which may not coincide with the general good nor, therefore, with the true good of any individual. But the same difficulty arises in determining the common good as in determining the general will. There may in fact be no general agreement about the nature of the common good, and no apparent reason, apart from more general support, why one view of its nature should be preferred to another. Rousseau specifically denies that the general will is simply the will of the majority, or that 'the majority is always right'. It is therefore very doubtful whether a general will, which is distinct both from a universal will and from a majority will, can exist, or whether the 'common good' at which that will is said to aim can be defined except in terms of what the majority of people believe the common good to be. The achievement of what the majority believes to be the common good may, and probably will, mean the sacrifice of what the minority believes to be the common good.

As was previously observed, Rousseau's theory of the general will is neither defensible nor even intelligible unless the general will is understood as the will of a collective *individual*. It is by no means clear that such a collective individual exists. Individuals in the ordinary sense-men and women of flesh and blood with their desires and prejudices and convictions-are easily recognised. It may be true that these desires, prejudices, and convictions are largely conditioned by the relationship of such individuals to other individuals, but this is far from saying that a truly collective individual does or could exist. It is not therefore surprising that the nature and existence of the collective individual should be matters of speculation; and that the attempt to make its alleged 'will' the standard of morality for a community should attract those who desire to provide some apparent 'justification' for an exercise of power which is really dictated by quite different motives.

12.3 ROUSSEAU'S MORAL THEORY

To modern philosophers the most important question, which can be asked about Rousseau's moral theory, is whether it is naturalistic. When he says that the general will is necessarily a good will does he mean simply that 'good' means 'general' (in the same way that 'equilateral' means 'with equal sides'), or does he mean that 'generality' and 'goodness' are different qualities, although when one characterises a will the other always does so as well? If he means that 'goodness' and 'generality' are synonymous, he is defending a moral theory which is just as naturalistic as that of Hobbes, although he differs from Hobbes in identifying 'the good' with 'the general' instead of with 'the desired'. And this interpretation is consistent with much of what he says.

Whatever may have been Rousseau's view of the relation between the goodness and the generality of the will; he thought that its generality could be defined in objective terms:

Each individual, as a man, may have a particular will contrary or dissimilar to the general will which he has as a citizen. His particular interest may speak to him quite differently from the common interest: his absolute and naturally independent existence may make him look upon what he owes to the common cause as a gratuitous contribution. The loss of which will do less harm to others than the payment of it is burdensome to him.

There is often a great deal of difference between the will of all and the general will; the latter considers only the common interest, while the former takes private interest into account, and is no more than a sum of particular wills: but take away from these same wills the pluses and minuses that cancel one another, and the general will remains as the sum of the differences.

Given the appropriate conditions, Rousseau believes that a general will, so conceived, will always emerge:

If, when the people, being furnished with adequate information, held its deliberations, the citizens had no communication one with another, the grand total of the small differences would always give the general will, and the decision would always be good.

But in a later passage he recognises that in practice the people may be misguided:

Of it the people wills always the good, but of itself it by no means always sees it. The general will is always in the right, but the judgement which guides it is not always enlightened. It must be got to see objects as they are, and sometimes as they ought to appear to it.

Rousseau therefore appears to hold that the general will can be identified as the will, which wills the common interest. The particular wills of individuals aim at particular interests, which may, and often do, conflict with the common interest of the community, and therefore with the true interest of its individual members. But a theory of this sort must show how the common interest can be defined in terms, which are not purely arbitrary. Rousseau himself does not provide any assurance that a general will, conceived as he conceives it, can exist. For there will always be differences of opinion among the individual members of a community about the nature of the common interest and the extent to which their particular interests conflict with it.

Indeed, the last sentence of the passage just quoted, with its reference to making the general will see objects 'as they ought to appear to it' raises the obvious question as to why objects ought to appear differently from how they do appear, and who is to determine how they ought to appear. The truth is that behind Rousseau's romanticism lies the extremely rationalist assumption that it is more *reasonable* to desire some objects than others, and that the general will is really the rational will. Only so is it possible to conceive of a will, which is neither the will of an individual. Nor of a majority neither of individuals, nor even of all the individuals in the society whose will it is said to be.

It is, of course, necessary to agree with Rousseau that an important distinction can be drawn between the apparent and the real interests of individuals-between that which appears likely to afford them the maximum of satisfaction and that which would really do so if they took account of all the relevant factors and calculated rightly. But the fact that this distinction can be drawn does not imply that there is only one way in which the real interest of an individual or the common interest of a society can be defined-unless it is defined, as Rousseau defines it, without reference to the actual wills of individuals, and in terms of a 'rational' will which is not necessarily related to any actual will at all.

12.4 ROUSSEAU'S THEORY IN PRACTICE

Apart from these general difficulties inherent in Rousseau's theory it is clear that its application in practice is very limited. For a general will can be achieved only in a community where every citizen participates actively in the work of legislation, and it cannot therefore be achieved in large communities with representative governments legislating on behalf of the people as a whole. It was for this reason that Rousseau considered that the Greek city-states exemplified the form, which the ideal state must always take. He held that; even if a representative government were to achieve a general would, this would not be the general will of the community but only of the representative government.

Again, Rousseau thought that the existence of associations within the state, such as churches, trade unions, and political parties, is a serious obstacle in the way of achieving a general will for the community as a whole, since they tend to influence the spontaneous expression of the individual's will, without which a general will cannot be formed. Rousseau therefore thought that if such associations are to be permitted at all they should be kept as small and as numerous as possible so as to cancel out each other's influence and not rival the influence of the general will.

12.5 THE FUNCTION OF GOVERNMENT

Since Rousseau holds that the general will should be the sovereign power in a community it follows that the function of government is purely executive. As he says:

Sovereignty, for the same reason as makes it inalienable, cannot be represented; it lies essentially in the general will, and will does not admit of representation: it is either the same, or other; there is no intermediate possibility. The deputies of the people, therefore, are not and cannot be its representatives: they are merely its stewards, and can carry through no definitive acts. Every law the people have not ratified in person is null and void-is, in fact, not a law. The people of England regard itself as free; but it is grossly mistaken; it is free only during the election of members of parliament.'

It is therefore clear that, whatever parallel may be drawn between Rousseau's ideal state and the totalitarian states of today, Rousseau would have emphatically denied the claim of any government to express the general will of the community. For Rousseau the general will is the spontaneous will of the 'body politic', constituted by the organic union of all citizens, and no government can govern in accordance with that will unless it is continually directed by it. And in the ideal state, modelled on the city states of Ancient Greece, Rousseau believes that the people would always have a general will on all major issues of policy, and would always make it abundantly clear what that will was. There would therefore be no need for a government to interpret it.

All this might possibly be true in a small and intimate community of the sort which Rousseau seems to have had in mind, but the dominating political forces of the modem world are large states in which representative government is, for practical reasons, inevitable and in which, according to Rousseau, it is therefore impossible to achieve a general will, still more to govern in accordance with it. Yet something closely resembling the general will as conceived by Rousseau does seem to operate in liberal democracies. On major constitutional principles, such as the maintenance of a constitutional monarchy, parliamentary government, a free press, and an independent judiciary there would appear to be virtually unanimous agreement among all sections of the population in modem Britain, and without such a general measure of agreement it is doubtful whether democracy would survive. Within that general agreement about the way in which government should govern there is, of course, abundant scope for disagreement about the policy which it should pursue; but agreement about the way in which government should resolve these disagreements is the condition on which alone democracy can survive, and this general agreement appears in many ways to be a spontaneous expression of a will which is 'general' in the literal sense, and therefore bears an important resemblance to Rousseau's basic conception.

There is, however, a fundamental difference between democratic theory and Rousseau's doctrine, for the former is an individualist and the latter an organic theory of the state. Democratic theory asserts that the general agreement among members of a democracy on broad constitutional issues is simply an important empirical fact which justifies the overriding of conflicting minority opinions on grounds of practical expediency; whereas Rousseau would have said that the unity of an organic state is based upon a general will which is moral in character and justifies the over-riding of minority opinions on moral grounds.

Rousseau would have said that the dissentients from the general will do not know what their 'real' will is and should be 'forced to be free'; whereas the democrat holds that the dissentients are under no delusion about what they want but must, as a matter of practical necessity, be forced to conform to the will of the majority.

On a superficial examination it might appear that modern totalitarian states come much nearer than the democracies to accepting the theory of the general will in the frequent references which are made in them to the 'will of the people' as the justification of governmental acts. But there is the fundamental difference that in such states no machinery exists for the direct and frequent ascertainment of the public will, and Rousseau would have said that without this no general 'will' in the true sense could exist. Indeed, the methods of controlling and organising public opinion which are such conspicuous features of modem totalitarian states are the direct antithesis of the relationship between government and people which, in Rousseau's view, gives government a moral sanction for its acts.

It is, therefore, in democratic rather than in authoritarian states that a force, which in some ways resembles the 'general will', seems to be found. While Rousseau would have said that no truly 'general' will can emerge in a state with a representative government, there is something remarkably like it to be found in the strong and united expressions of what is called 'public opinion', which are evoked in liberal democracies from time to time, and which usually have a decisive influence on governmental policy. But too much must not be made of this comparison for unless the state is assumed to be a genuine organism these expressions of public opinion must represent the 'will of the majority' or the 'will of all' rather than the general will in Rousseau's sense.

The truth is that Rousseau's refusal to identify the general will with the actual will of any individual or group of individual's shows that it is not an empirical concept at all. It is the rational will - the will that ought to be shared by everybody even if it is actually possessed by none.

13 HUME AND BURKE

13.1 CONSERVATISM

While Edmund Burke (1729-1797) has usually been regarded as the leading philosopher of political conservatism, David Hume (1711-1776) was, by general admission, a more profound philosopher, and his Empiricism is the logical basis of the Conservative creed. Moreover, he did not, like Burke, live into an age when revolution threatened the foundations of society, and when political conservatism was therefore a natural reaction to contemporary conditions. Hume's conservatism was founded on the more permanent basis of logical empiricism and utilitarian ethics, although it was no doubt encouraged to some extent by the stable political conditions under which he lived.

Hume's life was relatively uneventful, although he held the posts of Secretary to the British Ambassador in Paris and Under Secretary of State during the years 1763-1769. For the rest, he lived the life of a philosopher and historian. After unsuccessful attempts to settle down in the profession of law and in commerce, he went to France in the year I735, and spent the next few years in study and writing. The three Books of the *Treatise of Human* Nature appeared in I739 and I740. This work comprised a full exposition of Hume's metaphysical and moral philosophy, but the originality of his ideas and the complex nature of much of the argument restricted the book's appeal, and, as Hume himself said, 'it fell dead born from the press without reaching such a distinction as even to excite a murmur among the zealots'.

Hume felt that this failure to attract attention 'had proceeded more from the manner than the matter', and he set himself to expound his theories in a simpler and more readable style in his *Enquiry into the Human Understanding* (I748), the *Enquiry concerning the Peoples of Morals* (1751) and the *Dissertation on the Passions* (1757). He had published in 1741 and 1742 two volumes *of Essays Moral and Political,* which was immediately successful, and these were followed in I752 by a volume of *Political Discourses.* He also published a *History of Great Britain* and a *History of England under the House of Tudor. His Dialogues on Natural Religion* was published posthumously.

Although the *Treatise* was completed when Hume was only twenty-five years of age, it contains all the essential principles of his metaphysical and moral philosophy, and its supreme importance is now generally appreciated. It was the book, which awoke Kant from his 'dogmatic slumber' and inspired him to work out his own 'critical philosophy' as an answer to Hume's sceptical conclusions. It embodies the basic ideas, which have recently emerged in a new guise in the modern doctrine known as Logical Positivism.

The general theory expounded by Hume in the *Treatise and the Enquiries* is a form of Empiricism, in the sense in which this term was defined earlier. It is the doctrine that the only propositions, which are certainly true, are those which describe 'relations of ideas', i.e. are analytic; and that those which proceed beyond the mere analysis of an idea to assert something about its application to reality are without rational necessity and can be justified only by direct observation. Such propositions are synthetic, and Hume's Empiricism can be summed up in the axiom that a synthetic proposition can never be *a priori.*

13.2 HUME'S MORAL THEORY

As was shown earlier, Empiricism thus understood implies that the generalisations of both science and morality are empirical and devoid of rational necessity. They may be universally true, but they need not be, and whether they are or not can be ascertained only by observation. There is therefore no ground for assuming that there is a universal 'Natural' or Moral law standing independent of experience and prescribing the form which experience ought to take. The moral norms which apply to experience must be found within experience itself, and must therefore be subject to its contingent character and variations. What ought to be must ultimately be determined by what is, and the sense of duty must ultimately be a kind of feeling or desire.

In Hume's view these conclusions necessarily follow once we recognise that an act is an event, that its occurrence cannot be understood except in so far as it is caused by (i.e. regularly follows) another event, and that an act is always ultimately caused by a 'passion', i.e. a feeling or desire, although cognition and reason may play an important part in determining the form which that passion takes by showing what the conditions and consequences of realising its end are likely to be. Moral feelings of approval or disapproval are recognised by Hume to be among the most important and influential of the passions. But they are no more than passions and it is for experience to ascertain when, and in what circumstances, they occur.

There is no basis for any *a priori* claim that certain acts ought to be approved under all circumstances, for such a generalisation is itself simply the empirical proposition that a feeling of approval is excited in someone by all such acts.

Hume thinks that these conclusions necessarily follow from the consideration that moral approval and disapproval influence action, and frequently in a very marked degree. They cannot, for this reason, be acts of apprehension or judgement because the latter cannot (by themselves) influence action in any way. The judgement that 'the fire is out' does not result in any action on my part *unless* it is accompanied by a desire, such as the desire to keep warm.

Similarly, the judgement that 'stealing is wrong' would not dissuade people from stealing unless at the same time they desired to avoid doing what is wrong. Moral approval and disapproval must, therefore, in some sense express desires in view of the influence, which they have on action. The disinterested contemplation of good and evil could not have any such practical effects.

Hume thinks that it is inconceivable that acts should be directly influenced by reason, although reason may play an important part in determining the nature of the objects, which excite desire. He set forth his views on this fundamental question in his important chapter 'On the Influencing Motives of the Will',' where he claimed to prove *'first,* that reason alone can never be a motive to any action of the will; and, *secondly,* that it can never oppose passion in the direction of the will'.

Since moral experience must therefore be of an emotional and co native character, moral judgements must be about this emotional and co native experience and cannot, as is commonly assumed, be about external and objective facts. Actions, feelings and characters are not good or bad, right or wrong, in virtue of some quality, which they possess, but as Hume put it:

An action, sentiment, or character is virtuous or vicious, because its view causes a pleasure or uneasiness of a particular kind.

The words 'of a particular kind' are of great importance, because they mean that Hume is not advocating a theory of egoistic hedonism. As he says later in the same chapter:

The good qualities of an enemy are hurtful to us, but might still command our esteem and respect. It is only when a character is considered in general, without reference to our particular interest, that it causes such a feeling or sentiment as denominates it morally 'good or evil'.

Hume does not think that there is any universal law according to which the moral sentiments occur; but he thinks that the majority of those, which are not mere expressions of habitual attitudes, are based upon estimates of utility. Thus he says:

These sentiments may arise either from the mere species or appearance of characters and passions, or from reflections on their tendency to the happiness of mankind, and of particular persons. My opinion is, that both these causes are intermixed in our morals . . . I am also of opinion that reflections, tendencies of actions have by far the greatest influence and determine all the great lines of duty.

Judgements of utility, i.e. of the tendency of an act to promote happiness or diminish pain, are, therefore, in Hume's opinion, the usual basis of the moral principles which we habitually accept, or which we arrive at in cases of dispute. Hume recognises that this is a purely empirical generalisation to which there may be exceptions, but he thinks that it applies to the great majority of moral laws and is the generalisation, which gives them a large measure of systematic coherence. He recognises, however, that in a rapidly changing society moral laws, which could formerly be justified on a utilitarian basis, may, through the force of habit and tradition, survive long after they have ceased to serve their utilitarian purpose.

13.3 HUME'S POLITICAL THEORY

Hume believes that utility is similarly the foundation of the state. The way in which governments originated has, he thinks, no relevance to the utilitarian reasons, which now exist for obeying them, and he thinks that the doctrine of the social contract is without either historical or logical justification.

As he says:

If the reason be asked of that obedience, which we are bound to pay to government, I readily answer, *because society could not otherwise sub-sit;* and this answer is clear and intelligible to all mankind. Your answer is, *because we should keep our word.* But besides that nobody, till trained in a philosophical system, can either comprehend or relish this answer, besides this, I say, you find yourself embarrassed when it is asked, *why we are bound to keep our ward?* Nor can you give any answer, but that would, immediately, without any circuit, have accounted for our obligation to allegiance.

All governments have a special responsibility for the security of personal property, and this, too, is based on considerations of utility:

By the laws of society, this coat, this horse is mine, and *ought* to remain perpetually in my possession: I reckon on the secure enjoyment of it: by depriving me of it, you disappoint my expectations, and doubly displease me, and offend every bystander.

Hume, in short, agrees with Hobbes that the primary function of government is the maintenance of personal security, and that so long as a government fulfils this purpose there are utilitarian grounds for giving it allegiance whether it originally derived its power from force or from consent. Hume thinks that in practice the allegiance which people give to their government is, as a rule, simply an expression of habit, although such a habit, if challenged, can always be justified on grounds of utility. Thus Hume takes his place on the Conservative side of politics as a respecter of tradition and habit. In his view, radical innovation and violent revolution have consequences which can never be justified on utilitarian grounds, since on balance they diminish the general happiness, and are therefore opposed to the general objective of moral approbation.

Hume believed that there were also sound reasons for supporting the sort of government, which ruled in England during his lifetime. These reasons derive from his theory that the ultimate cause of all action must necessarily be 'passion', i.e. feeling or desire, and that reason, from its very nature, can never be a sufficient motive of any act. But, although passion is therefore the ultimate cause of all action, a distinction can be drawn between acts resulting from the impulse to satisfy a desire and those resulting from a rational calculation how it may be best satisfied.

Hence, although reason cannot by itself determine the objectives of action it can influence the course of action by drawing attention to the probable consequences of alternative courses of action and thus altering the action, which is taken. A distinction can therefore be drawn between unreflective passions on the one hand and those upon which reason has been brought to bear in the way just described. Hume called the uncontrolled passions 'violent' and those which had been influenced by reason calm'.

It is in terms of this distinction between calm and violent passions that Hume tried to defend aristocratic government. For he thinks that experience shows that the calm passions are most likely to replace the violent passions in people whose powers of reasoning have been developed by education and whose economic security makes them less likely to succumb to the temptation of seeking 'immediate, at the expense of lasting, advantage.

Thus, he believed that the most general and enduring happiness for all is most likely to be realised in a community where power is placed in the hands of a prosperous and educated minority. He also believed that drastic political changes are likely to disrupt the operation of the social traditions, which have proved most useful in the past, and to weaken the force of habit, which is the main source of allegiance to a government.

Hume's defence of political conservatism is, therefore based directly on his Empiricist Theory of Morality. If he is right in holding that the ultimate object of men's desires is happiness and that moral approval and disapproval are generally based upon an estimate of the extent to which the act which is approved or disapproved tends to promote or diminish the general happiness, then it follows that the form of government which men ought to support is that which experience has shown most likely to promote the general happiness.

It is true that the anthropological knowledge on which Hume based his political theory was somewhat limited and that he proceeded on the assumption that the conditions of life in the Britain which he knew were representative of conditions elsewhere and were likely to endure. He did not contemplate a future, in which the education and culture, which were then confined to a privileged minority, would be enjoyed by the entire population, and might thus; make the calm passions more general than they were when he lived.

Although Hume's political conservatism is therefore based on assumptions, which do not universally, apply, it remains an interesting and important example of a theory which attempts to justify a specific form of government on the ground of its utility in promoting the general happiness. Most political philosophers have based their justification of government on an *a priori* set of moral principles and have thus submitted a justification of a categorical nature.

As Hume's justification is based on empirical premises it is necessarily hypothetical in character. If people desire the general happiness, and if government by a cultivated minority is the best way of promoting such happiness, it necessarily follows that this form of government ought to be supported. But, if the truth of these premises can be disputed on empirical grounds (as it well may be) the conclusion does not follow.

Hume's defence of Conservatism, like his defence of any practical creed, is therefore based on the principle of utility. A respect for tradition, the avoidance of violent change, and the repudiation of all precise and uncompromising dogmas are, in Hume's view, the principles which are shown by experience to be the most effective in promoting the happiness of a community, and are thereby justified. For the general happiness is the ultimate aim of all human activity, and government is therefore justified in so far as it contributes to this end.

13.4 BURKE'S CONTRIBUTION TO POLITICAL THOUGHT

Edmund Burke (1729-1797) could be more accurately described as a philosophical politician than as a political philosopher, but his work deserves consideration in view of the influence, which he exercised on his contemporaries and the fact that he is usually held to have formulated the basic principles underlying the Conservative tradition in British politics. His exposition of these principles is rhetorical rather than logical, but he was able for that reason to reach a far wider circle than Hume, and beneath the rhetoric it is easy to discern the same empirical principles, which were defined so precisely by the Scottish philosopher.

Burke was educated at Trinity College, Dublin, and came to England at the age of twenty-one to keep his terms at the Temple and prepare himself for the English Bar. It was not long, however, before he realised that the study of law would stifle his urge to creative thinking in the field of politics, and he soon decided to abandon a legal career for the more congenial, if more hazardous, profession of letters.

In 1755 Burke achieved fame and acquired friendships by the publication of his *Vindication of Natural Society.* He became Private Secretary to the Marquis of Rockingham, who later became Prime Minister. Burke himself entered the House of Commons in I766 and held several high offices of State.

Burke belonged to the Whig Party, from which the Liberal tradition subsequently developed, but this does not make it inconsistent to regard him as a defender of Conservative principles, for the Whigs of his time differed from the Tories mainly on details of policy, and Burke's philosophy was applicable to both. In fact, he was not deeply interested in the transient issues of party politics, and was more concerned to defend traditions and principles, which he thought vital to the survival of the British Constitution.

Burke's theories are expounded in three principal writings, each of which was inspired by a contemporary issue. His *Thoughts on the Cause of the Present Discontents,* published in I770, was provoked by the attempt of George III to limit the powers of Parliament and extend the royal influence in politics. Burke sought to mobilise both public then and the nation at large against what he called 'a faction ruling by the private instructions of a Court against the general sense of the people', and his essential argument was that, although Parliamentary government had developed from obscure origins in a way, which was not wholly intelligible. Burke expressed his opposition to such attempts to interfere with the natural course of development in a memorable passage:

Our constitution stands on a nice equipoise with steep precipices and deep waters upon all sides of it. In removing it from a dangerous leaning towards one side there may be a risk of over-setting it on the other. Every project of a material change in a Government so complicated as ours is a matter of difficulties, in which a considerate man will not be too ready to decide, a prudent man too ready to undertake, or m honest man too ready to promise.

In these words Burke gave vivid expression to his basic conviction that a state is not a man-made machine but an immensely complicated organism, which the efforts of individuals have helped to shape, but whose evolution and destiny any individual cannot wholly understand. Burke believed that the way in which a state evolves and develops is largely determined by forces which no individual can fully comprehend, and that when men make changes they should do so with restraint and caution, since the consequences of their actions cannot be foreseen and may conflict with the most fundamental interests of the community as a whole.

Burke's next great work was his *Speech on Conciliation with America* (1775), in which he sought to avert the tragedy of war with the American colonists.

But the event, which made the deepest impression on Burke, and called forth the most eloquent exposition of his theory, was the French Revolution. Here, he felt, was a clear example of men confident in their own insight and judgement and determined to reconstitute society in accordance with their ideals and without thought for the lessons of history or respect for the accumulated wisdom of the centuries embodied in the existing constitution of France. Burke was not without sympathy for the practical objectives of the French Revolution, but he felt that the violent and unconstitutional method adopted by the revolutionaries was not the way to achieve them, and would have disastrous consequences for the community as a whole. He predicted that, although the Revolution might temporarily remove some of the more glaring injustices in French society, it would fail to achieve the real liberty at which it aimed, and would culminate, as in fact it did in a military dictatorship. These views were eloquently expounded in Burke's *Reflections on the Revolution in France* (I790), which had a wide sale both at home and abroad, and exercised a considerable influence in confirming the opposition of the vast majority of British people to the methods, and even the ideals, of the revolutionaries.

Burke's writings are, for the most part, variations on a single theme, and were addressed more to the public at large than to those whose interest lay in the philosophical foundations of political theory. Moreover, the exposition of his theory is too diffuse and rhetorical to make it clear exactly what his assumptions and deductions are. Yet it seems clear that the fundamental principle underlying the arguments which he applied to contemporary problems is the principle of utility-the principle that both in public and in private life the greatest happiness of the greatest number is the ultimate standard by which duty and justice must be determined, and that arbitrary assumptions about 'natural rights' must not be allowed to stand in th4jway of this overriding objective. The stress which he laid on the limitations of the individual's understanding of social and political laws was not, as has been sometimes suggested, because he thought of society as an organic individual with a general will but because he recognised the empirical character of the problem of achieving the greatest happiness of the greatest number, and repudiated all suggestions that it could be solved by some simple and self evident process that did not need to be tested in practice and could ignore the accumulated wisdom of tradition

13.5 EMPIRICISM AND CONSERVATISM

Burke's writings and speeches may therefore be justly regarded as the application of empiricism to the leading political issues of his age. It is because Empiricism is the logical and philosophical basis of modern Conservatism that Burke has been commonly regarded as the leading philosopher of the Conservative faith.

For Empiricism cannot justify change except where experience gives ground for supposing that change will increase the general happiness. Today, Burke's principles do not appear to be specifically the principles of Conservatism so much as the principles of constitutional democracy in general. He would clearly have opposed the revolutionary methods of modern Communism and extolled the fidelity of both the Conservative and Liberal Parties to constitutional traditions.

As to whether the record of recent Socialist Governments in Britain would have equally satisfied him, is more open to doubt. In so far as these Governments have worked through the traditional machinery of Parliament they would have met with his approval, but he would almost certainly have viewed with suspicion, if not active disapproval, their ambitious schemes of social reform and industrial reorganisation inspired by the abstract ideal of social equality.

When Burke died the industrial revolution had scarcely begun, and these problems had not arisen. If he had witnessed the consequences of that revolution in the nineteenth century he might have adopted a more progressive attitude to social reform than in fact he did. None the less, he would probably still have adhered to his view that 'the nature of man is intricate, the objects of society are of the greatest possible complexity, and therefore no simple disposition or direction of power can be suitable either to man's nature or to the quality of his affairs'.

Such cautious Empiricism is in marked contrast to the uncritical dogmatism, which Rationalism tends to encourage, and it remains a conspicuous feature of the Conservative outlook at the present day.

14 HEGEL

14.1 IDEALISM

Georg Wilhelm Friedrich Hegel (1770-1831) was born at Stuttgart and received his early education in the local grammar school. In the autumn of 1788 he proceeded to the University of Tubingen as a student of theology, but did not achieve any distinction. Subsequently, he worked for a time as a private tutor, first at Berne and later at Frankfort, where he was able to devote considerable time to study, and to work out the outlines of his general philosophy.

The death of his father in January 1799 gave him a modest inheritance, and he was able to give up his tutoring and go to Jena. There he became a close friend and collaborator of the philosopher Schelling, and was soon appointed to lecture at the University in an honorary capacity. In 1805 he was appointed to an extraordinary professorship at Jena, but he drew little money from the post, and had to look for other work when Napoleon's invasion in 1806 brought the life of the University to a standstill. After working for a year as a newspaper editor he became Rector of the Aegidien-Gymnasilim in Nuremberg, a post that he discharged with considerable success until August 1816. During the eight years, which he spent at Nuremberg, Hegel had been working steadily at his philosophy, and the first two volumes of his *Logic* appeared in 1812. In 1816 he was appointed as a Professor of Philosophy at Heidelberg. In 1821, he published his theory of moral and political philosophy in the *Philosophy of Right.*

Hegel's fame spread far and wide during his tenure of the Chair at Berlin, and a Hegelian school of disciples soon began to form. In 1830 he was made Rector of the University, and in 1831 he was decorated by Frederick William III. But the revolution of 1831 was a great shock to him, and he viewed the prospect of more democratic forms of government with deep anxiety. His whole philosophy was based on the principle that the state is more important and more real than the individual, and prescribes the ideals of individual conduct. Hegel was not, however, destined to witness the aftermath of the revolution, for he fell a victim to the cholera epidemic which attacked Europe in 1831, and died, after one day's illness, on 14 November in that year.

Hegel's political theory has been variously referred to as an 'Idealist' or 'Metaphysical' or 'Philosophical' Theory of the State. Of these adjectives, the most specific and illuminating is 'Idealist', since it describes one of the characteristic features of the general philosophy upon which Hegel's political theory is based. The adjectives 'Metaphysical' and 'Philosophical' indicate that this political theory depends, in a particularly direct and obvious way, upon a general 'metaphysical' or 'philosophical' theory of the universe; and a brief outline of its essential features must first be given if the foundations of the political theory are to be properly appreciated.

14.2 HEGEL'S IDEALISM AND KANT

Hegel's idealism is essentially the logical development of Kant's doctrine of the categories. Kant had been convinced that certain synthetic judgements - in particular, causal and moral judgements - are *a priori,* and had traced this *a priori* character to the operation of the categories in terms of which the mind was, in his view, bound to synthesise the raw material of its experience if that experience was to take a significant form. The validity of the categories had therefore to be postulated as a necessary condition of significant experience.

But in Kant's theory the categories were only the *formal* conditions of experience; its *material* conditions were constituted by unknowable things-in-themselves. Hegel rejected the notion of a thing-in-itself, which lies behind and does not enter into experience, on the ground that it is a self-contradictory notion; for it seemed to him obviously self-contradictory to speak of that which, by definition, cannot be known. Hegel therefore concluded that the categories must constitute the material as well as the formal conditions of experience, i.e. must determine both the raw material of experience and its relational characteristics.

For if the matter of experience is not determined by something which lies outside experience it must be determined, like the form of experience, by the necessary pattern of experience itself. There can be no external realm of 'things' or 'facts' by which the judgements which constitute experience can be accounted for or their truth confirmed. Indeed, the usual conception of truth as a sort of correspondence between judgement and reality must be replaced by a new conception according to which the truth of a judgement is defined in terms of its relationship to the only entities to which it can be related, namely other judgements.

Truth, according to this latter view, means *coherence,* i.e. a judgement is true in so far as it is consistent with other judgements, and more true the wider the range of judgements with which it is consistent. The only judgement which is wholly true is therefore a judgement asserting everything about everything,' for only such a judgement embodies, and is thus consistent with, the numerous judgements which, viewed from a narrower perspective, appear to be in some measure inconsistent with each other.

Thus Hegel rejected the distinction commonly drawn between knowledge and reality. Knowledge is reality and reality is knowledge, for if the two were separate reality would be unknowable and knowledge would be illusory. Since this implies that reality could not be other than it is-for it embraces everything in space and time, in imagination and in conception-knowledge could not be other than it is, and the contradictions which exist at the level of finite experience must disappear when viewed from the universal perspective of the Absolute. Hence, in Hegel's famous words, the real is rational.

14.3 IDENTITY OF KNOWLEDGE AND REALITY

The basic difference between Hegel's Rationalism and Empiricism obviously lies in the denial of a 'reality' outside experience. The possibility of such a reality is denied on the ground that its assertion would be self-contradictory. For, Hegel maintains, reality is necessarily part of experience in so far as any assertion whatsoever is made about it; and, if nothing is asserted about it, it does not in any intelligible sense exist. From this general premise the Coherence Theory of Truth necessarily follows; for if the truth of a judgement cannot be defined in terms of its relationship to that which is not a judgement, then its truth must be defined in terms of its relationship to another judgement or judgements.

It will be true in so far as it is consistent with other judgements assumed to be true, but the truth of these other judgements will in turn depend upon their relationship to yet other judgements, and so on *ad infinitum.* Hegel denied that this process involves a 'vicious circle'; on the contrary, he maintained that if it *were* pushed to infinity by asserting every judgement which is consistent with every other judgement the result would be one coherent system of judgements which could not be other than it is, and which would thus constitute absolute and *a priori* truth or the Absolute, as he called it.

While it is in practice impossible for a finite mind to achieve this absolute coherence, it is possible, by applying the test of coherence to an ever widening sphere of experience, to approach more closely to it, and thus achieve a higher degree of truth.

This amounts to saying that the conception of thinking held by the earlier rationalists was fundamentally mistaken. According to them thinking is a process of linear inference from *a priori* premises by *a priori* inferences to *a priori* conclusions.

Hume had effectively refuted this theory by pointing out that, where the premises afford grounds for drawing valid conclusions about the nature of the experienced world, they must necessarily assume a synthetic form and thus be without any *a priori* necessity themselves. Kant tried to save something of the older Rationalism by arguing that the more important synthetic generalisations (such as the laws of causality and morality) are necessary in a transcendental, though not in a logical, sense, meaning that their necessity is a necessity of experience though not of logic.

It was, however, left to Hegel to recognise the full implications of Hume's analysis and, in particular, to recognise that since the truth of a synthetic proposition is never an inherent characteristic of such a proposition it must be determined by the relationship of that proposition to other propositions. This, Hegel believed, is the only self-consistent conception of truth which can be applied to synthetic propositions, for any attempt to define their truth in terms of correspondence to 'facts' or other alleged features of reality' conceals within itself the very concept which is supposed to be defined.'

Hegel would have agreed that purely analytic propositions are, in a different sense, necessarily true, namely in the sense of being tautologies; but he saw that human thinking cannot be reduced to the repetition of tautologies, and he set himself to show how thinking can be at once rational and constructive. This, as already observed, he claimed to do by giving truth a novel interpretation in terms of coherence, and by arguing that such an interpretation is the only one which can avoid some form of self-contradiction.

Hegel thus claimed to show how can be at once rational and fruitful by defining truth in ten of the logical relationship of propositions to one another and by portraying thinking as a process, not of linear inference, but of dialectical evolution. He thought it obvious that the greater part of human thinking does not consist in the assertion of tautologies but in the opposition of thesis and antithesis, and the evolution of a synthesis which marks a genuine advance on the thesis, and does not merely assert it in-different language.

But he differed from empiricists like Hume in holding that, although such thinking is not tautologous, neither is it the completely irrational sequence with which they identified it. On the contrary, he believed that the apparently contingent features of the history of thought would, if viewed as a whole by an infinite mind, appear as the partial revelation of a logically necessary whole - the Absolute.

Hegel's theory is therefore something of a compromise between the older type of Rationalism and Hume's Empiricism. Like the earlier rationalists, Hegel believed that 'the real is rational', but he agreed with the empiricists that its rationality is not apparent at the finite level of human experience, and that thinking does not start from self-evident and *a priori* premises. The novelty of his theory lies in his contention that human experience can be made progressively less irrational by making it more comprehensive and coherent, and that beyond it there lies the unattainable ideal of an infinite experience from which the last vestige of irrationality would be removed. If, in other words, we knew everything about everything we should recognise that everything must be exactly as, it is.

14.4 Fallacies In Hegel's Theory Of Knowledge

Hegel's claim that human experience can be made progressively less irrational obviously requires the postulation of an 'Absolute' embodying absolute truth since otherwise there would be no standard by which to measure the relative truth of judgements made at the level of finite experience. Yet it is just this ultimate postulate which he fails to justify. However comprehensive an experience may become there is no rational ground for saying that it could not have been otherwise.

It may, indeed, be conceded that an infinite experience, in virtue of its infinite comprehension, must be coherent, but this does not rule out the possibility that it could take an indefinite number of different forms, and could therefore be completely coherent in an indefinite number of different ways. In claiming that the whole truth about anything would be necessarily true Hegel is, in fact, asserting a purely analytic proposition.

He is saying that, if the universe is defined as the object A possessing the characteristics X, Y, Z, etc., then the judgement that A is X is necessarily true; but this is obviously an analytic judgement of the form 'A-which-is-X-

Y-Z etc. is X'. Thus Hegel's theory that all truths would be recognised as necessarily true by an infinite mind is nothing more than an assertion of the truism that if the Absolute is defined as the whole truth about everything then it necessarily implies the partial truth about everything. But there is no categorical reason why the Absolute should be constituted as it is constituted.

For these reasons Hegel failed to provide a foundation for experience which is at once synthetic and necessary even at the level of infinite experience. All he showed is that human thinking at the finite level does, in fact, follow a certain pattern and that this is explained by the fact that all thinking takes the hypothetical form familiar in the natural sciences, and proceeds by formulating progressively more comprehensive hypotheses to account for the more primitive judgements known as the 'facts of experience'. This, Hegel believed, was the real nature of all the philosophical systems which had preceded his; hence his famous dictum that 'philosophy is the history of philosophy'. But he failed to show why the history of philosophy should have taken just the course which it has taken, or why the Absolute Spirit should have manifested itself in just the way that it has.

If the foregoing criticism of Hegel's theory is valid it is fatal to his whole system, for it is essential to the latter to maintain not only that the whole of experience implies any part of experience but that from any part of experience it is possible to proceed by dialectical thinking to the whole. This is what Hegel failed to establish. In so far as his dialectical process extends beyond the limits of analytic inference it is a synthetic process which widens experience only in so far as it proceeds beyond what is necessarily implied on *a priori* grounds. In so doing the dialectical process may constitute a useful and culminating account of how the Absolute is constituted, but it can never show how the Absolute *must be* constituted, and if it cannot do this it cannot provide any real alternative to Hume's Empiricism.

The fundamental inadequacy of Hegel's dialectical method for the task which he sets it to accomplish can be illustrated by an analysis of the very first triad in his deduction of the categories. These 'categories' are the most general characteristics which apply to the whole of reality, and the dialectical method can therefore be applied most plausibly to the deduction of their relationships. If this application is found to be invalid it will be safe to conclude that the method cannot be used to deduce the truth about the more concrete and less general features of experience.

Now Hegel's first triad consists of *Being* as the thesis, *Nothing* as the antithesis, and *Becoming* as the synthesis. Hegel regards *Being* as the original thesis because it is the most general and universal characteristic of everything in experience. Everything in experience necessarily is in the most general sense of the word 'is'. But, Hegel argues, something which merely 'is' without further specification would be nothing at all. Everything which 'is' must have some further determination - must, for example, be material or mental, animate or inanimate, and so on. Hence, he argues, mere *Being* would be the same as *Nothing.*

The synthesis of the opposition between *Being and Nothing is Becoming.* By this Hegel means that *Being* 'passes into' *Nothing and Nothing,* in turn, 'passes into' *Being.* Such 'passing into' is not, of course, a temporal but a logical process. What Hegel means is that the thought of 'Being' is identical with the thought of 'Nothing' and that the thought of 'Nothing' is identical with the thought of 'Being'. The two categories are therefore at one and the same time identical and different, and the synthesis of the dialectical triad to which their opposition leads is called *Becoming. Becoming* is the unity which contains within itself the difference found within the identity of *Being and Nothing.* Because it contains and preserves this difference it is a relatively *concrete* universal - in contrast to the *abstract* universals of traditional philosophy which specifically exclude what is not common to all the members of a class.

This initial triad of Hegel's dialectic introduces two of his most important and characteristic doctrines. In the first place, it shows that Hegel believed that even the most complete opposition-that of *Being and Nothing* is an underlying unity; and, in the second place, it introduces the important doctrine of the concrete universal, according to which universals of the most abstract character contain within themselves, and logically imply, the most specific characteristics of their concrete instances.

It is obvious that this doctrine of the concrete universal is the key to Hegel's whole philosophy, for if it is valid it implies that it is possible to deduce species from genus progressively until the most specific determinations of experience are reached. This is what Hegel claimed to do. But the very first triad illustrates though not so obviously as some later triads-the fallacy which vitiates the whole process. It is true that *Being* is equivalent to *Nothing* in the sense that Being in itself has no specific determinations such as mental being, physical being, animal being, etc.; but this could not be deduced from reflection upon Being unless we were already aware of some of the concrete manifestations of Being. It is only because we have already experienced some of these manifestations-that we can say that mere Being is not equivalent to any of them, i.e. is Nothing; but this is an analytic inference from concrete experience and not, as Hegel contends, a synthetic inference from mere Being.

Examination of any of the other triads in the dialectic would illustrate the same point, namely that in so far as Hegel's deductions proceed from the relatively abstract to the relatively concrete they are invalid unless the relatively concrete is already experienced as that which the relatively abstract characterises. We cannot infer that mere Being is equivalent to Nothing unless we already know that Being frequently characterises something; and what it characterises cannot be logically deduced from it.

14.5 HEGEL'S MORAL AND STATE PHILOSOPHY

These conclusions have an important application in Hegel's philosophy, which is an attempt to use the dialectical process to demonstrate the comparative morality of different types of political institution. If his logic can be defined as an exposition of the principle that 'the real is the rational', then his political philosophy can be defined in corresponding terms as an exposition of the principle that 'the right is the rational'.

According to Hegel, the essence of moral conduct is found when the individual acts not in accordance with particular impulses and desires but in accordance with universal reason-the reason which is shared by all rational beings. Hence Hegel rejects as wholly false all forms of a Utilitarian Theory of the State on the ground that they find the ultimate sanction of policy in the desires and interests of individuals. According to Hegel the 'will of the state' represents the true will of the individual, and only in so far as the latter coincides with the former is the individual acting morally.

Thus Hegel draws a sharp distinction between Civil Society and the state. Civil Society is that form of political organisation which follows logically from the disruption of the family due to children growing up and becoming independent persons. At that stage they become dependent for various necessities upon other people, and thus accept a form of organisation which embodies appropriate arrangements for mutual support. But Hegel believes that no rational man can rest content with such a form of political organisation since it assumes that every individual is seeking his own personal ends and regarding others simply as means to these ends. He can only be finally content with the higher form of organisation, called the state, which expresses the rational will of every individual contained within it, and in serving which every individual therefore finds the realisation of his true will.

Thus Hegel, like Rousseau, finds the criterion of political morality in the *general* will of the state. He readily admits that some states may not be perfect, and that it would be going too far to respect the authority of every ruler or government; but all contain at least an element of rationality in their fundamental purposes. Thus Hegel comments:

'Although a state may be declared to violate right principles, and to be defective in various ways, it always contains the essential moments of its existence, if, that is to say, it belongs to the full-formed states of our own time... Evil can doubtless disfigure it in many ways, but the ugliest man, the criminal, the invalid, the cripple, are living men.'

These observations certainly answer the criticism that Hegel held the will of any state to be a good will. But they give no indication how we may discriminate between good states and bad ones. If the dialectic process were really able-as Hegel thought it was - to provide valid deductions of the more determinate from the less determinate, then it might be possible to deduce from the conception of the state more specific criteria of its rationality. But, for the reasons already given, such deduction does not appear to be possible, and the conception of the 'will of the state' is therefore just as open to arbitrary interpretation and practical abuse as it was in Rousseau's theory.

14.6 THE RATIONAL WILL

The truth is that Hegel is no more able than was Kant to give the good will a 'content', i.e. specific objective, unless it is possible to deduce the more determinate from the less determinate. To say, as Hegel says, that the good will is the 'rational' and 'universal' will does not tell us *what* it wills unless it is possible to deduce from the concepts of 'rationality' and 'universality' the nature of the objectives at which the rational and universal will must aim.

This is impossible unless the dialectical deduction of the relatively determinate from the relatively indeterminate is possible. For the reasons set forth above, Hegel fails to show that such deduction is ever possible, and therefore his whole conception of morality is based on a fallacious assumption. In particular, he fails to provide any criterion for distinguishing between good states and bad ones, and thus makes it possible for the most arbitrary acts of government to be justified as the 'will of the state'.

Hegel, like Rousseau, distinguished the 'general will' or the 'will of the state' both from the 'will of the majority' and from the 'will of all'-in fact, from any actual will. They did so because by the 'general will' they meant the 'rational will', i.e. an ideal will which is not necessarily expressed by the will of the majority or, indeed, by any actual will at all. But while it is easy to talk of such a will it is impossible to define its objectives in a way that is not purely arbitrary, just because a will which is not, in the end, the expression of irrational desire is not a will at all. In other words, the conception of a will which may be nobody's will is self-contradictory and cannot therefore constitute a rational basis for morality or politics.

Hegel therefore fails, as Hume would have said he must fail to provide a rational basis for Morality and the State. His dialectical triad of Abstract Right-Morality-Social Ethics can at most claim to be a description of different manifestations of the moral sentiment. It cannot be, as Hegel thought it was the progressive evolution of a more rational conception of morality, since morality from its very nature is not of a rational character.

Similarly, Hegel's conception of world history as the progressive revelation of the Absolute Idea does not exhibit any rational necessity. It is impossible for a finite mind to deduce the future from the present, and to say that it would be possible to do so if only we knew the Absolute Idea in its entirety is equivalent to the analytic proposition that if the whole of history takes such and such a form, then any selected period of history necessarily takes a certain form. If history has, in fact, developed by a sort of dialectical process with sufficient regularity to justify a generalisation, that generalisation is an empirical and not a logical principle, for it is without any sort of logical necessity.

The final judgement on Hegel's philosophy must therefore be that, like Kant's philosophy, it fails to refute the Empiricism of Hume. In particular, it fails to establish that synthetic judgements can possess logical necessity. If it fails to do this it leaves the essential principles of Empiricism inviolate. For Hegel's Coherence Theory of Truth is just an alternative way of stating the empiricist principle that the only basis for a synthetic generalisation is a 'fact', but that the generalisation so reached is devoid of rational necessity. There is no reason why the empiricist should not accept the Hegelian definition of the truth of such a generalisation in terms of its consistency with the less general propositions which are said to describe the 'facts' upon which it is based.

Where Hegel claimed to have advanced on the empiricist position was in showing that the ultimate and all-inclusive generalisation - the Absolute Idea - is true in an absolute and categorical sense since it is both based upon, and in rum implies, every judgement included in total experience. But this, as previously shown, is simply equivalent to the tautology that if experience as a whole is constituted in a certain way, then every part of experience must be constituted in a certain way. It does not eliminate the ultimate hypothesis that experience is constituted in just that way, nor, therefore, does it constitute any reason why experience *as a whole* should not have been differently constituted.

This conclusion does not, of course, imply that Hegel's philosophy was not a powerful stimulus to fruitful speculation in the historical and social sciences, or that the processes of thought and history which his dialectic claims to express do not have a considerable basis in fact. But it does imply that those illuminating generalisations, which appear to correlate, and in some sense 'explain', the movements of human thought and history, are just the 'natural beliefs' of Hume's Empiricism, and are completely devoid of the rational necessity inherent in analytic thinking. Their application to reality is therefore of a hypothetical and not a categorical character, since it is conditional upon the assumption of their truth.

If the mental processes which result in these generalisations are to be described as 'thought', then it is necessary to draw a sharp distinction between such 'thought' and the very different type of thought to be found in logic and mathematics. The rational necessity inherent in the thing of logic and mathematics does not characterise the formulation of empirical generalisations, and Hegel's attempt to deduce the latter from an all - comprehensive and self-justifying generalisation must be pronounced a failure. In particular, he failed to provide a rational basis for the ultimate principles of morality, or for the doctrine that these principles are most perfectly expressed by the 'will of the state'.

The reader must bear in mind that, whatever the criticism, Hegel is the instigator of 'knowledge is reality and reality is knowledge'. As such, philosophers must not forget the meaning of his argument. Those responsible for the preparation of the curricula regarding the education and the training of managers must not forget that 'knowledge-reality' is applicable not only to the governments, but also to modern individuals. In consideration of the state and the leader who are in search of methods to improve the living of the citizens, and simultaneously, the corporate management who are in search of business improvement.

In both cases, the state leader and the business manager are in search of methods for the improvement of the living of the people.

15. UTILITARIANISM IN MANAGEMENT

15.1 BENTHAM AND MILL

This is the concept of an ethical doctrine expounded by Jeremy Bentham and refined by John Stuart Mill. In his *Introduction to the Principles of Morals and Legislation* (1789), Bentham identified the goal of morality as 'the greatest happiness of the greatest number', and, in consequentialist fashion, claimed that an action is right in so far as it tends to promote that goal. Bentham devoted much of his time to attacking the abuses in the legal system, but both he and his followers were to have a profound influence on all aspects of political and social reform in Britain during the 19th century. Acting as a pressure group on both Conservative and Liberal governments, they often gave a lead to public opinion. Mill's essay, *Utilitarianism* (1863), gave perhaps the clearest expression to the doctrine.

As a philosophical proposition, utilitarianism is hampered by the fundamental difficulty of comparing quantitatively the happiness of one person with that of another. Nevertheless, it has proved a remarkably persistent doctrine, which continues to attract adherents. Part of its appeal lies in its apparent clarity and simplicity: the concept of happiness seems much less obscure than rival moral concepts such as that of a natural right, and the rule, 'Maximize happiness', seems to offer a decisive and factual procedure for deciding what to do. Utilitarianism is particularly attractive as a method for public decision-making. Utilitarianism finds it hard, however, to explain why we value things other than happiness, such as equality and justice.

15.2 JURISPRUDENCE, THE PHILOSOPHY OR SCIENCE OF LAW

It entails philosophical and practical enquiry into law and legal systems and encompasses at least four broad types of study. First, there are studies of legal systems to identify their constituent elements such as rules, rights, and duties, and the bonds between them. There are different theories about the relationship between legal rules and morality (see justice). Legal positivists have regarded legal systems as distinct from systems of morality, while exponents of natural law have disagreed. Secondly, there are studies of the growth and social impact of law in such fields as medicine, business, and the environment. Thirdly, there are studies of the behaviour and beliefs of legal officers and institutions (police, legislatures, and juries, for example). We, 'legal realists', who argued that legal rules were often not the decisive factor in the outcome of cases pioneered this field. Other factors such as inter-organizational rivalry or public attitudes to a particular crime might outweigh them. Finally, there are studies, which look at all the social mechanisms, which we associate with the law, in particular those maintaining order and resolving, dispute. Studies by anthropologists of dispute resolution processes are increasingly influencing the use (notably in family law) of conciliation procedures alongside or instead of judicial decision-making. The term jurisprudence, derived from French usage, can also refer more narrowly to the case law built up by courts and especially by international law courts.

15.3 RATIONALISM IN MANAGEMENT

In a way a broad philosophical position characterized by the claim that reason is, in some way, a source of knowledge. This claim can mean either that reason provides us with a priori concepts (or innate ideas), which can give the content of knowledge, or, more simply, that sense-experience gives the content, which then has to be corrected, and justified, by reason. Rationalist is the common label for 17th-century continental philosophers such as Descartes, Leibniz, and Spinoza. In the works of these authors, much emphasis is put on systematic justification, and mathematics, especially geometry, is often taken to be the template of an ideal rationalist epistemology. Traditionally, rationalism stands opposed to empiricism, in which experience provides us with all of our concepts, and is the ultimate source of justification of knowledge claims. Philosophers such as Kant attempted to synthesize the insights of the two.

15.4 KIERKEGAARD, SOREN AABYE (1813-55), DANISH PHILOSOPHER.

Kierkegaard trained as a theologian and his writings, which border on ethics and theology and are often polemical, describe the human predicament in a way which is fiercely Protestant, highlighting themes of faith, choice, dread, and anguish, giving priority to man's relation to God. Hegel's optimistic and rational vision of the world figured as a target in many of Kierkegaard's works. Foremost among Kierkegaard's concepts are his idea of the 'existing individual', and his notion of 'subjective truth'. In *Either-Or* (1843) Kierkegaard described the radical choice to be made between the 'aesthetic' and the 'ethical' forms of human existence. He developed an 'existential dialectic', according to which the different stages of existence are aesthetic, ethical, and religious. Kierkegaard's writings were an important influence on existentialism.

15.5 THEORIES OF BENTHAM AND MILL

Jeremy Bentham (1748-1832,) and John Stuart Mill (1806-1873) are the outstanding exponents of the theory known as Utilitarianism, which was destined to exercise a profound influence upon both political and economic thought in England during the first three-quarters of the nineteenth century. The theory stands in sharp contrast to the idealism of Hegel in the stress which it lays upon the primacy of the individual and the artificial character of the state.

Bentham was born in London on 15 February, 1748, and was educated at Westminster School and Queen’s College, Oxford, which he entered at the age of thirteen. He was called to the Bar in 1769. At Oxford he had acquired a considerable interest in natural science, and he soon realised that his true inclination lay not in the practice of law but in the examination and criticism of its moral basis. He therefore decided to devote his life to working out a scientific system of jurisprudence and legislation. A private income made this possible, and he published a considerable number of books, of which the best known and most important is the *Introduction to the Principles of Morals and Legislation.*

In this work Bentham sought to work out a scientific basis for a legal code. The book brought him an international reputation, and his advice on legal codification was sought by several foreign governments. At home, apart from his literary interests, he was engaged for nearly twenty-five years in negotiations for the erection of a 'Panopticon', or model prison in which all convicts could be observed by an unseen inspector; and when this scheme was finally abandoned Bentham claimed, and received, £23,000 by way of compensation from the Government. Other varied activities engaged him in his later years. In 1823 he established *the Westminster Review,* and later put forward schemes for canals through the isthmus of Suez and the isthmus of Panama. He died on 6 June 1832 in his eighty-fifth year.

Mill was born on 20 May 1806, the eldest son of James Mill (1773-1836), historian and philosopher, who ultimately became head of India House, the head office of the East India Company. He was educated by his father, who was a strict disciplinarian, and subjected his son to an arduous training which involved starting the study of Greek at the age of three and Latin, Euclid and algebra at the age of eight. Mill's subsequent studies covered logic, psychology, political economy, and law. His father had intended that he should practise at the Bar, but in 1822 he entered India House, of which he became head in 1856. The company was dissolved in i858 and its powers transferred to the Government, notwithstanding Mill's eloquent and closely reasoned defence of its record.

Mill subsequently entered Parliament as Member for Westminster in 1865 after a highly unconventional election. In strict accordance with his principles, he refused to canvass, to pay agents to canvass for him, or to promise to attend to the local business of the constituency. Indeed, it was with considerable reluctance that he agreed to address a meeting of electors. Although he never held ministerial office, he made a certain impression in Parliament by his speeches, but he was defeated in the general election of 1868, and thereafter retired to a literary life in a cottage which he had acquired at Avignon.

In spite of his official duties, first in India House and subsequently in Parliament, Mill found time for writing throughout his life, and published a long series of books and articles on a variety of philosophical, political, and economic subjects. His most important philosophical work was his *System of Logic,* published in 1843, in which he sought to establish that induction the inference from particular instances to general principles - is the logical pattern which all fruitful thinking takes. He subsequently published a treatise on *Political Economy* in 1848, in which he propounded what was at that time the novel suggestion that, although the conditions of production depend on unalterable laws, the distribution of what is produced can with advantage be brought under human control. After that he devoted himself to the writing of three important political dissertations which are of fundamental interest to the philosopher - On Liberty (1859), Representative Government (186o), and Utilitarianism (1861). Mill died on 8 May 1873.

15.6 The Individual And Utilitarianism

The theories of Bentham and Mill mark a return to the individualist principle of which Hobbes and Locke were earlier exponents, and which still remains the dominating tradition of British political theory. It is the principle that the state exists for the sake of the individual, not the individual for the sake of the state, and that the justification of government is to be found in the service which it renders to the individual, whether in satisfying his desires or protecting his rights or realising his ideals. If, as usually happens, the desires of different individuals differ, then, as Locke realised, it is necessary for government to satisfy one desire rather than another, and the satisfaction of the desire of the majority of individuals is generally assumed, in these circumstances, to be both right and inevitable.

Bentham and Mill both held that the primary human desire is for pleasure or happiness, and that the primary duty of both individuals and governments is to increase pleasure, and to diminish pain, as much as possible. They therefore held that the rightness of an act is measured by its *usefulness* in promoting pleasure. It is for this reason that their theory is called *Utilitarianism.* It differs fundamentally from all forms of Intuitionism, which asserts that acts are intrinsically right or wrong without regard to their consequences.

According to Utilitarianism, an act should be approved or condemned according to whether it tends to promote or to diminish pleasure. Only an Intuitionist could consistently assert that it is always wrong to tell a lie. A Utilitarian believes that it is wrong to tell a lie if doing so is likely to diminish pleasure; but that it is right to tell a lie if this is likely to increase pleasure. On the Utilitarian Theory rightness and wrongness are thus definable in terms of the goodness or badness of the consequences of acts; and the goodness or badness of these consequences depends upon whether they are pleasant or painful.

The fundamental premise of Utilitarianism is therefore the proposition that pleasure alone is intrinsically good, i.e. good in itself and not merely as a means to something else which is intrinsically good. But although Utilitarian always accepts this proposition in some sense, they do not always make it clear whether they regard it as an analytic or as a synthetic proposition. Of the two Utilitarians whose theories are being discussed in the present chapter, Bentham makes a number of statements which suggest that he understood the proposition analytically and believed that when people call a thing ‘good’ they really mean that it is ‘pleasant’, and when they call a thing ‘bad’ they really mean that it is ‘painful’; whereas Mill appears to regard the two epithets as quite distinct in meaning, although synthetically connected.

15.7 Bentham’s Utilitarianism

Bentham introduces his theory in the following words:

'Nature has placed mankind under the governance of two sovereign masters, pain *and pleasure.* It is for them alone to point out what we ought to do, as well as to determine what we shall do... In words a man may pretend to abjure their empire: but in reality he will remain subject to it all the while. The *principle of utility* recognises this subjection, and assumes it for the foundation of that system, the object of which is to rear the fabric of felicity by the hands of reason and of law.'

The principle of utility is more specifically defined as follows:

'By the principle of utility is meant that principle which approves or disapproves of every action whatsoever, according to the tendency which it appears to have to augment or diminish the happiness of the party whose interest is in question.'

If Bentham means, as he seems to mean, that all action is determined by desire for pleasure or antipathy towards pain, the majority of modern psychologists would disagree with him. They would do so 'for substantially the same reasons as those put forward by Bishop Butler in his celebrated refutation of the doctrine in his *Sermons on Human Nature.* What Bishop Butler pointed out is that action is usually determined not by the desire for pleasure but by the desire for certain conditions, e.g. the satisfaction of hunger, or the achievement of power over others.

It may be that the satisfaction of these desires is in fact pleasant, but Butler maintained that the object of a desire is not the same thing as the pleasure which results from attaining it. For example, he said that the object of hunger is not pleasure but food, although the satisfaction of hunger does, in fact, result in pleasure. He would have recognised the existence of a direct desire for pleasure if a man had fasted deliberately in order to make his hunger more acute and thus cause the pleasure resulting from the satisfaction of his hunger to be more intense; but Butler held that the majority of human actions are in fact caused by the desire for certain things or conditions and not by desire for the pleasure which results from attaining these things or conditions.

There is, in short, an important distinction between the desire for pleasure and the desire for things or conditions which cause pleasure when attained; and it is now generally agreed that pleasure is not usually the direct object of desire, although it is a normal concomitant of the satisfaction of desire. But the recognition of this distinction does not mean that Bentham's theory is invalidated at its foundation.

For if it is admitted-as most psychologists would admit-that the satisfaction of desire is pleasant, then, even if pleasure is not usually the direct object of action, it is possible to make the pleasure which results from successful action and the pain which results from frustrated action serve equally well as criteria of moral conduct. It is no longer possible to say with Bentham that pleasure and pain always determine what we shall do, but it is still possible to make the pleasure or pain which results from an action the criterion by which the rightness or wrongness of that action is judged.

In any case, Bentham's principle of ethical hedonism-that all action ought to conform to the principle of utility-suggests that some actions do not conform to this principle and that the essence of moral conduct is to achieve this conformity; and it is this principle of ethical hedonism that is the really fundamental one in his system. Like Hobbes, who defined 'good' as 'the object of desire' and 'evil' as 'the object of aversion, Bentham defines the basic moral conceptions in terms of non-moral conceptions?

'Of an action that is conformable to the principle of utility one may always say either that it is one that ought to be done, or at least that it is not one that ought not to be done. One may also say that it is right it should be done; at least that it is not wrong it should be done: that it is a right action; at least that it is not a wrong action. When thus interpreted, the words *ought, and right and wrong,* and others of that stamp have a meaning: when otherwise, they have none.'

In other words, Bentham believes that to say that an action is 'right' means that it conforms to the principle of utility, i.e. augments (or at least does not diminish) the happiness of the party whose interest is in question; while when an action is said to be wrong this means that it does not conform to the principle of utility, i.e. diminishes the happiness of the party whose interest is in question. More shortly, a right action is, roughly speaking, one which increases or does not diminish happiness while a wrong action is one which diminishes happiness. Bentham admits that such an interpretation of the meaning of ethical terms may not appear to be consistent with the common usage of these terms, but he argues that this interpretation is the only possible one if moral terms are to have an objective significance. Only when morality is defined in terms of utility does it amount to more than the 'averment of unfounded sentiments'.

Bentham is here repudiating all claims that moral judgements express *a priori* knowledge and arguing that they are in fact empirical judgements of utility which must be verified by the scientific tests of observation and experiment. Morality, he contends, is a science, and its judgements are therefore subject to the usual criteria of the natural sciences. The contrary assumption that moral judgements are *a priory* judgements leads in practice to all sorts of inconsistent judgements being made without hope of reconciliation, and to all sorts of claims that certain practices are justified in the name of 'natural rights' or 'natural law'. And Bentham thinks that 'natural law' is just a name for irrational prejudice. His object is to replace it by the principle of utility and thus provide an empirical basis for human conduct and its reward or punishment.

In all this Bentham was rebelling against the prejudices and superstitions which he found embedded in the law and morality of his time. Both appeared to him to be irrational in origin; and his contention was that they would remain so until they became applications of the principle of utility. Law, in particular, would remain an incoherent collection of arbitrary conventions until it was subordinated to the ultimate purpose of promoting the greatest happiness of the greatest number.

15.8 PLEASURE AND PAIN

Bentham realised that it may frequently be difficult to calculate the quantity of pleasure or pain which will result from an act, but he argued that there is no insurmountable difficulty of principle in doing so, whereas there is no rational way whatsoever of ascertaining whether an act or law is right or wrong if 'right' and 'wrong' are not defined in terms of the resulting Pleasure or pain. And he thinks that the calculation of the quantity of pleasure or pain resulting from an act is sufficiently accurate to constitute a useful measure of that act's rightness of wrongness provided that account is taken of four respects in which pleasures and pains may vary, namely their:

(i) Intensity;

(ii) Duration;

(iii) Certainty or uncertainty; and

(iv) Propinquity or remoteness.

Bentham thinks that in measuring the utility of an act account must also be taken of the fecundity of the pleasure or pain in which it results, i.e. the chance which it has of being followed by sensations of the same kind; and its *purity,* i.e. the chance which it has of *not* being followed by sensations of the opposite kind. But all these characteristics are, Bentham thinks, essentially quantitative.

The qualitative distinction sometimes drawn between 'higher' and 'lower' pleasures is, in Bentham's view, quite irrelevant to the calculus of pleasures and the objective theory of morality which he is advancing. As he puts it succinctly, 'Quantity of pleasure being equal, pushpin is as good as poetry.' It is the balance of pleasure or pain resulting from an act which, Bentham thinks, is alone relevant to the determination of its rightness or wrongness.

Bentham does not suggest that an elaborate calculation of consequences must be made before every moral judgement or legislative or judicial operation; the rightness or wrongness of many acts is generally accepted in terms of their known pleasurable or painful consequences. What he thinks is important is that the calculus of pleasures, and not some arbitrary conception of 'moral law', should be appealed to when the rightness or wrongness of an act or law is in dispute.

For the same reason it is not any underlying 'moral' law which gives a binding force to the laws of a community. The latter are upheld by *sanctions,* by which Bentham means inducements to obey the laws or deterrents against disobeying them. Such sanctions must, he naturally thinks, be based on the only two motives for action which he recognises - pleasure and pain. For the only possible motives which, according to Bentham's psychology, can help to promote respect for these laws is the expectation of pleasure if they are obeyed and the fear of pain if they are disobeyed.

Such rewards and punishments Bentham calls sanctions, and he thinks that they may take either a physical or a political or a popular or a religious form according as the anticipated pleasure or pain would result from the operation of natural laws, or from judicial punishment, or from another individual's spontaneous reaction, or from the action of a superior invisible being. In other words, people are less likely to do something if they believe that this will bring them pain from one or other of these sources, and they are more likely to do something if they believe that by so doing they will be rewarded by pleasure from one or other of these sources.

15.9 THEORY OF PUNISHMENT

A punishment is obviously a familiar example of a sanction as conceived by Bentham, and, like sanctions generally, can be justified only by the principle of utility if the latter is accepted as the basis of morality. In particular, since punishment involves the infliction of pain it can be justified only if it prevents the occurrence of a greater pain. As Bentham expresses the point:

All punishment in itself is evil. Upon the principle of utility, if it ought at all to be admitted, it ought only to be admitted in as far as it promises to exclude some greater evil.

Bentham therefore rejects the theory that punishment ought to be retributive, i.e. that its justification lies in the moral propriety of making the sinner or criminal suffer on account of his sin or crime. In primitive societies this has always been the primary, if not the only, justification of punishment, whether or not it has also been held to have useful consequences in preventing the repetition of crime.

The so-called Retributive Theory of Punishment is therefore essentially a moral theory in its contention that a sinner or criminal deserves to suffer, and therefore ought to suffer, on account of his sin or crime. Bentham's fundamental objection to this theory of punishment is the same as his fundamental objection to conventional morality in general-that it is arbitrary and irrational without either objective basis or internal consistency.

Some may believe that a certain crime ought to be punished by flogging; others that it ought to be punished by five years' imprisonment; still others that a sentence of six months' imprisonment would be adequate; and Bentham believes that there is no possible way of justifying any of these arbitrary judgements until the purpose of punishment is defined in terms of utility, and the infliction of punishment therefore determined in accordance with the ultimate object of promoting the greatest happiness of the greatest number. Thus he concludes that the conception of punishment as retributive must be completely abandoned if any rational justification of its infliction is to be given, and that a new conception of punishment as a method of preventing the occurrence of a greater evil, i.e. more pain than is involved in the punishment itself, must be substituted.

Bentham works out the application of this principle in great detail. He lists the various kinds of pleasures and pains which may be experienced and thirty-two kinds of 'circumstances affecting sensibility" which must be taken account of if the effect of punishment is to be accurately estimated. No summary could give an adequate impression of the thoroughness with which Bentham works out this application of his principle of utility.

15.10 ASSESSMENT OF BENTHAM'S THEORY

To the therapeutic philosopher the question of primary interest is whether, in fact, utility is the only rational basis for conduct.

Certainly Bentham's argument that the judgements of ordinary morality are subjective and arbitrary is difficult to refute. But if it be admitted that the approbation or disapprobation of an act can be rational only if it is based on an estimate of the probable effects on happiness, the question arises whether such approbation or disapprobation does not depend upon the acceptance of an ultimate moral judgement, not based on the principle of utility, about the goodness or badness of the consequences.

It is by no means clear whether Bentham is, in fact, assuming the truth of an ultimate synthetic judgement that 'pleasure is good', or whether he holds that this judgement is analytic, i.e. that by calling a thing 'good' we simply *mean* that it is pleasant. If he held that the judgement is analytic then he was, by implication, reducing morality to the science of happiness, and judgements of approbation and disapprobation to scientific calculations about the probable consequences of actions.

But if he held that the judgement is synthetic he was retaining an irreducible element of morality in his analysis of experience and transferring to the judgements about the goodness and badness of ends all the arbitrary and subjective characteristics which he tried to remove from judgements about the rightness or wrongness of means. In other words, the judgement that a certain act is right may be verified objectively if by calling it 'right' we simply mean that it will increase human happiness; but there can be no genuinely moral sense in which *one ought* to do what is in this sense right unless it be assumed that human happiness is good in a genuinely moral sense. If this assumption is not made there can be no categorical reason why one ought to do anything, but only the hypothetical reason that one ought to do certain things *if* one wishes to promote happiness.

The conclusion to which Bentham's theory points-although he does not himself draw it-is that action can, indeed, only be justified by its consequences; but that these consequences cannot, in the end, themselves be rationally justified. The immediate consequences of an act may, of course, be justified as necessary means to the ultimate consequences which are aimed at. Preparing for war, for example, may be justified as a necessary means (if in certain circumstances it is a necessary means) to the preservation of peace. But there is no method by which, on Bentham's theory, the ultimate ends of action can be justified. They must be chosen, and the choice of ultimate ends is not a rational act.

The conclusion which Bentham could have drawn from these considerations, and which Mill did, perhaps unconsciously, draw, is that since the choice of ultimate ends cannot be rationally justified it cannot be rationally condemned either; that individuals should therefore be left free to choose their ends in so far as this freedom does not restrict the enjoyment of a similar freedom by others. This, of course, has become the basic assumption of political democracy.

If the people desire a society based upon free enterprise, then, according to democratic theory, they ought to get it; but if they desire a society based upon central planning and control, then they ought to get that. If, as often happens, they disagree about what they desire, then the will of the majority must prevail, as it represents what Locke called the 'greater force'. These are obviously the broad assumptions upon which a democratic society is based, and they all follow from the assumption that the ultimate ends of desire and action cannot be rationally justified and that action can be rational only in the sense that it is likely, in the light of scientific generations based upon previous experience, to promote the ends which are in fact desired.

It may be thought that Bentham's theory oversimplifies the ends of action in describing them as simply 'benefit, advantage, pleasure, good, or happiness' (all of which, as he says, 'comes to the same thing'). In so far as his theory is a psychological theory - as it is when he says that pleasure and pain alone 'determine what we shall do' - this criticism is justified. For it is a common observation that men desire many things besides pleasure, and that the attainment of some of the things which they desire does not bring them pleasure.

But as a philosopher Bentham is concerned not with what men actually desire but with what it would be rational for them to desire and the underlying assumption of his theory seems to be that it is rational to desire the things which satisfy desire, i.e. result in satisfaction or happiness. In other words, for the common moral distinction between what men desire and what men ought to desire Bentham substitutes the distinction between what they desire and what they would desire if they correctly estimated the consequences in terms of pleasure.

The difference between his analysis and that of many modern psychologists is that he asserts that pleasure and pain are always the objects of actual, as well as of rational, desire; whereas this seems plainly not to be the case.

It may be true that the only rational answer to the question 'Why do you desire to realise X?' is 'Because the realisation of X would be pleasant', and that the realisation of ends which do not cause pleasure does not satisfy desire; but that does not imply that people are incapable of desiring changes' which do not, in point of fact, prove to be pleasant. It does not, therefore, appear that Bentham was justified in saying that pleasure and pain alone 'determine what we shall do', although they may alone determine what it is rational for us to do. I.e. in Bentham's sense we 'ought' to do.

Pleasure and pain are the effects of certain conditions or changes, and it appears to be psychologically true that these conditions or changes are frequently the direct objects of desire, and that it is only at the reflective level, when an attempt is made to distinguish rational desires from actual desires, that it may be true to say that the object of every rational desire is pleasure. Bentham's principle of utility is simply recognition of the fact that the only objects which it is rational to desire for their own sake are the things which bring happiness, since desire is satisfied only when its fulfilment brings happiness.

These general principles can be illustrated by the following example. A shipwrecked family without supplies of fresh water may, as a matter of psychological fact, desire intensely to drink salty water; but past experience has shown that to do so would greatly aggravate their thirst, and that the realisation of this desire would therefore not bring happiness. It would therefore be irrational for them to drink salty water and if they behave rationally they will not do so. In other words the *immediate* object of desire may be distinguished from the *ultimate* object of desire, which is to increase pleasure and diminish pain. Action can therefore be defined as 'rational' when it takes the form which, in the light of scientific generalisations based on past experience, appears most likely to increase pleasure and reduce pain.

15.11 MILL'S UTILITARIAN PRINCIPLE

Mill's Utilitarian Theory is less consistent than Bentham's. Bentham recognised that if pleasure and pain alone determine what we ought to do, the source or quality of the pleasure is irrelevant to the determination of the rightness or wrongness of an act-that, as he put it, 'quantity of pleasure being equal, pushpin is as good as poetry'. But Mill rejected this doctrine. To him it appeared that some pleasures are 'higher', and therefore better, than others, even if, as pleasures, they are equal:

'It would be absurd that while, in estimating all other things, quality is considered as well as quantity, the estimation of pleasures should be supposed to depend upon quantity alone.'

It is clear from the examples which Mill gives to illustrate this principle that what he calls the 'quality' of a pleasure depends upon its source. This, however, is inconsistent with the principle of utility, which states that the quantity of pleasure in which an act results, and that alone, is the measure of its rightness. It is still clearer that Mill is, in effect, rejecting the principle of utility altogether when he asserts that some states of positive *dissatisfaction* are better than other states of satisfaction:

It is better to be a human being dissatisfied than a pig satisfied; better to be Socrates dissatisfied than a fool satisfied. If the fool or the pig is of a different opinion, it is because they only know their own side of the question. The other party to the comparison knows both sides.

It is obvious that if in certain circumstances it is better to be dissatisfied than to be satisfied, the principle of utility has been abandoned altogether and some new quality, quite distinct from the pleasantness of the situation, is being accepted as the moral criterion. The fact is that Mill was very conscious of the extent to which Bentham's utilitarian theory appeared to conflict with the austere morality of the Victorian Age, and he was anxious to effect a compromise which would reconcile them. But in making this attempt he abandoned the principle of utility, and returned in some measure to accept moral dogmas of the sort which Bentham had attempted to eliminate.

Apart from this attempted compromise with the outlook of contemporary morality, Mill's definition of the principle of utility is far from clear in view of the use which he makes of the word 'desirable':

Pleasure, and freedom from pain, are the only things desirable as ends; and ... all desirable things (which are as numerous in the utilitarian as in any other scheme) are desirable either for the pleasure inherent in themselves, or as means to the promotion of pleasure and the prevention of pain.'

For it is clear, when Mill goes on to offer an alleged proof of this principle, that he is using the word 'desirable' in two distinct senses. Thus he says:

'The only proof capable of being given is that an object is visible, is that people actually see it. The only proof that a sound is audible is that people hear it: and so of the other sources of our experience. In like manner, I apprehend, the sole evidence it is possible to produce that anything is desirable, is that people do actually desire it. . . . No reason can be given why the general happiness is desirable, except that each person, so far as he believes it to be attainable, desires his own happiness'.

This argument is vitiated by the ambiguous use of the word 'desirable', which may mean either 'capable of' or 'worthy of' being desired. The fact that people actually see an object proves that it is visible in the sense of 'capable of being seen'; and the fact that people hear a sound proves that it is audible in the sense of 'capable of being heard'. Similarly, the fact-if it be a fact that people desire happiness proves that happiness is desirable in the sense of 'capable of being desired'.

But it does not prove that happiness *ought* to be desired in any genuinely moral sense. The only proposition of practical importance which Mill could have 'validly inferred from the fact (if it be a fact) that everyone desires his own happiness is that everyone. ought (in the *rational* sense of 'ought') to desire the things which bring him happiness; but it does not follow from this that anyone would be acting wrongly, although he would be acting irrationally, if he sought the things which did not bring him happiness.

Having proven, to his satisfaction, that everyone desires happiness, Mill next tries to prove that nobody ultimately desires anything else, although, as he admits, 'it is palpable that they do desire things which, in common language, are decidedly distinguished from happiness. They desire, for example, virtue, and the absence of vice, no less really than pleasure and the absence of pain." But this consideration does not, in Mill's view, contradict the principle of utility:

'The principle of utility does not mean that any given pleasure, as music, for instance, or any given exemption from pain, as, for example, health, is to be looked upon as means to a collective something termed happiness, and to be desired on that account. They are desired and desirable in and for themselves; besides being means, they are a part of the end. Virtue, according to the utilitarian doctrine, is not naturally and originally part of the end, but it is capable of becoming so; and in those who love it disinterestedly it has become so, and is desired and cherished, not as a means to happiness, but as a part of their happiness.'

It is difficult to reconcile the foregoing argument with Mill's earlier statement that 'all desirable things - are desirable either for the pleasure inherent in them, or as means to the promotion of pleasure and the prevention of pain'. It may be psychologically true that virtue comes to be desired because it promotes happiness, but that does not make virtue part of happiness. What Mill is primarily concerned to establish is not a psychological theory about what people do desire but a philosophical theory about what it is rational for them to desire or (as he says) about what is desirable, namely the theory that 'pleasure, and freedom from pain, are the only things desirable as ends'.

Such a theory implies that, although people may actually desire other things, such as virtue or power or fame, these things are validly inferred from the fact (if it be a fact) that everyone desires his own happiness is that everyone ought (in the *rational* sense of 'ought') to desire the things which bring him happiness; but it does not follow from this that anyone would be acting wrongly, although he would be acting irrationally, if he sought the things which did not bring him happiness.

Having proved, to his satisfaction, that everyone desires happiness, Mill next tries to prove that nobody ultimately desires anything else, although, as he admits, 'it is palpable that they do desire things which, in common language, are decidedly distinguished from happiness. They desire, for example, virtue, and the absence of vice, no less really than pleasure and the absence of pain."

The principle of utility does not mean that any given pleasure, as music, for instance, or any given exemption from pain, as, for example, health, is to be looked upon as means to a collective something termed happiness, and to be desired on that account. They are desired and desirable in and for themselves; besides being means, they are a part of the end. Virtue, according to the utilitarian doctrine, is not naturally and originally part of the end, but it is capable of becoming so; and in those who love it disinterestedly it has become so, and is desired and cherished, not as a means to happiness, but as a part of their happiness.

It is difficult to reconcile the foregoing argument with Mill's earlier statement that 'all desirable things ... are desirable either for the pleasure inherent in themselves or as means to the promotion of pleasure and the prevention of pain'., It may be psychologically true that virtue comes to be desired because it promotes happiness, but that does not make virtue part of happiness. What Mill is primarily concerned to establish is not a psychological theory about what people do desire but a philosophical theory about what it is rational for them to desire or (as he says) about what is desirable, namely the theory that 'pleasure, and freedom from pain, are the only things desirable as ends'. Such a theory implies that, although people may actually desire other things, such as virtue or power or fame, these things are desirable only if, and in so far as, they promote happiness. To hold that they are desirable in themselves is to abandon the principle of utility.

The truth is that Mill's application of the principle of utility was less disinterested than Bentham's. To Bentham it was a standard by which the assumptions of conventional morality could be criticised and corrected; but Mill regarded it more as a principle which justified these assumptions and made clear their rational character. It is not therefore surprising that Mill's account of the principle is less consistent than Bentham's. For the principle of utility is, from its very nature, a potential challenge to conventional morality.

It repudiates all claims to the *a priori* certainty of moral judgements and assesses their truth by the empirical test of utility. It implies that whether an act is right or wrong never depends upon a 'knowledge' of right or wrong but only upon the tendency of that act to 'augment or diminish the happiness of the party whose interest is in question'.' Thus Mill's account of the principle of utility adds nothing of value to Bentham's more consistent exposition; on the contrary, it greatly obscures the meaning and significance of the principle by attempting to reconcile it at all costs with the assumptions of conventional morality.

15.12 MILL'S WORK 'ON LIBERTY'

It is in Mill's essay *On Liberty* that his most important and consistent contribution to the philosophy of individualism is to be found. For it is here that he draws some of the true implications of the principle of utility. These implications all follow, in the end, from the consideration that if happiness is the supreme good, and if happiness is found by different people in different ways, then in order to maximise happiness everyone must be left free to realise his desires as fully as possible so long as this freedom does not interfere with the enjoyment of a similar freedom by others. As Mill puts it:

'The object of this Essay is to assert one very simple principle ... that the sole end for which mankind are warranted, individually or collectively, in interfering with the liberty of action of any of their number, is self-protection'.

That the only purpose for which power can be rightfully exercised over any member of a civilised community, against his will, is to prevent harm to others. His own good, either physical or moral, is not a sufficient warrant. He cannot rightfully be compelled to do or forbear because it will be better for him to do so, because it will make him happier, because, in the opinions of others, to do so would be wise, or even right. Those are good reasons for remonstrating with him, or reasoning with him, or persuading him, or entreating him, but not for compelling him, or visiting him with any evil in case he do otherwise. To justify that, the conduct from which it is desired to deter him must be calculated to produce evil to someone else. A later passage in which the same point is emphasised is also worth quoting:

'The only freedom which deserves the name, is that of pursuing our own good in our own way, so long as we do not attempt to deprive others of theirs, or impede their efforts to obtain it. . . Mankind are greater gainers by suffering each other to live as seems good to themselves, than by compelling each to live as seems good to the rest.'

These passages set forth the essential features of Mill's defence of individual liberty, and show that he bases this doctrine on the utilitarian principle that happiness is the measure of goodness, and that action must therefore be justified or condemned by its tendency to increase or diminish the happiness of individuals. He emphasises that interference with individual liberty may result not only from the action of a tyrannical minority but also from the action of a government expressing the will of the majority. The 'tyranny of the majority' may, he thinks, be just as inimical to individual liberty as the tyranny exercised by a minority government maintaining itself by brute force, if the majority employ their weight of numbers to suppress the freedom of the individual. As he argues in a well known passage:

If all mankind minus one were of one opinion, and only one person were of the contrary opinion, mankind would be no more justified in silencing that one person, than he, if he had the power, would be justified in silencing mankind. Were an opinion a personal possession of no value except to the owner; if to be obstructed in the enjoyment of it were simply a private injury, it would make some difference whether the injury was inflicted only on a few persons or on many.

But the peculiar evil of silencing the expression of an opinion is that it is robbing the human race; posterity as well as the existing generation; those who dissent from the opinion, still more than those who hold it. If the opinion is right, they are deprived of the opportunity of exchanging error for truth: if wrong, they lose, what is almost as great a benefit, the clearer perception and livelier impression of truth, produced by its collision with error.'

Mill later sums up the case for toleration in two succinct sentences: 'All silencing of discussion is an assumption of infallibility' and 'The usefulness of an opinion is itself matter of opinion'. In short, however much the opinion and will of the majority must be followed because of their greater influence, it must never be forgotten that the majority is a majority of *individuals,* and that for the majority to suppress the opinions of the minority is to challenge the very foundation upon which majority rule is itself ultimately based.

It is clear that in these passages Mill is defining the basic assumptions upon which modern democracy is based. For the essence of such democracy is not the uncompromising application of the will of the majority but the insistence that this will, must be determined by the free expression of the wills of individuals, and must tolerate and recognise minority wills which diverge from the general consensus of desire.

It is for this reason that democracies sometimes tolerate the expression and propagation of opinions which, if generally accepted, might destroy democracy itself. In Britain, for example, Fascists and Communists have generally been accorded the same freedom of speech and political association as the parties which accept the democratic principle of toleration; and any special discrimination which has been exercised against them - such as the 18B Regulation during the Second World War and the more past restrictions on the employment of Communists in the Civil Service-has been regarded with considerable misgiving by many who were not affected by it.

It might, of course, be argued that a democracy has no obligation to tolerate those who are themselves intolerant of criticism and opposition, but democratic opinion in Britain at least has generally preferred to accord them the normal measure of toleration in the belief that the opinions and desires of individuals constitute the only standard by which the form and purpose of government ought to be determined.

Mill's plea for toleration was based on the belief that no one is infallible, and that all opinions-at least on matters of morals are liable to error. He did not, like Hume, raise the more fundamental question whether opinions on moral matters are subject to the criterion of truth and falsity at all. His language suggests that he believed that moral judgements are objectively true or false, but that men's minds are incapable of judging with certainty whether they are true or false.

But Hume would, of course, have said that such judgements do not describe an objective act or object but a subjective feeling; that they describe what people feel about certain acts or objects, and not how those acts or objects are characterised. If accepted, this analysis would clearly strengthen Mill's defence of individual liberty, for it would imply that the ultimate motives of action are desires; and that there is no rational ground for suppressing one desire in favour of another. On this analysis the problem which reason can help to solve is that of facilitating the maximum gratification of the maximum number of desires; and that is just an alternative way of describing the utilitarian ideal of the 'greatest happiness of the greatest number'.

15.13 UTILITARIANISM AND DEMOCRACY

Thus Bentham's theory of Utilitarianism and Mill's theory of Liberty together define the essential principles upon which liberal democracy is based. For the latter is a form of government under which, the policy is ultimately determined by the free expression of the individual's will. It is the antithesis of forms of government in which the will of the individual is held to be less real or less true than the will of a group of individuals, whether or not they are held to constitute an organic whole. On the democratic analysis the individual man or woman is the fundamental unit, and the expression of the individual's will is the ultimate force which, when combined with the expression of the wills of others, must determine policy.

Such an analysis clearly implies, although the implication is not always recognised, that there is no impersonal standard of morality to which the action of men or governments ought to conform.

Moral standards are created by groups of individuals, and while in practice it is necessary to determine policy in accordance with what Locke called the 'greater force' of the majority, the freedom of self-expression permitted to individuals or minorities who disagree with the majority is an implicit recognition that the will of the majority prevails only because it is the will of a majority, and not because it is in any objective sense 'right'. If the will of the majority were, in an objective sense, right or true, there would be no justification for tolerating opinions and movements constituting a potential challenge to it.

These are the general Principles embodied in the theories of Bentham and Mill, although neither philosopher fully appreciated their significance. The real meaning of Bentham's principle of utility is that there is no independent criterion of morality, that what brings happiness to an individual is right-in so far as it does not diminish the happiness of other individuals more-and that rightness and wrongness can be defined in terms of individual desire and happiness.

This, in turn, implies that there is no way of proving, on *a priori* grounds, that some forms of satisfaction are good and that others are bad; they are all good in so far as they promote happiness and do not diminish it; and the desire of the individual is therefore the ultimate criterion of morality and the ultimate justification of government. The problem of government is not, according to the Utilitarian Theory, to determine what ought to be desired-for the latter is a confused and misleading expression without objective significance-but to determine how the maximum number of desires can be most fully satisfied; and the complex machinery of government can be justified, in the end, only by its efficiency in realising this general aim.

Mill's plea for liberty of speech, thought and action is, as already observed, a direct implication of the utilitarian principle. For if the satisfaction of individual desires is the criterion of virtue and the justification of government, it follows that anything which diminishes such satisfaction must be condemned except where it is necessary to promote the maximum satisfaction on the whole.

If the satisfaction of individual desire is prevented for any other reason, the individualist basis of government is being abandoned and the way opened for government based upon force, exercised either arbitrarily or in the name of some alleged moral principle. To the utilitarian all such attempts to found government on moral law are attempts to base it on a foundation which cannot be rationally justified and are bound to conflict with the rational aim of maximising happiness, except where the moral law is itself an expression of the principle of utility.

16 KARL MARX

16.1 MARXISM, AN APPROACH TO SOCIAL PHILOSOPHY

Heinrich Karl Marx (18I8-1883) was born at Treves in Rhenish Prussia, the son of a Jewish lawyer. He was educated at the local High Grammar School, and at the Universities of Bonn and Berlin. It was at Berlin that he became closely associated with the young Hegelians and began to work out his adaptation of the Hegelian dialectic to a materialist theory of human society. Marx had originally hoped to teach at the University of Bonn, but his extreme political views made him unacceptable there, and he joined a radical newspaper, the *Rheinishe Zeitung,* becoming one of its editors in 1842.

It was, however, suppressed in 1843. He then went to Paris, where he met his future friend and collaborator, Friedrich Engels (1820 - 1895). Engels was the son of a rich cotton spinner, who owned a factory near Manchester, and he was thus able to make a close study of the English industrial system. His observations led him to conclusions very similar to those of Marx, and the two collaborated closely after their first meeting in 1844.

Marx's writings were soon viewed with disfavour by the authorities in Paris, and he went to Brussels, where Engels joined him. Both participated actively in the socialist working class movement and collaborated in the writing of the *Manifesto of the Communist Party,* which was published early in 1848. It had hardly appeared when the revolution of that year broke out in France.

Marx hoped and expected that this would be followed by a revolution in Germany, and he went with Engels to Cologne. There they founded a new daily paper to encourage revolutionary measures, and when the King of Prussia dissolved the National Assembly later in the year Marx and his associates advocated the non-payment of taxes and armed resistance to the King. Marx was subsequently acquitted at a trial for high treason, but was expelled from Germany in 1849. After a short stay in France he went to England, where he remained for the rest of his life.

Marx was a voluminous writer, and it is impracticable in a single chapter to do justice to all his works. But a general conception of his theory can be derived from his two most famous publications. One is the *Manifesto of the Communist Party,* originally published in February 1848, and reissued in Britain in 1948 on the occasion of its centenary with a new appreciation by the late Professor H. J. Laski. Its importance was rightly emphasised by Professor Laski in the following words:

It is admitted by every serious student of society to be one of the outstanding political documents of all time; in the influence it has exerted it compares with the American Declaration of Independence of 1776, and the French Declaration of Rights Of 1789. Its character is unique, not only because of the power with which it is written. But also because of the immense scope it covers in its intense brevity. It is a philosophy of history, a critical analysis of socialist doctrines and a passionate call to revolutionary action.'

The other book is the famous *Capital,* which develops in detail the economic theory briefly referred to in the *Manifesto.* The first volume of the *Capital* was published in 1867: the other two, which Marx had not completed when he died, were published posthumously.

16.2 DIALECTICAL MATERIALISM

The philosophy of Marx was largely inspired by Hegel's dialectical idealism. Marx agreed with Hegel that reality is a dialectical process, but differed in holding that this process is of a material, and not a logical, character. Hence Marx's philosophy is often referred to as dialectical materialism.

It is called materialism because Marx held that the dialectical process is a process, not of thought, but, of the material reality which thought reflects. Hegel was an idealist because he believed that thought is the fundamental reality, that there is no 'external' reality to which thought corresponds, and that the criterion of truth must therefore be found in the coherence of thoughts and not in their correspondence to 'things'.

Marx was a materialist in the sense that he repudiated this doctrine of the primacy of thought and believed that the nature of thought is determined by the material reality of which it is the reflection. By calling this reality 'material' he did not mean that it is 'physical' as distinct from 'mental'. His material reality embodies the whole universe of so-caned 'physical' and 'mental' processes, and the object of calling it material is to emphasise that it is that to which thought must correspond if it is to be valid. Thus Mm's theory is not a theory of physical determinism in the narrow sense, but a theory according to which the physical and mental interact in accordance with laws which must be empirically discovered.

The use of the word 'dialectical' to describe Marx's materialism suggests that the evolution of the material process is necessary, just as, according to Hegel, the dialectical evolution of thought is necessary.

Some of Marx's interpreters have taken this view. Thus Professor Sabine says that 'the question is whether dialectic, either idealist or materialist, can avoid Hume's proof that all necessity is merely conditional, and all value merely a relation to human propensities'. But there are two objections to this interpretation of Marx's theory. In the first place, Hegel failed to show that synthetic thinking can ever possess logical necessity, or therefore that dialectical thinking, which is synthetic thinking, can be logically necessary. Secondly, even if synthetic thinking were logically necessary it would not follow that a material process-which is not a logical process at all-could possess the essentially logical characteristic of necessity.

If Marx is a materialist he cannot consistently attribute necessity to the material process which, on his theory, constitutes reality. As materials process it is a process whose laws-if it conforms to laws-must be wholly empirical and devoid of any logical necessity. If the word 'dialectical' is used to describe the progress of its evolution it must be recognised that this does not imply that there is any necessity in the evolution so described.

So interpreted, Marx's theory is not a challenge to Hume's Empiricism but an expression of it. Like Hume, Marx is saying that no judgement claiming to be about the real world-no scientific or moral or religious judgement-has any logical necessity, and that the truth of such judgements depends on their correspondence to observable parts of the material process.

For Marx, as for Hume, necessity can characterise only analytic judgements and from these nothing can be deduced about the characteristics of the real world. Marx, however, has little interest in analytic judgements-except the fundamental one that reality is a material process-for such judgements do not, in his view, contribute anything to the shaping of history or the understanding of its laws. His object, as he once expressed it, was not to interpret the world (i.e. in the *a priori* sense) but to change it.

Thus for Marx it is science, and science alone, which can extend man's understanding of the real world. Other alleged sources of knowledge, such as religion and philosophy, are of no importance except in so far as they influence action, and provide data for scientific generalisations about action. Thus the religious belief in the existence of a Divine Being is, on Marx's view, without foundation or significance except in so far as it has a practical effect on the actions and reactions of those who accept it, or unless there is some scientific evidence for its truth. Similarly, moral convictions are without objective validity because there is no scientific way of demonstrating their truth.

There is no evidence by which the belief that 'X is right' may be verified or refuted: the fact that A believes that 'X is right' is not evidence that X is right but only that A believes that X is right. Thus all that the scientist can do in the field of morality is to discover what moral beliefs different people or groups of people hold and to ascertain whether there are general laws describing the causes and consequences of these beliefs. But these general laws, like all scientific laws, will be purely empirical and devoid of any rational necessity.

The implications of Marx's theory for philosophy are similar. He would have been in full agreement with modern Logical Positivists in denying the 'possibility of metaphysics'. That is to say, he would have denied that metaphysical generalisations about the universe claiming *a priori,* as distinct from scientific, validity can ever have objective significance.

For such generalisations are synthetic propositions and synthetic propositions can never be *a priori.* They can be justified only by experience, and there is no experience which can confirm or refute a metaphysical proposition. If a proposition can be confirmed or refuted by experience it must be a scientific, not a metaphysical, proposition. On the other hand, Marx would probably have raised no objection to the positivist's conception of philosophy as the study of the logical relationship of propositions, since these relationships are independent of actual experience and apply to experience only in a hypothetical sense.

If the foregoing interpretation of Marx's 'materialism' is correct the word 'dialectical', when applied to his theory, must simply mean 'causal' in the purely empirical sense. The purpose of using the word 'dialectical' is to emphasise that the causal process is one of *interaction* between what are usually referred to as the 'material' and 'mental' spheres, so that material conditions modify mental conditions, and mental conditions in turn react on material conditions.

But on the materialist hypothesis all such action and reaction is, of course, purely empirical. There is no *a priori* necessity in it, and it is for the scientist-the social scientist-to discover the empirical laws to which social evolution conforms. The main difficulty which confronts him in doing so is the obvious one that he himself participates in the social process which he is trying to describe, and may therefore find it difficult to take the detached view which is essential if his description is to be accurate.

Thus the fundamental difference between the theories of Hegel and Marx is that on Hegel's theory reality is a logical system while on Marx's theory it is a causal system, i.e. a system which develops in accordance with laws of a purely empirical character. To Hegel dialectical logic is the key to truth while to Marx the scientific method is the only one by which knowledge of the real world can be established.

Thus Marx's theory is, strictly speaking, not a philosophical but a scientific theory. Its only philosophical implication is that philosophy (except in the purely analytic sense) is impossible, and that science provides the key, and the only key, to the understanding of both nature and man-including the various moral and philosophical systems in which man has from time to time believed.

The validity of Marx's theory must therefore be judged by the criteria of science and, in particular, by its success in describing the facts of social and political evolution. It attempts to do so by the hypothesis that these facts are determined by economic relationships, and consideration must now be given to the basic principles of Marx's economic theory.

16.3 MARX'S ECONOMIC THEORY

Marx's economic theory is a development of the 'Labour Theory of Value' which was originally formulated by Locke and popularised by the economic writers of the early nineteenth century. Locke expressed the basic principle of the theory as follows:

Whatsoever, then, he [a man] removes out of the state that Nature hath provided and left it in, he bath mixed his labour with it, and joined to it something that is his own, and thereby makes it his property. It being by him removed from the common state Nature placed it in, it bath by this labour something annexed to it that excludes the common right of other men. For this 'labour' being the unquestionable property of the labourer, no man but he can have a right to what that is once joined to, at least where there is enough, and as good left in common for others.'

In short, by working on the raw materials of nature a man adds something to them which is unquestionably his own, and thus makes the finished product his personal property. It is also, Locke thinks, this labour which creates the greater part of the product's value:

If we will rightly estimate things as they come to our use, and cast up the several expenses about them-what in them is purely owing to Nature and what to labour-we shall find that in most of them ninety-nine hundredths are wholly to be put on the account of labour.

This was the principle which was accepted and developed by the early nineteenth century economists, who saw in a system of private enterprise, free from government interference and control, the most elective way of ensuring that every man received the proper return for his labour. The main qualification, which they introduced arose from reflection on the facts of exchange and from the observation that the prices at which goods are actually exchanged are determined by factors other than the labour which has contributed to the production.

Of these additional factors the most obvious are demand and monopoly. The price at which something can be purchased may be greatly increased both by an increased demand and by a monopoly of supply, but there are advantages in distinguishing that part of the price due to the labour expended in producing the article in question. Adam Smith called this part of the price the *natural* value, Macculloch called it the *real cost,* and Marx called it the *exchange value,* although he recognised that it is not the value at which goods usually exchange in existing societies.

In spite of his pretensions, however, Marx's economic theory is not purely scientific. A purely scientific economic theory would attempt to discover how economic value is determined and influenced. An examination of this sort would show that several factors besides the amount of labour expended in producing a manufactured article contribute to the determination of the price at which it is exchanged. But Marx, like many other economists, had a moral as well as a scientific object in view.

He was anxious to show not only how price is determined, but also how it ought to be determined, and his view, briefly stated, is that goods ought to be exchanged at their 'exchange value'. For only if this is done will the labourer receive a fair return for his labour, and each labourer own the wealth to which his labour entitles him. He may not, of course, retain the actual goods 'which his own work has produced, but he should, if he exchanges them, obtain an equivalent value of other goods in their place.

In thus arguing Marx is, of course, developing, in the light of the facts of exchange, the fundamental principle of Locke's theory-that the labourer creates value by working on his raw material, and that he has a right to the possession of the value so created. Marx is simply adding that, in a more advanced society where manufactured goods are exchanged, the labourer who sells the product of his labour should obtain in exchange something upon which an equivalent quantity of labour has been expended.

The Labour Theory of Value is, therefore, in part scientific and in part moral. It is in part moral because it does not merely state how price is determined in existing society but also how it would be determined in an ideal society; and this distinction rests upon the moral assumption that certain conditions would be ideal and that actual conditions may fall short of this ideal. Marx believed that in ideal conditions a man would receive, in exchange for the product of his labour, something on which an equivalent quantity of labour had been expended.

The early nineteenth century economists believed that this fair exchange of goods would be ensured by a system of *laisser-faire,* i.e. a system of completely free enterprise in which industry would be free from all forms of government restriction and private monopoly. In such circumstances they believed that the demand for goods would have the result that every man would obtain in return for the goods which he produced an equivalent value of goods produced by others. Marx believed that, on the contrary, a system of free enterprise would have just the opposite result. He thought that this would be due to two distinct, but related, factors, namely:

(i) the private ownership of *capital (i.e.* the means of social production), and

(ii) The practice of buying and selling labour power for the creation of new capital. These two factors Marx thought, would lead to a growing inequality of wealth which would in turn lead to class war between the bourgeoisie and the proletariat, whom Engels defined as follows in a footnote to the *Manifesto of the Communist Party:*

By bourgeoisie is meant the class of modem capitalists, owners of the means of social production and employers of wage labour. By proletariat, the class of modern wage labourers who, having no means of production of their own, are reduced to selling their labour power in order to live.

These definitions incidentally make it clear that by 'capital' Marx denotes 'the means of social production', i.e. the material equipment, such as land, factories, and machinery which are necessary to produce goods for which there is a social demand. He does not mean 'property' in the sense of personal possessions. Indeed, he specifically denies that Communists desire to abolish 'the right of personally acquiring property as the fruit of a man's labour'.

It is not property in this sense which Marx wishes to abolish but 'capital, i.e. that kind of property which exploits wage labour, and which cannot increase except upon conditions of begetting a new supply of wage labour for fresh exploitation'. Thus a man's garden is not by itself capital, but it becomes capital if he employs a gardener at a fixed wage to work it, and sells the produce at a profit to himself.

Marx thinks that the existence of capital prevents the labourer from securing the just reward for his labour because the owner of the capital, merely in virtue of that ownership, receives some of the value which the labourer has created. This is because under the capitalist system labour has itself an exchange value for the capitalist, who pays for it by wages, the level of these wages being determined by the cost of the food, shelter, clothing, etc. which the labourer and his family require in order to live.

Now Marx contends that under the capitalist system the labour-time necessary to provide the needs of the labourer may be, and usually is, less than the time which the labourer has to work in order to earn the wages with which to buy these necessities. If this is so the labourer must be working for only part of his day in producing the equivalent of his wages; during the remainder he must be producing what Marx calls *surplus value,* and this goes into his employer's pocket.

Surplus value may be shortly defined as 'the value produced by the labourer over and above the cost of his keep', commonly called *profit.* Such profit is usually shared by a number of capitalist addition to the owner or c the labourer over and identical with what is course, usually shared and landlords, in where the goods are being manufactured. But in all cases it constitutes, in Marx's view, a return to people who do not actually contribute to the work of producing the goods, which is the real process of creating value.

From these considerations Marx concludes that the capitalist and the labourer have opposite interests in industry. The capitalist's interest is to increase his profit by reducing wages or lengthening hours or intensifying the speed of work so that he gets a better return for the wages which he pays. The labourer's interest, on the other hand, is to secure higher wages or reduced hours or lowers productivity, so that his wages produce less surplus value.

This opposition of interests will, Marx believes, result sooner or later in a revolutionary attack by the proletariat upon the capitalist class, followed by the seizure of their capital, and the establishment of a proletarian dictatorship which 'sweeps away by force the old conditions of production'.

But it is not, in Marx's view, merely the opposing interests of capitalist and worker which make probable the transfer of power to the proletariat; the change is also determined by the fact that the worker's position becomes progressively worse owing to the acquisitive and competitive character of the capitalist system. Thus the capitalist keeps part of his profits to expand production by the purchase of new machinery, and this is liable to result in over-production leading to economic slumps and unemployment.

Again, the competition between capitalists necessitates the cutting of costs either by reducing wages or by intensive mechanisation or by the merging of several companies into combines. These latter measures are likely to create redundancy among the workers. Thus Marx believes that the capitalist system, if not controlled in the interest of the workers, will lead to a progressive worsening of their condition which will provoke them to seize power and organise the system of production in accordance with their interests.

It is here that the dialectical contradiction, which Marx believes to be inherent m the capitalist system, becomes manifest. For it is, according to

Marx's analysis, a system which prevents the majority of its members-the proletariat-from receiving the due reward for their labours, and, once this becomes apparent to them, they will, in Marx's view, inevitably condemn what they believe to be the injustice of their situation, and take the necessary steps to eradicate that injustice by placing capital, i.e. the means of social production, under the control of their own representatives.

Thus the evolution and ultimate collapse of the capitalist system is determined, in part, by a moral reaction to its economic consequences, and cannot be accounted for wholly in terms of economic factors, although the moral reaction is itself due to changed economic conditions.

This analysis shows why Marx does not mean by 'dialectical materialism' a system in which moral beliefs are the passive reflection of economic facts. On the contrary, he means that economic and moral factors interact so that, while the inequalities of wealth caused by the operation of the capitalist system lead to its moral condemnation, the latter in turn leads to the radical transformation of that system.

There is, however, no logical or *a priori* necessity in these interactions; their necessity is *de facto* and empirical, and is of exactly the same kind as the necessity of the generalisations of the natural sciences. The laws of social evolution are, in fact, themselves scientific generalisations, although those who participate in that evolution may be able to formulate these laws only in retrospect.

16.4 THE SOCIALIST REVOLUTION

Marx was not wholly consistent in working out this theory. He frequently implies, particularly in the *Manifesto,* that revolution in the form of civil insurrection is bound to be the culmination of the conflict between the bourgeoisie and the proletariat, and that this will therefore sooner or later be the fate of every capitalist community. But this conclusion does not follow from his theory of dialectical materialism, for there is nothing in that theory, which implies that the conflict must be resolved in the same way in every community.

It may be true that, if the capitalist class is uncompromising in defending its privileges without regard to the interests of the proletariat, a violent revolution is likely. But it is not obvious that economic justice cannot be achieved by constitutional and peaceful means in a democratic community if the capitalist class yields to the pressure exercised by the proletariat through the ballot box. Marx himself seems to recognise this when he writes:

The first step in the revolution by the working class is to raise the proletariat to the position of ruling class to win the battle of democracy.

The proletariat will use its political supremacy to wrest, by degrees, all capital from the bourgeoisie, to centralise all instruments of production in the hands of the state, i.e. of the proletariat organised as the ruling class; and to increase the total of productive forces as rapidly as possible.

It is obvious that these aims have already been partly achieved in Britain by a constitutionally elected Socialist Government, and further steps in the same direction may well be taken in the future if the majority of the electorate so desire. Indeed, it is interesting to note the extent to which the specific objectives of Communist policy as laid down in the *Manifesto* have already been achieved in Britain and other democratic countries, and the extent to which they would now be endorsed even by non-Socialist parties.

Marx listed these objectives, as follows:

- Abolition of property in land and application of all rents of land to public purposes.
- A heavy progressive or graduated income tax.
- Abolition of all right of inheritance.
- Confiscation of the property of all emigrants and rebels.
- Centralisation of credit in the hands of the state, by means of a national bank with state capital and an exclusive monopoly.
- Centralisation of the means of communication and transport in the hands of the state.
- Extension of factories and instruments of production owned by the state; the bringing into cultivation of waste lands, and the improvement of the soil generally in accordance with a common plan.
- Equal obligation of all to work. Establishment of industrial armies, especially for agriculture.
- Combination of agriculture with manufacturing industries; gradual abolition of all the distinction between town and country by a more equable distribution of the population over the country.
- Free education for all children in public schools. Abolition of children's factory labour in its present form. Combination of education with industrial production, etc.

However revolutionary these objectives may have appeared in the middle of the nineteenth century, the ordinary processes of Parliamentary democracy have already achieved many of them, in part at least. Indeed, the essence of the essence of the Marxist revolution is not that it should be violent but that it should be revolutionary - revolutionary in the change, which it brings about in the control of the means of social production. In capitalist society these means are owned by a privileged minority and (Marx believes) controlled to the disadvantage of the vast majority. The primary object of the social revolution, which he both desires and anticipates, is to place the means of social production under the control of the state, which he defines as the 'proletariat organised as the ruling class', with a view to ensuring that they are used in the interest of the proletariat. He describes the change succinctly as follows:

In bourgeois society, living labour is but a means to increase accumulated labour. In communist society, accumulated labour is but a means to widen, to enrich, and to promote the existence of the labourer.

In other words, Marx believes that in bourgeois society the surplus value created by the labourer goes into the pockets of the bourgeoisie, while in Communist society any value created by the labourer beyond what is returned to him as wages will be used, under the direction of society, to widen and enrich his life in various ways. He believes that the injustices of the capitalist system will be prevented only when the means of social production and the distribution of wealth are controlled by the state itself. During the first stage of the revolution he means by 'the state' simply 'the proletariat organised as the ruling classes. At this stage, therefore, all that the application of his theory involves is the substitution of government by the organised proletariat for government by the organised bourgeoisie.

16.5 THE CLASSLESS SOCIETY

But the stage of proletarian dictatorship is only transitional. and will, Marx believes, be followed by a classless society in which 'all production has been concentrated in the hands of a vast association of the whole nation'. When this happens 'the public power will lose its political character'. Marx elaborates this point in a passage which is worth quoting at length:

Political power, properly so called, is merely the organised power of one class for oppressing another. If the proletariat during its contest with the bourgeoisie is compelled, by the force of circumstances, to organise itself as a class; if, by means of a revolution, it makes itself the ruling class, and, as such, sweeps away by force the old conditions of production, then it will, along with these conditions, have swept away the conditions for the existence of class antagonisms and of classes generally, and will thereby have abolished its own supremacy as a class.

In place of the old bourgeois society, with its classes and class antagonisms, we shall have an association in which the free development of each is the condition for the free development of all.

This final stage has sometimes been described as one of anarchy, meaning not a condition of lawlessness but one in which a central government has become unnecessary. Some of Marx's followers undoubtedly understood it in this sense. But it is doubtful whether Marx himself thought that it would ever be possible to dispense with a central government. On the contrary, there are passages in the *Capital* which strongly suggest that in his opinion there will always be important functions for a central government, even if it ultimately loses its 'political' character. One of the most important of these functions he describes as follows:

Only when production will be under the conscious and prearranged control of society, will society establish a direct relation between the quantity of social labour time employed in the production of definite articles and the demand of society for them.

Under the capitalist system there is, in Marx's view, no such relationship between labour and social demand since the economic inequalities arising from the private ownership of capital, and the lack of any central planning of the use of capital, alike contribute to the perpetuation of an economic anarchy in which the idle demands of the rich may command labour more easily than the urgent needs of the poor simply because of the money which can be made available to pay for them.

It seems clear, then, that Marx anticipates a continuing need for a central government to draw up a list of what would now be called 'social priorities' and to ensure that the resources of the community, both material and human, are effectively utilised to satisfy these needs. He appears to believe that there will be general agreement about these social priorities and the measures necessary to satisfy them once the old conditions of production, i.e. the capitalist system, have been destroyed.

Once this has happened 'the public power will lose its political character' and a genuinely democratic basis for Communism will become possible. Opposition to Communism depends, Marx thinks, upon the continuance of the capitalist system, and will disappear as soon as that system has been abolished by the dictatorship of the proletariat. Indeed Marx believes that true democracy is impossible so long as capitalism survives, since capitalism is essentially a system of exploitation and inequality. Democratic equality will, he thinks, be achieved only when the economic organisation of the community is centrally planned and controlled.

In countries, such as Russia, where Communist governments were in control, this central planning and control of the economy was a conspicuous feature, but it was associated with an equally rigid control of speech and publication and political association which many would regard as a denial of the most fundamental of all democratic liberties. It seems probable that Marx would have defended these restrictions on the ground that the Communist states were still at the stage of dictatorship, and that it would be premature to dispense with this form of government until all vestiges of the capitalist system and the bourgeois mentality have been eliminated, and all danger of attack by other bourgeois countries has disappeared.

When, but only when, these conditions are satisfied, will there emerge the 'association in which the free development of each is the condition for the free development of all' and in which everyone freely accepts and supports the ideal of planned production for the satisfaction of social needs.

16.6 THE PLANNED SOCIETY

If the emotional prejudices associated with the word 'Communism' can be put aside, there is much in Marx's theory which is likely to attract those who recognise the inadequacy of *laisser-faire* and the need for some central planning of production for satisfying the needs of the individual in an equitable manner. They are likely to attach most weight not to Marx's theory of surplus value-which is generally recognised by economists to be based on an inadequate analysis of value-but to his theory that production is a co-operative process, that value is determined not only by the labour of those who work on the raw materials of nature but also by the extent to which the finished product satisfies the demand of the consumer, and that value is therefore partly determined by social relationships and is not an intrinsic quality of a manufactured article.

If these principles are true of a complex industrial community it follows that the Labour Theory of Value is inadequate to determine the just rewards of labour in such a community. In the simple society contemplated by Locke, where men supplied their own needs by working on the raw materials of nature, it appeared reasonable to say that a man had a right to the product of his labour; but in a complex industrial community, where several people generally co-operate in the production of manufactured goods, and manufacture them for the use of others, this simple definition of a just reward is quite inadequate, and a definition in terms of the social value of a man's labour must be substituted. But there is, of course, plenty of room for disagreement about what is socially valuable, since this conception cannot be defined in terms of individual desire, but only in terms of some general conception of how society ought to be constituted.

But who is to say how society ought to be constituted? Who is to specify the manner in which the free play of economic forces is to be restricted? The great theoretical attraction of the individualist theory of *laisser-faire* is that it does not raise these difficult and controversial questions but defines a thing's value in terms of what people will pay for it, and a worker's value in terms of what he can earn in a free and uncontrolled economy. Yet there is unanimous, or almost unanimous, agreement that some departure from *laisser-faire* is necessary in a modern industrial society, and this departure is justified on one or other of two grounds.

In the first place, it may be justified on the utilitarian ground that the majority of people will get more of what they want in a controlled than in a free economy. This is in principle the same argument as Hobbes used to justify government generally that the individual will, in general and in the long run, realise more of his desires under government than without government. It is just an application of Hobbes's argument to the specifically economic field for the purpose of justifying a measure of economic government.

Secondly, control of the economy may be justified on the moral ground that a free economy has consequences, e.g. great disparities of wealth, which are morally evil.

Marx makes no attempt to base his argument on utilitarian grounds, and it is the second principle which is the real ground for his condemnation of the capitalist system and of his plea for the substitution of a system in which 'the labour power of all the different individuals is consciously applied as one single social labour power'.' Without the assumption that economic inequality is morally bad Marx would have no ground for condemning the capitalist system as morally bad. Without moral assumptions about the sort of society which ought to be fashioned by the 'single social labour power' he would obviously have no moral ground for justifying the measures necessary to realise such a social order.

16.7 THE MORAL ASSUMPTIONS OF MARXISM

Thus moral assumptions are essential to Marx's theory on both its critical and constructive sides, yet as a materialist philosopher and a social scientist he cannot consistently make such assumptions. In making them he is himself becoming part of the material to describe, and he is failing to distinguish between the process and its description. His task, as a social scientist is to analyse and describe the process of social evolution and to formulate the laws in accordance with which that evolution appears to proceed; and the resulting description of the way in which society does evolve can never, by itself, be a valid basis for the inference that society ought to evolve in that way, and that people ought to promote that type of evolution.

The fact is that Marx, like Hegel, failed to adhere consistently to his own theory. Marx, as it has been said, was not a Marxist. He did not recognise that his own theories were subject to the relativity to which, on his materialist premises, all empirical generalisations are necessarily subject. He did not realise that his condemnation of the capitalist system was, on his own materialist premises, determined by the special features of that system during his lifetime.

Like many subsequent social scientists, he failed to recognise that, once idealism has been abandoned, there can be no rational way of justifying the ultimate ends of action. All that science can show is how certain ends can, in practice, be most quickly and efficiently attained; it cannot show that these ends, whether desired or not, *ought* to be desired; for science is exclusively interested in what is, not in what ought to be. It can show men how to do things, but not why they ought to do them.

Thus if Marx had remained true to his materialist outlook he would not have written as though there were a moral obligation to promote the realisation of a Communist society.' He would have been content to predict the probability of such a culmination, and, if he personally desired it, he might have utilised his scientific analysis to draw men's attention to the features of existing society which he believed would inspire them to revolutionise its character. This, in effect, is what he actually did. His economic analysis of the capitalist system underestimates the importance of several factors, such as monopoly and demand, which affect price, and places primary emphasis on the factor of surplus value and on the contention that in a capitalist society the worker is deprived of the just reward for his efforts.

There is no doubt that this emphasis has exercised an immense influence in politics which has extended far beyond the boundaries of official Communism. Indeed, much of Marx's analysis has become implicit in the outlook of liberal democracies. For example, the need for government control of the capitalist system in the interest of wage-camers has been generally accepted, and this has been largely due to the political pressure exercised by the wage-camers themselves in the belief that they have not been receiving a fair return for their labour.

16.8 THE LOGICAL BASIS OF MARXISM

If the moralising and propaganda in Marx's writings are discounted as inconsistent with his primary thesis, two distinct but interconnected questions must be considered: (i) Is Marx justified in his materialist assumption that the only possible knowledge about the real world, and the only possible ground for rational action in the real world, is scientific knowledge? (ii) If the preceding question is answered in the affirmative, does Marx provide a reasonably accurate and adequate scientific theory of social evolution?

The first of these questions is, of course, the fundamental question of all philosophy - that of the nature and scope of human knowledge. The answer to it closely depends on the answer to the second, for if Marx's scientific theory of social evolution appears to say all that can be said about human society with any pretence to objective truth, that will by itself be a weighty consideration in support of his materialist assumption that 'man's ideas, views, and conceptions, in one word, man's consciousness, changes with every change in the conditions of his material existence, in his social relations and in his social life',' and that moral and philosophical theories, far from having objective significance and providing rational guidance, are merely the causal by-products of an irrational process.

Marx himself does not appear to have appreciated these implications of a materialist philosophy. To him the ideal of human equality is obviously not just one possible ideal but the *right* ideal, to which all the strivings of mankind ought to be directed. Systems, such as the capitalist system, which prevent the attainment of equality ought, in his view, to be ruthlessly destroyed.

Yet the fact that Marx and the vast majority of human beings recoil from the moral nihilism which a materialist philosophy necessarily involves does not by itself imply that rational belief about the real world can be attained by other methods than those of science. The continuing difficulty of reaching any general agreement on the large issues of morality and metaphysics is by itself a standing challenge to all who reject the materialist view of the subjective nature of these controversies.

In considering the narrower question of the adequacy of Marx's economic theory, a distinction must be drawn between the validity and the influence of his principles. There can be no doubt that their influence has been immense. The theory that the capitalist system necessarily involves the exploitation of the real producers of value and the denial to them of an equitable return for the value which they produce has been one of the primary inspirations of Communist and Socialist movements everywhere.

But it is a distinct question whether these movements and their consequences have in practice confirmed Marx's predictions regarding the overthrow of the capitalist state and the ultimate evolution of a Communist society. If his predictions are understood to imply that every capitalist society will sooner or later suffer a violent revolution culminating in a proletarian dictator ship, they cannot be said to have been so far fulfilled except in Russia, China and some of the smaller states. But if the essence of Marx's theory is held to be that class distinctions, based upon economic inequality, will gradually disappear and all production be 'concentrated in the hands of a vast association of the whole nation', there is considerable evidence that a general movement of this character is taking place-admittedly in different ways-in the various capitalist societies.

For the extreme disparities of wealth which formerly existed are, in general, being progressively reduced by taxation, and business enterprise is being gradually brought under stricter control by government. While Marx appears to have thought that such changes could be brought about only by a bloody revolution, it is consistent with his own materialist principles to say that this was a reasonable expectation in the light of the economic and political situation in Britain in the middle of the nineteenth century, but that in the light of subsequent developments-and particularly the record of concessions obtained from capitalists through parliamentary procedure-it is no longer reasonable to predict that violence would be necessary to achieve the Communist State.

In other words, different material conditions may cause the bourgeoisie of different countries to react in different ways to the pressure of the proletariat, so that, while in some countries revolutionary action may be necessary to bring about the centralised control of industry, in others political pressure may be fully adequate.

If Marx's 'revolution' is interpreted in this wider sense it cannot be denied that the history of modem democracies provides considerable evidence of the tendency for private enterprise to be replaced by public control. In Britain, for example, the coal, gas and electricity industries, and a considerable section of the inland transport industry, have, since 1945, been placed in the ownership and under the control of the 'State'.

Whether Marx would have regarded the Boards, Commissions and Authorities which have been appointed to control these industries as satisfactory for the purpose in view may well be doubted, but at least the theoretical object of nationalising industries appears to be fundamentally the same as that of the revolution which Marx exhorted the 'workers of the world' to carry out, namely the planned control of industry for the purpose of ensuring that the economic resources of the community are fully exploited and effectively utilised for satisfying, on an equitable basis, the real needs of the people.

16.9 SOCIALISM

There is, however, an important difference between the two principal methods of achieving a planned society which proves, on analysis, to be the main factor distinguishing Communism from Socialism. The difference is that in a Socialist society the social ideals to which the central planning is directed are subject to the criticism and endorsement of a free electorate. In a Communist society, on the other hand, freedom of thought and association is denied and adverse criticism of the policy of the central government is condemned and punished. In such circumstances there can be no assurance that the aims of the government have a democratic foundation, and the claim that they represent the true 'will of the people' is pure presumption and is exposed to all the objections which can be made to an Organic Theory of the State.

To a democrat, indeed, the claim of a government to represent the 'will of the people' must appear wholly unjustified in the absence of democratic machinery through which that 'will' can be freely expressed. The fact is that Socialism, or at least the present British variety, seeks to reconcile the fundamental ideals of Marx with the democratic machinery based upon the individualist assumptions of the utilitarian tradition. In other words, it is attempting to create a society based upon social justice and the satisfaction of needs, while leaving to the people's judgement the ultimate decision whether, and how far, such a policy is to be carried out.

The Communist believes that the free judgement of the people cannot be trusted to endorse such ideals until they have been realised-that until they have been realised those who benefit from economic inequality and privilege will oppose these ideals, and may oppose them with a substantial measure of success. But to this criticism the Socialist may well reply that this is a smaller risk than the risk of sacrificing democracy for ever by denying the basic liberties of thought and political association.

16.10 MARXISM, COMMUNISM AND SOCIALISM

The three terms 'Marxism', 'Communism' and 'Socialism' have different meanings and are often confused. Marxism is a theory, partly philosophical but primarily scientific. It makes a general philosophical assumption, and thereafter proceeds to formulate the scientific, i.e. empirical, laws to which social evolution appears to conform. The philosophical assumption of Marxism is the assumption that the universe is a process of which the only possible knowledge is empirical or scientific knowledge.

Apart from this fundamental proposition-which is treated as an analytic proposition - Marxism consists of a series of scientific propositions, of which the most important is that 'man's ideas, views and conceptions, in one word, man's consciousness, changes with every change in the conditions of his material existence, in his social relations and in his social life" or, more briefly, that 'intellectual production changes its character in proportion as material production is changed'.

These are empirical generalisations, for which Marx claims no a priori certainty. He simply claims that dispassionate observation confirms their truth, and that- the way to understand men's ideas, i.e. their beliefs (particularly on political. moral and religious questions), is not to seek for some *a priori* necessity which they do not possess but to discover, by scientific enquiry, their empirical relationship to the material environment of those who profess them. He believes that observation shows that these relationships are of a constant character, so that laws may be formulated specifying the sort of ideas which will result from a given type of material environment. There is, according to Marx, no other sense in which these beliefs can be 'understood'.

Marxism may therefore be briefly defined as the theory that (a) the only possible knowledge about the universe is empirical knowledge, and (b) scientific investigation shows that the evolution of society is determined by the interaction between men's material conditions and their ideas in accordance with certain empirical laws which may be discovered by scientific investigation.

While Marxism is thus a philosophical and scientific theory about the nature of social evolution, 'Communism' and' 'Socialism' are words which are usually employed to designate certain political policies, i.e. programmes of action devised in order to achieve certain ends. The relationship between these policies and Marxism is that they aim, in varying degrees, at achieving the ends which Marxism is believed to justify. The difference, in so far as there is a difference, between Communists and Socialists is that Socialists accept the principle of achieving their ends through the machinery of a free democracy while Communists accept this only in so far as it is inevitable, and are ready to resort to unconstitutional means to attain their ends when such methods appear likely to be more successful.

But both policies are mainly shaped by the Marxist ideal of changing existing society into one in which 'the labour power of all the individuals is consciously applied as one single social labour power', i.e. in which the means of social production are placed under central control with a view to ensuring that these means are used for the maximum satisfaction of what are assumed to be the 'social needs' of the community. Both policies are directly opposed to the policy of free enterprise *or laisser-faire,* which they believe is bound to cause injustice and poverty.

But although these seem to be the ends of both Socialism and Communism, there is no ground for the belief that Marxism *justifies* these ends in a moral sense, i.e. shows that they ought to be pursued. All that Marxism as a scientific theory can say is that men do, or will, or must seek these ends because of the motives which determine their action. But to say that is quite different from saying that men *ought* to pursue such ends. A scientific proposition can never be the sole ground for a moral proposition, and according to Marxism moral propositions are in any case simply empirical propositions describing the reactions of men to their environment. They do not therefore provide a justification, but only an explanation, of men's actions. They show-in a purely empirical sense-why men *do* act in a certain way; for on an empirical theory the word *ought* must be defined in terms of empirical concepts, i.e. propositions containing the word 'ought' must be expressed in terms of propositions which are empirically verifiable.

Thus if Communism is based on certain moral ideals these ideals must be found elsewhere than in Marxism. The real relationship between

Communism and Marxism seems, indeed, to be that Communists assume that there is a moral obligation to promote the ends towards which Marxism asserts that society is in any case advancing. But Marxism itself provides no justification for this assumption.

Socialists, as already observed, aim at the same general ideals as Communists, but accept the necessity of achieving those ideals through the machinery of a free democracy. In other words, they accept the individualist and utilitarian theory that the object of government is to promote the good of the individual, and that the individual is the best judge of what his good is.

They assume, by implication that at least the majority of individuals in any society will, sooner or later, come to support freely the Socialist ideal of a planned society. Communists reject this assumption on the ground that until the ideals of Communism have been achieved the judgement of individuals will be perverted by the economic inequalities which surround them, and progress towards these ideals will therefore be impeded.

16.11 THE INFLUENCE OF MARXISM

It is clear from the foregoing discussion that the practical influence of Marx's theory has been the exact opposite of its logical implications. His materialist philosophy and scientific generalisations should have encouraged the dispassionate scientific analysis of practical problems and the rejection of all dogmatic claims that certain ideals are objectively right and that others are objectively wrong. But the practical influence of Marxism has been very different. Far from encouraging the dispassionate scientific analysis of practical problems, it has inspired the violent condemnation of certain features of existing society and a fanatical determination to destroy these features and replace them by a new order.

These two opposing tendencies are not least in evidence in Marx's own writings, where the clear enunciation of the materialist principle is followed by violent condemnation of the capitalist system. The truth is that in advocating the scientific study of society Marx forgot that his own emotional reactions to industrial conditions in the middle of the nineteenth century had no logical connection with his science, apart from being yet another illustration of the causal relationship between material conditions and human consciousness.

17. THE MORAL PHILOSOPHY JUSTIFICATION

17.1 HUMAN RELATIONS

Moral philosophy itself may be defined as the organisation of human relations in a community or, more briefly, as the organisation of personal situations; while philosophy, as commonly understood, is an attempt to define the principles prescribing what the methods and aims of society ought to be. But this, for the reasons given in this book, is a somewhat superficial conception of philosophy, for it ignores the underlying question whether these principles are *a priori* propositions of universal validity or whether they are empirical generalisations which can only justify hypothetical conclusions about what the methods and aims of ethics ought to be.

It is quite clear that many of the most important philosophers have assumed that the principles which justify ethics are either self-evident or capable of rational demonstration and therefore constitute a categorical basis for its justification. But such philosophers (of whom Plato and Locke are typical examples) have not, in general, considered the fundamental question whether propositions which are admittedly synthetic can be rationally justified.

Kant and Hegel and their followers are the only moral philosophers who have recognised the real significance of this question and have attempted to provide a rational justification of synthetic moral propositions. Hegel's solution, was to argue that the good will is the rational will, that the rational will is the will of the state, and that the nature of this rational will can be dialectically deduced from the notion of will as such.

Hegel's argument was explained at length and need not be reconsidered here. If the reasons there given for rejecting his conclusions are valid some form of Empiricism must necessarily be accepted, and this implies that the series of moral propositions which have often been accepted as adequate moral philosophies are, in fact, simply empirical generalisations which can have no universal application or validity and may vary from place to place and from time to time.

In short, Empiricism implies that the only justification which can be given for ethics is a hypothetical one and that there is no possible way of providing a categorical justification at any stage. The justification must take the form put forward by either Hobbes or Hume, namely that if certain ends are desired, or are held to be 'good', and if certain methods are the most effective for achieving those ends, then those methods ought to be adopted.

But the conclusion that those methods ought to be adopted is a hypothetical one depending on the validity of the two hypothetical propositions from which it is deduced; and the word 'ought' does not possess the categorical significance which is usually attached to it.

17.2 IMPLICATIONS OF EMPIRICISM

The most important implication of Empiricism is that there is no rational way of resolving ultimate differences regarding therapeutic ideals since the assertion that X (e.g. the general happiness) is such an ideal is, to Empiricism, necessarily a synthetic proposition and thus devoid of rational necessity. It does not follow from this that there is no rational way of resolving many differences which actually arise. It may often be possible to show that the opposing aims of two different types of morals are logically inconsistent with some more general aim which is accepted.

It might for example, be possible to resolve the differences between different psychological schools regarding the extent to which a person's moral beliefs should be controlled consistently to a more general aim, such as reducing stress and neuroses in general. For then it would be possible, in theory at least, to resolve the differences by showing that a specific form of treatment does, or does not, tend in practice to reduce the agony of living.

It is, in general, possible that many disagreements could be resolved by the rational process of drawing the logical implications of assumptions held in common by the many counselling versions to the dispute. But, unless Hegel's theory of reasoning is accepted, there is no ground for assuming that this process, however far it is carried, will lead to universal agreement on ultimate moral principles and, therefore, no ground for assuming that differences about such principles can ultimately be eliminated.

If Empiricism is accepted, it therefore follows that there is no rational assurance that disagreement about moral principles and ideals can be resolved. This in turn implies that there is no justification for the common assumption that the incompatible views of communities about the rights of the individual person cannot be true. Empiricism implies that, in the only sense in which such doctrines can be true, both may be true and that an ultimate and irresolvable difference may therefore exist.

If this conclusion is accepted, it follows that there is no *rational* way of eliminating ultimate differences of moral principle, and that in practice such conflicts must be resolved by one of three alternative methods, namely force, compromise, or toleration.

In other words, if the different principles accepted by different states result in the adoption of policies, which ultimately bring these states into conflict, then this conflict can be resolved only if one of these states succeeds in dominating the other; or if one meets the other half-way by some measure of compromise; or, finally, if they avoid conflict by 'agreeing to differ' in a spirit of mutual toleration. In any case, the acceptance of the Empiricist Theory, far from promoting conflict, might help to prevent it by showing that such a conflict would simply be a conflict of opposing forces and not, as is frequently assumed, a conflict between 'right' and 'might'.

17.3 Implications Of Rationalism

On the other hand, a Rationalist Theory of the kind defended by Hegel implies that in the will of the state there is an absolute standard of morality with which no compromise ought to be permitted. This in turn implies that between the wills of two states there may be a conflict which ought to be resolved by a trial of strength.

No doubt Hegel's theory also implies that states may fall short of perfection, and that their wills may not therefore be wholly good. He provides no criterion for showing how good states may be distinguished from bad ones; and the practical effect of his theory, when accepted, has been to strengthen the assumption that 'the state can do no wrong'. Hence when the wills of different states are in conflict the acceptance of the Hegelian theory tends to encourage the adoption of a rigid and uncompromising attitude and a resort to war.

To Hegel, war was far from being an unqualified evil. As he put it: 'War has the higher significance that by its agency the ethical health of peoples is preserved in their indifference to the stabilisation of finite institutions; just as the blowing of the winds preserves the sea from the foulness which would be the result of a prolonged calm, so also corruption in nations would be the product of prolonged, let alone "perpetual" peace. In other words, the conflict of states shows that none has achieved the ultimate good in its 'finite institutions', and war has the salutary consequence of promoting moral progress by preventing the perpetuation of existing imperfections.

Hegel's political theory has undoubtedly exercised its influence in this direction, although a proper understanding of it should have encouraged a more modest view of the powers of finite intelligence. But where Hegelianism has been influential, its insistence on the limitations of human judgement has been largely ignored, and the conception of the general will eagerly seized upon as providing an absolute standard of moral value.

This conception has been welcomed in the belief that it provides a universal and objective criterion of morality, and the problem of determining when a will is truly 'general' has been conveniently ignored.

17.4 HUME'S EMPIRICISM

The alternative analysis offered by Empiricism is not faced with the difficulty of establishing an absolute standard of morality. On the other hand, it need not, and as expounded by Hume does not, deny the reality of moral experience.

Hume took special care, particularly in the later exposition of his theory in the *Enquiry,* to emphasise that the 'pleasing sentiment of approbation' in which moral approval consists is pleasant' in quite a specific sense of that word, since it may enjoin the performance of acts which are far from 'pleasant' in the ordinary sense.

Thus Hume was able to account in purely empirical terms for the distinction commonly drawn between duty and inclination; and it is by no means obvious that such an analysis of moral experience is inadequate, even though it implies that the laws of morality are simply empirical generalisations about the moral feelings of individuals or groups of individuals.

If moral laws can be reduced in this way to empirical generalisations about the occurrence of the feelings of approbation and disapprobation, the question arises whether there is any general 'law' which describes the circumstances which normally evoke these feelings.

Hume believed that these feelings generally express a natural human tendency to feel pleased at what tends to promote happiness (whether in oneself or in others) and to feel displeased at what tends to diminish happiness (whether in oneself or in others).

But this, again, is a purely empirical generalisation, and Hume does not think that it is universally true. From instinct, habit, or tradition men sometimes approve acts which do not tend to promote the general happiness; and although Hume believed that if such men could be convinced by empirical evidence that such acts did not in fact promote the general happiness they would usually cease to approve them, he recognised that this, also, was a purely empirical generalisation, and that there is no reason why men must approve acts which tend to promote the general happiness.

As he said in a striking passage:

- 'Tis not contrary to reason to prefer the destruction of the whole world to the scratching of my finger.
- 'Tis not contrary to reason for me to choose my total ruin, to prevent the least uneasiness of an Indian or person wholly unknown to me.
- 'Tis as little contrary to reason to prefer even my own acknowledged lesser good to my greater, and have a more ardent affection for the former than the latter.

There is, in other words, no *reason* to explain why the vast majority of people would never entertain these preferences. The explanation is the purely empirical one that such preferences are determined not by reason but by feeling (or 'sentiment', as Hume says), and that the feelings implanted in human nature are such that the vast majority of people cannot help preferring a scratch on the finger to the destruction of the world, or the 'uneasiness of an Indian' to personal ruin, or a greater to a smaller personal good. In the same way,

Hume believed that the vast majority of people cannot help approving acts which are shown to be useful, or disapprovingly acts which are shown to be the contrary of useful. He recognise it hat in practice the feelings of approval and disapproval are largely determined by habit and convention, but he believed that the application of the principle of utility can do much to influence those feelings, and to ensure that acts which, under changed circumstances., cease to have the utilitarian value which they formerly possessed are no longer approved. For he held that few, if any, people would approve an act which they believed to be contrary to the principle of utility.

These considerations show where the ultimate difference between the Rationalist and Empiricist Moral Theories lies. The Rationalist Theory implies that virtue is its own reward and its own justification. The Empiricist Theory implies that moral judgements, as synthetic propositions, could conceivably have been other than they are, and offers an empirical explanation why they are what in fact they are. The explanation offered by Hume is that moral judgements are what they are because experience has shown that certain habits of conduct tend to promote the general happiness and because such conduct is the sort of conduct which usually evokes the feelings of moral approval.

One important consideration, which supports the Empiricist Theory, is that it can account so simply for the varying and often inconsistent moral judgements, which are actually made. Such inconsistencies are particularly striking when the moral codes of different communities or different epochs are compared, but they may be found within a single community as well.

In contemporary Britain, for example, different people take opposing views about the morality of abortion, gambling, divorce, and blood sports, and express these views in contradictory moral judgements. Such disagreements are easily explained by the Empiricist Theory, which asserts that they are based upon the different moral feelings aroused in different persons by contemplation of the same activity.

The Rationalist Theory, on the other hand, implies that such activities are either good or bad quite independently of the feelings, which they excite, and it must therefore provide some criterion for determining which of two contradictory moral judgements is true and which is false. This, of course, is just what Rationalist Theories from the time of Plato onwards have failed to do, and what; in Hume's opinion they could not conceivably succeed in doing.

The fact is that any moral theory which claims to be adequate must offer some explanation of the undeniable facts of moral controversy. People do frequently disagree about what are right and what is wrong, and the Rationalist Theory, which asserts that conflicting moral judgements are logically inconsistent, must obviously show how to distinguish between those which are true and those which are false.

On the other hand, the Empiricist Theory is not faced with this problem, if it regards these incompatible moral judgements as judgements describing the different feelings excited in different persons by contemplation of the same act or situation. The Empiricist Theory may, of course, indicate a method by which such differences may be eliminated if it can show that moral approval is generally excited by the contemplation of acts which tend to promote the general happiness, for it may then be possible to distinguish, in the light of well established empirical generalisations, between acts which really have this tendency and those which are falsely believed to have it.

17.5 MEANING OF 'JUSTIFICATION'

It follows from the foregoing considerations that the sort of 'justification' which can be offered for government takes a fundamentally different form according to whether a Rationalist or Empiricist Theory of Morality is adopted.

The Rationalist Theory implies that there are moral principles of an *a priori* character which constitute an objective and unconditional justification of certain forms of government.

The Empiricist Theory implies that moral principles are necessarily of a synthetic and empirical character, and that the justification of government which they provide is therefore conditional on the truth of these principles in the particular context to which they are applied. For, since these principles are synthetic propositions, they are devoid of rational necessity, and it is for experience to say whether, in a given context, they are, in fact, true.

For example, the moral principle-generally accepted in some form by democratic peoples-that a human being has certain absolute rights which any government ought to respect is, if true, an important criterion for determining whether a certain form of government is, or is not, justified. But the Empiricist Theory of Morality implies that this principle is without rational necessity, and may not be universally true. If in some contexts it is not true, it will be possible to justify forms of government which do not observe it.

But Empiricism need not, of course, take the form which was defended by Hume. It may, as in the theories of Machiavelli, Hobbes and Bentham, be combined with a Naturalistic Theory of Morality. Such a theory asserts that the basic moral concepts *of good, bad, right, and wrong* can be defined in terms of non-moral concepts such as *pleasant, painful, expedient and inexpedient.* It asserts, in other words, that moral terms are synonymous with non-moral terms, and that there is nothing specific or peculiar in what is commonly described as moral experience.

This naturalistic interpretation of morality does not, however, affect the issue of primary interest to the philosopher. Whether or not moral experience is unique and irreducible is a question for the psychologist to determine; and however he answers that question the issue which concerns the philosopher is whether moral or quasi-moral propositions are *a priori* or empirical. For, if they are empirical, they are without rational necessity, and cannot afford more than a hypothetical justification for action.

Whether or not 'the good' means simply 'the desired', the proposition 'X is good' cannot constitute more than a hypothetical justification for seeking X if it is an empirical proposition, for the justification will then be based on the hypothesis 'if X is good'. Only if the proposition 'X is good' is *a prim,* and thus necessarily true, will the justification for seeking X be categorical and unconditional.

Justification, in short, means moral justification, and like morality itself, has a meaning whether or not moral concepts can be defined in terms of non-moral concepts. Government is said to be justified if its methods are 'right' and its ends are 'good', whether or not 'right' and 'good' can be defined in non-moral terms.

The question of philosophical importance is whether a categorical or only a hypothetical justification of government can be given, and this, as already shown, depends on whether moral propositions-however interpreted-are *a priori* or empirical.

The justification of government can be an unconditional and categorical justification only if moral propositions are *a priori* in character. If these propositions are synthetic and empirical their truth in any given context cannot be assumed. Only experience can show whether they are true in a given context. What sort of experience is relevant to their truth depends, of course, on the nature of the moral experience which such propositions describe.

If Hume was right in holding that moral experience consists in the feelings of approval and disapproval which certain acts, characters or situations arouse, then a moral proposition will be true or false according to whether it accurately describes the moral feelings which are aroused in a given situation. Hume's theory therefore implies that the justification of government must depend on the moral feelings which it arouses, and that a specific form of government may be justified in the opinion of one individual or community and not in the opinion of another.

Hume thought that his theory was quite consistent with the fact that the members of a given community are, as a rule, in general agreement about the form of government which they approve, for he thought it only natural that the combined influence of tradition, habit and self-interest should tend to evoke in them the sentiments of approval and disapproval towards the same things. Where this general measure of agreement does not exist, he would have said that conditions are ripe for revolution, and that the latter is very likely to occur unless one of the opposing factions is of negligible strength and can be effectively suppressed.

It may be said in criticism of the Empiricist Theory that it bases the justification of government on moral principles which can be defined in the light of experience but which can never be justified by the necessity of reason; and that some form of Rationalist Theory must therefore be preferred in view of the final and categorical nature of the justification which it claims to give.

But to this the empiricist may reply that none of the attempts made by rationalists from Plato onwards have succeeded in demonstrating the rational necessity of moral propositions, or of resolving the existing conflict between the moral principles of different races, nations and individuals, except where they have shown that some of the accepted principles are logically inconsistent; and of course empiricists are equally entitled to say that logically inconsistent principles cannot all be true.

In short the empiricist can argue that the rationalist has not, in practice, been any more successful than the empiricist in finding ultimate and self-evident moral premises which are universally accepted, and that his failure to do so at once illustrates and justifies the empiricist's contention that such premises are, from their very nature, empirical in character and without rational necessity.

17.6 JUSTIFICATION OF DIFFERENT FORMS OF STATES

The essential distinction between authoritarian and democratic forms of government is the distinction between government by those who claim authority through superior knowledge and government by those who claim authority through popular support, and this distinction is, in the end, an expression of the distinction between the Rationalist and Empiricist Theories of Morality. For a Rationalist Theory of Morality implies that, a government ought to be authoritarian and an Empiricist Theory implies that it ought to be democratic in these senses.

A Rationalist Theory implies that government ought to be authoritarian because it implies that there are moral laws which are necessarily and universally true, and that anyone who apprehends those laws clearly and applies them consistently enjoys an authority which others ought to respect and obey. This was the form of government which Plato defended just because he believed that only a minority of people were capable of apprehending the *a priori* truths of morality. On the other hand, according to the Empiricist Theory of Morality, moral laws are empirical generalisations and no such general functions are necessarily universal. No one there can claim that his moral judgements are universally applicable and authoritative; for a different and apparently incompatible judgement made by someone else may be equally true in the only sense in which such judgements can be true.

The democratic practice of permitting the free expression of individual opinions, while accepting the opinion of the majority as the ultimate directive of policy, is an implicit recognition of these principles of Empiricism. It would, of course, be untrue to say that all supporters of democracy are aware of the underlying philosophical principle, but it is true to say that the Empiricist Theory of Morality implies that a moral judgement cannot be rejected as false on the ground that it is *prima fade* inconsistent with one which is accepted as true.

Two logically inconsistent judgements cannot, of course, both be true, but on the Empiricist Theory one man's judgement that X is good and another man's judgement that X is not good may both be true in the sense that the contemplation of X excites the feeling of moral approval in the one and excites the feeling of moral disapproval in the other, i.e. the two judgements are not really inconsistent. Thus the Empiricist Theory of Morality supplies the ultimate justification for the moral toleration which is the essential feature of the democratic way of life.

Which of the various moral judgements actually made is accepted as 'authoritative' depends, in a democracy, upon which receives the widest support. In other words, the judgement of the majority is accepted, in practice, as authoritative; but this does not imply that the judgement of a minority is not an equally true and valid moral judgement. and does not therefore justify

the suppression of a minority opinion on the ground that it is false. The authority of a democratic government is therefore quite different in character from that of an authoritarian government, which derives its authority from conformity to the *a priori* moral laws by which alone it can be justified. The authority of a democratic government originates in the support of the majority and is therefore based not on an assumed *a priori* right but on power on the recognition that, as Locke put it, 'it is necessary the body [community] should move that way whither the greater force carries it'. On the other hand, it may also be possible to justify the authority of a democratic government on grounds of utility if it is true that the realisation of the will of the majority promotes the greatest happiness of the greatest number.'

17.7 THEORY AND PRACTICE IN A STATE

A distinction was drawn at in this chapter between the exercise of government and its justification. The distinction is important, although the two aspects of government are closely related. The exercise of government always involves in some measure the control of the many by the few, and such control necessarily depends on the consent of the many. Such consent may be, and often is, wholly irrational, being based mainly upon habit and tradition. But questions have always been asked by some about the rational justification of the institutions and practices supported by these irrational forces, and it is to these questions that the philosopher attempts to give an answer.

Even if the answer is - as it must be for an empiricist - that government can be justified only by non-rational considerations, that is itself a rational proposition of the first importance, and there will remain for reason the important function of discovering and prescribing the most effective means by which the non-rational ends of government may be achieved. If, on the other hand, the answer is-as the rationalist believes-that there are rational norms by which government must be justified or condemned, there will be rational grounds for prescribing the ends of government as well as the means employed to realise them.

The broad alternatives in theory which have been distinguished in the preceding chapters are therefore based upon the Rationalist and Empiricist Theories of Morality respectively, and these alternative Theories of Morality are in rum based upon Rationalist and Empiricist Theories of Logic. It would, of course, be untrue to say that these alternatives have always been defined and distinguished in political theory; but they are the logical alternatives between which a choice must be made.

The justification of government is a moral justification, and the form which it takes therefore depends upon the form and logical status of moral propositions. If, as Plato, Aquinas, and Kant would all have said, moral propositions possess the rational necessity of mathematical propositions, a categorical justification of government can be given; but if such propositions are synthetic and empirical a hypothetical justification is all that can be looked for.

A categorical justification is the logical foundation of government by authority, while a hypothetical justification is the only possible justification of those forms of government which recognise the right to freedom of opinion and accept the need to govern within the limits of general consent. Which form of justification is valid depends, in the end, on whether moral propositions are *a priori* or empirical. Since such propositions are in any case synthetic, the issue ultimately turns on whether synthetic propositions can be *a priori.*

The ultimate question is therefore Kant's famous question: Are synthetic *a priori* propositions possible? The answer to that question must itself be an a priori proposition, for no empirical facts could be relevant to its truth. It is on this ground that the empiricist ultimately takes his stand. He contends that the conception of a synthetic *a priori* proposition is self-contradictory, and the assertion that a synthetic proposition can be *a priori* therefore necessarily false.

To the empiricist the synthetic, in virtue of its very meaning, excludes the necessary, and the necessary excludes the synthetic. For him a synthetic proposition *means* a proposition which can be denied without self-contradiction, and of which the truth can therefore be established only by experience. If these contentions are valid, the ultimate premise of rationalism must be rejected as self contradictory, and Empiricism accepted as the true account of the nature of thought. From this it will follow that the justification of government must be hypothetical in character, and conditioned by whatever moral assumptions are made about its proper aims and methods.

The empiricist maintains that it is only when, the inherent limitations of reason are recognised that it becomes possible to control action in a rational manner. It is only when reason, in Hume's words, is recognised to be the 'slave of the passions' that the rational control of action issuing from the 'Passions' becomes possible. Otherwise, in the view of the empiricist, reason is likely to be perverted to the futile task of seeking some *a* priori justification of the ends of action, when it is only possible function in the practical life is that of deducing the conditions and consequences of attaining specified ends, and thus perhaps modifying action by changing its anticipated results.

For the empiricist, therefore, the function of reason in the practical life is essentially utilitarian. It cannot, from its very nature, determine or prescribe the choice of ends. It can only specify, in the light of causal generalisations based on past experience, what means are likely to be most effective for the attainment of the ends desired, and what the attainment of these ends is likely to involve.

The problems of politics, to the empiricist.' are therefore scientific problems, and the true functions of the rational statesman those of a social scientist. The ends which he promotes must be discovered by a scientific study of human desires, and the means which he adopts by a scientific study of the conditions under which those desires can be most fully satisfied.

For the rationalist, on the other hand, reason has directive as well as instrumental functions, and can prescribe the ends which ought to be pursued as well as determine the means by which specified ends may be attained. To him the problems of politics are moral as well as scientific problems, for he recognises an *a priori* distinction between what is and what ought to be, between desires and duties; and he holds that the ideal statesman is one who is aware of this distinction, and who seeks to realise, as far as may be, the pattern of the ideal state.

18. MODERN MORAL CONCEPTS

18.1 THE NEW MILLENNIUM

Undoubtedly, the mass media of the late nineties have brought mankind forward into the uncertainty of the new millennium. The physical countdown of the clocks around the western world had begun. The closer the new millennium, the more mankind fell into a neurotic state. With such hysteria caused by the phobia of computing inabilities, humans no longer appeared to be the masters of the universe, or at least of the planet earth.

18.2 SOCIAL PRACTICES

Through the ages man has been pre-occupied with moral standards, probably more than other philosophical concepts. Societies through their various stages of evolution varied the theme with distinct differences in their demands on standards. These codes of behaviour were influenced by religions and the dogmas of each regional culture. What is acceptable in one tribe may be a fatal error in another society.

These variations of morality place a big demand on moral philosophers. Individuals from different cultures, social groups, of known and unknown social norms may occupy the professionals; the significance of this being the understanding demanded of the professions. A sophist would investigate the background, the beliefs, thoughts, religion and other circumstances which may constitute the personal philosophy of the individual.

18.3 LINGUISTIC EXPRESSIONS

“Language is the dress of thought,” said Samuel Johnson 200 years ago. The way we talk colours the way we think, and the way we think shapes the way we act. We are the unconscious prisoners of our language. Most of the time this matters little, but at times of change in culture or society, our inability to use new words to describe familiar things can hide the future from our eyes.

More positively, metaphors from other fields can help us to glimpse new possibilities in old scenes, just as they have helped scientists to think creatively about the things that they observe but cannot explain. "Relativity" was not a scientific word until Albert Einstein borrowed it to explain the oddities he saw in space.

The premise of this section of the book is that the complicated language of new schools of ideas no longer works as well as it should in modern society. It no longer describes what a person really is. It suggests the wrong priorities and screens out new possibilities. The terminology used is confusing because it does not make clear the individual’s personal philosophy. It is an affront to human behaviour in that it gives inadequate recognition to the people and their beliefs.

18.4 WORK RELATED PHILOSOPHY

First, however, we need a new language to release our thinking. It should be the language of polity. A public corporation has now to be regarded as a community not a piece of property, although a community created by a common purpose rather than a common place. The language of moral philosophy is then more appropriate for describing it than the language of business. No one owns a community. Formal communities need constitutions, which recognise the rights of the different constituencies and which lay down the method of governance. The core members of that community are more properly regarded as citizens than as employees or "human resources", citizens with responsibilities as well as rights.

Good businesses, some may say, already do this. It is only common sense to give proper recognition to those who work with you and for you. Customers are now everyone's central focus. Corporate governance, too, is in vogue as a discussion topic. The signs that some businesses are thinking like this only reinforce the contention that the time has come to update our concept of the corporation, to bring it into line with current practice and, not least, to fill the missing link in our idea of citizenship. For once, good practice can change bad language, rather than the other way round.

The law, in both Britain and the US, tends to follow best practice. The first step, therefore, towards a goal of giving legal status to the real company would be to change the practice of the best companies. That this is already happening should be an encouragement.

It needs to be reinforced, however, by the legitimacy that a proper theory of community and the mechanisms of citizenship would give it. We can even learn from the practices and the problems of countries where the concept of the corporation and the language are different.

It is dangerously xenophobic to believe that British capitalism is the only model that works. Corporations ought to be regarded as communities, as sovereign states within states. The key difference is that a community is something to which one belongs, while it, in turn, belongs to no one. A community is responsible for its future to its members, not its investors, who are entitled only to those due rewards. A community needs a purpose beyond itself in order to give it cohesion and motion.

18.5 MODERN ORGANISATIONS AND PEOPLE

Democratic institutions seek to balance power. Typically, they separate the institutions of legislation, execution and audit, or in political terms, the judiciary. The legislature is representative of the different constituencies or interest groups; the executive is accountable to the legislature but can and should also service it. The audit function needs to be an independent overseer of the executive and its workings, as well as a guardian of the agreed constitution.

With the notable exception of Britain, democracies have written constitutions that set down the common principles and purposes of the state, the methods of governance and the rights of interested parties. The new corporate model will have the same.

The operating units need to be represented in the legislature, or the policy-making body. At present in companies, this is done at the executive or management level. It should more properly be done at the board level where the main investors would also be represented. It is at this level that the different interest groups should be reconciled and the overall purpose of the corporation hammered out, for a compromise will always be required between the shorter-term needs of most investors and the longer-term requirements of the company to invest in its own future.

Such a board would inevitably be large. That would not matter as long as its role was clear. That role is to debate and ultimately to approve or reject policy proposals from the executive. Although proposals can, also, be put forward by other constituencies. It would meet less frequently than is the current practice because, under the new concept, the legislative and executive boards are separated although overlapping. The executive and audit functions of this corporate state would need no formal changes to current best practice.

The audit function should be independent of the executive, reporting to an audit committee of the board made up of outside directors. This is now common in the better organisations. It needs to become standard in order to encourage the corporation to take a broader and longer view of its activities.

Citizens typically have the right of residence, of free speech, fair trial and protection from unfair treatment. In every developed country, except Britain, these rights are guaranteed by a Bill of Rights. In most developed countries they are also entitled, as of right, to education and a minimum standard of living. The only really contentious item here, for businesses, is that of residence. It is no longer practical to offer permanent residence that is lifetime employment to anyone. Indeed, since the average lifetime of a Fortune 500 company is 40 years, the offer of a 50-year contract to new recruits has always been a rash promise.

In practice, we may be looking at a form of conditional and time-bonded tenure, or residence, as is now happening in some universities. The average job tenure in Britain is now 5.7 years. Ten-year renewable contracts might therefore be seen as a reasonable definition of residence for core employees.

The principle involved is that commitment follows commitment. Re-organisation has first to grant a form of citizenship before it can reasonably expect the responsibilities of citizenship from its people. Similarly, not all temporary immigrants can expect to be granted citizenship. They will have to earn their right to a corporate "green card" after a period of effective probation, in order to ensure that they are likely to be able to make a continuing contribution to this corporate society and are in tune with its values and priorities. Recruitment standards are the key to any effective policy of citizenship.

The more subtle but important change is the switch from being an employee or instrument to being a citizen, whose interests are intimately tied up with those of the corporation, or at least of one of its operating units. The board of the corporation is now accountable for the corporation and its future to all its citizens and interest groups, be they inside or outside the company.

Corporations are not, however, accidental communities of place. They are communities linked by a common purpose. The definition of that purpose becomes increasingly important. The enrichment of the shareholders, beyond the level necessary to keep their support, is unlikely to be sufficiently inspiring as an objective to all except a few at the top, whose rewards are often linked to the share price.

A larger and, if possible, a more noble cause is needed to keep the enthusiasm of the citizenry. This becomes the key challenge for the leadership under the community concept of the corporation. It is much easier, conceptually, to wrap it all up in a search for a "better bottom line". This, however, only begs the question of what you do with the money. Money-machines motivate only the few insiders who get most of the money. Great businesses have a purpose beyond their own survival.

18.6 THE PUBLIC AND THE STOCK MARKET

The great fear in this is that the investing public will lose interest and that the hope of personal financial gain, which is the driving force of capitalism, will wither and dies. If shareholders only get the dividend promised to them by the issuers of the shares, they are no more than bondholders or mortgage holders. Not so. There is nothing to prevent them buying and selling their stocks and shares in the hope that some will pay more for the ones that look safest or surest, much as they do now.

On the whole, investors are not buying dividends (which are usually minuscule compared with the market price), but prospects of capital gain. The only difference will be that they cannot vote to sell the company or to buy another. That is because they would not be citizens but non-resident outside agents.

Exceptions could be made for significant holders of the equity, say over five per cent, who might be assumed to be fully involved in the long-term health and prospects of the community. Venture capitalists and the entrepreneurs that we all need would therefore not be disenfranchised.

For understandable reasons, the investing community has always been opposed to the idea of non-voting shares. It reduces its power. More respectably, it argues that it makes companies too cosy, but that is because the voting shares are often held by a small, self-interested coterie. In the new language of polity the votes would be held by those with most to lose by bad performance - the workers and the major investors.

The stock market has always been largely a secondary market. This secondary market will continue as it always has, but it will not have a direct impact on the community, although the signals it gives out will contain important warnings or encouragement for the directors. It will be what it has always been, a casino. But, at long last, a casino without the power to affect the lives of the dice or the cards it is betting on.

18.7 CAPITALISM FOR THE INDIVIDUAL

Organisations will continue to be one of the major communities of society, although they may well be radically different in shape and structure. They must begin to take that responsibility seriously and to think of themselves as communities, for their own sake and for the sake of all who work for them. Because the better businesses are already heading this way, there is little doubt that community-thinking will lead to improved results as well as to a more decent capitalism.

In the not so distant past, the trade unions gathered more power unto themselves than was good for them or for the health of the communities where their members worked.

Now it is the turn of the financial community to see its powers reduced. It will turn out to be for the good of all. It needs no laws to make it start happening, just the creation of two types of stock and the enfranchisement of the real assets of any business these days - the people who work in it.

18.8 PHILOSOPHICAL CONTRIBUTIONS

In reading through these chapters, the reader will find that through the centuries, philosophy as a subject contributed more than any other subject in the shaping of our lives, how we exist and how we control our destiny.

It is true though to say that on occasions, philosophy together with the sciences (with all the technological discoveries, the theories of evolution and genetics, the space explorations) and the arts, have contributed to our defiance of nature.

Psychologist tried to explain the bad and the good experiences and how they shape the individual. Some moralists maintain that it is the bad points, rather than the glorious moments that are most influential in personality development - in building the behavioural characteristics.

The author prefers the explanation of the idealistic philosophers. Where *anthropos* to them is *kalos - man is good.* It is this good nature of man that constructed the states, the democracies, with all the liberties to explore the sciences and to think. Thus adopting concepts, which help with moving forward, in an ideal and positive manner.

'Story telling' through the electronic modes can only assist in preparing for the next decade, the new aeon, the new much awaited millennium. Computing and systems influenced our lives, only to speed and send further out the public stories of history, politics and philosophy. Information technology has and will have a bigger role to play in the education of the non-privileged and all the races. In turn, the new millennium can only benefit more people - thus helping the improvement of everything on this globe and giving new chances to mankind.

Politicians, in their patriotic moods, will ensure that everybody and everything in the environment will improve. Politicians are human, too. They are not always the egocentric individuals that the mass media try to interpret. They have families and they want their children and future generations to live in harmony.

Moral philosophy for the person, groups, society and the state (and the rest of the cosmos) will be well established in the new millennium. Problems will be understood and solutions will be easier to find. Moral philosophers will integrate the knowledge gained from a new way of living and the logic gained from the great thinkers.

Humanity has more than two and a half centuries of philosophy (as we know it from written books), which can be relied on - to take us safely into the next generation and their acceptable ethics. Neuroses, uncertainties, lack of confidence… will always be part of human nature. Moral philosophy with its vast thesaurus of assimilated knowledge will always assist in the harmonisation of people and the smooth running of the state.

18.9 INFLUENCES OF PHILOSOPHY THROUGH THE AGES

Historically, there are records of philosophical thoughts going back eight and a half thousand years. Recent excavations in Cyprus and parts of the Middle East show constructions of people living in a civilised manner; where the gathering of big communities held discussions on morality and acceptable (or prohibitive) modes of integration within their legal and accepted state boundaries.

Recorded thoughts, literature, poetry, art, religious beliefs, mathematical theorems and astronomical observations exist, proving that through the ages and since the Phoenicians, there have been influences on how humanity ought to behave and values which contributed to the evolution of thinking and the building of states. Individual standards, social norms and group deities helped with the setting up of laws within which the citizens found freedom.

People live in groups and humans choose to live in states, simply for what they can get out of society. Those who choose to live in solitude become recluse in monasteries and nunneries, or become thinkers in isolation high up in mountains. The remaining who wish to explore their interaction with others, integrate within the moral and legal demands of a government.

18.10 THE EMPIRES AND THEIR IMPACT

The Phoenicians, Assyrians, Egyptians, Greeks, Romans and the Israelites brought influence on how we live, think and behave, probably more than any other known races. In recent times, the biggest influence to occidental, oriental and African countries - also, the smaller and unknown nations - came from the powerful European empires of Britain, Spain, France, and Portugal…

The influence on thinking, believing, morality, language and the legal systems of the ancient, classical and modern powers on other peoples were not passed on peacefully. The people of lesser wealth did not (willingly) identify themselves with the leaders of the powerful nations. Changes in their way of living were done by force, oppression, slavery and exploitation. In doing so (for their own benefit), some European powers left a legacy for religion and some form of philosophical thinking.

It is universally acknowledged that the biggest influence came from the Hellenic states. The rest of Europe gained the lights of civilisation from the Greeks. Subsequently and based on the classical Greek civilisation, the rest of the Europeans spread the Grecian thoughts, in a diluted or in an altered version of rationalism which suited their needs. It is an acceptable fact that the Greek race has established the foundations of a holistic scientific knowledge and education, more than any other nation. This influence subsequently spread as far as India and the rest of the known world.

Obviously, the Greeks did not conquer the world with altruistic feelings and helping hands. Greece and all the states within Hellas were always poor. To sit back and think, to invent and to debate democratically, and to let their philosophers explore their logic, it meant that they had to exploit the material possessions of other races, or putting it more mildly, whenever necessary they had to trade with other people, or sell their know-how.

The Greeks, like many other powers, used strategic talents and polemic methods to obtain what they wanted in order to support their financial requirements back home. You cannot build a successful state unless you are prosperous. So for centuries the Greeks did just that.

Even during the Roman occupation - with the leadership of Constantine The Great, they built the Eastern Roman Empire - Byzantium and for a millennium they isolated themselves within their Orthodoxy. Their false feeling of superiority, their arrogance and their political isolation did not help; what with the Christian schism and the total separation away from the Catholics, the damage done by the Crusaders and subsequent Ottoman attacks, it made them kneel; the effect being their complete surrender and capitulation to the Turkish invaders. Thus, with the conquest of Constantinople, the glory that was Greece went down. With the Ottomans capturing Byzantium and the Greek islands, Greece has never recovered.

It is ironic that Greece with all its philosophy and past civilisation is in this new millennium in need of modern philosophical concepts, more than any other state in

Europe. The other two poor nations of the European Union, namely the old empires of Spain and Portugal are on the way to economic and social improvement. With the loss of their identity, the modern Greeks are still struggling to find their lost cause.

18.11 RECENT DEVELOPMENTS

A similar route for conquering other peoples was followed by the British and other European-based Empires. The British literature scene, the poetry, academia as a whole and philosophy, together with their language have contributed to the rest of the world's thinking, more than any other modern state.

Writers and poets such as Chaucer, Shakespeare, Milton, Dickens, Shaw, Wordsworth, Coleridge, Byron, Bacon… (Only a handful of authors are mentioned here), together with all the British Philosophers, their writings, thoughts and concepts have become household names around the world. In earlier chapters of this book, philosophers such as Hume, Burke, Mills, Locke, Hobbes, Bentham and their concepts on Utilitarianism, Rationalism, Conservatism, Socialism and Morality are extensively discussed.

The British have also influenced their colonies with the English language (which will continue to be universally influential in this new millennium), their parliamentary democracy, the legal system and of course the popular English sports; most of the ex-colonies play cricket and the rest of the world football. The Spanish and their inquisition spread Catholicism whether the American natives wanted it or not. The remaining of the European empires, as a legacy, they left mainly their linguistic communication and various dialects.

Germany and Russia only managed to conquer other European countries. It must be mentioned that, although Russia did not conquer any other nation beyond Eastern Europe, their political system has definitely made an impact on many third world countries.

The Soviet brand of communism influenced many other populations - East, West and African people. Although Leninism has failed, there are a few nations who still follow their own form of socialism.

The Teutonic race has given us Kant, Hegel, Marx, Rudolph Steiner and their modern engineering know-how. The German contribution to philosophy goes well beyond the two big European-wide wars. Such works on Philosophy can only be admired.

18.12 THE INTERNATIONAL SCENE

The United States of America with all their material wealth, they have not yet made an important enough impact to match the philosophy of their European ancestors - the idealistic philosophy. On the psychotherapeutic scene, they certainly contributed enormously. Having followed the psychoanalytical concepts for a generation or more, they expanded alternative methods of therapy and psychology in general, through Skinner on behaviourism, Carl Rogers on Eclecticism, on the modern form of counselling and similar academic and practical applications.

But, regarding philosophy - one can certainly accept that the American concept of consumerism has gone where no other materialism has gone before. It all started with cinematography and then with the active 'coca-cola-lisation' of the rest of the world, together with the silicon influence on technology.

Politically, their intervention in the Latin American countries, Vietnam, Laos, Iraq and the ex-Yugoslavian states has done little to improve the individual and the state, as is philosophically understood. Ironically, within the circles of political philosophy, it is accepted that the backing of Kuwait and other Moslem nations happened because of the empty Texan oil wells and the strategic geographical positions of Asia Minor, and not for the benefit of the people residing inside the warring regions.

18.13 MODERN PHILOSOPHICAL IMPACT

Philosophically speaking, the U.S.A.'s impact on the rest of the world is minimal in comparison with what the European philosophers have established. The U.S.A has been very successful in spreading the 'philosophy' of consumerism and the capitalistic freedom of trading. In an egocentric way, this is where the U.S.A. has excelled. With their vast natural resources and their technological success, the Americans will, for another generation or so, continue to influence the international political conflicts.

Consideration must be given to what some third world countries think of the existing political scene. That many members of the United Nations Organisation are influenced by the U.S.A. principles and self interests. More so now, because of the collapse of the Soviet block. But, with the re-formation and unification of Europe, the political influence of the European Union will show improvement to their international relationships - thus benefiting the smaller nations, the third world countries and the Eastern European countries. Economically, the E.U. will co-operate even more with the oriental, African and Latin American nations.

There are many other negotiated initiatives that the USA has taken, such as the Israeli-Arab conflicts. As yet, there is no solid progress. Certainly the U.S.A. initiative to resolve the long lasting Cypriot political conflict has reached a stale mate.

The U.S.A.'s willingness to engage in international disputes and problems was and remains patchy. But, the important point is that it will, in extremis, intervene in disputes; attempt to quash threats to global peace and stability and work to maintain the existence of international economic institutions. The United States of America, as a country, is not a true hegemon, in the sense of a power that seeks to impose its will on all

In any case, as this book is primarily interested in the influence of philosophy on individuals and the state, apart from the Hollywood and the remaining of the consumerism type of philosophy, which comes from America, it still remains to be seen how influential the Americans can be on the philosophy theme.

It is an undisputed fact that the Europeans cultures have established a philosophy that can be compassionate to other governments around the world and the people living within their own chosen morality. It still remains to be seen what other impact the Americans can have on the rest of the world, philosophically speaking.

18.14 CAPITALISM

Capitalism is what brought, directly or indirectly, the improvements in human welfare seen during the 20th century. Its resources and incentives produced the technological developments that altered our fives, from antibiotics to MRI scans, from telephones to computers, motor cars to jet airliners, oil refining to air-conditioning.

In countries that enjoy such developments, capitalism has paid for education, healthcare, welfare support, holidays and pensions. For most of the second half of the 20th century, especially the 1980s and 1990s, the lure of those benefits proved strong enough to make most people accept capitalism even if they could not bring themselves to love it.

The phenomenon of 'globalisation' is in truth simply the spread of this open, trading capitalism to countries around the world that had sought to shut themselves away from it. China, Vietnam, the Soviet Union and its eastern European satellites shut themselves away because they were communist; most of Latin America shut itself away because it wanted to be self-sufficient; India shut itself away because of a mixture of socialism and the urge for self-sufficiency.

During the past 20 years the governments of countries containing around 3 billion people - half the world's population - have sought either to adopt a basically capitalist economic system or to connect their existing domestic capitalism to international trade and capital flows by opening up their borders.

It is not necessary to be a professional economist to realise that this voluntary process is controversial, however. Protests against internationalised capitalism have erupted in many cities around the world, generally at times when international institutions (and thus the media) were holding their annual get-togethers. In domestic politics, too, trade unions and corporate bosses campaign for restrictions on imports or on foreign competition when their sales are suffering badly. This happens especially frequently in Europe and America in old industries such as steel, textiles and agriculture.

Environmentalists meanwhile seek restrictions on capitalism everywhere, regardless of whether the firms involved are domestic or international and whether the environmental damage is domestic (e.g. pollution or new dams) or international (e.g. global warming).

Since all the progress that has been (and will be) seen in technology and in general welfare has arisen from capitalist activities and since no alternative set of ideas has emerged to give hope to poorer countries that they can match the rich world's progress by adopting anything other than capitalist, it might seem reasonable to assume that capitalism is likely to be a given gift for the 21st century. One way or another it will be a feature of life during the next hundred years. That is surely true. But, all the difference in the world and for the world is contained in that phrase, 'one way or another'.

How much technology develops, how it develops, how well off we become in material terms, how big a problem the relative poverty of the underdeveloped world will pose for the developed countries, how the planet's environment serves to limit or enable our activities and circumscribe, or enhance our lives; all these questions depend on the way capitalism develops, or rather the way it is allowed to develop.

American policy from the beginning of the cold war until the fall of the Soviet Union, a decade ago, had clarity of purpose. It was to prevent communism from spreading around the globe and threatening the capitalist democracies and to ensure that the conditions, which had led to the Second World War were not repeated.

In overall terms it was a success. But, it also brought some vices. Chief among them was the fact that seeing the world through a single prism (containment of communism) can blind policy makers.

The Vietnam War is a classic case. America entered it with the best of anti-communist intentions, but left with more than 47,000 of its servicemen dead, 1.4m Vietnamese dead, its reputation and confidence shattered and its munitions littered all over Indochina.

The attacks of September 11 have again created a clear purpose, a single prism. The world's trouble spots are no longer just an irritant or embarrassment. They are seen to be potentially highly destructive threats to America itself.

The definition of the single prism is not quite as simple as it was during the cold war, however. It was initially described as a "war on terrorism", but that soon proved inadequate. In reality it is a war on threats to global security, which encompass threats to US security.

These arise principally from two separate quarters: international terrorist groups such as Al-Qaeda, who are ready and willing to commit atrocities across the globe; and from the efforts of unpredictable dictators to secure or develop weapons of mass destruction.

These are separate issues, which require different sorts of policies. But they combine to produce the fear and sense of urgency that a single prism requires if is to be maintained for long. One special nightmare is for an overlap between these two worries; a terrorist using nuclear, chemical or biological weapons with or without help from an unpredictable dictator.

How these challenges take place and are met will make all the difference in the 21st century.

Schumpeter writing in the first half of the 20th century, predicted capitalism's 'gales' of destruction would lead to socialism. Yet in America, where the gales have blown a lot more freely than elsewhere, this has not happened. Entrepreneurs can go bankrupt with little or no stigma, companies can hire people and fire them when they realise they have made a mistake. The result is an extraordinary capacity for innovation and reinvention, for pursuing new opportunities and new fortunes.

Will this capacity survive in the future? The answer boils down to some quite simple points:

- Ordinary Americans show no sign, for now, of rejecting this form of capitalism that some Europeans consider unacceptably brutal.
- There is a continuing supply of would-be Americans seeking to join this bracing environment.
- Inequality is tolerated, even welcomed in America because of its association with economic mobility and meritocracy.

What of the other sort of economic threat, that (as with Vietnam) the burden of America's world role could itself become so large as to distort and divert the country's economic course? This could certainly happen again, if efforts to contain terrorism or the spread of nuclear weapons give rise to lengthy wars.

Two mitigating points need to be borne in mind, though:

- The American economy has a very large load-bearing capacity before the strain begins to be felt.

- Today's less regulated, more flexible economy, operating in a world with freer trade and thus more international competition, is less prone to inflation than America's economy was in the 1970s.

If America has the economic strength, has it got the will to offer leadership? Are Americans, in President Kennedy's famous words of 1961, willing to "pay any price; bear any burden" for the sake of liberty and peace?

The most important thing is to try to understand the opportunities and risks that lie ahead. It ought to have been possible in 1900 to see the dangers posed by the growing rivalry between the most powerful countries and by the declining ability of Britain to maintain international order. It ought also to have been possible to see the danger that capitalism's instability and inbuilt tendency towards inequality could bring about a political and social backlash in the 20th century.

America is, and will continue to be, willing to use its military forces abroad, and even to accept casualties. It will also retain the ability to afford its international commitments, and is likely to remain economically vibrant. American leadership will persist and offers a crucial hope to the rest of the world.

Like Britain in the early 1900s, America does not have enough power to solve all the world's political and economic problems. But it does have enough military muscle to deter any country from seeking to impose its will on others.

There is a basic paradox about American leadership that is likely to make it essentially benign, at least until much later in the century. This is that the values it espouses and seeks to establish overseas would, if adopted by other countries, make those countries stronger. The United States is the first Pre-eminent power in history whose ideas, if they triumph, would bring about the loss of its own dominance. It is possible that as that moment comes closer, Americans will change their minds and seek to prevent their relative decline. But that is a long way off, and the possibility a remote one.

As for capitalism, there are reasons to be optimistic about the prospects in the early decades of the 21st century. Although it will never be loved, capitalism is already a lot better regulated in all the rich countries, than it was a hundred years ago.

18.15 POLITICAL PHILOSOPHY

The history of political philosophy from Plato until the present day makes plain that modern political philosophy is still faced with the basic problems defined by the Greeks. The need to re-deploy public power in order to maintain the survival and enhance the quality of human life, for example, has never been so essential. And, if the opportunities for promoting well-being are now far greater, the penalties for the abuse of power are nothing less than the destruction or gross degradation of all life on the planet. In these circumstances it is of no great importance that some analytical philosophers have declared themselves neutral; they have at least often discredited pretentious metaphysical myths.

On the empirical evidence, constitutionalism and the rule of law, with the ancient classic, medieval, and humanist traditions behind them, have proved themselves a more successful response to the environment than tyranny and repression. In the current and more sophisticated view, there are no shortcuts to the millennium. As Mosca points out, utopian ideas become dangerous when they succeed in bringing a large mass of intellectual and moral energies to bear upon an end that can never be achieved, and that in the day of purported achievement can mean nothing more than the triumph of the worst people and distress and disappointment for the good.

There will perhaps always be a struggle for pre-eminence in any society, and public laws are necessary to regulate it. Too much cannot be hoped of government, and the best society is that in which tyranny and caprice of power are prevented and in which men are free to create diverse and spontaneous institutions within the framework of law. Only within such a framework of a tolerably well-organized constitutionalism, gradually extended to relations between states, can the swiftly mounting opportunities provided by applied science be taken and the pattern of social life adjusted, so that the human species, instead of being thwarted and deformed by its institutions, can realize its full potentialities.

18.16 HUMANISTIC SOURCES

Though lacking permanence itself, humanism in large measure established the climate and provided the medium for the rise of modern thought. An impressive variety of major developments in literature, philosophy, art, religion, social science, and even natural science had their basis in humanism or were significantly nourished by it. Important spokesmen in all fields regularly made use of humanistic eloquence to further their causes.

More generally, the so-called modern awareness--that sense of alienation and freedom applied both to the individual and to the race--derives ultimately, for better or worse, from humanistic sources. But with humanism, as with every other historical subject, one should beware lest valid concern about changes, crises, sources, and influences obscure the even more important issues of human continuity and human value.

Whatever its weaknesses and inner conflicts, the humanistic movement was heroic in its breadth and energy, remarkable in its aspirations. For human development in all fields, it created a context of seldom-equalled fertility. Its characteristic modalities of thought, speech, and image lent themselves to the promptings of genius and became the media for enduring achievement. Its moral program formed the basis for lives that are remembered with admiration.

18.17 BIOETHICS

This is the discipline dealing with the ethical implications of both biological research and the applications of that research, especially in medicine. The first bioethics study institute, the Hastings Centre, was established in June 1969 and is now located in Briarcliff Manor, N.Y., U.S. In 1971 Georgetown University in Washington, D.C., established The Joseph and Rose Kennedy Institute of Ethics, which created a Centre for Bioethics and sponsored the publication of the first Encyclopaedia of Bioethics, 4 vol. (1978). By the 1990s there were well over a hundred bioethics organizations worldwide.

The rise of bioethics is traceable to several events. First, although ethical issues have been raised in medicine and biology since ancient times (witness, for instance, the Hippocratic oath), the large-scale introduction of biomedical and other technologies in the second half of the 20th century has intensified old problems and added new ones--such as issues over the definition of death and the withdrawal of life-sustaining medical treatment, prenatal diagnosis and abortion, the storage of frozen human embryos, the use of humans, animals, or foetal tissue for scientific research, the screening of persons for the AIDS virus or other infections, the disposition of toxic wastes, the expansion of genetic engineering, and the allocation of scarce health resources.

Second, awareness of bioethics and other moral issues has been dramatically raised; professionals and students now routinely raise ethical questions. In the course of such questioning, bioethics has affected philosophy, pushing it to pay more attention to practical problems. Finally, the growth of interdisciplinary and multidisciplinary work in academic institutions has facilitated dealing concurrently with biological research and with moral and social issues of human behaviour.

18.18 DEONTOLOGICAL ETHICS

In philosophy, these are the ethical theories that place special emphasis on the relationship between duty and the morality of human actions. Deontology (Greek deon, "duty," and logos, "science") consequently focuses on logic and ethics. No attempt is made in such theories to explicate specific moral obligations. In deontological ethics an action is considered morally good because of some characteristic of the action itself, not because the product of the action is good. Deontological ethics holds that at least some acts are morally obligatory regardless of their consequences for human welfare.

Descriptive of such ethics are such expressions as "Duty for duty's sake", "Virtue is its own reward", and "Let justice be done though the heavens fall". By contrast, teleological ethics holds that the basic standard of morality is precisely the value of what an action brings into being. Deontological theories have been termed formalistic because their central principle lies in the conformity of an action to some rule or law. The first great philosopher to define deontological principles was Immanuel Kant, the 18th-century German founder of critical philosophy, whose ethics were much influenced by Christianity as well as by the Rationalism of the Enlightenment. Kant held that nothing is good without qualification except a good will, which is one that wills to act in accord with the moral law and out of respect for that law, rather than out of natural inclinations.

He saw the moral law as a categorical imperative--i.e. an unconditional command--and believed that its content could be established by human reason alone. Reason begins with the principle "Act only on that maxim whereby thou canst at the same time will that it should become a universal law". Kant's critics, however, have questioned his view that all duties can be derived from this purely formal principle and have argued that, in his preoccupation with rational consistency; he neglected the concrete content of moral obligation.

The British philosopher W.D. Ross, who held that numerous "prima facie duties", rather than a single formal principle for deriving them, are themselves immediately self-evident, faced this objection in the 20th century. Ross distinguished these prima facie duties (such as promise keeping, reparation, gratitude, and justice) from actual duties, for "any possible act has many sides to it which are relevant to its rightness or wrongness"; and these facets have to be weighed before "forming a judgment on the totality of its nature" as an actual obligation in the given circumstances.

18.19 PHILOSOPHY OF PERSONAL IMMORTALITY

Many people believe that when the human body ceases to be a living system, there is not total annihilation of the person but that in some respect the person continues to exist.

The philosopher of mind can put aside the various watered-down versions of immortality in which the person continues to exist in the remote sense that people still remember him or his works or that his influence continues through history. The philosopher does look with interest, however, on the claim that there is an immortality in which a person, in his survival, meets the psychological criteria of personal identity, of inheritance of memory, beliefs, habits, and personality characteristics. It is clear that a person's view of immortality will be affected by opinions that he holds about the relation of mind to matter.

Given the versions of Materialism that urge the elimination of mental terms or their definition in bodily terms or that take bodily identity to be the basic criterion of personal identity, the very notion of survival after death is completely unintelligible. Many philosophers, however, reason that, since the notion of survival is intelligible, such versions of Materialism cannot be accepted. Central-state or identity theorists would admit survival to be an intelligible notion but would view it, like lightning without electricity, as something that never happens; they would thus be in agreement with many dualists, in particular epiphenomenalists and psychophysical parallelists.

Even an interactionist would be free to accept or reject survival, as would a neutral monist. If a philosopher holds that survival is an intelligible notion, he is still left with the further question of whether it ever happens. In the past there have been various a priori arguments for survival after death. Arguments based upon the nature of the self, such as its indivisibility, can be found in Plato's Phaedo.

Kant argued that man's moral principles require survival as a postulate. But among those today that hold that survival is intelligible, it is widely agreed that a priori arguments will not do. If there is survival, they say, it is a contingent fact and not a necessity; one must thus look to empirical data for guidance. A survey of the evidence shows that the case against survival, though strong, is by no means conclusive. One thing is clear: if there is survival, the survivors can theoretically give firsthand testimony to it, whereas if there is no survival, there will be no one to give such testimony.

18.20 CIVIL DISOBEDIENCE

Also called Passive Resistance, refusal to obey the demands or commands of a government or occupying power, without resorting to violence or active measures of opposition; its usual purpose is to force concessions from the government or occupying power. Civil disobedience has been a major tactic and philosophy of nationalist movements in Africa and India, in the civil rights movement of U.S. blacks, and of labour and anti-war movements in many countries.

Civil disobedience is a symbolic or ritualistic violation of the law, rather than a rejection of the system as a whole. The civil disobedient, finding legitimate avenues of change blocked or nonexistent, sees himself as obligated by a higher, extralegal principle to break some specific law. It is because civil disobedience is a crime, however, and known by actor and public alike to be punishable that the act serves as a protest. By submitting to punishment, the civil disobedient hopes to set a moral example that will provoke the majority or the government into effecting meaningful political, social, or economic change.

Under the imperative of setting a moral example, the major spokesmen of civil disobedience insists that the illegal actions be non-violent variety of criticisms has been directed against the philosophy and practice of civil disobedience.

The radical critique of the philosophy of civil disobedience condemns its acceptance of the existing political structure; conservative schools of thought, on the other hand, see the logical extension of civil disobedience as anarchy and the right of the individual to break any law he chooses, at any time.

Activists themselves are divided in interpreting civil disobedience either as a total philosophy of social change or as merely a tactic to be employed when the movement lacks other means. On a pragmatic level, the efficacy of civil disobedience hinges on the adherence of the opposition to a certain morality to which an appeal can ultimately be made.

The philosophical roots of civil disobedience lie deep in Western thought: Cicero, Saint Thomas Aquinas, John Locke, Thomas Jefferson, and Henry David Thoreau all sought to justify conduct by virtue of its harmony with some antecedent superhuman moral law.

The man who most clearly formulated the concept of civil disobedience for the modern world was Mohandas Gandhi. Drawing from Eastern and Western thought, Gandhi developed the philosophy of Satyagraha. First in the Transvaal of South Africa in 1906 and later in India, Gandhi led his people in Satyagraha to obtain equal rights and freedom.

Inspired by Gandhi's example, the civil-rights movement of the American blacks from the 1950s to the 1970s adopted the tactics and philosophy of civil disobedience, perhaps best expressed by Martin Luther King, Jr. Later the tactics of civil disobedience were employed by a variety of protest groups.

The principle of civil disobedience has achieved some standing in international law through the war crime trials at Nürnberg after World War II, which affirmed the principle that an individual may, under certain circumstances, be held accountable for failure to break the laws of his country.

18.21 DIFFERENCES AMONG COUNTRIES

Principles of legal ethics, whether written or unwritten, not only seek to control the conduct of legal practice but also reflect the basic assumptions, premises, and methods of the legal system within which the lawyer operates. They reflect as well the profession's conception of its own role in the administration of justice. In western European legal systems the role of the practitioner in both civil and criminal litigation differs from what it is in Anglo-American legal systems and this is reflected in the ethics of their legal professions.

Practitioners in countries having a Communist form of government are ordinarily salaried employees of the government, and their ethical obligations consequently have a focus different from that in countries where lawyers engage in independent practice or are employed by private firms. In England and to a certain extent in France, where the profession is divided into separate branches, the principles of professional ethics reflect the relationships incident to that division.

In western European and Anglo-American countries and others with similar systems of justice, such as Japan and India, in which the lawyer is not an employee of the state but engages in private practice to serve clients who employ him, professional ethics are addressed to two basic aspects of the lawyer's status. On the one hand, he is employed by clients to serve and represent their interests; on the other, he is participating in an important social function--the application of rules of law through advice, trial of cases, preparation of legal documents, and negotiation with others for his clients. Hence, the principles of legal ethics stress that the lawyer's chief interest lies in serving his client and in securing justice--not in increasing his own income. He is an agent of his client but deemed to retain a large measure of independent judgment as to the proper course to pursue. He represents his client's interests but may not engage in tactics that defeat the fair administration of justice.

The lawyer is engaged; it is said, in a profession and not in a business. Naturally the interests of client and society sometimes conflict, and the principles of legal ethics do not always indicate how these conflicts should be resolved.

Should a lawyer cross-examine an adverse witness in such a way as to undermine or destroy his testimony when the lawyer believes the witness is actually telling the truth? May he invoke rules of evidence to exclude points that would weigh against his case but that he considers being probably true? May he take advantage of the errors of an unskilled opponent? Should he demand a jury trial for purposes of delay when a jury trial has no advantage for his client? These questions may be answered differently in legal systems that operate on different premises.

A system in which a lawyer presents his client's case in the most favourable light permitted by law and in which the court must decide the merits of the case may well produce different answers than those produced in a system that assigns a higher priority to the lawyer's duty to the state to assure proper administration of justice.

18.22 LEGAL ETHICS, CRIMINAL CASES

Both the prosecution and the defence of criminal cases raise special ethical issues. The prosecutor represents the state, and the state's concern is not only in convicting the guilty but also in acquitting the innocent. The prosecutor also has an ethical and, in considerable measure, a legal duty to disclose to the defence any information known to him and unknown to the defence that might exonerate the defendant or mitigate the punishment. He must not employ trial tactics that may lead to unfair convictions, nor should he prosecute merely to enhance his political prospects. The defence counsel has different concerns. Under Anglo-American law an accused may compel the state to prove that he is guilty beyond a reasonable doubt.

The defence counsel, therefore, becomes ethically obligated to require the state to produce such proof, whether or not the attorney believes his client to be guilty. His client's guilt is for the tribunal to determine. The attorney may not, however, deliberately resort to perjured or other false testimony. Similar principles hold in civil-law countries. When the client, against the attorney's advice, insists on testifying falsely, the ethical course to be pursued has not been fully settled. Some maintain that the attorney should withdraw, if possible, or else merely permit the client to testify without aiding him or asserting the truth of the testimony given.

18.23 THE ETHICS OF INTEREST

The problem of the ethics of interest is still unresolved after many centuries of discussion, as long as the institution of private property is accepted, the usefulness of borrowing and lending can hardly be denied. In the long historic process of inheritance, widowhood, gain and loss, by which the distribution of the ownership of capital is determined, there is no reason to suppose that the actual ownership of capital falls into the hands of those best able to administer it.

Much of the capital of an advanced society, in fact, tends to be owned by elderly widows, simply because of the greater longevity of the female. Society, therefore, needs some machinery for separating the control of capital from its ownership. Financial instruments and financial markets are the principal agency for performing this function. If all securities took the form of stocks or equities, it might be argued that contractual obligations (bonds), and therefore interest as a form of income, would not be necessary. The case for bonds and interest, however, is the case for specialization.

There is a demand for many different degrees of ownership and responsibility, and interest-bearing obligations tap a market that would be hard to reach with equity securities; they are also peculiarly well adapted to the obligations of governments. The principal justification for interest and interest-bearing securities is that they provide an easy and convenient way for skilled administrators to control capital that they do not own and for the owners of capital to relinquish its control. The price society pays for this arrangement is interest. There remains the problem of the socially optimum rate of interest. It could be argued that there is no point in paying any higher price than one needs to and that the rate of interest should be as low as is consistent with the performance of the function of the financial markets.

This position, of course, would place all the burden of control of economic fluctuations on the fiscal system, and it is questionable whether this would be acceptable politically. The ancient problem of "usury", in the form of the exploitation of the ignorant poor by moneylenders, is still important in many parts of the world. The remedy is the development of adequate financial institutions for the needs of all classes of people rather than the attempt to prohibit or even to limit the taking of interest.

The complex structure of lending institutions in a developed society--banks, building societies, land banks, cooperative banks, credit unions, and so on--testifies to the reality of the service that the lender provides and that interest pays for. The democratisation of credit--that is, the extension of the power of borrowing to all classes in society--is one of the important social movements of the 20th century.

18.24 LEGAL ETHICS

Principles of conduct that members of the profession are expected to observe in the practice of law. They are an outgrowth of the development of the legal profession itself. Practitioners of law emerged when legal systems became too complex for those affected by them to understand and apply the law. Certain individuals with the required ability mastered the law and offered their skills for hire. No prescribed qualifications existed, and these specialists were not subject to legal controls.

The incompetent, unscrupulous, and dishonest charged exorbitant fees, failed to perform as promised, and engaged in delaying and obstructive tactics in the tribunals before which they appeared. Action to prevent such abuses was taken by legislation and by judicial and other governmental measures.

The right to practice law came to be limited to those who met prescribed qualifications. Expulsion from practice and criminal penalties were introduced for various types of misconduct. These measures did more than correct the abuses. They also gave recognition to the social importance of the functions performed by lawyers and identified those who were qualified to perform them. A consciousness developed within the profession of the need for standards of conduct.

This became the core of legal, or professional, ethics. Prior statutes, court rules, and other government directives remained in force along with the profession's self-imposed ethical standards. Taken together, they constituted the sum total of the restraints placed upon lawyers in regard to their professional conduct. This pattern has continued to the present time.

In many countries professional associations of lawyers have sought to commit the principles of ethical conduct to written form, but a written code is not essential. Ethical principles may exist by common understanding as well as in the literature and writings of the profession. This is the case in England. A code, however, makes ethically obligatory principles readily available to the practitioner and thus helps to assure greater observance of them.

When such a code does exist, it usually contains both statements of general ethical principles and particular rules governing specific problems of professional ethics. But no code can foresee every ethical problem that may arise in the practice of law. Hence, codes are supplemented by opinions rendered and published by committees of bar associations.

19. MODERN MANAGEMENT:

- THE PHILOSOPHICAL CONCEPTS

Modern Management and the philosophical concepts of morality, ethics, law, social, psychological, economics and other thoughts, as a whole group of activities have traditionally been concerned with finding effective solutions to specific political, State, government and other operational problems. The ideas brought forward in this book are those who proved themselves as great thinkers, which thoughts can assist in solving current management problems and new, better methods, techniques, and tools for processing new changes urgently required.

In the past, it has been found that too many of the solutions are not implemented and, of those that are, too few survive the inclination of management functional areas to return to familiar ways of doing things. Therefore, Management personnel have gradually come to realize that their tasks should not only include solving specific problems but also apply philosophical concepts that predict and prevent future problems, identify and solve current ones, and implement and maintain these solutions under changing conditions.

As an Executive in multi-national organisations and Government Departments, the author has come to realise that most problems do not arise in isolation but are part of an interacting system. The book, in principle, is seeking for a process of simultaneous interrelated solutions to a set of interdependent problems. Further on, substantial effort has been devoted in recommending a rational methodology for one, or the least possible management processes, for future changes in management. Businesses need to find better ways of doing things, is often not nearly as great as is the required to maximize use of what is already operational. This book, therefore, has been addressing itself more and more to determining how to produce the willingness to change procedures suitable to the way people are willing to work and with processes that they are familiar with.

The Author, who follows various consultancy assignments, suggests the additional, more detailed recommendations, including strategic changes, training, convincing resources, meetings with people, development of workshops and exchanges of new ideas. The reader, therefore, must consider such points that absorb resources, excessive costs and incur a heavy workload for existing staff.

In the areas in which technology advances fastest, new products and new materials are required in a constant flow, but there are many management areas in which the rate of change can be gentle. Although each process considered may be trivial, the total effect is many times as large as the margin between success and failure in an operational situation. These efforts to improve existing processes can be formalised to include the concepts explained in the various sections of this book.

The legacy processes and their procedures have had a dramatic impact on the management of businesses. The speed and data-handling capabilities of experienced staff, enables the realistic changes and because of their know-how they get meaningful solutions to those changes through the use of long standing techniques. There is still considerable difficulty, however, in drawing inferences from operational legacy processes to the real world of smooth management.

Additionally, the growing number of changes in the information-processing applications is currently on the increase. To this effect, the philosophical concepts explained in this book may be the optimum solution to the problems of adopting new processes. Awareness that possession of details on any changes is tantamount to a competitive edge is stimulating the gathering of information at national levels. Similarly, concern is mounting over the safeguarding and husbanding of changes to the proprietary and strategic information within the confines of a company, as well as within outsourcing companies. Management concepts in multi-national sites have as their objective the husbanding and optimisation of corporate resources, namely; employees and their activities, inventories of materials and equipment, facilities, and finances.

A corporation's administrative information systems and the Management Information Systems (MIS) focus primarily on resource administration and provide top management with reports of aggregate data. Executive information systems may be viewed as an evolution of administrative information systems in the direction of strategic tracking, modelling, and decision-making. Typically, Management consists of a number of processes, each supporting a particular function and changes, which may occur any day of the year.

Management processes concentrate on resource allocation and task completion of organized activities. They usually incorporate such scheduling methods as the Critical Path Method (CPM) or Program Evaluation and Review Technique (PERT).Their component parts sometimes interact so extensively that a change in one part is likely to affect many others. It is, therefore, of primary importance that all the Management processes interact with all the functionalities. Otherwise, Management as a human function is of no significance. Processes may also vary depending on the amount of human judgment that enters into their operation.

Management may have many responsibilities, but the most important of all is the ability to identify and positively execute plans to manage the changes threatening the objectives. Through a process of structured interviews and plans Assessment Analysis is used to highlight the specific requests for changes, which may turn into risks. During the interviews Assessment Analysis is used to capture the key changes from the interviewees. In turn, the Assessment Analysis provides a life-cycle process, which highlights the primary prioritisation of the changes. In large, complex and critical programmes, it is essential that a true prioritised report is available so that the imminent changes can be managed first.

The process commences by identifying the most important changes, which may become threats to a business at large. These are given priority, support and management expertise. Once the prioritisation exercise is completed, the participating people are notified and subsequently interviewed to bring out and capture any possible changes they may have.

Management allows the capture of collective knowledge and expertise from those involved on a project, in a form that facilitates the communication of changes, their assessments and the pro-active management of the changes required. The modern Executive attempts to merge the latest developments in human sciences and advanced technology. In many organisations, the major theme is the responsibility to the client, and the individual within the company. The Manager's role is to provide a service which will assist in developing skills, diagnose and treat discontinuities which affect the performance of the employee.

On the academic, educational and training aspect, the importance of a person as a professional must be emphasised, this being the major factor in dealing with organisational, system and personal problems. In the last few years, universities prepare their courses to suit the business environment and people's needs, which in turn lead to the professional accreditation of the appropriate management institutions. The whole venture of academia and the business world is seen by organisations as a benefit for a continuous human development policy. This ensures high quality employment opportunities, secured in growth industries at the forefront of technological changes.

It is now universally accepted that more and more top of the league universities are incorporating philosophical concepts in the subject of business management as a profession.

The future beckons for changing attitudes in understanding the management role and its varied requirements. It is a lengthy process of trials and discussions, but it will happen in some form. As a first step identify the training needs of individuals. This may include instructions on specific processes, as well as the understanding of the concepts pertaining to moral and political philosophy. To date, many businesses have been put off the philosophical aspects of modern management, because of misinformation and poor perception. Close levels of integration between the different forms of communicating is likely to drive a new generation of managers to choose new pathways for any given task.

Every business has its own working practices, requirements and tolerances, so a 'one-size-fits-all' approach is not appropriate. All business managers, however, would be wise to consider first and foremost people and their needs, as well as policies and procedures to suit the employee.

With the new mobile technology, during the next five years, our working lives will change fast. As with previous changes, electronic mobility will impact on our whole lifestyle. But unlike previous changes, this time round it will be fuelled by technologies that are coming out of the private world and into the corporate world.

The consumer will be driving changes in ways it never has before. Business people are increasingly being introduced to new technologies. The future will see the big ideas being more likely to come from senior managers, rather than from Information Technology managers and 'techies' who tended to be at the forefront of innovation in the past.

As such, the senior leaders, executives, managers and directors in order to succeed in their management performance, they must incorporate the philosophical thoughts and concepts of the acknowledged thinkers who, through the ages they have proven that the needs of the employees are of the uppermost importance for any business to be successful and profitable.

END

The process of managing a team involves the interaction of people where individuals contribute to the running or completion of a task. As in any State or country, under any government, people live together under various laws, rules, regulations and religions. The people elect or they follow a leader, be it a democratic or tyrannical leadership. People under such regimes follow a type of management. In a business environment such methods of management prevail. A Manager will delegate and lead one or more individuals within the organization by running the business or a system.

As in any government, the President or the Prime Minister will maintain the best possible methods for the running of the country and for improving the standards of living. A similar case prevails in the business world. Keeping your staff happy and motivated is an important part of leadership. Especially where a company is undergoing the technological change demanded by modern computing and the Information Technology systems involved. Think of the upheaval that can accompany the demands of a technological change.

Not everyone responds well to a change or the challenge. While one person may find change exciting, another may be scared rigid. Politically speaking, what is happening outside the country may also affect how an individual views change in politics. Keeping thoroughly abreast of how citizens are feeling is very important. The same exactly viewpoint will exist in an office. Far more important, however, is ensuring that staff know what is happening.

Management styles can, therefore, be considered as political systems where people participate in the smooth running of a country or a company, whether this is a global organization or a fruit stall in the back streets of London. Getting the people to work together, to manage or be managed is vital to the success of a business. Leadership is the key to success, yet not enough effort is being spent on helping to create effective leaders, whether political or business leaders, especially in addressing global issues.

ISBN: 978-1-84753-147-6

Author: ANDREAS SOFRONIOU

33 Marlborough Road, Swindon, Wilts. SN3 1PH, UK.

Phone: 07939 460013

The compilation of seven Management related books by
Andreas Sofroniou.

1. Information Technology

This section of the book aims to fill a gap in the current business and tutorial literature. It has been designed for the business individual, for the student and the computer professional who need a detailed overview of business information systems. It explores computing in general, the structured development of systems using processes and data analysis; object oriented and other methods. It includes the project planning and testing procedures for the Millennium thread.

2. Changes In I.T.

Change Management and the changes to Configuration, Release and Assets as a whole group of activities have traditionally been concerned with finding effective solutions to specific operational problems. The purpose of this book is to look at current problems and new, better methods, techniques, and tools for processing changes.

3. I.T. Risks

A risk is an uncertain event, which may have an adverse effect on the project's objectives. This book explains a proven risk management methodology, which should be very effective in the quest for identifying risks throughout the project lifecycle. It describes the processes, which commence by identifying the enterprise's most important and risky projects, as these must be given priority. The book is, essentially, dealing with a method that permits the collection of knowledge and experience from those involved.

4. Programmes Workshop

The Programme Management Workshop, as a manual and book, deals with the Management of Projects, where established

MANAGEMENT PROCEDURES AND VARIOUS DEVELOPMENT METHODS ARE EXPLAINED. THIS WORKSHOP IS INTENDED TO GIVE I.T. AND PROGRAMME MANAGEMENT STAFF AN OVERVIEW OF THE PROJECT DEVELOPMENT METHODS AND AN INDICATION OF HOW THESE RELATE TO THE VARIOUS PROJECT MANAGEMENT TECHNIQUES. THE WORKSHOP EXPLORES THE FUNDAMENTAL ASPECTS OF THE MANAGEMENT OF RISKS, PROGRAMMES, STRUCTURED SYSTEMS DEVELOPMENT, OPERATIONAL COMPUTING AND THE CONSTRUCTION OF NEW INFORMATION SYSTEMS.

5. EPISTEMOLOGY

THE PROCESS OF MANAGING A TEAM INVOLVES THE INTERACTION OF PEOPLE WHERE INDIVIDUALS CONTRIBUTE TO THE RUNNING OR COMPLETION OF A TASK. AS IN ANY STATE OR COUNTRY, UNDER ANY GOVERNMENT, PEOPLE LIVE TOGETHER UNDER VARIOUS LAWS, RULES, REGULATIONS AND RELIGIONS. THE PEOPLE ELECT OR THEY FOLLOW A LEADER, BE IT A DEMOCRATIC OR TYRANNICAL LEADERSHIP. PEOPLE UNDER SUCH REGIMES FOLLOW A TYPE OF MANAGEMENT. IN A BUSINESS ENVIRONMENT SUCH METHODS OF MANAGEMENT PREVAIL. A MANAGER WILL DELEGATE AND LEAD ONE OR MORE INDIVIDUALS WITHIN THE ORGANIZATION BY RUNNING THE BUSINESS OR A SYSTEM. MANAGEMENT STYLES CAN, THEREFORE, BE CONSIDERED AS POLITICAL SYSTEMS WHERE PEOPLE PARTICIPATE IN THE SMOOTH RUNNING OF A COUNTRY OR A COMPANY, WHETHER THIS IS A GLOBAL ORGANIZATION OR A FRUIT STALL IN THE BACK STREETS OF ANY CITY.

Andreas Sofroniou *DSc PhD PsD ExecMBA CEng FIoD, is a practising psychotherapist, an executive with international organisations and an adviser to governments. His published books include Information Technology, Management, Psychology, Poetry, Philosophy, and Fiction.*

Email: *sofroniou@aol.com*

Web Site: www.lulu.com/sofroniou

ISBN: ***978-1-84753-147-6***

www.ingramcontent.com/pod-product-compliance
Lightning Source LLC
Chambersburg PA
CBHW081431090925
32270CB00146B/6030
9781847531476